A CRITICAL COLLECTION

Ðrama

A CRITICAL COLLECTION

edited by

JAMES K. BOWEN
Southern Oregon College

RICHARD VAN DER BEETS
San Jose State College

with a foreword by
ANGUS BOWMER

HARPER & ROW, PUBLISHERS
New York, Evanston, San Francisco, London

CONTENTS

FOREWORD

BY ANGUS BOWMER

Since the beginning of Man's time on this earth, he has endeavored to formulate and communicate ideas concerning the relationships between man and man, man and the Universe, and man and God. He has done this in three ways: through religion, through philosophy, and through the arts. Religious concepts are based on faith; philosophy deals with purely intellectual concepts; while the arts combine the intellectual with the emotional.

Perhaps the most articulate of the arts, and certainly the most complex, is drama, involving as it does the appearance of colors, light, movement, proportion, and emotions to express theoretically postulated concepts of the nature of man and his environment.

We are hopefully emerging from a period in our cultural pattern which was dominated by basically Puritan concepts concerning the arts. These concepts, stemming from the philosophy of John Locke, negate the value of the aesthetic component in things, maintaining that material substance has certain primary characteristics, belonging to the atoms themselves, such as extension, mass, etc., but that the aesthetic characteristics, such as color, odors, sounds, and warmth do not belong to the atomic material at all, but are mere appearances projected upon the object by the observer. These latter qualities, along with sensed space and time were termed secondary qualities; while emotions, stemming as they do from these secondary, apparent qualities, were termed tertiary qualities.

The average American, then, without knowing why, has considered the only really important things (other than the purely unemotional mental substance) to be material substances such as the bridge over the river, the automobile in the garage, or the color television set in the living room. Therefore the engineer, the mechanic, and the manufacturer are necessary members of society because they produce material objects which are "practical," "real," which possess the primary characteristics of matter; while the artist, dealing with immediately experienced colors, sounds, and emotions, produces nothing "real," nothing primary, but only appearance.

Thus *Othello,* for instance, because it is concerned with theoretically postulated concepts of the nature of Man, has been considered a valid cultural artifact, in spite of the fact that the means of conveying these concepts is the aesthetic component composed of immediately perceived colors, movements, emotions, etc., as mere appearance. Following this line of thought it is not hard to see why the study of dramatic literature in the classroom has an older and firmer foothold in the American university than does theatre. For in the classroom, if the Lockean concept is accepted, it is possible to come more directly to the important theoretic component in the nature of Man and the Universe with a minimum of interference from the appearance of colors, light, movement, emotions, etc., of the aesthetic component, necessary to a theatrical production. This purely Lockean idea as to the place of drama in our culture pattern was expressed most simply and clearly by an English professor in a west coast university, who said to me, "The importance of Shakespeare has, thank God, nothing to do with theatre. In the drama of Shakespeare, the only thing that matters is significance."

There is now, however, widespread evidence of a revolution among a large section of our people, led by modern philosophers, maintaining that the aesthetic component in things is a positive good in itself, and that art has two functions: first, to present the aesthetic component of Man and his environment for its own sake; and, second, to use the aesthetic component symbolically to convey ideas concerning the theoretic component of the nature of things.

In reading the plays of this volume, then, there are certain techniques which must be employed if both the primary and secondary components are to be fully appreciated. These techniques are necessary because a play script is not the final form of the artifact. It is a means to the end which is the full performance of the play produced upon the stage.

To put the whole problem in another way, let us use Aristotle's six parts of a play:

1. PLOT: the overall architectonics of a play, i.e., the structure and shape, as well as the "story."
2. CHARACTER: the identification and differentiation of the personages involved in the plot.
3. THOUGHT: all ideas, expressed or implied.

4. DICTION: the language employed in conveying the plot, characters and thoughts of the play.
5. MUSIC: all the sounds, along with inflections, tones, volume, and their variations and contrasts, used to express the four previously mentioned parts.
6. SPECTACLE: everything seen on the stage, colors, forms, movements, and all their variations and combinations.

It is evident that the playwright can express the first four parts of a play, as listed by Aristotle, in a fairly concrete way. But the last two parts he can only suggest. This is why each production of a play is different. But the reader, like the director of a play, must, in his imagination, translate the diction, thought, character, and plot into what can be seen and heard, if he is to perceive the total impact of both the primary and secondary components.

Each reader, then, must become his own director. As he reads he must hear all the sounds, from the subtle inflection of an ironic syllable to the off-stage crash of sound-effect thunder. He must see all that takes place on the stage: the effect of a lifted eyebrow; the flash of a dagger snatched from concealment; the change in stage lighting as a lantern is extinguished.

Great dramatic literature read in this way may teach something of the nature of beauty as well as of the nature of Man.

Angus Bowmer

Producing/Director
Ashland Shakespeare Festival

PREFACE

The four abstracts of important critical studies appended to each play in this collection provide an engaging and challenging opportunity for the study of drama. Essentially, these abstracts present concise, readable, and accurate four-hundred-word summaries of some of the most outstanding critical judgments and aesthetic insights available in modern scholarship. Drawing from a wide scope of perspectives available to the drama scholar, these abstracts range from broad, sweeping assessments that examine the playwright's overall production to approaches that illustrate the benefits derived from a concentrated reading of a particular scene or passage. By offering thesis, method, and major points of substantiation, the abstracts not only indicate the basic positions of their respective authors, but they suggest also the general tone of the original essays. Moreover, the complete bibliographic citation, serving as a reliable reference source for the entire article, encourages the use of more detailed and fully developed scholarship.

The abstract as a critical tool is unique to the study of drama in collections of this kind. Because the abstracts render the substance of highly complex critical articles into language and terms readily understandable by the student, they lend themselves to a variety of classroom uses. The conciseness of the abstract permits a broad offering of material, which exposes the student to a substantial number of critical approaches to the drama. For example, the four abstracts that accompany *Everyman* serve to illustrate the manner in which distinct critical assessments complement one another. The first abstract centers on the relationship between the didactic nature of the play and its dramatic form; the second and third abstracts examine respectively the ways in which knowledge and friendship were understood in medieval times. The fourth, through its focus on theological priorities, maintains that the English version of *Everyman* does not keep with the Catholic view of redemption and salvation.

These are just some of the ways in which the abstract may be employed. Those who use this anthology will find that many more ways present themselves, as each set of abstracts offers unique themes for the study of particular plays.

In addition to the learning opportunities afforded by the abstract, the chronological ordering of the twelve plays provides an historical overview of the development of drama as an art form. By comparing and contrasting the dramatic techniques of one period of man's cultural development to another such period, insights into the creative process are revealed in a significantly demonstrable way. Moreover, this historical arrangement which spans more than two thousand years provides an opportunity for assessing imaginative approaches to many of man's perennial concerns. For example, the central contentions in Sophocles' *Oedipus Rex* are approached from a somewhat different perspective in Dürrenmatt's *The Visit,* thus providing added insights into both plays. O'Neill's use of Racine's *Phaedre* in creating *Desire Under the Elms* not only allows for a better comprehension of both plays, but aids in understanding the Phaedre legend as it has come down through man's literate history.

Drama: A Critical Collection substantially answers the need for a wide sampling of critical appraisal to inform the reader of the many ways drama may be read and enjoyed, and it places one of man's most complex and diverse art forms in an historical perspective. More importantly, however, the plays and attendant apparatus do not propose to merely fill in gaps in the reader's intellectual and aesthetic development—like all worthwhile texts, it offers a leading out to more and wider readings, which, in turn, will help him see himself and the world in more critical and humane ways.

The editors wish to thank especially James A. Hamby and Scott Hymain for their aid and advice.

JKB

RVDB

drama
A CRITICAL COLLECTION

OEDIPUS REX
SOPHOCLES

TRANSLATED BY
DUDLEY FITTS
and ROBERT FITZGERALD

CHARACTERS

OEDIPUS

A PRIEST

CREON

TEIRESIAS

IOCASTÊ

MESSENGER

SHEPHERD OF LAÏOS

SECOND MESSENGER

CHORUS OF THEBAN ELDERS

act one

THE SCENE: Before the palace of OEDIPUS, King of Thebes. A central door and two lateral doors open onto a platform which runs the length of the façade. On the platform, right and left, are altars; and three steps lead down into the "orchestra," or chorus-ground. At the beginning of the action these steps are crowded by suppliants who have brought branches and chaplets of olive leaves and who lie in various attitudes of despair, OEDIPUS enters.

prologue

OEDIPUS. My children, generations of the living
In the line of Kadmos, nursed at his ancient hearth:
Why have you strewn yourselves before these altars
In supplication, with your boughs and garlands?
The breath of incense rises from the city
With a sound of prayer and lamentation.

                                                    Children,
I would not have you speak through messengers,

And therefore I have come myself to hear you—
I, Oedipus, who bear the famous name.

    (*To a* PRIEST.)

You, there, since you are eldest in the company,
Speak for them all, tell me what preys upon you,
Whether you come in dread, or crave some blessing:
Tell me, and never doubt that I will help you
In every way I can; I should be heartless
Were I not moved to find you suppliant here.

    PRIEST. Great Oedipus, O powerful King of Thebes!
You see how all the ages of our people
Cling to your altar steps: here are boys
Who can barely stand alone, and here are priests
By weight of age, as I am a priest of God,
And young men chosen from those yet unmarried;
As for the others, all that multitude,
They wait with olive chaplet in the squares,
At the two shrines of Pallas, and where Apollo
Speaks in the glowing embers.

                            Your own eyes
Must tell you: Thebes is in her extremity
And can not lift her head from the surge of death.
A rust consumes the buds and fruits of the earth;
The herds are sick; children die unborn,
And labor is vain. The god of plague and pyre
Raids like detestable lightning through the city,
And all the house of Kadmos is laid waste,
All emptied, and all darkened: Death alone
Battens upon the misery of Thebes.
You are not one of the immortal gods, we know;
Yet we have come to you to make our prayer
As to the man of all men best in adversity
And wisest in the ways of God. You saved us
From the Sphinx, that flinty singer, and the tribute
We paid to her so long; yet you were never
Better informed than we, nor could we teach you:
It was some god breathed in you to set us free.

Therefore, O mighty King, we turn to you:

Find us our safety, find us a remedy,
Whether by counsel of the gods or men.
A king of wisdom tested in the past
Can act in a time of troubles, and act well.
Noblest of men, restore
Life to your city! Think how all men call you
Liberator for your triumph long ago;
Ah, when your years of kingship are remembered,
Let them not say *We rose, but later fell*—
Keep the State from going down in the storm!
Once, years ago, with happy augury,
You brought us fortune; be the same again!
No man questions your power to rule the land:
But rule over men, not over a dead city!
Ships are only hulls, citadels are nothing,
When no life moves in the empty passageways.

    OEDIPUS. Poor children! You may be sure I know
All that you longed for in your coming here.
I know that you are deathly sick; and yet,
Sick as you are, not one is as sick as I.
Each of you suffers in himself alone
His anguish, not another's; but my spirit
Groans for the city, for myself, for you.

I was not sleeping, you are not waking me.
No, I have been in tears for a long while
And in my restless thought walked many ways.
In all my search, I found one helpful course,
And that I have taken: I have sent Creon,
Son of Menoikeus, brother of the Queen,
To Delphi, Apollo's place of revelation,
To learn there, if he can,
What act or pledge of mine may save the city.
I have counted the days, and now, this very day,
I am troubled, for he has overstayed his time.
What is he doing? He has been gone too long.
Yet whenever he comes back, I should do ill
To scant whatever hint the god may give.

    PRIEST. It is a timely promise. At this instant

They tell me Creon is here.
  OEDIPUS. O Lord Apollo!
May his news be fair as his face is radiant!
  PRIEST. It could not be otherwise: he is crowned with bay,
The chaplet is thick with berries.
  OEDIPUS. We shall soon know;
He is near enough to hear us now.
  (*Enter* CREON.)

                                O Prince:

Brother, son of Menoikeus:
What answer do you bring us from the god?
  CREON. It is favorable. I can tell you, great afflictions
Will turn out well, if they are taken well.
  OEDIPUS. What with the oracle? These vague words
Leave me still hanging between hope and fear.
  CREON. Is it your pleasure to hear me with all these
Gathered around us? I am prepared to speak,
But should we not go in?
  OEDIPUS. Let them all hear it.
It is for them I suffer, more than for myself.
  CREON. Then I will tell you what I heard at Delphi.
In plain words
The god commands us to expel from the land of Thebes
An old defilement that it seems we shelter.
It is a deathly thing, beyond expiation.
We must not let it feed upon us longer.
  OEDIPUS. What defilement? How shall we rid ourselves of it?
  CREON. By exile or death, blood for blood. It was
Murder that brought the plague-wind on the city.
  OEDIPUS. Murder of whom? Surely the god has named him?
  CREON. My lord: long ago Laïos was our king,
Before you came to govern us.
  OEDIPUS. I know;
I learned of him from others; I never saw him.
  CREON. He was murdered; and Apollo commands us now
To take revenge upon whoever killed him.
  OEDIPUS. Upon whom? Where are they? Where shall we find a clue
To solve that crime, after so many years?
  CREON. Here in this land, he said.

                                        If we make enquiry,
We may touch things that otherwise escape us.

OEDIPUS. Tell me: Was Laïos murdered in his house,
Or in the fields, or in some foreign country?

CREON. He said he planned to make a pilgrimage.
He did not come home again.

OEDIPUS. And was there no one,
No witness, no companion, to tell what happened?

CREON. They were all killed but one, and he got away
So frightened that he could remember one thing only.

OEDIPUS. What was that one thing? One may be the key
To everything, if we resolve to use it.

CREON. He said that a band of highwaymen attacked them,
Outnumbered them, and overwhelmed the King.

OEDIPUS. Strange, that a highwayman should be so daring—
Unless some faction here bribed him to do it.

CREON. We thought of that. But after Laïos' death
New troubles arose and we had no avenger.

OEDIPUS. What troubles could prevent your hunting down the
    killers?

CREON. The riddling sphinx's song
Made us deaf to all mysteries but her own.

OEDIPUS. Then once more I must bring what is dark to light.
It is most fitting that Apollo shows,
As you do, this compunction for the dead.
You shall see how I stand by you, as I should,
To avenge the city and the city's god,
And not as though it were for some distant friend,
But for my own sake, to be rid of evil.
Whoever killed King Laïos might—who knows?—
Decide at any moment to kill me as well.
By avenging the murdered king I protect myself.

Come, then, my children: leave the altar steps,
Lift up your olive boughs!
                        One of you go
And summon the people of Kadmos to gather here.
I will do all that I can; you may tell them that.
    (*Exit a* PAGE.)

So, with the help of God,
We shall be saved—or else indeed we are lost.
 PRIEST. Let us rise, children. It was for this we came,
And now the King has promised it himself.
Phoibos has sent us an oracle; may he descend
Himself to save us and drive out the plague.
 (*Exeunt* OEDIPUS *and* CREON *into the palace by the central door.
The* PRIEST *and the* SUPPLIANTS *disperse R and L. After a short
pause the* CHORUS *enters the orchestra.*)

páronos

 CHORUS. What is the god singing in his profound (STROPHE 1.)
Delphi of gold and shadow?
What oracle for Thebes, the sunwhipped city?

Fear unjoints me, the roots of my heart tremble.
Now I remember, O Healer, your power, and wonder:
Will you send doom like a sudden cloud, or weave it
Like nightfall of the past?

Ah no: be merciful, issue of holy sound:
Dearest to our expectancy: be tender!

           (ANTISTROPHE 1.)
Let me pray to Athenê, the immortal daughter of Zeus,
And to Artemis her sister
Who keeps her famous throne in the market ring,
And to Apollo, bowman at the far butts of heaven—

O gods, descend! Like three streams leap against
The fires of our grief, the fires of darkness;
Be swift to bring us rest!

As in the old time from the brilliant house
Of air you stepped to save us, come again!

Now our afflictions have no end,   (STROPHE 2.)
Now all our stricken host lies down
And no man fights off death with his mind:

The noble plowland bears no grain,
And groaning mothers can not bear—

See, how our lives like birds take wing,
Like sparks that fly when a fire soars,
To the shore of the god of evening.

The plague burns on, it is pitiless,   (ANTISTROPHE 2.)
Though pallid children laden with death
Lie unwept in the stony ways,

And old gray women by every path
Flock to the strand about the altars
There to strike their breasts and cry
Worship of Zeus in wailing prayers:
Be kind, God's golden child!

There are no swords in this attack by fire,   (STROPHE 3.)
No shields, but we are ringed with cries.

Send the besieger plunging from our homes
Into the vast sea-room of that Atlantic
Or into the waves that foam eastward of Thrace—

For the day ravages what the night spares—

Destroy our enemy, lord of the thunder!
Let him be riven by lightning from heaven!   (ANTISTROPHE 3.)

Phoibos Apollo, stretch the sun's bowstring,
That golden cord, until it sing for us,
Flashing arrows in heaven!
                                    Artemis, Huntress,
Race with flaring lights upon our mountains!
O scarlet god, O golden-banded brow,
O Theban Bacchos in a storm of Maenads,
    (Enter OEDIPUS, CHORUS.)
Whirl upon Death, that all the Undying hate!
Come with blinding cressets, come in joy!

SCENE ONE.

OEDIPUS. Is this your prayer? It may be answered. Come,
Listen to me, act as the crisis demands,
And you shall have relief from all these evils.

Until now I was a stranger to this tale,
As I had been a stranger to the crime.
Could I track down the murderer without a clue?
But now, friends,
As one who became a citizen after the murder,
I make this proclamation to all Thebans:
If any man knows by whose hand Laïos, son of Labdakos,
Met his death, I direct that man to tell me everything,
No matter what he fears for having so long withheld it.
Let it stand as promised that no further trouble
Will come to him, but he may leave the land in safety.

Moreover: If anyone knows the murderer to be foreign,
Let him not keep silent: he shall have his reward from me.
However, if he does conceal it; if any man
Fearing for his friend or for himself disobeys this edict,
Hear what I propose to do:

I solemnly forbid the people of this country,
Where power and throne are mine, ever to receive that man
Or speak to him, no matter who he is, or let him
Join in sacrifice, lustration, or in prayer.
I decree that he be driven from every house,
Being, as he is, corruption itself to us: the Delphic
Voice of Zeus has pronounced this revelation.
Thus I associate myself with the oracle
And take the side of the murdered king.

As for the criminal, I pray to God—
Whether it be a lurking thief, or one of a number—
I pray that that man's life be consumed in evil and wretchedness.
And as for me, this curse applies no less
If it should turn out that the culprit is my guest here,
Sharing my hearth.
               You have heard the penalty.
I lay it on you now to attend to this
For my sake, for Apollo's, for the sick
Sterile city that heaven has abandoned.
Suppose the oracle had given you no command:
Should this defilement go uncleansed for ever?

You should have found the murderer: your king,
A noble king, had been destroyed!
                                        Now I,
Having the power that he held before me,
Having his bed, begetting children there
Upon his wife, as he would have, had he lived—
Their son would have been my children's brother,
If Laïos had had luck in fatherhood!
(But surely ill luck rushed upon his reign)—
I say I take the son's part, just as though
I were his son, to press the fight for him
And see it won! I'll find the hand that brought
Death to Labdakos' and Polydoros' child,
Heir of Kadmos' and Agenor's line.
And as for those who fail me,
May the gods deny them the fruit of the earth,
Fruit of the womb, and may they rot utterly!
Let them be wretched as we are wretched, and worse!

For you, for loyal Thebans, and for all
Who find my actions right, I pray the favor
Of justice, and of all the immortal gods.
    CHORUS. Since I am under oath, my lord, I swear
I did not do the murder, I can not name
The murderer. Might not the oracle
That has ordained the search tell where to find him?
    OEDIPUS. An honest question. But no man in the world
Can make the gods do more than the gods will.
    CHORUS. There is one last expedient—
    OEDIPUS. Tell me what it is.
Though it seem slight, you must not hold it back.
    CHORUS. A lord clairvoyant to the lord Apollo,
As we all know, is the skilled Teiresias.
One might learn much about this from him, Oedipus.
    OEDIPUS. I am not wasting time:
Creon spoke of this, and I have sent for him—
Twice, in fact: it is strange that he is not here.
    CHORUS. The other matter—that old report—seems useless.
    OEDIPUS. Tell me. I am interested in all reports.

CHORUS. The King was said to have been killed by highwaymen.

OEDIPUS. I know. But we have no witness to that.

CHORUS. If the killer can feel a particle of dread,
Your curse will bring him out of hiding!

OEDIPUS. No.
The man who dared that act will fear no curse.

(*Enter the blind seer* TEIRESIAS, *led by a* PAGE.)

CHORUS. But there is one man who may detect the criminal.
This is Teiresias, this is the holy prophet
In whom, alone of all men, truth was born.

OEDIPUS. Teiresias: seer: student of mysteries,
Of all that's taught and that no man tells,
Secrets of Heaven and secrets of the earth:
Blind though you are, you know the city lies
Sick with plague; and from this plague, my lord,
We find that you alone can guard or save us.

Possibly you did not hear the messengers?
Apollo, when we sent to him,
Sent us back word that this great pestilence
Would lift, but only if we established clearly
The identity of those who murdered Laïos.
They must be killed or exiled.

                          Can you use
Birdflight or any art of divination
To purify yourself, and Thebes, and me
From this contagion? We are in your hands.
There is no fairer duty
Than that of helping others in distress.

TEIRESIAS. How dreadful knowledge of the truth can be
When there's no help in truth! I knew this well,
But did not act on it: else I should not have come.

OEDIPUS. What is troubling you? Why are your eyes so cold?

TEIRESIAS. Let me go home. Bear your own fate, and I'll
Bear mine. It is better so: trust what I say.

OEDIPUS. What you say is ungracious and unhelpful
To your native country. Do not refuse to speak.

TEIRESIAS. When it comes to speech, your own is neither temperate
Nor opportune. I wish to be more prudent.

OEDIPUS. In God's name, we all beg you—

TEIRESIAS. You are all ignorant.

No; I will never tell you what I know.

Now it is my misery; then, it would be yours.

OEDIPUS. What! You do know something, and will not tell us?
You would betray us all and wreck the State?

TEIRESIAS. I do not intend to torture myself, or you.
Why persist in asking? You will not persuade me.

OEDIPUS. What a wicked old man you are! You'd try a stone's
Patience! Out with it! Have you no feeling at all?

TEIRESIAS. You call me unfeeling. If you could only see
The nature of your own feelings . . .

OEDIPUS. Why,
Who would not feel as I do? Who could endure
Your arrogance toward the city?

TEIRESIAS. What does it matter!
Whether I speak or not, it is bound to come.

OEDIPUS. Then, if "it" is bound to come, you are bound to tell me.

TEIRESIAS. No, I will not go on. Rage as you please.

OEDIPUS. Rage? Why not!

                                And I'll tell you what I think:
You planned it, you had it done, you all but
Killed him with your own hands: if you had eyes,
I'd say the crime was yours, and yours alone.

TEIRESIAS. So? I charge you, then,
Abide by the proclamation you have made:
From this day forth
Never speak again to these men or to me:
You yourself are the pollution of this country.

OEDIPUS. You dare say that! Can you possibly think you have
Some way of going free, after such insolence?

TEIRESIAS. I have gone free. It is the truth sustains me.

OEDIPUS. Who taught you shamelessness? It was not your craft.

TEIRESIAS. You did. You made me speak. I did not want to.

OEDIPUS. Speak what? Let me hear it again more clearly.

TEIRESIAS. Was it not clear before? Are you tempting me?

OEDIPUS. I did not understand it. Say it again.

TEIRESIAS. I say that you are the murderer whom you seek.

OEDIPUS. Now twice you have spat out infamy. You'll pay for it!

TEIRESIAS. Would you care for more? Do you wish to be really
angry?

OEDIPUS. Say what you will. Whatever you say is worthless.

TEIRESIAS. I say that you live in hideous love with her
Who is nearest you in blood. You are blind to evil.

OEDIPUS. It seems you can go on mouthing like this for ever.

TEIRESIAS. I can, if there is power in truth.

OEDIPUS. There is:
But not for you, not for you,
You sightless, witless, senseless, mad old man!

TEIRESIAS. You are the madman. There is no one here
Who will not curse you soon, as you curse me.

OEDIPUS. You child of endless night! You can not hurt me
Or any other man who sees the sun.

TEIRESIAS. True: it is not from me your fate will come.
That lies within Apollo's competence,
As it is his concern.

OEDIPUS. Tell me:
Are you speaking for Creon, or for yourself?

TEIRESIAS. Creon is no threat. You weave your own doom.

OEDIPUS. Wealth, power, craft of statesmanship!
Kingly position, everything admired!
What savage envy is stored up against these,
If Creon, whom I trusted, Creon my friend,
For this great office which the city once
Put in my hands unsought—if for this power
Creon desires in secret to destroy me!
He has bought this decrepit fortune-teller, this
Collector of dirty pennies, this prophet fraud—
Why, he is no more clairvoyant than I am!

                              Tell us:
Has your mystic mummery ever approached the truth?
When that hellcat the Sphinx was performing here,
What help were you to these people?
Her magic was not for the first man who came along:
It demanded a real exorcist. Your birds—
What good were they? or the gods, for the matter of that?
But I came by,
Oedipus, the simple man, who knows nothing—

I thought it out for myself, no birds helped me!
And this is the man you think you can destroy,
That you may be close to Creon when he's king!
Well, you and your friend Creon, it seems to me,
Will suffer most. If you were not an old man,
You would have paid already for your plot.

CHORUS. We can not see that his words or yours
Have been spoken except in anger, Oedipus,
And of anger we have no need. How can God's will
Be accomplished best? That is what most concerns us.

TEIRESIAS. You are a king. But where argument's concerned
I am your man, as much a king as you.
I am not your servant, but Apollo's.
I have no need of Creon to speak for me.

Listen to me. You mock my blindness, do you?
But I say that you, with both your eyes, are blind:
You can not see the wretchedness of your life,
Nor in whose house you live, no, nor with whom.
Who are your father and mother? Can you tell me?
You do not even know the blind wrongs
That you have done them, on earth and in the world below.
But the double lash of your parents' curse will whip you
Out of this land some day, with only night
Upon your precious eyes.
Your cries then—where will they not be heard?
What fastness of Kithairon will not echo them?

And that bridal-descant of yours—you'll know it then,
The song they sang when you came here to Thebes
And found your misguided berthing.
All this, and more, that you can not guess at now,
Will bring you to yourself among your children.
Be angry, then. Curse Creon. Curse my words.
I tell you, no man that walks upon the earth
Shall be rooted out more horribly than you.

OEDIPUS. Am I to bear this from him?—Damnation
Take you! Out of this place! Out of my sight!

TEIRESIAS. I would not have come at all if you had not asked me.

OEDIPUS. Could I have told that you'd talk nonsense, that

You'd come here to make a fool of yourself, and of me?
　　TEIRESIAS. A fool? Your parents thought me sane enough.
　　OEDIPUS. My parents again!—Wait: who were my parents?
　　TEIRESIAS. This day will give you a father, and break your heart.
　　OEDIPUS. Your infantile riddles! Your damned abracadabra!
　　TEIRESIAS. You were a great man once at solving riddles.
　　OEDIPUS. Mock me with that if you like; you will find it true.
　　TEIRESIAS. It was true enough. It brought about your ruin.
　　OEDIPUS. But if it saved this town?

　　　　　　　(*To the* PAGE.)
　　TEIRESIAS. Boy, give me your hand.
　　OEDIPUS. Yes, boy; lead him away.

　　　　　　　　　　　—While you are here
We can do nothing. Go; leave us in peace.
　　TEIRESIAS. I will go when I have said what I have to say.
How can you hurt me? And I tell you again:
The man you have been looking for all this time,
The damned man, the murderer of Laïos,
That man is in Thebes. To your mind he is foreign-born,
But it will soon be shown that he is a Theban,
A revelation that will fail to please.

　　　　　　　　　　　A blind man,
Who has his eyes now; a penniless man, who is rich now;
And he will go tapping the strange earth with his staff.
To the children with whom he lives now he will be
Brother and father—the very same; to her
Who bore him, son and husband—the very same
Who came to his father's bed, wet with his father's blood.
Enough. Go think that over.
If later you find error in what I have said,
You may say that I have no skill in prophecy.
　　　　　(*Exit* TEIRESIAS, *led by his* PAGE. OEDIPUS *goes into the palace.*)

ODE ONE

　　　CHORUS. The Delphic stone of prophecies　　　(STROPHE 1.)
　Remembers ancient regicide
　And a still bloody hand.

That killer's hour of flight has come.
He must be stronger than riderless
Coursers of untiring wind,
For the son of Zeus armed with his father's thunder
Leaps in lightning after him;
And the Furies follow him, the sad Furies.

Holy Parnassos' peak of snow   (ANTISTROPHE 1.)
Flashes and blinds that secret man,
That all shall hunt him down:
Though he may roam the forest shade
Like a bull gone wild from pasture
To rage through glooms of stone.
Doom comes down on him; flight will not avail him;
For the world's heart calls him desolate,
And the immortal Furies follow, for ever follow.

But now a wilder thing is heard   (STROPHE 2.)
From the old man skilled at hearing Fate in the wingbeat of a bird.
Bewildered as a blown bird, my soul hovers and can not find
Foothold in this debate, or any reason or rest of mind.
But no man ever brought—none can bring
Proof of strife between Thebes' royal house,
Labdakos' line, and the son of Polybos;
And never until now has any man brought word
Of Laïos' dark death staining Oedipus the King.

Divine Zeus and Apollo hold   (ANTISTROPHE 2.)
Perfect intelligence alone of all tales ever told;
And well though this diviner works, he works in his own night;
No man can judge that rough unknown or trust in second sight,
For wisdom changes hands among the wise.
Shall I believe my great lord criminal
At a raging word that a blind old man let fall?
I saw him, when the carrion woman faced him of old,
Prove his heroic mind! These evil words are lies.

SCENE TWO.

CREON. Men of Thebes:
I am told that heavy accusations

Have been brought against me by King Oedipus.

I am not the kind of man to bear this tamely.

If in these present difficulties
He holds me accountable for any harm to him
Through anything I have said or done—why, then,
I do not value life in this dishonor.
It is not as though this rumor touched upon
Some private indiscretion. The matter is grave.
The fact is that I am being called disloyal
To the State, to my fellow citizens, to my friends.
   CHORUS. He may have spoken in anger, not from his mind.
   CREON. But did you not hear him say I was the one
Who seduced the old prophet into lying?
   CHORUS. The thing was said; I do not know how seriously.
   CREON. But you were watching him! Were his eyes steady?
Did he look like a man in his right mind?
   CHORUS. I do not know.
I can not judge the behavior of great men.
But here is the King himself.
     (*Enter* OEDIPUS.)
   OEDIPUS. So you dared come back.
Why? How brazen of you to come to my house.
You murderer!
         Do you think I do not know
That you plotted to kill me, plotted to steal my throne?
Tell me, in God's name: am I coward, a fool,
That you should dream you could accomplish this?
A fool who could not see your slippery game?
A coward, not to fight back when I saw it?
You are the fool, Creon, are you not? hoping
Without support or friends to get a throne?
Thrones may be won or bought: you could do neither.
   CREON. Now listen to me. You have talked; let me talk, too.
You can not judge unless you know the facts.
   OEDIPUS. You speak well: there is one fact; but I find it hard
To learn from the deadliest enemy I have.
   CREON. That above all I must dispute with you.
   OEDIPUS. That above all I will not hear you deny.

CREON. If you think there is anything good in being stubborn
Against all reason, then I say you are wrong.

OEDIPUS. If you think a man can sin against his own kind
And not be punished for it, I say you are mad.

CREON. I agree. But tell me: what have I done to you?

OEDIPUS. You advised me to send for that wizard, did you not?

CREON. I did. I should do it again.

OEDIPUS. Very well. Now tell me:
How long has it been since Laïos—

CREON. What of Laïos?

OEDIPUS. Since he vanished in that onset by the road?

CREON. It was long ago, a long time.

OEDIPUS. And this prophet,
Was he practicing here then?

CREON. He was; and with honor, as now.

OEDIPUS. Did he speak of me at that time?

CREON. He never did;
At least, not when I was present.

OEDIPUS. But . . . the enquiry?
I suppose you held one?

CREON. We did, but we learned nothing.

OEDIPUS. Why did the prophet not speak against me then?

CREON. I do not know; and I am the kind of man
Who holds his tongue when he has no facts to go on.

OEDIPUS. There's one fact that you know, and you could tell it.

CREON. What fact is that? If I know it, you shall have it.

OEDIPUS. If he were not involved with you, he could not say
That it was I who murdered Laïos.

CREON. If he says that, you are the one that knows it!—
But now it is my turn to question you.

OEDIPUS. Put your questions. I am no murderer.

CREON. First, then: You married my sister?

OEDIPUS. I married your sister.

CREON. And you rule the kingdom equally with her?

OEDIPUS. Everything that she wants she has from me.

CREON. And I am the third, equal to both of you?

OEDIPUS. That is why I call you a bad friend.

CREON. No. Reason it out, as I have done.
Think of this first: Would any sane man prefer

Power, with all a king's anxieties,
To that same power and the grace of sleep?
Certainly not I.
I have never longed for the king's power—only his rights.
Would any wise man differ from me in this?
As matters stand, I have my way in everything
With your consent, and no responsibilities.
If I were king, I should be a slave to policy.
How could I desire a scepter more
Than what is now mine—untroubled influence?
No, I have not gone mad; I need no honors,
Except those with the perquisites I have now.
I am welcome everywhere; every man salutes me,
And those who want your favor seek my ear,
Since I know how to manage what they ask.
Should I exchange this ease for that anxiety?
Besides, no sober mind is treasonable.
I hate anarchy
And never would deal with any man who likes it.

Test what I have said. Go to the priestess
At Delphi, ask if I quoted her correctly.
And as for this other thing: if I am found
Guilty of treason with Teiresias,
Then sentence me to death! You have my word
It is a sentence I should cast my vote for—
But not without evidence!
                        You do wrong
When you take good men for bad, bad men for good.
A true friend thrown aside—why, life itself
Is not more precious!
                    In time you will know this well:
For time, and time alone, will show the just man,
Though scoundrels are discovered in a day.
    CHORUS. This is well said, and a prudent man would ponder it.
Judgments too quickly formed are dangerous.
    OEDIPUS. But is he not quick in his duplicity?
And shall I not be quick to parry him?
Would you have me stand still, hold my peace, and let

This man win everything, through my inaction?

    CREON. And you want—what is it, then? To banish me?

    OEDIPUS. No, not exile. It is your death I want,

So that all the world may see what treason means.

    CREON. You will persist, then? You will not believe me?

    OEDIPUS. How can I believe you?

    CREON. Then you are a fool.

    OEDIPUS. To save myself?

    CREON. In justice, think of me.

    OEDIPUS. You are evil incarnate.

    CREON. But suppose that you are wrong?

    OEDIPUS. Still I must rule.

    CREON. But not if you rule badly.

    OEDIPUS. O city, city!

    CREON. It is my city, too!

    CHORUS. Now, my lords, be still. I see the Queen,

Iocastê, coming from her palace chambers;

And it is time she came, for the sake of you both.

This dreadful quarrel can be resolved through her.

    (*Enter* IOCASTÊ.)

    IOCASTÊ. Poor foolish men, what wicked din is this?

With Thebes sick to death, is it not shameful

That you should rake some private quarrel up?

    (*To* OEDIPUS.)

Come into the house.

                  —And you, Creon, go now:

Let us have no more of this tumult over nothing.

    CREON. Nothing? No, sister: what your husband plans for me

Is one of two great evils: exile or death.

    OEDIPUS. He is right.

               Why, woman I have caught him squarely

Plotting against my life.

    CREON. No! Let me die

Accurst if ever I have wished you harm!

    IOCASTÊ. Ah, believe it, Oedipus!

In the name of the gods, respect this oath of his

For my sake, for the sake of these people here!

    CHORUS. Open your mind to her, my lord. Be ruled by her, I

beg you!

                                (STROPHE 1.)

OEDIPUS. What would you have me do?

CHORUS. Respect Creon's word. He has never spoken like a fool,
And now he has sworn an oath.

OEDIPUS. You know what you ask?

CHORUS. I do.

OEDIPUS. Speak on, then.

CHORUS. A friend so sworn should not be baited so,
In blind malice, and without final proof.

OEDIPUS. You are aware, I hope, that what you say
Means death for me, or exile at the least.

CHORUS. No, I swear by Helios, first in Heaven!   (STROPHE 2.)
May I die friendless and accurst,
The worst of deaths, if ever I meant that!
   It is the withering fields
     That hurt my sick heart:
  Must we bear all these ills,
    And now your bad blood as well?

OEDIPUS. Then let him go. And let me die, if I must,
Or be driven by him in shame from the land of Thebes.
It is your unhappiness, and not his talk,
That touches me.
         As for him—
Wherever he is, I will hate him as long as I live.

CREON. Ugly in yielding, as you were ugly in rage!
Natures like yours chiefly torment themselves.

OEDIPUS. Can you not go? Can you not leave me?

CREON. I can.
You do not know me; but the city knows me,
And in its eyes I am just, if not in yours.

  (*Exit* CREON.)

CHORUS. Lady Iocastê, did you not ask the King to go to his
    chambers?   (ANTISTROPHE 1.)

IOCASTÊ. First tell me what has happened.

CHORUS. There was suspicion without evidence: yet it rankled
As even false charges will

IOCASTÊ. On both sides?

CHORUS. On both.

IOCASTÊ. But what was said?

CHORUS. Oh let it rest, let it be done with!
Have you not suffered enough?
OEDIPUS. You see to what your decency has brought you:
You have made difficulties where my heart saw none.
CHORUS. Oedipus, it is not once only I have told you—

(ANTISTROPHE 2.)

You must know I should count myself unwise
To the point of madness, should I now forsake you—
    You, under whose hand,
      In the storm of another time,
    Our dear land sailed out free.
      But now stand fast at the helm!
IOCASTÊ. In God's name, Opedius, inform your wife as well:
Why are you so set in this hard anger?
OEDIPUS. I will tell you, for none of these men deserves
My confidence as you do. It is Creon's work,
His treachery, his plotting against me.
IOCASTÊ. Go on, if you can make this clear to me.
OEDIPUS. He charges me with the murder of Laïos.
IOCASTÊ. Has he some knowledge? Or does he speak from hearsay?
OEDIPUS. He would not commit himself to such a charge,
But he has brought in that damnable soothsayer
To tell his story.
IOCASTÊ. Set your mind at rest.
If it is a question of soothsayers, I tell you
That you will find no man whose craft gives knowledge
Of the unknowable.

Here is my proof:

An oracle was reported to Laïos once
(I will not say from Phoibos himself, but from
His appointed ministers, at any rate)
That his doom would be death at the hands of his own son—
His son, born of his flesh and of mine!
Now, you remember the story: Laïos was killed
By marauding strangers where three highways meet;
But his child had not been three days in this world
Before the King had pierced the baby's ankles
And had him left to die on a lonely mountain.

Thus, Apollo never caused that child
To kill his father, and it was not Laïos' fate
To die at the hands of his son, as he had feared.
This is what prophets and prophecies are worth!
Have no dread of them.
                     It is God himself
Who can show us what he wills, in his own way.

    OEDIPUS. How strange a shadowy memory crossed my mind,
Just now while you were speaking; it chilled my heart.

    IOCASTÊ. What do you mean? What memory do you speak of?

    OEDIPUS. If I understand you, Laïos was killed
At a place where three roads meet.

    IOCASTÊ. So it was said;
We have no later story.

    OEDIPUS. Where did it happen?

    IOCASTÊ. Phokis, it is called: at a place where the Theban Way
Divides into the roads toward Delphi and Daulia.

    OEDIPUS. When?

    IOCASTÊ. We had the news not long before you came
And proved the right to your succession here.

    OEDIPUS. Ah, what net has God been weaving for me?

    IOCASTÊ. Oedipus! Why does this trouble you?

    OEDIPUS. Do not ask me yet.
First, tell me how Laïos looked, and tell me
How old he was.

    IOCASTÊ. He was tall, his hair just touched
With white; his form was not unlike your own.

    OEDIPUS. I think that I myself may be accurst
By my own ignorant edict.

    IOCASTÊ. You speak strangely.
It makes me tremble to look at you, my king.

    OEDIPUS. I am not sure that the blind man can not see.
But I should know better if you were to tell me—

    IOCASTÊ. Anything—though I dread to hear you ask it.

    OEDIPUS. Was the King lightly escorted, or did he ride
With a large company, as a ruler should?

    IOCASTÊ. There were five men with him in all: one was a herald;
And a single chariot, which he was driving.

    OEDIPUS. Alas, that makes it plain enough!

                                                    But who—
Who told you how it happened?
    IOCASTÊ. A household servant.
The only one to escape.
    OEDIPUS. And is he still
A servant of ours?
    IOCASTÊ. No; for when he came back at last
And found you enthroned in the place of the dead king,
He came to me, touched my hand with his, and begged
That I would send him away to the frontier district
Where only the shepherds go—
As far away from the city as I could send him.
I granted his prayer; for although the man was a slave,
He had earned more than this favor at my hands.
    OEDIPUS. Can he be called back quickly?
    IOCASTÊ. Easily.
But why?
    OEDIPUS. I have taken too much upon myself
Without enquiry; therefore I wish to consult him.
    IOCASTÊ. Then he shall come.

                But am I not one also
To whom you might confide these fears of yours?
    OEDIPUS. That is your right; it will not be denied you,
Now least of all; for I have reached a pitch
Of wild foreboding. Is there anyone
To whom I should sooner speak?

Polybos of Corinth is my father.
My mother is a Dorian: Meropê.
I grew up chief among the men of Corinth
Until a strange thing happened—
Not worth my passion, it may be, but strange.

At a feast, a drunken man maundering in his cups
Cries out that I am not my father's son!

I contained myself that night, though I felt anger
And a sinking heart. The next day I visited
My father and mother, and questioned them. They stormed,
Calling it all the slanderous rant of a fool;

And this relieved me. Yet the suspicion
Remained always aching in my mind;
I knew there was talk; I could not rest;
And finally, saying nothing to my parents,
I went to the shrine at Delphi.

The god dismissed my question without reply;
He spoke of other things.
                              Some were clear,
Full of wretchedness, dreadful, unbearable:
As, that I should lie with my own mother, breed
Children from whom all men would turn their eyes;
And that I should be my father's murderer.

I heard all this, and fled. And from that day
Corinth to me was only in the stars
Descending in that quartet of the sky,
As I wandered farther and farther on my way
To a land where I should never see the evil
Sung by the oracle. And I came to this country
Where, so you say, King Laïos was killed.

I will tell you all that happened there, my lady.

There were three highways
Coming together at a place I passed;
And there a herald came towards me, and a chariot
Drawn by horses, with a man such as you describe
Seated in it. The groom leading the horses
Forced me off the road at his lord's command;
But as this charioteer lurched over towards me
I struck him in my rage. The old man saw me
And brought his double goad down upon my head
As I came abreast.
                          He was paid back, and more!
Swinging my club in this right hand I knocked him
Out of his car, and he rolled on the ground.
                                          I killed him.

I killed them all.
Now if that stranger and Laïos were—kin,
Where is a man more miserable than I?

More hated by the gods? Citizen and alien alike
Must never shelter me or speak to me—
I must be shunned by all.
                              And I myself.
Pronounced this malediction upon myself!
Think of it: I have touched you with these hands,
These hands that killed your husband. What defilement!

Am I all evil, then? It must be so,
Since I must flee from Thebes, yet never again
See my own countrymen, my own country,
For fear of joining my mother in marriage
And killing Polybos, my father.
                                    Ah,
If I was created so, born to this fate,
Who could deny the savagery of God?

O holy majesty of heavenly powers!
May I never see that day! Never!
Rather let me vanish from the race of men
Than know the abomination destined me!
    CHORUS. We too, my lord, have felt dismay at this.
But there is hope: you have yet to hear the shepherd.
    OEDIPUS. Indeed, I fear no other hope is left me.
    IOCASTÊ. What do you hope from him when he comes?
    OEDIPUS. This much:
If his account of the murder tallies with yours,
Then I am cleared.
    IOCASTÊ. What was it that I said
Of such importance?
    OEDIPUS. Why, "marauders," you said,
Killed the King, according to this man's story.
If he maintains that still, if there were several,
Clearly the guilt is not mine: I was alone
But if he says one man, singlehanded, did it,
Then the evidence all points to me.
    IOCASTÊ. You may be sure that he said there were several;
And can he call back that story now? He can not.
The whole city heard it as plainly as I.

But suppose he alters some detail of it:
He can not ever show that Laïos' death
Fulfilled the oracle: for Apollo said
My child was doomed to kill him; and my child—
Poor baby!—it was my child that died first.
No. From now on, where oracles are concerned,
I would not waste a second thought on any.
    OEDIPUS. You may be right.

                            But come: let someone go
For the shepherd at once. This matter must be settled.
    IOCASTÊ. I will send for him.
I would not wish to cross you in anything,
And surely not in this.—Let us go in.
    (*Exeunt into the palace.*)

ode two

    CHORUS. Let me be reverent in the ways of right,   (STROPHE 1.)
Lowly the paths I journey on;
Let all my words and actions keep
The laws of the pure universe
From highest Heaven handed down.
For Heaven is their bright nurse,
Those generations of the realms of light;
Ah, never of mortal kind were they begot,
Nor are they slaves of memory, lost in sleep:
Their Father is greater than Time, and ages not.

The tyrant is a child of Pride   (ANTISTROPHE 1.)
Who drinks from his great sickening cup
Recklessness and vanity,
Until from his high crest headlong
He plummets to the dust of hope.
That strong man is not strong.
But let no fair ambition be denied;
May God protect the wrestler for the State
In government, in comely policy,
Who will fear God, and on His ordinance wait.

Haughtiness and the high hand of disdain   (STROPHE 2.)
Tempt and outrage God's holy law;
And any mortal who dares hold
No immortal Power in awe
Will be caught up in a net of pain:
The price for which his levity is sold.
Let each man take due earnings, then,
And keep his hands from holy things,
And from blasphemy stand apart—
Else the crackling blast of heaven
Blows on his head, and on his desperate heart;
Though fools will honor impious men,
In their cities no tragic poet sings.

Shall we lose faith in Delphi's obscurities,   (ANTISTROPHE 2.)
We who have heard the world's core
Discredited, and the sacred wood
Of Zeus at Elis praised no more?
The deeds and the strange prophecies
Must make a pattern yet to be understood.
Zeus, if indeed you are lord of all,
Throned in light over night and day,
Mirror this in your endless mind:
Our masters call the oracle
Words on the wind, and the Delphic vision blind!
Their hearts no longer know Apollo,
And reverence for the gods has died away.

SCENE THREE.

(*Enter* IOCASTÊ.)

IOCASTÊ. Prince of Thebes, it has occurred to me
To visit the altars of the gods, bearing
These branches as a suppliant, and this incense.
Our King is not himself: his noble soul
Is overwrought with fantasies of dread,
Else he would consider
The new prophecies in the light of the old.
He will listen to any voice that speaks disaster,
And my advice goes for nothing.

(*She approaches the altar, R.*)

To you, then, Apollo,
Lycean lord, since you are nearest, I turn in prayer.
Receive these offerings, and grant us deliverance
From defilement. Our hearts are heavy with fear
When we see our leader distracted, as helpless sailors
Are terrified by the confusion of their helmsman.

(*Enter* MESSENGER.)

MESSENGER. Friends, no doubt you can direct me:
Where shall I find the house of Oedipus,
Or, better still where is the King himself?

CHORUS. It is this very place, stranger; he is inside.
This is his wife and mother of his children.

MESSENGER. I wish her happiness in a happy house,
Blest in all the fulfillment of her marriage.

IOCASTÊ. I wish as much for you: your courtesy
Deserves a like good fortune. But now, tell me:
Why have you come? What have you to say to us?

MESSENGER. Good news, my lady, for your house and your husband.

IOCASTÊ. What news? Who sent you here?

MESSENGER. I am from Corinth.
The news I bring ought to mean joy for you,
Though it may be you will find some grief in it.

IOCASTÊ. What is it? How can it touch us in both ways?

MESSENGER. The people of Corinth, they say,
Intend to call Oedipus to be their king.

IOCASTÊ. But old Polybos—is he not reigning still?

MESSENGER. No. Death holds him in his sepulchre.

IOCASTÊ. What are you saying? Polybos is dead?

MESSENGER. If I am not telling the truth, may I die myself.

(*To a* MAIDSERVANT.)

IOCASTÊ. Go in, go quickly; tell this to your master.
O riddlers of God's will, where are you now!
This was the man whom Oedipus, long ago,
Feared so, fled so, in dread of destroying him—
But it was another fate by which he died.

(*Enter* OEDIPUS, CHORUS.)

OEDIPUS. Dearest Iocastê, why have you sent for me?

IOCASTÊ. Listen to what this man says, and then tell me

What has become of the solemn prophecies.

    OEDIPUS. Who is this man? What is his news for me?

    IOCASTÊ. He has come from Corinth to announce your father's
      death!

    OEDIPUS. Is it true, stranger? Tell me in your own words.

    MESSENGER. I can say it more clearly: the King is dead.

    OEDIPUS. Was it by treason? Or by an attack of illness?

    MESSENGER. A little thing brings old men to their rest.

    OEDIPUS. It was sickness, then?

    MESSENGER. Yes, and his many years.

    OEDIPUS. Ah!

Why should a man respect the Pythian hearth, or
Give heed to the birds that jangle above his head?
They prophesied that I should kill Polybos,
Kill my own father; but he is dead and buried,
And I am here—I never touched him, never,
Unless he died of grief for my departure,
And thus, in a sense, through me. No. Polybos
Has packed the oracles off with him underground.
They are empty words.

    IOCASTÊ. Had I not told you so?

    OEDIPUS. You had; it was my faint heart that betrayed me.

    IOCASTÊ. From now on never think of those things again.

    OEDIPUS. And yet—must I not fear my mother's bed?

    IOCASTÊ. Why should anyone in this world be afraid,
Since Fate rules us and nothing can be foreseen?
A man should live only for the present day.
Have no more fear of sleeping with your mother:
How many men, in dreams, have lain with their mothers!
No reasonable man is troubled by such things.

    OEDIPUS. That is true; only—
If only my mother were not still alive!
But she is alive. I can not help my dread.

    IOCASTÊ. Yet this news of your father's death is wonderful.

    OEDIPUS. Wonderful. But I fear the living woman.

    MESSENGER. Tell me, who is this woman that you fear?

    OEDIPUS. It is Meropê, man; the wife of King Polybos.

    MESSENGER. Meropê? Why should you be afraid of her?

    OEDIPUS. An oracle of the gods, a dreadful saying.

MESSENGER. Can you tell me about it or are you sworn to silence?

OEDIPUS. I can tell you, and I will.

Apollo said through his prophet that I was the man
Who should marry his own mother, shed his father's blood
With his own hands. And so, for all these years
I have kept clear of Corinth, and no harm has come—
Though it would have been sweet to see my parents again.

MESSENGER. And is this the fear that drove you out of Corinth?

OEDIPUS. Would you have me kill my father?

MESSENGER. As for that
You must be reassured by the news I gave you.

OEDIPUS. If you could reassure me, I would reward you.

MESSENGER. I had that in mind, I will confess: I thought
I could count on you when you returned to Corinth.

OEDIPUS. No: I will never go near my parents again.

MESSENGER. Ah, son, you still do not know what you are doing—

OEDIPUS. What do you mean? In the name of God tell me!

MESSENGER. —If these are your reasons for not going home.

OEDIPUS. I tell you, I fear the oracle may come true.

MESSENGER. And guilt come upon you through your parents?

OEDIPUS. That is the dread that is always in my heart.

MESSENGER. Can you not see that all your fears are groundless?

OEDIPUS. How can you say that? They are my parents, surely?

MESSENGER. Polybos was not your father.

OEDIPUS. Not my father?

MESSENGER. No more your father than the man speaking to you.

OEDIPUS. But you are nothing to me!

MESSENGER. Neither was he.

OEDIPUS. Then why did he call me son?

MESSENGER. I will tell you:
Long ago he had you from my hands, as a gift.

OEDIPUS. Then how could he love me so, if I was not his?

MESSENGER. He had no children, and his heart turned to you.

OEDIPUS. What of you? Did you buy me? Did you find me by
chance?

MESSENGER. I came upon you in the crooked pass of Kithairon.

OEDIPUS. And what were you doing there?

MESSENGER. Tending my flocks.

OEDIPUS. A wandering shepherd?

MESSENGER. But your savior, son, that day.

OEDIPUS. From what did you save me?

MESSENGER. Your ankles should tell you that.

OEDIPUS. Ah, stranger, why do you speak of that childhood pain?

MESSENGER. I cut the bonds that tied your ankles together.

OEDIPUS. I have had the mark as long as I can remember.

MESSENGER. That was why you were given the name you bear.

OEDIPUS. God! Was it my father or my mother who did it? Tell
me!

MESSENGER. I do not know. The man who gave you to me
Can tell you better than I.

OEDIPUS. It was not you that found me, but another?

MESSENGER. It was another shepherd gave you to me.

OEDIPUS. Who was he? Can you tell me who he was?

MESSENGER. I think he was said to be one of Laïos' people.

OEDIPUS. You mean the Laïos who was king here four years ago?

MESSENGER. Yes; King Laoïs; and the man was one of the herds-
men.

OEDIPUS. Is he still alive? Can I see him?

MESSENGER. These men here
Know best about such things.

OEDIPUS. Does anyone here
Know this shepherd that he is talking about?
Have you see him in the fields, or in the town?
If you have, tell me. It is time things were made plain.

CHORUS. I think the man he means is that same shepherd
You have already asked to see. Iocastê perhaps
Could tell you something.

OEDIPUS. Do you know anything
About him, Lady? Is he the man we have summoned?
Is that the man this shepherd means?

IOCASTÊ. Why think of him?
Forget this herdsman. Forget it all.
This talk is a waste of time.

OEDIPUS. How can you say that,
When the clues to my true birth are in my hands?

IOCASTÊ. For God's love, let us have no more questioning!
Is your life nothing to you?
My own is pain enough for me to bear.

OEDIPUS. You need not worry. Suppose my mother a slave,
And born of slaves: no baseness can touch you.

IOCASTÊ. Listen to me, I beg you: do not do this thing!

OEDIPUS. I will not listen; the truth must be made known.

IOCASTÊ. Everything that I say is for your own good!

OEDIPUS. My own good
Snaps my patience, then; I want none of it.

IOCASTÊ. You are fatally wrong! May you never learn who you
are!

OEDIPUS. Go, one of you, and bring the shepherd here.
Let us leave this woman to brag of her royal name.

IOCASTÊ. Ah, miserable!
That is the only word I have for you now.
That is the only word I can ever have.

(*Exit into the palace.*)

CHORUS. Why has she left us, Oedipus? Why has she gone
In such a passion of sorrow? I fear this silence:
Something dreadful may come of it.

OEDIPUS. Let it come!
However base my birth, I must know about it.
The Queen, like a woman, is perhaps ashamed
To think of my low origin. But I
Am a child of Luck; I cannot be dishonored.
Luck is my mother; the passing months, my brothers,
Have seen me rich and poor.
                              If this is so,
How could I wish that I were someone else?
How could I not be glad to know my birth?

ODE THREE

CHORUS. If ever the coming time were known   (STROPHE.)
To my heart's pondering,
Kithairon, now by Heaven I see the torches
At the festival of the next full moon,
And see the dance, and hear the choir sing
A grace to your gentle shade:
Mountain where Oedipus was found,

O mountain guard of a noble race!
May the god who heals us lend his aid,
And let that glory come to pass
For our king's cradling-ground.   (ANTISTROPHE.)

Of the nymphs that flower beyond the years,
Who bore you, royal child,
To Pan of the hills of the timberline Apollo,
Cold in delight were the upland clears,
Or Hermês for whom Kyllenê's heights are piled?
Or flushed as evening cloud,
Great Dionysos, roamer of mountains,
He—was it he who found you there,
And caught you up in his own proud
Arms from the sweet god-ravisher
Who laughed by the Muses' fountains?

SCENE FOUR.

OEDIPUS. Sirs: though I do not know the man,
I think I see him coming, this shepherd we want:
He is old, like our friend here, and the men
Bringing him seem to be servants of my house.
But you can tell, if you have ever seen him.
    (*Enter* SHEPHERD *escorted by servants.*)
    CHORUS. I know him, he was Laïos man. You can trust him.
    OEDIPUS. Tell me first, you from Corinth: is this the shepherd we
were discussing?
    MESSENGER. This is the very man.
    (*To* SHEPHERD.)
    OEDIPUS. Come here. No, look at me. You must answer
Everything I ask.—You belonged to Laïos?
    SHEPHERD. Yes: born his slave, brought up in his house.
    OEDIPUS. Tell me: what kind of work did you do for him?
    SHEPHERD. I was a shepherd of his, most of my life.
    OEDIPUS. Where mainly did you go for pasturage?
    SHEPHERD. Sometimes Kithairon, sometimes the hills near-by.
    OEDIPUS. Do you remember ever seeing this man out there?
    SHEPHERD. What would he be doing there? This man?
    OEDIPUS. This man standing here. Have you ever seen him before?

SHEPHERD. No. At least, not to my recollection.

MESSENGER. And that is not strange, my lord. But I'll refresh
His memory: he must remember when we two
Spent three whole seasons together, March to September,
On Kithairon or thereabouts. He had two flocks;
I had one. Each autumn I'd drive mine home
And he would go back with his to Laïos' sheepfold.—
Is this not true, just as I have described it?

SHEPHERD. True, yes; but it was all so long ago.

MESSENGER. Well, then: do you remember, back in those days,
That you gave me a baby boy to bring up as my own?

SHEPHERD. What if I did? What are you trying to say?

MESSENGER. King Oedipus was once that little child.

SHEPHERD. Damn you, hold your tongue!

OEDIPUS. No more of that!
It is your tongue needs watching, not this man's.

SHEPHERD. My King, my Master, what is it I have done wrong?

OEDIPUS. You have not answered his question about the boy.

SHEPHERD. He does not know. . . . He is only making trouble. . . .

OEDIPUS. Come, speak plainly, or it will go hard with you.

SHEPHERD. In God's name, do not torture an old man!

OEDIPUS. Come here, one of you; bind his arms behind him.

SHEPHERD. Unhappy King! What more do you wish to learn?

OEDIPUS. Did you give this man the child he speaks of?

SHEPHERD. I did.
And I would to God I had died that very day.

OEDIPUS. You will die now unless you speak the truth.

SHEPHERD. Yet if I speak the truth, I am worse than dead.

OEDIPUS. Very well; since you insist upon delaying—

SHEPHERD. No! I have told you already that I gave him the boy.

OEDIPUS. Where did you get him? From your house? From some-
    where else?

SHEPHERD. Not from mine, no. A man gave him to me.

OEDIPUS. Is that man here? Do you know whose slave he was?

SHEPHERD. For God's love, my King, do not ask me any more!

OEDIPUS. You are a dead man if I have to ask you again.

SHEPHERD. Then . . . Then the child was from the palace of Laïos

OEDIPUS. A slave child? or a child of his own line?

SHEPHERD. Ah, I am on the brink of dreadful speech!

OEDIPUS. And I of dreadful hearing. Yet I must hear.

SHEPHERD. If you must be told, then . . .

They said it was Laïos' child;
But it is your wife who can tell you about that.

OEDIPUS. My wife!—Did she give it to you?

SHEPHERD. My lord, she did.

OEDIPUS. Do you know why?

SHEPHERD. I was told to get rid of it.

OEDIPUS. An unspeakable mother!

SHEPHERD. There had been prophecies . . .

OEDIPUS. Tell me.

SHEPHERD. It was said that the boy would kill his own father.

OEDIPUS. Then why did you give him over to this old man?

SHEPHERD. I pitied the baby, my King,
And I thought that this man would take him far away
To his own country.

He saved him—but for what a fate!
For if you are what this man says you are,
No man living is more wretched than Oedipus.

OEDIPUS. Oh God!
It was true!

All the prophecies!

—Now,
O Light, may I look on you for the last time!
I, Oedipus,
Oedipus, damned in his birth, in his marriage damned,
Damned in the blood he shed with his own hand!

(*He rushes into the palace.*)

Oꭇ foꭒꭇ

CHORUS. Alas for the seed of men.   (STROPHE 1.)

What measure shall I give these generations
That breathe on the void and are void
And exist and do not exist?

Who bears more weight of joy
Than mass of sunlight shifting in images,

Or who shall make his thoughts stay on
That down time drifts away?

Your splendor is all fallen.

O naked brow of wrath and tears,
O change of Oedipus!
I who saw your days call no man blest—
Your great days like ghosts gone.

That mind was a strong bow.   (ANTISTROPHE 1.)

Deep, how deep you drew it then, hard archer,
At a dim fearful range,
And brought dear glory down!

You overcame the stranger—
The virgin with her hooking lion claws—
And though death sang, stood like a tower
To make pale Thebes take heart.

Fortress against our sorrow!

Divine king, giver of laws.
Majestic Oedipus!
No prince in Thebes had ever such renown.
No prince won such grace of power.

And now of all men ever known   (STROPHE 2.)
Most pitiful is this man's story:
His fortunes are most changed, his state
Fallen to a low slave's
Ground under bitter fate.

O Oedipus, most royal one!
The great door that expelled you to the light
Gave at night—ah, gave night to your glory:
As to the father, to the fathering son.

All understood too late.

How could that queen whom Laïos won,
The garden that he harrowed at his height,
Be silent when that act was done?

But all eyes fail before time's eye,   (ANTISTROPHE 2.)
All actions come to justice there.
Though never willed, though far down the deep past,
Your bed, your dread sirings,
Are brought to book at last.

Child by Laïos to die,
Then doomed to lose that fortunate little death,
Would God you never took breath in this air
That with my wailing lips I take to cry:

For I weep the world's outcast.

Blind I was, and can not tell why;
Asleep, for you had given ease of breath;
A fool, while the false years went by.

éxodus

(*Enter, from the palace,* SECOND MESSENGER.)
SECOND MESSENGER. Elders of Thebes, most honored in this land,
What horrors are yours to see and hear, what weight
Of sorrow to be endured, if, true to your birth,
You venerate the line of Labdakos!
I think neither Istros nor Phasis, those great rivers,
Could purify this place of the corruption
It shelters now, or soon must bring to light—
Evil not done unconsciously, but willed.
The greatest griefs are those we cause ourselves.
CHORUS. Surely, friend, we have grief enough already;
What new sorrow do you mean?
SECOND MESSENGER. The Queen is dead.
CHORUS. Iocastê? Dead? But at whose hand?
SECOND MESSENGER. Her own.
The full horror of what happened you cannot know,
For you did not see it; but I, who did, will tell you
As clearly as I can how she met her death.
When she had left us,
In passionate silence, passing through the court,
She ran to her apartment in the house

Her hair clutched by the fingers of both hands.
She closed the doors behind her; then, by that bed
Where long ago the fatal son was conceived—
That son who should bring about his father's death—
We heard her call upon Laïos, dead so many years,
And heard her wail for the double fruit of her marriage,
A husband by her husband, children by her child.
Exactly how she died I do not know:
For Oedipus burst in moaning and would not let us
Keep virgil to the end: it was by him
As he stormed about the room that our eyes were caught.

From one to another of us he went, begging a sword,
Cursing the wife who was not his wife, the mother
Whose womb had carried his own children and himself.
I do not know: it was none of us aided him.
But surely one of the gods was in control!
For with a dreadful cry
He hurled his weight, as though wrenched out of himself,
At the twin doors: the bolts gave, and he rushed in.
And there we saw her hanging, her body swaying
From the cruel cord she had noosed about her neck.
A great sob broke from him, heartbreaking to hear,
As he loosed the rope and lowered her to the ground.

I would blot out from my mind what happened next!
For the King ripped from her gown the golden brooches
That were her ornament, and raised them, and plunged them down
Straight into his own eyeballs, crying, "No more,
No more shall you look on the misery about me,
The horrors of my own doing! Too long you have known
The faces of those whom I should never have seen,
Too long been blind to those for whom I was searching!
From this hour, go in darkness!" And as he spoke,
He struck at his eyes—not once, but many times;
And the blood spattered his beard,
Bursting from his ruined sockets like red hail.

So from the unhappiness of two this evil has sprung,
A curse on the man and woman alike. The old

Happiness of the house of Labdakos
Was happiness enough: where is it today?
It is all wailing and ruin, disgrace, death—all
The misery of mankind that has a name—
And it is wholly and for ever theirs.

    CHORUS. Is he in agony still? Is there no rest for him?
    SECOND MESSENGER. He is calling for someone to lead him to the
        gates
So that all the children of Kadmos may look upon
His father's murderer, his mother's—no,
I can not say it!

                And then he will leave Thebes,
Self-exiled, in order that the curse
Which he himself pronounced may depart from the house.
He is weak, and there is none to lead him.
So terrible is his suffering.

                But you will see:
Look, the doors are opening; in a moment
You will see a thing that would crush a heart of stone.

    (*The central door is opened;* OEDIPUS, *blinded, is led in.*)
    CHORUS. Dreadful indeed for men to see
Never have my own eyes
Looked on a sight so full of fear.

Oedipus!
What madness came upon you, what daemon
Leaped on your life with heavier
Punishment than a mortal man can bear?
No; I can not even
Look at you, poor ruined one.
And I would speak, question, ponder,
If I were able. No.
You make me shudder.

    OEDIPUS. God.   God.
Is there a sorrow greater?
Where shall I find harbor in this world?
My voice is hurled far on a dark wind.
What has God done to me?

    CHORUS. Too terrible to think of, or to see.

OEDIPUS. O cloud of night,   (STROPHE 1.)
Never to be turned away: night coming on,
I can not tell how: night like a shroud!

My fair winds brought me here.
                         O God. Again
The pain of the spikes where I had sight,
The flooding pain
Of memory, never to be gouged out.
   CHORUS. This is not strange.
You suffer it all twice over, remorse in pain,
Pain in remorse.
   OEDIPUS. Ah dear friend   (ANTISTROPHE 1.)
Are you faithful even yet, you alone?
Are you still standing near me, will you stay here,
Patient, to care for the blind?
                        The blind man!
Yet even blind I know who it is attends me,
By the voice's tone—
Though my new darkness hide the comforter.
   CHORUS. Oh fearful act!
What god was it drove you to rake black
Night across your eyes?
   OEDIPUS. Apollo. Apollo. Dear   (STROPHE 2.)
Children, the god was Apollo.
He brought my sick, sick fate upon me.
But the blinding hand was my own!
How could I bear to see
When all my sight was horror everywhere?
   CHORUS. Everywhere; that is true.
   OEDIPUS. And now what is left?
Images? Love? A greeting even,
Sweet to the senses? Is there anything?
Ah, no friends: lead me away.
Lead me away from Thebes.
                  Lead the great wreck
And hell of Oedipus, whom the gods hate.
   CHORUS. Your fate is clear, you are not blind to that.
Would God you had never found it out!

OEDIPUS. Death take the man who unbound   (ANTISTROPHE 2.)
My feet on that hillside
And delivered me from death to life! What life?
If only I had died,
This weight of monstrous doom
Could not have dragged me and my darlings down.
  CHORUS. I would have wished the same.
  OEDIPUS. Oh never to have come here
With my father's blood upon me! Never
To have been the man they call his mother's husband!
Oh accurst! Oh child of evil,
To have entered that wretched bed—

                              the selfsame one!
More primal than sin itself, this fell to me.
  CHORUS. I do not know how I can answer you.
You were better dead than alive and blind.
  OEDIPUS. Do not counsel me any more. This punishment
That I have laid upon myself is just.
If I had eyes,
I do not know how I could bear the sight
Of my father, when I came to the house of Death,
Or my mother: for I have sinned against them both
So vilely that I could not make my peace
By strangling my own life.

                    Or do you think my children,
Born as they were born, would be sweet to my eyes?
Ah never, never! Nor this town with its high walls,
Nor the holy images of the gods.

                        For I,
Thrice miserable!—Oedipus, noblest of all the line
Of Kadmos, have condemned myself to enjoy
These things no more, by my own malediction
Expelling that man whom the gods declared
To be a defilement in the house of Laïos.
After exposing the rankness of my own guilt,
How could I look men frankly in the eyes?
No, I swear it,
If I could have stifled my hearing at its source,
I would have done it and made all this body

A tight cell of misery, blank to light and sound:
So I should have been safe in a dark agony
Beyond all recollection.

Ah Kithairon!

Why did you shelter me? When I was cast upon you,
Why did I not die? Then I should never
Have shown the world my execrable birth.

Ah, Polybos! Corinth, city that I believed
The ancient seat of my ancestors: how fair
I seemed, your child; And all the while this evil
Was cancerous within me!

For I am sick

In my daily life, sick of my origin.
O three roads, dark ravine, woodland and way
Where three roads met: you, drinking my father's blood,
My own blood, spilled by my own hand: can you remember
The unspeakable things I did there, and the things
I went on from there to do?

O marriage, marriage!

The act that engendered me, and again the act
Performed by the son in the same bed—

Ah, the net

Of incest, mingling fathers, brothers, sons,
With brides, wives, mothers: the last evil
That can be known by men: no tongue can say
How evil!

No. For the love of God, conceal me

Somewhere far from Thebes; or kill me; or hurl me
Into the sea, away from men's eyes for ever.

Come, lead me. You need not fear to touch me.
Of all men, I alone can bear this guilt.

(*Enter* CREON.)

CHORUS. We are not the ones to decide; but Creon here
May fitly judge of what you ask. He only
Is left to protect the city in your place.

OEDIPUS. Alas, how can I speak to him? What right have I
To beg his courtesy whom I have deeply wronged?

CREON. I have not come to mock you, Oedipus.

Or to reproach you, either.
    (*To* ATTENDANTS.)

                          —You, standing there:
If you have lost all respect for man's dignity,
At least respect the flame of Lord Helios:
Do not allow this pollution to show itself
Openly here, an affront to the earth
And Heaven's rain and the light of day. No, take him
Into the house as quickly as you can.
For it is proper
That only the close kindred see his grief.

  OEDIPUS. I pray you in God's name, since your courtesy
Ignores my dark expectation, visiting
With mercy this man of all men most execrable:
Give me what I ask—for your good, not for mine.

  CREON. And what is it that you would have me do?

  OEDIPUS. Drive me out of this country as quickly as may be
To a place where no human voice can ever greet me.

  CREON. I should have done that before now—only,
God's will had not be wholly revealed to me.

  OEDIPUS. But his command is plain: the parricide
Must be destroyed. I am that evil man.

  CREON. —That is the sense of it, yes; but as things are,
We had best discover clearly what is to be done.

  OEDIPUS. You would learn more about a man like me?

  CREON. You are ready now to listen to the god.

  OEDIPUS. I will listen. But it is to you
That I must turn for help. I beg you, hear me.

The woman in there —
Give her whatever funeral you think proper:
She is your sister.

                —But let me go, Creon!
Let me purge my father's Thebes of the pollution
Of my living here, and go out to the wild hills,
To Kithairon, that has won such fame with me,
The tomb my mother and father appointed for me,
And let me die there, as they willed I should.
And yet I know

Death will not ever come to me through sickness
Or in any natural way: I have been preserved
For some unthinkable fate. But let that be.

As for my sons, you need not care for them.
They are men, they will find some way to live.
But my poor daughters, who have shared my table,
Who never before have been parted from their father—
Take care of them, Creon; do this for me.
And will you let me touch them with my hands
A last time, and let us weep together?
Be kind, my lord,
Great prince, be kind!
                          Could I but touch them,
They would be mine again, as when I had my eyes.
      (*Enter* ANTIGONE *and* ISMENE, *attended.*)
Ah, God!
Is it my dearest children I hear weeping?
Has Creon pitied me and sent my daughters?
      CREON. Yes, Oedipus: I knew that they were dear to you
In the old days, and know you must love them still.
      OEDIPUS. May God bless you for this—and be a friendlier
Guardian to you than he has been to me!

Children, where are you?
Come quickly to my hands: they are your brother's—
Hands that have brought your father's once clear eyes
To this way of seeing—
                          Ah dearest ones,
I had neither sight nor knowledge then, your father
By the woman who was the source of his own life!
And I weep for you—having no strength to see you—,
I weep for you when I think of the bitterness
That men will visit upon you all your lives.
What homes, what festivals can you attend
Without being forced to depart again in tears?
And when you come to marriageable age,
Where is the man, my daughters, who would dare
Risk the bane that lies on all my children?
Is there any evil wanting? Your father killed

His father; sowed the womb of her who bore him;
Engendered you at the fount of his own existence!

That is what they will say of you.
                                        Then, whom
Can you ever marry? There are no bridegrooms for you,
And your lives must wither away in sterile dreaming.

O Creon, son of Menoikeus!
You are the only father my daughters have,
Since we, their parents, are both of us gone for ever.
They are your own blood: you will not let them
Fall into beggary and loneliness;
You will keep them from the miseries that are mine!
Take pity on them; see, they are only children,
Friendless except for you. Promise me this,
Great Prince, and give me your hand in token of it.
    (*Creon clasps his right hand.*)

Children:
I could say much, if you could understand me,
But as it is, I have only this prayer for you:
Live where you can, be as happy as you can—
Happier, please God, than God has made your father!
    CREON. Enough. You have wept enough. Now go within.
    OEDIPUS. I must; but it is hard.
    CREON. Time eases all things.
    OEDIPUS. But you must promise—
    CREON. Say what you desire.
    OEDIPUS. Send me from Thebes!
    CREON. God grant that I may!
    OEDIPUS. But since God hates me . . .
    CREON. No, he will grant your wish.
    OEDIPUS. You promise?
    CREON. I can not speak beyond my knowledge.
    OEDIPUS. Then lead me in.
    CREON. Come now, and leave your children.
    OEDIPUS. No! Do not take them from me!
    CREON. Think no longer
That you are in command here, but rather think

How when you were, you served your own destruction.
   (*Exeunt into the house all but the* CHORUS; *the* CHORAGOS *chants*
   directly to the audience.)
   CHORUS. Men of Thebes: look upon Oedipus.
This is the king who solved the famous riddle
And towered up, most powerful of men.
No mortal eyes but looked on him with envy,
Yet in the end ruin swept over him.

Let every man in mankind's frailty
Consider his last day; and let none
Presume on his good fortune until he find
Life, at his death, a memory without pain.

SUNKEN IMAGERY IN SOPHOCLES' *OEDIPUS*

Image analysis of Sophocles' *Oedipus* can provide an understanding of the ancient art of poetic composition, but such a study must
be tempered by the realization that the multiple possibilities of
meaning for any given image must coincide with the meanings
given to that image during the work's historical environment.* With
this qualification, it is enlightening to utilize the technique of iconics
with *Oedipus* since Sophocles presents major and minor symbolic
images, as well as nonsymbolic elements, and then cultivates them to
deeper connotations throughout the drama. Five major images, the
plague, the ship, the harborhaven, the plough, and the vision-blindness
dialectic, provide the deepest levels of symbolism. Concerning the
plague image, it should be remembered that the ancient Greek word
for "plague" had no pathological denotation. Since the Theban plague
is accompanied by plant blight and puerperal fever, it affects all pro-
creation and is, therefore, a symbolic plague which serves as a punishment in direct relation to the divine relationship between offspring and
parents which Oedipus has unknowingly violated. Also operating on a
symbolic level, the image of the ship, a "sunken metaphor" since it
is not always clearly obvious, represents the city with Oedipus as
captain and finally clearly shifts to represent Oedipus himself as he
finds and seeks the harbor-haven. Functioning on three levels, the
harbor-haven is literally the Euxine Sea, but it symbolically relates
to the Oedipus-Jocasta marriage and to Jocasta's womb. Similarly
related to the mysteries of birth and fate, the plough, as the fourth
dominant image, has a motion on the land which is obviously
analogous to ship-sea motion, although there is no explicit connection in Sophocles' works. Nonetheless, the plough image directly
relates to the plague symbol through the common mystery of birth
and growth, and the four main images interweave to form a pre-
dominant image-chain. A fifth major image, equally present yet not
directly linked to the chain, is that of vision-blindness. Oedipus'

* Abstracted from Herbert Musurillo, "Sunken Imagery in Sophocles'
Oedipus," *American Journal of Philology*, LXXVII (1957), 36-51.

intelligence, highly praised in relationship to the Sphinx, eventually brings about his downfall. On a second level, Oedipus ironically taunts Teiresias by saying: "Night alone is your nurse, and hence you cannot harm me or anyone who sees the light." Ultimately, Oedipus' vision is blind, and blind Teiresias sees. On a third level, the vision-blindness image relates to Oedipus' eventual self-blinding since it becomes an exterior symbol of his interior blindness. The dominant images do not, however, provide the total unity for the drama. Certain minor images provide deeper levels of meaning: the animal hunt relates to Oedipus' search for the murderer and also symbolizes the god's pursuit of the guilty; the basanite touchstone, besides being a plot clue, is a means of determining the relative wisdom between Teirasias and Oedipus and is also a measure of actual prosperity as opposed to apparent well-being; the walls of the city, while representing Oedipus as a wall against the Theban plague, recalls Hybris' attempts to climb the walls and also symbolize Oedipus' apparent rise, even though he is actually falling. Finally, the inclination of the scales symbolizes Oedipus' guilt-innocence dialectic, the "tilt" affecting the elderly, and the relationship between Oedipus and the gods. Yet, intertwined with major and minor images, certain nonsymbolic elements provide further sublevels to the meaning of *Oedipus.* Surely the dictum of Solon, suggesting that life's happiness is only a semblance, is explified by Oedipus. A similar relationship exists between the "high-footed laws" spoken of by the Chorus and the divine violation which Oedipus unwittingly comments. The conflict between Oedipus' and Jocasta's interpretations of the oracles similarly relates to the previously mentioned bipolar vision-blindness image. There seems to be no focal point which provides thematic unity to the play. An interlocking image-sequence, initiated with the plague symbol and progressing to the exposure of Oedipus' crime, approaches a thematic center, yet even that chain cannot be fully appreciated without an understanding of the minor images and the nonsymbolic elements. Perhaps modern criticism's preoccupation with a single unified interpretation cannot justifiably span the time gap between us and ancient Greek poetic art. In that sense, it might be said that *Oedipus* has no unified interpretation; a dominant motif may not have been expected by the audience nor intended by the artist.

WHO KILLED LAIUS?

Critics have tended to overlook the obvious discrepancies concerning who killed Laius in Sophocles' *Oedipus Rex*.* Preferring to dismiss these differences as an oversight on Sophocles' part, such critics have done the author a disservice, for the differences are intentional and basic to interpretation. Although other evidence exists to point toward a single killer, Oedipus, Sophocles has Oedipus himself point out and comment upon the possibility of several killers, and when the Shepherd, the supposed eye-witness, is present, Oedipus fails to question the Shepherd in order to establish guilt or inocence beyond a doubt. These differences, once opened to speculation, present other far-reaching questions. If it is possible that Oedipus did not murder his father, then who did? Although the evidence is not definite as to the identity of the murderer, there is a textual possibility that the character, the Chorus, might be guilty. Suspicion of the Chorus arises due to its vascillating nature. Characterized by a rapid shift of allegiance concerning Oedipus, the Chorus lacks faith, requiring "the word/proved right beyond doubt." Although the Chorus, seeking moderation, backs Creon and negates Oedipus, this would also be the appropriate defensive action if the Chorus were guilty of the murder. The Chorus should be pleased upon hearing that Apollo, the healer, will cure the corruption in Thebes, but, instead, the Chorus reacts by saying, "I worship full of fears for what doom you will bring to pass." Such fear is unnatural but would be easily explainable if, being guilty, the Chorus anticipated receiving the punishment. To refer only to the Chorus as a suspicious vascillating character is, however, an oversimplification. If the Chorus is guilty, it would seem natural to anticipate a sly, defensive attitude in that character, but such is not the case. The Chorus honestly wants justice, and the motivation behind its desire is the key to understanding the play's various contradictions. As an example of normal psychoanalytic behavior, criminals usually experience guilt and even may become criminals in order to receive

* Abstracted from Karl Harshbarger, "Who Killed Laius?" *Tulane Drama Review*, IX (1965), 120-131.

punishment. The plague which comes over the city, being more than physical, can be seen as a symbol of the festering guilt within the Chorus. The actions of the Chorus thus become a means of alleviating guilt feelings. Faced with a dual problem, to avoid discovery and subsequent punishment and to gain relief from the pain of guilt, the Chorus finds relief through a scapegoat. Oedipus, already feeling guilt concerning his mother, perhaps realizes the dilemma of the Chorus and thus succumbs to the natural solution, a sacrifice.

WHY IS OEDIPUS CALLED *TYRANNOS?*

To ask why Oedipus is called *tyrannos* is not to ask why the play is entitled *tyrannos.** Historically, a *tyrannos* is not only a king but also a despot who, through friends, money, or influence, has risen to power. Thus, the term connotes tyranny as well as being a neutral term for "king," "empire," "royalty," etc. But, in what manner does Oedipus deserve to be called *tyrannos?* Oedipus does not rise to power in Thebes through traditional ascendency; his control arises from individual accomplishment and not heredity. In the opening scene, Creon carefully draws the distinction by referring to Laius as king, not *tyrannos.* In reply, Oedipus identifies Laius as *tyrannos,* a term more closely akin to the connotation of Oedipus' own title. Throughout the play, Oedipus maintains the use of *tyrannos* in reference to Laius except for one important deviation. Following the statement of the curse upon the murderer, Oedipus refers to Laius as *basileus* (king). Psychologically, Oedipus describes Laius on this occasion in the terms to which Oedipus would like to be related; whereas, Oedipus' early references were an attempt to bring Laius down to Oedipus' level of relationship to the throne. The interplay of terminology becomes doubly ironic when Oedipus discovers that he *is* king through lineage, for that discovery also highlights Oedipus' unforgiveable sin. Yet, the connotations of *tyrannos* go beyond even

* Abstracted from Bernard M. W. Knox, "Why is Oedipus Called *Tyrannos?" The Classical Journal,* L (December, 1954), 97-102.

that level of complexity. Shortly after declaring undying loyalty to Oedipus, the chorus states, "Violence and pride engender the *tyrannos*," and then goes on to verbally attack Oedipus. The change of attitude within the chorus is more involved than it might seem. Although Oedipus entered Thebes after a violent act, slaying the highwaymen, he is not a typical *tyrannos*. He fails to totally fulfill the political type since he does not rule in a tyrannical manner. The play cannot, therefore, be viewed as simply an attack on the institution of *tyrannos*. The key to political interpretation lies in an assessment of Athens itself. Thucydides has told how Pericles boasted of Athenians as having risen to power in the Greek world through their own efforts, as did Oedipus, not through inherited power. Similarly, Athens was offered power, as was Oedipus. Applying the word *tyrannos* to Oedipus in Thebes can thus suggest a parallel relationship between Athens and Greece. Viewed in this manner, Oedipus is a national figure who embodies numerous Athenian sources of pride as listed by Thucydides: strong willed, vigorous, experienced, courageous, reflective, self-confident, versatile, socially devoted, suspicious, and wrathful. The obvious parallels clearly reinforce the interpretation. More than simply a tragic hero, Oedipus *tyrannos* represents, through ascendency, character, and title, the *tyrannos* of Greece, Athens. Sophocles, through the manipulation of kingly terminology, thus adds a political dimension to the meaning of the play. Interpreted in that manner, he also adds an interesting dimension to Oedipus' fall.

SELF-DESTRUCTION IN *OEDIPUS REX*

Analytic critics have long regarded the self-destructive behavior of Oedipus as arising from his guilt over incest and patricide. However, the motivational dynamics of Oedipus' self-destruction are best understood in the light of the hero's *matricidal* urges.* When he

* Abstracted from M. D. Faber, "Self-Destruction in *Oedipus Rex*," *American Imago, XXVII* (Spring, 1970), 41-51.

discovers the truth about himself, Oedipus' first thought is that he
should not live any longer; but his first real impulse, as Sophocles'
text makes clear, is to murder Jocasta. When he bursts into his
mother's antechamber and finally into her bedroom Oedipus is bent
upon matricide, not suicide. The hero's matricidal urges arise from
his unconscious conviction that he has been *betrayed* and that it is
Jocasta who has betrayed him. The paradoxical twist that clarifies the
matter may be stated thus: when Jocasta ceases to be Oedipus' wife
she becomes, of a sudden, Oedipus' *mother again.* Now Oedipus, at
the deepest unconscious level, is particularly sensitive to maternal
rejection. As an infant he experienced abandonment at the hands of
the mother (Sophocles stresses Jocasta's role in the separation); as
a young man he was told by the drunken Corinthian that his parents
were not his parents; in this way, Oedipus' oldest and deepest psychic
wound opens under the stress of the play's events, and in psychic
fury he craves to destroy the betrayer. That Jocasta is already dead
when Oedipus discovers her only means that his matricidal wish
has magically come true. He desired her dead and now he finds her
so. Thus, when he stabs at his eyes, Oedipus is attempting to expiate
not only his past crimes, but the crimes he has committed in the now
of the tragedy. Expiation, however, is not Oedipus' sole aim; that is,
when he blinds himself he is attempting to deal with the future as
well as the past. If he is to meet his mother and his father in
another world he will meet them in a harmless condition. This will
prevent the reoccurrence of disastrous deeds. Oedipus' self-destruction, then, is predicated by *anxiety* as well as by guilt. As for Jocasta,
she commits suicide on her marriage bed, crying out to the husband,
Laius, who, as she sees it, has *abandoned* her to her incestuous union.
Her suicide expresses *anger* at Laius. The point is, while Jocasta
is the significant other for Oedipus in his self-destruction, Oedipus
is *not* the significant other for Jocasta in hers. This underscores the
whole thrust of the oedipal entanglement that is at the heart of
Sophocles' play. For the son it is the mother who is *the* significant
object; for the mother, however, the son is not the object, and can
never be, for it is the father upon whom *her* marriage oedipally
rests. Not only *must* the oedipal relationship not be in a moral,
societal way; it *cannot* ever fully or satisfactorily be in a human
emotive way. The deepest irony is the irony of our psychology. Our
psychology is our "fate."

lysistrata
ARISTOPHANES

CHARACTERS

TRANSLATED BY
CHARLES T. MURPHY

LYSISTRATA
CALONICE   } *Athenian women*
MYRRHINE
LAMPITO, *a Spartan woman*
LEADER *of the Chorus of Old Men*
CHORUS *of Old Men*
LEADER *of the Chorus of Old Women*
CHORUS *of Old Women*

ATHENIAN MAGISTRATE
THREE ATHENIAN WOMEN
CINESIAS, *an Athenian, husband of Myrrhine*
SPARTAN HERALD
SPARTAN AMBASSADORS
ATHENIAN AMBASSADORS
TWO ATHENIAN CITIZENS
CHORUS *of Athenians*
CHORUS *of Spartans*

As is usual in ancient comedy, the leading characters have significant names. LYSISTRATA is "She who disbands the armies"; MYRRHINE's name is chosen to suggest *myrton*, a Greek word meaning *pudenda muliebria;* LAMPITO is a celebrated Spartan name; CINESIAS, although a real name in Athens, is chosen to suggest a Greek verb *kinein, to move,* then *to make love, to have intercourse,* and the name of his deme, Paionidai, suggests the verb *paiein,* which has about the same significance.

SCENE: In Athens, beneath the Acropolis. In the center of the stage is the Propylaea, or gate-way to the Acropolis; to one side is a small grotto, sacred to Pan. The Orchestra represents a slope leading up to the gate-way. .
It is early in the morning. LYSISTRATA is pacing impatiently up and down.

LYSISTRATA. If they'd been summoned to worship the God of Wine, or Pan, or to visit the Queen of Love, why, you couldn't have pushed your way through the streets for all the timbrels. But now there's not a single woman here—except my neighbour; here she comes.

Lysistrata by Aristophanes, translated by Charles T. Murphy in Whitney J. Oates and Charles T. Murphy, *Greek Literature in Translation*. Used by permission of the publishers, David McKay Co., Inc.

(*Enter* CALONICE.)

Good day to you, Calonice.

CALONICE. And to you, Lysistrata. (*noticing* LYSISTRATA'S *impatient air*) But what ails you? Don't scowl, my dear; it's not becoming to you to knit your brows like that.

LYSISTRATA (*sadly*). Ah, Calonice, my heart aches; I'm so annoyed at us women. For among men we have a reputation for sly trickery—

CALONICE. And rightly too, on my word!

LYSISTRATA: —but when they were told to meet here to consider a matter of no small importance, they lie abed and don't come.

CALONICE. Oh, they'll come all right, my dear. It's not easy for a woman to get out, you know. One is working on her husband, another is getting up the maid, another has to put the baby to bed, or wash and feed it.

LYSISTRATA. But after all, there are other matters more important than all that.

CALONICE. My dear Lysistrata, just what is this matter you've summoned us women to consider? What's up? Something big?

LYSISTRATA. Very big.

CALONICE (*interested*). Is it stout, too?

LYSISTRATA (*smiling*). Yes indeed—both big and stout.

CALONICE. What? And the women still haven't come?

LYSISTRATA. It's not what you suppose; they'd have come soon enough for *that*. But I've worked up something, and for many a sleepless night I've turned it this way and that.

CALONICE (*in mock disappointment*). Oh, I guess it's pretty fine and slender, if you've turned it this way and that.

LYSISTRATA. So fine that the safety of the whole of Greece lies in us women.

CALONICE. In us women? It depends on a very slender reed then.

LYSISTRATA. Our country's fortunes are in our hands; and whether the Spartans shall perish—

CALONICE. Good! Let them perish, by all means.

LYSISTRATA. —and the Boeotians shall be completely annihilated.

CALONICE. Not completely! Please spare the eels.

LYSISTRATA. As for Athens, I won't use any such unpleasant words. But you understand what I mean. But if the women will meet here—the Spartans, the Boeotians, and we Athenians—then all together we will save Greece.

CALONICE. But what could women do that's clever or distinguished? We just sit around all dolled up in silk robes, looking pretty in our sheer gowns and evening slippers.

LYSISTRATA. These are just the things I hope will save us: these silk robes, perfumes, evening slippers, rouge, and our chiffon blouses.

CALONICE. How so?

LYSISTRATA. So never a man alive will lift a spear against the foe—

CALONICE. I'll get a silk gown at once.

LYSISTRATA. —or take up his shield—

CALONICE. I'll put on my sheerest gown!

LYSISTRATA. —or sword.

CALONICE. I'll buy a pair of evening slippers.

LYSISTRATA. Well then, shouldn't the women have come?

CALONICE. Come? Why, they should have *flown* here.

LYSISTRATA. Well, my dear, just watch: they'll act in true Athenian fashion—everything too late! And now there's not a woman here from the shore or from Salamis.

CALONICE. They're coming, I'm sure; at daybreak they were laying —to their oars to cross the straits.

LYSISTRATA. And those I expected would be the first to come— the women of Acharnae—they haven't arrived.

CALONICE. Yet the wife of Theagenes means to come: she consulted Hecate about it. (*seeing a group of women approaching*) But look! Here come a few. And there are some more over here. Hurrah! Where do they come from?

LYSISTRATA. From Anagyra.

CALONICE. Yes indeed! We've raised up quite a stink from Anagyra anyway.

(*Enter* MYRRHINE *in haste, followed by several other women.*)

MYRRHINE (*breathlessly*). Have we come in time, Lysistrata? What do you say? Why so quiet?

LYSISTRATA. I can't say much for you, Myrrhine, coming at this hour on such important business.

MYRRHINE. Why, I had trouble finding my girdle in the dark, But if it's so important, we're here now! tell us.

LYSISTRATA. No. Let's wait a little for the women from Boeotia and the Peloponnesus.

MYRRHINE. That's a much better suggestion. Look! Here comes Lampito now.

(*Enter* LAMPITO *with two other women.*)

LYSISTRATA. Greetings, my dear Spartan friend. How pretty you look, my dear. What a smooth complexion and well-developed figure! You could throttle an ox.

LAMPITO. Faith, yes, I think I could. I take exercises and kick my heels against my bum. (*She demonstrates with a few steps of the Spartan "bottom-kicking" dance.*)

LYSISTRATA. And what splendid breasts you have.

LAMPITO. La! You handle me like a prize steer.

LYSISTRATA. And who is this young lady with you?

LAMPITO. Faith, she's an Ambassadress from Boeotia.

LYSISTRATA. Oh yes, a Boeotian, and blooming like a garden too.

CALONICE (*lifting up her skirt*). My word!
How neatly her garden's weeded!

LYSISTRATA. And who is the other girl?

LAMPITO. Oh, she's a Corinthian swell.

MYRRHINE (*after a rapid examination*). Yes indeed. She swells very nicely (*pointing*) here and here.

LAMPITO. Who has gathered together this company of women?

LYSISTRATA. I have.

LAMPITO. Speak up, then. What do you want?

MYRRHINE. Yes, my dear, tell us what this important matter is.

LYSISTRATA. Very well, I'll tell you. But before I speak, let me ask you a little question.

MYRRHINE. Anything you like.

LYSISTRATA (*earnestly*). Tell me: don't you yearn for the fathers of your children, who are away at the wars? I know you all have husbands abroad.

CALONICE. Why, yes; mercy me! my husband's been away for five months in Thrace keeping guard on—Eucrates.

MYRRHINE. And mine for seven whole months in Pylus.

LAMPITO. And mine, as soon as ever he returns from the fray, readjusts his shield and flies out of the house again.

LYSISTRATA. And as for lovers, there's not even a ghost of one left. Since the Milesians revolted from us, I've not even seen an eight-inch dingus to be a leather consolation for us widows. Are you willing, if I can find a way, to help me end the war?

MYRRHINE. Goodness, yes! I'd do it, even if I had to pawn my dress and—get drunk on the spot!

CALONICE. And I, even if I had to let myself be split in two like a flounder.

LAMPITO. I'd climb up Mt. Taygetus if I could catch a glimpse of peace.

LYSISTRATA. I'll tell you, then, in plain and simple words. My friends, if we are going to force our men to make peace, we must do without—

MYRRHINE. Without what? Tell us.

LYSISTRATA. Will you do it?

MYRRHINE. We'll do it, if it kills us.

LYSISTRATA. Well then, we must do without sex altogether. (*general consternation*) Why do you turn away? Where go you? Why turn so pale? Why those tears? Will you do it or not? What means this hesitation?

MYRRHINE. I won't do it! Let the war go on.

CALONICE. Nor I! Let the war go on.

LYSISTRATA. So, my little flounder? Didn't you say just now you'd split yourself in half?

CALONICE. Anything else you like. I'm willing, even if I have to walk through fire. Anything rather than sex. There's nothing like it, my dear.

LYSISTRATA (*to* MYRRHINE). What about you?

MYRRHINE. (*sullenly*). I'm willing to walk through fire, too.

LYSISTRATA. Oh vile and cursed breed! No wonder they make tragedies about us: we're naught but "love-affairs and bassinets." But you, my dear Spartan friend, if you alone are with me, our enterprise might yet succeed. Will you vote with me?

LAMPITO. 'Tis cruel hard, by my faith, for a woman to sleep alone without her nooky; but for all that, we certainly do need peace.

LYSISTRATA. O my dearest friend! You're the only real woman here.

CALONICE. (*wavering*). Well, if we do refrain from—(*shuddering*) what you say (God forbid!), would that bring peace?

LYSISTRATA. My goodness, yes! If we sit at home all rouged and powdered, dressed in our sheerest gowns, and neatly depilated, our men will get excited and want to take us; but if you don't come to them and keep away, they'll soon make a truce.

LAMPITO. Aye; Menelaus caught sight of Helen's naked breast and dropped his sword, they say.

CALONICE. What if the men give us up?

LYSISTRATA. "Flay a skinned dog," as Pherecrates says.

CALONICE. Rubbish! These make-shifts are no good. But suppose they grab us and drag us into the bedroom?

LYSISTRATA. Hold on to the door.

CALONICE. And if they beat us?

LYSISTRATA. Give in with a bad grace. There's no pleasure in it for them when they have to use violence. And you must torment them in every possible way. They'll give up soon enough; a man gets no joy if he doesn't get along with his wife.

MYRRHINE. If this is your opinion, we agree.

LAMPITO. As for our own men, we can persuade them to make a just and fair peace; but what about the Athenian rabble? Who will persuade them not to start any more monkey-shines?

LYSISTRATA. Don't worry. We guarantee to convince them.

LAMPITO. Not while their ships are rigged so well and they have that mighty treasure in the temple of Athene.

LYSISTRATA. We've taken good care for that too: we shall seize the Acropolis today. The older women have orders to do this, and while we are making our arrangements, they are to pretend to make a sacrifice and occupy the Acropolis.

LAMPITO. All will be well then. That's a very fine idea.

LYSISTRATA. Let's ratify this, Lampito, with the most solemn oath.

LAMPITO. Tell us what oath we shall swear.

LYSISTRATA. Well said. Where's our Policewoman? (*to a Scythian slave*) What are you gaping at? Set a shield upside-down here in front of me, and give me the sacred meats.

CALONICE. Lysistrata, what sort of an oath are we to take?

LYSISTRATA. What oath? I'm going to slaughter a sheep over the shield, as they do in Aeschylus.

CALONICE. Don't, Lysistrata! No oaths about peace over a shield.

LYSISTRATA. What shall the oath be, then?

CALONICE. How about getting a white horse somewhere and cutting out its entrails for the sacrifice?

LYSISTRATA. White horse indeed!

CALONICE. Well then, how shall we swear?

MYRRHINE. I'll tell you: let's place a large black bowl upside-down and then slaughter—a flask of Thasian wine. And then let's swear— not to pour in a single drop of water.

LAMPITO. Lord! How I like that oath!

LYSISTRATA. Someone bring out a bowl and a flask.

(*A slave brings the utensils for the sacrifice.*)

CALONICE. Look, my friends! What a big jar! Here's a cup that 'twould give me joy to handle. (*She picks up the bowl.*)

LYSISTRATA. Set it down and put your hands on our victim. (*as* CALONICE *places her hands on the flask*) O Lady of Persuasion and dear Loving Cup, graciously vouchsafe to receive this sacrifice from us women. (*She pours the wine into the bowl.*)

CALONICE. The blood has a good colour and spurts out nicely.

LAMPITO. Faith, it has a pleasant smell, too.

MYRRHINE. Oh, let me be the first to swear, ladies!

CALONICE. No, by our Lady! Not unless you're allotted the first turn.

LYSISTRATA. Place all your hands on the cup, and one of you repeat on behalf of what I say. Then all will swear and ratify the oath. *I will suffer no man, be he husband or lover,*

CALONICE. *I will suffer no man, be he husband or lover,*

LYSISTRATA. *To approach me all hot and horny.* (*as* CALONICE *hesitates*) Say it!

CALONICE (*slowly and painfully*): *To approach me all hot and horny.* O Lysistrata, I feel so weak in the knees!

LYSISTRATA. *I will remain at home unmated,*

CALONICE. *I will remain at home unmated,*

LYSISTRATA. *Wearing my sheerest gown and carefully adorned,*

CALONICE. *Wearing my sheerest gown and carefully adorned,*

LYSISTRATA. *That my husband may burn with desire for me.*

CALONICE. *That my husband may burn with desire for me.*

LYSISTRATA. *And if he takes me by force against my will,*

CALONICE. *And if he takes me by force against my will,*

LYSISTRATA. *I shall do it badly and keep from moving.*

CALONICE. *I shall do it badly and keep from moving.*

LYSISTRATA. *I will not stretch my slippers toward the ceiling,*

CALONICE. *I will not stretch my slippers toward the ceiling,*

LYSISTRATA. *Nor will I take the posture of the lioness on the knife-handle.*

CALONICE. *Nor will I take the posture of the lioness on the knife-handle.*

LYSISTRATA. *If I keep this oath, may I be permitted to drink from this cup,*

CALONICE. *If I keep this oath, may I be permitted to drink from this cup,*

LYSISTRATA. *But if I break it, may the cup be filled with water.*

CALONICE. *But if I break it, may the cup be filled with water.*

LYSISTRATA. Do you all swear to this?

ALL. I do, so help me!

LYSISTRATA. Come then, I'll just consummate this offering.

(*She takes a long drink from the cup.*)

CALONICE (*snatching the cup away*). Shares, my dear! Let's drink to our continued friendship.

(*A shout is heard from off-stage.*)

LAMPITO. What's that shouting?

LYSISTRATA. That's what I was telling you; the women have just seized the Acropolis. Now, Lampito, go home and arrange matters in Sparta; and leave these two ladies here as hostages. We'll enter the Acropolis to join our friends and help them lock the gates.

CALONICE. Don't you suppose the men will come to attack us?

LYSISTRATA. Don't worry about them. Neither threats nor fire will suffice to open the gates, except on the terms we've stated.

CALONICE. I should say not! Else we'd belie our reputation as unmanageable pests.

(LAMPITO *leaves the stage. The other women retire and enter the Acropolis through the Propylaea.*)

(*Enter the* CHORUS OF OLD MEN, *carrying fire-pots and a load of heavy sticks.*)

LEADER OF MEN. Onward, Draces, step by step, though your shoulder's aching.

Cursèd logs of olive-wood, what a load you're making!

FIRST SEMI-CHORUS OF OLD MEN (*singing*). Aye, many surprises await a man who lives to a ripe old age;

For who could suppose, Strymodorus my lad, that the women we've nourished (alas!),

Who sat at home to vex our days,

Would seize the holy image here,

And occupy this sacred shrine,

With bolts and bars, with fell design,

To lock the Propylaea?

LEADER OF MEN. Come with speed, Philourgus, come! to the temple hast'ning.
There we'll heap these logs about in a circle round them,
And whoever has conspired, raising this rebellion,
Shall be roasted, scorched, and burnt, all without exception,
Doomed by one unanimous vote—but first the wife of Lycon.

SECOND SEMI-CHORUS (*singing*).
No, no! by Demeter, while I'm alive, no woman shall mock at me.
Not even the Spartan Cleomenes, our citadel first to seize,
Got off unscathed; for all his pride
And haughty Spartan arrogance,
He left his arms and sneaked away,
Stripped to his shirt, unkempt, unshav'd
With six years' filth still on him.

LEADER OF MEN. I besieged that hero bold, sleeping at my station,
Marshalled at these holy gates sixteen deep against him.
Shall I not these cursèd pests punish for their daring,
Burning these Euripides-and-God-detested women?
Aye! or else may Marathon overturn my trophy.

FIRST SEMI-CHORUS (*singing*).
There remains of my road
Just this brow of the hill;
There I speed on my way.
Drag the logs up the hill, though we've got no ass to help.
(God! my shoulder's bruised and sore!)
Onward still must we go.
Blow the fire! Don't let it go out
Now we're near the end of our road.

ALL (*blowing on the fire-pots*).
Whew! Whew! Drat the smoke!

SECOND SEMI-CHORUS (*singing*).
Lord, what smoke rushing forth
From the pot, like a dog
Running mad, bites my eyes!
This must be Lemnos-fire. What a sharp and stinging smoke!
Rushing onward to the shrine
Aid the gods. Once for all
Show your mettle, Laches my boy!
To the rescue hastening all!

ALL (*blowing on the fire-pots*). Whew!
Whew! Drat the smoke!
(*The chorus has now reached the edge of the Orchestra nearest the stage, in front of the Propylaea. They begin laying their logs and fire-pots on the ground.*)
LEADER OF MEN. Thank heaven, this fire is still alive. Now let's first put down these logs here and place our torches in the pots to catch; let's make a rush for the gates with a battering-ram. If the women don't unbar the gate at our summons, we'll have to smoke them out.

Let me put down my load. Ouch! That hurts! (*to the audience*) Would any of the generals in Samos like to lend a hand with this log? (*throwing down a log*) Well, *that* won't break my back any more, at any rate. (*turning to his fire-pot*) Your job, my little pot, is to keep those coals alive and furnish me shortly with a red-hot torch.

O mistress Victory, be my ally and grant me to rout these audacious women in the Acropolis.

(*While the men are busy with their logs and fires, the* CHORUS OF OLD WOMEN *enters, carrying pitchers of water.*)
LEADER OF WOMEN. What's this I see? Smoke and flames? Is that a fire ablazing?
Let's rush upon them. Hurry up! They'll find us women ready.
FIRST SEMI-CHORUS OF OLD WOMEN (*singing*).
With wingèd foot onward I fly,
Ere the flames consume Neodice;
Lest Critylla be overwhelmed
By a lawless, accurst herd of old men.
I shudder with fear. Am I too late to aid them?
At break of the day filled we our jars with water
Fresh from the spring, pushing our way straight through the crowds.
    Oh, what a din!
Mid crockery crashing, jostled by slave-girls,
Sped we to save them, aiding our neighbours,
Bearing this water to put out the flames.
SECOND SEMI-CHORUS OF OLD WOMEN (*singing*).
Such news I've heard: doddering fools
Come with logs, like furnace-attendants,
Loaded down with three hundred pounds,

Breathing many a vain, blustering threat,
That all these abhorred sluts will be burnt to charcoal.
O goddess, I pray never may they be kindled;
Grant them to save Greece and our men; madness and war help them
    to end.
With this as our purpose, golden-plumed Maiden,
Guardian of Athens, seized we thy precinct.
Be my ally, Warrior-maiden,
'Gainst these old men, bearing water with me.

(*The women have now reached their position in the Orchestra, and their* LEADER *advances toward the* LEADER OF THE MEN.)

LEADER OF WOMEN. Hold on there! What's this, you utter scoundrels? No decent, God-fearing citizens would act like this.

LEADER OF MEN. Oho! Here's something unexpected: a swarm of women have come out to attack us.

LEADER OF WOMEN. What, do we frighten you? Surely you don't think we're too many for you. And yet there are ten thousand times more of us whom you haven't even seen.

LEADER OF MEN. What say, Phaedria? Shall we let these women wag their tongues? Shan't we take our sticks and break them over their backs?

LEADER OF WOMEN. Let's set our pitchers on the ground; then if anyone lays a hand on us, they won't get in our way.

LEADER OF MEN. By God! If someone gave them two or three smacks on the jaw, like Bupalus, they wouldn't talk so much!

LEADER OF WOMEN. Go on, hit me, somebody! Here's my jaw! But no other bitch will bite a piece out of you before me.

LEADER OF MEN. Silence; or I'll knock out your—senility!

LEADER OF WOMEN. Just lay one finger on Stratyllis, I dare you!

LEADER OF MEN. Suppose I dust you off with this first? What will you do?

LEADER OF WOMEN. I'll tear the living guts out of you with my teeth.

LEADER OF MEN. No poet is more clever than Euripides: "There is no beast so shameless as a woman."

LEADER OF WOMEN. Let's pick up our jars of water, Rhodippe.

LEADER OF MEN. Why have you come here with water, you detestable slut?

LEADER OF WOMEN. And why have you come with fire, you funeral vault? To cremate yourself?

LEADER OF MEN. To light a fire and singe your friends.

LEADER OF WOMEN. And I've brought water to put out your fire.

LEADER OF MEN. What? You'll put out my fire?

LEADER OF WOMEN. Just try and see!

LEADER OF MEN. I wonder: shall I scorch you with this torch of mine?

LEADER OF WOMEN. If you've got any soap, I'll give you a bath.

LEADER OF MEN. Give *me* a bath, you stinking hag?

LEADER OF WOMEN. Yes—a bridal bath!

LEADER OF MEN. Just listen to her! What crust!

LEADER OF WOMEN. Well, I'm a free citizen.

LEADER OF MEN. I'll put an end to your bawling. (*The men pick up their torches.*)

LEADER OF WOMEN. You'll never do jury-duty again. (*The women pick up their pitchers.*)

LEADER OF MEN. Singe her hair for her!

LEADER OF WOMEN. Do your duty, water!

(*The women empty their pitchers on the men.*)

LEADER OF MEN. Ow! Ow! For heaven's sake!

LEADER OF WOMEN. Is it too hot?

LEADER OF MEN. What do you mean "hot"? Stop! What are you doing?

LEADER OF WOMEN. I'm watering you, so you'll be fresh and green.

LEADER OF MEN. But I'm all withered up with shaking.

LEADER OF WOMEN. Well, you've got a fire; why don't you dry yourself?

(*Enter an Athenian* MAGISTRATE, *accompanied by four Scythian policemen.*)

MAGISTRATE. Have these wanton women flared up again with their timbrels and their continual worship of Sabazius? Is this another Adonis-dirge upon the roof-tops—which we heard not long ago in the Assembly? That confounded Demostratus was urging us to sail to Sicily, and the whirling women shouted, "Woe for Adonis!" And then Demostratus said we'd best enroll the infantry from Zacynthus, and a tipsy woman on the roof shrieked, "Beat your breasts for

Adonis!" And that vile and filthy lunatic forced his measure through. Such license do our women take.

LEADER OF MEN. What if you heard of the insolence of these women here? Besides their other violent acts, they threw water all over us, and we have to shake out our clothes just as if we'd leaked in them.

MAGISTRATE. And rightly, too, by God! For we ourselves lead the women astray and teach them to play the wanton; from these roots such notions blossom forth. A man goes into the jeweler's shop and says, "About that necklace you made for my wife, goldsmith: last night, while she was dancing, the fastening-bolt slipped out of the hole. I have to sail over to Salamis today; if you're free, do come around tonight and fit in a new bolt for her." Another goes to the shoe-maker, a strapping young fellow with manly parts, and says, "See here, cobbler, the sandal-strap chafes my wife's little—toe; it's so tender. Come around during the siesta and stretch it a little, so she'll be more comfortable." Now we see the results of such treatment: here I'm a special Councillor and need money to procure oars for the galleys; and I'm locked out of the Treasury by these women.

But this is no time to stand around. Bring up crow-bars there! I'll put an end to their insolence. (*to one of the policemen*) What are you gaping at, you wretch? What are you staring at? Got an eye out for a tavern, eh? Set your crowbars here to the gates and force them open. (*retiring to a safe distance*) I'll help from over here.

(*The gates are thrown open and* LYSISTRATA *comes out followed by several other women.*)

LYSISTRATA. Don't force the gates; I'm coming out of my own accord. We don't need crow-bars here; what we need is good sound common-sense.

MAGISTRATE. Is that so, you strumpet? Where's my policeman? Officer, arrest her and tie her arms behind her back.

LYSISTRATA. By Artemis, if he lays a finger on me, he'll pay for it, even if he is a public servant.

(*The policeman retires in terror.*)

MAGISTRATE. You there, are you afraid? Seize her round the waist—and you, too. Tie her up, both of you!

FIRST WOMAN (*as the second policeman approaches* LYSISTRATA).

By Pandrosus, if you but touch her with your hand, I'll kick the stuffings out of you.

(*The second policeman retires in terror.*)

MAGISTRATE. Just listen to that: "kick the stuffings out." Where's another policeman? Tie *her* up first, for her chatter.

SECOND WOMAN. By the Goddess of the Light, if you lay the tip of your finger on her, you'll soon need a doctor.

(*The third policeman retires in terror.*)

MAGISTRATE. What's this? Where's my policeman? Seize *her* too. I'll soon stop your sallies.

THIRD WOMAN. By the Goddess of Tauros, if you go near her, I'll tear out your hair until it shrieks with pain.

(*The fourth policeman retires in terror.*)

MAGISTRATE. Oh, damn it all! I've run out of policemen. But women must never defeat us. Officers, let's charge them all together. Close up your ranks!

(*The policemen rally for a mass attack.*)

LYSISTRATA. By heaven, you'll soon find out that we have four companies of warrior-women, all fully equipped within!

MAGISTRATE (*advancing*). Twist their arms off, men!

LYSISTRATA (*shouting*). To the rescue, my valiant women!

O sellers-of-barley-green-stuffs-and-eggs,
O sellers-of-garlic, ye keepers-of-taverns, and vendors-of-bread,
     Grapple! Smite! Smash!
Won't you heap filth on them? Give them a tongue-lashing!

(*The women beat off the policemen.*)
Halt! Withdraw! No looting on the field.

MAGISTRATE. Damn it! My police-force has put up a very poor show.

LYSISTRATA. What did you expect? Did you think you were attacking slaves? Didn't you know that women are filled with passion?

MAGISTRATE. Aye, passion enough—for a good strong drink!

LEADER OF MEN. O chief and leader of this land, why spend your words in vain?
Don't argue with these shameless beasts.
You know not how we've fared:
A soapless bath they've given us; our clothes are soundly soaked.

LEADER OF WOMEN. Poor fool! You never should attack or strike
a peaceful girl.
But if you do, your eyes must swell.
For I am quite content
To sit unmoved, like modest maids, in peace and cause no pain;
But let a man stir up my hive, he'll find me like a wasp.
CHORUS OF MEN *(singing)*.

O God, whatever shall we do with creatures like Womankind?
This can't be endured by any man alive.
   Question them!
   Let us try to find out what this means.
   To what end have they seized on this shrine,
     This steep and rugged, high and holy,
       Undefiled Acropolis?

LEADER OF MEN. Come, put your questions: don't give in, and
probe her every statement.
For base and shameful it would be to leave this plot untested.
MAGISTRATE. Well then, first of all I wish to ask her this: for what
purpose have you barred us from the Acropolis?
LYSISTRATA. To keep the treasure safe, so you won't make war
on account of it.
MAGISTRATE. What? Do we make war on account of the treasure?
LYSISTRATA. Yes, and you cause all our other troubles for it, too.
Peisander and those greedy office-seekers keep things stirred up so
they can find occasions to steal. Now let them do what they like:
they'll never again make off with any of this money.
MAGISTRATE. What will you do?
LYSISTRATA. What a question! We'll administer it ourselves.
MAGISTRATE. *You* will administer the treasure?
LYSISTRATA. What's so strange in that? Don't we administer the
household money for you?
MAGISTRATE. That's different.
LYSISTRATA. How is it different?
MAGISTRATE. We've got to make war with this money.
LYSISTRATA. But that's the very first thing: you mustn't make war.
MAGISTRATE. How else can we be saved?
LYSISTRATA. We'll save you.
MAGISTRATE. *You*?

LYSISTRATA. Yes, we!

MAGISTRATE. God forbid!

LYSISTRATA. We'll save you, whether you want it or not.

MAGISTRATE. Oh! This is terrible!

LYSISTRATA. You don't like it, but we're going to do it none the less.

MAGISTRATE. Good God! it's illegal!

LYSISTRATA. We *will* save you, my little man!

MAGISTRATE. Suppose I don't want you to?

LYSISTRATA. That's all the more reason.

MAGISTRATE. What business have you with war and peace?

LYSISTRATA. I'll explain.

MAGISTRATE (*shaking his fist*). Speak up, or you'll smart for it.

LYSISTRATA. Just listen, and try to keep your hands still.

MAGISTRATE. I can't. I'm so mad I can't stop them.

FIRST WOMAN. Then you'll be the one to smart for it.

MAGISTRATE. Croak to yourself, old hag! (*to* LYSISTRATA) Now then, speak up.

LYSISTRATA. Very well. Formerly we endured the war for a good long time with our usual restraint, no matter what you men did. You wouldn't let us say "boo," although nothing you did suited us. But we watched you well, and though we stayed at home we'd often hear of some terribly stupid measure you'd proposed. Then, though grieving at heart, we'd smile sweetly and say, "What was passed in the Assembly today about writing on the treaty-stone?" "What's that to you?" my husband would say. "Hold your tongue!" And I held my tongue.

FIRST WOMAN. But I wouldn't have—not I!

MAGISTRATE. You'd have been soundly smacked, if you hadn't kept still.

LYSISTRATA: So I kept still at home. Then we'd hear of some plan still worse than the first; we'd say, "Husband, how could you pass such a stupid proposal?" He'd scowl at me and say, "If you don't mind your spinning, your head will be sore for weeks. *War shall be the concern of Men.*"

MAGISTRATE. And he was right, upon my word!

LYSISTRATA. Why right, you confounded fool, when your pro-posals were so stupid and we weren't allowed to make suggestions?

"There's not a *man* left in the country," says one. "No, not one," says another. Therefore all we women have decided in council to make a common effort to save Greece. How long should we have waited? Now, if you're willing to listen to our excellent proposals and keep silence for us in your turn, we still may save you.

MAGISTRATE. We men keep silence for you? That's terrible; I won't endure it!

LYSISTRATA. Silence!

MAGISTRATE. Silence for *you,* you wench, when you're wearing a snood? I'd rather die!

LYSISTRATA. Well, if that's all that bothers you—here! take my snood and tie it round your head. (*During the following words the women dress up the* MAGISTRATE *in women's garments.*) And *now* keep quiet! Here, take this spinning-basket, too, and card your wool with robes tucked up, munching on beans. *War shall be the concern of Women*!

LEADER OF WOMEN. Arise and leave your pitchers, girls; no time is this to falter.

We too must aid our loyal friends; our turn has come for action.

CHORUS OF WOMEN (*singing*).

I'll never tire of aiding them with song and dance; never may
Faintness keep my legs from moving to and fro endlessly.
For I yearn to do all for my friends;
They have charm, they have wit, they have grace,
With courage, brains, and best of virtues—
Patriotic sapience.

LEADER OF WOMEN. Come, child of manliest ancient dames, off-spring of stinging nettles,

Advance with rage unsoftened; for fair breezes speed you onward.

LYSISTRATA. If only sweet Eros and the Cyprian Queen of Love shed charm over our breasts and limbs and inspire our men with amorous longing and priapic spasms, I think we may soon be called Peacemakers among the Greeks.

MAGISTRATE. What will you do?

LYSISTRATA. First of all, we'll stop those fellows who run madly about the Marketplace in arms.

FIRST WOMAN. Indeed we shall, by the Queen of Paphos.

LYSISTRATA. For now they roam about the market, amid the pots and greenstuffs, armed to the teeth like Corybantes.

MAGISTRATE. That's what manly fellows ought to do!

LYSISTRATA. But it's so silly: a chap with a Gorgon-emblazoned shield buying pickled herring.

FIRST WOMAN. Why, just the other day I saw one of those long-haired dandies who command our cavalry ride up on horseback and pour into his bronze helmet the egg-broth he'd bought from an old dame. And there was a Thracian slinger too, shaking his lance like Tereus; he'd scared the life out of the poor fig-peddler and was gulping down all her ripest fruit.

MAGISTRATE. How can you stop all the confusion in the various states and bring them together?

LYSISTRATA. Very easily.

MAGISTRATE. Tell me how.

LYSISTRATA. Just like a ball of wool, when it's confused and snarled: we take it thus, and draw out a thread here and a thread there with our spindles; thus we'll unsnarl this war, if no one prevents us, and draw together the various states with embassies here and embassies there.

MAGISTRATE. Do you suppose you can stop this dreadful business with balls of wool and spindles, you nit-wits?

LYSISTRATA. Why, if *you* had any wits, you'd manage all affairs of state like our wool-working.

MAGISTRATE. How so?

LYSISTRATA. First you ought to treat the city as we do when we wash the dirt out of a fleece: stretch it out and pluck and thrash out of the city all those prickly scoundrels; aye, and card out those who conspire and stick together to gain office, pulling off their heads. Then card the wool, all of it, into one fair basket of good-will, mingling in the aliens residing here, any loyal foreigners, and any-one who's in debt to the Treasury; and consider that all our colonies lie scattered round about like remnants; from all of these collect the wool and gather it together here, wind up a great ball, and then weave a good stout cloak for the democracy.

MAGISTRATE. Dreadful! Talking about thrashing and winding balls of wool, when you haven't the slightest share in the war!

LYSISTRATA. Why, you dirty scoundrel, we bear more than twice as much as you. First, we bear children and send off our sons as soldiers.

MAGISTRATE. Hush! Let bygones be bygones!

LYSISTRATA. Then, when we ought to be happy and enjoy our youth, we sleep alone because of your expeditions abroad. But never mind us married women: I grieve most for the maids who grow old at home unwed.

MAGISTRATE. Don't men grow old too?

LYSISTRATA. For heaven's sake! That's not the same thing. When a man comes home, no matter how grey he is, he soon finds a girl to marry. But woman's bloom is short and fleeting; if she doesn't grasp her chance, no man is willing to marry her and she sits at home a prey to every fortune-teller.

MAGISTRATE (*coarsely*). But if a man can still get it up—

LYSISTRATA. See here, you: what's the matter? Aren't you dead yet? There's plenty of room for you. Buy yourself a shroud and I'll bake you a honey-cake. (*handing him a copper coin for his passage across the Styx*) Here's your fare! Now get yourself a wreath.

(*During the following dialogue the women dress up the* MAGISTRATE *as a corpse.*)

FIRST WOMAN. Here, take these fillets.

SECOND WOMAN. Here, take this wreath.

LYSISTRATA. What do you want? What's lacking? Get moving; off to the ferry! Charon is calling you; don't keep him from sailing.

MAGISTRATE. Am I to endure these insults? By God! I'm going straight to the magistrates to show them how I've been treated.

LYSISTRATA. Are you grumbling that you haven't been properly laid out? Well, the day after tomorrow we'll send around all the usual offerings early in the morning.

(*The* MAGISTRATE *goes out still wearing his funeral decorations.* LYSISTRATA *and the women retire into the Acropolis.*)

LEADER OF MEN. Wake, ye sons of freedom, wake! 'Tis no time for sleeping. Up and at them, like a man! Let us strip for action.

(*The* CHORUS OF MEN *remove their outer cloaks.*)

CHORUS OF MEN (*singing*).

Surely there is something here greater than meets the eye;
For without a doubt I smell Hippias' tyranny.
Dreadful fear assails me lest certain bands of Spartan men,
Meeting here with Cleisthenes, have inspired through treachery

All these god-detested women secretly to seize
Athens' treasure in the temple, and to stop that pay
Whence I live at my ease.

LEADER OF MEN. Now isn't it terrible for them to advise the state
and chatter about shields, being mere women?

And they think to reconcile us with the Spartans—men who hold
nothing sacred any more than hungry wolves. Surely this is a web
of deceit, my friends, to conceal an attempt at tyranny. But they'll
never lord it over me; I'll be on my guard and from now on,
    "The blade I bear
    A myrtle spray shall wear."
I'll occupy the market under arms and stand next to Aristogeiton.
    Thus I'll stand beside him. (*He strikes the pose of the famous
statue of the tyrannicides, with one arm raised.*) And here's my
chance to take this accurst old hag and—(*striking the* LEADER OF
WOMEN) smack her on the jaw!

LEADER OF WOMEN. You'll go home in such a state your Ma
won't recognize you! Ladies all, upon the ground let us place these
garments.

    (*The* CHORUS OF WOMEN *remove their outer garments.*)
    CHORUS OF WOMEN (*singing*).

Citizens of Athens, hear useful words for the state.
Rightfully; for it nurtured me in my youth royally.
As a child of seven years carried I the sacred box;
Then I was a Miller-maid, grinding at Athene's shrine;
Next I wore the saffron robe and played Brauronia's Bear;
And I walked as Basket-bearer, wearing chains of figs,
As a sweet maiden fair.

LEADER OF WOMEN. Therefore, am I not bound to give good
advice to the city?

Don't take it ill that I was born a woman, if I contribute something better than our present troubles. I pay my share; for I contribute MEN. But you miserable old fools contribute nothing, and
after squandering our ancestral treasure, the fruit of the Persian
Wars, you make no contribution in return. And now, all on account
of you, we're facing ruin.

What, muttering, are you? If you annoy me, I'll take this hard,

rough slipper and— (*striking the* LEADER OF MEN) smack you on
the jaw!

CHORUS OF MEN. (*singing*).

This is outright insolence! Things go from bad to worse.
If you're men with any guts, prepare to meet the foe.
Let us strip our tunics off! We need the smell of male
Vigour. And we cannot fight all swaddled up in clothes.

(*They strip off their tunics.*)

Come then, my comrades, on to the battle, ye who once to Leipsy-
    drion came;
Then ye were MEN. Now call back your youthful vigour.
With light, wingèd footstep advance,
Shaking old age from your frame.

LEADER OF MEN. If any of us gives these wenches the slightest
hold, they'll stop at nothing: such is their cunning.

They will even build ships and sail against us, like Artemisia. Or
if they turn to mounting, I count our Knights as done for: a woman's
such a tricky jockey when she gets astraddle, with a good firm seat
for trotting. Just look at those Amazons that Micon painted, fighting
on horseback against men!

But we must throw them all in the pillory— (*seizing and choking
the* LEADER OF WOMEN) grabbing hold of yonder neck!

CHORUS OF WOMEN (*singing*).

'Ware my anger! Like a boar 'twill rush upon you men.
Soon you'll bawl aloud for help, you'll be so soundly trimmed!
Come, my friends, let's strip with speed, and lay aside these robes;
Catch the scent of women's rage. Attack with tooth and nail!

(*They strip off their tunics.*)

Now then, come near me, you miserable man! you'll never eat garlic
    or black beans again.
And if you utter a single hard word, in rage I will "nurse" you as
    once
The beetle requited her foe.

LEADER OF WOMEN. For you don't worry me; no, not so long as
my Lampito lives and our Theban friend, the noble Ismenia.

You can't do anything, not even if you pass a dozen—decrees!
You miserable fool, all our neighbours hate you. Why, just the other

day when I was holding a festival for Hecate, I invited as playmate
from our neighbours the Boeotians a charming, wellbred Copaic—
eel. But they refused to send me one on account of your decrees.

And you'll never stop passing decrees until I grab your foot and—
(*tripping up the* LEADER OF MEN) toss you down and break your
neck!

(*Here an interval of five days is supposed to elapse.* LYSISTRATA
comes out from the Acropolis.)

LEADER OF WOMEN. (*dramatically*). Empress of this great em-
prise and undertaking,
Why come you forth, I pray, with frowning brow?

LYSISTRATA. Ah, these cursèd women! Their deeds and female
notions make me pace up and down in utter despair.

LEADER OF WOMEN. Ah, what sayest thou?

LYSISTRATA. The truth, alas! the truth.

LEADER OF WOMEN. What dreadful tale hast thou to tell thy
friends?

LYSISTRATA. 'Tis shame to speak, and not to speak is hard.

LEADER OF WOMEN. Hide not from me whatever woes we suffer.

LYSISTRATA. Well then, to put it briefly, we want—laying!

LEADER OF WOMEN. O Zeus, Zeus!

LYSISTRATA. Why call on Zeus? That's the way things are. I can
no longer keep them away from the men, and they're all deserting.
I caught one wriggling through a hole near the grotto of Pan,
another sliding down a rope, another deserting her post; and yesterday I found one getting on a sparrow's back to fly off to Orsilo-
chus and had to pull her back by the hair. They're digging up all
sorts of excuses to get home. Look, here comes one of them now.
(*A woman comes hastily out of the Acropolis.*) Here you! Where
are you off to in such a hurry?

FIRST WOMAN. I want to go home. My very best wool is being
devoured by moths.

LYSISTRATA. Moths? Nonsense! Go back inside.

FIRST WOMAN. I'll come right back; I swear it. I just want to
lay it out on the bed.

LYSISTRATA. Well, you won't lay it out, and you won't go home,
either.

FIRST WOMAN. Shall I let my wool be ruined?

LYSISTRATA. If necessary, yes. (*Another woman comes out.*)

SECOND WOMAN. Oh dear! Oh dear! My precious flax! I left it at home all unpeeled.

LYSISTRATA. Here's another one, going home for her "flax." Come back here!

SECOND WOMAN. But I just want to work it up a little and then I'll be right back.

LYSISTRATA. No indeed! If you start this, all the other women will want to do the same. (*A third woman comes out.*)

THIRD WOMAN. O Eilithyia, goddess of travail, stop my labour till I come to a lawful spot!

LYSISTRATA. What's this nonsense?

THIRD WOMAN. I'm going to have a baby—right now!

LYSISTRATA. But you weren't even pregnant yesterday.

THIRD WOMAN. Well, I am today. O Lysistrata, do send me home to see a midwife, right away.

LYSISTRATA. What are you talking about? (*putting her hand on her stomach*) What's this hard lump here?

THIRD WOMAN. A little boy.

LYSISTRATA. My goodness, what have you got there? It seems hollow; I'll just find out. (*pulling aside her robe*) Why, you silly goose, you've got Athene's sacred helmet there. And you said you were having a baby!

THIRD WOMAN. Well, I *am* having one, I swear!

LYSISTRATA. Then what's this helmet for?

THIRD WOMAN. If the baby starts coming while I'm still in the Acropolis, I'll creep into this like a pigeon and give birth to it there.

LYSISTRATA. Stuff and nonsense! It's plain enough what you're up to. You just wait here for the christening of this—helmet.

THIRD WOMAN. But I can't sleep in the Acropolis since I saw the sacred snake.

FIRST WOMAN. And I'm dying for lack of sleep: the hooting of the owls keeps me awake.

LYSISTRATA. Enough of these shams, you wretched creatures. You want your husbands, I suppose. Well, don't you think they want us? I'm sure they're spending miserable nights. Hold out, my friends, and endure for just a little while. There's an oracle that we shall conquer, if we don't split up. (*producing a roll of paper*) Here it is.

FIRST WOMAN. Tell us what it says.

LYSISTRATA. Listen.

"When in the length of time the Swallows shall gather together,
Fleeing the Hoopoe's amorous flight and the Cockatoo shunning,
Then shall your woes be ended and Zeus who thunders in heaven
Set what's below on top—"

FIRST WOMAN. What? Are we going to be on top?

LYSISTRATA. "But if the Swallows rebel and flutter away from the
temple,
Never a bird in the world shall seem more wanton and worthless."

FIRST WOMAN. That's clear enough, upon my word!

LYSISTRATA. By all that's holy, let's not give up the struggle now.
Let's go back inside. It would be a shame, my dear friends, to disobey
the oracle.

(*The women all retire to the Acropolis again.*)

CHORUS OF MEN (*singing*).

I have a tale to tell,
Which I know full well.
  It was told me
  In the nursery.

Once there was a likely lad,
  Melanion they name him;
The thought of marriage made him mad,
  For which I cannot blame him.

So off he went to mountains fair;
  (No woman to upbraid him!)
A mighty hunter of the hare,
  He had a dog to aid him.

He never came back home to see
  Detested women's faces.
He showed a shrewd mentality.
  With him I'd fain change places!

ONE OF THE MEN (*to one of the women*). Come here, old dame;
give me a kiss.

WOMAN. You'll ne'er eat garlic, if you dare!

MAN. I want to kick you—just like this!

WOMAN. Oh, there's a leg with bushy hair!

MAN. Myronides and Phormio

Were hairy—and they thrashed the foe.
CHORUS OF WOMEN. (*singing*).

I have another tale,
With which to assail
    Your contention
    'Bout Melanion.

Once upon a time a man
    Named Timon left our city,
To live in some deserted land.
    (We thought him rather witty.)

He dwelt alone amidst the thorn;
    In solitude he brooded.
From some grim Fury he was born:
    Such hatred he exuded.

He cursed you men, as scoundrels through
    And through, till life he ended.
He couldn't stand the sight of YOU!
    But women he befriended.

WOMAN (*to one of the men*). I'll smash your face in, if you like.
MAN. Oh no, please don't! You frighten me.
WOMAN. I'll lift my foot—and thus I'll strike.
MAN. Aha; Look there! What's that I see?
WOMAN. Whate'er you see, you cannot say
That I'm not neatly trimmed today.

(LYSISTRATA *appears on the wall of the Acropolis.*)
LYSISTRATA. Hello! Hello! Girls, come here quick!
(*Several women appear beside her.*)
WOMAN. What is it? Why are you calling?
LYSISTRATA. I see a man coming: he's in a dreadful state. He's
mad with passion. O Queen of Cyprus, Cythera, and Paphos, just
keep on this way!
WOMAN. Where is the fellow?
LYSISTRATA. There, beside the shrine of Demeter.
WOMAN. Oh yes, so he is. Who is he?
LYSISTRATA. Let's see. Do any of you know him?
MYRRHINE. Yes indeed. That's my husband, Cinesias.
LYSISTRATA. It's up to you, now: roast him, rack him, fool him,

love him—and leave him! Do everything, except what our oath forbids.

MYRRHINE. Don't worry; I'll do it.

LYSISTRATA. I'll stay here to tease him and warm him up a bit. Off with you.

(*The other women retire from the wall. Enter* CINESIAS *followed by a slave carrying a baby.* CINESIAS *is obviously in great pain and distress.*)

CINESIAS (*groaning*). Oh-h! Oh-h-h! This is killing me! O God, what tortures I'm suffering!

LYSISTRATA (*from the wall*). Who's that within our lines?

CINESIAS. Me.

LYSISTRATA. A *man?*

CINESIAS (*pointing*). A *man,* indeed!

LYSISTRATA. Well, go away!

CINESIAS. Who are you to send me away?

LYSISTRATA. The captain of the guard.

CINESIAS. Oh, for heaven's sake, call out Myrrhine for me.

LYSISTRATA. Call Myrrhine? Nonsense! Who are you?

CINESIAS. Her husband, Cinesias of Paionidai.

LYSISTRATA (*appearing much impressed*). Oh, greetings, friend. Your name is not without honour here among us. Your wife is always talking about you, and whenever she takes an egg or an apple, she says, "Here's to my dear Cinesias!"

CINESIAS (*quivering with excitement*). Oh, ye gods in heaven!

LYSISTRATA. Indeed she does! And whenever our conversations turn to men, your wife immediately says, "All others are mere rubbish compared with Cinesias."

CINESIAS (*groaning*). Oh! Do call her for me.

LYSISTRATA. Why should I? What will you give me?

CINESIAS. Whatever you want. All I have is yours—and you see what I've got.

LYSISTRATA. Well then, I'll go down and call her. (*She descends.*)

CINESIAS. And hurry up! I've had no joy of life ever since she left home. When I go in the house, I feel awful: everything seems so empty and I can't enjoy my dinner. I'm in such a state all the time!

MYRRHINE (*from behind the wall*). I *do* love him so. But he won't let me love him. No, no! Don't ask me to see him!

CINESIAS. O my darling, O Myrrhine honey, why do you do this to me? (MYRRHINE *appears on the wall.*) Come down here!

MYRRHINE. No, I won't come down.

CINESIAS. Won't you come, Myrrhine, when *I* call you?

MYRRHINE. No; you don't want me.

CINESIAS. *Don't want you?* I'm in agony!

MYRRHINE. I'm going now.

CINESIAS. Please don't! At least, listen to our baby. (*to the baby*) Here you, call your mamma! (*pinching the baby*)

BABY. Ma-ma! Ma-ma! Ma-ma!

CINESIAS (*to* MYRRHINE). What's the matter with you? Have you no pity for your child, who hasn't been washed or fed for five whole days?

MYRRHINE. Oh, poor child; your father pays no attention to you.

CINESIAS. Come down then, you heartless wretch, for the baby's sake.

MYRRHINE. Oh, what it is to be a mother! I've got to come down, I suppose. (*She leaves the wall and shortly reappears at the gate.*)

CINESIAS (*to himself*). She seems much younger, and she has such a sweet look about her. Oh, the way she teases me! And her pretty, provoking ways make me burn with longing.

MYRRHINE (*coming out of the gate and taking the baby*). O my sweet little angel! Naughty papa! Here, let Mummy kiss you, Mamma's little sweetheart! (*She fondles the baby lovingly.*)

CINESIAS (*in despair*). You heartless creature, why do you do this? Why follow these other women and make both of us suffer so? (*He tries to embrace her.*)

MYRRHINE. Don't touch me!

CINESIAS. You're letting all our things at home go to wrack and ruin.

MYRRHINE. I don't care.

CINESIAS. You don't care that your wool is being plucked to pieces by the chickens?

MYRRHINE. Not in the least.

CINESIAS. And you haven't celebrated the rites of Aphrodite for ever so long. Won't you come home?

MYRRHINE. Not on your life, unless you men make a truce and stop the war.

CINESIAS. Well then, if that pleases you, we'll do it.

MYRRHINE. Well then, if that pleases *you,* I'll come home—afterwards! Right now I'm on oath not to.

CINESIAS. Then just lie down here with me for a moment.

MYRRHINE. No— (*in a teasing voice*) and yet, I won't say I don't love you.

CINESIAS. You love me? Oh, do lie down here, Myrrhine dear!

MYRRHINE. What, you silly fool! in front of the baby?

CINESIAS (*hastily thrusting the baby at the slave*). Of course not. Here—home! Take him, Manes! (*The slave goes off with the baby.*) See, the baby's out of the way. Now won't you lie down?

MYRRHINE. But where, my dear?

CINESIAS. Where? The grotto of Pan's a lovely spot.

MYRRHINE. How could I purify myself before returning to the shrine?

CINESIAS. Easily: just wash here in the Clepsydra.

MYRRHINE. And then, shall I go back on my oath?

CINESIAS. On my head be it! Don't worry about the oath.

MYRRHINE. All right, then, Just let me bring out a bed.

CINESIAS. No, don't. The ground's all right.

MYRRHINE. Heavens, no! Bad as you are, I won't let you lie on the bare ground. (*She goes into the Acropolis.*)

CINESIAS. Why, she really loves me; it's plain to see.

MYRRHINE (*returning with a bed*). There! Now hurry up and lie down. I'll just slip off this dress. But—let's see: oh yes, I must fetch a mattress.

CINESIAS. Nonsense! No mattress for me.

MYRRHINE. Yes indeed! It's not nice on the bare springs.

CINESIAS. Give me a kiss.

MYRRHINE (*giving him a hasty kiss*). There! (*She goes.*)

CINESIAS (*in mingled distress and delight*). Oh-h! Hurry back!

MYRRHINE (*returning with a mattress*). Here's the mattress; lie down on it. I'm taking my things off now—but—let's see: you have no pillow.

CINESIAS. I don't *want* a pillow!

MYRRHINE. But I do. (*She goes.*)

CINESIAS. Cheated again, just like Heracles and his dinner!

MYRRHINE (*returning with a pillow*). Here, lift your head. (*to herself, wondering how else to tease him*) Is that all?

CINESIAS. Surely that's all! Do come here, precious!

MYRRHINE. I'm taking off my girdle. But remember: don't go back on your promise about the truce.

CINESIAS. Hope to die, if I do.

MYRRHINE. You don't have a blanket.

CINESIAS (*shouting in exasperation*). I don't want one! I WANT TO—

MYRRHINE. Sh-h! There, there, I'll be back in a minute. (*She goes.*)

CINESIAS. She'll be the death of me with these bed-clothes.

MYRRHINE (*returning with a blanket*). Here, get up.

CINESIAS. I've got *this* up!

MYRRHINE. Would you like some perfume?

CINESIAS. Good heavens, no! I won't have it!

MYRRHINE. Yes, you shall, whether you want it or not. (*She goes.*)

CINESIAS. O lord! Confound all perfumes anyway!

MYRRHINE (*returning with a flask*). Stretch out your hand and put some on.

CINESIAS (*suspiciously*). By God, I don't much like this perfume. It smacks of shilly-shallying, and has no scent of the marriage-bed.

MYRRHINE. Oh dear! This is Rhodian perfume I've brought.

CINESIAS. It's quite all right, dear. Never mind.

MYRRHINE. Don't be silly! (*She goes out with the flask.*)

CINESIAS. Damn the man who first concocted perfumes!

MYRRHINE (*returning with another flask*). Here, try this flask.

CINESIAS. I've got another one all ready for you. Come, you wretch, lie down and stop bringing me things.

MYRRHINE. All right; I'm taking off my shoes. But, my dear, see that you vote for peace.

CINESIAS (*absently*). I'll consider it. (MYRRHINE *runs away to the Acropolis.*) I'm ruined! The wench has skinned me and run away! (*chanting, in a tragic style*) Alas! Alas! Deceived, deserted by this fairest of women, whom shall I—lay? Ah, my poor little child, how shall I nurture thee? Where's Cynalopex? I needs must hire a nurse.

LEADER OF MEN (*chanting*). Ah, wretched man, in dreadful wise beguiled, betrayed, thy soul is sore distressed. I pity thee, alas! alas! What soul, what loins, what liver could stand this strain? How firm and unyielding he stands, with naught to aid him of a morning.

CINESIAS. O lord! O Zeus! What tortures I endure!

LEADER OF MEN. This is the way she's treated you, that vile and cursèd wanton.

LEADER OF WOMEN. Nay, not vile and cursèd, but sweet and dear.

LEADER OF MEN. Sweet, you say? Nay, hateful, hateful!

CINESIAS. Hateful indeed! O Zeus, Zeus!
Seize her and snatch her away,
Like a handful of dust, in a mighty,
Fiery tempest! Whirl her aloft, then let her drop
Down to the earth, with a crash, as she falls—
On the point of this waiting
    Thingummybob! (*He goes out.*)

(*Enter a Spartan* HERALD, *in an obvious state of excitement, which he is doing his best to conceal.*)

HERALD. Where can I find the Senate or the Prytanes? I've got an important message. (*The Athenian* MAGISTRATE *enters.*)

MAGISTRATE. Say there, are you a man or Priapus?

HERALD (*in annoyance*). I'm a herald, you lout! I've come from Sparta about the truce.

MAGISTRATE. Is that a spear you've got under your cloak?

HERALD. No, of course not!

MAGISTRATE. Why do you twist and turn so? Why hold your cloak in front of you? Did you rupture yourself on the trip?

HERALD. By gum, the fellow's an old fool.

MAGISTRATE (*pointing*). Why, you dirty rascal, you're all excited.

HERALD. Not at all. Stop this tom-foolery.

MAGISTRATE. Well, what's that I see?

HERALD. A Spartan message-staff.

MAGISTRATE. Oh, certainly! That's just the kind of message-staff I've got. But tell me the honest truth: how are things going in Sparta?

HERALD. All the land of Sparta is up in arms—and our allies are up, too. We need Pellene.

MAGISTRATE. What brought this trouble on you? A sudden Panic?

HERALD. No, Lampito started it and then all the other women in Sparta with one accord chased their husbands out of their beds.

MAGISTRATE. How do you feel?

HERALD. Terrible. We walk around the city bent over like men lighting matches in a wind. For our women won't let us touch them until we all agree and make peace throughout Greece.

MAGISTRATE. This is a general conspiracy of the women; I see it now. Well, hurry back and tell the Spartans to send ambassadors here with full powers to arrange a truce. And I'll go tell the Council to choose ambassadors from here; I've got a little something here that will soon persuade them!

HERALD. I'll fly there; for you've made an excellent suggestion.

(*The* HERALD *and the* MAGISTRATE *depart on opposite sides of the stage.*)

LEADER OF MEN. No beast or fire is harder than womankind to tame,

Nor is the spotted leopard so devoid of shame.

LEADER OF WOMEN. Knowing this, you dare provoke us to attack? I'd be your steady friend, if you'd but take us back.

LEADER OF MEN. I'll never cease my hatred keen of womankind.

LEADER OF WOMEN. Just as you will. But now just let me help you find

That cloak you threw aside. You look so silly there

Without your clothes. Here, put it on and don't go bare.

LEADER OF MEN. That's very kind, and shows you're not entirely bad.

But I threw off my things when I was good and mad.

LEADER OF WOMEN. At last you seem a man, and won't be mocked, my lad.

If you'd been nice to me, I'd take this little gnat

That's in your eye and pluck it out for you, like that.

LEADER OF MEN. So that's what's bothered me and bit my eye so long!

Please dig it out for me. I own that I've been wrong.

LEADER OF WOMEN. I'll do so, though you've been a most ill-natured brat.

Ye gods! See here! A huge and monstrous little gnat!

LEADER OF MEN. Oh, how that helps! For it was digging wells in me.

And now it's out, my tears can roll down hard and free.

LEADER OF WOMEN. Here, let me wipe them off, although you're such a knave,

And kiss me.

LEADER OF MEN. No!

LEADER OF WOMEN. Whate'er you say, a kiss I'll have. (*She kisses him.*)

LEADER OF MEN. Oh, confound these women!
They've a coaxing way about them.
He was wise and never spoke a truer word, who said,
"We can't live with women, but we cannot live without them."
Now I'll make a truce with you. We'll fight no more; instead,
    I will not injure you if you do me no wrong.
    And now let's join our ranks and then begin a song.
COMBINED CHORUS (*singing*).

Athenians, we're not prepared,
To say a single ugly word
About our fellow-citizens.
Quite the contrary: we desire but to say and to do
Naught but good. Quite enough are the ills now on hand.

Men and women, be advised:
    If anyone requires
Money—minae two or three—
    We've got what he desires.

My purse is yours, on easy terms:
When Peace shall reappear,
Whate'er you've borrowed will be due.
    So speak up without fear.

You needn't pay me back, you see,
If you can get a cent from me!

We're about to entertain
    Some foreign gentlemen;
We've soup and tender, fresh-killed pork.
    Come round to dine at ten.

Come early; wash and dress with care,
    And bring the children, too.
Then step right in, no "by your leave."
    We'll be expecting you.

Walk in as if you owned the place.
You'll find the door—shut in your face!

(*Enter a group of Spartan Ambassadors; they are in the same
desperate condition as the Herald in the previous scene.*)

LEADER OF CHORUS. Here come the envoys from Sparta, sprouting
long beards and looking for all the world as if they were carrying
pig-pens in front of them.

Greetings, gentlemen of Sparta. Tell me, in what state have you
come?

SPARTAN. Why waste words? You can plainly see what state we've
come in!

LEADER OF CHORUS. Wow! You're in a pretty high-strung condition, and it seems to be getting worse.

SPARTAN. It's indescribable. Won't someone please arrange a
peace for us—in any way you like.

LEADER OF CHORUS. Here come our own, native ambassadors,
crouching like wrestlers and holding their clothes in front of them;
this seems an athletic kind of malady.

(*Enter several Athenian Ambassadors.*)

ATHENIAN. Can anyone tell us where Lysistrata is? You see our
condition.

LEADER OF CHORUS. Here's another case of the same complaint.
Tell me, are the attacks worse in the morning?

ATHENIAN. No, we're always afflicted this way. If someone doesn't
soon arrange this truce, you'd better not let me get my hands on—
Cleisthenes!

LEADER OF CHORUS. If you're smart, you'll arrange your cloaks so
none of the fellows who smashed the Hermae can see you.

ATHENIAN. Right you are; a very good suggestion.

SPARTAN. Aye, by all means. Here, let's hitch up our clothes.

ATHENIAN. Greetings, Spartan. We've suffered dreadful things.

SPARTAN. My dear fellow, we'd have suffered still worse if one of
those fellows had seen us in this condition.

ATHENIAN. Well, gentlemen, we must get down to business.
What's your errand here?

SPARTAN. We're ambassadors about peace.

ATHENIAN. Excellent; so are we. Only Lysistrata can arrange
things for us; shall we summon her?

SPARTAN. Aye, and Lysistratus too, if you like.

LEADER OF CHORUS. No need to summon her, it seems. She's
coming out of her own accord.

(*Enter* LYSISTRATA *accompanied by a statue of a nude female figure, which represents Reconciliation.*)
Hail noblest of women; now must thou be
A judge shrewd and subtle, mild and severe,
Be sweet yet majestic: all manners employ.
The leaders of Hellas, caught by thy love-charms,
Have come to thy judgment, their charges submitting.

LYSISTRATA. This is no difficult task, if one catch them still in amorous passion, before they've resorted to each other. But I'll soon find out. Where's Reconciliation? Go, first bring the Spartans here, and don't seize them rudely and violently, as our tactless husbands used to do, but as befits a woman, like an old, familiar friend; if they won't give you their hands, take them however you can. Then go fetch these Athenians here, taking hold of whatever they offer you. Now then, men of Sparta, stand here beside me, and you Athenians on the other side, and listen to my words.

I am a woman, it is true, but I have a mind; I'm not badly off in native wit, and by listening to my father and my elders, I've had a decent schooling.

Now I intend to give you a scolding which you both deserve. With one common font you worship at the same altars, just like brothers, at Olympia, at Thermopylae, at Delphi—how many more might I name, if time permitted;—and the Barbarians stand by waiting with their armies; yet you are destroying the men and towns of Greece.

ATHENIAN. Oh, this tension is killing me!

LYSISTRATA. And now, men of Sparta,—to turn to you—don't you remember how the Spartan Pericleidas came here once as a suppliant, and sitting at our altar, all pale with fear in his crimson cloak, begged us for an army? For all Messene had attacked you and the god sent an earthquake too? Then Cimon went forth with four thousand hoplites and saved all Lacedaemon. Such was the aid you received from Athens, and now you lay waste the country which once treated you so well.

ATHENIAN (*hotly*). They're in the wrong, Lysistrata, upon my word, they are!

SPARTAN (*absently, looking at the statue of Reconciliation*). We're in the wrong. What hips! How lovely they are!

LYSISTRATA. Don't think I'm going to let you Athenians off. Don't you remember how the Spartans came in arms when you were wearing the rough, sheepskin cloak of slaves and slew the host of Thessalians, the comrades and allies of Hippias? Fighting with you on that day, alone of all the Greeks, they set you free and instead of a sheepskin gave your folk a handsome robe to wear.

SPARTAN (*looking at* LYSISTRATA). I've never seen a more distinguished woman.

ATHENIAN (*looking at Reconciliation*). I've never seen a more voluptuous body!

LYSISTRATA. Why then, with these many noble deeds to think of, do you fight each other? Why don't you stop this villainy? Why not make peace? Tell me, what prevents it?

SPARTAN (*waving vaguely at Reconciliation*). We're willing, if you're willing to give up your position on yonder flank.

LYSISTRATA. What position, my good man?

SPARTAN. Pylus; we've been panting for it for ever so long.

ATHENIAN. No, by God! You shan't have it!

LYSISTRATA. Let them have it, my friend.

ATHENIAN. Then what shall we have to rouse things up?

LYSISTRATA. Ask for another place in exchange.

ATHENIAN. Well, let's see: first of all (*pointing to various parts of Reconciliation's anatomy*) give up Echinus here, this Maliac Inlet in back there, and these two Megarian legs.

SPARTAN. No, by heavens! You can't have *everything,* you crazy fool!

LYSISTRATA. Let it go. Don't fight over a pair of legs.

ATHENIAN (*taking off his cloak*). I think I'll strip and do a little planting now.

SPARTAN (*following suit*). And I'll just do a little fertilizing, by gosh!

LYSISTRATA. Wait until the truce is concluded. Now if you've decided on this course, hold a conference and discuss the matter with your allies.

ATHENIAN. Allies? Don't be ridiculous! They're in the same state we are. Won't all our allies want the same thing we do—to jump in bed with their women?

SPARTAN. Ours will, I know.

ATHENIAN. Especially the Carystians, by God!

LYSISTRATA. Very well. Now purify yourselves, that your wives may feast and entertain you in the Acropolis; we've provisions by the basketfull. Exchange your oaths and pledges there, and then each of you may take his wife and go home.

ATHENIAN. Let's go at once.

SPARTAN. Come on, where you will.

ATHENIAN. For God's sake, let's hurry!

(*They all go into the Acropolis.*)

CHORUS (*singing*).

Whate'er I have of coverlets
   And robes of varied hue
And golden trinkets,—without stint
   I offer them to you.

Take what you will and bear it home,
   Your children to delight,
Or if your girl's a Basket-maid;
   Just choose whate'er's in sight.

There's naught within so well secured
   You cannot break the seal
And bear it off; just help yourselves;
   No hesitation feel.

But you'll see nothing, though you try,
Unless you've sharper eyes than I!

If anyone needs bread to feed
   A growing family,
I've lots of wheat and full-grown loaves;
   So just apply to me.

Let every poor man who desires
   Come round and bring a sack
To fetch the grain; my slave is there
To load it on his back.

But don't come near my door, I say:
Beware the dog, and stay away!

(*An* ATHENIAN *enters carrying a torch; he knocks at the gate.*)

ATHENIAN. Open the door! (*to the* CHORUS, *which is clustered around the gate*) Make way, won't you! What are you hanging around for? Want me to singe you with this torch? (*to himself*)

No; it's a stale trick, I won't do it! (*to the audience*) Still, if I've got to do it to please *you,* I suppose I'll have to take the trouble.

(*A* SECOND ATHENIAN *comes out of the gate.*)

SECOND ATHENIAN. And I'll help you.

FIRST ATHENIAN (*waving his torch at the* CHORUS). Get out! Go bawl your heads off! Move on here, so the Spartans can leave in peace when the banquet's over.

(*They brandish their torches until the* CHORUS *leaves the Orchestra.*)

SECOND ATHENIAN. I've never seen such a pleasant banquet: the Spartans are charming fellows, indeed they are! And we Athenians are very witty in our cups.

FIRST ATHENIAN. Naturally: for when we're sober we're never at our best. If the Athenians would listen to me, we'd always get a little tipsy on our embassies. As things are now, we go to Sparta when we're sober and look around to stir up trouble. And then we don't hear what they say—and as for what they *don't* say, we have all sorts of suspicions. And then we bring back varying reports about the mission. But this time everything is pleasant; even if a man should sing the Telamon-song when he ought to sing "Cleitagoras," we'd praise him and swear it was excellent.

(*The two* CHORUSES *return, as a* CHORUS OF ATHENIANS *and a* CHORUS OF SPARTANS.)

Here they come back again. Go to the devil, you scoundrels!

SECOND ATHENIAN. Get out, I say! They're coming out from the feast.

(*Enter the Spartan and Athenian envoys, followed by* LYSISTRATA *and all the women.*)

SPARTAN (*to one of his fellow-envoys*). My good fellow, take up your pipes; I want to do a fancy two-step and sing a jolly song for the Athenians.

ATHENIAN. Yes, do take your pipes, by all means. I'd love to see you dance.

SPARTAN (*singing and dancing with the* CHORUS OF SPARTANS). These youths inspire

To song and dance, O Memory;
Stir up my Muse, to tell how we
And Athens' men, in our galleys clashing

At Artemisium, 'gainst foemen dashing in godlike ire,
Conquered the Persian and set Greece free.
    Leonidas

Led on his valiant warriors
Whetting their teeth like angry boars.
Abundant foam on their lips was flow'ring,
A stream of sweat from their limbs was show'ring.
The Persian was
Numberless as the sand on the shores.

O Huntress who slayest the beasts in the glade,
O Virgin divine, hither come to our truce,
Unite us in bonds which all time will not loose.
Grant us to find in this treaty, we pray,
An unfailing source of true friendship today,
And all of our days, helping us to refrain
From weaseling tricks which bring war in their train.
    Then hither, come hither! O huntress maid.

LYSISTRATA. Come then, since all is fairly done, men of Sparta,
lead away your wives, and you, Athenians, take yours. Let every man
stand beside his wife, and every wife beside her man, and then, to
celebrate our fortune, let's dance. And in the future, let's take care
to avoid these misunderstandings.
CHORUS OF ATHENIANS (*singing and dancing*).

Lead on the dances, your graces revealing.
Call Artemis hither, call Artemis' twin,
Leader of dances, Apollo the Healing,
Kindly God—hither! let's summon him in!

    Nysian Bacchus call,
Who with his Maenads, his eyes flashing fire,
    Dances, and last of all
Zeus of the thunderbolt flaming, the Sire,
    And Hera in majesty,
    Queen of prosperity.

    Come, ye Powers who dwell above
Unforgetting, our witnesses be
Of Peace with bonds of harmonious love—

The Peace which Cypris has wrought for me.
   Alleluia! Io Paean!
   Leap in joy—hurrah! hurrah!
   'Tis victory—hurrah! hurrah!
   Euoi! Euoi! Euai! Euai!

LYSISTRATA *(to the Spartans).* Come now, sing a new song to cap ours.

CHORUS OF SPARTANS *(singing and dancing).*

Leaving Taygetus fair and renown'd
Muse of Laconia, hither come:
Amyclae's god in hymns resound,
Athene of the Brazen Home,
And Castor and Pollux, Tyndareus' sons,
Who sport where Eurotas murmuring runs.

   On with the dance! Heia! Ho!
      All leaping along,
   Mantles a-swinging as we go!
      Of Sparta our song.
There the holy chorus ever gladdens,
There the beat of stamping feet,
As our winsome fillies, lovely maidens,
Dance, beside Eurotas' banks a-skipping,—
   Nimbly go to and fro
Hast'ning, leaping feet in measures tripping,
Like the Bacchae's revels, hair astreaming.
Leda's child, divine and mild,
Leads the holy dance, her fair face beaming.
   On with the dance! as your hand
      Presses the hair
   Streaming away unconfined.
      Leap in the air
   Light as the deer; footsteps resound
   Aiding our dance, beating the ground.
Praise Athene, Maid divine, unrivalled in her might,
Dweller in the Brazen Home, unconquered in the fight.
(All go out singing and dancing.)

THE END

THE POLITICAL BACKGROUND OF *LYSISTRATA*

Evidence shows *Lysistrata* to have been written in the second half of the year 412 B.C.; consequently, it is in the events of that year or in those which slightly precede it that an explanation of the intention and dispositions of the poet must be sought.* When word came to Athens of the disaster that had befallen the army in Sicily in September of 413, it produced an explosion of anger followed by a profound stupor; and yet, the energetic spirit of Athens reacted almost at once. No one at that time proposed to make peace; by common consent, preparations were made for vigorous resistance, and the sense of danger had the effect of allaying discussion and of making the masses more tractable. The military events of 412 did not alter the situation, and careful politicians could not consider the possibility of negotiating a peace. How did it happen then that Aristophanes, just at this time, conceived the idea of writing a comedy in favor of peace? A comic poet might, in case of need, antagonize a prevailing opinion, but evidently only if he could rely upon at least a considerable and influential minority. There was no such minority favoring peace in the Athenian masses in 411, the year in which *Lysistrata* was first performed. What Aristophanes tried to do in this comedy was to appeal to deep-seated opinions that were for the moment kept back and restrained by urgent considerations, but which only awaited an opportunity to gain the upper hand. He fully shared these opinions and tried to show, in his own fashion, that their realization was not so far distant nor so impossible as people about him commonly thought. Aristophanes did this independently of all party influence and placed himself above party considerations by the choice of his representatives: there is no aristocratic chorus, nor any spokesman for the rural democracy; the mouthpieces of the poet are women, and foremost of all Lysistrata, drawn together by a common interest which is not that of any party or of any city in particular. By his choice of representatives, Aristophanes gives us to understand that he is devoted to a more

* Abstracted from Maurice Croiset, *Aristophanes and the Political Parties at Athens,* translated by James Loeb, London, 1909, 115-143.

general and truly human concern than political interest. Everything in *Lysistrata* combines to characterize his political tendency as absolutely independent, and if he aims at any domestic reform it is only the allaying of hatred, the surrender of prejudices, and the cooperation of citizens in a spirit of mutual good will.

PEACE, POLITICS, AND THE GODS IN *LYSISTRATA*

Although the peace in *Lysistrata* seems at first glance to be the work of Aphrodite, it is in fact brought about by the action of the women in the play, unhindered and unhelped by the gods.* Further, no character represents the poet or is a spokesman for the poet. Because the poet does not act within *Lysistrata,* the women must act; and must act like men because war must become the business of women. They must bring peace not through the deeds of Aphrodite, but by emulating the virgin goddesses Artemis and Athena; these two goddesses are more implicitly present in *Lysistrata* than in any other play. At the end of the play, the emphasis is wholly on the warlike Athena who, having neither given birth nor even having been born herself, embodies denial of life. Peace is brought about, then, by Lysistrata through the effect of the wives' strike against the husbands. The strike would be ineffective if the husbands were not at home and if the wives did not have greater self-control than their husbands (this is supported by the very existence of the goddesses Artemis and Athena). Lysistrata's plan is based upon an unnatural coincidence of *physis* (nature) and *nomos* (law) by which war would be against nature since it damns men and women to sexual starvation or blocks the generation of offspring. More significantly, all of this is merely preparatory to the women's taking political power; Lysistrata's design ultimately requires a change of regime as well as a sex strike. If one assumes that the women in *Lysistrata* represent those men who favor peace and that the men in

* Abstracted from Leo Strauss, *Socrates and Aristophanes,* New York, 1966, 195-213.

the play represent those men who favor war, then the play suggests that the best way to achieve peace under the circumstances is by a change in the Athenian regime. The laughable aspect of the play's action is limited to the sex strike; perhaps the change of regime is the poet's serious proposal. If so, *Lysistrata* comes closer than any of Aristophanes' plays to suggesting a serious political proposal. Through the women's actions, Aristophanes may be commenting on the actions of higher and more dangerous beings.

PROLOGUE, AGON, AND THE STRUCTURE OF *LYSISTRATA*

The Aristophanic Prologue consists of three divisions: parade, recitation, and exposition.* In the first, two characters of lesser importance discuss the situation in general terms without revealing details. In the recitation, an explanation of the plot is given either directly to the audience or is disclosed as the dialogue develops. The exposition comprises several short scenes that further develop the plot and prepare the way for the imminent entrance of the chorus. With but few exceptions, Aristophanic Prologues, including that of *Lysistrata,* show these divisions; two other plays that open directly with the recitation are parodies of Euripides' use of the Prologue as an undramatic program (with its features of invocation of the land and the genealogical tree). The Agon, or argument, is a highly formal debate in which the chorus delivers odes but is excluded from actual participation in the contest. The agonists, or contestants, often share the action with a third figure—a buffoon who provides comic relief with humorous irrelevancies. In Aristophanes' hands, the Agon is of great importance: his comedies center on some absurdly brilliant and quite impracticable proposition conceived by the hero at

* Abstracted from M. Whittaker, "The Comic Fragments in Their Relation to the Structure of Old Attic Comedy," *Classical Quarterly, XXIX* (1935), 181-191.

the beginning of the play; he is then forced to contend against opposition, which generally crystallizes in the Agon and forms the crux of the play. The Agon, consequently, is a real debate both in form and content. In *Lysistrata,* Aristophanes also uses the Agon as a convenient frame to conceal what is actually a scene of pure exposition, as opposed to the rather acrimonious debates of other plays. In his plays, Aristophanes uses the Agon to deal with a variety of subjects: education, literature, rhetoric, and comparatively normal politics; *Lysistrata,* however, takes for its subject in the Agon a political innovation of the fantastic type.

LYSISTRATA: THE PLAY

Regular translation, adaptation, production (and occasionally, confiscation) have made *Lysistrata* the modern favorite of all Aristophanes' comedies.* Yet this eminence is not without its dangers: specifically, the widespread but misguided view of the play as a kind of treasure-trove of applied salaciousness. *Lysistrata* is not Aristophanes' most popular play because it is obscene—it is not—or his most prurient—Aristophanes is never prurient—but because it is, to a contemporary reader or viewer, his most cogent and comprehensible. The play's treatment of sex is, in fact, more soothing than shocking; and those aspects of the subject that perhaps make us most uneasy, homosexuality and scatology, are subordinated to the central concern of pleasant ribaldry, heterosexual intercourse. And it is love, not simply sex, that is at the heart of the play; the basic relationship is not unthinking sexual gratification, but the fundamental link between husband and wife—love in its civic embodiment. This is identified with the city of Athens itself: the Akropolis, the heart of the city, is connected with the desired objects, and its restoration represents the achievement of love (the connection between the sex strike and the seizure of the Akropolis is suggested by the old men's attack on the gate with logs they are unable to lift and with fires they are unable to light). The sexual urge is but the beginning; the

* Abstracted from Douglass Parker, *Aristophanes' Lysistrata,* Ann Arbor, 1964, 1-6.

ultimate objective is a unified city and a united, peaceful Hellas. The play ends, significantly, not with an orgy but with an invocation of the whole pantheon; sex and wisdom combine to form the civilizing force of love. Modern readers, with a myopia developed over the centuries, are perhaps too prone to misconstrue this play by viewing the revolt of the women as less fantasy than possibility, by succumbing to sentimentality. *Lysistrata* is not simply a mediocre polemic; it is a great play.

EVERYMAN
ANONYMOUS

TRANSLATED BY
C. G. CHILD

Here beginneth a treatise how the High Father of Heaven sendeth Death to summon every creature to come and give an account of their lives in this world, and is in manner of a moral play.

(*The* MESSENGER *enters.*)
MESSENGER. I pray you all give your audience,
And hear this matter with reverence,
  In form a moral play.
The Summoning of Everyman it is called so,
That of our lives and ending maketh show
  How transitory we be every day.
This matter is wondrous precious,
But the meaning of it is more gracious
  And sweet to bear away.
The story saith: Man, in the beginning
Watch well, and take good heed of the ending,
  Be you never so gay!
Ye think sin in the beginning full sweet,
Which, in the end, causeth the soul to weep,
  When the body lieth in clay.
Here shall you see how Fellowship and Jollity,
Both Strength, Pleasure, and Beauty,
  Will fade from thee as flower in May,
For ye shall hear how our Heaven's King
Calleth Everyman to a general reckoning.
  Give audience and hear what he doth say.
  (*The* MESSENGER *goes*).
GOD SPEAKETH. I perceive, here in my majesty,
  How that all creatures be to me unkind,
Living, without fear, in worldly prosperity.

Everyman, in *Everyman and Other Early Plays,* translated by C. G. Child. Used by permission of Houghton Mifflin Company.

In spiritual vision the people be so blind,
Drowned in sin, they know me not for their God;
   In worldly riches is all their mind.
They fear not my righteousness, the sharp rod.
   My law that I disclosed, when I for them died,
They clean forget, and shedding of my blood red.
   I hung between two it cannot be denied,
To get them life I suffered to be dead,
I healed their feet, with thorns was hurt my head.
   I could do no more than I did truly,
   And now I see the people do clean foresake me;
They use the seven deadly sins damnable
   In such wise that pride, covetousness, wrath, and lechery,
Now in this world be made commendable,
   And thus they leave of angels the heavenly company.
Every man liveth so after his own pleasure,
And yet of their lives they be nothing sure.
The more I them forbear, I see
The worse from year to year they be;
All that live grow more evil apace;
Therefore I will, in briefest space,
From every man in person have a reckoning shown.
For, if I leave the people thus alone
In their way of life and wicked passions to be,
They will become much worse than beasts, verily.
Now for envy would one eat up another, and tarry not,
Charity is by all clean forgot.
I hoped well that every man
In my glory should make his mansion,
And thereto I made them all elect,
But now I see, like traitors abject,
They thank me not for the pleasure that I for them meant,
Nor yet for their being that I them have lent.
I proffered the people great multitude of mercy,
And few there be that ask it heartily.
They be so cumbured with worldly riches, thereto
I must needs upon them justice do,—
On every man living without fear.
Where art thou, Death, thou mighty messenger?

(DEATH *enters.*)

DEATH. Almighty God, I am here at your will,
Your commandment to fulfil.

GOD. Go thou to Everyman,
And show him in my name
A pilgrimage he must on him take,
Which he in no wise may escape,
And that he bring with him a sure reckoning
Without delay or any tarrying.

DEATH. Lord, I will in the world go run over all,
And cruelly search out both great and small.
Every man will I beset that liveth beastly
Out of God's law, and doth not dread folly.
He that loveth riches I will strike with my dart
His sight to blind and him from heaven to part—
Except if Alms be his good friend—
In hell for to dwell, world without end.
Lo, yonder I see Everyman walking.
Full little he thinketh on my coming!
His mind is on fleshly lusts and his treasure,
And great pain it shall cause him to endure
Before the Lord, of Heaven the King.
Everyman, stand still! Wither art thou going
Thus gayly? Hast thou thy Maker forgot?

(EVERYMAN *enters.*)

EVERYMAN. Why askest thou?
Wouldest thou know? For what?

DEATH. Yea, sir, I will show you now.
In great haste I am sent to thee
From God, out of his majesty.

EVERYMAN. What, sent to me!

DEATH. Yea, certainly.
Though thou hast forgot him here,
He thinketh on thee in the heavenly sphere,
As, ere we part, thou shalt know.

EVERYMAN. What desireth God of me?

DEATH. That shall I show thee.
A reckoning he will needs have
    Without any longer respite.

EVERYMAN. To give a reckoning longer leisure I crave.
This blind matter troubleth my wit.

DEATH. Upon thee thou must take a long journey,
Therefore, do thou thine accounting-book with thee bring.
For turn again thou canst not by no way,
And look thou be sure in thy reckoning.
For before God thou shalt answer, and show true
Thy many bad deeds and good but a few,
How thou hast spent thy life and in what wise
Before the Chief Lord of Paradise.
Get thee prepared that we may be upon that journey,
For well thou knowest thou shalt make none for thee attorney.

EVERYMAN. Full unready I am such reckoning to give.
I know thee not. What messenger art thou?

DEATH. I am Death that no man fear,
For every man I arrest and no man spare.
For it is God's commandment
That all to me should be obedient.

EVERYMAN. O Death, thou comest when I had thee least in mind!
In thy power it lieth to save me yet;—
Thereto of my goods will I give thee, if thou wilt be kind,—
Yea, a thousand pounds shalt thou get!—
And defer this matter till another day.

DEATH. Everyman, it may not be in any way.
I set no store by gold, silver, riches, or such gear,
Nor by pope, emperor, king, prince, or peer.
For, if I would receive gifts great,
All the world I might get,
But my custom is clean the contrary way.
I give thee no respite. Come hence, nor delay!

EVERYMAN. Alas, shall I have no longer respite!
I may say Death giveth no warning!
To think on thee, it maketh my heart sick,
For all unready is my book of reckoning.
But if I might have twelve years of waiting,
My accounting-book I would make so clear
That my reckoning I should not need to fear.
Wherefore, Death, I pray thee, for God's mercy,
Spare me till I be provided with a remedy!

DEATH. It availeth thee not to cry, weep, and pray,
But haste thee lightly, that thou mayest be on thy journey,
And make proof of thy friends, if thou can,
For, know thou well, time waiteth for no man,
And in the world each living creature
Because of Adam's sin must die by nature.

EVERYMAN. Death, if I should this pilgrimage take,
And my reckoning duly make,
Show me, for Saint Charity,
Should I not come again shortly?

DEATH. No, Everyman, if once thou art there,
Thou mayest nevermore come here,
Trust me, verily.

EVERYMAN. O gracious God, in the high seat celestial,
Have mercy on me in this utmost need!
Shall I no company have from this vale terrestrial
Of mine acquaintance that way me to lead?

DEATH. Yea, if any be so hardy
As to go with thee and bear thee company.
Haste thee that thou mayest be gone to God's magnificence,
Thy reckoning to give before his presence.
What, thinkest thou thy life is given thee,
And thy worldly goods also?

EVERYMAN. I had thought so, verily.

DEATH. Nay, nay, it was but lent to thee,
For, as soon as thou dost go,
Another a while shall have it and then even so,
Go therefore as thou hast done.
Everyman, thou art mad! Thou hast thy wits five,
And here on earth will not amend thy life,
For suddenly I do come!

EVERYMAN. O wretched caitiff, whither shall I flee
That I may escape this endless sorrow!
Nay, gentle Death, spare me until to-morrow
That I may amend me
With good advisement!

DEATH. Nay, thereto I will not consent,
Nor no man respite, if I might,
But to the heart suddenly I shall smite

Without any "advisement."
And now out of thy sight I will me hie,
See that thou make thee ready speedily,
For thou mayest say this is the day
Wherefrom no man living may escape away.
    EVERYMAN. Alas, I may well weep with sighs deep!
    Now have I no manner of company
To help me on my journey and me to keep,
    And also my writing is all unready.
What can I do that may excuse me!
    I would to God I had never been begot!
To my soul a full great profit it would be.
    For now I fear pains huge and great, God wot!
The time passeth—help, Lord, that all things wrought!
For, though I mourn, yet it availeth naught.
The day passeth and is almost through,
I wot not well of aught that I may do.
To whom were it best that I my plaint should make?
What if to Fellowship I thereof spake,
And what this sudden chance should mean disclosed?
For surely in him is all my trust reposed—
We have in the world so many a day
Been good friends in sport and play.
I see him yonder certainly—
I trust that he will bear me company;
Therefore to him will I speak to ease my sorrow.
Well met, good Fellowship, and a good morrow!
    (*Enter* FELLOWSHIP)
    FELLOWSHIP *speaketh,* I wish thee good morrow, Everyman, by
this day!
    Sir, why lookest thou so piteously?
If anything be amiss, prithee to me it say
    That I may help in remedy.
    EVERYMAN. Yea, good Fellowship, yea,
    I am in great jeopardy!
    FELLOWSHIP. My true friend, show to me your mind.
I will not forsake thee to my live's end,
    In the way of good company.
    EVERYMAN. That was well spoken and lovingly.

FELLOWSHIP. Sir, I must needs know your heaviness.
I have pity to see you in any distress.
If any have wronged you, revenged ye shall be,
Though I upon the ground be slain for thee,
Even should I know before that I should die.
 EVERYMAN. Verily, Fellowship, gramercy!
 FELLOWSHIP. Tush! By thy thanks I set not a straw.
Show me your grief and say no more.
 EVERYMAN. If I my heart should you unfold,
  And you then were to turn your heart from me,
And no comfort would give when I had told,
  Then should I ten times sorrier be.
 FELLOWSHIP. Sir, I say as I will do indeed!
 EVERYMAN. Then you be a good friend at need.
I have found you true heretofore.
 FELLOWSHIP. And so ye shall evermore,
For, in faith, if thou goest to hell,
  I will not forsake thee by the way.
 EVERYMAN. Ye speak like a good friend—I believe you well.
  I shall deserve it, if so I may!
 FELLOWSHIP. I speak of no deserving, by this day.
For he that will say, and nothing do,
Is not worthy with good company to go.
Therefore show me the grief of your mind,
As to your friend most loving and kind.
 EVERYMAN. I shall show you how it is:
  Commanded I am to go a journey,
A long way hard and dangerous,
  And give a strict account without delay
  Before the High Judge, Adonai.
Wherefore, I pray you, bear me company.
As we have promised, on this journey.
 FELLOWSHIP. That is matter, indeed! Promise is duty—
But if I should take such a voyage on me,
I know well it should be to my pain;
Afeard also it maketh me, for certain.
But let us take counsel here as well as we can,
For your words would dismay a strong man.
 EVERYMAN. Why, if I had need, ye said

Ye would never forsake me, quick nor dead,
Though it were to hell truly!

FELLOWSHIP. So I said certainly,
But such pleasant things be set aside, the truth to say;
And also, if we took such a journey,
When should we come again?

EVERYMAN. Nay, never again till the day of doom.

FELLOWSHIP. In faith, then, will I not come there.
Who hath you these tidings brought?

EVERYMAN. Indeed, Death was with me here.

FELLOWSHIP. Now, by God that all hath bought,
If Death were the messenger,
For no man living here below
I will not that loathly journey go—
Not for the father that begat me!

EVERYMAN. Ye promised otherwise, pardy!

FELLOWSHIP. I know well I do say so, truly,
And still, if thou wilt eat and drink and make good cheer,
Or, haunt of women the merry company,
I would not forsake you while the day is clear,
Trust me, verily.

EVERYMAN. Yea, thereto ye would be ready!
To go to mirth, solace, and play,
Your mind would sooner persuaded be
Than to bear me company on my long journey.

FELLOWSHIP. Now, in good sooth, I have no will that way—
But if thou would'st murder, or any man kill,
In that I will help thee with a good will.

EVERYMAN. Oh, that is simple advice, indeed!
Gentle Fellowship, help me in my necessity!
We have loved long, and now I am in need!
And now, gentle Fellowship, remember me!

FELLOWSHIP. Whether ye have loved me or no,
By Saint John, I will not with thee go!

EVERYMAN. Yea, I pray thee, take this task on thee and do so
much for me,
As to bring me forward on my way for Saint Charity,
And comfort me till I come without the town.

FELLOWSHIP. Nay, if thou wouldest give me a new gown,

I will not a foot with thee go.
But, if thou hadst tarried, I would not have left thee so.
And so now, God speed thee on thy journey,
For from thee I will depart as fast as I may!

EVERYMAN. Whither away, Fellowship? Will you forsake me?

FELLOWSHIP. Yea, by my faith! I pray God take thee.

EVERYMAN. Farewell, good Fellowship,—for thee my heart is sore.
Adieu forever, I shall see thee no more!

FELLOWSHIP. In faith, Everyman, farewell now at the ending.
For you I will remember that parting is grieving.

(FELLOWSHIP goes.)

EVERYMAN. Alack! Shall we thus part indeed?
Ah, Lady, help! Lo, vouchsafing no more comfort,
Fellowship thus forsaketh me in my utmost need.
For help in this world whither shall I resort?
Fellowship heretofore with me would merry make,
And now little heed of my sorrow doth he take.
It is said in prosperity men friends may find
Which in adversity be full unkind.
Now whither for succor shall I flee,
Since that Fellowship hath forsaken me?
To my kinsmen will I truly,
Praying them to help me in my necessity.
I believe that they will do so
For "Nature will creep where it may not go."

(KINDRED and COUSIN enter.)

I will go try, for yonder I see them go.
Where be ye now, my friends and kinsmen, lo?

KINDRED. Here we be now at your commandment.
Cousin, I pray you show us your intent
In any wise and do not spare.

COUSIN. Yea, Everyman, and to us declare
If ye be disposed to go any whither,
For, wit you well, we will live and die together!

KINDRED. In wealth and woe we will with you hold,
For "with his own kin a man may be bold."

EVERYMAN. Gramercy, my friends and kinsmen kind!
Now shall I show you the grief of my mind.
I was commanded by a messenger

That is a High King's chief officer.
He bade me go a pilgrimage to my pain,
And I know well I shall never come again;
And I must give a reckoning strait,
For I have a great enemy that lieth for me in wait,
Who intendeth me to hinder.

KINDRED. What account is that which you must render?—
That would I know.

EVERYMAN. Of all my works I must show
How I have lived and my days have spent,
    Also of evil deeds to which I have been used
In my time, since life was to me lent,
    And of all virtues that I have refused.
Therefore, I pray you, go thither with me
To help to make my account, for Saint Charity!

COUSIN. What, to go thither? Is that the matter?
Nay, Everyman, I had liefer fast on bread and water
All this five year and more!

EVERYMAN. Alas, that ever my mother me bore!
For now shall I never merry be,
If that you forsake me!

KINDRED. Ah, sir, come! Ye be a merry man!
    Pluck up heart and make me moan.
But one thing I warn you, by Saint Anne,
    As for me, ye shall go alone!

EVERYMAN. My cousin, will you not with me go?

COUSIN. No, by our Lady! I have the cramp in my toe.
Trust not to me, for, so God me speed,
I will deceive you in your utmost need.

KINDRED. It availeth not us to coax and court.
    Ye shall have my maid, with all my heart.
She loveth to go to feasts, there to make foolish sport
    And to dance, and in antics to take part.
To help you on that journey I will give her leave willingly,
If so be that you and she may agree.

EVERYMAN. Now show me the very truth within your mind—
Will you go with me or abide behind?

KINDRED. Abide behind? Yea, that I will, if I may—
Therefore farewell till another day!

EVERYMAN. How shall I be merry or glad?—
For fair promises men to me make,
But, when I have most need, they me forsake!
I am deceived—that maketh me sad!
COUSIN. Cousin Everyman, farewell now, lo!
For, verily, I will not with thee go.
Also of mine own an unready reckoning,
I have to give account of, therefore I make tarrying.
Now God keep thee, for now I go!
    (KINDRED *and* COUSIN *go.*)
EVERYMAN. Ah, Jesus, is all to this come so?
Lo, "fair words make fools fain,"
They promise, and from deeds refrain.
My kinsmen promised me faithfully
For to abide by me stedfastly,
And now fast away do they flee.
Even so Fellowship promised me.
What friend were it best for me to provide?
I am losing my time longer here to abide.
Yet still in my mind a thing there is,
All my life I have loved riches.
If that my Goods now help me might,
He would make my heart full light.
To him will I speak in my sorrow this day.
My Goods and Riches, where art thou, pray?
    (GOODS *is disclosed hemmed in by chests and bags.*)
GOODS. Who calleth me? Everyman? Why this haste thou hast?
I lie here in corners trussed and piled so high,
And in chests I am locked so fast,
    Also sacked in bags, thou mayest see with thine eye,
I cannot stir; in packs, full low I lie.
What ye would have, lightly to me say.
EVERYMAN. Come hither, Goods, with all the haste thou may,
For counsel straightway I must ask of thee.
GOODS. Sir, if ye in this world have sorrow or adversity,
That can I help you to remedy shortly.
EVERYMAN. It is another disease that grieveth me;
In this world it is not, I tell thee so,
I am sent for another way to go,

To give a strict account general
Before the highest Jupiter of all.
And all my life I have had joy and pleasure in thee,
Therefore I pray thee go with me,
For, peradventure, thou mayest before God Almighty on high
My reckoning help to clean and purify,
For one may hear ever and anon
That "money maketh all right that is wrong."
 GOODS. Nay, Everyman, I sing another song—
I follow no man on such voyages,
For, if I went with thee,
Thou shouldest fare much the worse for me,
For, because on me thou didst set thy mind,
Thy reckoning I have made blotted and blind,
So that thine account thou canst not make truly—
And that hast thou for the love of me.
 EVERYMAN. That would be to me grief full sore and sorrowing,
When I should come that fearful answering.
Up, let us go thither together!
 GOODS. Nay, not so! I am too brittle, I may not endure,
I will follow no man one foot, be ye sure.
 EVERYMAN. Alas! I have thee loved, and had great pleasure
All the days of my life in goods and treasure.
 GOODS. That is to thy damnation, I tell thee a true thing,
For love of me is to the love everlasting contrary.
But if thou hadst the while loved me moderately,
In such wise as to give the poor a part of me,
Then would'st thou not in this dolor be,
Nor in this great sorrow and care.
 EVERYMAN. Lo, now was I deceived ere I was ware,
And all I may blame to misspending of time.
 GOODS. What, thinkest thou I am thine?
 EVERYMAN. I had thought so.
 GOODS. Nay, Everyman, I say no.
Just for a while I was lent to thee,
A season thou hast had me in prosperity.
My nature it is man's soul to kill,
If I save one, a thousand I do spill.
Thinkest thou that I will follow thee?

Nay, from this world not, verily!

EVERYMAN. I had thought otherwise.

GOODS. So it is to thy soul Goods is a thief,
For when thou art dead I straightway devise
Another to deceive in the same wise
    As I have done thee, and all to his soul's grief.

EVERYMAN. O false Goods, cursed may thou be!
Thou traitor to God that hast deceived me,
And caught me in thy snare.

GOODS. Marry, thou broughtest thyself to this care,—
Whereof I am glad!
I must needs laugh, I cannot be sad!

EVERYMAN. Ah, Goods, thou hast had long my hearty love.
I gave thee that which should be the Lord's above.
But wilt thou not go with me, indeed?—
    I pray thee truth to say!

GOODS. No, so God me speed!
    Therefore farewell, and have good-day.
    (GOODS *is hidden from view.*)

EVERYMAN. Oh, to whom shall I make my moan
    For to go with me on that heavy journey!
First Fellowship, so he said, would have with me gone,
    His words were very pleasant and gay,
But afterwards he left me alone;
Then spake I to my kinsmen, all in despair,
And they also gave me words fair,
They lacked not fair speeches to spend,
But all forsook me in the end;
Then went I to my Goods that I loved best,
In hope to have comfort, but there had I least,
For my Goods sharply did me tell
That he bringeth many into hell.
Then of myself I was ashamed,
And so I am worthy to be blamed.
Thus may I well myself hate.
Of whom shall I now counsel take?
I think that I shall never speed
Till I go to my Good Deeds.
But, alas! she is so weak,

That she can neither move nor speak.

Yet will I venture on her now.

My Good Deeds, where be you?

   (GOOD DEEDS *is shown.*)

   GOOD DEEDS. Here I lie, cold in the ground.

Thy sins surely have me bound

That I cannot stir.

   EVERYMAN. O Good Deeds, I stand in fear!

I must pray you for counsel,

For help now would come right well!

   GOOD DEEDS. Everyman, I have understanding

   That ye be summoned your account to make

Before Messias, of Jerusalem King.

   If you do my counsel, that journey with you will I take.

   EVERYMAN. For that I come to you my moan to make.

I pray you that ye will go with me.

   GOOD DEEDS. I would full fain, but I cannot stand, verily.

   EVERYMAN. Why, is there something amiss that did you befall?

   GOOD DEEDS. Yea, Sir, I may thank you for all.

If in every wise ye had encouraged me,

Your book of account full ready would be.

Behold the books of your works and your deeds thereby.

Ah, see, how under foot they lie

   Unto your soul's deep heaviness.

   EVERYMAN. Our Lord Jesus his help vouchsafe to me,

For one letter here I cannot see.

   GOOD DEEDS. There is a blind reckoning in time of distress!

   EVERYMAN. Good Deeds, I pray you help me in this need,

Or else I am forever damned indeed.

Therefore help me to make reckoning

Before him, that Redeemer is of everything,

That is, and was, and shall ever be, King of All.

   GOOD DEEDS. Everyman, I am sorry for your fall,

And fain would I help you, if I were able.

   EVERYMAN. Good Deeds, your counsel, I pray you, give me.

   GOOD DEEDS. That will I do, verily.

Though on my feet I may not go,

I have a sister that shall with you be, also,

Called Knowledge, who shall with you abide,

To help you to make that dire reckoning.
(KNOWLEDGE *enters*.)
KNOWLEDGE. Everyman, I will go with thee and be thy guide,
In thy utmost need to go by thy side.
EVERYMAN. In good condition I am now in every thing,
And am wholly content with this good thing.
Thanks be to God, my creator!
GOOD DEEDS. And when he hath brought thee there,
Where thou shalt heal thee of thy smart,
Then go with thy reckoning and thy good deeds together,
For to make thee joyful at heart
Before the Holy Trinity.
EVERYMAN. My Good Deeds, gramercy!
I am well content, certainly,
With your words sweet.
KNOWLEDGE. Now go we together lovingly
To Confession, that cleansing river fair.
EVERYMAN. For joy I weep—I would we were there!
But, I pray you, give me cognition,
Where dwelleth that holy man, Confession?
KNOWLEDGE. In the House of Salvation.
We shall find him in that place,
That shall us comfort by God's grace.
(CONFESSION *enters*.)
Lo, this is Confession. Kneel down, and ask mercy,
For he is in good favor with God Almighty.
EVERYMAN. O glorious fountain that all uncleanness doth clarify,
Wash from me the spots of vice unclean,
That on me no sin be seen!
I come with Knowledge for my redemption,
Redeemed with heartfelt and full contrition,
For I am commanded a pilgrimage to take,
And great accounts before God to make.
Now I pray you, Shrift, Mother of Salvation,
Help my good deeds because of my piteous exclamation!
CONFESSION. I know your sorrow well, Everyman.
Because with Knowledge ye come to me.
I will you comfort as well as I can,
And a precious stone will I give thee,

Called penance, voice-voider of adversity.
Therewith shall your body chastened be
Through abstinence and perseverance in God's service.
Here shall you receive that scourge of me
That is penance strong, that ye must endure,
To remember thy Saviour was scourged for thee
With sharp scourges, and suffered it patiently—
So must thou ere thou escape from that painful pilgrimage.
Knowledge, do thou sustain him on this voyage,
And by that time Good Deeds will be with thee.
But in any case be sure of mercy,
For your time draweth on fast, if ye will saved be.
Ask God mercy, and he will grant it truly.
When with the scourge of penance man doth him bind,
The oil of forgiveness then shall he find.

   (CONFESSION *goes.*)

   EVERYMAN. Thanked be God for his gracious work,
     For now will I my penance begin.
This hath rejoiced and lightened my heart,
     Though the knots be painful and hard within.
   KNOWLEDGE. Everyman, see that ye your penance fulfil,
     Whatever the pains ye abide full dear,
And Knowledge shall give you counsel at will,
     How your account ye shall make full clear.
   EVERYMAN. O eternal God, O heavenly being,
O way of righteousness, O goodly vision,
Which descended down into a virgin pure
Because he would for every man redeem
     That which Adam forfeited by his disobedience—
O blessed God, elect and exalted in thy divinity,
     Forgive thou my grievous offence!
     Here I cry thee mercy in this presence.

O spiritual treasure, O ransomer and redeemer,
Of all the world the hope and the governor,
Mirror of joy, founder of mercy,
Who illumineth heaven and earth thereby,
Hear my clamorous complaint, though late it be,
Receive my prayers, unworthy in this heavy life!

Though I be a sinner most abominable,
Yet let my name be written in Moses' table.

O Mary, pray to the Maker of everything
To vouchsafe me help at my ending,
And save me from the power of my enemy,
For Death assaileth me strongly!—
And, Lady, that I may, by means of thy prayer,
In your Son's glory as partner share,
Through the mediation of his passion I it crave.
I beseech you, help my soul to save!

Knowledge, give me the scourge of penance;
My flesh therewith shall give acquittance.
I will now begin, if God give me grace.
   KNOWLEDGE. Everyman, God give you time and space!
Thus I bequeath you into the hands of our Saviour,
Now may you make your reckoning sure.
   EVERYMAN. In the name of the Holy Trinity,
My body sorely punished shall be.
Take this, body, for the sin of the flesh.
As thou delightest to go gay and fresh,
And in the way of damnation thou didst me bring.
Therefore suffer now the strokes of punishing.
Now of penance to wade the water clear I desire,
To save me from purgatory, that sharp fire.
   GOOD DEEDS. I thank God now I can walk and go,
And am delivered of my sickness and woe!
Therefore with Everyman I will go and not spare;
His good works I will help him to declare.
   KNOWLEDGE. Now, Everyman, be merry and glad,
Your Good Deeds cometh now, ye may not be sad.
Now is your Good Deeds whole and sound,
Going upright upon the ground.
   (GOOD DEEDS *rises and walks to them.*)
   EVERYMAN. My heart is light and shall be evermore.
Now will I smite faster than I did before.
   GOOD DEEDS. Everyman, pilgrim, my special friend,
Blessed be thou without end!
For thee is prepared the eternal glory.

Now thou hast made me whole and sound this tide,
In every hour I will by thee abide.

EVERYMAN. Welcome, my Good Deeds! Now I hear thy voice,
I weep for sweetness of love.

KNOWLEDGE. Be no more sad, but ever rejoice!
God seeth thy manner of life on his throne above.
Put on this garment to thy behoof,

Which wet with the tears of your weeping is,
Or else in God's presence you may it miss,
When ye to your journey's end come shall.

EVERYMAN. Gentle Knowledge, what do you it call?

KNOWLEDGE. A garment of sorrow it is by name,

From pain it will you reclaim.
Contrition it is,
That getteth forgiveness,
Passing well it doth God please.

GOOD DEEDS. Everyman, will you wear it for your soul's ease?

(EVERYMAN *puts on the robe of contrition.*)

EVERYMAN. Now blessed be Jesu, Mary's son,

For now have I on true contrition!
And let us go now without tarrying.
Good Deeds, have we all clear our reckoning?

GOOD DEEDS. Yea, indeed, I have them here.

EVERYMAN. Then I trust we need not fear.

Now, friends, let us not part in twain!

KNOWLEDGE. Nay, Everyman, that will we not, for certain.

GOOD DEEDS. Yet must thou lead with thee
Three persons of great might.

EVERYMAN. Who should they be?

GOOD DEEDS. Discretion and Strength they hight.

And thy Beauty may not abide behind.

KNOWLEDGE. Also ye must call to mind

Your Five Wits as your counsellors beside.

GOOD DEEDS. You must have them ready at every tide.

EVERYMAN. How shall I get them hither?

KNOWLEDGE. You must call them all together.

And they will hear you immediately.

EVERYMAN. My friends, come hither and present be,

Discretion, Strength, my Five Wits, and Beauty.

(*They enter.*)

BEAUTY. Here at your will be we all ready.
What will ye that we should do?

GOOD DEEDS. That ye should with Everyman go,
And help him in his pilgrimage.
Advise you—will you with him or not, on that voyage?

STRENGTH. We will all bring him thither,
To help him and comfort, believe ye me!

DISCRETION. So will we go with him all together.

EVERYMAN. Almighty God, beloved mayest thou be!
I give thee praise that I have hither brought
Strength, Discretion, Beauty, Five Wits—lack I nought—
And my Good Deeds, with Knowledge clear,
All be in my company at my will here.
I desire no more in this my anxiousness.

STRENGTH. And I, Strength, will stand by you in your distress.
Though thou wouldest in battle fight on the ground.

FIVE WITS. And though it were through the world round,
We will not leave you for sweet or sour.

BEAUTY. No more will I unto Death's hour,
Whatsoever thereof befall.

DISCRETION. Everyman, advise you first of all.
Go with a good advisement and deliberation.
We all give you virtuous monition
That all shall be well.

EVERYMAN. My friends, hearken what I will tell.
I pray God reward you in his heavenly sphere.
Now hearken all that be here,
For I will make my testament
Here before you all present.
   In alms, half my goods will I give with my hands twain,
In the way of charity with good intent,
   And the other half still shall remain
In bequest to return where it ought to be.
This I do in despite of the fiend of hell,
Out of his peril to quit my well
For ever after and this day.

KNOWLEDGE. Everyman, hearken what I say.
Go to Priesthood, I you advise,

And receive of him in any wise
The Holy Sacrament and Unction together,
Then see ye speedily turn again hither.
We will all await you here, verily.
    FIVE WITS. Yea, Everyman, haste thee that ye may ready be.
There is no emperor, king, duke, nor baron bold,
That from God such commission doth hold
As he doth to the least priest in this world consign,
For of the Blessed Sacraments, pure and benign,
He beareth the keys, and thereof hath the cure
For man's redemption, it is ever sure,
Which God as medicine for our souls' gain
Gave us out of his heart with great pain,
Here in this transitory life for thee and me.
Of the Blessed Sacraments seven there be,
Baptism, Confirmation, with Priesthood good,
And the Sacrament of God's precious Flesh and Blood,
Marriage, the Holy Extreme Unction, and Penance.
These seven are good to have in remembrance,
Gracious Sacraments of high divinity.
    EVERYMAN. Fain would I receive that holy body.
And meekly to my spiritual father will I go.
    FIVE WITS. Everyman, that is best that ye can do.
God will you to salvation bring,
For Priesthood exceedeth every other thing.
To us Holy Scripture they do teach,
And convert men from sin, heaven to reach.
God hath to them more power given
Than to any angel that is in heaven.
With five words he may consecrate
God's body in flesh and blood to make,
And handleth his Maker between his hands.
The priest bindeth and unbindeth all bands
Both in earth and heaven.—
Thou dost administer all the Sacraments seven.
Though we should kiss thy feet, yet thereof thou worthy wert.
Thou art the surgeon that doth cure of mortal sin the hurt.
Remedy under God we find none

Except in Priesthood alone.—
Everyman, God gave priests that dignity,
And setteth them in his stead among us to be,
Thus be they above angels in degree.

    KNOWLEDGE. If priests be good, it is so surely;
But when Jesus hung on the cross with grievous smart,
There he gave out of his blessed heart
That same Sacrament in grievous torment.—
He sold them not to us, that Lord omnipotent.
Therefore Saint Peter the apostle doth say
That Jesus' curse have all they
Which God their Saviour do buy or sell,
Or if they for any money do "take or tell."
Sinful priests give sinners bad example in deed and word,
Their children sit by other men's fires, I have heard,
And some haunt of women the company,
With life unclean as through lustful acts of lechery—
These be with sin made blind.

    FIVE WITS. I trust to God no such may we find.
Therefore let us do Priesthood honor,
And follow their doctrines for our souls' succor.
We be their sheep, and they shepherds be,
By whom we all are kept in security.
Peace! for yonder I see Everyman come,
Who unto God hath made true satisfaction.

    GOOD DEEDS. Methinketh it is he indeed.

    EVERYMAN. Now may Jesus all of you comfort and speed!
I have received the Sacrament for my redemption,
And also mine extreme unction.
Blessed be all they that counselled me to take it!
And now, friends, let us go without longer respite.
I thank God ye would so long waiting stand.
Now set each of you on this rood your hand,
And shortly follow me.
I go before where I would be.
God be our guide!

    STRENGTH. Everyman, we will not from you go,
    Till ye have gone this voyage long.

DISCRETION. I, Discretion, will abide by you also.

KNOWLEDGE. And though of this pilgrimage the hardships be
never so strong,
No turning backward in me shall you know.
Everyman, I will be as sure by thee,
As ever I was by Judas Maccabee.

EVERYMAN. Alas! I am so faint I may not stand,
    My limbs under me do fold.
Friends, let us not turn again to this land,
    Not for all the world's gold,
For into this cave must I creep,
And turn to the earth, and there sleep.

BEAUTY. What—into this grave! Alas! Woe is me!

EVERYMAN. Yea, there shall ye consume utterly.

BEAUTY. And what,—must I smother here?

EVERYMAN. Yea, by my faith, and never more appear!
In this world we shall live no more at all,
But in heaven before the highest lord of all.

BEAUTY. I cross out all this! Adieu, by Saint John!
I take "my tap in my lap" and am gone.

EVERYMAN. What, Beauty!—whither go ye?

BEAUTY. Peace! I am deaf, I look not behind me,
Not if thou wouldest give me all the gold in thy chest.
    (BEAUTY goes, followed by the others, as they speak in turn.)

EVERYMAN. Alas! in whom may I trust!
Beauty fast away from me doth hie.
She promised with me to live and die.

STRENGTH. Everyman, I will thee also forsake and deny,
Thy game liketh me not at all!

EVERYMAN. Why, then ye will forsake me all!
Sweet Strength, tarry a little space.

STRENGTH. Nay, Sir, by the rood of grace,
I haste me fast my way from thee to take,
Though thou weep till thy heart do break.

EVERYMAN. Ye would ever abide by me, ye said.

STRENGTH. Yea, I have you far enough conveyed.
Ye be old enough, I understand,
Your pilgrimage to take in hand.
I repent me that I thither came.

EVERYMAN. Strength, for displeasing you I am to blame.
Will ye break "promise that is debt"?
STRENGTH. In faith, I care not!
Thou art but a fool to complain,
You spend your speech and waste your brain.
Go, thrust thyself into the ground!
EVERYMAN. I had thought more sure I should you have found,
But I see well, who trusteth in his Strength,
She him deceiveth at length.
Both Strength and Beauty have forsaken me,
Yet they promised me fair and lovingly.
DISCRETION. Everyman, I will after Strength be gone—
As for me, I will leave you alone.
EVERYMAN. Why, Discretion, will ye forsake me!
DISCRETION. Yea, in faith, I will go from thee,
For when Strength goeth before
I follow after, evermore.
EVERYMAN. Yet, I pray thee, for love of the Trinity
Look in my grave once in pity of me.
DISCRETION. Nay, so nigh will I not come, trust me well!
Now I bid you each farewell.
EVERYMAN. Oh, all things fail save God alone—
Beauty, Strength, and Discretion!
For when Death bloweth his blast,
They all run from me full fast.
FIVE WITS. Everyman, my leave now of thee I take.
I will follow the others, for here I thee forsake.
EVERYMAN. Alas! then may I wail and weep,
For I took you for my best friend.
FIVE WITS. I will thee no longer keep.
Now farewell, and here's an end!
EVERYMAN. O Jesu, help! All have forsaken me.
GOOD DEEDS. Nay, Everyman, I will abide by thee,
I will not forsake thee indeed!
Thou wilt find me a good friend at need.
EVERYMAN. Gramercy, Good Deeds, now may I true friends see.
They have forsaken me everyone,
I loved them better than my Good Deeds alone.
Knowledge, will ye forsake me also?

KNOWLEDGE. Yea, Everyman, when ye to death shall go,
But not yet, for no manner of danger.

EVERYMAN. Gramercy, Knowledge, with all my heart!

KNOWLEDGE. Nay, yet will I not from hence depart,
Till whereunto ye shall come, I shall see and know.

EVERYMAN. Methinketh, alas! that I must now go
To make my reckoning, and my debts pay,
For I see my time is nigh spent away.
Take example, all ye that this do hear or see,
How they that I love best do forsake me,
Except my Good Deeds that abideth faithfully.

GOOD DEEDS. All earthly things are but vanity.
Beauty, Strength and Discretion do man forsake,
Foolish friends and kinsmen that fair spake,
All flee away save Good Deeds, and that am I!

EVERYMAN. Have mercy on me, God most mighty,
And stand by me, thou Mother and Maid, holy Mary!

GOOD DEEDS. Fear not, I will speak for thee.

EVERYMAN. Here I cry God mercy!

GOOD DEEDS. Shorten our end and minish our pain,
Let us go and never come again.

EVERYMAN. Into thy hands, Lord, my soul I commend —
Receive it, Lord, that it be not lost!
As thou didst me buy, so do thou me defend,
And save me from the fiend's boast
That I may appear with that blessed host
That shall be saved at the day of doom.
In manus tuas, of mights the most,
Forever *commendo spiritum meum.*

(EVERYMAN *goes into the grave.*)

KNOWLEDGE. Now that he hath suffered that we all shall endure,
The Good Deeds shall make all sure;
Now that he hath made ending,
Methinketh that I hear angels sing,
And make great joy and melody,
Where Everyman's soul shall received be!

(THE ANGEL *appears.*)

THE ANGEL. Come, excellent elect spouse to Jesu!
Here above shalt thou go,

Because of thy singular virtue.
  Now thy soul from thy body is taken, lo!
Thy reckoning is crystal clear.
Now shalt thou into the heavenly sphere,
Unto which ye all shall come
That live well before the day of doom.
   (THE ANGEL *goes and the* DOCTOR *enters.*)
   DOCTOR. This moral men may have in mind,—
  Ye hearers, take it as of worth, both young and old,
And forsake Pride, for he deceiveth you in the end, as ye will find,
  And remember Beauty, Five Wits, Strength and Discretion all told,
They all at the last do Everyman forsake
Save that his Good Deeds there doth he take
But beware, if they be small,
Before God he hath no help at all,
None excuse for Everyman may there then be there.
Alas how shall he then do and fare!
For after death amends may no man make,
For then Mercy and Pity do him forsake.
If his reckoning be not clear when he doth come,
God will say, *Ite, maledicti, in ignem æternum.*
And he that hath his account whole and sound,
High in heaven he shall be crowned,
Unto which place God bring us all thither
That we may live, body and soul, together!
Thereto their aid vouchsafe the Trinity—
Amen, say ye, for holy Charity!

FINIS

Thus endeth this moral play of Everyman.

DOCTRINE AND DRAMATIC STRUCTURE IN *EVERYMAN*

The fifteenth-century morality *Everyman* is a didactic work in dramatic form.* Yet it has never been analyzed adequately from the point of view of the relationship between its dramatic form and its didactic purpose. In attempting to explain what every man must do to be saved, the preacher-playwright had to reduce the complex answer to this question to terms of simple dramatic representation without falsifying or obscuring the doctrine. In both respects he succeeded, conveying his teaching through apt "characterizations," through simultaneously occurring emotional and doctrinal climaxes, through action that brings into harmony the dramatic and theological elements of Everyman's experience. But the lesson involved is not simply "Do good deeds and you will be saved." Rather, attentive reading reveals with what admirably economy the play dramatizes orthodox Medieval Christian doctrine: to achieve salvation one must do good deeds, but these may be done efficaciously by redeemed Christians only. The man who is saved is the man who repents his sin and places his trust in God. Structurally, the play turns on two climactic desertions of the protagonist by two theologically and dramatically distinct groups of "friends" in whom he has placed his confidence. The first set—Fellowship, Kindred, and Cousin—personify the human associations upon which men expect to be able to rely in times of crisis. The second group personifies the qualities that help man to realize his natural perfection—Beauty, Strength, Discretion, and Five Wits. But they too at length desert him, in the natural order in which such qualities would fade away from a dying man, leaving only Good Deeds to accompany him into the grave. When Everyman finally remembers to call upon his Good Deeds, she is powerless to help until her "sister," Knowledge, comes to the rescue. Past critics have misinterpreted the play by not recognizing that Knowledge stands, not for learning or comprehension of truth, but rather for contrition, or "acknowledgment of one's sin." Knowledge leads the hero to Confession, then to receiving the Eucharist.

* Abstracted from Lawrence V. Ryan, "Doctrine and Dramatic Structure in *Everyman,*" *Speculum,* XXXII (1957), 722-735.

The significance is that only the repentant sinner, with grace channeled to him through the sacraments of the church, may perform deeds that grow out of true charity and hence are profitable to salvation. In conveying this lesson *Everyman* is successful because its author made the doctrinal and dramatic orders coincide perfectly so that what the audience learns grows directly out of the action represented in this finest of English moralities.

THE MEANING OF THE CHARACTER KNOWLEDGE IN *EVERYMAN*

The problem that has troubled scholars for years is whether in the medieval morality play *Everyman* the important character Knowledge really signifies "knowledge."* She is designated as the guide and counselor of Everyman in his journey to salvation, but what kind of knowledge could possibly help Everyman, now summoned by Death? Critics have held that she signifies "contrition" or "acknowledgement of one's sins" or "confession," citing evidence from the *NED* that the word "knowledge" had these meanings in the fourteenth and fifteenth centuries. They overlook the frequent use of the word to mean "acquaintance with truths" in such fourteenth-, fifteenth-, and sixteenth-century works as the *Cursor Mundi* (*ca.* 1300-1350); Barbour's *Bruce* (1375); Caxton's *Fables of Alfonce* (1484); Chaucer's *Parson's Tale; The Court of Sapience* (*ca.* 1465); Caxton's *Royal Book* (1484); Caxton's *Doctrinal of Sapience* (1489); *Ratis Raving; Mundus et Infans* (printed 1522); John Bale's *The Preaching of John the Baptist* (1538); and Sir Thomas Elyot's *Of the Knowledge Which Maketh a Wise Man* (1533). What kind of knowledge does Knowledge, sister of Good Deeds, signify? The answer may be found in the many medieval allegorical moral treatises written about man's journey to the Celestial Jeru-

* Abstracted from Helen S. Thomas, "The Meaning of the Character Knowledge in *Everyman*," *Mississippi Quarterly*, XIV (Winter, 1961), 3-13.

salem. Always there is a Wisdom figure such as the Parson in Chaucer's *Parson's Tale;* Christ in Hoccleve's dialogue *How to Learn to Die,* the *Orologium Sapientiae,* and the morality play *Wisdom;* Grace Dieu in Lygate's *The Pilgramage of the Life of Man;* Dame Nature and Reason in Lygate's *Reason and Sensuallyte;* and Dame Sapience in *The Court of Sapience.* In this last named treatise, Dame Sapience, attended by Intellygence and Science, represents the knowledge of things divine and human necessary for man's salvation, or as she states: "I am the trew propyr knowledge certayn/Of erthely thyng, and eke of thyng diuyne." As a Sapience or Wisdom figure, Knowledge in *Everyman* represents two well-defined aspects of the medieval personification of Wisdom: knowledge and good counsel. She is obligated, as a Wisdom figure, to give comfort and counsel to the man near death—Everyman. He begs for counsel and she, unlike his other friends, gives him good counsel. She thus represents not only knowledge of the correct path to salvation through the Church, including proper shrift or a thorough knowledge of one's sins to be confessed, but also good counsel, which, as one of the spiritual works of mercy, should proceed from such knowledge.

THE DOCTRINE OF FRIENDSHIP IN *EVERYMAN*

The plot of *Everyman* obviously consists of a test of friendship made by a worldly young man when he suddenly learns that God has summoned him to his reckoning.* The doctrine of friendship in this morality is accordingly worth examining even though our conclusion can be anticipated, namely, that this doctrine consists of the essential commonplaces of the medieval doctrine of friendship. As in certain of the Faithful Friend analogues, these commonplaces have been adapted to the plot in keeping with two articles of faith in particular: (1) the necessity, for salvation, of good works, and (2) divine judgment after death. One of these common-

* Abstracted from John Conley, "The Doctrine of Friendship in *Everyman*," *Speculum,* XLIV (1969), 374-382.

places is that no one should be accounted a friend whose friendship
has not been tested. This ancient precept, which has been called
"the first law of friendship," occurs, for instance, in Ecclesiasticus
vi:7: "If thou wouldst get a friend, try him before thou takest him,
and do not credit him easily." In *Everyman* this precept is introduced
in effect almost at the onset, when God's messenger, Death, ad-
monishes Everyman to "preue thy frendes yf thou can." Interestingly,
this admonition is lacking in the corresponding passage in *Elckerlijc;*
indeed, *Everyman* may be said to have the more emphatic treatment
of friendship. The ancient test par excellence of friendship is adversity, a commonplace expressed, for example, by the formula *In
necessitate probatur amicus* (A friend is proven in time of need).
The source of this formula is evidently Proverbs xvii:17: "He that
is a friend loveth at all times, and a brother is proved in distress." In
the end all of Everyman's friends fail him with the exception of
Good Deeds, his one true friend. True friendship, then, is lasting.
The Biblical *locus classicus* is again Proverbs xvii:17. False friendship, correspondingly, is transitory. True friendship is also virtuous,
as the ancients tell us; in fact, to paraphrase Aristotle (*Nicomachean
Ethics,* viii, c. 3, 1156b), it is lasting precisely because it is virtuous.
In Christian thought, however, true friendship is not simply virtuous
—or natural—but supernatural, for man's relation to God is involved. The *locus classicus* for the doctrine of Christian friendship
is John xv:15: "I will not now call you servants, for the servant
knoweth not what his lord doth. But I have called you friends,
because all things whatsoever I have heard of my Father, I have
made known to you." Similarly, the friendship of Good Deeds is
supernaturally virtuous; dependent on grace and performed in the
state of grace, good deeds, as the play reminds us, enable every man
to save his soul provided that he be free from mortal sin at the
moment of death. If lasting and virtuous, true friendship is obviously
precious, or in the words of Ecclesiasticus vi:14-15, "he that hath
found" a true friend "hath found a treasure"; indeed, "nothing can
be compared to a faithful friend. . ." In *Everyman* true friendship
is implicitly classified as a lasting good, exemplified by only one
of Everyman's friends, Good Deeds (cf. *Speculum S. Edmundi—
Mirror of Saint Edmund*—by Edmund Rich, Archbishop of Canter-
bury). Finally, true friendship provides counsel and comfort per-
taining not only to this life but also to the next life. In the Christian

tradition the *locus classicus* is Ecclesiasticus vi:16: "A faithful friend is the medicine of life and immortality." Fittingly it is Good Deeds, rather than Knowledge, who of Everyman's friends speaks the last words of counsel, beginning," All erthly thynges is but vanyte. . . ." Fittingly, too, Good Deeds is the first one of Everyman's friends to give him comfort, and it is she who says to Everyman, lying in the grave and forsaken by all except her, "Fere not; I wyll speke for the."

ELCKERLIJC – EVERYMAN: THE QUESTION OF PRIORTY

Continual controversy has centered around the Dutch *Elckerlijc* and the English *Everyman* as to which is the original version and which is the translation.* This problem in originality can be unquestionably resolved by examining the authorship of each work. Knowing the cultural milieu which existed at the time of authorship, it is safe to assume that the author was aware of the doctrines of Catholicism as well as the contents of the *Bible*. Utilizing this premise, it is possible to examine the theological and biblical knowledge evidenced in each text as a means of ascertaining priority. Since the play is primarily a religious allegory concerning Everyman's (Elckerlijc's) salvation, and since Catholicism was the religion of the time, the fundamental plot should parallel Catholic doctrine regarding salvation. As early as the Council of Florence in 1439, the Catholic Church has maintained that a baptized believer who has slipped from the path of righteousness can only regain favor through the orderly process of guilt recognition, confession, and the subsequent realization of guilt removal (satisfaction). The English version states that knowledge led Everyman to confession, while the Dutch version states that Kennisse (contrition) led Elckerlijc to penance. Thus, in the first instance, the Dutch version more appro-

---

* Abstracted from Francis A. Wood. *"Elckerlijc–Everyman:* The Question of Priority." *Modern Philology, VIII* (1910), 279-302.

priately parallels Catholic morality regarding guilt recognition leading to the need for confession. Still more differences between the two
works can be found concerning biblical knowledge regarding the
process of confession. In the English version, Everyman cries for
help, and Goodes (wealth) replies that he is there in abundance.
In the Dutch version, Goet (wealth) responds by admonishing
Elckerlijc that he can help in any worldly matter but would create
his utter damnation in a confrontation with God. The response in
the English version is inconsistent with the biblical teaching that
"riches profit not in the day of wrath." The Dutch version preserves
the temporality of wealth, while the English version does not. Concerning the relief from sin afforded by confession, further significant
differences are apparent. Everyman desires cleansing in order to
avoid punishment in the future; Elckerlijc seeks an immediate reward in that Duecht (Virtue) will join him as righteousness once
he is cleansed. Again, the Dutch version is more in keeping with
Catholic doctrine concerning the righteous life. The obvious differences between the Catholic and biblical knowledge operating in
each version provide conclusive evidence regarding priority. *Everyman* is theologically incorrect, faulty in biblical allusions, and inconsistent with its allegorical purpose; it is definitely a translation
of the original Dutch version, and a poor translation at that.

Othello
WILLIAM SHAKESPEARE

DRAMATIS PERSONAE

DUKE OF VENICE

BRABANTIO, *a Senator*

OTHER SENATORS

GRATIANO, *brother to Brabantio*

LODOVICO, *kinsman to Brabantio*

OTHELLO, *a noble Moor in the service of the Venetian state*

CASSIO, *his lieutenant*

IAGO, *his ancient*

MONTANO, *Othello's predecessor in the government of Cyprus*

RODERIGO, *a Venetian gentleman*

CLOWN, *servant to Othello*

DESDEMONA, *daughter of Brabantio and wife to Othello*

EMILIA, *wife to Iago*

BIANCA, *mistress to Cassio*

SAILOR, MESSENGER, HERALD, OFFICERS, GENTLEMEN, MUSICIANS, *and* ATTENDANTS

SCENE: *Venice: a seaport in Cyprus.*

act one
SCENE ONE. VENICE. A STREET.

(*Enter* RODERIGO *and* IAGO)

ROD. Tush, never tell me. I take it much unkindly
That thou, Iago, who hast had° my purse
As if the strings were thine, shouldst know of this.

IAGO. 'Sblood,° but you will not hear me.
If ever I did dream of such a matter,   5
Abhor me.

ROD. Thou told'st me thou didst hold him in thy hate.

IAGO. Despise me if I do not. Three great ones of the city,
In personal suit° to make me his Lieutenant,
Off-capped° to him. And, by the faith of man,   10

From *Shakespeare: The Complete Works,* edited by G. B. Harrison, copyright 1948, 1952, by Harcourt, Brace Jovanovich, Inc., and reprinted with their permission.

Act I, Sc. i: 2. *had:* i.e., used.   **4.** *'Sblood:* by God's blood.   **9.** *In . . . suit:* making this request in person.   **10.** *Off-capped:* stood cap in hand.

I know my price, I am worth no worse a place.
But he, as loving his own pride and purposes,
Evades them, with a bombast circumstance°
Horribly stuffed with epithets of war.°
And, in conclusion,   15
Nonsuits° my mediators, for "Certes,"° says he,
"I have already chose my officer."
And what was he?
Forsooth, a great arithmetician,°
One Michael Cassio, a Florentine,   20
A fellow almost damned in a fair wife,°
That never set a squadron in the field,
Nor the division of a battle° knows
More than a spinster, unless the bookish theoric,°
Wherein the toged° Consuls° can propose
As masterly as he—mere prattle without practice
Is all his soldiership. But he, sir, had the election.
And I, of whom his eyes had seen the proof
At Rhodes, at Cyprus, and on other grounds
Christian and heathen, must be beleed° and calmed   30
By debitor and creditor. This countercaster,°
He, in good time,° must his Lieutenant be,
And I—God bless the mark!°—his Moorship's Ancient.°
    ROD. By Heaven, I rather would have been his hangman.

13. *bombast circumstance:* bombastic phrases. Bombast is cotton padding used
to stuff out a garment.   14. *stuffed . . . war:* padded out with military terms.
16. *Nonsuits:* rejects the petition of.   *Certes:* assuredly.   19. *arithmetician:*
Contemporary books on military tactics are full of elaborate diagrams and
numerals to explain military formations. Cassio is a student of such books.
21. *almost . . . wife:* A much-disputed phrase. There is an Italian proverb. "You
have married a fair wife? You are damned." If Iago has this in mind, he means
by *almost* that Cassio is about to marry.   23. *division . . . battle:* organization
of an army.   24. *bookish theoric:* student of war; not a practical soldier.   25.
toged: wearing a toga.   *Consuls:* councilors. Cf. I.ii.43.   30. *beleed:* placed
on the lee (or unfavorable) side.   31. *countercaster:* calculator (repeating the
idea of arithmetician). Counters were used in making calculations.   32. *in . . .*
time: A phrase expressing indignation.   33. *God . . . mark:* An exclamation
of impatience.   *Ancient:* ensign, the third officer in the company of which
Othello is Captain and Cassio Lieutenant.

IAGO. Why, there's no remedy. 'Tis the curse of service,   35
Preferment goes by letter and affection,
And not by old gradation,° where each second
Stood heir to the first. Now, sir, be judge yourself
Whether I in any just term am affined°
To love the Moor.
    ROD.   I would not follow him, then.   40
    IAGO. Oh, sir content you,
I follow him to serve my turn upon him.
We cannot all be masters, nor all masters
Cannot be truly followed. You shall mark
Many a duteous and knee-crooking knave   45
That doting on his own obsequious bondage
Wears out his time, much like his master's ass,
For naught but provender, and when he's old, cashiered.°
Whip me such honest knaves. Others there are
Who, trimmed in forms and visages of duty,°   50
Keep yet their hearts attending on themselves,
And throwing but shows of service° on their lords
Do well thrive by them, and when they have lined their coats
Do themselves homage.° These fellows have some soul,
And such a one do I profess myself. For, sir,   55
It is as sure as you are Roderigo,
Were I the Moor, I would not be Iago.
In following him, I follow but myself.
Heaven is my judge, not I for love and duty,
But seeming so, for my peculiar° end.   60
For when my outward action doth demónstrate
The native act and figure of my heart°

36–37. *Preferment . . . gradation:* promotion comes through private recommendation and favoritism and not by order of seniority.   **39.** *affined:* tied by
affection.   **48.** *cashiered:* dismissed. The word at this time did not imply dishonorable discharge.   **50.** *trimmed . . . duty:* decking themselves out with the
outward forms of loyal service.   **52.** *throwing . . . service:* serving merely in
outward show.   **54.** *Do . . . homage:* serve themselves.   *homage:* an outward
act signifying obedience.   **60.** *peculiar:* particular, personal.   **62.** *native . . .*
heart: natural actions and shape of my secret designs.

In compliment extern,° 'tis not long after
But I will wear my heart upon my sleeve
For daws° to peck at. I am not what I am.°   65
  ROD. What a full fortune° does the thick-lips owe°
If he can carry 't thus!°
  IAGO.   Call up her father,
Rouse him. Make after him, poison his delight,
Proclaim him in the streets. Incense her kinsmen,
And though he in a fertile climate dwell,   70
Plague him with flies. Though that his joy be joy,
Yet throw such changes of vexation on 't
As it may lose some color.°
  ROD. Here is her father's house, I'll call aloud.
  IAGO. Do, with like timorous° accent and dire yell   75
As when, by night and negligence, the fire
Is spied in populous cities.
  ROD. What ho, Brabantio! Signior Brabantio, ho!
  IAGO. Awake! What ho, Brabantio! Thieves!
    Thieves! Thieves!
Look to your house, your daughter and your bags!°   80
Thieves! Thieves!
      (BRABANTIO *appears above, as a window.*)
  BRA. What is the reason of this terrible summons?
What is the matter there?
  ROD. Signior, is all your family within?
  IAGO. Are your doors locked?
  BRA.   Why, wherefore ask you this?   85
  IAGO. 'Zounds,° sir, you're robbed. For shame,
    put on your gown,°
Your heart is burst, you have lost half your soul.
Even now, now, very now, an old black ram
Is tupping° your white ewe. Arise, arise,
Awake the snorting° citizens with the bell,   90

---

63. *extern:* outward. 65. *daws:* jackdaws; i.e., fools. *I . . . am:* i.e., I am in secret a devil. 66. *full fortune:* overflowing good luck. *owe:* own. 67. *carry't thus:* i.e., bring off this marriage. 72–73. *throw . . . color:* cause him some annoyance by way of variety to tarnish his joy. 75. *timorous:* terrifying. 80. *bags:* moneybags. 86. *'Zounds:* by God's wounds. *gown:* dressing gown. 89. *tupping:* covering. 90. *snorting:* snoring.

Or else the Devil° will make a grandsire of you,
Arise, I say.

    BRA.   What, have you lost your wits?

    ROD. Most reverend signior, do you know my voice?

    BRA. Not I. What are you?

    ROD. My name is Roderigo.

    BRA.   The worser welcome.   95
I have charged thee not to haunt about my doors.
In honest plainness thou hast heard me say
My daughter is not for thee, and now, in madness,
Being full of supper and distempering draughts,°
Upon malicious bravery° dost thou come   100
To start° my quiet,

    ROD. Sir, sir, sir ——

    BRA.   But thou must needs be sure
My spirit and my place have in them power
To make this bitter to thee.

    ROD.   Patience, good sir.

    BRA. What tell'st thou me of robbing? This is Venice,   105
My house is not a grange.°

    ROD.   Most grave Brabantio,
In simple and pure soul I come to you.

    IAGO. 'Zounds, sir, you are one of those that will not serve
God if the Devil bid you. Because we come to do you service
and you think we are ruffians, you'll have your daughter covered   110
with a Barbary° horse, you'll have your nephews° neigh to
you, you'll have coursers for cousins,° and jennets° for germans.°

    BRA. What profane wretch art thou?   115

    IAGO. I am one, sir, that comes to tell you your daughter and
the Moor are now making the beast with two backs.

    BRA. Thou art a villain.

---

91. *Devil:* The Devil in old pictures and woodcuts was represented as black.
99. *distempering draughts:* liquor that makes senseless.   100. *bravery:* defiance.   101. *start:* startle.   106. *grange:* lonely farm.   111. *Barbary:* Moorish.
112. *nephews:* grandsons.   113. *cousins:* near relations.   *jennets:* Moorish
ponies.   114. *germans:* kinsmen.

IAGO.   You are—a Senator.

BRA. This thou shalt answer. I know thee, Roderigo.   120

ROD. Sir, I will answer anything. But I beseech you
If 't be your pleasure and most wise consent,
As partly I find it is, that your fair daughter,
At this odd-even° and dull° watch o' the night,
Transported with no worse nor better guard   125
But with a knave of common hire, a gondolier,
To the gross of clasps of a lascivious Moor—
If this be known to you, and your allowance,°
We then have done you bold and saucy wrongs.
But if you know not this, my manners tell me   130
We have your wrong rebuke. Do not believe
That from the sense of all civility°
I thus would play and trifle with your reverence.
Your daughter, if you have not given her leave,
I say again, hath made a gross revolt,°   135
Tying her duty, beauty, wit, and fortunes
In an exaravagant° and wheeling° stranger
Of here and everywhere. Straight satisfy yourself.
If she be in her chamber or your house,
Let loose on me the justice of the state   140
For thus deluding you.

BRA.   Strike on the tinder,° ho!
Give me a taper!° Call up all my people!
This accident is not unlike my dream.
Belief of it oppresses me already.
Light, I say! Light!   (*Exit above.*)

IAGO.   Farewell, for I must leave you.   145

---

124. *odd-even:* about midnight.   *dull:* heavy, sleepy.   128. *your allowance:* by
your permission.   132. *from . . . civility:* disregarding all sense of decent behavior.   135. *gross revolt:* indecent rebellion.   137. *extravagant:* vagabond.
wheeling: wandering.   141. *tinder:* the primitive method of making fire, used
before the invention of matches. A spark, made by striking flint on steel, fell
on the tinder, some inflammable substance such as charred linen, which was
blown into flame.   142. *taper:* candle.

It seems not meet, nor wholesome to my place,°
To be produced—as if I stay I shall—
Against the Moor. For I do know the state,
However this may gall° him with some check,°
Cannot with safety cast° him. For he's embarked   150
With such loud reason to the Cyprus wars,
Which even now stand in act,° that, for their souls,
Another of his fathom° they have none
To lead their business. In which regard,
Though I do hate him as I do Hell pains,   155
Yet for necessity of present life
I must show out a flag° and sign of love,
Which is indeed but sign. That you shall surely find him,
Lead to the Sagittary° the raisèd search,
And there will I be with him. So farewell.   (*Exit.*)   160

(*Enter, below,* BRABANTIO, *in his nightgown, and*
SERVANTS *with torches.*)

BRA. It is too true an evil. Gone she is,
And what's to come of my despisèd time°
Is naught but bitterness. Now, Roderigo,
Where didst thou see her? Oh, unhappy girl!
With the Moor, say'st thou? Who would be a father!   165
How didst thou know 'twas she? Oh, she deceives me
Past thought! What said she to you? Get more tapers.
Raise all my kindred. Are they married, think you?
     ROD. Truly, I think they are.
     BRA. Oh Heaven! How got she out? Oh, treason of the
          blood!°   170
Fathers, from hence trust not your daughters' minds

---

146. *place:* i.e., as Othello's officer.   149. *gall:* make sore.   *check:* rebuke.
150. *cast:* dismiss from service.   152. *stand in act:* are on the point of beginning.   153. *fathom:* depth.   157. *flag:* a sign of welcome.   159. *Sagittary:*
presumably some building in Venice, not identified, used as a meeting place for
the Council.   162. *what's . . . time:* the rest of my wretched life.   170. *treason
. . . blood:* treachery of my own child.

By what you see them act. Are there not charms°
By which the property° of youth and maidhood
May be abused?° Have you not read, Roderigo,
Of some such thing?
   ROD.   Yes, sir, I have indeed.   175
   BRA. Call up my brother. Oh, would you had had her!
Some one way, some another. Do you know
Where we may apprehend her and the Moor?
   ROD. I think I can discover him, if you please
To get good guard and go along with me.   180
   BRA. Pray you, lead on. At every house I'll call,
I may command° at most. Get weapons, ho!
And raise some special officers of night.
On, good Roderigo, I'll deserve your pains.°

                              (*Exeunt.*)

SCENE TWO. ANOTHER STREET.

(*Enter* OTHELLO, IAGO, *and* ATTENDANTS *with torches.*)
   IAGO. Though in the trade of war I have slain men,
Yet do I hold it very stuff° o' the conscience
To do no contrivèd° murder. I lack iniquity
Sometimes to do me service. Nine or ten times
I had thought to have yerked° him here under the ribs.   5
   OTH. 'Tis better as it is.
   IAGO.   Nay, but he prated
And spoke such scurvy and provoking terms
Against your honor
That, with the little godliness I have,
I did full hard forbear him.° But I pray you, sir,   10
Are you fast° married? Be assured of this,

---

172. *charms:* magic spells. 173. *property:* nature. 174. *abused:* deceived.
182. *command:* find supporters. 184. *deserve . . . pains:* reward your labor.
   Sc. ii: 2. *stuff:* material, nature. 3. *contrived:* deliberately planned. 5.
yerked: jabbed. 10. *full . . . him:* had a hard job to keep my hands off him.
11. *fast:* securely.

That the Magnifico° is much beloved,
And hath in his effect° a voice potential
As double as° the Duke's. He will divorce you,
Or put upon you what restraint and grievance   15
The law, with all his might to enforce it on,
Will give him cable.°

    OTH.   Let him do his spite.
My services which I have done the signiory°
Shall outtongue his complaints. 'Tis yet to know°—
Which, when I know that boasting is an honor,   20
I shall promulgate°—I fetch my life and being°
From men of royal siege,° and my demerits°
May speak unbonneted° to as proud a fortune
As this that I have reached. For know, Iago,
But that I love the gentle Desdemona,   25
I would not my unhousèd° free condition
Put into circumscription and confine°
For the sea's worth. But look! What lights come yond?

    IAGO. Those are the raisèd father and his friends.
You were best go in.

    OTH.   Not I, I must be found.   30
My parts,° my title, and my perfect° soul
Shall manifest me rightly. Is it they?

    IAGO. By Janus,° I think no.

        (*Enter* CASSIO, *and certain* OFFICERS *with torches.*)

    OTH. The servants of the Duke, and my Lieutenant.
The goodness of the night upon you, friends!   35
What is the news?

---

12. *Magnifico:* the title of the chief men of Venice.   13. *in . . . effect:* what he can do.   13–14. *potential . . . as:* twice as powerful as.   17. *cable:* rope. 18. *signiory:* the state of Venice.   19. *'Tis . . . know:* it has still to be made known.   21. *promulgate:* proclaim.   *fetch . . . being:* am descended.   22. *royal siege:* throne.   *demerits:* deserts.   23. *unbonneted:* A disputed phrase. Usually it means "without a cap"; i.e., in sign that the wearer is standing before a superior. But Othello means that his merits are such that he need show deference to no man.   26. *unhoused:* unmarried.   27. *confine:* confinement. 31. *parts:* abilities.   *perfect:* ready.   33. *Janus:* the two-faced God of the Romans, an appropriate deity for Iago.

CAS.   The Duke does greet you, General,
And he requires your haste-posthaste° appearance,
Even on the instant.

    OTH.   What is the matter, think you?

    CAS. Something from Cyprus, as I may divine.
It is a business of some heat. The galleys°   40
Have sent a dozen sequent° messengers
This very night at one another's heels,
And many of the consuls, raised and met,
Are at the Duke's already. You have been hotly called for
When, being not at your lodging to be found,   45
The Senate hath sent about three several° quests
To search you out.

    OTH. 'Tis well I am found by you.
I will but spend a word here in the house
And go with you.   (*Exit.*)

    CAS.   Ancient, what makes he here?

    IAGO. Faith, he tonight hath boarded a land carrack.°   50
If it prove lawful prize, he's made forever.

    CAS. I do not understand.

    IAGO.   He's married.

    CAS.   To who?

             (*Re-enter* OTHELLO.)

    IAGO. Marry,° to —— Come, Captain, will you go?

    OTH.   Have with you.

    CAS. Here comes another troop to seek for you.

    IAGO. It is Brabantio. General, he advised,°   55
He comes to bad intent.

---

37. *haste-posthaste:* with the quickest possible speed. When it was necessary to urge the postboy to greater speed than usual, the letter or dispatch was inscribed "haste, posthaste." The Earl of Essex once inscribed a letter "haste, haste, haste posthaste, haste for life." 40. galleys: Venetian ships manned and rowed by slaves; the fastest of craft. 41. *sequent:* following one after another. 46. *several:* separate. 50. *carrack:* the largest type of Spanish merchant ship. 53. *Marry:* Mary, by the Virgin—with a pun. 55. *advised:* careful.

(*Enter* BRABANTIO, RODERIGO, *and* OFFICERS *with*
torches and weapons.)

OTH.   Holloa! Stand there!

ROD. Signior, it is the Moor.

BRA.   Down with him, thief!
                      (*They draw on both sides.*)

IAGO. You, Roderigo! Come, sir, I am for you.

OTH. Keep up° you bright swords, for the dew will rust
them.

Good signor, you shall more command with years   60
Than with your weapons.

BRA. O thou foul thief, where hast thou stowed my
daughter?

Damned as thou art, thou hast enchanted her.
For I'll refer me to all things of sense°
If she in chains of magic were not bound,   65
Whether a maid so tender, fair, and happy,
So opposite to marriage that she shunned
The wealthy curlèd darlings of our nation,
Would ever have, to incur a general mock,
Run from her guardage° to the sooty bosom   70
Of such a thing as thou, to fear, not to delight.
Judge me the world if 'tis not gross in sense°
That thou hast practiced on her with foul charms,
Abused her delicate youth with drugs or minerals
That weaken motion.° I'll have 't disputed on,°   75
'Tis probable, and palpable° to thinking.
I therefore apprehend and do attach° thee
For an abuser of the world, a practicer
Of arts inhibited and out of warrant.°
Lay hold upon him. If he do resist,   80

---

59. *Keep up:* sheathe.   64. *refer . . . sense:* i.e., by every rational consideration.
70. *guardage:* guardianship.   72. *gross in sense:* i.e., plain to the perception.
75. *motion:* sense.   *disputed on:* argued in the courts of law.   76. *palpable:*
clear.   77. *attach:* arrest.   79. *arts . . . warrant:* forbidden and illegal acts;
i.e., magic and witchcraft.

Subdue him at his peril.

OTH.   Hold your hands,
Both you of my inclining and the rest.
Were it my cue to fight, I should have known it
Without a prompter. Where will you that I go
To answer this your charge?

BRA.   To prison, till fit time   85
Of law and course of direct session°
Call thee to answer.

OTH.   What if I do obey?
How may the Duke be therewith satisfied,
Whose messengers are here about my side
Upon some present° business of the state   90
To bring me to him?

1. OFF.   'Tis true, most worthy signior.
The Duke's in Council, and your noble self
I am sure is sent for.

BRA.   How! The Duke in Council!
In this time of the night! Bring him away.
Mine's not an idle° cause. The Duke himself,   95
Or any of my brothers of the state,
Cannot but feel this wrong as 'twere their own.
For if such actions may have passage free,°
Bondslaves and pagans shall our statesmen be.

                                        (*Exeunt.*)

SCENE THREE. A COUNCIL CHAMBER.

(*The* DUKE *and* SENATORS *sitting at a table,* OFFICERS
attending.)

DUKE. There is no composition° in these news°
That gives them credit.

1. SEN.   Indeed they are disproportioned.

---

86. *course . . . session:* trial in the ordinary courts, where witches and other
criminals are tried—and not by special commission as a great man.   **90.** *present:* immediate.   **95.** *idle:* trivial.   **98.** *have . . . free:* be freely allowed.
      Sc. iii: 1. *composition:* agreement.   *news:* reports.

My letters say a hundred and seven galleys.

    DUKE. And mine, a hundred and forty.

    2. SEN.   And mine, two hundred.

But though they jump not on a just account°—   5

As in these cases, where the air reports,°

'Tis oft with difference—yet do they call confirm

A Turkish fleet, and bearing up° to Cyprus.

    DUKE. Nay, it is possible enough to judgment.

I do not so secure me in the error,°   10

But the main article° I do approve

In fearful° sense.

    SAILOR. (*Within*) What ho! What ho! What ho!

    1. OFF. A message from the galleys.

                  (*Enter* SAILOR.)

    DUKE.   Now, what's the business?

    SAIL. The Turkish preparation makes for Rhodes.

So was I bid report here to the state   15

By Signior Angelo.

    DUKE. How say you by this change?

    1. SEN.   This cannot be,

By no assay of reason.° 'Tis a pageant°

To keep us in false gaze.° When we consider

The importancy of Cyprus to the Turk,   20

And let ourselves again but understand

That as it more concerns the Turk than Rhodes,

So may he with more facile question bear° it,

For that it stands not in such warlike brace°

But altogether lacks the abilities   25

That Rhodes is dressed° in—if we make thought of this,

We must not think the Turk is so unskillful

---

5. *jump . . . account:* do not agree with an exact estimate. 6. *aim reports:* i.e., intelligence reports of an enemy's intention often differ in the details. 8. *bearing up:* making course for. 10. *I . . . error:* I do not consider myself free from danger, because the reports may not all be accurate. 11. *main article:* general purport. 12. *fearful:* to be feared. 18. *assay of reason:* reasonable test. *pageant:* show. 19. *false gaze:* looking the wrong way. 23. *with . . . bear:* take it more easily. 24. *brace:* state of defense. 26. *dressed:* prepared.

To leave that latest which concerns him first,
Neglecting an attempt of ease and gain
To wake and wage° a danger profitless.   30
    DUKE. Nay, in all confidence, he's not for Rhodes.
    1. OFF. Here is more news.
                (*Enter a* MESSENGER.)
    MESS. The Ottomites,° Reverend and Gracious,
Steering with due course toward the isle of Rhodes,
Have there injointed° them with an after-fleet.°   35
    1. SEN. Aye, so I thought. How many, as you guess?
    MESS. Of thirty sail. And now they do restem°
Their backward course, bearing with frank appearance°
Their purposes toward Cyprus. Signior Montano,
Your trusty and most valiant servitor,   40
With his free duty recommends you thus,°
And prays you to believe him.
    DUKE. 'Tis certain then for Cyprus.
Marcus Luccicos, is not he in town?
    1. SEN. He's now in Florence.   45
    DUKE. Write from us to him, post-posthaste dispatch.
    1. SEN. Here comes Brabantio and the valiant Moor.
        (*Enter* BRABANTIO, OTHELLO, IAGO, RODERIGO,
                and OFFICERS.)
    DUKE. Valiant Othello, we must straight employ you.
Against the general enemy Ottoman.
(*To* BRABANTIO) I did not see you. Welcome, gentle signior,   50
We lacked your counsel and your help tonight.
    BRA. So did I yours. Good your Grace, pardon me,
Neither my place nor aught I heard of business
Hath raised me from my bed, nor doth the general care
Take hold on me. For my particular° grief   55
Is of so floodgate° and o'erbearing nature
That it engluts° and swallows other sorrows,

---

30. *wage:* risk. 33. *Ottomites:* Turks. 35. *injointed:* joined. *after-fleet:*
following, second fleet. 37. *restem:* steer again. 38. *frank appearance:* no
attempt at concealment. 41. *With . . . thus:* with all due respect thus advises.
55. *particular:* personal. 56. *floodgate:* i.e., like water rushing through an
opened sluice. 57. *engluts:* swallows.

And it is still itself.

DUKE. Why, what's the matter?

BRA. My daughter! Oh, my daughter!

ALL. Dead?

BRA. Aye, to me.

She is abused, stol'n from me and corrupted 60
By spells and medicines bought of mountebanks.°
For nature so preposterously to err,
Being not deficient, blind, or lame of sense,
Sans° witchcraft could not.

DUKE. Who'er he be that in this foul proceeding 65
Hath thus beguiled your daughter of herself°
And you of her, the bloody book of law
You shall yourself read in the bitter letter
After your own sense—yea, though our proper° son
Stood in your action.

BRA. Humbly I thank your Grace. 70
Here is the man, this Moor, whom now, it seems,
Your special mandate for the state affairs
Hath hither brought.

ALL. We are very sorry for 't.

DUKE. (*To* OTHELLO) What in your own part can you
say to this?

BRA. Nothing but this is so. 75

OTH. Most potent, grave, and reverend signiors,
My very noble and approved° good masters,
That I have ta'en away this old man's daughter,
It is most true—true, I have married her.
The very head and front° of my offending 80
Hath this extent, no more. Rude° am I in my speech,
And little blest with the soft phrase of peace.
For since these arms of mine had seven years' pith°
Till now some nine moons wasted, they have used

---

61. *mountebanks:* quack doctors, who dealt in poisons and love potions. Cf.
Haml, IV.vii.142. 64. *Sans:* without. 66. *beguiled . . . herself:* cheated
your daughter of herself; i.e., caused her to be "beside herself." 69. *proper:*
own. 77. *approved:* tested; i.e., found good masters by experience. 80. *front:*
forehead. 81. *Rude: rough,* uncultured. 83. *pith:* marrow.

Their dearest° action in the tented field.   85
And little of this great world can I speak,
More than pertains to feats of broil and battle,
And therefore little shall I grace my cause
In speaking for myself. Yet, by your gracious patience,
I will a round unvarnished tale° deliver   90
Of my whole course of love—what drugs, what charms,
What conjuration and what mighty magic—
For such proceeding I am charged withal—
I won his daughter.
    BRA.   A maiden never bold,
Of spirit so still and quiet that her motion   95
Blushed at herself,° and she—in spite of nature,
Of years, of country, credit,° everything—
To fall in love with what she feared to look on!
It is a judgment maimed and most imperfect
That will confess° perfection so could err   100
Against all rules of nature, and must be driven
To find out practices° of cunning Hell
Why this should be. I therefore vouch° again
That with some mixtures° powerful o'er the blood,°
Or with some dram conjured° to this effect,   105
He wrought upon her.
    DUKE.   To vouch this is no proof
Without more certain and more overt° test
Than these thin habits° and poor likelihoods°
Of modern seeming° do prefer° against him.
    1. SEN. But, Othello, speak.   110
Did you by indirect and forcèd° courses

---

85. *dearest:* most important.   90. *round . . . tale:* direct, unadorned account.
95–96. *Of . . . herself:* she was so shy that she blushed at the slightest cause.
motion: outward behavior.   97. *credit:* reputation.   100. *will confess:* would
believe.   102. *practices:* plots.   103. *vouch:* declare.   104. *mixtures:* drugs.
blood: passions.   105. *conjured:* mixed with spells.   107. *overt:* open.   108.
thin habits: slight evidence; lit., thin clothes.   *poor likelihoods:* unconvinc-
ing charges.   109. *modern seeming:* slight suspicion.   *prefer:* make a charge
against.   111. *forced:* unnatural.

Subdue and poison this young maid's affections?
Or came it by request, and such fair question
As soul to soul affordeth?

OTH.   I do beseech you
Send for the lady to the Sagittary,   115
And let her speak of me before her father.
If you do find me foul in her report,
The trust, the office I do hold of you,
Not only take away, but let your sentence
Even fall upon my life.

DUKE.   Fetch Desdemona hither.   120

OTH. Ancient, conduct them, you best know the place
                         (*Exeunt* IAGO *and* ATTENDANTS.)
And till she come, as truly as to Heaven
I do confess the vices of my blood,
So justly to your grave ears I'll present
How I did thrive in this fair lady's love   125
And she in mine.

DUKE.   Say it, Othello.

OTH. Her father loved me, oft invited me,
Still° questioned me the story of my life
From year to year, the battles, sieges, fortunes,   130
That I have passed.
I ran it through, even from my boyish days
To the very moment that he bade me tell it.
Wherein I spake of most disastrous chances,°
Of moving accidents° by flood and field,   135
Of hairbreadth 'scapes i' the imminent deadly breach,°
Of being taken by the insolent foe
And sold to slavery, of my redemption thence,
And portance° in my travels' history.
Wherein of antres° vast and deserts idle,°   140
Rough quarries, rocks, and hills whose heads touch heaven,
It was my hint° to speak—such was the process.°

---

129. *Still:* always, continually. 134. *chances:* accidents. 135. *accidents:* occurrences. 136. *breach:* assault on a city. 139. *portance:* bearing. 140. *antres:* caves. *idle:* worthless. 142. *hint:* occasion. *process:* proceeding, order.

And of the cannibals that each other eat,
The anthropophagi,° and men whose heads
Do grow beneath their shoulders.° This to hear   145
Would Desdemona seriously incline.
But still the house affairs would draw her thence,
Which ever as she could with haste dispatch,
She'd come again, and with a greedy ear
Devour up my discourse. Which I observing,   150
Took once a pliant° hour and found good means
To draw from her a prayer of earnest heart
That I would all my pilgrimage dilate,°
Whereof by parcels° she had something heard,
But not intentively.° I did consent,   155
And often did beguile her of° her tears
When I did speak of some distressful stroke
That my youth suffered. My story being done,
She gave me for my pains a world of sighs.
She swore, in faith, 'twas strange, 'twas passing strange,   160
'Twas pitiful, 'twas wondrous pitiful.
She wished she had not heard it, yet she wished
That Heaven had made her° such a man. She thanked me,
And bade me, if I had a friend that loved her,
I should but teach him how to tell my story   165
And that would woo her. Upon this hint I spake.
She loved me for the dangers I had passed,
And I loved her that she did pity them.
This only is the witchcraft I have used.
Here comes the lady, let her witness it.   170
          (*Enter* DESDEMONA, IAGO, *and* ATTENDANTS.)
     DUKE. I think this tale would win my daughter too.
Good Brabantio,
Take up this mangled matter at the best.°

144. *anthropophagi:* cannibals. 144–45. *men . . . shoulders:* See *Temp,*
III,iii.46–47,n. 151. *pliant:* suitable. 153. *dilate:* relate at length. 154.
parcels: portions. 155. *intentively:* intently. 156. *beguile . . . of:* draw from
her. 163. *her:* for her. 173. *Take . . . best:* make the best settlement you
can of this confused business.

Men do their broken weapons rather use
Than their bare hands.

  BRA.   I pray you hear her speak.   175
If she confess that she was half the wooer,
Destruction on my head if my bad blame
Light on the man! Come hither, gentle mistress.
Do you perceive in all this noble company
Where most you owe obedience?

  DES.   My noble Father,   180
I do perceive here a divided duty.
To you I am bound for life and education,
My life and education both do learn° me
How to respect you, you are the lord of duty,°
I am hitherto your daughter. But here's my husband,   185
And so much duty as my mother showed
To you, preferring you before her father
So much I challenge that I may profess
Due to the Moor my lord.

  BRA.   God be with you! I have done.
Please it your Grace, on to the state affairs.   190
I had rather to adopt a child than get° it.
Come hither, Moor.
I here do give thee that with all my heart
Which, but thou hast already, with all my heart
I would keep from thee. For your sake, jewel,   195
I am glad at soul I have no other child,
For thy escape would teach me tyranny,
To hang clogs on them. I have done, my lord.

  DUKE. Let me speak like yourself, and lay a sentence°
Which, as a grise° or step, may help these lovers   200
Into your favor.
When remedies are past, the griefs are ended
By seeing the worst, which late on hopes depended°
To mourn a mischief that is past and gone

---

183. *learn:* teach. 184. *lord of duty:* the man to whom I owe duty. 181. *get:*
beget. 199. *sentence:* proverbial saying. 200. *grise:* degree, step. 202–03.
When . . . depended: our anxieties end when the feared event happens.

Is the next way to draw new mischief on.   205
What cannot be preserved when fortune takes,
Patience her injury a mockery makes.°
The robbed that smiles steals something from the thief.
He robs himself that spend a bootless° grief.
    BRA. So° let the Turk of Cyprus us beguile,   210
We lose it not so long as we can smile.
He bears the sentence well that nothing bears
But the free comfort which from thence he hears.
But he bears both the sentence and the sorrow
That, to pay grief, must of poor patience borrow.   215
These sentences, to sugar or to gall,
Being strong on both sides, are equivocal.
But words are words. I never yet did hear
That the bruisèd heart was piercèd through the ear.
I humbly beseech you, proceed to the affairs of state.   220
    DUKE. The Turk with a most mighty preparation makes for
Cyprus. Othello, the fortitude of the place is best known to
you, and though we have there a substitute° of most allowed°
sufficiency,° yet opinion, a sovereign mistress of effects, throws
a more safer voice on you.° You must therefore be content to   225
slubber° the gloss of your new fortunes with this more stub-
born and boisterous expedition.
    OTH. The tyrant custom, most grave Senators,
Hath made the flinty and steel couch of war
My thrice-driven° bed of down. I do agnize°   230
A natural and prompt alacrity

---

207. *Patience . . . makes:* i.e., when we are not unduly disturbed by our misfortunes, we mock Fortune. 209. *bootless:* vain. 210–19. *So . . . ear:* Brabantio retaliates sarcastically with a few "sentences" of his own: Let the Turk
take Cyprus; it is no loss if we smile at it. It is easy enough to produce senten-
tious consolation, it costs nothing; but the man who has to endure both consolation and the sorrow itself must needs be patient. These sentences work
both ways; mere words hurt no one. Cf. Leonato's similar outburst, *M Ado,*
V.i.3–38. 223. *substitute:* deputy commander. *allowed:* admitted. 224.
sufficiency: efficiency. 224–25. *yet . . . you:* yet public opinion, which controls
our actions, is such that we regard you as a safer choice. 226. *slubber:* tarnish.
230. *thrice-driven:* three times refined. *agnize:* confess.

I find in hardness,° and do undertake
These present wars against the Ottomites.
Most humbly therefore bending to your state,
I crave fit disposition for my wife,   235
Due reference of place° and exhibition,°
With such accommodation and besort°
As levels with her breeding.°
    DUKE.   If you please,
Be 't at her father's.
    BRA.   I'll not have it so.
    OTH. Nor I
    DES.   Nor I. I would not there reside,   240
To put my father in impatient thoughts
By being in his eye. Most gracious Duke,
To my unfolding° lend your prosperous° ear,
And let me find a charter° in your voice
To assist my simpleness.   245
    DUKE. What would you, Desdemona?
    DES. That I did love the Moor to live with him,
My downright violence and storm of fortunes
May trumpet to the world. My heart's subdued
Even to the very quality of my lord.°   250
I saw Othello's visage in his mind,
And to his honors and his valiant parts
Did I my soul and fortunes consecrate.
So that, dear lords, if I be left behind,
A moth of peace,° and he got to the war,   255
The rites for which I love him are bereft me,
And I a heavy interim° shall support
By his dear absence. Let me go with him.

232. *hardness:* hardship. 236. *Due . . . place:* i.e., that she shall be treated as becomes my wife. *exhibition:* allowance. 237. *besort:* attendants. 238. *levels . . . breeding:* as suits her birth. 243. *unfolding:* plan; lit., revealing. *prosperous:* favorable. 244. *charter:* privilege. 247–50. *That . . . lord:* my love for the Moor is publicly shown by the way in which I have violently taken my fortunes in my hands; my heart has become a soldier like my husband. *quality:* profession. 255. *moth of peace:* a useless creature living in luxury. 257. *interim:* interval.

OTH. Let her have your voices.

Vouch° with me, Heaven, I therefore beg it not   260
To please the palate of my appetite,
Nor to comply with heat—the young affects
In me defunct°—and proper satisfaction,
But to be free and bounteous° to her mind.°
And Heaven defend° your good souls, that you think   265
I will your serious and great business scant
For she is with me. No, when light-winged toys°
Of feathered Cupid seel° with wanton dullness
My speculative and officed instruments,°
That my disports° corrupt and taint my business,   270
Let housewives make a skillet° of my helm,
And all indign° and base adversities
Make head against° my estimation!°

  DUKE. Be it as you shall privately determine,
Either for her stay or going. The affair cries haste,   275
And speed must answer 't. You must hence tonight.

  DES. Tonight, my lord?

  DUKE.   This night.

  OTH.   With all my heart.

  DUKE. At nine i' the morning here we'll meet again.
Othello, leave some officer behind,
And he shall our commission° bring to you,   280
With such things else of quality and respect
As doth import you.°

  OTH.   So please your Grace, my Ancient,
A man he is of honesty and trust.
To his conveyance I assign my wife,

260. *Vouch:* certify.   262–63. *young . . . defunct:* in me the passion of youth
is dead.   264. *bounteous:* generous. *to . . . mind:* Othello repeats Desdemona's claim that this is a marriage of minds.   265. *defend:* forbid.   267.
toys: trifles.   268. *seel:* close up; a technical term from falconry.   269.
speculative . . . instruments: powers of sight and action; i.e., my efficiency
as your general.   270. *disports:* amusements.   271. *skillet:* saucepan.   272.
indign: unworthy.   273. *Make . . . against:* overcome. *estimation:* reputation.   280. *commission:* formal document of appointment.   281–82. *With
. . . you:* with other matters that concern your position and honor.

With what else needful your good grace shall think   285
To be sent after me.

    DUKE.   Let it be so.

Good night to everyone. (*To* BRABANTIO) And, noble signior,
If virtue no delighted beauty lack,
Your son-in-law is far more fair than black.°

    1. SEN. Adieu, brave Moor. Use Desdemona well.   290

    BRA. Look to her, Moor, if thou hast eyes to see.
She has deceived her father, and may thee.°

             (*Exeunt* DUKE, SENATORS, OFFICERS, *etc.*)

    OTH. My life upon her faith! Honest Iago,
My Desdemona must I leave to thee.
I prithee, let thy wife attend on her,   295
And bring them after in the best advantage.°
Come, Desdemona, I have but an hour
Of love, of worldly matters and direction,
To spend with thee. We must obey the time.

             (*Exeunt* OTHELLO *and* DESDEMONA.)

    ROD. Iago!   300

    IAGO. What say'st thou, noble heart?

    ROD. What will I do, thinkest thou?

    IAGO. Why, go to bed and sleep.

    ROD. I will incontinently° drown myself.

    IAGO. If thou dost, I shall never love thee after. Why, thou   305
silly gentleman!

    ROD. It is silliness to live when to live is torment, and then
have we a prescription to die when death is our physician.

    IAGO. Oh, villainous! I have looked upon the world for four
times seven years, and since I could distinguish betwixt a   310
benefit and an injury I never found man that knew how to
love himself. Ere I would say I would drown myself for the
love of a guinea hen, I would change my humanity with a
baboon.

288–89. *If . . . black:* if worthiness is a beautiful thing in itself, your son-in-
law, though black, has beauty.   **291–92.** *Look . . . thee:* Iago in the background takes note of these words, and later reminds Othello of them with
deadly effect. See III.iii.206.   **296.** *in . . . advantage:* at the best opportunity.
304. *incontinently:* immediately.

ROD. What should I do? I confess it is my shame to be so   315
fond,° but it is not in my virtue° to amend it.

IAGO. Virtue! A fig! 'Tis in ourselves that we are thus or
thus. Our bodies are gardens, to the which our wills° are
gardeners. So that if we will plant nettles or sow lettuce, set
hyssop and weed up thyme, supply it with one gender° of   320
herbs or distract it with many, either to have it sterile with
idleness or manured with industry—why, the power and cor-
rigible° authority of this lies in our wills. If the balance of our
lives had not one scale of reason to poise° another of sensuality, the blood and baseness of our natures would conduct   325
us to most preposterous conclusions. But we have reason to
cool our raging motions, our carnal stings,° our unbittered°
lusts, whereof I take this that you call love to be a sect or
scion.°

ROD. It cannot be.   330

IAGO. It is merely a lust of the blood and a permission of
the will. Come, be a man. Drown thyself! Drown cats and
blind puppies. I have professed me thy friend, and I confess
me knit to thy deserving with cables of perdurable° toughness.
I could never better stead° thee than now. Put money in thy   335
purse, follow thou the wars, defeat thy favor with an usurped
beard°—I say put money in thy purse. It cannot be that Desdemona should long continue her love to the Moor— put
money in thy purse—nor he his to her. It was a violent com-
mencement, and thou shalt see an answerable sequestration°—   340
put but money in thy purse. These Moors are changeable in
their wills.—Fill thy purse with money. The food that to him
now is as luscious as locusts° shall be to him shortly as bitter
as coloquintida.° She must change for youth. When she is

316. *fond:* foolishly in love. *virtue:* manhood. 318. *wills:* desires. 320.
gender: kind. 322. *corrigible:* correcting, directing. 324. *poise:* weigh.
327. *carnal stings:* fleshly desires. *unbitted:* uncontrolled. 329. *sect or
scion:* Both words mean a slip taken from a tree and planted to produce a
new growth. 334. *perdurable:* very hard. 335. *stead:* help. 336–37. *defeat . . . beard:* disguise your face by growing a beard. 340. *answerable se-
questration:* corresponding separation; i.e., reaction. 343. *locusts:* It is not
known what fruit was called a locust. 344. *coloquintida:* known as "bitter
apple," a form of gherkin from which a purge was made.

sated with his body, she will find the error of her choice. She   345
must have change, she must—therefore put money in thy
purse. If thou wilt needs damn thyself, do it a more delicate
way than drowning. Make all the money thou canst.° If santi-
mony and a frail vow betwixt an erring° barbarian and a
supersubtle Venetian be not too hard for my wits and all the   350
tribe of Hell, thou shalt enjoy her—therefore make money.
A pox of drowning thyself! It is clean out of the way. Seek
thou rather to be hanged in compassing° thy joy than to be
drowned and go without her.

    ROD. Wilt thou be fast to my hopes if I depend on the issue?   355
    IAGO. Thou art sure of me. Go, make money. I have told
thee often, and I retell thee again and again, I hate the Moor.
My cause is hearted,° thine hath no less reason. Let us be con-
junctive° in our revenge against him. If thou canst cuckold°
him, thou dost thyself a pleasure, me a sport. There are many   360
events in the womb of time, which will be delivered. Traverse,° go, provide thy money. We will have more of this
tomorrow, Adieu.

    ROD. Where shall we meet i' the morning?
    IAGO. At my lodging.   365
    ROD. I'll be with thee betimes.°
    IAGO. Go to, farewell. Do you hear, Roderigo?
    ROD. What say you?
    IAGO. No more of drowning, do you hear?
    ROD. I am changed. I'll go see all my land. (*Exit.*)   370
    IAGO. Thus do I ever make my fool my purse,
For I mine own gained knowledge should profane
If I would time expend with such a snipe
But for my sport and profit. I hate the Moor,
And it is thought abroad that 'twixt my sheets   375
He has done my office. I know not if 't be true,
But I for mere suspicion in that kind
Will do as if for surety. He holds me well,
The better shall my purpose work on him.

---

348. *Make . . . canst:* turn all you can into ready cash.   **349.** *erring:* vagabond.
353. *compassing:* achieving.   **358.** *hearted:* heartfelt.   **359.** *conjunctive:*
united.   **359.** *cuckold:* make him a cuckold.   **362.** *Traverse:* quickstep.
366. *betimes:* in good time, early.

Cassio's a proper° man. Let me see now,   380
To get his place, and to plume up° my will
In double knavery——How, how?—Let's see.—
After some time, to abuse Othello's ear
That he is too familiar with his wife.
He hath a person and a smooth dispose   385
To be suspected,° framed to make women false.
The Moor is of a free and open nature
That thinks men honest that but seem to be so,
And will as tenderly be led by the nose
As asses are.   390
I have 't. It is engendered.° Hell and night
Must bring this monstrous birth to the world's light. (*Exit.*)

act two

SCENE ONE. A SEAPORT IN CYPRUS. AN OPEN PLACE NEAR THE WHARF.

(*Enter* MONTANO *and two* GENTLEMEN.)

MON. What from the cape can you discern at sea?
1. GENT. Nothing at all. It is a high-wrought flood.°
I cannot 'twixt the heaven and the main°
Descry a sail.
MON. Methinks the wind hath spoke aloud at land,   5
A fuller blast ne'er shook our battlements.
If it hath ruffianed° so upon the sea,
What ribs of oak, when mountains melt on them,
Can hold the mortise?° What shall we hear of this?
2. GENT. A segregation° of the Turkish fleet.   10
For do but stand upon the foaming shore,
The chidden billow seems to pelt the clouds,
The wind-shaked surge, with high and monstrous mane,

---

380. *proper:* handsome.   381. *plume up:* glorify.   385–86. *He . . . suspected:* an easy way with him that is naturally suspected.   391. *engendered:* conceived.
Act. II, Sc. i: 2. *high-wrought flood:* heavy sea.   3. *main:* sea.   7. *ruffianed:* played the ruffian.   9. *hold . . . mortise:* remain fast joined.   10. *segregation:* separation.

Seems to cast water on the burning Bear,°
And quench the guards of the ever-fixèd Pole,°   15
I never did like molestation° view
On the enchafèd flood.
    MON.   If that the Turkish fleet
Be not ensheltered and embayed,° they are drowned.
It is impossible to bear it out.
                (*Enter a* THIRD GENTLEMEN.)
    3. GENT. News, lads! Our wars are done.   20
The desperate tempest hath so banged the Turks
That their designment halts.° A noble ship of Venice
Hath seen a grievous wreck and sufferance°
On most part of their fleet.
    MON. How! Is this true?
    3. GENT.   The ship is here put in,   25
A Veronesa, Michael Cassio,
Lieutenant to the warlike Moor Othello,
Is come on shore, the Moor himself at sea,
And is in full commission° here for Cyprus.
    MON. I am glad on 't. 'Tis a worthy governor.   30
    3. GENT. But this same Cassio, though he speaks of comfort
Touching the Turkish loss, yet he looks sadly
And prays the Moor be safe, for they were parted
With foul and violent tempest.
    MON.   Pray Heaven he be,
For I have served him, and the man commands   35
Like a full° soldier. Let's to the seaside, ho!
As well to see the vessel that's come in
As to throw out our eyes for brave Othello,
Even till we make the main and the aerial blue
An indistinct regard.°
    3. GENT.   Come, let's do so.   40

---

14. *Bear:* the Great Bear.   15. *guards . . . Pole:* stars in the "tail" of the Little
Bear constellation.   16. *molestation:* disturbance.   17. *enchafed:* angry.   18.
embayed: anchored in some bay.   22. *designment halts:* plan is made lame.
23. *sufferance:* damage.   29. *in . . . commission:* with full powers. See.
I.iii.281–82.   36. *full:* perfect.   39–40. *Even . . . regard:* until we can no
longer distinguish between sea and sky.

For every minute is expectancy
Of more arrivance.°

(Enter CASSIO.)

CAS. Thanks, you the valiant of this warlike isle
That so approve the Moor! Oh, let the heavens
Give him defense against the elements,   45
For I have lost him on a dangerous sea.
   MON. Is he well shipped?°
   CAS. His bark is stoutly timbered, and his pilot
Of very expert and approved allowance.°
Therefore my hopes, not surfeited° to death,   50
Stand in bold cure.°   (A cry within:
                                "A sail, a sail, a sail!")

(Enter a FOURTH GENTLEMAN.)

   CAS. What noise?
   4. GENT. The town is empty. On the brow o' the sea
Stand ranks of people, and they cry "A sail!"
   CAS. My hopes do shape° him for the governor.   55
                                      (Guns heard)
   2. GENT. They do discharge their shot of courtesy.
Our friends, at least.
   CAS.   I pray you, sir, go forth,
And give us truth who 'tis that is arrived.
   2. GENT. I shall.   (Exit.)
   MON. But, good Lieutenant, is your General wived?   60
   CAS. Most fortunately. He hath achieved° a maid
That paragons° description and wild fame,
One that excels the quirks of blazoning pens
And in the essential vesture of creation
Does tire the ingener.°
(Re-enter SECOND GENTLEMAN.) How now! Who has put in?   65

41–42. *For . . . arrivance:* every minute more arrivals are expected.   **47.** *well shipped:* in a good ship.   **49.** *approved allowance:* proved skill.   **50.** *surfeited:* sickened.   **51.** *Stand . . . cure:* have every hope of cure.   **55.** *shape:* imagine.   **61.** *achieved:* won.   **62.** *paragons:* surpasses.   **63–65.** *One . . . ingener:* one that is too good for the fancy phrases (*quirks*) of painting pens (i.e., poets) and in her absolute perfection wearies the artist (i.e., the painter). (Cassio is full of gallant phrases and behavior, in contrast to Iago's bluntness.) *ingener:* inventor.

2. GENT. 'Tis one Iago, Ancient to the General.

CAS. He has had most favorable and happy speed.
Tempests themselves, high seas, and howling winds,
The guttered° rocks, and congregated sands,
Traitors ensteeped° to clog the guiltless keel,   70
As having sense of beauty, do omit
Their mortal natures,° letting go safely by
The divine Desdemona.

MON.   What is she?

CAS. She that I spake of, our great Captain's captain,
Left in the conduct° of the bold Iago,   75
Whose footing° here anticipates our thoughts
A sennight's° speed. Great Jove, Othello guard,
And swell his sail with thine own powerful breath,
That he may bless this bay with his tall ship,
Make love's quick pants in Desdemona's arms,   80
Give renewed fire to our extincted° spirits,
And bring all Cyprus comfort.

(*Enter* DESDEMONA, EMILIA, IAGO, RODERIGO,
and ATTENDANTS.)

Oh, behold,
The riches of the ship is come on shore!
Ye men of Cyprus, let her have your knees.
Hail to thee, lady! And the grace of Heaven,   85
Before, behind thee, and on every hand,
Enwheel° thee round!

DES.   I thank you, valiant Cassio.
What tidings can you tell me of my lord?

CAS. He is not yet arrived, nor know I aught
But that he's well and will be shortly here.   90

DES. Oh, but I fear——How lost you company?

CAS. The great contention of the sea and skies
Parted our fellowship.°—But, hark! A sail.

(*A cry within:* "A sail, a sail!" *Guns heard.*)

---

69. *guttered:* worn into channels.   70. *ensteeped:* submerged.   71–72. *omit
. . . natures:* forbear their deadly nature.   75. *conduct:* escort.   76. *footing:*
arrival.   77. *sennight:* week.   81. *extincted:* extinguished.   87. *Enwheel:* en-
compass.   93. *fellowship:* company.

2. GENT. They give their greeting to the citadel.
This likewise is a friend.

    CAS.   See for the news.

                         (*Exit* GENTLEMAN.)

Good Ancient, you are welcome. (*To* EMILIA) Welcome,
    mistress.
Let it not gall your patience, good Iago,
That I extend my manners.° 'Tis my breeding°
That gives me this bold show of courtesy.°   100

                      (*Kissing her.*)

    IAGO. Sir, would she give you so much of her lips
As of her tongue she oft bestows on me,
You'd have enough.

    DES.   Alas, she has no speech.

    IAGO. In faith, too much,
I find it still° when I have list° to sleep.   105
Marry, before your ladyship, I grant,
She puts her tongue a little in her heart
And chides with thinking.

    EMIL. You have little cause to say so.

    IAGO. Come on, come on. You are pictures° out of doors,   110
Bells° in your parlors, wildcats in your kitchens,
Saints in your injuries,° devils being offended,
Players in your housewifery, and housewives in your beds.

    DES. Oh, fie upon thee, slanderer!

    IAGO. Nay, it is true, or else I am a Turk.°   115
You rise to play, and go to bed to work.

    EMIL. You shall not write my praise.

    IAGO.   No, let me not.

    DES. What wouldst thou write of me if thou shouldst
    praise me?

    IAGO. O gentle lady, do not put me to 't,
For I am nothing if not critical.°   120

---

99. *extend my manners:* i.e., salute your wife. *breeding:* bringing up. **100.**
bold . . . courtesy: i.e., of saluting your wife with a kiss—a piece of presumptuous behavior which indicates that Cassio regards himself as Iago's social
superior. **105.** *still:* continuously. *list:* desire. **110.** *pictures:* i.e., painted
and dumb. **111.** *Bells:* i.e., ever clacking. **112.** *Saints . . . injuries:* saints
when you hurt anyone else. **115.** *Turk:* heathen. **120.** *critical:* bitter.

DES. Come on, assay.°—There's one gone to the harbor?

IAGO. Aye, madam.

DES. I am not merry, but I do beguile
The thing I am by seeming otherwise.
Come, how wouldst thou praise me?   125

IAGO. I am about it, but indeed my invention
Comes from my pate as birdlime does from frieze°—
It plucks out brains and all. But my Muse labors,
And thus she is delivered.
If she be fair and wise, fairness and wit,   130
The one's for use, the other useth it.

DES. Well praised! How if she be black and witty?

IAGO. If she be black, and thereto have a wit,
She'll find a white° that shall her blackness fit.

DES. Worse and worse.   135

EMIL. How if fair and foolish?

IAGO. She never yet was foolish that was fair,
For even her folly helped her to an heir.

DES. These are old fond paradoxes° to make fools laugh
i' the alehouse. What miserable praise hast thou for her that's   140
foul and foolish?

IAGO. There's none so foul, and foolish thereunto,
But does foul pranks which fair and wise ones do.

DES. Oh, heavy ignorance! Thou praisest the worst best. But
what praise couldst thou bestow on a deserving woman in-   145
deed, one that in the authority of her merit did justly put on
the vouch of very malice itself?°

IAGO. She that was ever fair and never proud,
Had tongue at will° and yet was never loud,
Never lacked gold and yet went never gay,   150
Fled from her wish and yet said "Now I may."
She that, being angered, her revenge being nigh,
Bade her wrong stay and her displeasure fly.

---

121. *assay:* try.   126–27. *my . . . frieze:* my literary effort (*invention*) is as
hard to pull out of my head as frieze (cloth with a nap) stuck to birdlime.
134. *white:* with a pun on *wight* (1.158), man, person.   139. *fond paradoxes:*
foolish remarks, contrary to general opinion.   146–47. *one . . . itself:* one so
deserving that even malice would declare her good.   149. *tongue . . . will:* a
ready flow of words.

She that in wisdom never was so frail
To change the cod's head for the salmon's tail.°   155
She that could think and ne'er disclose her mind,
See suitors following and not look behind.
She was a wight, if ever such wight were——
    DES. To do what?
    IAGO. To suckle fools and chronicle small beer.°   160
    DES. Oh, most lame and impotent conclusion! Do not learn
of him, Emilia, though he be thy husband. How say you, Cassio? Is he not a most profane and liberal° counselor?
    CAS. He speaks home,° madam. You may relish° him more
in the soldier than in the scholar.   165
    IAGO. (*Aside*) He° takes her by the palm. Aye, well said,
whisper. With as little a web as this will I ensnare as great a
fly as Cassio. Aye, smile upon her, do, I will gyve° thee in
thine own courtship. You say true, 'tis so indeed. If such tricks
as these strip you out of your Lieutenantry, it had been better   170
you had not kissed your three fingers° so oft, which now again
you are most apt to play the sir° in. Very good, well kissed!
An excellent courtesy! 'Tis so indeed. Yet again your fingers
to your lips? Would they were clyster pipes° for your sake!
(*Trumpet within.*) The Moor! I know his trumpet.   175
    CAS. 'Tis truly so.
    DES. Let's meet him and receive him.
    CAS. Lo where he comes!
        (*Enter* OTHELLO *and* ATTENDANTS.)
    OTH. O my fair warrior!°
    DES.   My dear Othello!
    OTH. It gives me wonder great as my content   180
To see you here before me. O my soul's joy!

---

155. *To . . . tail:* to prefer the tail end of a good thing to the head of a poor
thing.   160. *chronicle . . . beer:* write a whole history about trifles (*small beer:*
thin drink).   163. *liberals:* gross.   164. *home:* to the point.   *relish:* appreciate.   166–75. *He . . . sake:* As so often, Shakespeare without using elaborate
stage directions exactly indicates the action of the dialogue. Cf. *W Tale,*
I.ii.111–18.   168. *gyve:* fetter.   171. *kissed . . . fingers:* a gesture of gallantry.
172. *play . . sir:* act the fine gentleman   174. *clyster pipes:* an enema syringe.
179. *warrior:* because she is a soldier's wife. See I.iii249.

If after every tempest come such calms,
May the winds blow till they have wakened death!
And let the laboring bark climb hills of seas
Olympus high,° and duck again as low   185
As Hell's from Heaven! If it were now to die,
'Twere now to be most happy, for I fear
My soul hath her content so absolute
That not another comfort like to this
Succeeds in unknown fate.
    DES.   The Heavens forbid   190
But that our loves and comforts should increase,
Even as our days do grow!
    OTH.   Amen to that, sweet powers!
I cannot speak enough of this content.
It stops me here,° it is too much of joy.
And this, and this, the greatest discords be   195
                     (*Kissing her*)
That e'er our hearts shall make!
    IAGO. (*Aside*)   Oh, you are well tuned now,
But I'll set down the pegs° that make this music,
As honest as I am.
    OTH.   Come, let us to the castle.
News, friends. Our wars are done, the Turks are drowned.
How does my old acquaintance of this isle?   200
Honey, you shall be well desired in Cyprus,
I have found great love amongst them. O my sweet,
I prattle out of fashion,° and I dote
In mine own comforts. I prithee, good Iago,
Go to the bay and disembark my coffers.°   205
Bring thou the master° to the citadel.
He is a good one, and his worthiness
Does challenge° much respect. Come, Desdemona,
Once more well met Cyprus.
            (*Exeunt all but* IAGO *and* RODERIGO.)

185. *Olympus-high:* high as Olympus, the highest mountain in Greece. 194. *here:* i.e., in the heart. 197. *set . . . pegs:* i.e., make you sing a different key. A stringed instrument was tuned by the pegs. 203. *prattle . . . fashion:* talk idly. 205. *coffers:* trunks. 206. *master:* captain of the ship. 208. *challenge:* claim.

IAGO. Do thou meet me presently° at the harbor. Come   210
hither. If thou beest valiant—as they say base men being in
love have then a nobility in their natures more than is native
to them—list me. The Lieutenant tonight watches on the
court of guard.° First, I must tell thee this. Desdemona is directly in love with him.   215
  ROD. With him! Why, 'tis not possible.
  IAGO. Lay thy finger thus,° and let thy soul be instructed.
Mark me with what violence she first loved the Moor, but
for° bragging and telling her fantastical lies. And will she
love him still for prating? Let not thy discreet heart think it. 220
Her eyes must be fed, and what delight shall she have to look
on the Devil?° When the blood is made dull with the act of
sport, there should be, again to inflame it and to give satiety
a fresh appetite, loveliness in favor,° sympathy in years, manners and beauties, all which the Moor is defective in. Now, for 225
want of these required conveniences, her delicate tenderness
will find itself abused, begin to heave the gorge,° disrelish
and abhor the Moor. Very nature will instruct her in it and
compel her to some second choice. Now, sir, this granted—as
it is a most pregnant and unforced position°—who stands so   230
eminently in the degree of this fortune as Cassio does? A
knave very voluble, no further conscionable° than in putting
on the mere form of civil and humane seeming° for the better
compassing of his salt° and most hidden loose affection? Why,
none, why, none. A slipper° and subtle knave, a finderout of   235
occasions, that has an eye can stamp and counterfeit advantages,° though true advantage never present itself. A devilish
knave! Besides, the knave is handsome, young, and hath all
those requisites in him that folly and green° minds look after.

---

210. *presently:* immediately.   213–14. *watches . . . guard:* is on duty with
the guard. The court of guard meant both the guard itself and the guardroom.
217. *finger thus:* i.e., on the lips.   218–19. *but for:* only for.   222. *Devil:* See
I.i.91,n.   224. *favor:* face.   227. *heave . . . gorge:* retch.   *gorge:* throat.
230. *pregnant . . . position:* very significant and probable argument.   232. *no
. . . conscionable:* who has no more conscience.   233. *humane seeming:* cour-
teous appearance.   234. *salt:* lecherous.   235. *slipper:* slippery.   236–37.
stamp . . . advantages: forge false opportunities.   239. *green:* inexperienced,
foolish.

A pestilent complete knave, and the women hath found him 240
already.

ROD. I cannot believe that in her. She's full of most blest
condition.°

IAGO. Blest fig's-end!° The wine she drinks is made of
grapes. If she had been blest, she would never have loved the 245
Moor. Blest pudding! Didst thou not see her paddle° with the
palm of his hand? Didst not mark that?

ROD. Yes, that I did, but that was but courtesy.

IAGO. Lechery, but this hand, an index° and obscure prologue to the history of lust and foul thoughts. They met so 250
near with their lips that their breaths embraced together. Villainous thoughts, Roderigo! When these mutualities° so marshal the way, hard at hand comes the master and main exercise,
the incorporate° conclusion. Pish! But, sir, be you ruled by
me. I have brought you from Venice. Watch you tonight. 255
For the command, I'll lay 't upon you. Cassio knows you not.
I'll not be far from you. Do you find some occasion to anger
Cassio, either by speaking too loud, or tainting° his discipline,
or from what other course you please which the time shall
more favorably minister.° 260

ROD. Well.

IAGO. Sir, he is rash and very sudden in choler,° and haply°
may strike at you. Provoke him, that he may, for even out of
that will I cause these of Cyprus to mutiny, whose qualifica-
tion° shall come into no true taste again but by the displant- 265
ing° of Cassio. So shall you have a shorter journey to your
desires by the means I shall then have to prefer° them, and
the impediment most profitably removed without the which
there were no expectation of our prosperity.

ROD. I will do this, if I can bring it to my opportunity. 270

---

243. *condition:* disposition. 244. *Blest fig's-end:* blest nonsense, a phrase used
as a substitute in contempt for a phrase just used, as is also *blest pudding*
(1.246). 246. *paddle:* play. 249. *index:* table of contents. 252. *mutuali-
ties:* mutual exchanges. 254. *incorporate:* bodily. 258. *tainting:* disparag-
ing. 260. *minister:* provide. 262. *choler:* anger. *haply:* perhaps. 265.
qualifications: appeasement. 265–66. *displanting:* removal. 267. *prefer:*
promote.

IAGO. I warrant thee. Meet me by and by at the citadel. I
must fetch his necessaries ashore. Farewell.

    ROD. *Adieu.*   (*Exit.*)

    IAGO. That Cassio loves her, I do well believe it.

That she loves him, 'tis apt and of great credit.°   275

The Moor, howbeit that I endure him not,

Is of a constant, loving, noble nature,

And I dare think he'll prove to Desdemona

A most dear husband. Now, I do love her too,

Not out of absolute lust, though peradventure   280

I stand accountant for as great a sin,

But partly led to diet° my revenge

For that I do suspect the lusty Moor

Hath leaped into my seat. The thought whereof

Doth like a poisonous mineral° gnaw my inwards.   285

And nothing can or shall content my soul

Till I am evened with him, wife for wife.

Or failing so, yet that I put the Moor

At least into a jealousy so strong

That judgment° cannot cure. Which thing to do,   290

If this poor trash of Venice, whom I trash°

For his quick hunting,° stand the putting-on,°

I'll have our Michael Cassio on the hip,

Abuse him to the Moor in the rank garb°—

For I fear Cassio with my nightcap too—   295

Make the Moor thank me, love me, and reward me

For making him egregiously° an ass

And practicing upon° his peace and quiet

Even to madness. 'Tis here, but yet confused.

Knavery's plain face is never seen till used.   (*Exit.*) 300

---

275. *apt . . . credit:* likely and very credible.   282. *diet:* feed.   285. *poisonous
mineral:* corrosive poison. See I.ii.74.   290. *judgment:* reason.   291. *trash
. . . trash:* rubbish . . . discard.   291–92. *trash . . . hunting:* FI reads "trace"
and Q1 "crush." If the emendation "trash" is correct, it means "hold back from
outrunning the pack." Cf. *Temp.* I.ii.81,n.   292. *putting-on:* encouraging.
294. *rank garb:* gross manner; i.e., by accusing him of being Desdemona's
lover.   297. *egregiously:* notably.   298. *practicing upon:* plotting against.

SCENE TWO. A STREET.

(Enter a HERALD *with a proclamation,* PEOPLE
following.)

HER. It is Othello's pleasure, our noble and valiant General,
that upon certain tidings now arrived, importing the mere
perdition° of the Turkish fleet, every man put himself into
triumph°—some to dance, some to make bonfires, each man
to what sport and revels his addiction° leads him. For, besides   5
these beneficial news, it is the celebration of his nuptial. So
much was his pleasure should be proclaimed. All offices° are
open, and there is full liberty of feasting from this present
hour of five till the bell have told eleven. Heaven bless the
isle of Cyprus and our noble General Othello!   *(Exeunt.)*   10

SCENE THREE. A HALL IN THE CASTLE.

(Enter OTHELLO, DESDEMONA, CASSIO, *and*
ATTENDANTS.*)*

OTH. Good Michael, look you to the guard tonight.
Let's teach ourselves that honorable stop,
Not to outsport discretion.°
    CAS. Iago hath direction what to do,
But notwithstanding with my personal eye   5
Will I look to 't.
    OTH.   Iago is most honest.
Michael, good night. Tomorrow with your earliest°
Let me have speech with you, Come, my dear love,
The purchase made, the fruits are to ensue—
That profit's yet to come 'tween me and you.   10
Good night.

Sc. ii: 3. *mere perdition:* absolute destruction.   3–4. *put . . . triumph:* celebrate.   5. *addiction:* inclination.   7. *offices:* the kitchen and buttery—i.e.,
free food and drink for all.
    Sc. iii: 3. *outsport discretion:* let the fun go too far.   7. *with . . . earliest:*
very early.

(*Exeunt* OTHELLO, DESDEMONA, *and* ATTENDANTS.)
(*Enter* IAGO.)

CAS. Welcome, Iago. We must to the watch.

IAGO. Not this hour. Lieutenant, 'tis not yet ten o' the clock. Our General cast° us thus early for the love of his Desdemona, who let us not therefore blame. He hath not yet made wanton the night with her, and she is sport for Jove.

CAS. She's a most exquisite lady.

IAGO. And, I'll warrant her, full of game.

CAS. Indeed she's a most fresh and delicate creature.

IAGO. What an eye she has. Methinks it sounds a parley to provocation.°

CAS. An inviting eye, and yet methinks right modest.

IAGO. And when she speaks, is it not an alarum° to love?

CAS. She is indeed perfection.

IAGO. Well, happiness to their sheets! Come, Lieutenant, I have a stoup° of wine, and here without are a brace of Cyprus gallants that would fain° have a measure to the health of black Othello.

CAS. Not tonight, good Iago. I have very poor and unhappy brains for drinking. I could well wish courtesy would invent some other customs of entertainment.

IAGO. Oh, they are our friends. But one cup—I'll drink for you.

CAS. I have drunk but one cup tonight, and that was craftily qualified° too, and behold what innovation° it makes here. I am unfortunate in the infirmity, and dare not task° my weakness with any more.

IAGO. What, man! 'Tis a night of revels. The gallants desire it.

CAS. Where are they?

IAGO. Here at the door. I pray you call them in.

CAS. I'll do 't, but it dislikes me.   (*Exit.*)

IAGO. If I can fasten but one cup upon him,
With that which he hath drunk tonight already

14. *cast:* dismissed.   20–21. *sounds . . . provocation:* invites to a love talk. 23. *alarum:* call to arms.   26. *stoup:* large drinking vessel.   27. *fain:* gladly. 34–35. *craftily qualified:* cunningly mixed.   35. *innovation:* revolution, disturbance.   36. *task:* burden.   42. *dislikes:* displeases.

He'll be as full of quarrel and offense   45
As my young mistress' dog. Now my sick fool Roderigo,
Whom love hath turned almost the wrong side out,
To Desdemona hath tonight caroused°
Potations pottle-deep,° and he's to watch.
Three lads of Cyprus, noble swelling° spirits   50
That hold their honors in a wary distance,°
The very elements° of this warlike isle,
Have I tonight flustered with flowing cups,
And they watch too. Now, 'mongst this flock of drunkards,
Am I to put our Cassio in some action   55
That may offend the isle. But here they come.
If consequence do but approve my dream,°
My boat sails freely, both with wind and stream.

> (*Re-enter* CASSIO, *with him* MONTANO *and* GENTLEMEN,
> SERVANTS *following with wine.*)

CAS. 'Fore God, they have given me a rouse° already.

MON. Good faith, a little one—not past a pint, as I am a   60
soldier.

IAGO. Some wine, ho! (*Sings.*)
"And let me the cannikin° clink, clink,
And let me the cannikin clink.
A soldier's a man,   65
A life's but a span.°
Why, then let a soldier drink."
Some wine, boys!

CAS. 'Fore God, an excellent song.

IAGO. I learned it in England, where indeed they are most   70
potent in potting.° Your Dane, your German, and your swag-
bellied° Hollander—Drink, ho!—are nothing to your English.

CAS. Is your Englishman so expert in his drinking?

---

48. *caroused:* drunk healths. 49. *pottle-deep:* "bottom up"; a pottle held
two quarts. 50. *swelling:* bursting with pride. 51. *hold . . . distance:* "have
a chip on their shoulders." 52. *very elements:* typical specimens. 57. *If . . .
dream:* if what follows proves my dream true. 59. *rouse:* a deep drink.
63. *cannikin:* drinking pot. 66. *span:* lit., the measure between the thumb
and little finger of the outstretched hand; about 9 inches. 71. *potent in
potting:* desperate drinkers. 71–72. *swag-bellied:* with loose bellies. Germans
and Dutchmen were almost as famous for drinking as the Danes.

IAGO. Why, he drinks you with facility your Dane dead
drunk, he sweats not° to overthrow your Almain,° he gives   75
your Hollander a vomit° ere the next pottle can be filled.

CAS. To the health of our General!

MON. I am for it, Lieutenant, and I'll do you justice.

IAGO. O sweet England! (*Sings.*)

"King Stephen was a worthy peer,   80
    His breeches cost him but a crown.
He held them sixpence all too dear,°
    With that he called the tailor lown.°

"He was a wight of high renown,
    And thou art but of low degree.   85
'Tis pride that pulls the country down.
    Then take thine auld cloak about thee."

Some wine, ho!

CAS. Why, this is a more exquisite song than the other.

IAGO. Will you hear 't again?   90

CAS. No, for I hold him to be unworthy of his place that
does those things. Well, God's above all, and there be souls
must be saved and there be souls must not be saved.

IAGO. It's true, good Lieutenant.

CAS. For mine own part—no offense to the General, nor any 95
man of quality°—I hope to be saved.

IAGO. And so do I too, Lieutenant.

CAS. Aye, but, by your leave, not before me. The Lieutenant
is to be saved before the Ancient. Let's have no more of this,
let's to our affairs. God forgive us our sins! Gentlemen, let's 100
look to our business. Do not think, gentlemen, I am drunk.
This is my Ancient, this is my right hand and this is my left.
I am not drunk now, I can stand well enough and speak well
enough.

ALL. Excellent well.   105

CAS. Why, very well, then, you must not think then that I
am drunk.   (*Exit.*)

---

75. *sweats not:* has no need to labor excessively. *Almain:* German.   **75–76.**
gives . . . vomit: drinks as much as will make a Dutchman throw up.   **82.** *six-*
pence . . . dear: too dear by sixpence.   **83.** *lown:* lout.   **96.** *quality:* rank.

MON. To the platform,° masters. Come, let's set the watch.°

IAGO. You see this fellow that is gone before.
He is a soldier to fit to stand by Caesar   110
And give direction. And do but see his vice.
'Tis to his virtue a just equinox,°
The one as long as the other. 'Tis pity of him.
I fear the trust Othello put him in
On some odd time° of his infirmity   115
Will shake this island.

MON.   But is he often thus?

IAGO. 'Tis evermore the prologue to his sleep.
He'll watch the horologe a double set,°
If drink rock not his cradle.

MON.   It were well
The General were put in mind of it.   120
Perhaps he sees it not, or his good nature
Prizes the virtue that appears in Cassio
And looks not on his evils. Is not this true?

(Enter RODERIGO.)

IAGO. (*Aside to him*). How now, Roderigo! I pray you,
after the Lieutenant. Go.   (*Exit* RODERIGO.) 125

MON. And 'tis great pity that the noble Moor
Should hazard such a place as his own second
With one of an ingraft° infirmity.
It were an honest action to say
So to the Moor.

IAGO.   Not I, for this fair island.   130
I do love Cassio well, and would do much
To cure him of this evil—But, hark! What noise?

(A cry within: "Help! help!")

(Re-enter CASSIO, *driving in* RODERIGO.)

CAS. 'Zounds! You rogue! You rascal!

MON.   What's the matter, Lieutenant?

---

108. *platform:* the level place on the ramparts where the cannon were mounted.
set . . . watch: mount guard.   112. *just equinox:* exact equal.   115. *some . . .
time:* some time or other.   118. *watch . . . set:* stay awake the clock twice
round.   128. *ingraft:* engrafted, firmly fixed.

CAS. A knave teach me my duty!

But I'll beat the knave into a wicker bottle.°   135

  ROD. Beat me!

  CAS. Dost thou prate, rogue?   (*Striking* RODERIGO.)

  MON.   Nay, good Lieutenant,   (*Staying him.*)

I pray you, sir, hold your hand.

  CAS.   Let me go, sir,

Or I'll knock you o'er the mazzard.°

  MON.   Come, come, you're drunk.

  CAS. Drunk!   (*They fight.*)   140

  IAGO. (*Aside to* RODERIGO) Away, I say. Go out and cry a

    mutiny.°   (*Exit* RODERIGO.)

Nay, good Lieutenant! God's will, gentlemen!

Help, ho!—Lieutenant—sir—Montano—sir—

Help, masters!—Here's a goodly watch indeed!

                    (*A bell rings.*)

Who's that that rings the bell?—Diablo,° ho!

The town will rise. God's will, Lieutenant, hold—   145

You will be shamed forever.

      (*Re-enter* OTHELLO *and* ATTENDANTS.)

  OTH.   What is the matter here?

  MON. 'Zounds, I bleed still, I am hurt to the death. (*Faints.*)

  OTH. Hold, for your lives!

  IAGO. Hold, ho! Lieutenant—sir—Montano—gentlemen—

Have you forgot all sense of place and duty?   150

Hold! The General speaks to you. Hold, hold, for shame!

  OTH. Why, how now, ho! From whence ariseth this?

Are we turned Turks, and to ourselves do that

Which Heaven hath forbid the Ottomites?

For Christian shame, put by this barbarous brawl.   155

He that stirs next to carve for his own rage°

---

135. *But . . . bottle:* One of those bad-tempered threatening phrases which have no very exact meaning, like "I'll knock him into a cocked hat." *wicker bottle:* large bottle covered with wicker, demijohn. 139. *mazzard:* head, a slang word. 141. *cry . . . mutiny:* cry that a mutiny has broken out; i.e., raise a riot. 144. *Diablo:* the Devil. 156. *carve . . . rage:* to satisfy his hunger for rage.

Holds his soul light, he dies upon his motion.°
Silence that dreadful bell. It frights the isle
From her propriety.° What is the matter, masters?
Honest Iago, that look'st dead with grieving,   160
Speak, who began this? On thy love, I charge thee.
   IAGO. I do not know. Friends all but now, even now,
In quarter and in terms like bride and groom
Devesting° them for bed. And then, but now,
As if some planet had unwitted men,°   165
Swords out, and tilting° one at other's breast
In opposition bloody. I cannot speak
Any beginning to this peevish odds,°
And would in action glorious I had lost
Those legs that brought me to a part of it!   170
   OTH. How comes it, Michael, you are thus forgot?°
   CAS. I pray you, pardon me, I cannot speak.
   OTH. Worthy Montano, you were wont be civil.°
The gravity and stillness° of your youth
The world hath noted, and your name is great   175
In mouths of wisest censure.° What's the matter
That you unlace° your reputation thus,
And spend your rich opinion° for the name
Of a night brawler? Give me answer to it.
   MON. Worthy Othello, I am hurt to danger.   180
Your officer, Iago, can inform you—
While I spare speech, which something now offends me—
Of all that I do know. Nor know I aught
By me that's said or done amiss this night,
Unless self-charity° be sometimes a vice,   185
And to defend ourselves it be a sin
When violence asails us.

157. *upon . . . motion:* at his first movement.   159. *propriety:* natural behavior.   164. *Devesting:* taking off their clothes.   165. *planet . . . men:* as if some evil star had made men mad.   166. *tilting:* thrusting.   169. *peevish odds:* silly disagreement.   171. *are . . . forgot:* have so forgotten yourself.   173. *civil:* well behaved.   174. *stillness:* staid behavior.   176. *censure:* judgment.   177. *unlace:* undo.   178. *spend . . . opinion:* lose your good reputation.   185. *self-charity:* love for oneself.

OTH.   Now, by Heaven,
My blood begins my safer guides to rule,
And passion, having my best judgment collied,°
Assays to lead the way. If I once stir,   190
Or do but lift this arm, the best of you
Shall sink in my rebuke. Give me to know
How this foul rout° began, who set it on,
And he that is approved° in this offense,   195
Though he had twinned with me, both at a birth,
Shall lose me. What! In a town of war,
Yet wild, the people's hearts brimful of fear,
To manage° private and domestic quarrel,
In night, and on the court and guard of safety!   200
'Tis monstrous. Iago, who began 't?
    MON. If partially affined, or leagued in office,
Thou dost deliver° more or less than truth,
Thou are no soldier.
    IAGO.   Touch me not so near.
I had rather have this tongue cut from my mouth   205
Than it should do offense to Michael Cassio.
Yet I persuade myself to speak the truth
Shall nothing wrong him. Thus it is, General.
Montano and myself being in speech,
There comes a fellow crying out for help,   210
And Cassio following him with determined sword
To execute upon him. Sir, this gentleman
Steps in to Cassio and entreats his pause.°
Myself the crying fellow did pursue,
Lest by his clamor—as it so fell out—   215
The town might fall in fright. He, swift of foot,
Outran my purpose, and I returned the rather
For that I heard the clink and fall of swords,
And Cassio high in oath, which till tonight
I ne'er might say before. When I came back—   220

---

189. *collied:* darkened. 194. *rout:* riot, uproar. 195. *approved:* proved
guilty. 199. *manage:* be concerned with. 202–03. *If . . . deliver:* if, because you are influenced by partiality or because he is your fellow officer, you
report. *affined:* bound. 213. *entreats . . . pause:* begs him to stop.

For this was brief—I found them close together,
At blow and thrust, even as again they were
When you yourself did part them.
More of this matter cannot I report.
But men are men, the best sometimes forget.   225
Though Cassio did some little wrong to him,
As men in rage strike those that wish them best,
Yet surely Cassio, I believe, received
From him that fled some strange indignity,
Which patience could not pass.

OTH.   I know, Iago,   230
Thy honesty and love doth mince this matter,
Making it light to Cassio. Cassio, I love thee,
But never more be officer of mine.
(*Re-enter* DESDEMONA, *attended.*) Look, if my gentle love be
    not raised up!
I'll make thee an example.

DES.   What's the matter?   235

OTH. All's well now, sweeting.° Come away to bed. (*To*
    MONTANO, *who is led off*)
Sir, for your hurts, myself will be your surgeon.
Lead him off.
Iago, look with care about the town,
And silence those whom this vile brawl distracted.   240
Come, Desdemona. 'Tis the soldiers' life
To have their balmy slumbers waked with strife.

(*Exeunt all but* IAGO *and* CASSIO.)

IAGO. What, are you hurt, Lieutenant?

CAS. Aye, past all surgery.

IAGO. Marry, Heaven forbid!   245

CAS. Reputation, reputation, reputation! Oh, I have lost my
reputation! I have lost the immortal part of myself, and what remains is bestial. My reputation, Iago, my reputation!

IAGO. As I am an honest man, I thought you had received
some bodily wound. There is more sense in that than in repu-   250
tation. Reputation is an idle and most false imposition,° oft

---

236. *sweeting:* sweetheart.   251. *imposition:* a quality laid on a man by others.

DRAMA: A CRITICAL COLLECTION

got without merit and lost without deserving. You have lost no
reputation at all unless you repute yourself such a loser. What,
man! There are ways to recover the General again. You are
but now cast in his mood,° a punishment more in policy°   255
than in malice—even so as one would beat his offenseless dog
to affright an imperious lion.° Sue to him again and he's yours.

    CAS. I will rather sue to be despised than to deceive so good
a commander with so slight, so drunken, and so indiscreet an
officer. Drunk? And speak parrot?° And squabble? Swagger?   260
Swear? And discourse fustian° with one's shadow? O thou invisible spirit of wine, if thou hast no name to be known by,
let us call thee devil!

    IAGO. What was he that you followed with your sword?
What had he done to you?   265

    CAS. I know not.

    IAGO. Is 't possible?

    CAS. I remember a mass of things, but nothing distinctly—
a quarrel, but nothing wherefore. Oh God, that men should
put an enemy in their mouths to steal away their brains! That 270
we should, with joy, pleasance,° revel, and applause, transform
ourselves into beasts!

    IAGO. Why, but you are now well enough. How came you
thus recovered?

    CAS. It hath pleased the devil drunkeness to give place to   275
the devil wrath. One unperfectness shows me another, to make
me frankly despise myself.

    IAGO. Come, you are too severe a moraler.° As the time, the
place, and the condition of this country stands, I could heartily
wish this had not befallen. But since it is as it is, mend it for   280
your own good.

    CAS. I will ask him for my place again, he shall tell me I am
a drunkard! Had I as many mouths as Hydra,° such an answer
would stop them all. To be now a sensible man, by and by a

---

255. *cast . . . mood:* dismissed because he is in a bad mood. *in policy:* i.e.,
because he must appear to be angry before the Cypriots. 256–57. *even . . .
lion:* a proverb meaning that when the lion sees the dog beaten, he will know
what is coming to him. 260. *speak parrot:* babble. 261. *fustian:* nonsense;
lit., cheap cloth. 271. *pleasance:* a gay time. 278. *moraler:* moralizer.
283. *Hydra:* a hundred-headed beast slain by Hercules.

fool, and presently a beast! Oh strange! every inordinate° cup   285
is unblest, and the ingredient is a devil.

IAGO. Come, come, good wine is a good familiar creature,
if it be well used. Exclaim no more against it. And, good Lieutenant, I think you think I love you.

CAS. I have well approved it, sir. I drunk!   290

IAGO. You or any man living may be drunk at some time,
man. I'll tell you what you shall do. Our General's wife is now
the General. I may say so in this respect, for that he hath devoted and given up himself to the contemplation, mark, and
denotement° of her parts and graces. Confess yourself freely   300
to her, importune her help to put you in your place again.
She is of so free, so kind, so apt,° so blessed a disposition, she
holds it a vice in her goodness not to do more than she is
requested. This broken joint between you and her husband
entreat her to splinter° and, my fortunes against any lay°   305
worth naming, this crack of your love shall grow stronger than
it was before.

CAS. You advise me well.

IAGO. I protest, in the sincerity of love and honest kindness.

CAS. I think it freely, and betimes in the morning I will   310
beseech the virtuous Desdemona to undertake for me. I am
desperate of my fortunes if they check me here.°

IAGO. You are in the right. Good night, Lieutenant, I must
to the watch.

CAS. Good night, honest Iago.   (*Exit.*)   315

IAGO. And what's he then that says I play the villain?
When this advise is free I give and honest,
Probal° to thinking, and indeed the course
To win the Moor again? For 'tis most easy
The inclining Desdemona to subdue   320
In any honest suit. She's framed° as fruitful
As the free elements.° And then for her
To win the Moor, were 't to renounce his baptism,
All seals and symbols of redeemèd sin,

285. *inordinate:* excessive. 300. *denotement:* careful observation. 302. *apt:*
ready. 305. *splinter:* put in splints. *lay:* bet. 311–12. *I . . . here:* I despair of my future if my career is stopped short here. 318. *Probal:* probable.
321. *framed:* made. 322. *free elements:* i.e., the air.

His soul is so enfettered to her love   325
That she may make, unmake, do what she list,
Even as her appetite shall play the god
With his weak function.° How am I then a villain
To counsel Cassio to this parallel course,
Directly to his good? Divinity of Hell!   330
When devils will the blackest sins put on,
They do suggest° at first with heavenly shows,
As I do now. For whiles this honest fool
Plies° Desdemona to repair his fortunes,
And she for him pleads strongly to the Moor,   335
I'll pour this pestilence into his ear,
That she repeals° him for her body's lust.
And by how much she strives to do him good,
She shall undo her credit with the Moor.
So will I turn her virtue into pitch,   340
And out of her own goodness make the net
That shall enmesh them all.
(*Enter* RODERIGO.)   How now, Roderigo!

     ROD. I do follow here in the chase, not like a hound that
hunts but one that fills up the cry.° My money is almost spent,
I have been tonight exceedingly well cudgeled, and I think the   345
issue will be I shall have so much experience for my pains and
so, with no money at all and a little more wit, return again to
Venice.

     IAGO. How poor are they that have not patience!
What wound did ever heal but by degrees?   350
Thou know'st we work by wit and not by witchcraft,
And wit depends on dilatory Time°
Does 't not go well? Cassio hath beaten thee,
And thou by that small hurt hast cashiered Cassio.
Though other things grow fair against the sun,   355
Yet fruits that blossom first will first be ripe.°

---

328. *function:* intelligence.   332. *suggest:* seduce.   334. *Plies:* vigorously
urges.   337. *repeals:* calls back.   344. *one . . . cry:* See *MND,* IV.i.127–28,n.
352. *And . . . Time:* and cleverness must wait for Time, who is in no hurry.
355–56. *Though . . . ripe:* though the fruit ripens in the sun, yet the first fruit
to ripen will come from the earliest blososms; i.e., our first plan—to get Cassio
cashiered—has succeeded, the rest will soon follow.

Content thyself awhile. By the mass, 'tis morning.
Pleasure and action makes the hours seem short.
Retire thee, go where thou art billeted.
Away, I say. Thou shalt know more hereafter.   360
Nay, get thee gone. (*Exit* RODERIGO.) Two things are to be
    done:
My wife must move for° Cassio to her mistress,
I'll set her on,
Myself the while to draw the Moor apart
And bring him jump° when he may Cassio find   365
Soliciting his wife. Aye, that's the way.
Dull not device° by coldness and delay.   (*Exit.*)

act three

SCENE ONE. BEFORE THE CASTLE.

(*Enter* CASSIO *and some* MUSICIANS.)
CAS. Masters, play here, I will content your pains°—
Something that's brief, and bid "Good morrow, General."°

                          (*Music.*)
          (*Enter* CLOWN.)
CLO. Why, masters, have your instruments been in Naples,°
that they speak i' the nose thus?
1. MUS. How, sir, how?   5
CLO. Are these, I pray you, wind instruments?
1. MUS. Aye, marry are they, sir.
CLO. Oh, thereby hangs a tail.
1. MUS. Whereby hangs a tale, sir?
CLO. Marry, sir, by many a wind instrument that I know.   10
But, masters, here's money for you. And the General so likes

---

362. *move for:* petition for.   365. *jump:* at the moment, just.   367. *Dull*
. . . *device:* do not spoil the plan.
    Act III, Sc. i: 1. *content . . . pains:* reward your labor.   1. *bid . . . General:*
It was a common custom to play or sing a song beneath the bedroom window
of a distinguished guest or of a newly wedded couple on the morning after
their wedding night.   3. *in Naples:* a reference to the Neapolitan (i.e., ve-
nereal) disease.

your music that he desires you, for love's sake, to make no
more noise with it.

1. MUS. Well, sir, we will not.

CLO. If you have any music that may not be heard, to 't   15
again. But, as they say, to hear music the General does not
greatly care.

1. MUS. We have none such, sir.

CLO. Then put up your pipes in your bag, for I'll away. Go,
vanish into air, away!   (*Exeunt* MUSICIANS.)   20

CAS. Dost thou hear, my honest friend?

CLO. No, I hear not your honest friend, I hear you.

CAS. Prithee keep up thy quillets.° There's a poor piece of
gold for thee. If the gentlewoman that attends the General's
wife be stirring, tell her there's one Cassio entreats her a little   25
favor of speech. Wilt thou do this?

CLO. She is stirring, sir. If she will stir hither, I shall seem
to notify unto her.

CAS. Do, good my friend.   (*Exit* CLOWN.)

(*Enter* IAGO.) In happy time,° Iago.   30

IAGO. You have not been abed, then?

CAS. Why, no, the day had broke
Before we parted. I have made bold, Iago,
To send in to your wife. My suit to her
Is that she will to virtuous Desdemona   35
Procure me some access.

IAGO.   I'll send her to you presently,
And I'll devise a mean to draw the Moor
Out of the way, that your convérse and business
May be more free.

CAS. I humbly thank you for 't. (*Exit* IAGO.) I never knew   40
A Florentine more kind° and honest.

(*Enter* EMILIA.)

EMIL. Good morrow, good Lieutenant. I am sorry
For your displeasure,° but all will sure be well.

---

23. *keep . . . quillets:* put away your wisecracks.   30. *In . . . time:* i.e., I am
glad to see you.   41. *Florentine . . . kind:* Iago is a Venetian. Cassio means:
even one of my own people could not have been kinder.   43. *your displeasure:*
i.e., that Othello is displeased with you.

The General and his wife are talking of it,
And she speaks for you stoutly. The Moor replies   45
That he you hurt is of great fame in Cyprus
And great affinity,° and that in wholesome wisdom
He might not but° refuse you. But he protests he loves you,
And needs no other suitor but his likings°
To take the safest occasion by the front   50
To bring you in° again.

CAS.   Yet I beseech you
If you think fit, or that it may be done,
Give me advantage of some brief discourse
With Desdemona alone.

EMIL.   Pray you, come in.
I will bestow you where you shall have time.   55
To speak your bosom freely.°

CAS.   I am much bound to you.   (*Exeunt.*)

SCENE TWO. A ROOM IN THE CASTLE.

(*Enter* OTHELLO, IAGO, *and* GENTLEMEN.)

OTH. These letters give, Iago, to the pilot,
And by him do my duties° to the Senate.
That done, I will be walking on the works.°
Repair there to me.

IAGO.   Well, my good lord, I'll do 't.

OTH. This fortification, gentlemen, shall we see 't?   5

GENT. We'll wait upon your lordship.   (*Exeunt.*)

47. *affinity:* kindred. 48. *might . . . but:* i.e., he must. 49. *likings:* affections. 50–51. *safest . . . in:* to take the first opportunity to restore you to your position. *front:* forehead; i.e., to take Time by the forelock. 56. *speak . . . freely:* declare what is on your mind.

Sc. ii: 2. *do . . . duties:* express my loyalty. 3. *works:* fortifications.

SCENE THREE. THE GARDEN OF THE CASTLE.

(*Enter* DESDEMONA, CASSIO, *and* EMILIA.)

DES. Be thou assured, good Cassio, I will do
All my abilities in thy behalf.

EMIL. Good madam, do. I warrant it grieves my husband
As if the case were his.

DES. Oh, that's an honest fellow. Do not doubt Cassio,   5
But I will have my lord and you again
As friendly as you were.

CAS.   Bounteous madam,
Whatever shall become of Michael Cassio,
He's never anything but your true servant.

DES. I know 't. I thank you. You do love my lord.   10
You have known him long, and be you well assured
He shall in strangeness stand no farther off
Than in a politic distance.°

CAS.   Aye, but, lady,
That policy may either last so long,
Or feed upon such nice and waterish diet,°   15
Or breed itself so out of circumstance,°
That, I being absent and my place supplied,°
My General will forget my love and service.

DES. Do not doubt° that. Before Emila here
I give thee warrant of thy place.° Assure thee,   20
If I do vow a friendship, I'll perform it
To the last article. My lord shall never rest.
I'll watch him tame° and talk him out of patience,
His bed shall seem a school, his board a shrift.°
I'll intermingle every thing he does   25
With Cassio's suit. Therefore be merry, Cassio,

Sc. iii: 12–13. *He . . . distance:* i.e., his apparent coldness to you shall only be so much as his official position demands for reasons of policy. **15.** *nice . . . diet:* have such weak encouragement. **16.** *breed . . . circumstance:* become so used to the situation. **17.** *supplied:* filled by another. **19.** *doubt:* fear. **20.** *give . . . place:* guarantee that you will be restored to your position. **23.** *watch . . . tame:* as wild hawks are made tame by keeping them from sleep. **24.** *shrift:* place of confession and absolution.

For thy solicitor shall rather die
Than give thy cause away.
> (*Enter* OTHELLO *and* IAGO, *at a distance.*)

EMIL. Madam, here comes my lord.

CAS. Madam, I'll take my leave.   30

DES. Nay, stay and hear me speak.

CAS. Madam, not now. I am very ill at ease,
Unfit for mine own purposes.°

DES. Well, do your discretion.   (*Exit* CASSIO.)

IAGO. Ha! I like not that.

OTH. What dost thou say?   35

IAGO. Nothing, my lord. Or if—I know not what.

OTH. Was not that Cassio parted from my wife?

IAGO. Cassio, my lord! No, sure, I cannot think it,
That he would steal away so guilty-like,
Seeing you coming.

OTH.   I do believ 'twas he.   40

DES. How now, my lord!
I have been talking with a suitor here,
A man that languishes in your displeasure.

OTH. Who is 't you mean?

DES. Why, your Lieutenant, Cassio. Good my lord,   45
If I have any grace or power to move you,
His present reconciliation take.°
For if he be not one that truly loves you,
That errs in ignorance and not in cunning,°
I have no judgment in an honest face.   50
I prithee call him back.

OTH.   Went he hence now?

DES. Aye, sooth, so humbled
That he hath left part of his grief with me,
To suffer with him, Good love, call him back.

OTH. Not now, sweet Desdemona, some other time.   55

DES. But shall 't be shortly?

OTH.   The sooner, sweet for you.

---

33. *Unfit . . . purposes:* in no condition to plead my own cause.   47. *His . . . take:* accept his immediate apology and forgive him.   49. *in cunning:* knowingly.

DES. Shall 't be tonight at supper?

OTH.   No, not tonight.

DES. Tomorrow dinner then?

OTH.   I shall not dine at home.
I meet the captains at the citadel.

DES. Why, then tomorrow night or Tuesday morn,   60
On Tuesday noon, or night, on Wednesday morn.
I prithee name the time, but let it not
Exceed three days. In faith, he's penitent,
And yet his trespass, in our common reason°—
Save that, they say, the wars must make examples   65
Out of their best—is not almost° a fault
To incur a private check.° When shall he come?
Tell me, Othello. I wonder in my soul
What you would ask me that I should deny,
Or stand so mammering° on. What! Michael Cassio,   70
That came a-wooing with you, and so many a time
When I have spoke of you dispraisingly
Hath ta'en your part—to have so much to do
To bring him in! Trust me, I could do much——

OTH. Prithee, no more. Let him come when he will.   75
I will deny thee nothing.

DES.   Why, this is not a boon.°
'Tis as I should entreat you wear your gloves,
Or feed on nourishing dishes, or keep you warm,
Or sue to you to do a peculiar° profit
To your own person. Nay, when I have a suit   80
Wherein I mean to touch your love indeed,
It shall be full of poise° and difficult weight,°
And fearful to be granted.°

OTH.   I will deny thee nothing.
Whereon I do beseech thee grant me this,
To leave me but a little to myself.   85

DES. Shall I deny you? No. Farewell, my lord.

---

64. *common reason:* common sense. 66. *not almost:* hardly. 67. *check:* rebuke. 70. *mammering:* hesitating. 76. *boon:* great favor. 79. *peculiar:*
particular. 82. *poise:* weight in the scales. *difficult weight:* hard to estimate.
83. *fearful . . . granted:* only granted with a sense of fear.

OTH. Farewell, my Desdemona. I'll come to thee straight.
DES. Emilia, come. Be as your fancies teach you.°
Whate'er you be, I am obedient.
                    (*Exeunt* DESDEMONA *and* EMILIA.)
  OTH. Excellent wretch! Perdition catch my soul   90
But I do love thee! And when I love thee not,
Chaos° is come again.
  IAGO. My noble lord——
  OTH.   What dost thou say, Iago?
  IAGO. Did Michael Cassio,° when you wooed my lady,
Know of your love?   95
  OTH. He did, from first to last. Why dost thou ask?
  IAGO. But for a satisfaction of my thought,
No further harm.
  OTH.   Why of thy thought, Iago?
  IAGO. I did not think he had been acquainted with her.
  OTH. Oh yes, and went between us very oft.   100
  IAGO. Indeed!
  OTH. Indeed! Aye, indeed. Discern'st thou aught in that?
Is he not honest?
  IAGO. Honest, my lord!
  OTH. Honest! Aye, honest.
  IAGO. My lord, for aught I know.
  OTH. What dost thou think?
  IAGO. Think, my lord!   105
  OTH. Think, my lord! By Heaven, he echoes me
As if there were some monster in his thought
Too hideous to be shown. Thou dost mean something.
I heard thee say even now thou likedst not that
When Cassio left my wife. What didst not like?   110
And when I told thee he was of my counsel
In my whole course of wooing, thou criedst "Indeed!"
And didst contract and purse thy brow together
As if thou then hadst shut up in they brain
Some horrible conceit.° If thou dost love me,   115

88. *Be . . . you:* please yourself. 92. *Chaos:* the utter confusion that existed before order was established in the universe. The idea of order and chaos is worked out elaborately in *Tr & Cr.* I.iii.83–124. 115. *conceit:* conceptions, notion.

Show me thy thought.

    IAGO. My lord, you know I love you.

    OTH.   I think thou dost,

And for° I know thou'rt full of love and honesty

And weigh'st thy words before thou givest them breath,

Therefore these stops of thine fright me the more.   120

For such things in a false disloyal knave

Are tricks of custom, but in a man that's just

They're close delations,° working from the heart,

That passion cannot rule.

    IAGO.   For Michael Cassio,

I dare be sworn I think that he is honest.   125

    OTH. I think so too.

    IAGO.   Men should be what they seem,

Or those that be not, would they might seem none!°

    OTH. Certain, men should be what they seem.

    IAGO. Why, then I think Cassio's an honest man.

    OTH. Nay, yet there's more in this.   130

I prithee speak to me as to thy thinkings,

As thou dost ruminate, and give thy worst of thoughts

The worst of words.

    IAGO.   Good my lord, pardon me.

Thought I am bound to every act of duty,

I am not bound to that all slaves are free to.   135

Utter my thoughts? Why, say they are vile and false,

As where's that palace whereinto foul things

Sometimes intrude not? Who has a breast so pure

But some uncleanly apprehensions

Keep leets and law days, and in session sit   140

With meditations lawful?°

    OTH. Thou dost conspire against thy friend, Iago,

If thou but think'st him wronged and makest his ear

A stranger to thy thoughts.

---

118. *for:* since. 123. *close delations:* concealed accusations. 127. *seem none:*
i.e., not seem to be honest men.   138–41. *Who . . . lawful:* whose heart is
so pure but that some foul suggestion will sit on the bench alongside lawful
thoughts; i.e., foul thoughts will rise even on the most respectable occasions.
leet: court held by the lord of the manor. *law days:* days when courts sit.
session: sitting of the court.

IAGO.   I do beeseech you—
Though I perchance am vicious in my guess,   145
As, I confess, it is my nature's plague
To spy into abuses, and oft my jealousy°
Shapes faults that are not—that your wisdom yet,
From one that so imperfectly conceits,°
Would take no notice, nor build yourself a trouble   150
Out of his scattering° and unsure observance.°
It were not for your quiet nor your good,
Nor for my manhood, honesty, or wisdom,
To let you know my thoughts.
    OTH.   What dost thou mean?
    IAGO. Good name in man and woman, dear my lord,   155
Is the immediate° jewel of their souls.
Who steals my purse steals trash—'tis something, nothing,
'Twas mine, 'tis his, and has been slave to thousands—
But he that filches from me my good name
Robs me of that which not enriches him   160
And makes me poor indeed.
    OTH. By Heaven, I'll know thy thoughts.
    IAGO. You cannot if my heart were in your hand,
Nor shall not whilst 'tis in my custody.
    OTH. Ha!
    IAGO.   Oh, beware, my lord, of jealousy.   165
It is the green-eyed monster which doth mock°
The meat° it feeds on. That cuckold lives in bliss
Who, certain of his fate, loves not his wronger.°
But, oh, what damnèd minutes tells he o'er
Who dotes, yet doubts, suspects, yet strongly loves!   170
    OTH. Oh, misery!
    IAGO. Poor and content is rich, and rich enough,
But riches fineless° is as poor as winter
To him that ever fears he shall be poor.

---

147. *jealousy:* suspicion. 149. *conceits:* conceives, imagines. 151. *scattering:* scattered, casual. *observance:* observation. 156. *immediate:* most valuable. 166. *doth mock:* makes a mockery of. 167. *meat:* i.e., victim. 167–68. *That . . . wronger:* i.e., the cuckold who hates his wife and knows her falseness is not tormented by suspicious jealousy. 173. *fineless:* limitless.

Good Heaven, the souls of all my tribe defend   175
From jealousy!
   OTH.   Why, why is this?
Think'st thou I'd make a life of jealousy,
To follow still the changes of the moon
With fresh suspicions? No, to be once in doubt
Is once to be resolved.° Exchange me for a goat   180
When I shall turn the business of my soul
To such exsufflicate and blown surmises,
Matching thy inference.° 'Tis not to make me jealous
To say my wife is fair, feeds well, loves company,
Is free of speech, sings, plays, and dances well.   185
Where virtue is, these are more virtuous.
Nor from mine own weak merits will I draw
The smallest fear or doubt of her revolt,°
For she had eyes, and chose me. No, Iago,
I'll see before I doubt, when I doubt, prove,   190
And on the proof, there is no more but this—
Away at once with love or jealousy!
   IAGO. I am glad of it, for now I shall have reason
To show the love and duty that I bear you
With franker spirit. Therefore, as I am bound,   195
Receive it from me. I speak not yet of proof.
Look to your wife. Observe her well with Cassio.
Wear your eye thus, not jealous nor secure.°
I would not have your free and noble nature
Out of self-bounty° be abused, look to 't.   200
I know our country disposition well.
In Venice° they do let Heaven see the pranks
They dare not show their husbands. Their best conscience
Is not to leave 't undone, but keep 't unknown.

179–80. *to . . . resolved:* whenever I find myself in doubt I at once seek out the
truth.   181–83. *When . . . inference:* when I shall allow that which concerns
me most dearly to be influenced by such trifling suggestions as yours. *exsuf-
ficate:* blown up, like a bubble.   188. *revolt:* faithlessness.   198. *secure:* over-
confident.   200. *self-bounty:* natural goodness.   202. *In Venice:* Venice was
notorious for its loose women; the Venetian courtesans were among the sights
of Europe and were much commented upon by travelers.

OTH. Dost thou say so?   205
IAGO. She did deceive her father,° marrying you,
And when she seemed to shake and fear your looks,
She loved them most.
OTH.   And so she did.
IAGO.   Why, go to, then.
She that so young could give out such a seeming
To seel° her father's eyes up close as oak——   210
He thought 'twas witchcraft—but I am much to blame.
I humbly do beseech you of your pardon
For too much loving you.
OTH.   I am bound to thee forever.
IAGO. I see this hath a little dashed your spirits.
OTH. Not a jot, not a jot.
IAGO.   I' faith, I fear it has.   215
I hope you will consider what is spoke
Comes from my love, but I do see you're moved.
I am to pray you not to strain my speech
To grosser issues° nor to larger reach°
Than to suspicion.   220
OTH. I will not.
IAGO.   Should you do so, my lord,
My speech should fall into such vile success°
As my thoughts aim not at. Cassio's my worthy friend.—
My lord, I see you're moved.
OTH.   No, not much moved.
I do not think but Desdemona's honest.°   225
IAGO. Long live she so! And long live you to think so!
OTH. And yet, how nature erring from itself——
IAGO. Aye, there's the point. As—to be bold with you—
Not to affect° many proposed matches°

206. *She . . . father:* Iago deliberately echoes Brabantio's parting words. See
I.iii.293–94. **210.** *seel:* blind. See I.iii.270,n. **219.** *grosser issues:* worse
conclusions. *larger reach:* i.e., more widely. **222.** *success:* result. **225.** *honest:* When applied to Desdemona, "honest" means "chaste," but applied to
Iago it has the modern meaning of "open and sincere." **229.** *affect:* be inclined to. *proposed matches:* offers of marriage.

Of her own clime, complexion, and degree,   230
Whereto we see in all things nature tends°——
Foh! One may smell in such a will most rank,°
Foul disproportion, thoughts unnatural.
But pardon me. I do not in position
Distinctly speak of her, though I may fear   235
Her will, recoiling to her better judgment,
May fall to match° you with her country forms,°
And happily° repent.
   OTH.   Farewell, farewell.
If more thou dost perceive, let me know more.
Set on thy wife to observe. Leave me, Iago.   240
   IAGO. (*Going*) My lord, I take my leave.
   OTH. Why did I marry? This honest creature doubtless
Sees and knows more, much more, than he unfolds.
   IAGO. (*Returning*) My lord, I would I might entreat your
      honor
To scan this thing no further. Leave it to time.   245
Though it be fit that Cassio have his place,
For sure he fills it up with great ability,
Yet if you please to hold him off awhile,
You shall by that perceive him and his means.
Note if your lady strain his entertainment°   250
With any strong or vehement importunity—
Much will be seen in that. In the meantime,
Let me be thought too busy in my fears—
As worthy cause I have to fear I am—
And hold her free, I do beseech your Honor.   255
   OTH. Fear not my government.°
   IAGO. I once more take my leave.   (*Exit.*)
   OTH. This fellow's of exceeding honesty,

---

231. *in . . . tends:* i.e., a woman naturally marries a man of her own country, color, and rank. 232. *will . . . rank:* desire most lustful. 237. *match:* compare. *country forms:* the appearance of her countrymen; i.e., white men. 238. *happily:* haply, by chance. 250. *strain . . . entertainment:* urge you to receive him. 256. *government:* self-control.

And knows all qualities,° with a learned spirit,
Of human dealings.° If I do prove her haggard,   260
Though that her jesses were my dear heartstrings,
I'd whistle her off and let her down the wind
To prey at fortune.° Haply, for I am black
And have not those soft parts of conversation
That chamberers° have, or for I am declined   265
Into the vale of years—yet that's not much—
She's gone, I am abused, and my relief
Must be to loathe her. Oh, curse of marriage,
That we can call these delicate creatures ours,
And not their appetites! I had rather be a toad   270
And live upon the vapor of a dungeon
Than keep a corner in the thing I love
For others' uses. Yet, 'tis the plague of great ones,
Prerogatived° are they less the base.
'Tis destiny unshunnable, like death.   275
Even then this forkèd plague° is fated to us
When we do quicken.° Desdemona comes.
(*Re-enter* DESDEMONA *and* EMILIA.) If she be false, oh, then
        Heaven mocks itself!
I'll not believe 't.
    DES.   How now, my dear Othello!
Your dinner, and the generous° islanders   280
By you invited, do attend your presence.
    OTH. I am to blame.
    DES.   Why do you speak so faintly?
Are you not well?
    OTH. I have a pain upon my forehead here.
    DES. Faith, that's with watching,° 'twill away again.   285

---

259. *qualities:* different kinds.   259–60. *with . . . dealings:* with wide experience of human nature.   260–63. *If . . . fortune:* Othello keeps up the imagery of falconry throughout. He means: If I find that she is wild, I'll whistle her off the game and let her go where she will, for she's not worth keeping. *haggard:* a wild hawk.   *jesses:* the straps attached to a hawk's legs.   265. *chamberers:* playboys.   274. *Prerogatived:* privileged.   276. *forked plagues:* i.e., to be a cuckold.   277. *quickens:* stir in our mother's womb.   280. *generous:* noble, of gentle blood.   285. *watching:* lack of sleep.

Let me but bind it hard, within this hour
It will be well.
    OTH.   Your napkin° is too little,
      (*He puts the handkerchief from him, and she drops it.*)
Let it alone. Come, I'll go in with you.
    DES. I am very sorry that you are not well.
               (*Exeunt* OTHELLO *and* DESDEMONA.)
    EMIL. I am glad I have found this napkin.   290
This was her first remembrance from the Moor.
My wayward° husband hath a hundred times
Wooed me to steal it, but she so loves the token,
For he conjured° her she should ever keep it,
That she reserves it evermore about her   295
To kiss and talk to. I'll have the work ta'en out,°
And give 't Iago. What he will do with it
Heaven knows, not I.
I nothing but to please his fantasy.°
               (*Re-enter* IAGO.)
    IAGO. How now! What do you here alone?   300
    EMIL. Do not you chide, I have a thing for you.
    IAGO. A thing for me? It is a common thing——
    EMIL. Ha!
    IAGO. To have a foolish wife.
    EMIL. Oh, is that all? What will you give me now   305
For that same handkerchief?
    IAGO.   What handkerchief?
    EMIL. What handkerchief!
Why, that the Moor first gave to Desdemona,
That which so often you did bid me steal.
    IAGO. Hast stol'n it from her?   310
    EMIL. No, faith, she let it drop by negligence,
And, to the advantage,° I being here took 't up.
Look, here it is.
    IAGO.   A good wench. Give it me.

---

287. *napkin:* handkerchief.   292. *wayward:* unaccountable.   294. *conjured:*
begged with an oath.   296. *work . . . out:* pattern copied.   299. *fantasy:*
whim.   312. *to . . . advantage:* thereby giving me the opportunity.

   EMIL. What will you do with 't, that you have been so
     earnest
To have me filch it?
   IAGO. (*Snatching it*) Why, what's that to you?   315
   EMIL. If 't be not for some purpose of import,
Give 't me again. Poor lady, she'll run mad
When she shall lack it.
   IAGO: Be not acknown on 't,° I have use for it.
Go, leave me.   (*Exit* EMILIA.)   320
I will in Cassio's lodging lose this napkin,
And let him find it. Trifles light as air
Are to the jealous confirmations strong
As proofs of Holy Writ. This may do something.
The Moor already changes with my poison.   325
Dangerous conceits are in their natures poisons,
Which at the first are scarce found to distaste,°
But with a little° act upon the blood
Burn like the mines of sulphur. I did say so.°
Look where he comes!
(*Re-enter* OTHELLO.) Not poppy,° nor mandragora,°   330
Nor all the drowsy syrups of the world,
Shall ever medicine thee to that sweet sleep
Which thou owedst° yesterday.
   OTH.   Ha! Ha! False to me?
   IAGO. Why, how now, General! No more of that.
   OTH. Avaunt!° Be gone! Thou hast set me on the rack.°   335
I swear 'tis better to be much abused
Than but to know 't a little.
   IAGO.   How now, my lord!
   OTH. What sense had I of her stol'n hours of lust?
I saw 't not, thought it not, it harmed not me.
I slept the next night well, was free and merry.   340
I found not Cassio's kisses on her lips.

---

319. *Be . . . on't:* know nothing about it.   327. *distaste:* taste unpleasantly.
328. *with a little:* in a little while.   329. *I . . . so:* As Iago says this, Othello
is seen approaching, with all the signs of his agitation outwardly visible.
330. *poppy:* opium. *mandragora:* called also mandrake, a root used as a drug
to bring sleep. *owedst:* owned, possessed. 335. *Avaunt:* be off! *on . . .
rack:* i.e., in torment.

He that is robbed, not wanting° what is stol'n,
Let him not know 't and he's not robbed at all.
   IAGO. I am sorry to hear this.
   OTH. I had been happy if the general camp,   345
Pioners° and all, had tasted her sweet body,
So I had nothing known. Oh, now forever
Farewell the tranquil mind! Farewell content!
Farewell the plumèd° troop and the big wars
That make ambition virtue! Oh, farewell,   350
Farewell the neighing steed and the shrill trump,
The spirit-stirring drum, the ear-piercing fife,
The royal banner and all quality,°
Pride, pomp, and circumstance of glorious war!
And, O you mortal engines,° whose rude throats   355
The immortal Jove's dread clamors counterfeit,°
Farewell! Othello's occupation's gone!
   IAGO. Is 't possible, my lord?
   OTH. Villain, be sure thou prove my love a whore,
Be sure of it, give me the ocular proof.   360
Or by the worth of man's eternal soul,
Thou hadst been better have been born a dog
Than answer my waked wrath!
   IAGO.   Is 't come to this?
   OTH. Make me to see 't, or at the least so prove it
That the probation° bear no hinge nor loop   365
To hang a doubt on, or woe upon thy life!
   IAGO. My noble lord——
   OTH. If thou dost slander her and torture me,
Never pray more, abandon all remorse.°
On horror's head horrors accumulate,   370
Do deeds to make Heaven weep, all earth amazed,
For nothing canst thou to damnation add
Greater than that.
   IAGO.   Oh, grace! Oh, Heaven defend me!

342. *wanting:* missing. 346. *Pioners:* pioneers, the lowest type of soldier.
349. *plumed:* wearing plumes in the helmet. 353. *quality:* military rank.
355. *mortal engines:* deadly cannon. 356. *counterfeit:* imitate. 365. *probation:* proof. 369. *remorse:* pity.

Are you a man? Have you a soul or sense?
God be wi' you, take mine office. O wretched fool,   375
That livest to make thine honesty a vice!
O monstrous world! Take note, take note, O world,
To be direct and honest is not safe.
I thank you for this profit,° and from hence
I'll love no friend, sith° love breeds such offense.   380
   OTH. Nay, stay. Thou shouldst be honest.
   IAGO. I should be wise, for honesty's a fool,
And loses that it works for.
   OTH.   By the world,
I think my wife be honest, and think she is not.
I think that thou art just, and think thou art not.   385
I'll have some proof. Her name, that was as fresh
As Dian's° visage, is now begrimed and black
As mine own face. If there be cords, or knives,
Poison, or fire, or suffocating streams,
I'll not endure it. Would I were satisfied!   390
   IAGO. I see, sir, you are eaten up with passion.
I do repent me that I put it to you.
You would be satisfied?
   OTH.   Would! Nay, I will.
   IAGO. And may, but how? How satisfied, my lord?
Would you, the supervisor,° grossly gape on?   395
Behold her topped?
   OTH.   Death and damnation! Oh!
   IAGO. It were a tedious difficulty, I think,
To bring them to that prospect.° Damn them then,
If ever mortal eyes do see them bolster°
More than their own! What then? How then?   400
What shall I say? Where's satisfaction?
It is impossible you should see this,
Were they as prime° as goats, as hot as monkeys,
As salt° as wolves in pride,° and fools as gross
As ignorance made drunk. But yet I say   405

---

379. *profit:* profitable lesson. 380. *sith:* since. 387. *Dian:* Diana, goddess
of chastity. 395. *supervisor:* looker-on. 398. *prospect:* sight. 399. *bolster:*
sleep together. 403. *prime:* lustful. 404. *salt:* eager. *in pride:* in heat.

If imputation° and strong circumstances,
Which lead directly to the door of truth,
Will give you satisfaction, you may have 't.
    OTH. Give me a living° reason she's disloyal.
    IAGO. I do not like the office.   410
But sith I am entered in this cause so far,
Pricked° to 't by foolish honesty and love,
I will go on. I lay with Cassio lately,
And being troubled with a raging tooth,
I could not sleep.   415
There are a kind of men so loose of soul
That in their sleeps will mutter their affairs.
One of this kind is Cassio.
In sleep I heard him say "Sweet Desdemona,
Let us be wary, let us hide our loves."   420
And then, sir, would he gripe° and wring my hand,
Cry "O sweet creature!" and then kiss me hard,
As if he plucked up kisses by the roots
That grew upon my lips. Then laid his leg
Over my thigh, and sighed and kissed, and then   425
Cried "Cursed fate that gave thee to the Moor!"
    OTH. Oh, monstrous! Monstrous!
    IAGO.   Nay, this was but his dream.
    OTH. But this denoted a foregone conclusion.
'Tis a shrewd doubt,° though it be but a dream.
    IAGO. And this may help to thicken other proofs   430
That do demónstrate thinly.
    OTH.   I'll tear her all to pieces.
    IAGO. Nay, but be wise. Yet we see nothing done.
She may be honest yet. Tell me but this:
Have you not sometimes seen a handkerchief
Spotted with strawberries° in your wife's hand?   435
    OTH. I gave her such a one, 'twas my first gift.
    IAGO. I know not that. But such a handkerchief—
I am sure it was your wife's—did I today

---

406. *imputation:* probability.   409. *living:* tangible.   412. *Pricked:* spurred
on.   421. *gripe:* grip.   429. *shrewd doubt:* bitter suspicion.   435. *with strawberries:* with a pattern of strawberries.

See Cassio wipe his beard with.
   OTH.   If it be that——
   IAGO. If it be that, or any that was hers,   440
It speaks against her with the other proofs.
   OTH. Oh, that the slave had forty thousand lives!
One is too poor, too weak, for my revenge.
Now do I see 'tis true. Look here, Iago,
All my fond love thus do I blow to Heaven—   445
'Tis gone.
Arise, black Vengeance, from thy hollow cell!
Yield up, O Love, thy crown and hearted° throne
To tyrannous hate! Swell, bosom, with thy fraught,°
For 'tis of aspics'° tongues!
   IAGO.   Yet be content.   450
   OTH. Oh, blood, blood, blood!
   IAGO. Patience, I say. Your mind perhaps may change.
   OTH. Never, Iago. Like to the Pontic Sea,
Whose icy current and compulsive course
Ne'er feels retiring ebb but keeps due on   455
To the Propontic and the Hellespont;°
Even so my bloody thoughts, with violent pace,
Shall ne'er look back, ne'er ebb to humble love,
Till that capable° and wide revenge
Swallow them up. Now, by yond marble Heaven, 460
In the due reverence of a sacred vow   (Kneels.)
I here engage° my words.
   IAGO.   Do not rise yet.   (Kneels.)
Witness, you ever burning lights above,
You elements that clip° us round about,
Witness that here Iago doth give up   465
The execution of his wit, hands, heart,

---

448. *hearted:* in my heart. 449. *fraught:* freight, load. 450. *aspic:* asp, a small poisonous snake. See *Ant & Cleo,* V.ii.351–56. 453–56. *Like . . . Hellespont:* In Pliny's *Natural History,* translated by Philemon Holland in 1601, it was noted that "the sea Pontus (Black Sea) evermore floweth and runneth out into Propontis (Sea of Marmora) but the sea never returneth back again within Pontus." *Hellespont:* the Dardanelles. 459. *capable:* comprehensive, complete. 462. *engage:* pledge. 464. *elements . . . clip:* skies that embrace, surround.

To wronged Othello's service! Let him command,
And to obey shall be in me remorse,°
What bloody business ever.   (*They rise.*)
  OTH.   I greet thy love,
Not with vain thanks, but with acceptance bounteous,   470
And will upon the instant put thee to 't.°
Within these three days let me hear thee say
That Cassio's not alive.
  IAGO. My friend is dead. 'Tis done at your request. But let
her live.
  OTH. Damn her, lewd minx! Oh, damn her!   475
Come, go with me apart. I will withdraw,
To furnish me with some swift means of death
For the fair devil. Now art thou my Lieutenant.
  IAGO. I am your own forever.   (*Exeunt.*)

SCENE FOUR. BEFORE THE CASTLE.

(*Enter* DESDEMONA, EMILIA, *and* CLOWN.)
  DES. Do you know, sirrah, where Lieutenant Cassio lies?
  CLO. I dare not say he lies anywhere.
  DES. Why, man?
  CLO. He's a soldier, and for one to say a soldier lies is
stabbing.   5
  DES. Go to. Where lodges he?
  CLO. To tell you where he lodges is to tell you where I lie.
  DES. Can anything be made of this?
  CLO. I know not where he lodges, and for me to devise a
lodging, and say he lies here or he lies there, were to lie in   10
mine own throat.
  DES. Can you inquire him out and be edified by report?°
  CLO. I will catechize the world for him; that is, make ques-
tions and by them answer.

---

468. *remorse:* solemn obligation. **471.** *put . . . to't:* put you to the proof.
  Sc. iv: **12.** *edited by report:* enlightened by the information. Desdemona
speaks with mock pomposity.

DES. Seek him, bid him come hither. Tell him I have moved   15
my lord on his behalf and hope all will be well.

CLO. To do this is within the compass of man's wit, and
therefore I will attempt the doing it.   (*Exit.*)

DES. Where should I lose that handkerchief, Emilia?

EMIL. I know not, madam.   20

DES. Believe me, I had rather have lost my purse
Full of crusados.° And, but my noble Moor
Is true of mind and made of no such baseness
As jealous creatures are, it were enough
To put him to ill thinking.

EMIL.   Is he not jealous?   25

DES. Who, he? I think the sun where he was born
Drew all such humors° from him.

EMIL.   Look where he comes.

DES. I will not leave him now till Cassio
Be called to him.

(*Enter* OTHELLO.) How is 't with you, my lord?

OTH. Well, my good lady. (*Aside*) Oh, hardness to dis-
    semble!
                                                            30
How do you, Desdemona?

DES.   Well, my good lord.

OTH. Give me your hand. This hand is moist,° my lady.

DES. It yet has felt no age nor known no sorrow.

OTH. This argues fruitfulness and liberal heart.
Hot, hot, and moist—this hand of yours requires   35
A sequester° from liberty, fasting and prayer,
Much castigation, exercise devout.
For here's a young and sweating devil here,
That commonly rebels. 'Tis a good hand,
A frank one.

DES.   You may indeed say so,   40
For 'twas that hand that gave away my heart.

22. *crusados:* small gold Portuguese coins. 27. *humors:* moods; lit., damp-
nesses. 32. *moist:* a hot moist palm was believed to show desire. 36. *se-
quester:* separation.

OTH. A liberal° hand. The hearts of old gave hands,
But our new heraldry is hands, not hearts.°
   DES. I cannot speak of this. Come now, your promise.
   OTH. What promise, chuck?°   45
   DES. I have sent to bid Cassio come speak with you.
   OTH. I have a salt and sorry rheum° offends me.
Lend me thy handkerchief.
   DES. Here, my lord.
   OTH. That which I gave you.   50
   DES. I have it not about me.
   OTH. Not?
   DES. No indeed, my lord.
   OTH. That's a fault. That handkerchief
Did an Egyptian° to my mother give.   55
She was a charmer, and could almost read
The thoughts of people. She told her while she kept it
'Twould make her amiable and subdue my father
Entirely to her love, but if she lost it
Or made a gift of it, my father's eye   60
Should hold her loathed and his spirits should hunt
After new fancies. She dying gave it me,
And bid me, when my fate would have me wive,
To give it her. I did so. And take heed on 't,
Make it a darling like your precious eye.   65
To lose 't or give 't were such perdition
As nothing else could match.
   DES.   Is 't posible?
   OTH. 'Tis true. There's magic in the web of it.

---

42. *liberal:* overgenerous.   42–43. *The . . . hearts:* once love and deeds went together, but now it is all deeds (i.e., faithlessness) and no love. This phrase has been taken as a reference to the order of baronets created by James I in 1611, who bore on their heraldic coats of arms the device of the "bloody hand of Ulster." If so, the lines are a later addition; but the reference is very doubtful. The contrast between hearts (true love and faith) and hands (actions) is natural (see *Lear* I.ii. 72–73). As Othello's passions rise, he ceases to be entirely coherent.   45. *chuck:* a term of affection, but not the kind of word with which a person of Othello's dignity would normally address his wife. He is beginning to treat her with contemptuous familiarity. See IV.ii.24.   47. *rheum:* common cold.   55. *Egyptian:* gypsy.

A sibyl° that had numbered in the world
The sun to course two hundred compasses   70
In her prophetic fury° sewed the work.
The worms were hallowed that did breed the silk,
And it was dyed in mummy° which the skillful
Conserved° of maidens' hearts.

DES.   Indeed! Is 't true?
OTH. Most veritable, therefore look to 't well.   75
DES. Then would to God that I had never seen 't.
OTH. Ha! Wherefore?
DES. Why do you speak so startlingly and rash?
OTH. Is 't lost? Is 't gone? Speak, is it out o' the way?
DES. Heaven bless us!   80
OTH. Say you?
DES. It is not lost, but what an if it were?
OTH. How!
DES. I say it is not lost.
OTH. Fetch 't, let me see it.   85
DES. Why, so I can, sir, but I will not now.
This is a trick to put me from my suit.
Pray you let Cassio be received again.
OTH. Fetch me the handkerchief. My mind misgives.
DES. Come, come.   90
You'll never meet a more sufficient man.
OTH. The handkerchief!
DES.   I pray talk me of Cassio.
OTH. The handkerchief!
DES.   A man that all his time
Hath founded his good fortunes on your love,
Shared dangers with you——   95
OTH. The handkerchief!
DES. In sooth, you are to blame.
OTH. Away!   (Exit.)
EMIL. Is not this man jealous?
DES. I ne'er saw this before.   100
Sure there's some wonder in this handkerchief.

---

69. *sibyl:* prophetess.   71. *fury:* inspiration.   73. *mummy:* a concoction made
from Egyptian mummies.   74. *Conserved:* prepared.

I am most unhappy in the loss of it.

EMIL. 'Tis not a year or two shows us a man.°
They are all but stomachs and we all but food.
They eat us hungerly, and when they are full   105
They belch us. Look you, Cassio and my husband.

(*Enter* CASSIO *and* IAGO.)

IAGO. There is no other way, 'tis she must do 't.
And, lo, the happiness!° Go and impórtune her.

DES. How now, good Cassio! What's the news with you?

CAS. Madam, my former suit. I do beseech you   110
That by your virtuous means I may again
Exist, and be a member of his love
Whom I with all the office of my heart
Entirely honor. I would not be delayed.
If my offense be of such mortal kind   115
That nor my service past nor present sorrows
Nor purposed merit in futurity°
Can ransom me into his love again,
But to know so must be my benefit.
So shall I clothe me in a forced content   120
And shut myself up in some other course
To Fortune's alms.°

DES.   Alas, thrice-gentle Cassio!
My advocation° is not now in tune.
My lord is not my lord, nor should I know him
Were he in favor as in humor altered.°   125
So help me every spirit sanctified,
As I have spoken for you all my best
And stood within the blank° of his displeasure
For my free speech! You must awhile be patient.

---

103. *'Tis . . . man:* it does not take a couple of years for us to discover the nature of a man; i.e., he soon shows his real nature.   108. *And . . . happiness:* what good luck, here she is.   117. *Nor . . . futurity:* nor my good resolutions for the future.   119–22. *But . . . alms:* if I know that Othello will not restore me to my position, it will have this benefit: I shall force myself to be contented and try my luck elsewhere. *Fortune's alms:* what Fortune may give me.   123. *advocation:* advocacy, pleading.   125. *favor . . . altered:* as changed in face as in mood.   128. *blank:* aim. The blank is the bull's-eye of a target.

What I can do I will, and more I will   130
Than for myself I dare. Let that suffice you.
   IAGO. Is my lord angry?
   EMIL.   He went hence but now,
And certainly in strange unquietness.
   IAGO. Can he be angry? I have seen the cannon
When it hath blown his ranks into the air,   135
And, like the Devil, from his very arm
Puffed his own brother, and can he be angry?
Something of moment then. I will go meet him.
There's matter in 't indeed if he be angry.
   DES. I prithee do so. (*Exit* IAGO.) Something sure of state,   140
Either from Venice, or some unhatched practice
Made demonstrable° here in Cyprus to him,
Hath puddled° his clear spirit. And in such cases
Men's natures wrangle with inferior things,
Though great ones are their object.° 'Tis even so,   145
For let our finger ache and it indues°
Our other healthful members even to that sense
Of pain. Nay, we must think men are not gods,
Nor of them look for such observancy
As fits the bridal.° Beshrew me° much, Emilia,   150
I was, unhandsome warrior° as I am,
Arraigning his unkindness with my soul,
But now I find I had suborned the witness,°
And he's indicted falsely.
   EMIL. Pray Heaven it be state matters, as you think,   155
And no conception nor no jealous toy°
Concerning you.
   DES. Alas the day, I never gave him cause!
   EMIL. But jealous souls will not be answered so.

141–42. *unhatched . . . demonstrable:* some plot, not yet matured, which has
been revealed. 143. *puddled:* muddied, stirred up. 143–45. *in . . . objects:*
when men are disturbed by great matters, they show their temper in small
things. 146. *indues:* endows, pervades. 150. *bridal:* honeymoon. *Beshrew
me:* plague on me. 151. *unhandsome warrior:* clumsy soldier. Desdemona
continually thinks of herself as Othello's companion in arms. Cf. I.iii.249ff.
153. *suborned . . . witness:* corrupted the evidence; i.e., it is my fault, not his.
156. *jealous toy:* silly suspicion.

They are not ever jealous for the cause,   160
But jealous for they are jealous. 'Tis a monster
Begot upon itself, born on itself.
   DES. Heaven keep that monster from Othello's mind!
   EMIL. Lady, amen.
   DES. I will go seek him. Cassio, walk hereabout.   165
If I do find him fit, I'll move your suit,
And seek to effect it to my uttermost.
   CAS. I humbly thank your ladyship.
               (*Exeunt* DESDEMONA *and* EMILIA.)
               (*Enter* BIANCA.)
   BIAN. Save you, friend Cassio!
   CAS.   What make you from° home?
How is it with you, my most fair Bianca?   170
I' faith, sweet love, I was coming to your house.
   BIAN. And I was going to your lodging, Cassio.
What, keep a week away? Seven days and nights?
Eightscore eight hours? And lovers' absent hours,
More tedious than the dial eightscore times?°   175
Oh, weary reckoning!
   CAS.   Pardon me, Bianca.
I have this while with leaden thoughts been pressed,
But I shall in a more continuate time°
Strike off this score of absence. Sweet Bianca,
          (*Giving her* DESDEMONA'S *handkerchief*)
Take me this work out.°
   BIAN.   O Cassio, whence came this?   180
This is some token from a newer friend.
To the felt absence now I feel a cause.
Is 't come to this? Well, well.
   CAS.   Go to, woman!
Throw your vile guesses in the Devil's teeth,
From whence you have them. You are jealous now   185
That this is from some mistress, some remembrance.

---

169. *make . . . from:* are you doing away from.   174–75. *And . . . times:*
when one's lover is absent for a week does it not seem far longer than a hundred and sixty clock hours?   178. *continuate time:* i.e., when my time is not
continually being interrupted.   180. *Take . . . out:* copy this pattern.

No, by my faith, Bianca.
    BIAN.   Why, whose is it?
    CAS. I know not, sweet. I found it in my chamber.
I like the work well. Ere it be demanded—
As like enough it will—I'd have it copied.   190
Take it, and do 't, and leave me for this time.
    BIAN. Leave you! Wherefore?
    CAS. I do attend here on the General,
And think it no addition,° nor my wish,
To have him see me womaned.°
    BIAN.   Why, I pray you?   195
    CAS. Not that I love you not.
    BIAN.   But that you do not love me.
I pray you bring me on the way a little,
And say if I shall see you soon at night.
    CAS. 'Tis but a little way that I can bring you,
For I attend here. But I'll see you soon.   200
    BIAN. 'Tis very good, I must be circumstanced.°   (*Exeunt.*)

act four

SCENE ONE. CYPRUS. BEFORE THE CASTLE.

(*Enter* OTHELLO *and* IAGO.)

    IAGO. Will you think so?
    OTH.   Think so, Iago!
    IAGO.   What,
To kiss in private?
    OTH.   An unauthorized kiss.
    IAGO. Or to be naked with her friend in bed
An hour or more, not meaning any harm?
    OTH. Naked in bed, Iago, and not mean harm!   5
It is hypocrisy against the Devil.°
They that mean virtuously and yet do so,

---

194. *addition:* honor.   195. *womaned:* with a girl.   201. *circumstanced:* put
off.
    Act. IV, Sc. i: 6. *hypocrisy . . . Devil:* "double-crossing the Devil"; i.e.,
they are behaving in a most suspicious way.

The Devil their virtue tempts and they tempt Heaven.°
    IAGO. So° they do nothing, 'tis a venial° slip.
But if I give my wife a handkerchief——   10
    OTH. What then?
    IAGO. Why, then, 'tis hers, my lord, and being hers,
She may, I think, bestow 't on any man.
    OTH. She is protectress of her honor too.
May she give that?   15
    IAGO. Her honor is an essence that's not seen.
They have it very oft that have it not.°
But for the handkerchief——
    OTH. By Heaven, I would most gladly have forgot it.
Thou said'st—oh, it comes o'er my memory,   20
As doth the raven o'er the infected house,°
Boding° to all—he had my handkerchief.
    IAGO. Aye, what of that?
    OTH.   That's not so good now.
    IAGO.   What,
If I had said I had seen him do you wrong?
Or heard him say—as knaves be such abroad,   25
Who having, by their own importunate suit,
Or voluntary dotage° of some mistress,
Convincèd or supplied° them, cannot choose
But they must blab——
    OTH.   Hath he said anything?
    IAGO. He hath, my lord, but be you well assured,   30
No more than he'll unswear.
    OTH.   What hath he said?
    IAGO. Faith, that he did——I know not what he did.
    OTH. What? What?
    IAGO. Lie——
    OTH.   With her?
    IAGO.   With her, on her, what you will.

7–8. *They . . . Heaven:* i.e., those who go to bed together and mean no harm
are asking the Devil to tempt them, and they make God suspect their innocence. 9. *So:* so long as. *venial:* pardonable. 17. *They . . . not:* i.e.,
many are honored who have no honor. 21. *As . . . house:* i.e., as a bird of
prey waits for its victim to die. 22. *Boding:* foretelling evil. 27. *dotage:*
infatuation. 28. *Convinced or supplied:* overcome or satisfied their desires.

OTH. Lie° with her! Lie on her!—We say lie on her when   35
they belie her.—Lie with her! 'Zounds, that's fulsome!° Hand-
kerchief—confessions—handkerchief!—To confess, and be
hanged for his labor. First to be hanged, and then to confess.
I tremble at it. Nature would not invest herself in such
shadowing passion without some instruction.° It is not words   40
that shake me thus. Pish! Noses, ears, and lips. Is 't possible?
—Confess?—Handkerchief?—Oh, devil!   (*Falls in a trance.*)
IAGO. Work on,
My medicine, work! Thus credulous fools are caught,
And many worthy and chaste dames even thus,   45
All guiltless, meet reproach. What ho! My lord!
My lord, I say! Othello! (*Enter* CASSIO.) How now, Cassio!
CAS. What's the matter?
IAGO. My lord is fall'n into an epilepsy.
This is his second fit, he had one yesterday.   50
CAS. Rub him about the temples.
IAGO.   No, forbear,
The lethargy° must have his quiet course.
If not, he foams at mouth and by and by
Breaks out to savage madness. Look, he stirs.
Do you withdraw yourself a little while,   55
He will recover straight. When he is gone,
I would on great occasion speak with you.   (*Exit* CASSIO.)
How is it, General? Have you not hurt your head?°
OTH. Does thou mock me?
IAGO.   I mock you! No, by Heaven.
Would you would bear your fortune like a man!   60
OTH. A hornèd man's a monster and a beast.
IAGO. There's many a beast, then, in a populous city,
And many a civil° monster.
OTH. Did he confess it?
IAGO.   Good sir, be a man.

35–42. *Lie . . . devil:* Othello breaks into incoherent muttering before he falls
down in a fit. 36. *fulsome:* disgusting. 39–40. *Nature . . . instruction:*
nature would not fill me with such overwhelming emotion unless there was
some cause. 52. *lethargy:* epileptic fit. Cf. *II Hen IV*, I.ii.127–29. 58. *Have
. . . head:* With brutal cynicism Iago asks whether Othello is suffering from
cuckold's headache. 63. *civil:* sober, well-behaved citizen.

Think every bearded fellow that's but yoked°   65
May draw with you.° There's millions now alive
That nightly lie in those unproper beds
Which they dare swear peculiar.° Your case is better.
Oh, 'tis the spite of Hell, the Fiend's archmock,
To lip° a wanton in a secure couch°   70
And to suppose her chaste! No, let me know,
And knowing what I am, I know what she shall be.
    OTH. Oh, thou art wise, 'tis certain.
    IAGO.   Stand you awhile apart,
Confine yourself but in a patient list.°
Whilst you were here o'erwhelmèd with your grief—   75
A passion most unsuiting such a man—
Cassio came hither. I shifted him away,
And laid good 'scuse upon your ecstasy,°
Bade him anon return and here speak with me,
The which he promisèd. Do but encave° yourself,   80
And mark the fleers,° the gibes, and notable scorns,
That dwell in every region of his face.
For I will make him tell the tale anew,
Where, how, how oft, how long ago, and when
He hath and is again to cope° your wife.   85
I say but mark his gesture. Marry, patience,
Or I shall say you are all in all in spleen,°
And nothing of a man.
    OTH.   Dost thou hear, Iago?
I will be found most cunning in my patience,
But—dost thou hear?—most bloody.
    IAGO.   That's not amiss,   90
But yet keep time in all. Will you withdraw?
                          (OTHELLO *retires.*)
Now will I question Cassio of Bianca,

---

65. *yoked:* married. 66. *draw . . . you:* lit., be your yoke fellow, share your
fate. 67–68. *That . . . peculiar:* that lie nightly in beds which they believe
are their own but which others have shared. 70. *lip:* kiss. *secure couch:* lit.,
a carefree bed; i.e., a bed which has been used by the wife's lover, but secretly.
74. *patient list:* confines of patience. 78. *ecstasy:* fit. 80. *encave:* hide. 81.
fleers: scornful grins. 85. *cope:* encounter. 87. *spleen:* hot temper. Cf. *I
Hen* IV, V.ii.19.

A housewife° that by selling her desires
Buys herself bread and clothes. It is a creature
That dotes on Cassio, as 'tis the strumpet's plague   95
To beguile many and be beguiled by one.
He, when he hears of her, cannot refrain
From the excess of laughter. Here he comes.
(*Re-enter* CASSIO.) As he shall smile, Othello shall go mad,
And his unbookish° jealousy must construe°   100
Poor Cassio's smiles, gestures, and light behavior
Quite in the wrong. How do you now, Lieutenant?

   CAS. The worser that you give me the addition°
Whose want even kills me.

   IAGO. Ply° Desdemona well, and you are sure on 't.   105
Now, if this suit lay in Bianca's power,
How quickly should you speed!

   CAS.   Alas, poor caitiff!°

   OTH. Look how he laughs already!

   IAGO. I never knew a woman love man so.

   CAS. Alas, poor rogue! I think, i' faith, she loves me.   110

   OTH. Now he denies it faintly and laughs it out.

   IAGO. Do you hear, Cassio?

   OTH.   Now he impórtunes him
To tell it o'er. Go to. Well said, well said.

   IAGO. She gives it out that you shall marry her.
Do you intend it?   115

   CAS. Ha, ha, ha!

   OTH. Do you triumph, Roman?° Do you triumph?

   CAS. I marry her! What, a customer!° I prithee bear some
charity to my wit. Do not think it so unwholesome. Ha, ha, ha!

   OTH. So, so, so, so. They laugh that win.°   120

   IAGO. Faith, the cry goes that you shall marry her.

   CAS. Prithee say true.

   IAGO. I am a very villain else.

---

93. *housewife:* hussy. 100. *unbookish:* unlearned, simple. *construe:* interpret. 103. *addition:* title (Lieutenant) which he has lost. 105. *Ply:* urge.
107. *caitiff:* wretch. 117. *triumph, Roman:* The word "triumph" suggests
"Roman" because the Romans celebrated their victories with triumphs, elaborate shows, and processions. Cf. *Caesar,* I.i.56. 118. *customer:* harlot. 120.
They . . . win: a proverbial saying. See *Temp.* II.i.33.

OTH. Have you scored° me? Well.

CAS. This is the monkey's own giving out. She is persuaded   125
I will marry her out of her own love and flattery, not out of
my promise.

OTH. Iago beckons me, now he begins the story.

CAS. She was here even now. She haunts me in every place.
I was the other day talking on the sea bank with certain Vene-   130
tians, and thither comes the bauble,° and, by this hand, she
falls me thus about my neck——

OTH. Crying "O dear Cassio!" as it were. His gesture imports it.

CAS. So hangs and lolls and weeps upon me, so hales° and   135
pulls me. Ha, ha, ha!

OTH. Now he tells how she plucked him to my chamber.
Oh, I see that nose of yours, but not that dog I shall throw it to.

CAS. Well, I must leave her company.

IAGO. Before me!° Look where she comes.   140

CAS. 'Tis such another fitchew!° Marry, a perfumed one.
(*Enter* BIANCA.) What do you mean by this haunting of me?

BIAN. Let the Devil and his dam° haunt you! What did you
mean by that same handkerchief you gave me even now? I
was a fine fool to take it. I must take out the work? A likely   145
piece of work, that you should find it in your chamber and not
knew who left it there! This is some minx's token, and I must
take out the work? There, give it your hobbyhorse.° Whereso-
ever you had it, I'll take out no work on 't.

CAS. How now, my sweet Bianca! How now! How now!   150

OTH. By Heavens, that should be my handkerchief!

BIAN. An° you'll come to supper tonight, you may, An you
will not, come when you are next prepared for.   (*Exit.*)

IAGO. After her, after her.

CAS. Faith, I must, she'll rail i' the street else.   155

IAGO. Will you sup there?

CAS. Faith, I intend so.

---

124. *scored:* marked, as with a blow from a whip.   131. *bauble:* toy, plaything.   135. *hales:* hauls, drags.   140. *Before me:* by my soul, a mild oath.
141. *fitchew:* polecat, a creature most demonstrative in the mating season.
143. *dam:* mother.   148. *hobbyhorse:* harlot.   152. *An:* if.

IAGO. Well, I may chance to see you, for I would very fain°
speak with you.

CAS. Prithee, come, will you?   160

IAGO. Go to. Say no more.   (*Exit* CASSIO.)

OTH. (*Advancing*) How shall I murder him, Iago?

IAGO. Did you perceive how he laughed at his vice?

OTH. Oh, Iago!

IAGO. And did you see the handkerchief?   165

OTH. Was that mine?

IAGO. Yours, by this hand. And to see how he prizes the
foolish woman your wife? She gave it him, and he hath given
it his whore.

OTH. I would have him nine years a-killing. A fine woman!   170
A fair woman! A sweet woman!

IAGO. Nay, you must forget that.

OTH. Aye, let her rot, and perish, and be damned tonight,
for she shall not live. No, my heart is turned to stone, I strike
it and it hurts my hand. Oh, the world hath not a sweeter   175
creature. She might lie by an emperor's side, and command
him tasks.

IAGO. Nay, that's not your way.°

OTH. Hang her! I do but say what she is, so delicate with
her needle, an admirable musician—oh, she will sing the sav-   180
ageness out of a bear—of so high and plenteous wit and invention——

IAGO. She's the worse for all this.

OTH. Oh, a thousand times. And then, of so gentle a condition!°
                                                               185
IAGO. Aye, too gentle.

OTH. Nay, that's certain. But yet the pity of it, Iago! O Iago,
the pity of it, Iago!

IAGO. If you are so fond° over her iniquity, give her patent°
to offend, for if it touch not you, comes near nobody.   190

OTH. I will chop her into messes.° Cuckold me!

IAGO. Oh, 'tis foul in her.

OTH. With mine officer!

---

158. *fain:* gladly. 178. *Nay . . . way:* i.e., don't get soft thoughts about her.
184–85. *condition:* nature. 189. *fond:* foolish. *patent:* a grant by the King
of some special privilege. 191. *messes:* little pieces.

IAGO. That's fouler.

OTH. Get me some poison, Iago, this night. I'll not expostu- 195
late° with her, lest her body and beauty unprovide° my mind
again. This night, Iago.

IAGO. Do it not with poison, strangle her in her bed, even
the bed she hath contaminated.

OTH. Good, good. The justice of it pleases. Very good.   200

IAGO. And for Cassio, let me be his undertaker.°
You shall hear more by midnight.

OTH. Excellent good. (*A trumpet within.*) What trumpet
is that same?

IAGO. Something from Venice, sure, 'Tis Lodovico   205
Come from the Duke. And see, your wife is with him.

      (*Enter* LODOVICO, DESDEMONA, *and* ATTENDANTS.)

LOD. God save the worthy General!

OTH.   With all my heart, sir.

LOD. The Duke and Senators of Venice greet you.
                                 (*Gives him a letter.*)

OTH. I kiss the instrument° of their pleasures.
                                 (*Opens the letter, and reads.*)

DES. And what's the news, good Cousin Lodovico?   210

IAGO. I am very glad to see you, signior.
Welcome to Cyprus.

LOD. I thank you. How does Lieutenant Cassio?

IAGO. Lives, sir.

DES. Cousin, there's fall'n between him and my lord.   215
An unkind breach, but you shall make all well.

OTH. Are you sure of that?

DES. My lord?

OTH. (*Reads.*) "This fail you not to do, as you will——"

LOD. He did not call, he's busy in the paper.   220
Is there division 'twixt my lord and Cassio?

DES. A most unhappy one. I would do much
To atone° them, for the love I bear to Cassio.

195–96. *expostulate:* argue. **196.** *unprovide:* weaken. **201.** *be . . . undertaker:* undertake to manage his business. In Shakespeare's plays the word does
not mean "mortician." **209.** *instrument:* i.e., the official letter which he has
just received. **223.** *atone:* reconcile.

OTH. Fire and brimstone!

DES.   My lord?

OTH.   Are you wise?°

DES. What, is he angry?

LOD.   Maybe the letter moved him,   225
For, as I think, they do command him home,
Deputing Cassio in his government.°

DES. By my troth,° I am glad on 't.

OTH.   Indeed!

DES.   My lord?

OTH. I am glad to see you mad.

DES.   Why, sweet Othello?

OTH. Devil!   *(Striking her.)*   230

DES. I have not deserved this.

LOD. My lord, this would not be believed in Venice
Though I should swear I saw 't. 'Tis very much.°
Make her amends, she weeps.

OTH.   O devil, devil!
If that the earth could teem with a woman's tears,   235
Each drop she falls would prove a crocodile.°
Out of my sight!

DES.   I will not stay to offend you.   *(Going.)*

LOD. Truly, an obedient lady.
I do beseech your lordship, call her back.

OTH. Mistress!   240

DES. My lord?

OTH. What would you with her, sir?

LOD.   Who, I, my lord?

OTH. Aye, you did wish that I would make her turn.
Sir, she can turn and turn, and yet go on
And turn again. And she can weep, sir, weep.   245
And she's obedient, as you say, obedient,

---

224. *Are . . . wise:* i.e., in saying you bear love to Cassio.   227. *in . . . government:* in his place as governor.   228. *troth:* truth.   233. *'Tis . . . much:* this is too much.   235–36. *If . . . crocodile:* if the earth could breed from woman's ears, each tear that she lets fall would become a crocodile. It was believed that the crocodile would cry and sob to attract the sympathetic passer-by, who was then snapped up.

Very obedient. Proceed you in your tears.
Concerning this, sir—oh, well-painted passion!°—
I am commanded home. Get you away.
I'll send for you anon. Sir, I obey the mandate,   250
And will return to Venice. Hence, avaunt!

                             (*Exit* DESDEMONA.)

Cassio shall have my place. And, sir, tonight,
I do entreat that we may sup together.
You are welcome, sir, to Cyprus. Goats and monkeys! (*Exit.*)
    LOD. Is this the noble Moor whom our full Senate   255
Call all-in-all sufficient? This the nature
Whom passion could not shake? Whose solid virtue
The shot of accident nor dart of chance
Could neither graze nor pierce?
    IAGO.   He is much changed.   260
    LOD. Are his wits safe? Is he not light of brain?
    IAGO. He's that he is. I may not breathe my censure°
What he might be. If what he might he is not,
I would to Heaven he were!°
    LOD.   What, strike his wife!
    IAGO. Faith, that was not so well, yet would I knew   265
That stroke would prove the worst!
    LOD.   Is it his use?°
Or did the letters work upon his blood,
And new-create this fault?
    IAGO.   Alas, alas!
It is not honesty in me to speak
What I have seen and known. You shall observe him,   270
And his own courses° will denote him so
That I may save my speech. Do but go after,
And mark how he continues.
    LOD. I am sorry that I am deceived in him.   (*Exeunt.*)

---

248. *well-painted passion:* cleverly imitated emotion; *passion* is any violent emotion.   262. *censure:* opinion, judgment.   264. *I . . . were:* I wish he were the man he ought to be. Once more Iago hints that he is holding back some unpleasant fact.   266. *Is . . . use:* does he always behave like this?   271. *courses:* ways, behavior.

SCENE TWO. A ROOM IN THE CASTLE.

(*Enter* OTHELLO *and* EMILIA.)

OTH. You have seen nothing, then?

EMIL. Nor ever heard, nor ever did suspect.

OTH. Yes, you have seen Cassio and she together.

EMIL. But then I saw no harm, and then I heard

Each syllable that breath made up between them.   5

OTH. What, did they never whisper?

EMIL.   Never, my lord.

OTH. Nor send you out o' the way?

EMIL. Never.

OTH. To fetch her fan, her gloves, her mask, nor nothing?

EMIL. Never, my lord.   10

OTH. That's strange.

EMIL. I durst, my lord, to wager she is honest,

Lay down my soul at stake.° If you think other,

Remove your thought, it doth abuse your bosom.

If any wretch have put this in your head,   15

Let Heaven requite it with the serpent's curse!°

For if she be not honest, chaste, and true,

There's no man happy, the purest of their wives

Is foul as slander.

OTH. Bid her come hither. Go.   (*Exit* EMILIA.)

She says enough. Yet she's a simple bawd°   20

That cannot say as much. This is a subtle whore,

A closet° lock and key of villainous secrets.

And yet she'll kneel and pray, I have seen her do 't.

(*Enter* DESDEMONA *with* EMILIA.)

DES. My lord, what is your will?

OTH.   Pray, chuck,° come hither.

DES. What is your pleasure?

OTH.   Let me see your eyes.   25

Look in my face.

Sc. ii: 13. *at stake:* as the stake, the bet.   16. *serpent's curse:* i.e., the curse
laid on the serpent in the Garden of Eden.   20. *bawd:* keeper of a brothel.
22. *closet:* box in which secret papers are kept.   24. *chuck:* See III.iv.45,n.

DES.   What horrible fancy's this?

OTH. (*To* EMILIA) Some of your function,° mistress.
Leave procreants alone and shut the door,
Cough, or cry hem, if anybody come.
Your mystery,° your mystery. Nay, dispatch.° (*Exit* EMILIA.)   30
     DES. Upon my knees, what doth your speech import?
I understand a fury in your words,
But not the words.
     OTH. Why, what art thou?
     DES. Your wife, my lord, your true and loyal wife.

     OTH. Come, swear it, damn thyself,   35
Lest, being like one of Heaven,° the devils themselves
Swear thou art honest.
     DES.   Heaven doth truly know it.
     OTH. Heaven truly knows that thou art false as Hell.
     DES. To whom, my lord? With whom? How am I false?   40
     OTH. O Desdemona! Away! Away! Away!
     DES. Alas the heavy day! Why do you weep?
Am I the motive of these tears, my lord?
If haply you my father do suspect
An instrument of this your calling-back,   45
Lay not your blame on me. If you have lost him,
Why, I have lost him too.
     OTH.   Had it pleased Heaven
To try me with affliction, had they rained
All kinds of sores and shames on my bare head,
Steeped me in poverty to the very lips,   50
Given to captivity me and my utmost hopes,
I should have found in some place of my soul
A drop of patience. But, alas, to make me
A fixèd figure for the time of scorn
To point his slow unmoving finger at!°   55

---

27. *Some . . . function:* get about your business; i.e., prostitution. Othello pretends that Emilia is keeper of a brothel and Desdemona one of the women. 30. *mystery:* profession. *dispatch:* be quick. 36. *being . . . Heaven:* because you look like an angel. 54–55. *A . . . at:* A difficult image, much discussed. F1 reads "slow and moving finger"; Q1 reads "slow unmoving." Probably it means "a perpetual mark for scorn to point at which motionless finger." *time of scorn:* (perhaps) scorn for all time.

Yet could I bear that too, well, very well.
But there where I have garnered up my heart,°
Where either I must live or bear no life,
The fountain from the which my current runs
Or else dries up—to be discarded thence!   60
Or keep it as a cistern for foul toads
To knot and gender° in! Turn thy complexion there,
Patience, thou young and rose-lipped churubin—
Aye, there, look grim as Hell!
    DES. I hope my noble lord esteems me honest.   65
    OTH. Oh, aye, as summer flies are in the shambles,°
That quicken even with blowing.° O thou weed,
Who are so lovely fair and smell'st so sweet
That the sense aches at thee, would thou hadst ne'er been born!
    DES. Alas, what ignorant sin have I committed?   70
    OTH. Was this fair paper,° this most goodly book,
Made to write "whore" upon? What committed!
Committed! O thou public commoner!°
I should make very forges of my cheeks°
That would to cinders burn up modesty   75
Did I but speak thy deeds. What committed!
Heaven stops the nose at it, and the moon winks.
The bawdy wind, that kisses all it meets,
Is hushed within the hollow mine° of earth
And will not hear it. What committed!   80
Impudent strumpet!
    DES.   By Heaven, you do me wrong.
    OTH. Are not you a strumpet?
    DES.   No, as I am a Christian.
If to preserve this vessel for my lord
From any other foul unlawful touch
Be not to be a strumpet, I am none.   85
    OTH. What, not a whore?

---

57. *garnered . . . heart:* stored the harvest of my love. 62. *gender:* mate.
66. *shambles:* slaughterhouse. 67. *quicken . . . blowing:* come to life as soon
as the eggs are laid. 71. *fair paper:* i.e., her white body. 73. *public commoner:* one who offers herself to all comers. 74. *I . . . cheeks:* i.e., my cheeks
would be as hot as a forge if I told the truth. 79. *hollow mine:* i.e., the cave
where the winds were supposed to be kept.

DES.   No, as I shall be saved.
OTH. Is 't possible?
DES. Oh, Heaven forgive us!
OTH.   I cry you mercy, then.
I took you for that cunning whore of Venice
That married with Othello.   (*Raising his voice.*)
    You, mistress,   90
That have the office opposite to Saint Peter,°
And keep the gate of Hell!
(*Re-enter* EMILIA.) You, you, aye, you!
We have done our course, there's money for your pains.
I pray you turn the key, and keep our counsel.°   (*Exit.*)
    EMIL. Alas, what does this gentleman conceive?°   95
How do you, madam? How do you, my good lady?
    DES. Faith, half-asleep.
    EMIL. Good madam, what's the matter with my lord?
    DES. With who?
    EMIL. Why, with my lord, madam.   100
    DES. Who is thy lord?
    EMIL.   He that is yours, sweet lady.
    DES. I have none. Do not talk to me, Emilia.
I cannot weep, nor answer have I none
But what should go by water.° Prithee tonight
Lay on my bed my wedding sheets. Remember,   105
And call thy husband hither.
    EMIL.   Here's a change indeed!   (*Exit.*)
    DES. 'Tis meet I should be used so, very meet.
How have I been behaved that he might stick
The small'st opinion on my least misuse?°
                (*Re-enter* EMILIA *with* IAGO.)
    IAGO. What is your pleasure, madam? How is 't with you? 110
    DES. I cannot tell Those that do teach young babes
Do it with gentle means and easy tasks.

---

91. *office . . . Peter:* St. Peter kept the keys to Heaven.   94. *counsel:* i.e., secret.
95. *conceive:* imagine.   104. *should . . . water:* be expressed in tears.   108–
09. *How . . . misuse:* what have I done that he could find the smallest reason to
find fault with my least mistake?

He might have chid me so, for, in good faith,
I am a child to chiding.

    IAGO.   What's the matter, lady?

    EMIL. Alas, Iago, my lord hath so bewhored her,   115
Thrown such despite and heavy terms upon her,
As true hearts cannot bear.

    DES. Am I that name, Iago?

    IAGO.   What name, fair lady?

    DES. Such as she says my lord did say I was.

    EMIL. He called her whore. A beggar in his drink   120
Could not have laid such terms upon his callet.°

    IAGO. Why did he so?

    DES. I do not know. I am sure I am none such.

    IAGO. Do not weep, do not weep. Alas the day!

    EMIL. Hath she forsook so many noble matches,   125
Her father and her country and her friends,
To be called whore? Would it not make one weep?

    DES. It is my wretched fortune.

    IAGO.   Beshrew him for 't!
How comes this trick upon him?

    DES.   Nay, Heaven doth know.

    EMIL. I will be hanged if some eternal villain,   130
Some busy and insinuating rogue,
Some cogging, cozening° slave, to get some office,
Have not devised this slander. I'll be hanged else.

    IAGO. Fie, there is no such man, it is impossible.

    DES. If any such there be, Heaven pardon him!   135

    EMIL. A halter pardon him! And Hell gnaw his bones!
Why should he call her whore? Who keeps her company?
What place? What time? What form? What likelihood
The Moor's abused by some most villainous knave,
Some base notorious knave, some scurvy fellow.   140
O Heaven, that such companions° Thou'dst unfold,°
And put in every honest hand a whip
To lash the rascals naked through the world

---

121. *laid . . . callet:* used such words about his moll.   132. *cogging, cozening:*
deceiving, cheating.   141. *companions:* low creatures.   *unfold:* bring to light.

Even from the east to the west!

IAGO.   Speak withindoor.°

EMIL. Oh, fie upon them! Some such squire° he was   145
That turned your wit the seamy side without,
And made you to suspect me with the Moor.

IAGO. You are a fool. Go to.°

DES.   O good Iago,
What shall I do to win my lord again
Good friend, go to him, for, by this light of Heaven,   150
I know not how I lost him. Here I kneel.
If e'er my will did trespass 'gainst his love
Either in discourse of thought or actual deed,
Or that mine eyes, mine ears, or any sense
Delighted them in any other form,   155
Or that I do not yet, and ever did,
And ever will, though he do shake me off
To beggarly divorcement, love him dearly,
Comfort forswear° me! Unkindness may do much,
And his unkindness may defeat° my life,   160
But never taint my love. I cannot say "whore,"
It doth abhor me now I speak the word.
To do the act that might the addition° earn
Not the world's mass of vanity° could make me.

IAGO. I pray you be content, 'tis but his humor.   165
The business of the state does him offense,
And he does chide with you.

DES. If 'twere no other——

IAGO. 'Tis but so, I warrant.   (*Trumpets within.*)
Hark how these instruments summon to supper!   170
The messengers of Venice stay the meat.°
Go in, and weep not, all things shall be well.

                    (*Exeunt* DESDEMONA *and* EMILIA.)

(*Enter* RODERIGO.) How now, Roderigo!

ROD. I do not find that thou dealest justly with me.

---

144. *Speak withindoor:* don't shout so loud that all the street will hear you.
145. *squire:* fine fellow.   148. *Go to:* An expression of derision.   159. *forswear:* repudiate.   160. *defeat:* destroy.   163. *addition:* title. Cf. IV.i.105.
164. *vanity:* i.e., riches.   171. *meat:* serving of supper.

IAGO. What in the contrary?   175

ROD. Every day thou daffest° me with some device, Iago,
and rather, as it seems to me now, keepest from me all con-
veniency° than suppliest me with the least advantage of hope.
I will indeed no longer endure it, nor am I yet persuaded to
put up in peace what already I have foolishly suffered.   180

IAGO. Will you hear me, Roderigo?

ROD. Faith, I have heard too much, for your words and performances are no kin together.

IAGO. You charge me most unjustly.

ROD. With naught but truth. I have wasted myself out of   185
my means. The jewels you have had from me to deliver to
Desdemona would half have corrupted a votarist.° You have
told me she hath received them, and returned me expectations
and comforts of sudden respect and acquaintance, but I find
none.   185

IAGO. Well, go to, very well.

ROD. Very well! Go to! I cannot go to, man, nor 'tis not
very well. By this hand, I say 'tis very scurvy, and begin to find
myself fopped° in it.

IAGO. Very well.   190

ROD. I tell you 'tis not very well. I will make myself known
to Desdemona. If she will return me my jewels, I will give
over my suit and repent my unlawful solicitation. If not, assure
yourself I will seek satisfaction of you.

IAGO. You have said now.°   195

ROD. Aye, and said nothing but what I protest intendment
of doing.

IAGO. Why, now I see there's mettle° in thee, and even from
this instant do built on thee a better opinion than ever before.
Give me thy hand, Roderigo. Thou has taken against me a   200
most just exception,° but yet I protest I have dealt most
directly in thy affair.

ROD. It hath not appeared.

---

176. *thou daffest:* you put me aside. Cf. *I Hen IV,* IV.i.96.   177–78. *con-*
veniency: opportunity.   187. *votarist:* one who has taken a vow, here a nun.
189. *fopped:* fooled.   195. *You . . . now:* or in modern slang, "Oh yeah."
198. *mettle:* metal, good stuff.   201. *just exception:* reasonable grievance.

IAGO. I grant indeed it hath not appeared, and your suspicion is not without wit° and judgment. But, Roderigo, if   210
thou hast that in thee indeed which I have greater reason to
believe now than ever—I mean purpose, courage, and valor—
this night show it. If thou the next night following enjoy not
Desdemona, take me from this world with treachery and
devise engines° for my life.   215

ROD. Well, what is it? Is it within reason and compass?

IAGO. Sir, there is especial commission come from Venice to
depute Cassio in Othello's place.

ROD. Is that true? Why, then Othello and Desdemona return
again to Venice.   220

IAGO. Oh, no. He goes into Mauritania, and takes away with
him the fair Desdemona, unless his abode be lingered here by
some accident. Wherein none can be so determinate° as the
removing of Cassio.

ROD. How do you mean, "removing of" him?   225

IAGO. Why, by making him uncapable° of Othello's place,
knocking out his brains.

ROD. And that you would have me to do?

IAGO. Aye, if you dare do yourself a profit and a right. He
sups tonight with a harlotry,° and thither will I go to him.   230
He knows not yet of his honorable fortune. If you will watch
his going thence, which I will fashion to fall out between
twelve and one, you may take him at your pleasure. I will be
near to second your attempt, and he shall fall between us.
Come, stand not amazed at it, but go along with me. I will   235
show you such a necessity in his death that you shall think
yourself bound to put it on him. It is now high suppertime,
and the night grows to waste. About it.

ROD. I will hear further reason for this.

IAGO. And you shall be satisfied.   (*Exeunt.*)   240

---

210. *wit:* wisdom.   215. *engines:* instruments of torture.   223. *determinate:*
decisive.   226. *uncapable:* unable to take.   230. *harlotry:* harlot.

SCENE THREE. ANOTHER ROOM
IN THE CASTLE.

(*Enter* OTHELLO, LODOVICO, DESDEMONA,
EMILIA, *and* ATTENDANTS.)

LOD. I do beseech you, sir, trouble yourself no further.

OTH. Oh, pardon me, 'twill do me good to walk.

LOD. Madam, good night. I humbly thank your ladyship.

DES. Your Honor is most welcome.

OTH.   Will you walk, sir?

Oh—Desdemona——   5

DES. My lord?

OTH. Get you to bed on the instant, I will be returned forth-
with. Dismiss your attendant there. Look it be done.

DES. I will, my lord.   10

(*Exeunt* OTHELLO, LODOVICO, *and* ATTENDANTS.)

EMIL. How goes it now? He looks gentler than he did.

DES. He says he will return incontinent.°

He hath commanded me to go to bed,

And bade me to dismiss you.

EMIL.   Dismiss me!

DES. It was his bidding, therefore, good Emilia,   15

Give me my nightly wearing,° and adieu.

We must not now displease him.

EMIL. I would you had never seen him!

DES. So would not I. My love doth so approve° him

That even his stubbornness, his checks, his frowns—   20

Prithee, unpin me—have grace and favor in them.

EMIL. I have laid those sheets you bade me on the bed.

DES. All's one. Good faith, how foolish are our minds!

If I do die before thee, prithee shroud me

In one of those same sheets.

EMIL.   Come, come, you talk.   25

DES. My mother had a maid called Barbara.

She was in love, and he she loved proved mad

Sc. iii: 12. *incontinent:* immediately. 16. *nightly wearing:* nightgown.
19. *approve:* commend.

And did forsake her. She had a song of "willow"°—
An old thing 'twas, but it expressed her fortune,
And she died singing it. That song tonight   30
Will not go from my mind. I have much to do
But to go hang my head all at one side
And sing it like poor Barbara. Prithee, dispatch.
    EMIL. Shall I go fetch your nightgown?
    DES.   No, unpin me here.
This Lodovico is a proper man.   35
    EMIL. A very handsome man.
    DES. He speaks well.
    EMIL. I know a lady in Venice would have walked barefoot
to Palestine for a touch of his nether° lip.
    DES. (*Singing*)

"The poor soul sat sighing by a sycamore tree,   40
    Sing all a green willow.
Her hand on her bosom, her head on her knee,
    Sing willow, willow, willow.
The fresh streams ran by her, and murmured her moans,
    Sing willow, willow, willow.   45
Her salt tears fell from her, and softened the stones—"

Lay by these—(*Singing*)
               "Sing willow, willow, willow."
Prithee, hie thee, he'll come anon.°—(*Singing*)

"Sing all a green willow must be my garland.   50
Let nobody blame him, his scorn I approve——"

Nay, that's not next. Hark! Who is 't that knocks?
    EMIL. It's the wind.
    DES. (*Singing*)

"I called my love false love, but what said he then?
    Sing willow, willow, willow.   55
If I court moe° women, you'll couch with moe men."

So get thee gone, good night. Mine eyes do itch.

---

28. *willow:* the emblem of the forlorn lover. **39.** *nether:* lower. **49.** *anon:*
soon. **56.** *moe:* more.

Doth that bode weeping?
    EMIL.   'Tis neither here nor there.
    DES. I have heard it said so. Oh, these men, these men!
Dost thou in conscience think—tell me, Emilia—   60
That there be women do abuse their husbands
In such gross kind?
    EMIL.   There be some such, no question.
    DES. Wouldst thou do such a deed for all the world?
    EMIL. Why, would not you?
    DES.   No, by this heavenly light!
    EMIL. Nor I neither by this heavenly light. I might do 't as 65
well i' the dark.
    DES. Wouldst thou do such a deed for all the world?
    EMIL. The world's a huge thing. It is a great price
For a small vice.
    DES.   In troth, I think thou wouldst not.
    EMIL. In troth, I think I should, and undo 't when I had 70
done. Marry, I would not do such a thing for a joint ring,°
nor for measures of lawn,° nor for gowns, petticoats, nor caps,
nor any petty exhibition;° but for the whole world—why, who
would not make her husband a cuckold to make him a monarch? I should venture Purgatory for 't.   75
    DES. Beshrew me if I would do such a wrong
For the whole world.
    EMIL. Why, the wrong is but a wrong i' the world, and
having the world for your labor, 'tis a wrong in your own
world and you might quickly make it right.   80
    DES. I do not think there is any such woman.
    EMIL. Yes, a dozen, and as many to the vantage° as would
store° the world they played for.
But I do think it is their husbands' faults
If wives do fall. Say that they slack their duties   85
And pour our treasures into foreign laps,
Or else break out in peevish jealousies,

71. *joint ring:* ring made in two pieces, a lover's gift. 72. *measures of lawn:*
lengths of finest lawn, or as a modern woman would say, "sheer nylon."
73. *petty exhibition:* small allowance of money. 82. *as . . . vantage:* and
more too; *vantage* is that added to the exact weight to give generous measure.
83. *store:* stock, fill up.

Throwing restraint° upon us, or say they strike us,
Or scant our former having in despite,°
Why, we have galls,° and though we have some grace,   90
Yet have we some revenge. Let husbands know
Their wives have sense like them. They see and smell
And have their palates both for sweet and sour,
As husbands have. What is it that they do
When they change us for others? Is it sport?   95
I think it is. And doth affection breed it?
I think it doth. Is 't frailty that thus errs?
It is so too. And have not we affections,
Desires for sport, and frailty, as men have?
Then let them use us well. Else let them know   100
The ills we do, their ills instruct us so.

    DES. Good night, good night. Heaven me such uses° send,
Not to pick bad from bad, but by bad mend!   (*Exeunt.*)

act five

SCENE ONE. CYPRUS. A STREET.

        (*Enter* IAGO *and* RODERIGO.)

    IAGO. Here, stand behind this bulk,° straight° will he come.
Wear thy good rapier bare, and put it home.
Quick, quick, fear nothing, I'll be at thy elbow.
It makes us, or it mars us. Think on that,
And fix most firm thy resolution.   5

    ROD. Be near at hand, I may miscarry in 't.

    IAGO. Here, at thy hand. Be bold, and take thy stand.

                        (*Retires.*)

    ROD. I have no great devotion to the deed,
And yet he hath given me satisfying reasons.
'Tis but a man gone. Forth, my sword. He dies.   10

    IAGO. I have rubbed this young quat° almost to the sense,°

---

88. *Throwing restraint:* putting restraints.   89. *scant . . . despite:* for spite cut
down our allowance.   90. *galls:* bile, the cause of bitterness.   102. *uses:*
practices.
    Act V, Sc. i: 1. *bulk:* stall outside a shop.   *straight:* straightway.   11. *quat:*
pimple.   *to . . . sense:* to the quick, to the raw.

And he grows angry. Now, whether he kill Cassio,
Or Cassio him, or each do kill the other,
Every way makes my gain. Live Roderigo,
He calls me to a restitution large°   15
Of gold and jewels that I bobbed° from him
As gifts to Desdemona.
It must not be. If Cassio do remain,
He hath a daily beauty in his life
That makes me ugly,° and besides, the Moor   20
May unfold° me to him. There stand I in much peril.
No, he must die. Be 't so. I hear him coming.
     (*Enter* CASSIO.)
 ROD. I know his gait, 'tis he. Villain, thou diest!
      (*Makes a pass at* CASSIO.)
 CAS. That thrust had been mine enemy indeed
But that my coat is better than thou know'st.°   25
I will make proof of thine.
     (*Draws, and wounds* RODERIGO.)
 ROD.   Oh, I am slain!
     (IAGO *from behind wounds* CASSIO
       in the leg, and exit.)
 CAS. I am maimed for ever. Help, ho! Murder! Murder!
          (*Falls.*)
     (*Enter* OTHELLO.)
 OTH. The voice of Cassio. Iago keeps his word.
 ROD. Oh, villain that I am!
 OTH.   It is even so.
 CAS. Oh, help, ho! Light! A surgeon!   30
 OTH. 'Tis he. O brave Iago, honest and just,
That hast such noble sense of thy friend's wrong!
Thou teachest me. Minion,° your dear lies dead,
And your unblest fate hies.° Strumpet, I come!
Forth of my heart those charms, thine eyes, are blotted.   35
Thy bed lust-stained shall with lust's blood be spotted. (*Exit.*)

---

15. *large:* full. 16. *bobbed:* cheated. 19–20. *He . . . ugly:* by comparison
with him I am a poor thing. Iago is conscious of his lack of social graces.
21. *unfold:* expose. 25. *coat . . . know'st:* i.e., I wear mail under my coat.
33. *Minion:* darling, in a bad sense. 34. *hies:* comes on quickly.

(*Enter* LODOVICO *and* GRATIANO.)

CAS. What ho! No watch?° No passage?° Murder! Murder!

GRA. 'Tis some mischance, the cry is very direful.

CAS. Oh, help!

LOD. Hark!   40

ROD. Oh, wretched villain!

LOD. Two or three groan. It is a heavy° night.
These may be counterfeits.° Let's think 't unsafe
To come in to the cry without more help.

ROD. Nobody come? Then shall I bleed to death.

LOD. Hark!   45

(*Re-enter* IAGO, *with a light.*)

GRA. Here's one comes in his shirt, with light and weapons.

IAGO. Who's there? Whose noise is this that cries on°
    murder?

LOD. We do not know.

IAGO.   Did not you hear a cry?

CAS. Here, here! For Heaven's sake, help me!

IAGO.   What's the matter?   50

GRA. This is Othello's Ancient, as I take it.

LOD. The same indeed, a very valiant fellow.

IAGO. What are you here that cry so grievously?

CAS. Iago? Oh, I am spoiled, undone by villains!
Give me some help.   55

IAGO. Oh me, Lieutenant! What villains have done this?

CAS. I think that one of them is hereabout,
And cannot make away.

IAGO.   Oh, treacherous villains!
(*To* LODOVICO *and* GRATIANO.) What are you there?
    Come in and give some help.   60

CAS. That's one of them.

IAGO. Oh, murderous slave! Oh, villain! (*Stabs* RODERIGO.)

ROD. Oh, damned Iago! Oh, inhuman dog!

IAGO. Kill men i' the dark! Where be these bloody thieves?
How silent is this town! Ho! Murder! Murder!
What may you be? Are you of good or evil?   65

---

37. *watch:* police. *No passage:* nobody passing.   42. *heavy:* thick.   43.
counterfeits: fakes.   47. *cries on:* cries out.

LOD. As you shall prove us, praise us.

IAGO. Signior Lodovico?

LOD. He, sir.

IAGO. I cry you mercy. Here's Cassio hurt by villains.

GRA. Cassio!   70

IAGO. How is 't, brother?

CAS. My leg is cut in two.

IAGO.   Marry, Heaven forbid!

Light, gentlemen. I'll bind it with my shirt.   (*Enter* BIANCA.)

BIAN. What is the matter ho? Who is 't that cried?

IAGO. Who is 't that cried!   75

BIAN. Oh, my dear Cassio! My sweet Cassio! Oh,
Cassio, Cassio, Cassio!

IAGO. Oh, notable strumpet! Cassio, may you suspect
Who they should be that have thus mangled you?

CAS. No.   80

GRA. I am sorry to find you thus. I have been to seek you.

IAGO. Lend me a garter. So. Oh, for a chair,
To bear him easily hence!

BIAN. Alas, he faints! Oh, Cassio, Cassio, Cassio!

IAGO. Gentlemen all, I do suspect this trash   85
To be a party in this injury.
Patience awhile, good Cassio. Come, come,
Lend me a light. Know we this face or no?
Alas, my friend and my dear countryman
Roderigo? No—yes, sure. Oh Heaven! Roderigo.   90

GRA. What, of Venice?

IAGO. Even he, sir. Did you know him?

GRA.   Know him! Aye.

IAGO. Signior Gratiano? I cry you gentle pardon.°
These bloody accidents must excuse my manners,
That so neglected you.

GRA.   I am glad to see you.   95

IAGO. How do you, Cassio? Oh, a chair, a chair!

GRA. Roderigo!

IAGO. He, he, 'tis he. (*A chair brought in*) Oh, that's well
    said, the chair.

93. *I . . . pardon:* I beg you kindly pardon me.

Some good man bear him carefully from hence.
I'll fetch the General's surgeon. (*To* BIANCA) For you, mistress,   100
Save you your labor. He that lies slain here, Cassio,
Was my dear friend. What malice was between you?
   CAS. None in the world, nor do I know the man.
    IAGO. (*To* BIANCA) What, look you pale? Oh, bear him out
     o' the air.   (CASSIO *and* RODERIGO *are borne off.*)
Stay you, good gentlemen. Look you pale, mistress?   105
Do you perceive the gastness° of her eye?
Nay, if you stare, we shall hear more anon.
Behold her well, I pray you look upon her.
Do you see, gentlemen? Nay, guiltiness will speak,
Though tongues were out of use.   110
            (*Enter* EMILIA.)
   EMIL. 'Las, what's the matter? What's the matter, husband?
   IAGO. Cassio hath here been set on in the dark
By Roderigo, and fellows that are 'scaped.
He's almost slain, and Roderigo dead.
   EMIL. Alas, good gentlemen! Alas, good Cassio!   115
   IAGO. This is the fruit of whoring. Prithee, Emilia,
Go know of Cassio where he supped tonight.
What, do you shake at that?
   BIAN. He supped at my house, but I therefore shake not.
   IAGO. Oh, did he so? I charge you, go with me.   120
   EMIL. Fie, fie upon thee, strumpet!
   BIAN. I am no strumpet, but of life as honest
As you that thus abuse me.
   EMIL.   As I! Foh! Fie upon thee!
   IAGO. Kind gentlemen, let's go see poor Cassio dressed.°
Come, mistress, you must tell 's another tale,   125
Emilia, run you to the citadel,
And tell my lord and lady what hath happed!
Will you go on? I pray. (*Aside*) This is the night
That either makes me or fordoes° me quite.   (*Exeunt.*)

---

106. *gastness:* ghastly look.   **124.** *dressed:* i.e., his wound dressed.   **129.** *fordoes:* ruins.

SCENE TWO. A BEDCHAMBER IN THE CASTLE.
DESDEMONA IN BED ASLEEP, A LIGHT BURNING.

(*Enter* OTHELLO.)

OTH. It is the cause,° it is the cause, my soul.
Let me not name it to you, you chaste stars!
It is the cause. Yet I'll not shed her blood,
Nor scar that whiter skin of hers than snow
And smooth as monumental alabaster.°   5
Yet she must die, else she'll betray more men.
Put out the light, and then put out the light.
If I quench thee, thou flaming minister,°
I can again thy former light restore,
Should I repent me. But once put out thy light,   10
Thou cunning'st° pattern of excelling nature,
I know not where is that Promethean heat°
That can thy light relume.° When I have plucked the rose,
I cannot give it vital growth again,
It needs must wither. I'll smell it on the tree.   15

(*Kissing her*)

Ah, balmy breath, that dost almost persuade
Justice to break her sword! One more, one more.
Be thus when thou art dead, and I will kill thee,
And love thee after. One more, and this the last.
So sweet was ne'er so fatal. I must weep,   20
But they are cruel tears. This sorrow's heavenly,
It strikes where it doth love. She wakes.

DES. Who's there? Othello?

OTH.   Aye, Desdemona.

DES. Will you come to bed, my lord?

Sc. ii: 1. *It . . . cause:* The meaning of the opening lines of this speech has
been much discussed. The *cause* is Desdemona's supposed faithlessness; Othello, at this moment, sees himself as embodied vengeance, the venger of man
betrayed by woman.   5. *monumental alabaster:* Alabaster is white translucent
stone, much used for memorial effigies on Elizabethan tombs.   8. *minister:*
servant.   11. *cunning'st:* most skillfully made.   12. *Promethean heat:* fire
from Heaven. Prometheus stole fire from Heaven and first gave it to man.
13. *relume:* relight.

OTH. Have you prayed tonight, Desdemona?   25

DES. Aye, my lord.

OTH. If you bethink yourself of any crime
Unreconciled as yet to Heaven and grace,
Solicit for it straight.

DES. Alas, my lord, what may you mean by that?   30

OTH. Well, do it, and be brief. I will walk by.
I would not kill thy unpreparèd spirit.
No, Heaven forfend! I would not kill thy soul.°

DES. Talk you of killing?

OTH. Aye, I do.   35

DES. Then Heaven have mercy on me!

OTH. Amen, with all my heart!

DES. If you say so, I hope you will not kill me.

OTH. Hum!

DES. And yet I fear you, for you are fatal° then   40
When your eyes roll so. Why I should fear I know not,
Since guiltiness I know not, but yet I feel I fear,

OTH. Think on thy sins.

DES.   They are loves I bear you.

OTH. Aye, and for that thou diest.

DES. That death's unnatural that kills for loving.   45
Alas, why gnaw you so your nether lip?
Some bloody passion shakes your very frame.
These are portents,° but yet I hope, I hope,
They do not point on me.

OTH.   Peace, and be still!

DES. I will so. What's the matter?   50

OTH. That handkerchief which I so loved and gave thee
Thou gavest to Cassio.

DES.   No, by my life and soul!
Send for the man, and ask him.

OTH.   Sweet soul, take heed,
Take heed of perjury, thou art on thy deathbed.

DES. Aye, but not yet to die.

27–33. *If . . . soul:* Othello will be a merciful murderer. *Cf. Haml,* I.v.76–80.
forfend: forbid. **40.** *fatal:* deadly. **48.** *portents:* signs foretelling disaster.

OTH.   Yes, presently.°   55
Therefore confess thee freely of thy sin,
For to deny each article with oath
Cannot remove nor choke the strong conception°
That I do groan withal. Thou art to die.
   DES. Then Lord have mercy on me!
   OTH.   I say amen.   60
   DES. And have you mercy too! I never did
Offend you in my life, never loved Cassio
But with such general warranty° of Heaven
As I might love. I never gave him token.
   OTH. By Heaven, I saw my handkerchief in 's hand.   65
O perjured woman! Thou dost stone° my heart,
And makes me call what I intend to do
A murder, which I thought a sacrifice.
I saw the handkerchief.
   DES.   He found it, then,
I never gave it him. Send for him hither.   70
Let him confess a truth.
   OTH.   He hath confessed.
   DES. What, my lord?
   OTH. That he hath used thee.
   DES.   How! Unlawfully?
   OTH. Aye.
   DES. He will not say so.
   OTH.   No, his mouth is stopped.   75
Honest Iago hath ta'en order for 't.
   DES. Oh, my fear interprets! What, is he dead?
   OTH. Had all his hairs been lives, my great revenge
Had stomach for them all.
   DES. Alas, he is betrayed, and I undone!   80
   OTH. Out, strumpet! Weep'st thou for him to my face?
   DES. Oh, banish me, my lord, but kill me not!
   OTH. Down, strumpet!
   DES. Kill me tomorrow, let me live tonight!
   OTH. Nay, if you strive——   85

---

55. *presently:* at once. 58. *conception:* thought. 63. *warranty:* permission.
66. *stone:* turn to stone.

DES. But half an hour!

OTH.   Being done, there is no pause.

DES. But while I say one prayer!

OTH.   It is too late.

(He stifles her.)

EMIL. (*Within*) My lord, my lord! What ho! My lord, my lord!

OTH. What noise is this? Not dead? Not yet quite dead?

I that am cruel am yet merciful,   90

I would not have thee linger in thy pain.

So, so.

EMIL. (*Within*) What ho! My lord, my lord!

OTH.   Who's there?

EMIL. (*Within*) Oh, good my lord, I would speak a word with you!

OTH. Yes, 'tis Emilia. By and by. She's dead.   95

'Tis like she comes to speak of Cassio's death.

The noise was here. Ha! No more moving?

Still as the grave. Shall she come in? Were 't good?

I think she stirs again. No. What's best to do?

If she come in, she'll sure speak to my wife.   100

My wife! My wife! What wife? I have no wife.

Oh, insupportable! Oh, heavy hour!

Methinks it should be now a huge eclipse

Of sun and moon, and that the affrighted globe

Should yawn at alteration.°

EMIL.   (*Within*) I do beseech you   105

That I may speak with you, O good my lord!

OTH. I had forgot thee. Oh, come in, Emilia.

Soft, by and by. Let me the curtains° draw.

Where art thou?   *(Unlocks the door.)*

(*Enter* EMILIA.) What's the matter with thee now?   110

EMIL. Oh, my good lord, yonder 's foul murders done!

OTH. What, now?

EMIL. But now, my lord.

OTH. It is the very error° of the moon.

---

105. *yawn at alteration:* gape with wonder at some monstrous change.
108. *curtains:* i.e., of the bed.   114. *error:* wandering out of her proper course.

She comes more nearer each than she was wont   115
And makes men mad.
    EMIL. Cassio, my lord, hath killed a young Venetian
Called Roderigo.
    OTH.   Roderigo killed!
And Cassio killed!
    EMIL.   No, Cassio is not killed.
    OTH. Not Cassio killed! Then murder's out of tune,   120
And sweet revenge grows harsh.
    DES. Oh, falsely, falsely murdered!
    EMIL.   Alas, what cry is that?
    OTH. That! What?
    EMIL. Out and alas! That was my lady's voice.
Help! Help, ho! Help! O lady, speak again!   125
Sweet Desdemona! O sweet mistress, speak!
    DES. A guiltless death I die.
    EMIL. Oh, who hath done this deed?
    DES. Nobody, I myself. Farewell
Commend me to my kind lord. Oh, farewell!   (*Dies.*) 130
    OTH. Why, how should she be murdered?
    EMIL. Alas, who knows?
    OTH. You heard her say herself it was not I.
    EMIL. She said so. I must needs report the truth.
    OTH. She's like a liar gone to burning Hell.   135
'Twas I that killed her.
    EMIL.   Oh, the more angel she,
And you the blacker devil!
    OTH. She turned to folly,° and she was a whore.
    EMIL. Thou dost belie her, and thou art a devil.
    OTH. She was false as water.
    EMIL.   Thou art rash as fire to say   140
That she was false. Oh, she was heavenly true!
    OTH. Cassio did top her, ask thy husband else.
Oh, I were damned beneath all depth in Hell.
But that I did proceed upon just grounds.
To this extremity. Thy husband knew it all.   145
    EMIL. My husband!

138. *folly:* lewdness.

OTH. Thy husband.

EMIL. That she was false to wedlock?

OTH. Aye, with Cassio. Nay, had she been true,
If Heaven would make me such another world   150
Of one entire and perfect chrysolite,°
I'd not have sold her for it.

EMIL. My husband!

. OTH.   Aye, 'twas he that told me first.
An honest man he is, and hates the slime
That sticks on filthy deeds.

EMIL.   My husband!   155

OTH. What needs this iteration° woman? I say thy husband.

EMIL. Oh, mistress, villainly hath made mocks with love!
My husband say that she was false!

OTH.   He, woman.
I say thy husband. Dost understand the word?
My friend, thy husband, honest, honest Iago.   160

EMIL. If he say so, may his pernicious soul
Rot half a grain a day! He lies to the heart.
She was too fond of her most filthy bargain.

OTH. Ha!

EMIL. Do thy worst.   165
This deed of thine is no more worthy Heaven
Than thou wast worthy her.

OTH.   Peace, you were best.

EMIL. Thou hast not half that power to do me harm
As I have to be hurt. O gull!° O dolt!°
As ignorant as dirt! Thou hast done a deed——   170
I care not for thy sword, I'll make thee known,
Though I lost twenty lives. Help! Help, ho! Help!
The Moor hath killed my mistress! Murder! Murder!
      (*Enter* MONTANO, GRATIANO, IAGO, *and others.*)

MON. What is the matter? How now, General!

EMIL. Oh, are you come, Iago? You have done well,   175
That men must lay their murders on your neck.

GRA. What is the matter?

---

151. *chrysolite:* a semiprecious stone, usually green in color.   156. *iteration:*
repetition.   169. *gull:* dupe.   *dolt:* dull-witted ass.

EMIL. Disprove this villain, if thou be'st a man.
He says thou told'st him that his wife was false.
I know thou didst not, thou'rt not such a villain.   180
Speak, for my heart is full.
   IAGO. I told him what I thought, and told no more
Than what he found himself was apt° and true.
   EMIL. But did you ever tell him she was false?
   IAGO. I did.   185
   EMIL. You told a lie, an odious, damnèd lie,
Upon my soul, a lie, a wicked lie!
She false with Cassio! Did you say with Cassio!
   IAGO. With Cassio, mistress. Go to, charm your tongue.°
   EMIL. I will not charm my tongue, I am bound to speak   190
My mistress here lies murdered in her bed.
   ALL. Oh, Heavens forefend!
   EMIL. And your reports have set the murder on.
   OTH. Nay, stare not, masters. It is true indeed.
   GRA. 'Tis a strange truth.   195
   MON. Oh, monstrous act!
   EMIL.   Villainy, villainy, villainy!
I think upon 't. I think I smell 't. Oh, villainy!
I thought so then.° I'll kill myself for grief.
Oh, villainy, villainy!
   IAGO. What, are you mad? I charge you, get you home.   200
   EMIL. Good gentlemen, let me have leave to speak.
'Tis proper I obey him, but not now.
Perchance, Iago, I will ne'er go home.
   OTH. Oh! Oh! Oh!   (*Falling on the bed.*)
   EMIL.   Nay, lay thee down and roar,
For thou hast killed the sweetest innocent   205
That e'er did lift up eye.
   OTH.   (*Rising*) Oh, she was foul!
I scarce did know you, Uncle. There lies your niece,
Whose breath indeed these hands have newly stopped.
I know this act shows horrible and grim.

183. *apt:* likely. 189. *charm . . . tongue:* be silent. 198. *I . . . then:* i.e.,
I suspected this earlier—as for example when Iago took the handkerchief. See
III.iii.313.

GRA. Poor Desdemona! I am glad thy father's dead.   210
Thy match was mortal° to him, and pure grief
Shore his old thread in twain.° Did he live now,
This sight would make him do a desperate turn—
Yes, curse his better angel from his side,
And fall to reprobation.°   215
    OTH. 'Tis pitiful, but yet Iago knows
That she with Cassio hath the act of shame
A thousand times committed. Cassio confessed it.
And she did gratify his amorous works
With that recognizance° and pledge of love   220
Which I first gave her, I saw it in his hand.
It was a handkerchief, an antique token
My father gave my mother.
    EMIL. Oh, Heaven! Oh, heavenly powers!
    IAGO. 'Zounds! Hold your peace.
    EMIL.   'Twill out, 'twill out. I peace!   225
No, I will speak as liberal as the north.°
Let Heaven and men and devils, let them all,
All, all, cry shame against me, yet I'll speak.
    IAGO. Be wise, and get you home.
    EMIL.   I will not. (IAGO *offers to stab* EMILIA.)
    GRA.   Fie!
Your sword upon a woman!   230
    EMIL. O thou dull Moor! That handkerchief thou speak'st of
I found by fortune and did give my husband,
For often with a solemn earnestness,
More than indeed belonged to such a trifle,
He begged of me to steal it.
    IAGO.   Villainous whore!   235
    EMIL. She give it Cassio! No, alas, I found it,
And I did give 't my husband.
    IAGO.   Filth, thou liest!
    EMIL. By Heaven, I do not, I do not, gentlemen.

---

211. *match . . . mortal:* i.e., grief at this marriage killed him. 212. *Shore . . .
twain:* cut his thread of life in two. 215. *reprobation:* damnation; i.e., by
self-murder. 220. *recognizance:* badge, token. 226. *liberal . . . north:* as
freely as the north wind, which is loud and bitter.

Oh, murderous coxcomb!° What should such a fool
Do with so good a wife?

OTH.   Are there no stones° in Heaven   240
But what serve for the thunder? Precious villain!

     (*He runs at* IAGO. IAGO, *from behind,*
        stabs EMILIA, *and exit.*)

GRA. The woman falls. Sure, he hath killed his wife.

EMIL. Aye, aye. Oh, lay me by my mistress' side.

GRA. He's gone, but his wife's killed.

MON. 'Tis a notorious villain. Take you this weapon,   245
Which I have here recovered from the Moor.
Come, guard the door without, let him not pass,
But kill him rather. I'll after that same villain,
For 'tis a damnèd slave.

    (*Exeunt all but* OTHELLO *and* EMILIA.)

OTH.   I am not valiant neither.
But every puny whipster° gets my sword.   250
But why should honor outlive honesty?
Let it go all.

EMIL.   What did thy song bode, lady?
Hark, canst thou hear me? I will play the swan,
And die in music.° (*Singing*)

    "Willow, willow, willow."

Moor, she was chaste. She loved thee, cruel Moor,   255
So come my soul to bliss as I speak true.
So speaking as I think, I die, I die.   (*Dies.*)

OTH. I have another weapon in this chamber.
It is a sword of Spain,° the ice brook's temper.°—
Oh, here it is. Uncle, I must come forth.   260

GRA. (*Within*) If thou attempt it, it will cost thee dear.
Thou hast no weapon, and perforce must suffer.

OTH. Look in upon me then, and speak with me,
Or, naked° as I am, I will assault thee.

---

239. *coxcomb:* conceited fool. 240. *stones:* thunderbolts. 250. *whipster:*
whippersnapper. 253–54. *play . . . music:* i.e., I will sing at my death. It was
believed that swans sang once only, just before they died. 259. *sword of
Spain:* Spanish swords and rapiers, from Toledo or Bilbao, were famous. *ice
. . . temper:* hardened in ice-cold water. 264. *naked:* unarmed.

(*Re-enter* GRATIANO.)

GRA. What is the matter?

OTH.   Behold, I have a weapon,   265
A better never did itself sustain
Upon a soldier's thigh. I have seen the day
That with this little arm and this good sword
I have made my way through more impediments
That twenty times your stop. But, oh, vain boast!   270
Who can control his fate? 'Tis not so now.
Be not afraid, though you do see me weaponed.
Here is my journey's end, here is my butt°
And very sea mark of my utmost sail.°
Do you go back dismayed? 'Tis a lost fear.   275
Man but a rush° against Othello's breast,
And he retires. Where should Othello go?
Now, how dost thou look now? O ill-starred wench!
Pale as thy smock! When we shall meet at compt,°
This look of thine will hurl my soul from Heaven   280
And fiends will snatch at it. Cold, cold, my girl!
Even like thy chastity. Oh, cursèd slave!
Whip me, ye devils,
From the possession of this heavenly sight!
Blow me about in winds! Roast me in sulphur!   285
Wash me in steep-down gulfs° of liquid fire!
O Desdemona! Desdemona! Dead!
Oh! Oh! Oh!

      (*Enter* LODOVICO, MONTANO, CASSIO *carried in a chair,
              and* OFFICERS *with* IAGO, *prisoner.*)

LOD. Where is this rash and most unfortunate man?

OTH. That's he that was Othello. Here I am.   290

LOD. Where is that viper? Bring the villain forth.

OTH. I look down toward his feet,° but that's a fable.

---

273. *butt:* aim.   274. *And . . . sail:* the mark that I have reached the end of
my voyage.   *sea mark:* a conspicuous object by which the mariner checks his
course.   276. *Man . . . rush:* attack with only a reed.   279. *compt:* account;
i.e., the Day of Judgment.   286. *steep-down gulfs:* sheer whirlpools.   292. *toward . . . feet:* i.e., to see if he has the cloven hoof of a devil.

If that thou be'st a devil,° I cannot kill thee.

(*Wounds* IAGO.)

LOD. Wrench his sword from him.

IAGO.   I bleed, sir, but not killed.

OTH. I am not sorry neither. I'd have thee live,   295
For, in my sense, 'tis happiness to die.

LOD. O thou Othello, that wert once so good,
Fall'n in the practice° of a damnèd slave,
What shall be said to thee?

OTH.   Why, anything.

An honorable murderer, if you will,   300
For naught did I in hate, but all in honor.

LOD. This wretch hath part confessed his villainy.
Did you and he consent in Cassio's death?

OTH. Aye.

CAS. Dear General, I never gave you cause.   305

OTH. I do believe it, and I ask your pardon.
Will you, I pray, demand that demidevil
Why he hath thus ensnared my soul and body?

IAGO. Demand me nothing. What you know, you know.
From this time forth I never will speak word.   310

LOD. What, not to pray?

GRA.   Torments will ope your lips.

OTH. Well, thou dost best.

LOD. Sir, you shall understand what hath befall'n,
Which, as I think, you know not. Here is a letter
Found in the pocket of the slain Roderigo,   315
And here another. The one of them imports
The death of Cassio to be undertook
By Roderigo.

OTH. Oh, villain!

CAS.   Most heathenish and most gross!

LOD. Now here's another discontented paper,   320
Found in his pocket too. And this, it seems,
Roderigo meant to have sent this damnèd villain
But that, belike, Iago in the interim
Came in and satisfied him.

293. *If . . . devil:* if you are an evil spirit and no man. **298.** *Fall'n . . . practice:* destroyed by the plotting.

OTH.   Oh, the pernicious caitiff!
How came you, Cassio, by that handkerchief   325
That was my wife's?
  CAS.   I found it in my chamber.
And he himself confessed but even now
That there he dropped it for a special purpose
Which wrought to his desire.
  OTH.   O fool! Fool! Fool!
  CAS. There is besides in Roderigo's letter   330
How he upbraids Iago, that he made him
Brave° me upon the watch, whereon it came
That I was cast.° And even but now he spake
After long seeming dead, Iago hurt him,
Iago set him on.   335
  LOD. You must forsake this room, and go with us.
Your power and your command is taken off,
And Cassio rules in Cyprus. For this slave,
If there be any cunning cruelty
That can torment him much and hold him long,°   340
It shall be his. You shall close prisoner rest
Till that the nature of your fault be known
To the Venetian state. Come, bring away.
  OTH. Soft you,° a word or two before you go.
I have done the state some service, and they know 't.   345
No more of that. I pray you, in your letters,
When you shall these unlucky deeds relate,
Speak of me as I am, nothing extenuate,
Nor set down aught in malice. Then must you speak
Of one that loved not wisely but too well,   350
Of one not easily jealous, but, being wrought,
Perplexed in the extreme, of one whose hand,
Like the base Indian, threw a pearl away
Richer than all his tribe°—of one whose subdued eyes,

332. *Brave:* dare, insult.   333. *cast:* dismissed.   340. *hold . . . long:* i.e., in dying.   344. *Soft you:* pause awhile.   353–54. *base . . . tribe:* A much discussed passage. F1 reads "Iudean" (Judean), and if correct it would refer to Judas Iscariot, who betrayed Jesus. Shakespeare does not elsewhere use the word "Judean," and he does associate India with pearls, as in *Tr & Cr,* I.i.105: "Her bed is India, There she lies a pearl."

Albeit unusèd to the melting mood,   355
Drop tears as fast as the Arabian trees
Their medicinal gum. Set you down this,   ˙
And say besides that in Aleppo once,
Where a malignant and a turbaned Turk
Beat a Venetian and traduced° the state,   360
I took by the throat the circumcisèd dog
And smote him, thus.   (*Stabs himself.*)
    LOD. Oh, bloody period!
    GRA.   All that's spoke is marred.°
    OTH. I kissed thee ere I killed thee. No way but this,
Killing myself, to die upon a kiss.   365
                (*Falls on the bed, and dies.*)
    CAS. This did I fear, but thought he had no weapon.
For he was great of heart.
    LOD.   (*To* IAGO) O Spartan° dog,
More fell° than anguish, hunger, or the sea!
Look on the tragic loading° of this bed,
This is thy work. The object poisons sight,   370
Let it be hid.° Gratiano, keep the house,
And seize upon the fortunes of the Moor,
For they succeed on you. To you, Lord Governor,
Remains the censure of this hellish villain,
The time, the place, the torture.   375
Oh, enforce it!
Myself will straight aboard, and to the state
This heavy act with heavy heart relate.   (*Exeunt.*)

---

360. *traduced:* insulted.   363. *marred:* spoiled.   367. *Spartan:* i.e., hard-hearted.   368. *fell:* cruel.   369. *loading:* burden—the bodies of Desdemona and Othello.   371. *Let . . . hid:* At these words the curtains are closed across the inner stage (or chamber, if this scene was acted aloft), concealing all three bodies.

THE INDISCRETIONS
OF DESDEMONA

Iago's speech of II.ii.340–342 is central because it gives a precise statement of satanically clever policy:

So will I turn her virtue into pitch,
And out of her own goodness make the net
That shall enmesh them all.

The explanation of this method is to be found in a careful study of Elizabethan and Jacobean attitudes toward women in general and marriage in particular.* Throughout the play Iago states what was supposed to be the ideal behavior for a married woman, according to the strictures of such diverse sources as the Bible, the homilies, broadside ballads, Renaissance compendia of knowledge, and courtesy books. Then, having set up the ideal in jocular style in II.ii, he proceeds to show the discrepancy between it and the conduct of Desdemona. Careful misconstruction of her actions thus makes her appear a wanton, while the so-called evidence of misconduct springs in fact from the lady's virtues of sympathy, kindheartedness, and fidelity in friendship. This background of religio-social conventions concerning matrimony was probably familiar to a Jacobean audience who would then have seen Othello as less gullible than modern playgoers consider him. Iago is able to mount his campaign with ammunition innocently and virtuously supplied by Desdemona because of her failure to observe the "rules." As a maiden, Desdemona offended against those strictures which insisted upon maidenly modesty, silence in wooing, and total dependence on parental choice in the negotiation of a marriage contract. In addition, she married for love, something that modern playgoers would approve, but an action which sixteenth-century writers warned against, believing that love without adequate financial support would soon turn to hate. Thus she has, according to Brabantio, made a "gross revolt," something that Iago later capitalizes on. Then, after marriage, she

* Abstracted from Margaret Loftus Ranald, "The Indiscretions of Desdemona," *Shakespeare Quarterly, XIV* (1963), 127-139.

allows the claims of friendship to supersede those of matrimonial duty and violates the exceedingly strict code of conduct laid down for wives by the writers of moralistic courtesy books, to say nothing of the writers of Sunday sermons. She fails to occupy herself solely with domesticity and household economy; she meddles in her husband's business, openly disobeying him by continuing her pleas for Cassio. She even vows to nag Othello into submission to her will and thus ensure the reinstatement of the Lieutenant. Finally, she talks alone with the disgraced Cassio, a very indiscreet act, since he is a secret visitor whom Othello would consider unwelcome in his house. It is this situation that Iago exploits fully, compounding Desdemona's innocent fault by suggestively recalling that Cassio had acted as go-between before the elopement of Othello and his wife. In thus showing the wifely faults of Desdemona, which arise from her warmhearted impulsiveness, Shakespeare runs the risk of alienating the sympathies of the moralistic. However, in the last two acts, he shows that Desdemona is more than the perfect wife according to conduct-book strictures, and certainly not the creature of duplicitous cunning that Iago makes Othello believe through skilful lies and misconstructions. Desdemona herself accidentally stumbles on the truth when she asks "Alas, what ignorant sin have I committed?" Finally, she proves her complete and self-sacrificing love by a deathbed lie in an attempt to save Othello from paying for his crime of murder. Therefore in death Desdemona is remembered for her loving generosity and her errors seem minor indeed. But in indicating that Desdemona is not faultless according to a well-known code of feminine behavior, Shakespeare manages to explain the character and to some extent exculpate the actions of Othello. Like Caesar's wife, Desdemona should have kept herself above suspicion, but her virtuous love of justice and her sympathy in friendship both contribute to the innocent indiscretions which corroborate Iago's allegations and increase the reluctant suspicions of the valorous and socially inexperienced Othello.

GOOD NAME IN *OTHELLO*

Many interpretations have been offered concerning the importance placed on a man's reputation in Shakespeare's *Othello*.* Although these various interpretations have proved enlightening, they
have not been exhaustive. A more ancient morality, stemming from
Roman law, can, through the importance of fame, provide new
insights regarding Othello's reputation and Iago's relationship to it.
Under Roman law the reputation afforded a man through his dignity
was considered a natural right. That dignity could, however, become
tainted in either of two ways. If the individual stained his dignity
through a criminal act, he incurred legal infamy, a loss of good name.
Similarly, if any doubts were cast upon an individual's good name,
even by false rumor, the resulting loss of dignity was the same. Even
though both types of infamy could be legally released, by a papal
edict or a swearing of innocence respectively, the community's
opinion of the man might never actually be changed. The ultimate
extension of the Roman morality concerning reputation is that, since
good name is a natural consequence of being a man, loss of good
name is the equivalent of loss of self. On the positive side of dignity
and fame, the inherent fame which a man has through his character
can be increased by lineage, good deeds, or virtuous behavior on the
part of his wife; conversely, a breakdown in any of these areas can
yield a proportionate loss of fame. All of these variations of fame
are present in Othello's reputation. Since good name is so highly
valued, loss of good name becomes especially evil. Traditionally,
slander, the tool for destruction of reputation, arises out of Envy.
Often equated with the Devil's evilness, Envy's attack on good name
was used by Spenser, Chaucer, Gower, Virgil, and Ovid. Thus,
Shakespeare follows traditional motivation by having Iago's plot
grow out of envy. Yet, Iago's motivation is especially evil for Iago
is sinister. Utilizing his reputation for honesty, his technique of
innuendo coupled with hesitancy, and his ability to predict future

* Abstracted from Madeleine Doran, "Good Name in *Othello*," *Studies in
English Literature, VII* (1967), 195-217.

events, which he structures, Iago is clearly an evil villain. Shakespeare introduces his main character, Othello, through slanderous comments made by Roderigo and Iago. Othello then appears, making comments such as: "My parts, my title, and my perfect soul/shall manifest me rightly." It soon becomes obvious that Othello is of good reputation and character and that accusations against him are false. Iago's intended victim is thus Othello, and, by slandering Othello's friend, Cassio, Iago tricks Othello into crimes which will make the lies true. It is ironic that Iago's reputation for honesty is a primary device used to slander the reputation of both Cassio and Othello, as well as Desdemona. Dramatic irony concerning good name is further intensified when, following a confrontation with Othello, Desdemona seeks help from Iago, her undoer. Emilia stands beside Iago and comments that the slander must be brought about by "some eternal villain/some busy and insinuating rogue." Othello's final speech becomes a swearing of innocence, as in the traditional Roman morality. He seeks to be released from a charge of bad fame, since he possessed no malice as did Iago. A clear distinction is made between the possible types of loss of good name by the final forgiveness granted by Cassio. Stating that Othello was "great of heart," Cassio absolves Othello of any loss of good name arising from innate evil and thus shows the loss of reputation to be the result of an act of passion only.

A TIME SCHEME FOR *OTHELLO*

Shakespeare's numerous and confusing references to time in *Othello* have fostered many critical attempts to relate these references to a single time scheme.* The Double Time theory of Wilson and Halpin, suggesting a True Historic Time of thirty-six hours for the main action and a Dramatic Time of approximately two months for other irreconcilable references, has been the most widely accepted scheme. Yet, all time references in *Othello* can be reconciled

* Abstracted from Albert Frederick Sproule, "*A Time Scheme for Othello*," *Shakespeare Quarterly, VII* (1956), 217-226.

to a three-day scheme. The first day at Cyprus carries through to Scene III of Act II. The action of Act II has traditionally been assumed to begin on Saturday, yet the time of day on Saturday has been misunderstood. In response to Montano, the second Gentleman makes reference to the stars; such a reference is only meaningful if the time is early morning when the stars are visible. Cassio's reference to "se'nnights speed" in Scene I is frequently misinterpreted; the comment does not necessarily suggest a passage of seven days. It could easily refer to Iago's arrival as being seven days sooner than expected. Similarly, geographic specialists have pointed out that a fourteen-hundred mile trip could not be completed in four days, yet the question should be whether or not Shakespeare was concerned with geographic accuracy. In any event, Iago's comment in Scene III, "In troth 'tis morning," marks the end of the first day. The second day, beginning in Act III, ends in Scene II of that same act. In Act II Cassio stated that he intended to contact Desdemona in the morning. When Desdemona subsequently asks Othello to invite Cassio to dinner, she sets a maximum three-day limit for the dinner date, and, since nothing in the play suggests the expiration of those three days, three days stands also as the maximum amount of time for the remainder of the play's action. Othello subsequently reinforces that time limit by admonishing Iago to silence Cassio in that time; later, Othello says, "Iago keeps his word." Although Act III, concludes the second day, many events during that night provide action for the third day. The third day begins in Scene iv of Act III. The use of comic interruptions in *Othello* has been noted in many studies as a means of showing the passage of time. Desdemona's conversation with the Clown can be interpreted in that manner, just as the comic interruption at the second day's beginning. Scene III of Act III ends in darkness; no indication of darkness is present in Scene IV, and it is thus quite natural that the women are holding long conversations outside the castle. Since time is also needed for Emilia and Desdemona to find the handkerchief, afternoon is a conceivable time for the beginning of the action of the third day. The comment made by Iago in Act IV, Scene I, refers to Othello's fit as his second, having had one yesterday. Since no such fit occurs on the first day, Act IV, Scene I, must be in the third day. Cassio accepts Iago's comments without disagreement. The action of Act V occurs in darkness and is related to the darkness action of

Scene III in Act IV; this is thus the night of the third day. If one last major problem is reconcilable, the three-day time scheme is complete. Bianca's reference to "seven days and nights," made in Act III, Scene IV, is the basis for interpretations which suggest a longer play action. Since her comment is made on the third day, four days need to be explained. It is possible that she too made the Venice-Cyprus trip. When deriding Cassio for his lack of affection, Cassio responds to her by remarking that he has been pressed by leaden thoughts "this while." "This while" could easily include the trip with Bianca in company. It has often been noted that Bianca fulfills the description of a Venetian courtezan, and this occupation would explain her likelihood in going to Venice and helps account for the seven-day reference. *Othello* has often been criticized for not providing sufficient time to allow for a climax of such a tragedy. If, however, Shakespeare intended a three-day time scheme, such criticisms lose their justification. *Othello* is a tragedy which depends on the interplay of black and white. Night brings tragic fears; the daylight brings a hope for happiness and often includes comic action. The day-night conflict moves to its ultimate tragedy on the third night as the doom of darkness overcomes its daylight opposition.

THE CHRISTIANNESS
OF *OTHELLO*

Although Othello is plainly Christian in some sense, it will not bear such an extreme interpretation that Othello is damned for his sins and that the audience must understand as much.* Many of the biblical allusions and analogues that various critics find in the play to support their contentions of its Christianness are dubious, and the interpretations made of them are extreme. For instance, the assumption that Lear's wanderings and his return to Cordelia are an analogue of the wanderings and return home of the Prodigal Son is

* Abstracted from Robert H. West, "The Christianness of *Othello*," *Shakespeare Quarterly*, XV (1964), 333-343.

a real strain on the dramatic fabric. Almost as much a strain is to suppose that the fall of Othello is a sufficient analogue to the fall of Adam for us to view Othello's fall securely as a decline into a literal hell. Nor can we safely conclude of Othello's evil acts that by Renaissance theological standards they are so surely mortal sin that they must be thought to damn him. The theology is abstract and discursive whereas the action of the play is concrete and immediate and theologically unexplicit. Still, *Othello* is Christian in a way. It makes the sort of appeal to the transcendental that may come from conviction that the universe is God's. We see love and guilt in *Othello* and a sort of justice. The characters often speak of them in Christian terms, refer them to divinity or to hell; and in a way the action sustains the reference. From Desdemona's love we cannot infer deity, nor hell from Othello's fault, but the love and the fault are positive all the same, dramatically absolute. Through them we sense divine justice. None of this requires, however, that the dramatist proclaim the eternal outcome of Othello's faults or establish an orthodox supernal ground for the tragedy. To make *Othello* a stamped and certified *exemplum* of Christian sin and punishment is to take half the art out of it and much of the honesty and most of the mystery.

the misanthrope
JEAN MOLIÈRE

TRANSLATED BY
HANS P. GUTH

CHARACTERS

ALCESTE, *the misanthrope*
PHILINTE, *until recently* ALCESTE'S *friend*
ORONTE, *gentleman of rank and part-time poet*
CÉLIMÈNE, *loved (with certain reservations) by* ALCESTE
ÉLIANTE, *friend and cousin of* CÉLIMÈNE
ACASTE ⎱ *men of distinction*
CLITANDRE ⎰
ARSINOÉ, *reputed to be a prude*
SERVANTS
AN OFFICER

act one
SCENE ONE. PHILINTE, ALCESTE.

PHILINTE. How now? What is wrong?
ALCESTE.   Please leave me alone.
PHILINTE. But please do explain your abruptness of tone . . .
ALCESTE. Please leave me, I say, and shame on your head.
PHILINTE. At least you should hear me without turning red . . .
ALCESTE. I *want* to turn red, and refuse you my ear.
PHILINTE. Well, I don't understand your temper, I fear,
And though we are friends, I must say at long last . . .

The Misanthrope by Molière, translated by Hans P. Guth, copyright 1961 by Hans P. Guth, and reprinted with his permission.

A NOTE ON THE TRANSLATION. Molière's play is familiar to most English readers in prose translations. These radically change the tone of the original, preserving the strongly satirical element but removing the playful elegance of Molière's verse. What in a prose translation is merely dull insistence on a point already made, in the original is often a high-spirited playing off of variations on a theme. On the other hand, a verse translation using the five-beat line of the familiar closed couplet ("Love in these labyrinths his slaves detains,/And mighty hearts are held in slender chains") makes Molière

ALCESTE (*rises abruptly*). Who, I? and your friend? That's a
thing of the past.
Up to now, it is true, to my heart you were dear,
But the traits that of late in your nature appear
Make me solemnly state that our friendship has ceased.
From a tainted attachment you see me released.
PHILINTE. I am then, Alceste, to blame in your eyes?
ALCESTE. All standards of honor your conduct defies.
For what you have done, no excuse can be found.
For remorse you should weep and your tears stain the ground.
I see how you greet like a dear, long-lost friend
A man on whose every word you attend;
You flatter and banter and put him at ease
And give to his hand the most violent squeeze;
And when I inquire: Who is he? For shame!
You hardly so much as remember his name!
As he leaves, your tender affections depart;
His back turned, your remarks strike a chill to the heart.
Just heavens! What cowardly, infamous role
To degrade and betray thus one's innermost soul.
And if, inadvertent, I had done the same,
I would hang myself straight and blot out my name.
PHILINTE. Myself, I don't think the offense merits hanging,
And respectfully hope, despite your haranguing,
That, a merciful judge, you will grant a delay
And let me stay clear of the noose, if I may.
ALCESTE. Your irony, Sir, is badly misplaced.
PHILINTE. How should I repair, then, my lapses of taste?
ALCASTE. Be sincere; by a strict code of honor abide;
Let in all that you say your heart be your guide.

---

sound like a French Alexander Pope, depriving him of his colloquial raciness
and nonchalance. The following translation uses a four-beat line that lends
itself both to conversational ease and to occasional flights of rhetoric. As with
other French verse drama of the seventeenth century, the reader of Molière's
Misanthrope must learn not to be hypnotized by the regularity of meter and
rhyme. He must learn to read not in couplets but in paragraphs, abandoning
himself freely to the rhetorical drive provided by indignation or malice. Once
meter and rhyme become familiar enough to be natural, they provide a delightful and unobtrusive counterpoint to the caprice, the sparkle, and the
exuberant good humor of Molière's play. [Hans P. Guth]

PHILINTE. When someone accosts me in glad-handed ease
I have to repay him in kind, if you please,
Respond as seems best to his jovial tirade
And pay compliments back for each compliment paid.

ALCESTE. No, no! I won't stand for this cowardly way
That with people of your persuasion bears sway,
And I hate from the heart the false front you describe,
The hollow routines of a frivolous tribe:
The cordial conveyors of untruths that flatter,
Obliging dispensers of valueless chatter,
Who warmly converse while the heart remains cool
And treat thus alike the sage and the fool.
What boots it if people receive me with zeal
And tenderly talk of the friendship they feel
And commend the way I talk and behave
And then do the same for an errant knave?
No, no! And no! Such a prostitute smile
Will never a true man of honor beguile.
Our friendship turns cheap if we ever intend
To cherish the world at large as our friend.
Esteem must select from the common run—
Esteem for all is esteem for none.
And since you adopt this vice of our age,
My affections from you I must disengage.
I refuse the promiscuous warmth of a soul
That denies to merit its central role.
To accept wholesale friendship I firmly decline;
Who befriends one and all is no friend of mine.

PHILINTE. But the world expects that we give to our acts
The civil exterior that custom exacts.

ALCESTE. No, no! We should chastise, upon its detection,
With merciless rigor all bogus affection.
We should speak man to man, and strive to reveal
In the words we pronounce the convictions we feel;
The heart should ever be heard; in no case
Should empty phrases our feelings debase.

PHILINTE. But to practice strict candor, you'll have to agree,
Would quite often be foolish, and painful to see,
And at times, whatever strict honor requires,

We must mask the feelings the world inspires.
Now, would it be fitting, or make people like us,
To let one and all know just how they strike us?
And if someone merits dislike or disgrace,
Should we tell him so openly, straight to his face?

   ALCESTE. Yes, indeed.

   PHILINTE.   You would want me to tell Colette
At her age she is foolish to play the coquette?
That her make-up is shocking beyond belief?

   ALCESTE. That's right.

   PHILINTE.   I would plunge vain Jacques into grief
And call his accounts, all heard before,
Of his family's glory a crashing bore?

   ALCESTE. Just so.

   PHILINTE.   But, surely you jest.

   ALCESTE.   I do not.
I refuse to spare the fool and the sot.
My eyes are offended; the court and the town
Are too full of the sights that compel me to frown.
My mood turns black, and my anger mounts
To hear of men's actions the daily accounts.
I find vile flattery ever in season—
Injustice, deception, selfishness, treason;
I quiver with rage, and feel strongly inclined
To challenge to battle all humankind.

   PHILINTE. Your high indignation is somewhat naïve
And I smile to see you thus chafe and grieve.
The world for you will not change its way—
And since you believe in frankness, today
I'll be frank myself, and thus let you know
You amuse those you meet, wherever you go;
And your fiery anger at custom's mild yoke
Has made you the butt of many a joke.

   ALCESTE. Of that I am glad. That tribute I treasure.
It's a very good sign, and gives me great pleasure.
The men of our times are so vile to my eyes
That I would be disturbed if they thought me wise.

   PHILINTE. Your displeasure at human nature is great.

   ALCESTE. I've developed for it a terrible hate.

PHILINTE. And all poor mortals, of every station,
Must equally share in this condemnation?
But you surely admit, there are those who call . . .
ALCESTE. I make no exception. I hate them all.
For some are actively bad and do wrong,
And the others still suffer this poisonous throng
And treat them with none of that vigorous scorn
That vice should inspire in the virtuous-born.
Such tolerance of the most vicious sort
Extends to the scoundrel I battle in court.
From behind his mask the traitor shines through,
And everyone knows what the rascal can do;
His obsequious manner, so clearly contrived,
Deceives only those who have newly arrived.
It is known that this crook, who to hell should be hurled,
Through dirty employment moved up in the world,
That his fortune, now grown so tall and so lush,
Causes merit to groan and virtue to blush.
Whatever opprobrious names he is called
Hardly anyone seems by his presence appalled!
Call him criminal, coward, rogue, and thief
And no one will register disbelief—
Yet his leer is welcomed without dismay;
Into every circle he worms his way.
The reward that should be some honest man's prize
Through intrigue he will snatch from under his eyes.
God help and protect us! I'm hurt to the quick
When people condone the shady and slick.
And at times the desire for being alone
Makes me yearn for a desert where man is unknown.
PHILINTE. O dear! Let us cease to mourn the world's plight
And see human nature in friendlier light;
As the rigorous critic its workings dissects
Let him make some allowance for venial defects.
A flexible virtue is what the world needs:
Strict wisdom too often due measure exceeds.
Good sense shuns extravagance even in honor
And bids us *love* virtue, not dote upon her.
A code austere and unforgiving

Is at odds with the mores of modern living;
It asks too much of mortal man.
We must follow the times as best we can.
Only foolish presumption would start a movement
To impose on the world a scheme for improvement.
Like yours, any day my eyes notice much
That could have been this way or might have been such;
But in spite of what daily thus crosses my way,
I do not (as would you) ever anger display.
I simply take men as they are; unlike you,
I accustom my soul to accept what they do.
Philosophical calm I aim to acquire
While you must breathe forth philosophical ire.

 ALCESTE. But this calm, dear Sir, who argue so well,
Will it never allow your anger to swell?
If a bosom friend to be false is shown,
If one schemes to despoil you of all that you own,
If one spreads ugly rumors to murder your name—
Will your equable temper stay ever the same?

 PHILINTE. I regard the defects of which you've complained
As vices in human nature ingrained,
And am no more incensed at the cold-blooded look
Of a self-seeking man, a rogue, or a crook
Than at vultures I see in their natural shapes,
Or ferocious wolves, or malicious apes.

 ALCESTE. I must then submit to be cheated and sold
Without that I should . . . but the views that you hold
Are so lax they leave me speechless with rage.

 PHILINTE. Indeed, to speak less you would be most sage.
To discuss your opponent in public forbear
And devote to your lawsuit all possible care.

 ALCESTE. I shall devote nothing; that much should be clear.

 PHILINTE. But to argue your case, who's been asked to appear?

 ALCESTE. Only Justice and Reason—no venal drudge.

 PHILINTE. You won't arrange to have lunch with the judge?

 ALCESTE. No. Why? Is my case maybe doubtful or wrong?

 PHILINTE. Not at all. But the schemer's resources are strong,
And . . .

 ALCESTE. No. I am firmly resolved to stand pat.

I am right, or I'm wrong.

PHILINTE.   Don't trust in that.

ALCESTE. I won't stir.

PHILINTE.   But your foe is cunning; prepare
To see him maneuver and plot . . .

ALCESTE.   I don't care.

PHILINTE. You're deceived.

ALCESTE.   Maybe so. I'll do as I choose.

PHILINTE. And yet . . .

ALCESTE.   I would rather be right and lose.

PHILINTE. But at least . . .

ALCESTE.   No more. I shall learn through this case
If it's true that men are criminal, base,
Perverse, and corrupt to such a degree
As to treat me unjustly for all to see.

PHILINTE. What a man!

ALCESTE.   I'd prefer, no matter the cost
To have proved my point, though the suit was lost.

PHILINTE. Ah, people would snigger and laugh with disdain
If they could but hear you hold forth in this vein.

ALCESTE. The worse for the scoffers.

PHILINTE.   But tell me, Alceste,
The standard that passes your rigorous test—
That unflinching honor to which you aspire—
Is it found in the woman you love and admire?
I'm astonished, for one, that although it seems
You denounce mankind, its customs and schemes,
Though you claim it is steeped in all you decry,
You have found in its ranks what charms your eye.
And one thing surprises me even more:
Your remarkable choice of a girl to adore.
Sincere Éliante has a weakness for you;
Arsinoé, the prude, but waits for her cue:
Your heart receives them with frigid reserve
While Célimène makes it her private preserve—
Whose malicious wit and coquettish play
Are much in accord with the trends of the day.
If you hate our age, does your lady fair
Of your vehement censure receive her share?

Do these faults lose their taint in a shape so sweet?
Are you blind as a lover, or merely discreet?

ALCESTE. No. The love this young widow inspires me to feel
Has not blinded my eyes to the faults you reveal.
I am, whatever my heart objects,
The first one to see and condemn her defects.
But despite all this my love does not cease.
I confess my weakness: she knows how to please.
I may notice in her what is worthy of blame,
But in spite of her faults to my heart she lays claim.
Her appeal is too strong, and my love will cast out
These faults of the times from her heart no doubt.

PHILINTE. If in that you succeed, you'll be famed among men.—
She returns your love, I may take it then?

ALCESTE. Of course, or else I would not be here.

PHILINTE. But if she has shown whom she clearly prefers,
Why then do your rivals annoy you so much?

ALCESTE. A true loving heart can share nothing with such.
And my coming here today is designed
To allow me to tell her this weighs on my mind.

PHILINTE. As for me, if I yearned for love's sweet prize,
I'd address to Éliante, her cousin, my sighs.
Her heart (which esteems you) is loyal and true;
Such a choice would be happy and fitting for you.

ALCESTE. You are right. And my reason agrees every day.
But then reason in love holds but little sway.

PHILINTE. I'm disturbed, and fear for the hope you show.

SCENE TWO. ORONTE, ALCESTE, PHILINTE.

ORONTE. When I asked for them, I was told below
That Éliante is out, and Célimène too;
But since I was told I would still find you,
I've come up to express with sincerest zeal
The enormous esteem that for you I feel.
I have always hoped you would in the end
Know my ardent desire to become your friend.
My heart is eager to recognize worth
And would trade for your friendship all else on this earth;

And you, I am sure without condition
Will accept a friend of my position.

(*During* ORONTE's *speech,* ALCESTE *seems absent-minded and acts as if he does not realize he is being addressed. He takes notice only when* ORONTE *says to him*)
It is you, if you please, who are thus addressed.

ALCESTE. I, Sir?

ORONTE.   Yes, you. You are not distressed?

ALCESTE. Not at all. But I'm struck by surprise, I must say,
And I did not expect to be honored this way.

ORONTE. You should not be surprised at the love you inspire;
In your presence, the world cannot help but admire.

ALCESTE. Dear Sir . . .

ORONTE.   You surpass in merit, I claim,
The bearer of many a famous name.

ALCESTE. Dear Sir . . .

ORONTE.   Yes, indeed. To me you're endeared
As much as the finest the country has reared.

ALCESTE. Dear Sir . . .

ORONTE.   I really mean every word.
Allow me to show you how deeply I'm stirred,
To clasp to my bosom a long-cherished friend
And ask you forever on me to depend.
Take my hand, I beg you. May I, with respect
Call you brother and friend?

ALCESTE.   Dear Sir . . .

ORONTE.   You object?

ALCESTE. To accept such generous praise I am loath;
And friendship requires a more gradual growth—
One surely profanes its holy name
When friend and acquaintance are one and the same.
Such knots should be tied with forethought and care;
To get better acquainted we ought to prepare:
We might differ so widely in standards or taste
As to make us too late repent of our haste.

ORONTE. How well you put it! How wise and true!
Your words but increase my regard for you.
Let us leave it to time then to strengthen our bond;
But meanwhile I'm yours, and hope you'll respond

By leaving to me your concerns in high places.
As you know, I enjoy the King's good graces.
He listens to me, and indeed, I must say
Is most kind to me in every way.
In short, I am yours with all my might;
And because you will judge profoundly and right,
I am going to show you, to strengthen our ties,
A sonnet I've written and as you advise
It shall perish or see the light of day.

ALCESTE. Dear Sir, I am hardly the man to say.
Please excuse me.

ORONTE.   But why?

ALCESTE.   I have the defect
To be somewhat franker than people expect.

ORONTE. That is just what I want. And I would complain
If when asked for your candid response you should feign
Approval or pleasure, just to be kind.

ALCESTE. If such is your wish, I shall speak my mind.

ORONTE. "A Sonnet . . ." (it's a sonnet). "To Hope . . ." (I allude
To hope inspired by a lady I wooed).
"To Hope . . ." These verses aren't meant to be grand
But tender and sweet, you will understand.

ALCEST. We shall see.

ORONTE.   "To Hope . . ." I'm afraid that the style
By its awkward spots might cause you to smile,
And I hope you will find the thoughts well phrased.

ALCESTE. We shall shortly know.

ORONTE.   I was much amazed
It took but a quarter hour, I recall.

ALCESTE. The time is not the issue at all.

ORONTE. (*Reads*) Hope, it is true, gives solace
And beguiles a few moments with laughter,
But Phyllis, what unhappy comfort,
If nothing follows thereafter!

PHILINTE. Ah, how these verses charm and delight!

ALCESTE (*aside to* PHILINTE). Can you shamelessly tolerate stuff
    so trite?

ORONTE. At first you were gracious to me,
But why did you thus incline

If it was your cruel will
With mere hope to let me repine?

 PHILINTE. How elegantly these phrases are turned!

 ALCESTE. (*aside to* PHILINTE). Great God! Vile dissembler! Such
  stuff should be burned.

 ORONTE. If such eternal waiting
   Should push my zeal to extremes
   To expire I calmly prepare.
   Your concern would be unavailing:
   Such desperate hope, it seems,
   Dear Phyllis, make hope despair.

 PHILINTE. The close is tender and not at all lame.

 ALCESTE. (*aside*). A plague on your close, in the devil's name!
I wish you were safely confined and enclosed!

 PHILINTE. I've never heard verses so well composed.

 ALCESTE (*aside*). The nerve!

 ORONTE (*to* PHILINTE).   You flatter, and if I may say . . .

 PHILINTE. I do not.

 ORONTE (*aside*). Yes, you do! and cheat and betray.

 ORONTE (*to* ALCESTE). But you, Sir, remember to what you agreed.
Tell us frankly, I pray, what your taste has decreed.

 ALCESTE. Here indeed a delicate question is raised.
Creative talents desire to be praised.
But once to a person (whose name I won't mention)
I said when his verses came to my attention
That a man must be armed against the bite
Of the sudden passion he feels to write;
That he must control the importunate urge
In the flood of his verses his friends to submerge;
That the would-be author in quest of his goal
Runs the risk of playing an unfitting role.

 ORONTE. Are you trying to say that the verses I read
Would have better remained . . .

 ALCESTE.   That's not what I said.
Him I told: frigid writing is cold-blooded crime,
And just this one fault is enough in our time
To lower the worthiest man in all eyes—
It is just such defects that the world decries.

 ORONTE. Do you find that my verses are not for these times?

ALCESTE. That's not what I said. But, to help stop his rhymes,
I reminded him strongly that now and then
Such thirst for glory has spoiled able men.

ORONTE. Are my verses then bad? Do you class me with these?

ALCESTE. That's not what I said. *Him* I asked: if you please,
What brings to your eye the ominous glint,
What devil compels you to break into print?
The only bad authors who find us forgiving
Are unfortunate wretches who write for a living.
So take my advice: resist the temptation;
Don't expose yourself to such recrimination;
And do not exchange so rashly your claim
To solid repute and an honest name
For the title some publishers gladly purvey
Of a poor foolish author sans praise and sans pay.
This was what I tried to make him see.

ORONTE. Very well. You indeed are candid with me.
But if you were asked how my poem would rank . . .

ALCESTE. I would quietly file it, to be quite frank.
You have followed bad models, as authors are prone,
And your phrases quite lack a natural tone.
For what do you mean: "beguiles with laughter,"
Or what about this: "Nothing follows thereafter."

> (*Mimics*) To expire I calmly prepare.
> Such desperate hope, it seems,
> Dear Phyllis, makes hope despair.

This flowery style of which people are fond
Is far from true feeling and nature's bond.
You are playing with words; it's quite insincere,
And nature knows no such affected leer.
The awful taste of our time gives one pause;
Our parents more wisely bestowed their applause,
And I prize much less what all now admire
Than an old-fashioned song I learned from my sire:

> If the king were to say,
> "Take Paris; it's thine"
> And asked me to leave
> My sweetheart behind,

> I would say, "Sir King,
> Not for me your bequest;
> My girl I love best, heigh ho!
> My girl I love best."

The rhyme is defective, the style somewhat old,
But surely it's better, a hundred fold,
Than these trivial rhymes where good sense is alseep,
And surely here feeling is pure and deep?

> (*Hums or sings sotto voce*)
> If the king were to say,
> "Take Paris; it's thine"
> And asked me to leave
> My sweetheart behind,
> I would say, "Sir King,
> Not for me your bequest;
> My girl I love best, heigh ho!
> My girl I love best."

Yes, such is the language that comes from the heart.
(*To* PHILINTE, *who is smiling*) You sophisticates laugh at its lack
    of art.
Yet I treasure these simple lines much more
Than the glittering trifles that all adore.

ORONTE. As for me, I maintain that my verses are fine.

ALCESTE. For good cause you no doubt to this verdict incline.
But for other good cause, which I hope you'll respect
Such a flattering judgment you see me reject.

ORONTE. While others praise them, I'm pleased with my lot.

ALCESTE. They know how to flatter, and I do not.

ORONTE. You pride yourself on your agile wit.

ALCESTE. To find cause for praise, I'd need plenty of it.

ORONTE. I can do quite well *without* your acclaim.

ALCESTE. You will have to, because I won't furnish the same.

ORONTE. What verses could you, if faced with the task,
Produce on this theme, I should like to ask.

ALCESTE. I could, if I would, write lines just as poor,
Though I would not expose them to view, I am sure.

ORONTE. You are most self-assured; your superior tone . . .

ALCESTE. Let others adore you; leave *me* alone.

ORONTE. But, my dear little man, come off your high horse.

ALCESTE. I'll stay on, my big boy, and pursue my own course.

PHILINTE (*comes between them*): But please, my dear Sirs, that's
enough for today.

ORONTE. I am leaving right now. I did wrong to stay.
Please accept, dear Sir, my most humble respect.

ALCESTE. And receive, dear Sir, my regards most abject.

(ORONTE *leaves.*)

SCENE THREE. PHILINTE, ALCESTE.

PHILINTE. There you have it! Be ranker than men can bear
And at once you're embroiled in a tedious affair.
The vanity of Oronte is such . . .

ALCESTE. Don't say any more.

PHILINTE.   But . . .

ALCESTE.   I've had too much.

PHILINTE. But indeed . . .

ALCESTE.   Please leave me.

PHILINTE.   But let . . .

ALCESTE.   No talk.

PHILINTE. But at least . . .

ALCESTE.   I won't listen.

PHILINTE.   The way you balk . . .

ALCESTE. Don't follow me, Go! Stop pulling my sleeve.

PHILINTE. You are not yourself. I refuse to leave.

act two

SCENE ONE. ALCESTE, CÉLIMÈNE.

ALCESTE. You must, dear friend, give me leave to complain.
The way you behave gives me reason for pain:
Too often your thoughtlessness raises my gall;
Some day we shall separate once and for all.
I shall not deceive you with sugared pretense—
I feel I'll be forced with your love to dispense,
And in spite of all promises you would have heard
I might not be able to honor my word.

CÉLIMÈNE. It's to quarrel with me, I note with dismay,
That you've wanted to come and see me today.
    ALCESTE. I don't quarrel at all. But your generous soul
To all comers, dear Madam, presents itself whole.
Too many suitors beleaguer your door;
I won't share you with every officious bore.
    CÉLIMÈNE. Why should I be blamed for the suitors you see?
Can I stop all these people from taking to me?
And if someone pleads for a share of my time
Should I reach for a stick to punish his crime?
    ALCESTE. A stick, dear Madam, is not what you need
But a heart from too facile a tenderness freed.
True, your charms go with you wherever you walk,
But those lured by your looks are egged on by your talk;
And your kind reception (of those I despise)
Completes the conquest begun by your eyes.
The radiant smile you offer to each
Gives hope to every diligent leech.
If you were to appear more discreetly wise
You would soon extinguish their amorous sighs.
But at least, dear Madam, do tell in what way
Your Clitandre so pleases and charms you, I pray.
On what solid foundation of worth and of skill
Do you build the esteem you are granting him still?
Is his letting his graceful fingernails grow
The cause of the signal fondness you show?
Have you joined those victims of fashion's cant
Whom the dazzling charms of his wig enchant?
Does his dandyish garb assure him of grace?
Does he conquer with masses of ribbon and lace?
Has he earned by the elegant cut of his pants
That servitude sweet that a woman grants?
Have his oily smile, his falsetto voice
Been attractive enough to determine your choice?
    CÉLIMÈNE. How unjustly you censure the course I pursue!
Why I humor the man is no secret to you;
For he and his friends will lend me support
To help win the case I have pending in court.
    ALCESTE. It were better to lose, if it came to the test,

Than to humor a rival I must detest.

CÉLIMÈNE. The whole world now attracts your jealous abuse!

ALCESTE. The whole world shares alike in your kindness profuse.

CÉLIMÈNE. Just that point should appease your tempestuous soul
Since my tender regard goes to none as a whole.
There would be juster cause for all this ado
If I spread it less widely than now I do.

ALCESTE. But I whom excessively jealous you call,
What is mine, may I ask, that's not shared by them all?

CÉLIMÈNE. The bliss of knowing my love for you.

ALCESTE. How can I convince my heart it is true?

CÉLIMÈNE. I think if I say as much to your face
My word should be more than enough in this case.

ALCESTE. But how do I know that as part of the game
All the others might not have been told the same?

CÉLIMÈNE. Your style as a lover is sweet indeed!
And how highly you think of the life that I lead!
Well then! just to grant you relief from your care
I deny the esteem I've been rash to declare;
Now none will deceive you but you alone.
Good luck!

ALCESTE. Oh, why isn't my heart made of stone?
If only my soul could regain its ease
I would thank and bless the gods on my knees.
I admit it freely. I ever try
To set myself free from this terrible tie,
But my strongest efforts are all in vain:
For my sins, I am sure, I thus groan and complain.

CÉLIMÈNE. Your ardor, indeed, is an unequaled one.

ALCESTE. Yes, it is. On this point I will yield to none.
For no one can fathom my love for you,
And never has anyone loved as I do.

CÉLIMÈNE. Your method is startling and new, I agree,
For it seems that you court me to quarrel with me.
Your love takes the form of tantrum and whim
And never before was passion so grim.

ALCESTE. But it is in your power to stop all my grief.
Let us bury right now our disputes; and in brief
Let us open our hearts, and at once let's begin. . . .

SCENE TWO. CÉLIMÈNE, ALCESTE, BASQUE.

CÉLIMÈNE. What is it?
BASQUE.   Acaste is below.
CÉLIMÈNE.   Show him in.

SCENE THREE. CÉLIMÈNE, ALCESTE.

ALCESTE. Indeed! Are we ever alone at all?
Forever you're ready to see those who call!
For this once, it seems you might change your routine
And inform your Acaste you're not to be seen.
    CÉLIMÈNE. And affront him by having him sent away?
    ALCESTE. Your concern as usual is aimed the wrong way.
    CÉLIMÈNE. He's a man who would never forgive me the slight
Of my having denied myself to his sight.
    ALCESTE. But why should you care about what he may feel . . .
    CÉLIMÈNE. Why indeed! His good will is worth a great deal.
He is one of those who—I don't know how or why—
Count for much in the King's and the public's eye.
Their constant meddling I watch with alarm;
They do us no good, but they *can* do us harm.
And no matter what other support we may find,
We should never offend loud-mouthed men of his kind.
    ALCESTE. Well and good. As I only too well recall
You find reasons to suffer the presence of all;
And your pretexts, albeit transparently thin . . .

SCENE FOUR. ALCESTE, CÉLIMÈNE, BASQUE.

BASQUE. Clitandre has come, if you please.
CÉLIMÈNE.   Show him in.
    (*To* ALCESTE, *who is leaving*) You are off?
ALCESTE.   Yes indeed.
CÉLIMÈNE.   Please remain.
ALCESTE.   But why?
CÉLIMÈNE. Please stay.
ALCESTE.   But I can't.
CÉLIMÈNE.   I insist.
ALCESTE.   I won't try.

You are set for a long conversational bout.
It's unfair to require me to sweat it out.

CÉLIMÈNE. I insist, I insist!

ALCESTE.   I'll be bored to tears.

CÉLIMÈNE. All right, leave! You must have your way, it appears.

SCENE FIVE. ÉLIANTE, PHILINTE, ACASTE, ALCESTE, CLITANDRE, CÉLIMÈNE, BASQUE.

ÉLIANTE (*to* CÉLIMÈNE). I have brought two distinguished friends, as you see.
But you knew we were here.

CÉLIMÈNE.   Yes, indeed (*To* BASQUE) Chairs for three.
(*To* ALCESTE) Still not gone?

ALCESTE.   No, not yet. I shall leave on condition
That for them or for me you announce your decision.

CÉLIMÈNE. Oh, be still.

ALCESTE.   Today you'll announce who will lose.

CÉLIMÈNE. You are out of your mind.

ALCESTE.   Not at all. You shall choose.

CÉLIMÈNE. Indeed!

ALCESTE.   You'll declare to whom you belong.

CÉLIMÈNE. You are pleased to be gay.

ALCESTE.   I've been patient too long.

CLITANDRE. I have just seen Cléonte, no sage as a rule,
In full view of the King act the absolute fool.
Let us hope a kind friend will one of these days
Point out to the man his impossible ways.

CÉLIMÈNE. It is true, his manners amaze and amuse;
And his bumbling behavior is hard to excuse.
And the passage of time, it is to be feared,
Far from softening his traits only makes them more weird.

ACASTE. Good grief! Since we're speaking of men who appall,
I have just shaken off the most tiresome of all:
Damon, the great talker, an hour or more
Made me roast in the sun at my carriage door.

CÉLIMÈNE. Strange creature, who always crosses one's way
And though making great speeches has nothing to say!
His weighty pronouncements lack meaning; and hence

One hears the noise but misses the sense.

ÉLIANTE (*to* PHILINTE). Not bad for a start; in this gay little chat
One's neighbors are treated as mice by the cat.

CLITANDRE. Timante, dear Madam, is also quite queer.

CÉLIMÈNE. The desire for importance has spoiled him, poor dear.
With preoccupied air he strides into view
And acts always most busy—with nothing to do.
Whatever he says, he looks solemn and grave,
Frowns and hems fit to kill—what a way to behave!—
Forever butts in to confide something awful
(What's a scandal to him as a rule is quite lawful).
He makes secrets of trifles and will by and by
Confidentially whisper "hello" and "good-by."

ACASTE. And Gerald, dear Madam?

CÉLIMÈNE.   What teller of tales!
He has always just dined with the Prince of Wales.
In his talk, he frequents the great of this earth;
If one isn't a duchess, one has little worth.
He is charmed by a title, and talks without end
Of the horses and dogs of some blue-blooded friend.
The most noble and rich are "Dear Marge" and "Old Jim";
As if "Sir" and "Mylady" were noxious to him.

CLITANDRE. With Bélise, it is said, he gets along well.

CÉLIMÈNE. Oh, how lacking in wit and how tongue-tied a belle!
Her calls are ordeals for whose passing I pray.
In cold sweat one searches for something to say;
Her lack of the powers of communication
Effectively stifles all conversation.
Her silence is solid, and, dumb as a wall,
She resists all clichés that the mind can recall.
The sun, the rain, or the wintry blast—
One tries hard to make their discussion last,
But her visit, which calls for all of one's strength,
Stretches out to the most unbearable length.
One yawns like a person about to expire,
And yet like a log she stays put by the fire.

ACASTE. And what of Adraste?

CÉLIMÈNE.   Presumption extreme!
He's a person inflated with self-esteem.

He forever claims virtues the world fails to see
And reviles for their blindness the powers that be.
No matter what post someone else obtains
He claims he was slighted and mopes and complains.

CLITANDRE. And what of Cleon, at whose house you may meet
All the people who count—don't you think he is sweet?

CÉLIMÈNE. He has hired a cook who's unusually able,
And the people who visit him visit his table.

ÉLIANTE. He *does* provide most magnificent food.

CÉLIMÈNE. But the last course of all quite ruins one's mood:
The poor fool, by presenting himself for dessert,
Quite spoils all the pleasure the chef has conferred.

PHILINTE. On his uncle Damis a man can depend.
What of him?

CÉLIMÈNE. I have always esteemed him my friend.

PHILINTE. He seems wise and enjoys universal respect.

CÉLIMÈNE. He tries hard to seem witty—which is a defect.
In the absence of any genuine spark
He labors and strains for the clever remark.
He decided that brilliance through scorn best is shown
And his every word turned sardonic in tone.
With all that he reads, he finds fault; I believe
He assumes that to praise is passé and naïve,
That one proves one's acumen by withering looks,
That only a fool would *enjoy* reading books,
And that by sophisticates he is preferred
Who looks down on what pleases the common herd.
Yes, even mere chit-chat incurs his disdain;
One's passing remarks he finds banal and vain;
And crossing his arms, his answers most terse,
With infinite pity he lets one converse.

ACASTE. I'll be damned. That's him! That's the man to a *T!*

CLITANDRE (*to* CÉLIMÈNE). How precisely you paint the people
you see!

ALCESTE. That's it, my dear friends! Strike again! Twist the knife!
Let everyone join; and spare no one's life.
Yet as soon as your victim but shows his face,
You hasten to offer your cordial embrace;
And pumping his arm, you swear and protest

How you love and prefer him to all the rest.

CLITANDRE. Why blame *us?* If these lively portraits offend
You should aim your complaint at your charming friend.

ALCESTE. No, it's you that I blame. Your gleeful assent
Draws her out and confirms her satirical bent.
Her malicious tongue grows more agile and pert
As you cheer whatever she's pleased to assert.
In her acid critiques she'd be certain to pause
If for once she should notice a dearth of applause.
Those who flatter, like you, are always to blame
For the vices that earn us dishonor and shame.

PHILINTE. But why take the side of the people we mention,
Who fare worse when they come to *your* attention?

CÉLIMÈNE. Very true! How forever he must contradict!
Where all are agreed he states views that conflict;
He must always give voice to that obstinate pride
That at once makes him champion the opposite side.
The ideas of others are bound to displease;
Dissent is with him a chronic disease.
He assumes that the world would value him less
If he ever should falter and simply say "yes."
He loves contradiction as misers their pelf
And will often in fact contradict himself.
He will charge at his own opinions with force
If ever he hears them when others discourse.

ALCESTE. As always the scoffers applaud what you say.
You are pleased to taunt me, and well you may.

PHILINTE. However, it's true, you are quick to slap down
Whatever one says; and you equally frown
At whatever one showers with ample applause
And whatever one censures, though both with good cause.

ALCESTE. That's because men won't ever base judgments on reason;
One's anger against them is always in season.
To whatever profession or trade they belong,
Their praise and their censures are equally wrong.

CÉLIMÈNE. But . . .

ALCESTE.   No, dear Madam, and come what may,
You amuse yourself in a blameable way;
And it's wrong to encourage in you with glee

Those deplorable flaws that all can see.

CLITANDRE. I don't know about that—and indeed I object
That to me, for one, she's without a defect.

ACASTE. I can see she is blessed with charm and with grace;
If she has any flaws, they don't show in her face.

ALCESTE. They show clearly enough. And rather than hide them
The more that I love her, the more I must chide them.
A suitor does wrong to be meek as a dove:
To chastise is truly a labor of love.
And I'd spurn any lover—as everyone ought—
Who'd officiously echo my every thought,
Who would always appease me, and flatter, and coo,
And praise to the skies whatever I do.

CÉLIMÈNE. In effect, if to change us but lay in your power,
We would in true love turn all sweet into sour,
And to show tender passion it would be quite right
To insult those we love, with all our might.

ÉLIANTE. As a rule, true love takes a different course.
From passing their choice, our lovers turn hoarse.
Their passion affects their vision, it seems,
And all is most fair in the girl of their dreams.
Her very defects are transformed in this game
And often assume a most flattering name.
The pale one is "white as a lily"; and yet
The swarthy one is "an attractive brunette,"
The skinny one "slender" or "girlish of figure,"
The fat one "majestic" (the more so the bigger).
The untidy one, void of what stimulates passion,
Is a girl whose "beauty departs from the fashion."
The tall one looks down with a goddess's face;
The short one looks up with most delicate grace.
The insolent one has a "noble mind";
The rogue is "vivacious"; the stupid one "kind."
The gossipy one shows "a sociable heart";
The tongue-tied one's "modesty" sets her apart.
And thus our lovers, their ardor extreme,
Love us not as we are but such as we seem.

ALCESTE. And yet . . .

CÉLIMÈNE.   Why persist in this line of thought?

Shall we move and look at some pictures I bought?
You're not going, my friends?

CLITANDRE AND ACASTE.   Oh, no. We shall stay.

ALCESTE (*to* CÉLIMÈNE). You're terribly worried they'll leave, I must say.
(*To the others*) Whatever your plans, I should like you to know
That *I* shall remain until after you go.

ACASTE. Unless I should be in our hostess's way
It so happens, dear friend, that I have all day.

CLITANDRE. Except to attend on the King tonight
I don't think I've a single appointment in sight.

CÉLIMÈNE (*to* ALCESTE). You're being facetious.

ALCESTE.   Of those you receive
We shall find if it's me that you'd like to see leave.

SCENE SIX. ALCESTE, CÉLIMÈNE, ÉLIANTE, ACASTE, PHILINTE, CLITANDRE, BASQUE.

BASQUE. Someone asked for you, Sir, and insists you must know
What his message is before you go.

ALCESTE. Reply that I'm busy; his message can wait.

BASQUE. His uniform's gay with tassel and plait,
And his badge shines like gold.

CÉLIMÈNE (*to* ALCESTE).   You had better go see.
Or let him come in.

SCENE SEVEN. ALCESTE, CÉLIMÈNE, ACASTE, PHILINTE, CLITANDRE, A UNIFORMED OFFICER.

ALCESTE (*to the* OFFICER). You are looking for me?

OFFICER. Let us step aside, if you will be so kind.

ALCESTE. Please speak up and inform me of what's on your mind.

OFFICER. Well, then; you will see that my summons is clear:
In front of the Marshal you'll have to appear,
Dear sir.

ALCESTE.   Who me?

OFFICER.   That's correct.

ALCESTE.   To what end?

PHILINTE. It's the quarrel you had with your poet-friend.

CÉLIMÈNE (*to* PHILINTE). What's that?

PHILINTE. He insulted Oronte when distraught
By some little verses the latter had brought.
If now settled, their feud won't come to a head.

ALCESTE. I shall not retract one word that I said.

PHILINTE. But you'll have to appear; you had better go.

ALCESTE. But what is there to settle, I'd like to know?
And shall I be made, by official constraint,
To admire the poem that caused this complaint?
On this point I have not at all changed my mind;
It is thoroughly bad.

PHILINTE. You could try to be kind . . .

ALCESTE. I refuse to retreat. The lines were absurd.

PHILINTE. You'll express your regret and admit that you erred.
Come along.

ALCESTE. I'll go, but no words you might waste
Can make me recant.

PHILINTE. We had better make haste.

ALCESTE. Unless a royal decree is proclaimed
To make me approve of the verses I blamed,
I'll maintain, so help me! they're void of all worth
And that poets so bad should be wiped off the earth.
(*To* CLITANDRE *and* ACASTE, *who are laughing*) The devil! What
    laughter, my friends, and what sport
At my humble expense.

CÉLIMÈNE. Be off, and report
Where you must.

ALCESTE. I am going there now. After that
I'll return so we two can finish our chat.

act three

SCENE ONE. CLITANDRE, ACASTE.

CLITANDRE. Dear Marquis, old man, you appear well at ease;
All strive to amuse you, and none to displease.
But tell me at once, wishful thinking aside,
Do you have solid grounds for your joy and your pride?

ACASTE. God knows, I don't see when I look at my fate
The slightest occasion for grumbling or hate.

I am rich, I am young, and descend, as you know,
From a house whose rank is indeed far from low;
And my family's name is such that with ease
I could aim at whatever position I please.
As for stoutness of heart—which all must admire—
I am hardly deficient in generous fire.
I have shown, I may say, if it comes to the test
I can manfully shoot it out with the best.
I have wit and good taste, so much so indeed
I discuss and condemn even books I don't read.
A new play makes me haunt foyer and backstage,
Where I shine in my role of critic and sage.
In a beautiful passage when actors excel
I will clap and shout bravo! to break the spell.
I am clever, look handsome; my smile is heartfelt,
My teeth brilliant white, my hips strong but svelte.
In matters of dress, I can say without fear
You'd be hard put indeed to discover my peer.
That I'm highly esteemed by all you can tell:
The women pursue me; the King likes me well.
With such traits, I believe, dear Marquis, old man,
One can live in content one's allotted span.

CLITANDRE. Hm—but sure elsewhere of all women's applause,
Why expend your sighs here, in a hopeless cause?

ACASTE. I—and hopeless? Well, well! I assure you I don't
Breathe passionate love if I'm sure that *she* won't.
No, a man of mean talents and meaner fame
May in anguish adore a disdainful dame,
Go down on his knees when his suit is delayed,
Draw on tears and on amorous sighs for aid,
And attempt to obtain through a siege long drawn out
What at first was denied the presumptuous lout.
But the man of distinction has far too much sense
To present his love free and bear all the expense.
No matter how dazzling a beauty may be,
I believe that, thank God! I'm as precious as she.
And if she is destined to conquer my heart,
It appears only fair that she should do her part;
And at least, to conform to the rules of fair play,

She had better be ready to meet me halfway.

CLITANDRE. And you think Célimène will be glad to conform?

ACASTE. I've no reason to think she departs from the norm.

CLITANDRE. To see you so wrong I'm sincerely aggrieved.
You are blind to the truth and are badly deceived.

ACASTE. It is true, I'm deceived, and I'm blind, as you say.

CLITANDRE. Let me ask what has bolstered your hopes, if I may.

ACASTE. I'm deceived.

CLITANDRE.   What inspires this exuberant mood?

ACASTE. I am blind.

CLITANDRE.   Have you proofs of how well you have wooed?

ACASTE. As I say, I'm a fool.

CLITANDRE.   What did she reveal?
Has she told you in secret just how she may feel?

ACASTE. She maltreats me.

CLITANDRE.   Be frank to a friend true and tried.

ACASTE. I'm forever repulsed.

CLITANDRE.   All joking aside:
Let me know at once what mine you have struck.

ACASTE. I'm the desolate one, and you are in luck.
Her aversion for me is indeed without measure,
And some day I shall hang myself just for her pleasure.

CLITANDRE. Well, well. But, my friend, befall what may,
Let us settle this matter the amiable way:
Whoever can show certain proof on his part
That he's clearly preferred in Célimène's heart,
Let the other make way; let it be understood
He'll remove himself from the contest for good.

ACASTE. Ah, well put! Thus speaks the voice of true love.
I agree to the terms as listed above.
But quiet!

SCENE TWO. CÉLIMÈNE, ACASTE, CLITANDRE.

CÉLIMÈNE. Still here?

CLITANDRE.   Love forbids us to go.

CÉLIMÈNE. I think I just heard a carriage below.
Who is it?

CLITANDRE. Who knows?

SCENE THREE. CÉLIMÈNE, ACASTE, CLITANDRE, BASQUE.

BASQUE.   Arsinoé would fain
Have a word with you.
    CÉLIMÈNE.   That woman again?
    BASQUE. Éliante below entertains your guest.
    CÉLIMÈNE. What on earth does she want? What attracts this pest?
    ACASTE. She's renowned as a terrible prude, you know,
And her high moral zest . . .
    CÉLIMÈNE.   Yes, indeed—all for show!
In her heart she is worldly; her greatest desire
Is to hook some poor man, though her schemes all misfire.
When another of numerous lovers makes light,
She can't help turning green with sheer envious spite.
That her pitiful person's ignored by the world
Is the clue to the angry indictments she's hurled;
And in vain with the prude's censorious speech
Does she cover the fact she's avoided by each.
To protect her poor person from slighting attacks
She denounces as vile the appeal that she lacks;
And yet she would welcome a lover with zest!
And has even been known to make eyes at Alceste.
The fact that he loves me annoys her no end,
And she feels I have stolen her predestined friend.
Her jealous dislike, which she hides very ill,
Shows in many a token of spite and ill-will;
And where I am concerned, she turns stupid with rage.
Her impertinent tricks would fill many a page,
And . . .

SCENE FOUR. ARSINOÉ, CÉLIMÈNE, CLITANDRE, ACASTE.

    CÉLIMÈNE. How nice you could come! If you only knew
How warmly I often have thought of you.
    ARSINOÉ. I've come over to tell you some things you should hear.
    CÉLIMÈNE. What a genuine pleasure to see you appear!
    (CLITANDRE *and* ACASTE *walk off, laughing.*)

SCENE FIVE. ARSINOÉ, CÉLIMÈNE.

ARSINOÉ. Their leaving just now is most opportune.
CÉLIMÈNE. Please sit down.
ARSINOÉ.   No thanks, I'll be going quite soon.
Dear Madame, our friendship, if earnest and great,
Must show in the things that carry most weight.
And since there's no need that could be more acute
Than to safeguard one's honor and good repute,
I shall mention your own reputation to you
As a service I feel as a friend is your due;
For among some very fine people last night
Your person by chance did some comment incite.
And your conduct, dear Madam—the splash that you make—
Was regrettably thought to be quite a mistake.
The crowd that seems never for long to depart,
Your constant flirtations, the rumors they start—
All these found their critics, by virtue inspired,
And rather more strict than I could have desired.
As you well can imagine, I felt dismayed
And did all that I could to come to your aid.
I protested that all your intentions were pure,
That we all of your goodness of heart could be sure;
Even so, you admit, there are things in our lives
That are hard to excuse, though one earnestly strives;
And I found myself forced to make the concession
That your conduct creates a—dubious impression.
It appears to all in unfortunate light,
And one hears the unpleasantest stories recite;
And if ever your sober judgment prevails
You will give less occasion to bearers of tales.
I am sure there is nothing unethical—No!
May heaven protect me from wronging you so!
But it's easy to think of one's neighbor as vicious;
Private virtue is wasted when all are suspicious.
Dear Madam, I know you're too just and too kind
Not to view this advice with an equable mind,
To ascribe it to aught but the diligent zeal
Of a friend whose devotion is such as I feel.

CÉLIMÈNE. Dear Madam, I'm heartily grateful for this,
And so far from my taking your warning amiss,
I shall hasten to show my sincere appreciation
And in turn shall discuss with you *your* reputation.
Since you show your devotion by saving each word
Of the rumors about me you chance to have heard,
Let me follow your kind example. I, too,
Hear such tales—I'll repeat what they say about *you*.
Not too long ago, for a visit, I went
To a house that the very best people frequent.
They discussed what manner of life is the best,
And your name, as it happened, was dropped by a guest.
But none of those present, alas! seemed to feel
Of your noisy crusades the inherent appeal.
The grave airs you put on, and the tedious vein
In which of our low moral tone you complain,
The finicky taste by which you are spurred
To find vaguely suggestive an innocent word,
Your complacent belief that *you* pass every test,
And those looks full of pity you cast on the rest,
Your continual lectures, the faults that you find
In what's harmless and pure to the well-balanced mind—
Dear Madam, all these, if I may be so candid,
Were censured more strictly than justice demanded.
What's the point (so they said) of that virtuous mien
That's belied by the deeds we recall to have seen?
What's the point of appearing in church every day
When she's beating her maids and denies them their pay?
By her pious harangues she wears men to a frazzle,
But she's coated with rouge and is eager to dazzle.
She's the fig-leaf's best friend, and will valiantly strive
To ban nudes from the arts (though she loves them when live).
As you well can imagine I came to your aid
And attacked the malicious charges there made;
But they all with one voice overruled my plea
And concluded by saying how good it would be
If you'd leave the concerns of your neighbors alone
And invest the time saved in minding your own.
One should contemplate well one's own conduct and mind

Before one would rashly condemn all mankind;
The full weight of a blameless life is required
So that men can by words *and* by deeds be inspired;
And in fact, it is wisest to leave inspiration
To the men who have made it their chief occupation.
Dear friend, I'm convinced you're too just and too kind
Not to view this advice with an equable mind,
To ascribe it to aught but the fervor and zeal
Of a friend whose devotion is such as I feel.

ARSINOÉ. Though just censure may irk an ungrateful mind,
I did not quite expect a reply of this kind.
I see clearly, dear friend, in your bitter tirade,
You've been hurt to the quick by the points I just made.

CÉLIMÈNE. The reverse is the truth, dear Madam, the fact is
I would make these exchanges a permanent practice.
We could thus destroy and make utterly perish
The delusions concerning ourselves that we cherish.
If you were of my mind, with commendable zeal
We could loyally aim to unmask and reveal,
Conscientiously gather and store for review
All the things we might hear, you of me, I of you.

ARSINOÉ. Ah, dear friend! Who would censure *your* innocent life?
It's in me that faults and defects are rife.

CÉLIMÈNE. Praise and blame are capricious like sunshine and rain,
And our age helps decide what we like and disdain.
There's a season in life for love and flirtations
And another that's fitted for prudish orations.
It is perfectly wise to subscribe to the latter
When at last one's mirror refuses to flatter.
Thus one puts a good front on defeat. I don't claim
That some unpleasant day I won't do just the same.
In due course, time runs out; but right now I have plenty—
It's too soon to turn prude for a woman of twenty.

ARSINOÉ. But indeed, my dear friend, how you harp on your age!
To exult in one's birthday would hardly seem sage.
Too, dear Madam, what little we differ in years
Can hardly seem reason for joy or for tears;
And I still do not see why you go to such length
To drive home an attack so deficient in strength.

CÉLIMÈNE. And I, for my part, do not see why you aim
Wherever you go to destroy my good name.
Why must you work off your frustrations on *me?*
Can I help it if you make men falter and flee?
And if *I* chance to kindle in men ardent passion,
If I'm plagued with attentions of every fashion,
With avowals you wish should be lavished elsewhere—
Pray, what should I do to assure you your share?
In this struggle, all women are comrades-in-arms;
I do nothing to thwart the effect of your charms.

ARSINOÉ. How sad if you think that one longs night and day
For the amorous crowd you so proudly display!
As if people weren't able to judge with great ease
At what price one can readily garner all these.
Would you claim that the men who pursue you in shoals
Are the kind who admire our beautiful souls?
That they burn with the fire of honest devotion?
That the fame of your virtues explains this commotion?
Few are quite *that* naïve; and the world, though reputed
To nod, is not blind; there are women well suited
To kindle the flame of true love in men's minds
Who yet are not followed by males of all kinds.
From all this it is easy to draw the conclusion:
Platonic devotion remains an illusion;
And it's certain it's not our beautiful eyes
That these lovers will yearn for with armorous sighs.
Is this then the glory with which you're inflated?
Your triumphs indeed seem much overrated.
To vaunt your attractions you're too much inclined—
You've no cause to look down on the rest of mankind.
If one envied the conquests that fill you with pride
One would easily top your success if one tried
And attract, with tangible signs of esteem,
As many pursuers as you, it would seem.

CÉLIMÈNE. I hope you will try, and report to me then
The results of this secret of how to please men.
And without . . .

ARSINOÉ.   Let's break off this fruitless debate.
It might strain both our tempers until it's too late.

I'd have left your apartments some minutes ago
If my carriage had only arrived below.
   CÉLIMÈNE. As long as you wish please feel free to remain;
Let no hurry disturb the poise you maintain.
Not to tire you with more than politeness demands
I am leaving you in more congenial hands.
And our friend here, whom chance has just caused to come by,
Will, I'm sure, entertain you much better than I.

SCENE SIX. ALCESTE, CÉLIMÈNE, ARSINOÉ.

   CÉLIMÈNE. Alceste, I must finish a letter today
That it would be most awkward and rude to delay.
Please stay with our friend. My regrets most sincere
To you, dear Madam, for leaving you here.

SCENE SEVEN. ALCESTE, ARSINOÉ.

   ARSINOÉ. By her wish, as you see, we'll converse while I wait,
Dearest friend, for my carriage to come to the gate.
I admit that of all the kindness she shows
I'm most charmed by the pleasure this meeting bestows.
How true that a man of moral perfection
Can command of us all both respect and affection!
Your merit, I'm sure, has some secret charm
That is ever at work to persuade and disarm.
I am sure if at court one were of my mind,
To your virtue one would be a little less blind.
You have cause for complaint; and I note with dismay
How seldom due praise or reward comes your way.
   ALCESTE. Comes *my* way, dear Madam? What claim could I enter?
What service to country has made me the center
Of public regard? And in what respect
Could I justly complain at court of neglect?
   ARSINOÉ. A man that is worthy of royal reward
Need not to such eminent heights have soared;
Occasion wanting, with virtue imbued,
He shows a potential recitude.
Your merit . . .

ALCESTE.   But please, leave my merit aside;
For the court wouldn't know if I cheated and lied.
What a tedious job, what a task to inherit,
To unearth one's subjects' potential merit!
ARSINOÉ. True merit, believe me, unearths itself;
And the world won't let yours gather dust on the shelf.
In circles the most select, to be frank,
I have heard you commended by people of rank.
ALCESTE. Ah, Madam, today one commends left and right
And praises whatever appears to one's sight.
When the merit of all is extolled beyond measure,
To be recognized ceases to cause one much pleasure.
My grocer was knighted, and soon, I would guess,
My chambermaid's name will appear in the press.
ARSINOÉ. Yet I wish that to give to your talents free scope
You would fix on some post of distinction your hope.
Though little you now seem to covet the role,
There are means of smoothing your way to this goal.
I've connections I'd use in promoting your case.
Who could have you advanced at the most rapid pace.
ALCESTE. And then, dear Madam, what am I to do?
How little I'm suited for public view!
When first I was born, though otherwise whole,
One thing that I lacked was a courtier's soul.
I don't have whatever it takes to succeed
In a cold-blooded world of ambition and greed.
Being frank to a fault is a weakness of mine;
For to polish the apple I firmly decline.
And whoever is weak in this versatile art
Cannot play in this world a conspicuous part.
Thus removed from the public's eye, it is true,
He lacks titles and pensions him otherwise due;
But the loss of these benefits leaves me quite cool
If it saves me the trouble of playing the fool:
I escape disappointments that sour one's kindness
And the tedium of conversation that's mindless,
The compulsion to flatter society belles
Or hear verses against which my stomach rebels.
ARSINOÉ. I see you're determined. Before I depart,

Let me touch one more subject that's close to my heart.
How my feelings take part in your troubled affection—
If your love could but take a propitious direction!
You deserve to fare better by far than you do,
And the person you love is unworthy of you.

ALCESTE. Whatever kind office to me you intend,
You recall that the person you mean is your friend?

ARSINOÉ. Yes, I do. But my conscience has suffered too long
To pass over in silence such palpable wrong.
To see you thus slighted I'm hurt and dismayed,
And I feel you should know that your love is betrayed.

ALCESTE. Your remarks show a most considerate trend,
And such news obliges a lover no end.

ARSINOÉ. Be she three times my friend, she is, I repeat,
Unworthy to have a true man at her feet;
And she has only lukewarm affection for you.

ALCESTE. It could be—since our hearts are hidden from view;
But your role, I must say, would have been much more kind
Not to plant such a thought in a lover's mind.

ARSINOÉ. If you willingly let yourself be deluded,
Your friends must be still—I regret I intruded.

ALCESTE. On this subject, dear Madam, it must be plain
It's one's doubts that cause one the greatest pain;
And therefore a friend should remain aloof
Until he can furnish convincing proof.

ARSINOÉ. Very well! Fair enough. On this point you shall find
The evidence ample and clearly defined.
I want you to see there is cause for alarm.
If you will be so kind as to give me your arm
I'll be glad to produce the proof you desire
Of the faithless heart of the one you admire—
And to offer instead, if thus you should choose
What could amply console you for what you will lose.

act four
SCENE ONE. ÉLIANTE, PHILINTE.

PHILINTE. Was ever a soul so hardened in virtue
Or retraction so strained that just watching it hurt you?
No matter what argument we would invent
In his righteous disdain we made hardly a dent;
And never a quarrel so weird in its kind
Arose to disturb the juridical mind.
"No, Your Honor," he said, "I am glad to retract
Whatever you wish, except obvious fact.
What was my offense? What is his complaint?
Is one's honor at stake if one's wit is but faint?
My opinion hurts neither his name nor his purse:
One can live like a saint and write damnable verse.
It is not his honor that's touched, I am sure:
I am glad to pronounce his motives most pure
And proclaim his merit to all who would know it;
He is noble of soul—but a pitiful poet.
I will praise, if you wish, his large house and expenses,
The way he rides horses and dances and fences;
But to praise his verse I politely refuse
And maintain that a person unkissed by the muse
Should restrain his impulse to rhyme and compose
To escape the just censure of friends and of foes."
At last, the extreme of sweetness and light
To which he would bend his pursuit of the right
Was to say in a tone of but ill-feigned ease,
"Dear Sir, I regret I am hard to please.
For your sake, I could wish, from the depth of my heart,
To have found you more skilled in the poet's art."
And with this much concession and saving of face
One there made them shake hands and dismissed the case.
ÉLIANTE. It is true that his manner departs from the norm;
Yet I cherish his failure to bend and conform.
That frankness and candor he prizes so much
Has a noble and truly heroic touch.

In our time, these his virtues are far too rare;
I would wish to encounter them everywhere.

    PHILINTE. The more that I know him, the more above all
I'm surprised by the passion that holds him in thrall.
When a man is endowed with his frame of mind,
I don't see how his heart could to love have inclined;
And I grasp even less how your cousin became
The person who kindled this amorous flame.

    ÉLIANTE. This merely confirms that love doesn't wait
To select for itself a compatible mate;
And what love to congenial souls is imputed
In this instance at least is amply refuted.

    PHILINTE. Is he loved in return, from what you can see?

    ÉLIANTE. To judge in this case is not easy for me.
How decide if she'll render his passion in kind?
In these matters it's rare that she knows her own mind.
She will love and not know it unless she is told,
Or else *think* she's in love when her heart is quite cold.

    PHILINTE. Our friend with this cousin of yours, I believe,
Will find ample occasion to suffer and grieve.
If I were in his place, to bare you my soul,
I should fasten my eyes on a different goal,
And with juster discernment I should take my clue
To respond to the kindness long proffered by you.

    ÉLIANTE. On this point, I won't speak with a feigned modest air:
Above all in this matter I want to be fair
In no way would I meddle to dampen his zeal,
But rather I share in all he must feel.
As far as the outcome depends on my view
To unite them I gladly do all I can do.
However, if things turn from bad to still worse
And his love should encounter a serious reverse,
If another must serve to respond to his passion,
I would hardly object in too vigorous fashion.
The refusal that severed his previous ties
Would not lower the man at all in my eyes.

    PHILINTE. In my turn, I, dear Madam, from meddling desist
To let you be patient and kind as you list.

He himself, if he wishes it, may let you hear
What I have on this point taken care to make clear.
But if at long last, through their being united,
Your love should be caused to remain unrequited,
For that favor extreme I should fervently pray
That your heart now bestows in such one-sided way.

    ÉLIANTE. You are speaking in jest.

    PHILINTE.   I'm in earnest as never.
At this juncture I have no desire to be clever.
I am ready to offer myself to you whole,
And I yearn for that moment with all of my soul.

SCENE TWO. ALCESTE, ÉLIANTE, PHILINTE.

    ALCESTE. Ah, Madam, I hurry to you to obtain
Redress for an evil I cannot sustain.

    ÉLIANTE. What has happened? What could have excited you so?

    ALCESTE. I fear I have suffered a fatal blow.
I'd be less overwhelmed, I assure you, dear friend,
If in chaos all nature had come to its end.
All is over. . . . My love. . . . It's too awful to say.

    ÉLIANTE. But collect yourself and be calm, I pray.

    ALCESTE. Just heavens! Why send us such odious vice
In a package that seems all sugar and spice?

    ÉLIANTE. But, dear Sir, what event . . .

    ALCESTE.   All is lost . . . beyond aid.
I am hurt unto death—I am lost and betrayed!
Célimène . . . (could such terrible news be believed?)
Célimène is unfaithful, and I am deceived.

    ÉLIANTE. And you have just support for this grave supposition?

    PHILINTE. Perhaps this is merely a passing suspicion;
And your jealous temper at times make you see . . .

    ALCESTE. Please be silent; you've nothing to do with me.
    (*To* ÉLIANTE) The written proof of her treacherous spite
Is right here in my pocket in black and white.
Yes, a letter she wrote to Oronte—of all men—
Shows my shame and her guilt in the strokes of her pen.
Oronte—whom I thought she for sure would despise,

Who most harmless a rival appeared to my eyes!
    PHILINTE. At first glance by a letter we may be misled;
It may seem less conclusive when later reread.
    ALCESTE. Please withhold the advice to which you are prone
And expend your concern on affairs of your own.
    ÉLIANTE. But restrain your emotions; be calm, I ask . . .
    ALCESTE. It is you who will have to perform this task;
It's to you that I turn in this hour of smart
To help me set free a suffering heart.
Help punish your faithless, ungrateful relation,
Who rewards with betrayal a man's dedication.
Help avenge what makes weep the angels above.
    ÉLIANTE. Avenge? But how?
    ALCESTE.   By accepting my love.
Accept the heart that I snatch from her hand,
And avenge thus an act that bears treason's brand.
I shall punish her by the sincere devotion,
The passionate ardor, the urgent emotion,
The respectful attention, and dutiful care
Which will hallow the love that for you I declare.
    ÉLIANTE. I share, I am sure, in the pain that you feel
And disdain not at all the love you reveal;
But perhaps on reflection the evil might shrink
And your need for revenge be less clear than you think.
When one's injured by someone so full of attractions,
Quite often one's plans are not followed by actions;
One may threaten and show all the anger you feel,
Yet the verdict of guilt is reversed on appeal.
Indignation will pass like a shower in May—
And such quarrels of lovers one sees every day.
    ALCESTE. No, Madam. No, no. Her offense is too rank.
There's no prospect of peace; I must tell her point-blank.
To abandon the course that I take would be sin;
I would hate myself always if I should give in.
Here she is. My anger revives at her sight.
I shall strongly denounce her corruption and spite,
Confound and destroy her, and offer you then
A heart disengaged from this temptress of men.

SCENE THREE. CÉLIMÈNE, ALCESTE.

ALCESTE (*aside*). O heavens! How can I control my rage?
CÉLIMÈNE. O dear! What is this performance you stage?
What disaster explains these mournful sighs?
And what causes this somber look in your eyes?
ALCESTE. The lowest betrayal a soul can embrace—
Your behavior the most disloyal and base;
An evil more rank than could ever produce
A malicious fiend or an angry Zeus.
CÉLIMÈNE. As ever, my tender and loving Alceste.
ALCESTE. Do not laugh. This is hardly the time for jest.
To blush and to weep you have every reason;
I have certain proofs of your horrible treason.
Here's the fruit of forebodings my mind would have curbed;
For it wasn't in vain that my heart was disturbed.
My frequent suspicions, at which you had snorted,
Have finally shown themselves amply supported;
For in spite of your skill and deceitful charm
I could read in my stars I had cause for alarm.
But please do not assume I'll allow this crime
To go unrevenged and be mellowed by time.
I know well that affection cannot be constrained,
That as nature commands one is loved or disdained,
That one does not invade a heart by force,
That each soul in love must pursue its own course.
And thus I'd have judged it but fair enough
If I had at your hands had an open rebuff.
If at first you'd extinguished my passionate flame,
I would only have had my own fate to blame.
But to nourish that flame with deceitful smile
Is most treacherous and perfidious guile.
No punishment ever could be too severe;
I shall shrink from nothing, I make it quite clear.
Prepare yourself for the worst, if you're sage—
I am not myself; I'm distilled into rage.
The mortal blow that has pierced my defenses
Has made reason surerender its rule of my senses.

I abandon myself to my wrath; I warn all:
I declare I won't answer for what may befall.
    CÉLIMÈNE. To what cause should this furious tirade be assigned?
At long last, if you please, are you out of your mind?
    ALCESTE. I was out of my mind when I suffered your face
To entice me to court contempt and disgrace,
When I thought that the line of your waist and your bust
Was sufficient as proof of a heart I could trust.
    CÉLIMÈNE. And what is this treason of which you complain?
    ALCESTE. Ah, how well you dissemble, how glibly you feign!
But to counter your wiles I am fully prepared.
Please look at this note: here your baseness is bared.
Behold here a proof that you cannot refute;
Face to face with this witness you'll have to stand mute.
    CÉLIMÈNE. Is this then the object you find so exciting?
    ALCESTE. Can you bear without blushing to look at your writing?
    CÉLIMÈNE. What is there for me to blush about?
    ALCESTE. Will you be so bold as to brazen it out,
To disown it because it's an unsigned note?
    CÉLIMÈNE. But why should I disown a letter I wrote?
    ALCESTE. And yet you can see it without any shame
For the crime against me that its phrases proclaim?
    CÉLIMÈNE. It must be admitted: You're one of a kind.
    ALCESTE. You defy then a proof to convince the most blind?
The regard for Oronte that you show as you write
Should not make me indignant nor you contrite?
    CÉLIMÈNE. Oronte! And who says it's to him it was sent?
    ALCESTE. The people I had it from knew where it went.
But suppose it was meant for another—What then?
Should I pardon the faults revealed by your pen?
In what way would this fact serve to lessen your shame?
    CÉLIMÈNE. But suppose the address was a *woman's* name—
Why should you be hurt, and where is my crime?
    ALCESTE. Ah, how clever! You thought of this ruse just in time!
I admit, this gambit I did not expect,
And you see me at once convinced and checked.
Do you mean to rely on deception so crude?
Do you think me so easy to gull and delude?
Let us see in what way, by what means you would try

To maintain and support such a palpable lie,
And how, for a female recipient, you fashion
The words of a note so torrid with passion.
Now twist, if you please to conform to your aims
What I'm going to read . . .

CÉLIMÈNE.   I refuse to play games.
I am tired of your ludicrous bullying ways
And the arrogant temper your conduct displays.

ALCESTE. Let us not get excited—please look at this note
And explain then the phrases I'm going to quote.

CÉLIMÈNE. No, thanks. And I'm sure that in any event
I could hardly care less what you think that it meant.

ALCESTE. But please, convince me, to put me to rest,
How this not could have been to a woman addressed.

CÉLIMÈNE. It was meant for Oronte—You were perfectly right.
I receive his attentions with joy and delight;
His talk I admire and his smile I imbibe
And confess to whatever crimes you describe.
Now do as you please, ignore all restraints,
But stop setting my teeth on edge with complaints.

ALCESTE (aside). O God! Was more cruel a creature created?
Was ever a heart so abused and berated?
By righteous anger my fury is fed;
I come to complain, and am nagged instead!
Instead of abating my sorrows and fears,
She confirms all my charges, and does so with sneers!
Yet my heart is so weak I endeavor in vain
To break loose from so galling and shameful a chain,
To forswear in anger all further devotion
To the unworthy object of futile emotion.

(To CÉLIMÈNE.) Perfidious woman, how always you seem
To employ against me my weakness extreme,
And exploit for your ends the prodigious excess
Of the fatal love that for you I profess.
Deny at least the charges I brought;
Cease pretending you give to your guilt any thought.
Show, I ask, that this note is free of all blame,
And I'm urged by my passion to clear your name.
Try to act the faithful lover's part

And I'll try to believe you with all my heart.

CÉLIMÈNE. Go on, you are mad in your jealous delusions,
And you do not deserve a lover's effusions.
I would like to find out how you could have concluded
I would stoop to deception to keep you deluded.
Why on earth, if my heart had inclined as you say,
Would I fail to admit it the very same day?
Does the open assurance of tender esteem
Fail to counter suspicions as vague as a dream?
When compared with such candor, what weight do they bear?
Why insult me by even admitting they're there?
Since we stretch our good will to its utmost span
In deciding to own our love for a man;
Since a woman's honor, that bridle to feeling,
Is opposed to admissions so frankly revealing;
Dare the lover, for whom these risks are incurred,
Contest unpunished the oracle's word?
He's to blame if he is not completely consoled
By what after a long inner struggle he's told.
Your suspicions well merit my high indignation,
And you've lost all your title to consideration.
It is stupid of me, and simple of mind,
To continue to be even partially kind;
I should save my regard for a different face
And make sure your complaints have a solid base.

ALCESTE. Ah, temptress! My weakness for you is absurd.
You deceive me, no doubt, with each candied word.
But no matter, I must submit to my fate;
My heart is yours to love or to hate.
I shall see in the end what you really feel
And what treason or steadfastness time will reveal.

CÉLIMÈNE. I must say that your love defies every rule.

ALCESTE. But compared with my ardor all passion is cool.
In my wish to make known to all its strength
You will see I have gone to unusual length,
For I'm wishing that no one would think you fair,
That you'd suffered a fate the most meager and bare,
That at birth you'd been placed in the poorest condition,
Deprived of your wealth, without rank or position,

So that then by my love and most generous trust
I could start to repair a fate so unjust
And rejoice and give thanks to the powers above
To see you owe all to the man that you love.

   CÉLIMÈNE. Your good will, I must say, takes the strangest form,
And I hope I'll be spared the chance to conform. . . .
But here is your servant, in strange disguise.

SCENE FOUR. CÉLIMÈNE, ALCESTE, DUBOIS.

   ALCESTE. What's this masquerade? Why these rolling eyes?
What ails you?
   DUBOIS.   Dear Sir . . .
   ALCESTE.   What's your news?
   DUBOIS.   I can't tell.
   ALCESTE. What on earth . . .
   DUBOIS.   Believe me, Sir, all is not well.
   ALCESTE. Why? and how?
   DUBOIS.   Can I talk?
   ALCESTE.   Yes—right now, if you please.
   DUBOIS. Will nobody hear?
   ALCESTE.   How this fellow will tease!
Speak up!
   DUBOIS. Well, Sir, we must beat a retreat.
   ALCESTE. What's this?
   DUBOIS.   It is time to be quick on our feet.
   ALCESTE. But why?
   DUBOIS.   As I say, we will have to depart.
   ALCESTE. For what cause?
   DUBOIS.   There's no time for good-bys; we must start.
   ALCESTE. But *why,* I still ask, do you talk this way?
   DUBOIS. Because we must pack and depart today.
   ALCESTE. I shall cudgel your obstinate head, you lout,
If you will not explain what all this is about.
   DUBOIS. A person in black and gloomy of face
Has come to present to you at your place
A paper so crowded with legal "whereases"
That to read it the devil would call for his glasses.
It's to do with your lawsuit, that much I can tell,

Though to read it would baffle a fiend out of hell.

ALCESTE. What has that got to do, kindly tell without stumbling,
With this hurried departure of which you were mumbling?

DUBOIS. Some time later, a man—if you'll let me explain—
Who's your guest quite often in times of less strain
Arrived at your house in the greatest hurry,
And since you were gone, with an air of great worry
He asked me (a trust loyal service can claim)
To inform you—now wait, what *is* the man's name?

ALCESTE. Be damned to the name! What is it he said?

DUBOIS. Well, he's one of your friends—why trouble my head?
To see urgent reason for flight he professed;
You are threatened, he said, with immediate arrest.

ALCESTE. He did! He explained in detail, I should think?

DUBOIS. No. He asked, it is true, for some paper and ink
And has wirtten a note which, I'm sure, will declare
In all points what's behind this mysterious affair.

ALCESTE. Hand it over at once!

CÉLIMÈNE.   What can all this mean?

ALCESTE. I don't know, but the truth shall shortly be seen.
Will it take you all day, in the devil's name?

DUBOIS (*after taking a long time to search for the note*). On my
word, I left it at home when I came.

ALCESTE. I don't know what restrains me . . .

CÉLIMÈNE.   Be calm, I pray,
And be off to clear up what caused this affray.

ALCESTE. My fate, it appears, whatever I do
Has vowed to prevent me from talking to you;
But permit your suitor to thwart its spite,
And return to you, Madam, before tonight.

act five

SCENE ONE. ALCESTE, PHILINTE.

ALCESTE. As I stated before, I am firmly resolved.

PHILINTE. But must you, whatever the hardship involved . . .

ALCESTE. No, however you may insist or upbraid me,
From what I have said you shall never dissuade me.

This our age has become iniquity's den,
And I mean to retire from the commerce of men.
My foe arraigned against him and his cause
Integrity, decency, shame, and the laws;
The strength of my case all were quick to cite;
I was calm in the knowledge I was in the right—
And yet all my hopes bear most bitter fruit:
I've the right on my side, but I lose my suit.
Yes, a scoundrel, known for his unsavory past,
Scores a triumph that leaves honest men aghast!
His guile thwarts good faith, and, instead of resistance,
In cutting my throat he gains legal assistance!
His crafty eye, whose mere glance corrodes,
Overturns plainest justice and time-honored codes!
One rewards his offense by judicial decree!
Not content yet with what he has done to me,
He refers to a book of most scurrilous type,
Consisting of mere pornographical tripe
That makes one regret that the laws are not tighter—
And whispers to all that I am the writer!
And Oronte his devious malice now shows
By spreading this slander wherever he goes!
Oronte, a man of repute and of rank
Whom I've injured by being sincere and frank,
Who comes to me, full of most urgent zeal,
To read me his verses and ask what I feel;
And since I respond with unblinking eye
And refuse to deceive him by telling a lie,
He repays me by stooping to slander, and so
Now my would-be friend is my bitterest foe!
And it seems that no pardon could ever be had
For just once pointing out that his sonnet was bad.
Are these the high aims that men pursue?
Do these acts represent the things that they do?
Here indeed good faith and a virtuous course
And justice and honor are shown in full force.
Too severe are the wounds that the heart here receives;
Let us leave then this den of cutthroats and thieves;
Since you men to be wolf among wolves are proud,

I shall gladly secede from your treacherous crowd.

PHILINTE. For so rash a decision you would be to blame;
And all evils are not so intense as you claim.
Your foe, in spreading a lie so abject,
Has yet to produce any serious effect.
His libelous charges fall back on his head;
In the end he will suffer for what he has said.

ALCESTE. You think so? Such slanders are greatly in vogue:
He has license to be a most unabashed rogue;
And this scheme, so far from destroying his name,
Is bound to procure him still wider acclaim.

PHILINTE. At least, it remains little heed has been paid
To the spiteful rumor by which you're dismayed;   .
And in this respect you have nothing to fear.
In your lawsuit, whose issue I'm sorry to hear,
The decree of the court should be promptly appealed.
The verdict . . .

ALCESTE.   No thanks. I shall readily yield.
The injustice here done is such obvious fact
I refuse to allow them a chance to retract.
Too clearly it shows how right is ignored,
And in future ages it shall be abhorred
As a famous milestone, a signal mark
Of the evils that render out times so dark.
I know well that the cost may well bleed me white,
But it is not too high if it gives me the right
To expose and denounce the injustice of man
And to hate human nature as hard as I can.

PHILINTE. But consider . . .

ALCESTE.   Consider your efforts as wasted.
What can sweeten the bitter defeats I have tasted?
Can you be so brash as intend to my face
To belittle man's vice and gloss over disgrace?

PHILINTE. Not at all. Your judgment agrees with mine.
All moves through intrigue and ulterior design.
Only schemers succeed, and it's easy to see
That man is quite other than what he should be.
But should their so patent iniquity then

Make us want to retire from the haunts of men?
All these human defects but give us a chance
To develop a more philosophical stance—
And this exercise shows a man at his best;
For if all were with equal integrity blessed,
And if all were as honest and just as they should,
Where would be the distinction of those who are good?
Their most notable mark is a temper that smothers
Our chafing resentment at wrongs done by others.
And just as a heart of virtue profound . . .
   ALCESTE. How well you talk. Your speeches abound
With impeccable logic and graces sublime.
Yet, Sir, you are wasting your breath and your time,
For my safety, my reason enjoins my retreat.
My tongue has not learned to be smooth and discreet;
I can't vouch for my words, since I say what I think,
And the feuds I might cause make me shudder and shrink.
I shall see Célimène, and when she arrives
She will have to agree to my plan for our lives.
I shall see if her passion for me is sincere;
Her reply will at once make all doubt disappear.
   PHILINTE. Let us go upstairs, and wait for her there.
   ALCESTE. No, my soul is too restless and troubled by care.
Please go first and leave me; and I shall remain
Alone with the bleakness of heart that's my bane.
   PHILINTE. I wish you had company less apt to chill.
I shall ask Éliante to come down, if she will.

SCENE TWO. CÉLIMÈNE, ORONTE, ACASTE.

   ORONTE. Yes, Madam, you must now decide if it's true
That so tender a union will tie me to you.
The assurance I want you should quickly dispense;
A lover is irked to be kept in suspense.
If my passion has wakened responsive chords,
Do not grudge me the pleasure the knowledge affords.
As your proof (need for proof was never acuter)
You must cease to acknowledge Alceste as your suitor.

This tangible token of love I exact;
I insist you refuse to receive him, in fact.

CÉLIMÈNE. But what is the reason you suddenly flout him
After all the to-do you at first made about him?

ORONTE. I'm afraid it's not *my* turn for interrogation.
It is *you* whose behavior needs clarification.
You shall choose which one you prefer of us two;
And once you are resolved, I shall shortly be too.

ALCESTE (*emerging from his corner*). Yes, for once he is right.
You will have to decide.
By the sentence we crave we agree to abide.
Like him, I insist you shall not stay aloof;
For my love now demands unmistakable proof.
This affair has moved far too slow from the start,
And right now is the time to lay bare your whole heart.

ORONTE. I am sorry with passion so inopportune
To disturb, Sir, your chance to obtain such a boon.

ALCESTE. I am sorry to share with you, jealous or not.
To the slightest extent, Sir, what heart she has got.

ORONTE. If your love she to mine should turn out to prefer . . .

ALCESTE. If the least in your favor her judgment should err . . .

ORONTE. I here swear to extinguish all amorous fire.

ALCESTE. I here swear to be cured from all loving desire.

ORONTE. Dear Madam, be frank; it is your turn to speak.

ALCESTE. Dear Madam, deliver the verdict we seek.

ORONTE. Let us know whom you choose for your love; please begin.

ALCESTE. Put an end to suspense; may the better man win.

ORONTE. Can you question with whom you long since should have sided?

ALCESTE. Can it be that you falter? You seem undecided!

CÉLIMÈNE. My word! How unwelcome the choice you exact,
And how little you show of good sense or of tact!
I am sure of my stand on the question you raise,
And it's not that my heart is lost in a maze.
The case is too clear to perplex or confuse,
And nothing is easier for me than to choose.
However, it's terribly awkward, I find,
To announce to you two a choice of this kind.

Whenever we have something painful to broach,
We should surely employ a more subtle approach.
There are less drastic methods of communication
Than to shout from the rooftops the heart's inclination.
In short, there are pleasanter means to explain
To a dutiful lover he's burning in vain.

ORONTE. Not at all. A frank statement is just what we need.
At this point, we should find it most welcome.

ALCESTE.   .   Agreed.
It's exactly this drastic effect I desire;
Of your tactful maneuvers I easily tire.
To please all mankind is your driving ambition;
But let's have no more trifling—pronounce your decision.
You must openly state and reveal your affection,
Or I'll see in your silence a tacit rejection.
I would know how to take your refusal to speak
And would thus see confirmed premonitions most bleak.

ORONTE. I'm sincerely obliged to your firmness, dear Sir;
And in what you have said I most gladly concur.

SCENE THREE. ÉLIANTE, PHILINTE,
CÉLIMÈNE, ORONTE, ALCESTE.

CÉLIMÈNE. Dear cousin, I'm treated extremely ungently
By two men who've conspired to tease and torment me.
In turn, each insists at the top of his voice
That at once to them both I should publish my choice,
That I ask one of them, in effect, to his face
His affection for me to subdue and erase.
Please confess: Is it thus that such things should be done?

ÉLIANTE. To provide such advice I am hardly the one.
You have chosen your arbiter rashly, I fear;
I prefer that one's words should be candid and clear.

ORONTE. No avenue, Madam, remains for retreat.

ALCESTE. Your evasions, dear Madam, are doomed to defeat.

ORONTE. You must open your heart; you must cast the dice.

ALCESTE. And if not, your silence alone will suffice.

ORONTE. But a single word will unravel the knot.

ALCESTE. By your failure to speak I shall know my lot.

SCENE FOUR. ARSINOÉ, CÉLIMÈNE, ÉLIANTE, ALCESTE, PHILINTE, ACASTE, CLITANDRE, ORONTE.

ACASTE (*to* CÉLIMÈNE). We have come here because we both
felt we should mention
A little affair that deserves your attention.

CLITANDRE (*to* ORONTE *and* ALCESTE). It is fortunate that we
encounter you here,
For you both are involved, as will shortly appear.

ARSINOÉ (*to* CÉLIMÈNE). To see me, dear friend, your surprise
may be keen,
But these gentlemen asked me to witness this scene.
They both came to my house to voice their complaints
Of a trait that would weary the patience of saints.
Your esteemed elevation of soul is a pledge
You can *not* have committed the crime they allege.
On their proofs I bestowed the most searching attention,
And, my friendship forgetting our little—dissension,
I accompanied them in the hope, by and large,
To see you deny such a slanderous charge.

ACASTE. Yes, Madam, let's see with an open mind,
What you say to these comments by you undersigned.
To Clitandre, from you, this letter was sent.

CLITANDRE. And this sweet little note for Acaste was meant.

ACASTE (*to* ORONTE *and* ALCESTE). You will find that the hand
is familiar, I trust;
For, polite as she is, I am sure that she must
On many occasions have written to you.
But to read her own words—it's no more than her due:

> "It is ironical that you should condemn my ways and allege that
> I never enjoy myself as much as when you are away. You are
> most unjust; and if you don't appear shortly to demand my
> pardon, I may decide never to forgive you for your offense.
> Hulking Tom the Count . . ."

He ought to be here.

> "Hulking Tom the Count, who heads your list of undesirable
> rivals, is not even in the running; and since I have seen him
> spend three quarters of an hour spitting into a puddle in order

to make circles in the water, he has suffered somewhat in my esteem. As for our little marquis . . ."

That's me, I'm afraid.

"As for our little marquis, who insists on holding my hand for hours on end, he is the most diminutive person I ever saw, and his appearance owes as much to his tailor as to his creator. As for my morose friend . . ."

(*To* ALCESTE) Your turn, Sir.

"As for my morose friend, I am at times amused by his abrupt and uncouth behavior, but as a rule he bores me to distraction. As for the maker of sonnets . . ."

(*To* ORONTE) You have not been overlooked.

"As for the maker of sonnets, who trembles with the urge to create and defies mankind to call him author, it is asking too much of me to make me listen to what he is saying; and I find his prose as boring as his verse. Please admit the thought into your head that I don't always enjoy myself as much as you think, that I miss you—more than I care to admit—at the parties to which I am dragged, and that the true seasoning of life's enjoyments is the presence of those one loves."

CLITANDRE. And here is a relevant excerpt from the other:

"Your Clitandre, who seems to annoy you by his saccharine allusions, would be the last man on earth to attract my regard. He is badly mistaken to hope for my love—just as you are badly mistaken to *lack* hope. To come closer to the truth, you two should trade expectations. Come to see me as often as you can, to help me alleviate the affliction of his continual presence."

Revealing bequests of a notable mind—
And a label that fits would be easy to find.
Enough. We are leaving. Wherever you go
We shall publish the traits that these documents show.

ACASTE. I have plenty to tell you, and if I refrain
It's because I must think you beneath my disdain.
And I'll show you that people as little as I
Can find solace in worthiest hearts, if they try.

SCENE FIVE. CÉLIMÈNE, ÉLIANTE, ARSINOÉ, ALCESTE, ORONTE, PHILINTE.

ORONTE. Is this how you use your fangs on your betters,
After all the sweet phrases you put in *my* letters!
And your heart, which so coyly pretended to yearn,
To all the male sex is promised in turn!
I have acted the fool, but I'm tired of the role;
You have done me a favor in baring your soul.
I retrieve here the heart you so lightly regard,
And I'm amply revenged now that thence you are barred.
(*To* ALCESTE) I shall cease, Sir, to stand in the way of your passion;
I am sure she'll respond in most ladylike fashion.

SCENE SIX. CÉLIMÈNE, ÉLIANTE, ARSINOÉ, ALCESTE, PHILINTE.

ARSINOÉ (*to* CÉLIMÈNE). Without doubt, your behavior is vicious and low;
Indignation compels me to label it so.
Was ever like course by a woman pursued?
I say nothing of others to whom you were rude.
(*Points to* ALCESTE) But this man, who aspired to make you his wife,
A true pillar of honor and upright life,
Who worshiped you with an idolatrous zeal,
Must he bear . . .
ALCESTE.   But excuse me, dear Madam, I feel
I myself should handle my own affairs.
Why thus charge yourself with superfluous cares?
Though so warmly you are to my side inclined,
I shall be quite unable to pay you in kind.
It's not *you* I shall call on with passionate voice
If I look for redress in a different choice.
ARSINOÉ. Do you think I am yearning for such a match?
You must feel, Sir, you are a most precious catch.
How inflated your spirit must be, and how vain,
If this is the sort of belief you sustain!
What our friend here leaves over is hardly a prize

Of a kind to be yearned for with passionate sighs.
Please be undeceived, and revise your pretensions.
On a woman like me you would waste your attentions.
Sigh for *her*, as before, till your love is requited;
I can't wait to behold you content and united.

SCENE SEVEN. CÉLIMÈNE, ÉLIANTE,
ALCESTE, PHILINTE.

ALCESTE (*to* CÉLIMÈNE). I've been silent, you see, despite what occurred.
I have calmly stood by until all have been heard.
Have I curbed my temper enough today?
May I now . . .
CÉLIMÈNE. . . . I agree with all you can say.
You are quite in your rights to heap scorn on my action;
I shall patiently bear all blame and detraction.
I've done wrong, I admit it. Contrition and shame
Would make any excuses seem vapid and lame.
I have scorned the anger the others have shown;
But my crime toward you I am ready to own.
I have shown all the traits that you justly despise,
And I know just how guilty I seem in your eyes.
In your charge of betrayal all proofs bear you out;
And you have every reason to hate me, no doubt.
Go ahead, vent your ire.
ALCESTE.   I wish that I could!
I am forced by my love to neglect my own good.
Though my reason decided to hate and detest,
Would my heart be prepared to obey its request?
(*To* ÉLIANTE *and* PHILINTE) Here you see what an unworthy passion can do.
You have witnessed what weakness has made me go through,
But the terrible truth is, you haven't seen all:
You shall watch me play still more abjectly her thrall.
We're too rashly called sage—that my fate will illumine;
The austerest of men are at heart all too human.
(*To* CÉLIMÈNE.) Yes, then! I'm prepared to forgive you; and hence
I shall try to excuse and forget your offense;

I shall call it a weakness to which your young mind
By corrupting examples was led and inclined—
Provided you give your wholehearted consent
To the break with mankind upon which I am bent
And determine to follow me to the retreat
Where I've sworn I shall live in seclusion complete.
This heroic decision no doubt in all eyes
Soon will clear you of spite and malicious lies;
And thus cleared of a scandal that causes me pain
You'll be worthy again of a love without stain.

    CÉLIMÈNE. To renounce the world at my age! Must your wife
Be buried alive far from civilized life?

    ALCESTE. If your love finds its longed-for object in mine,
Why on earth should you ever for others repine?
Can't we find in each other contentment in plenty?

    CÉLIMÈNE. But solitude frightens a woman of twenty.
I don't feel I can marshal the grandeur of soul
That would make me resolve to pursue such a goal.
If a love sealed in marriage can make you content,
I could muster the courage to give my consent;
And our union will . . .

    ALCESTE.   No! You are all I detest.
This refusal alone is far worse than the rest.
In effect, since you will not, throughout wedded life,
Let your husband be all (as *I* would my wife),
I here spurn and reject you. This offer you scorn
At long last makes me break the chains I have worn.

SCENE EIGHT. ÉLIANTE, ALCESTE, PHILINTE.

    ALCESTE (*to* ÉLIANTE). Your virtues set off your external graces;
You have, Madam, that candor that nothing replaces.
You have long inspired admiration extreme;
But allow me to hold you thus still in esteem
And consent that my heart, bruised by scorn and defiance,
Should no more court the honor of closer alliance.
Too unworthy I feel; and my reason suspects
As a lover I suffer from innate defects.
Too, the courtship you merit should not be a sequel

To the wooing of one who's in no way your equal.
In effect . . .

    ÉLIANTE. Please do what your feelings command,
Since I'm not at a loss where to grant my hand;
And here is your friend, who in case of need,
To accept such an offer has kindly agreed.

    PHILINTE. Ah! That honor, dear Madam, is all that I sigh for,
And a prize I am eager to live and to die for.

    ALCESTE. May you both find the bliss that will banish dejection
And forever preserve an untarnished affection!
For myself—deeply wronged, maligned, and betrayed—
I shall leave the abyss where all vices parade
And search for a place remote from the crowd
Where a life full of honor is still allowed.

    PHILINTE. Let us try, dear Madam, let's do all we can
To dissuade from such steps this remarkable man.

SOCIETY IN *LE MISANTHROPE*

The action of *Le Misanthrope* reveals the self-absorption of seventeenth-century aristocratic society, its talk—boasting, flattery, ridicule, slander—its scramble for prestige, and its debasement of love and friendship.* These are also topics of discussion in the play. Molière characterizes the observer and the thing observed. Alceste, Célimène, and Philinte view society; we view them, and society through them. The gradations between characters on stage, characters described in "portraits" and the anonymous "les gens" (people) convey the sense of a closed, self-conscious society in which everybody knows everybody else. People try hard to make an impression on one another and usually fail. The last portrait is that of the viscount who spends three quarters of an hour spitting into a well to watch the circles. His activity epitomizes the idleness, stupidity, and futility of the society to which he belongs. Love is the most engrossing activity of this idle and bored society. It is social pastime which provides ample opportunities for the satisfaction of personal vanity. Orante in his sonnet, Acaste in his attitude toward Célimène, Arsinoë in her remarks about her, all look on love as a commercial transaction. The man who courts a woman expects a fair return on his investment. Both have the same goal: to be admired by members of the opposite sex. They aspire to the reputation of irresistibility. As vanity motivates love, so self-interest motivates friendship. Alceste with his rigoristic ideal of friendship and love is continuously exposed to the debased and corrupt versions of these qualities presented by Orante, Célimène, and Arsinoë. He urges total sincerity —but he is furious when criticized. His failure to live up to the standards he sets for others makes his indignation comic. The public reading of Célimène's letters brings about the destruction of her clique, and points to the destructiveness of a society which depends for its sense of its own cleverness or righteousness on others. Alceste too is dependent on others. His misanthropy is closer to Célimène's gossip than he realizes. He may seem to resemble the tragic hero whose painful search ends in self-discovery, but in fact he learns nothing from his experience, and is still possessed by self-

* Abstracted from Quentin M. Hope, "Society in *Le Misanthrope*," *French Review* XXXII (1959), 329-336.

pity and self-regard when he leaves the stage. The play is as hard on
the misanthrope as it is on the society he despises. Yet neither stands
wholly condemned. Alceste and Célimène remain magnetic characters. Éliante and Philinte live in society and are uncorrupted by it.
Philinte has the last word: he will bring Alceste back into the company of his fellow-man. That, in the view of comedy, is where man
belongs.

FUTILITY AND SELF-DECEPTION IN *LE MISANTHROPE*

Le Misanthrope contains a series of scathing portraits, serving to
expose the futility and self-deception of seventeenth-century salon
society rather than its viciousness.* Célimène's portrayal of a courtier, spitting for three quarters of an hour in a well to make rings,
is most revealing in this respect. Alceste, who suffers from this
futility, dreams of more virile and heroic times. Unfortunately, he is
vain, childish, egotistic and, worst of all, blind to his own short-
comings. He jousts against humanity at large in order to forget his
own absurdity. Because of his self-deception, he does not realize
that he desperately needs the company of all these fops he considers
his inferiors. No less than they, he is the victim of his own idleness:
they are all domesticated oppressors quite incapable of justifying
their own existence. Alceste's superiority stems from the fact that,
in spite of his self-deception, he has an inkling of his true situation.
This situation stands out more clearly when Alceste is compared to
Don Garcie from whom he has borrowed several speeches: their
heroic, passionate tones not only are out of place in the salon of a
coquette, but show that Alceste lives in an imaginary world. Instead
of battling against a powerful evil like Don Garcie, Alceste must
cope with nothing more heroic than a lawsuit and a poetaster. Within Célimène's salon, it is not the language of passion but that of the

* Abstracted from Judd D. Hubert, "Futility and Self-Deception in *Le
Misanthrope," Studies in Seventeenth Century French Literature,* XXXIII
(1963), 165-184.

market place that prevails. The *petits marquis* express their love or
friendship in terms of barter and exchange; but their warmest protestations are nothing but counterfeit tender. Indeed, only Alceste,
in his unsuccessful lawsuit, loses real money. The contrast between
his archaic lyric and Oronte's *précieux* sonnet measures the gap
between the misanthrope and the other suitors. Alceste expresses
his refusal of the world—of the King's offer, Paris, and any other
form of exchange; the sonnet wittily plays with the themes of commerce and complacency, typical of the rest of the comedy. Thus, the
unsubstantiality of Alceste's private universe clashes with the super-
ficiality of Oronte's worldliness. Illusion is pitted against illusion—
or words against words. Éliante alone has found an alternative, for
she notices only the good qualities of her acquaintances. Instead of
sketching satirical portraits in the manner of Célimène, she charit-
ably uses her imagination in order to transfigure and idealize, with
the help of appreciative words, quite ordinary people, living in a
devitalized society.

ACTION AND ILLUSION IN *LE MISANTHROPE*

Le Misanthrope, Molière's greatest of comedies of manners, suggests at first acquaintance that it has a straightforward moral message because of the clash between the apparent moral rectitude of
Alceste and the various shades of falseness of the other characters.*
A closer study of the play gives rise to doubts as to where morality
lies. A basic tenet of Molière's comedies is that a healthy social
order must be preserved, no matter what ruse or nonsense is used for
this purpose, and so it is necessary to seek a thematic central action
which bears upon a threat to the social fabric. Instead of seeing a
lack of total honesty as the threat to society (Alceste's view of
things), we perceive that the world of Célimène's salon functions

* Abstracted from Hallam Walker, "Action and Illusion in *Le Misanthrope*," *Kentucky Foreign Language Quarterly,* IX (1962), 150-161.

through and by a mutual preservation of personal illusions by the
habitués, with the true threat being anything which destroys illusions about self or one's social image. Each character works seriously
at acting out a chosen role which offers scope for indulgence of a
cherished illusion, nor does this exclude a truly modest or virtuous
role. This concept of a sophisticated society turning upon such behavior, and a comedy based upon it, is theatrical in the extreme.
With this unifying theme Molière devises variations on game playing or play acting in a plot about love and social status. The key rule
of the game and of the play's action is that the ego is permitted
self-indulgence up to the point where it harms the chances of others
to enjoy the same pleasure. The "morality," the theme, and the action
of *Le Misanthrope* are thus really one, and the seventeenth-century
audience probably found this evident and natural. Alceste is a mis-
anthropist not so much in his talk of leaving human society as in
his antisocial refusal to play a proper part, choosing for himself
the role of paragon of virtue which it is impossible for the others
to support. Worse, perhaps, his ego demands a starring role. He
insists upon taking himself seriously, taking with literal force his
vocabulary studded with words such as "treason" and "shame."
Molière places him in love with the flirtatious Célimène, a situation
leading to a marvelous counterpoint of motives and language. The
plot has Alceste making repeated efforts to see his love alone and
to get her to pledge her hand in marriage. Social pressures conspire
to frustrate his attempts, and each act ends with an exit by him. The
play's overall rhythmic pattern of movement of approach and retreat
is amplified by the influx and withdrawal of Célimène's friends,
suitors, and enemies, all of whom leave her at the end of the play.
She, who at first seems to be the opposite of Alceste in her enthusias-
tic play with illusions, finally commits the crime of "lèse-illusion" by
her satirical portraits of everyone in her circle, and this is not forgiven. The force of *Le Misanthrope* lies in its brilliant coordination
of theme and actions on stage. It is a tightly constructed piece of
theater on the seemingly illusory acceptance of poses and masks for
reality, yet we see that this theatricality observed in life by Molière
is an important and valid social principle. It is as if this great comedy
said "all the world's a stage" and that this is not idle vanity but an
essential strength of human society.

THE ACTOR'S ALCESTE: EVOLUTION OF *LE MISANTHROPE*

The enigmatic nature of Alceste in *Le Misanthrope* of Molière has been the subject of endless discussion among literary critics.* Since the actor also is required to interpret the work of a dramatic author, it should be interesting to examine the various manners in which Alceste has been played. The purpose of this abstract, then, is to discuss the transformations in the role of Alceste from Molière's time to the mid-eighteenth century. We have no direct evidence of the way Molière interpreted the role on stage. We do, however, know that Alceste is a complex character, and that Molière, in *La Critique de l'Ecole des femmes,* defended the presentation of such complexity. Judging from his reputation as a comic actor, it is reasonable to assume that Molière exaggerated Alceste's oddities in as amusing a manner as possible, while at the same time maintaining his ambiguities. The first important interpreter of Alceste after Molière was Baron, who returned to the theater in 1720, after a long retirement. An extremely egoistic and independent man, Baron was so obsessed with the desire to show off the lordly manners he had learned by frequenting the nobility of the time, that he often took great liberties with texts, and in the case of Alceste, transformed him into a completely sympathetic and dignified character. Grandval played Alceste much in the manner of his illustrious predecessor, but stressed his violent and impatient side. This interpretation also was justifiable in terms of contemporary society since noble and haughty violence was typical of the courtier of Louis XV. In short, the conscious imitation of the eighteenth-century "petits maîtres" is probably the most important element in the interpretation of the *Misanthrope.* Rousseau's famous criticism of Molière coincided with Grandval's interpretation of Alceste as a noble gentleman. His

---

* Abstracted from E. D. Sullivan, "The Actor's Alceste: Evolution of *The Misanthrope*," *Modern Language Quarterly,* IX (1948), 492-496.

attack on Molière's intentions in creating the character, while having nothing to do with contemporary performances, gave such authority to the Baron-Grandval version, that it came to be regarded as Molière's own. Baron's interpretation made Alceste a completely sympathetic character by emphasizing his nobility and dignity at the expense of his ridiculous elements. Rousseau's persecution complex led him to attack Molière for making Alceste a comic figure. The authority of these two great egoists succeeded in stripping the role of its comic traits both on the stage and in the mind of the literary critic or casual reader of the play.

phaedra
JEAN RACINE

TRANSLATED BY
ROBERT LOWELL

CHARACTERS

THESEUS, *son of Aegeus and King of Athens*

PHAEDRA, *wife of Theseus and daughter of Minos and Pasiphaë*

HIPPOLYTUS, *son of Theseus and Antiope, Queen of the Amazons*

ARICIA, *princess of the royal blood of Athens*

OENONE, *nurse of Phaedra*

THERAMENES, *tutor of Hippolytus*

ISMENE, *friend of Aricia*

PANOPE, *waiting-woman of Phaedra*

Guards

Pronunciation:

Phaedra=Pheédra
Oenone=Eenónee
Ismene=Ismeénee
Aricia=Arísha

Theramenes=Therámeneés
Panope=Pánopeé
Pasiphaë=Pásiphá-ee

act one
SCENE ONE. HIPPOLYTUS, THERAMENES.

HIPPOLYTUS. No, no, my friend, we're off! Six months have passed
since Father heard the ocean howl and cast
his galley on the Aegean's skull-white froth.
Listen! The blank sea calls us—off, off, off!
I'll follow Father to the fountainhead
and marsh of hell. We're off. Alive or dead,
I'll find him.

THERAMENES. Where, my lord? I've sent a host
of veteran seamen up and down the coast;

each village, creek and cove from here to Crete
has been ransacked and questioned by my fleet;
my flagship skirted Hades' rapids, furled
sail there a day, and scoured the underworld.
Have you fresh news? New hopes? One even doubts
if noble Theseus wants his whereabouts
discovered. Does he need helpers to share
the plunder of his latest love affair;
a shipload of spectators and his son
to watch him ruin his last Amazon—
some creature, taller than a man, whose tanned
and single bosom slithers from his hand,
when he leaps to crush her like a waterfall
of honeysuckle?

    HIPPOLYTUS. You are cynical,
my friend. Your insinuations wrong a king,
sick as myself of his philandering.
His heart is Phaedra's and no rivals dare
to challenge Phaedra's sole possession there.
I sail to find my father. The command
of duty calls me from this stifling land.

    THERAMENES. This stifling land? Is that how you deride
this gentle province where you used to ride
the bridle-paths, pursuing happiness?
You cured your orphaned childhood's loneliness
and found a peace here you preferred to all
the blaze of Athens' brawling protocol.
A rage for exploits blinds you. Your disease
is boredom.

    HIPPOLYTUS. Friend, this kingdom lost its peace,
when Father left my mother for defiled
bull-serviced Pasiphaë's child. The child
of homicidal Minos is our queen!

    THERAMENES. Yes, Phaedra reigns and rules here. I have seen
you crouch before her outbursts like a cur.
When she first met you, she refused to stir
until your father drove you out of court.
The news is better now; our friends report
the queen is dying. Will you cross the seas,

desert your party and abandon Greece?
Why flee from Phaedra? Phaedra fears the night
less than she fears the day that strives to light
the universal ennui of her eye—
this dying woman, who desires to die!

    HIPPOLYTUS. No, I despise her Cretan vanity,
hysteria and idle cruelty.
I fear Aricia; she alone survives
the blood-feud that destroyed her brothers' lives.

    THERAMENES. Prince, Prince, forgive my laughter. Must you fly
beyond the limits of the world and die,
floating in flotsam, friendless, far from help,
and clubbed to death by Tartars in the kelp?
Why arm the shrinking violet with a knife?
Do you hate Aricia, and fear for your life,
Prince?

    HIPPOLYTUS. If I hated her, I'd trust myself
and stay.

    THERAMENES. Shall I explain you to yourself?
Prince, you have ceased to be that hard-mouthed, proud
and pure Hippolytus, who scorned the crowd
of common lovers once and rose above
your wayward father by despising love.
Now you justify your father, and you feel
love's poison running through you, now you kneel
and breathe the heavy incense, and a god
possesses you and revels in your blood!
Are you in love?

    HIPPOLYTUS. Theramenes, when I call
and cry for help, you push me to the wall.
Why do you plague me, and try to make me fear
the qualities you taught me to revere?
I sucked in prudence with my mother's milk.
Antiope, no harlot draped in silk,
first hardened me. I was my mother's son
and not my father's. When the Amazon,
my mother, was dethroned, my mind approved
her lessons more than ever. I still loved
her bristling chastity. Later, you told

stories about my father's deeds that made me hold
back judgment—how he stood for Hercules,
a second Hercules who cleared the Cretan seas
of pirates, throttled Scirron, Cercyon,
Procrustes, Sinnis, and the giant man
of Epidaurus writhing in his gore.
He pierced the maze and killed the Minotaur.
Other things turned my stomach: that long list
of women, all refusing to resist.
Helen, caught up with all her honeyed flesh
from Sparta; Periboea, young and fresh,
already tired of Salinis. A hundred more,
their names forgotten by my father—whore
and virgin, child and mother, all deceived,
if their protestations can be believed!
Ariadne declaiming to the rocks,
her sister, Phaedra, kidnapped. Phaedra locks
the gate at last! You know how often I
would weary, fall to nodding and deny
the possibility of hearing the whole
ignoble, dull, insipid boast unroll.
And now I too must fall. The gods have made me creep.
How can I be in love? I have no specious heap
of honors, friend. No mastered monsters drape
my shoulders—Theseus' excuse to rape
at will. Suppose I chose a woman. Why
choose an orphan? Aricia is eternally
cut off from marriage, lest she breed
successors to her fierce brothers, and seed
the land with treason. Father only grants
her life on one condition. This—he wants
no bridal torch to burn for her. Unwooed
and childless, she must answer for the blood
her brothers shed. How can I marry her,
gaily subvert our kingdom's character,
and sail on the high seas of love?
    THERAMENES. You'll prove
nothing by reason, for you are in love.
Theseus' injustice to Aricia throws

her in the light; your eyes he wished to close
are open. She dazzles you. Her pitiful
seclusion makes her doubly terrible.
Does this innocent passion freeze your blood?
There's sweetness in it. Is your only good
the dismal famine of your chastity?
You shun your father's path? Where would you be,
Prince, if Antiope had never burned
chastely for Theseus? Love, my lord, has turned
the head of Hercules, and thousands—fired
the forge of Vulcan! All your uninspired,
cold moralizing is nothing, Prince. You have changed!
Now no one sees you riding, half-deranged
along the sand-bars, where you drove your horse
and foaming chariot with all your force,
tilting and staggering upright through the surf—
far from their usual course across the turf.
The woods are quiet . . . How your eyes hang down!
You often murmur and forget to frown.
All's out, Prince. You're in love; you burn. Flames, flames,
Prince! A dissimulated sickness maims
the youthful quickness of your daring. Does
lovely Aricia haunt you?
    HIPPOLYTUS. Friend, spare us.
I sail to find my father.
    THERAMENES. Will you see
Phaedra before you go?
    HIPPOLYTUS. I mean to be
here when she comes. Go, tell her. I will do
my duty. Wait, I see her nurse. What new
troubles torment her?

SCENE TWO. HIPPOLYTUS,
THERAMENES, OENONE.

    OENONE. Who has griefs like mine,
my lord? I cannot help the queen in her decline.
Although I sit beside her day and night,
she shuts her eyes and withers in my sight.

An eternal tumult roisters through her head,
panics her sleep, and drags her from her bed.
Just now she fled me at the prime
of day to see the sun for the last time.
She's coming.
    HIPPOLYTUS. So! I'll steal away. My flight
removes a hateful object from her sight.

SCENE THREE. PHAEDRA, OENONE.

    PHAEDRA. Dearest, we'll go no further. I must rest.
I'll sit here. My emotions shake my breast,
the sunlight throws black bars across my eyes.
My knees give. If I fall, why should I rise,
Nurse?
    OENONE. Heaven help us! Let me comfort you.
    PHAEDRA. Tear off these gross, official rings, undo
these royal veils. They drag me to the ground.
Why have you frilled me, laced me, crowned me, and wound
my hair in turrets? All your skill torments
and chokes me. I am crushed by ornaments.
Everything hurts me, and drags me to my knees!
    OENONE. Now this, now that, Madam. You never cease
commanding us, then cancelling your commands.
You feel your strength return, summon all hands
to dress you like a bride, then say you choke!
We open all the windows, fetch a cloak,
rush you outdoors. It's no use, you decide
that sunlight kills you, and only want to hide.
    PHAEDRA. I feel the heavens' royal radiance cool
and fail, as if it feared my terrible
shame has destroyed its right to shine on men.
I'll never look upon the sun again.
    OENONE. Renunciation or renunciation!
Now you slander the source of your creation.
Why do you run to death and tear your hair?
    PHAEDRA. Oh God, take me to some sunless forest lair . . .
There hoof-beats raise a dust-cloud, and my eye
follows a horseman outlined on the sky!

OENONE. What's this, my lady?

PHAEDRA. I have lost my mind.
Where am I? Oh forget my words! I find
I've lost the habit now of talking sense.
My face is red and guilty—evidence
of treason! I've betrayed my darkest fears,
Nurse, and my eyes, despite me, fill with tears.

OENONE. Lady, if you must weep, weep for your silence
that filled your days and mine with violence.
Ah deaf to argument and numb to care,
you have no mercy. Spare me, spare
yourself. Your blood is like polluted water,
fouling a mind desiring its own slaughter.
The sun has died and shadows filled the skies
thrice now, since you have closed your eyes;
the day has broken through the night's content
thrice now, since you have tasted nourishment.
Is your salvation from your terrified
conscience this passive, servile suicide?
Lady, your madness harms the gods who gave
you life, betrays your husband. Who will save
your children? Your downfall will orphan them,
deprive them of their kingdom, and condemn
their lives and future to the discipline
of one who abhors you and all your kin,
a tyrant suckled by an amazon,
Hippolytus . . .

PHAEDRA. Oh God!

OENONE. You still hate someone;
thank heaven for that, Madam!

PHAEDRA. You spoke his name!

OENONE. Hippolytus, Hippolytus! There's hope
in hatred, Lady. Give your anger rope.
I love your anger. If the winds of love
and fury stir you, you will live. Above
your children towers this foreigner, this child
of Scythian cannibals, now wild
to ruin the kingdom, master Greece, and choke
the children of the gods beneath his yoke.

Why dawdle? Why deliberate at length?
Oh, gather up your dissipated strength.
    PHAEDRA. I've lived too long.
    OENONE. Always, always agonized!
Is your conscience still stunned and paralyzed?
Do you think you have washed your hands in blood?
    PHAEDRA. Thank God, my hands are clean still. Would to God
my heart were innocent!
    OENONE. Your heart, your heart!
What have you done that tears your soul apart?
    PHAEDRA. I've said too much. Oenone, let me die;
by dying I shall escape blasphemy.
    OENONE. Search for another hand to close your eyes.
Oh cruel Queen, I see that you despise
my sorrow and devotion. I'll die first,
and end the anguish of this service cursed
by your perversity. A thousand roads
always lie open to the killing gods.
I'll choose the nearest. Lady, tell me how
Oenone's love has failed you. Will you allow
your nurse to die, your nurse, who gave up all—
nation, parents, children, to serve in thrall.
I saved you from your mother, King Minos' wife!
Will your death pay me for giving up my life?
    PHAEDRA. What I could tell you, I have told you. Nurse,
only my silence saves me from the curse
of heaven.
    OENONE. How could you tell me anything
worse than watching you dying?
    PHAEDRA. I would bring
my life and rank dishonor. What can I say
to save myself, or put off death a day.
    OENONE. Ah Lady, I implore you by my tears,
and by your suffering body. Heaven hears,
and knows the truth already. Let me see.
    PHAEDRA. Stand up.
    OENONE. Your hesitation's killing me!
    PHAEDRA. What can I tell you? How the gods reprove
me!

OENONE. Speak!

PHAEDRA. Oh Venus, murdering Venus! love
gored Pasiphaë with the bull.

OENONE. Forget
your mother! When she died, she paid her debt.

PHAEDRA. Oh Ariadne, oh my Sister, lost
for love of Theseus on that rocky coast.

OENONE. Lady, what nervous languor makes you rave
against your family; they are in the grave.

PHAEDRA. Remorseless Aphrodite drives me. I,
my race's last and worst love-victim, die.

OENONE. Are you in love?

PHAEDRA. I am insane with love!

OENONE. Who is he?

PHAEDRA. I'll tell you. Nothing love can do
could equal . . . Nurse, I am in love. The shame
kills me. I love the . . . Do not ask his name.

OENONE. Who?

PHAEDRA. Nurse, you know my old loathing for the son
of Theseus and the barbarous amazon?

OENONE. Hippolytus! My God, oh my God!

PHAEDRA. You,
not I, have named him.

OENONE. What can you do,
but die? Your words have turned my blood to ice.
Oh righteous heavens, must the blasphemies
of Pasiphaë fall upon her daughter?
Her Furies strike us down across the water.
Why did we come here?

PHAEDRA. My evil comes from farther off. In May,
in brilliant Athens, on my marriage day,
I turned aside for shelter from the smile
of Theseus. Death was frowning in an aisle—
Hippolytus! I saw his face, turned white!
My lost and dazzled eyes saw only night,
capricious burnings flickered through my bleak
abandoned flesh. I could not breathe or speak.
I faced my flaming executioner,
Aphrodite, my mother's murderer!

I tried to calm her wrath by flowers and praise,
I built her a temple, fretted months and days
on decoration. I even hoped to find
symbols and stays for my distracted mind,
searching the guts of sacrificial steers.
Yet when my erring passions, mutineers
to virtue, offered incense at the shrine
of love, I failed to silence the malign
Goddess. Alas, my hungry open mouth,
thirsting with adoration, tasted drouth—
Venus resigned her altar to my new lord—
and even while I was praying, I adored
Hippolytus above the sacred flame,
now offered to his name I could not name.
I fled him, yet he stormed me in disguise,
and seemed to watch me from his father's eyes.
I even turned against myself, screwed up
my slack courage to fury, and would not stop
shrieking and raging, till half-dead with love
and the hatred of a stepmother, I drove
Hippolytus in exile from the rest
and strenuous wardship of his father's breast.
Then I could breathe, Oenone; he was gone;
my lazy, nerveless days meandered on
through dreams and daydreams, like a stately carriage
touring the level landscape of my marriage.
Yet nothing worked. My husband sent me here
to Troezen, far from Athens; once again the dear
face shattered me; I saw Hippolytus
each day, and felt my ancient, venomous
passion tear my body limb from limb;
naked Venus was clawing down her victim.
What could I do? Each moment, terrified
by loose diseased emotions, now I cried
for death to save my glory and expel
my gloomy frenzy from this world, my hell.
And yet your tears and words bewildered me,
and so endangered my tranquillity,
at last I spoke. Nurse, I shall not repent,

if you will leave me the passive content
of dry silence and solitude.

SCENE FOUR. PHAEDRA, OENONE, PANOPE.

PANOPE. My heart breaks. Would to God, I could refuse
to tell your majesty my evil news.
The King is dead! Listen, the heavens ring
with shouts and lamentations for the King.
  PHAEDRA. The King is dead? What's this?
  PANOPE. In vain
you beg the gods to send him back again.
Hippolytus has heard the true report,
he is already heading for the port.
  PHAEDRA. Oh God!
  PANOPE. They've heard in Athens. Everyone
is joining factions—some salute your son,
others are calling for Hippolytus;
they want him to reform and harden us—
even Aricia claims the loyalty
of a fanatical minority.
The Prince's captains have recalled their men.
His flag is up and now he sails again
for Athens. Queen, if he appear there now,
he'll drag the people with him!
  OENONE. Stop, allow
the Queen a little respite for her grief.
She hears you, and will act for our relief.

SCENE FIVE. PHAEDRA, OENONE.

OENONE. I'd given up persuading you to live;
death was your refuge, only death could give
you peace and save your troubled glory. I
myself desired to follow you, and die.
But this catastrophe prescribes new laws:
the king is dead, and for the king who was,
fate offers you his kingdom. You have a son;
he should be king! If you abandon
him, he'll be a slave. The gods, his ancestors,

will curse and drive you on your fatal course.
Live! Who'll condemn you if you love and woo
the Prince! Your stepson is no kin to you,
now that your royal husband's death has cut
and freed you from the throttling marriage-knot.
Do not torment the Prince with persecution,
and give a leader to the revolution;
no, win his friendship, bind him to your side.
Give him this city and its countryside.
He will renounce the walls of Athens, piled
stone on stone by Minerva for your child.
Stand with Hippolytus, annihilate
Aricia's faction, and possess the state!
    PHAEDRA. So be it! Your superior force has won.
I will live if compassion for my son,
devotion to the Prince, and love of power
can give me courage in this fearful hour.

act two

SCENE ONE. ARICIA, ISMENE.

    ARICIA. What's this? The Prince has sent a messenger?
The Prince begs me to wait and meet him here?
The Prince begs! Goose, you've lost your feeble wits!
    ISMENE. Lady, be calm. These are the benefits
of Theseus' death: first Prince Hippolytus
comes courting favors; soon the populous
cities of Greece will follow—they will eat
out of your hand, Princess, and kiss your feet.
    ARICIA. This felon's hand, this slave's! My dear, your news
is only frivolous gossip, I refuse
to hope.
    ISMENE. Ah Princess, the just powers of hell
have struck. Theseus has joined your brothers!
    ARICIA. Tell
me how he died.
    ISMENE. Princess, fearful tales
are circulating. Sailors saw his sails,

his infamous black sails, spin round and round
in Charybdis' whirlpool; all hands were drowned.
Yet others say on better evidence
that Theseus and Pirithoüs passed the dense
darkness of hell to rape Persephone.
Pirithoüs was murdered by the hound;
Theseus, still living, was buried in the ground.

ARICIA. This is an old wives' tale. Only the dead
enter the underworld, and see the bed
of Queen Persephone. What brought him there?

ISMENE. Princess, the King is dead—dead! Everywhere
men know and mourn. Already our worshipping
townsmen acclaim Hippolytus for their king;
in her great palace, Phaedra, the self-styled
regent, rages and trembles for her child.

ARICIA. What makes you think the puritanical
son of Theseus is human. Will he recall
my sentence and relent?

ISMENE. I know he will.

ARICIA. You know nothing about him. He would kill
a woman, rather than be kind to one.
That wolf-cub of a fighting amazon
hates me above all women. He would walk
from here to hell, rather than hear me talk.

ISMENE. Do you know Hippolytus? Listen to me.
His famous, blasphemous frigidity,
what is it, when you've seen him close at hand?
I've watched him like a hawk, and seem him stand
shaking beside you—all his reputation
for hating womenkind bears no relation
to what I saw. He couldn't take his eyes
off you! His eyes speak what his tongue denies.

ARICIA. I can't believe you. Your story's absurd!
How greedily I listen to each word!
Ismene, you know me, you know how my heart
was reared on death, and always set apart
from what it cherished—can this plaything of
the gods and furies feel the peace of love?
What sights I've seen, Ismene! "Heads will roll,"

my brothers told me, "we will rule." I, the sole
survivor of those fabulous kings, who tilled
the soil of Greece, have seen my brothers killed,
six brothers murdered! In a single hour,
the tyrant, Theseus, lopped them in their flower.
The monster spared my life, and yet decreed
the torments of this childless life I lead
in exile, where no Greek can look on me;
my forced, perpetual virginity
preserves his crown; no son shall bear my name
or blow my brothers' ashes into flame.
Ismene, you know how well his tyranny
favors my temperament and strengthens me
to guard the honor of my reputation;
his rigor fortified my inclination.
How could I test his son's civilities?
I'd never even seen him with my eyes!
I'd never seen him. I'd restrained my eye,
that giddy nerve, from dwelling thoughtlessly
upon his outward grace and beauty—on mere
embellishments of nature, a veneer
the Prince himself despises and ignores.
My heart loves nobler virtues, and adores
in him his father's hard intelligence.
He has his father's daring and a sense
of honor his father lacks. Let me confess,
I love him for his lofty haughtiness
never submitted to a woman's yoke.
How could Phaedra's splendid marriage provoke
my jealousy? Have I so little pride,
I'd snatch at a rake's heart, a heart denied
to none—all riddled, opened up to let
thousands pass in like water through a net?
To carry sorrows to a heart, alone
untouched by passion, inflexible as stone,
so fasten my dominion on a force
as nervous as a never-harnessed horse—
this stirs me, this enflames me. Devilish Zeus
is easier mastered than Hippolytus;

heaven's love-infatuated emperor
confess less glory on his conqueror!
Ismene, I'm afraid. Why should I boast?
His very virtues I admire most
threaten to rise and throw me from the brink
of hope. What girlish folly made me think
Hippolytus could love Aricia?
    ISMENE. Here
he is. He loves you, Princess. Have no fear.

SCENE TWO. ARICIA, ISMENE, HIPPOLYTUS.

    HIPPOLYTUS. Princess, before
I leave here, I must tell you what's in store
for you in Greece. Alas, my father's dead.
The fierce forebodings that disquieted
my peace are true. Death, only death, could hide
his valor from this world he pacified.
The homicidal Fates will not release
the comrade, friend and peer of Hercules.
Princess, I trust your hate will not resent
honors whose justice is self-evident.
A single hope alleviates my grief,
Princess, I hope to offer you relief.
I now revoke a law whose cruelty
has pained my conscience. Princess, you are free
to marry. Oh enjoy this province, whose
honest, unhesitating subjects choose
Hippolytus for king. Live free as air,
here, free as I am, much more free!
    ARICIA. I dare
not hope. You are too gracious. Can you free
Aricia from your father's stern decree?
    HIPPOLYTUS. Princess, the Athenian people, torn in two
between myself and Phaedra's son, want you.
    ARICIA. Want me, my Lord!
    HIPPOLYTUS. I've no illusions. Lame
Athenian precedents condemn my claim,
because my mother was a foreigner.

But what is that? If my only rival were
my younger brother, his minority
would clear my legal disability.
However, a better claim than his or mine
now favors you, ennobled by the line
of great Erectheus. Your direct descent
sets you before my father; he was only lent
this kingdom by adoption. Once the common
Athenian, dazed by Theseus' superhuman
energies, had no longing to exhume
the rights that rushed your brothers to their doom.
Now Athens calls you home; the ancient feud
too long has stained the sacred olive wood;
blood festers in the furrows of our soil
to blight its fruits and scorch the farmer's toil.
This province suits me; let the vines of Crete
offer my brother a secure retreat.
The rest is yours. All Attica is yours;
I go to win you what you right assures.
   ARICIA. Am I awake, my lord? Your sayings seem
like weird phantasmagoria in a dream.
How can your sparkling promises be true?
Some god, my lord, some god, has entered you!
How justly you are worshiped in this town;
oh how the truth surpasses your renown!
You wish to endow me with your heritage!
I only hoped you would not hate me. This rage
your father felt, how can you put it by
and treat me kindly?
   HIPPOLYTUS. Princess, is my eye
blind to beauty? Am I a bear, a bull, a boar,
some abortion fathered by the Minotaur?
Some one-eyed Cyclops, able to resist
Aricia's loveliness and still exist?
How can a man stand up against your grace?
   ARICIA. My lord, my lord!
   HIPPOLYTUS. I cannot hide my face,
Princess! I'm driven. Why does my violence
so silence reason and intelligence?

Must I be still, and let my adoration
simmer away in silent resignation?
Princess, I've lost all power to restrain
myself. You see a madman, whose insane
pride hated love, and hoped to sit ashore,
watching the galleys founder in the war;
I was Diana's liegeman, dressed in steel.
I hoped to trample love beneath my heel—
alas, the flaming Venus burns me down,
I am the last dependent on her crown.
What left me charred and writhing in her clutch?
A single moment and a single touch.
Six months now, bounding like a wounded stag,
I've tried to shake this poisoned dart, and drag
myself to safety from your eyes that blind
when present, and when absent leave behind
volleys of burning arrows in my mind.
Ah Princess, shall I dive into the sea,
or steal the wings of Icarus to flee
love's Midas' touch that turns my world to gold?
Your image drives me stumbling through the cold,
floods my deserted forest caves with light,
darkens the day and dazzles through my night.
I'm grafted to your side by all I see;
all things unite us and imprison me.
I have no courage for the Spartan exercise
that trained my hand and steeled my energies.
Where are my horses? I forget their names.
My triumphs with my chariot at the games
no longer give me strength to mount a horse.
The ocean drives me shuddering from its shores.
Does such a savage conquest make you blush?
My boorish gestures, headlong cries that rush
at you like formless monsters from the sea?
Ah, Princess, hear me! Your serenity
must pardon the distortions of a weak
and new-born lover, forced by you to speak
love's foreign language, words that snarl and yelp . . .
I never could have spoken without your help.

SCENE THREE. ARICIA, ISMENE,
HIPPOLYTUS, THERAMENES.

THERAMENES. I announce the Queen. She comes hurriedly,
looking for you.

HIPPOLYTUS. For me!

THERAMENES. Don't ask me why;
she insisted. I promised I'd prevail
on you to speak with her before you sail.

HIPPOLYTUS. What can she want to hear? What can I say?

ARICIA. Wait for her, here! You cannot turn away.
Forget her malice. Hating her will serve
no purpose. Wait for her! Her tears deserve
your pity.

HIPPOLYTUS. You're going, Princess? And I must go
to Athens, far from you. How shall I know
if you accept my love.

ARICIA. My lord, pursue
your gracious promise. Do what you must do,
make Athens tributary to my rule
Nothing you offer is unacceptable;
yet this empire, so great, so glorious,
is the least precious of your gifts to us.

SCENE FOUR. HIPPOLYTUS, THERAMENES.

HIPPOLYTUS. We're ready. Wait, the Queen's here. I need you.
You must interrupt this tedious interview.
Hurry down to the ship, then rush back, pale
and breathless. Say the wind's up and we must sail.

SCENE FIVE. HIPPOLYTUS, OENONE, PHAEDRA.

PHAEDRA. He's here! Why does he scowl and look away
from me? What shall I do? What shall I say?

OENONE. Speak for your son, he has no other patron.

PHAEDRA. Why are you so impatient to be gone
from us, my lord? Stay! we will weep together.
Pity my son; he too has lost his father.

My own death's near. Rebellion, sick with wrongs,
now like a sea-beast, lifts its slimey prongs,
its muck, its jelly. You alone now stand
to save the state. Who else can understand
a mother? I forget. You will not hear
me! An enemy deserves no pity. I fear
your anger. Must my son, your brother, Prince,
be punished for his cruel mother's sins?
    HIPPOLYTUS. I've no such thoughts.
    PHAEDRA. I persecuted you
blindly, and now you have good reason to
return my impudence. How could you find
the motivation of this heart and mind
that scourged and tortured you, till you began
to lose the calm composure of a man,
and dwindle to a harsh and sullen boy,
a thing of ice, unable to enjoy
the charms of any civilized resource
except the heavy friendship of your horse,
that whirled you far from women, court and throne,
to course the savage woods for wolves alone?
You have good reason, yet if pain's a measure,
no one has less deserved your stern displeasure.
My lord, no one has more deserved compassion.
    HIPPOLYTUS. Lady, I understand a mother's passion,
a mother jealous for her children's rights.
How can she spare a first wife's son? Long nights
of plotting, devious ways of quarrelling—
a madhouse! What else can remarriage bring?
Another would have shown equal hostility,
pushed her advantage more outrageously.
    PHAEDRA. My lord, if you had known how far my love
and yearning have exalted me above
this usual weakness . . . Our afflicting kinship
is ending . . .
    HIPPOLYTUS. Madam, the precious minutes slip
by, I fatigue you. Fight against your fears.
Perhaps Poseidon has listened to our tears,
perhaps your husband's still alive. He hears

us, he is surging home—only a short
day's cruise conceals him, as he scuds for port.

    PHAEDRA. That's folly, my lord. Who has twice visited
black Hades and the river of the dead
and returned? No, the poisonous Acheron
never lets go. Theseus drifts on and on,
a gutted galley on that clotted waste—
he woos, he wins Persephone, the chaste . . .
What am I saying? Theseus is not dead.
He lives in you. He speaks, he's taller by a head,
I see him, touch him, and my heart—a reef . . .
Ah Prince, I wander. Love betrays my grief . . .

    HIPPOLYTUS. No, no, my father lives. Lady, the blind
furies release him; in your loyal mind,
love's fullness holds him, and he cannot die.

    PHAEDRA. I hunger for Theseus. Always in my eye
he wanders, not as he appeared in hell,
lascivious eulogist of any belle
he found there, from the lowest to the Queen;
no, faithful, airy, just a little mean
through virtue, charming all, yet young and new,
as we would paint a god—as I now see you!
Your valiant shyness would have graced his speech,
he would have had your stature, eyes, and reach,
Prince, when he flashed across our Cretan waters,
the loved enslaver of King Minos' daughters.
Where were you? How could he conscript the flower
of Athens' youth against my father's power,
and ignore you? You were too young, they say;
you should have voyaged as a stowaway.
No dawdling bypath would have saved our bull,
when your just vengeance thundered through its skull.
There, light of foot, and certain of your goal,
you would have struck my brother's monstrous soul,
and pierced our maze's slow meanders, led
by Ariadne and her subtle thread.
By Ariadne? Prince, I would have fought
for precedence; my every flaming thought,
love-quickened, would have shot you through the dark,

straight as an arrow to your quaking mark.
Could I have waited, panting, perishing,
entrusting your survival to a string,
like Ariadne, when she skulked behind,
there at the portal, to bemuse her mind
among the solemn cloisters of the porch?
No, Phaedra would have snatched your burning torch,
and lunged before you, reeling like a priest
of Dionysus to distract the beast.
I would have reached the final corridor
a lap before you, and killed the Minotaur!
Lost in the labyrinth, and at your side,
would it have mattered, if I lived or died?

    HIPPOLYTUS. What are you saying, Madam? You forget
my father is your husband!

    PHAEDRA. I have let
you see my grief for Theseus! How could I
forget my honor and my majesty,
Prince?

    HIPPOLYTUS. Madam, forgive me! My foolish youth
conjectured hideous untruths from your truth.
I cannot face my insolence. Farewell . . .

    PHAEDRA. You monster! You understood me too well!
Why do you hang there, speechless, petrified,
polite! My mind whirls. What have I to hide?
Phaedra in all her madness stands before you.
I love you! Fool, I love you, I adore you!
Do not imagine that my mind approved
my first defection, Prince, or that I loved
your youth light-heartedly, and fed my treason
with cowardly compliance, till I lost my reason.
I wished to hate you, but the gods corrupt
us; though I never suffered their abrupt
seductions, shattering advances, I
too bear their sensual lightnings in my thigh.
I too am dying. I have felt the heat
that drove my mother through the fields of Crete,
the bride of Minis, dying for the full
magnetic April thunders of the bull.

I struggled with my sickness, but I found
no grace or magic to preserve my sound
intelligence and honor from this lust,
plowing my body with its horny thrust.
At first I fled you, and when this fell short
of safety, Prince, I exiled you from court.
Alas, my violence to resist you made
my face inhuman, hateful. I was afraid
to kiss my husband lest I love his son.
I made you fear me (this was easily done);
you loathed me more, I ached for you no less.
Misfortune magnified your loveliness.
I grew so wrung and wasted, men mistook
me for the Sibyl. If you could bear to look
your eyes would tell you. Do you believe my passion
is voluntary? That my obscene confession
is some dark trick, some oily artifice?
I came to beg you not to sacrifice
my son, already uncertain of his life.
Ridiculous, mad embassy, for a wife
who loves her stepson! Prince, I only spoke
about myself! Avenge yourself, invoke
your father; a worse monster threatens you
than any Theseus ever fought and slew.
The wife of Theseus loves Hippolytus!
See, Prince! Look, this monster, ravenous
for her execution, will not flinch.
I want your sword's spasmodic final inch.
   OENONE. Madam, put down this weapon. Your distress
attracts the people. Fly these witnesses.
Hurry! Stop kneeling! What a time to pray!

SCENE SIX. THERAMENES, HIPPOLYTUS.

   THERAMENES. Is this Phaedra, fleeing, or rather dragged away
sobbing? Where is your sword? Who tore
this empty scabbard from your belt?
   HIPPOLYTUS. No more!
Oh let me get away! I face disaster.

Horrors unnerve me. Help! I cannot master
my terror. Phaedra . . . No, I won't expose
her. No! Something I do not dare disclose . . .

THERAMENES. Our ship is ready, but before you leave,
listen! Prince, what we never would believe
has happened: Athens has voted for your brother.
The citizens have made him king. His mother
is regent.

HIPPOLYTUS. Phaedra is in power!

THERAMENES. An envoy sent from Athens came this hour
to place the scepter in her hands. Her son is king.

HIPPOLYTUS. Almighty gods, you know this woman!
Is it her spotless virtue you reward?

THERAMENES. I've heard a rumor. Someone swam aboard
a ship off Epirus. He claims the King
is still alive. I've searched. I know the thing
is nonsense.

HIPPOLYTUS. Search! Nothing must be neglected.
If the king's dead, I'll rouse the disaffected
people, crown Aricia, and place our lands,
our people, and our lives in worthy hands.

act three

SCENE ONE. PHAEDRA, OENONE.

PHAEDRA. Why do my people rush to crown me queen?
Who can even want to see me? They have seen
my downfall. Will their praise deliver me?
Oh bury me at the bottom of the sea!
Nurse, I have said too much! Led on by you,
I've said what no one should have listened to.
He listened. How could he pretend my drift
was hidden? Something held him, and made him shift
his ground . . . He only wanted to depart
and hide, while I was pouring out my heart.
Oh how his blushing multiplied my shame!
Why did you hold me back! You are to blame,
Oenone. But for you, I would have killed

myself. Would he have stood there, iron-willed
and merciless, while I fell upon his sword?
He would have snatched it, held me, and restored
my life. No! No!

    OENONE. Control yourself! No peace
comes from surrendering to your disease,
Madam. Oh daughter of the kings of Crete,
why are you weeping and fawning at the feet
of this barbarian, less afraid of fate
than of a woman? You must rule the state.

    PHAEDRA. Can I, who have no courage to restrain
the insurrection of my passions, reign?
Will the Athenians trust their sovereignty
to me? Love's despotism is crushing me,
I am ruined.

    OENONE. Fly!

    PHAEDRA. How can I leave him?

    OENONE. Lady, you have already banished him.
Can't you take flight?

    PHAEDRA. The time for flight has passed.
He knows me now. I rushed beyond the last
limits of modesty, when I confessed.
Hope was no longer blasting through my breast;
I was resigned to hopelessness and death,
and gasping out my last innocent breath,
Oenone, when you forced me back to life.
You thought I was no longer Theseus' wife,
and let me feel that I was free to love.

    OENONE. I would have done anything to remove
your danger. Whether I'm guilty or innocent
is all the same to me. Your punishment
should fall on one who tried to kill you, not
on poor Oenone. Lady, you must plot
and sacrifice this monster, whose unjust
abhorrence left you dying in the dust.
Oh humble him, undo him, oh despise
him! Lady, you must see him with my eyes.

    PHAEDRA. Oenone, he was nourished in the woods;
he is all shyness and ungracious moods

because the forests left him half-inhuman.
He's never heard love spoken by a woman!
We've gone too far. Oenone, we're unwise;
perhaps the young man's silence was surprise.
 OENONE. His mother, the amazon, was never moved by men.
 PHAEDRA. The boy exists. She must have loved!
 OENONE. He has a sullen hatred for our sex.
 PHAEDRA. Oh, all the better; rivals will not vex
my chances. Your advice is out of season;
now you must serve my frenzy, not my reason!
You tell me love has never touched his heart;
we'll look, we'll find an undefended part.
He's turned his bronze prows seaward; look, the wind
already blows like a trumpeter behind
his bulging canvas! The Acropolis
of Athens and its empire shall be his!
Hurry, Oenone, hunt the young man down,
blind him with dazzling visions of the crown.
Go tell him I relinquish my command,
I only want the guidance of his hand.
Let him assume these powers that weary me,
he will instruct my son in sovereignty.
Perhaps he will adopt my son, and be
the son and mother's one divinity!
Oenone, rush to him, use every means
to bend and win him; if he fears the Queen's
too proud, he'll listen to her slave. Plead, groan,
insist, say I am giving him my throne . . .
No, say I'm dying!

SCENE TWO. PHAEDRA.

 PHAEDRA. Implacable Aphrodite, now you see
the depths to which your tireless cruelty
has driven Phaedra—here is my bosom;
every thrust and arrow his struck home!
Oh Goddess, if you hunger for renown,
rise now, and shoot a worthier victim down!
Conquer the barbarous Hippolytus,

who mocks the graces and the power of Venus,
and gazes on your godhead with disgust.
Avenge me, Venus! See, my cause is just,
my cause is yours. Oh bend him to my will! . . .
You're back, Oenone? Does he hate me still?

SCENE THREE. PHAEDRA, OENONE.

OENONE. Your love is folly, dash it from your soul,
gather your scattered pride and self-control,
Madam! I've seen the royal ship arrive.
Theseus is back, Theseus is still alive!
Thousands of voices thunder from the docks.
People are waving flags and climbing rocks.
While I was looking for Hippolytus . . .
    PHAEDRA. My husband's living! Must you trouble us
by talking? What am I living for?
He lives, Oenone, let me hear no more
about it.
    OENONE. Why?
    PHAEDRA. I told you, but my fears
were stilled, alas, and smothered by your tears.
Had I died this morning, I might have faced
the gods. I heeded you and die disgraced!
    OENONE. You are disgraced!
    PHAEDRA. Oh Gods of wrath,
how far I've travelled on my dangerous path!
I go to meet my husband; at his side
will stand Hippolytus. How shall I hide
my thick adulterous passion for this youth,
who has rejected me, and knows the truth?
Will the stern Prince stand smiling and approve
the labored histrionics of my love
for Theseus, see my lips, still languishing
for his, betray his father and his King?
Will he not draw his sword and strike me dead?
Suppose he spares me? What if nothing's said?
Am I a gorgon, or Circe, or the infidel
Medea, stifled by the flames of hell,

yet rising like Aphrodite from the sea,
refreshed and radiant with indecency?
Can I kiss Theseus with dissembled poise?
I think each stone and pillar has a voice.
The very dust rises to disabuse
my husband—to defame me and accuse!
Oenone, I want to die. Death will give
me freedom; oh it's nothing not to live;
death to the unhappy's no catastrophe!
I fear the name that must live after me,
and crush my son until the end of time.
Is his inheritance his mother's crime,
his right to curse me, when my pollution stains
the blood of heaven bubbling in his veins?
The day will come, alas, the day will come,
when nothing will be left to save him from
the voices of despair. If he should live
he'll flee his subjects like a fugitive.

    OENONE. He has my pity. Who has ever built
firmer foundations to expose her guilt?
But why expose your son? Is your contribution
for his defense to serve the prosecution?
Suppose you kill yourself? The world will say
you fled your outraged husband in dismay.
Could there be stronger evidence and proof
than Phaedra crushed beneath the horse's hoof
of blasphemous self-destruction to convince
the crowds who'll dance attendance on the Prince?
The crowds will mob your children when they hear
their defamation by a foreigner!
Wouldn't you rather see earth bury us?
Tell me, do you still love Hippolytus?

      PHAEDRA. I see him as a beast, who'd murder us.

      OENONE. Madam, let the positions be reversed!
You fear the Prince; you must accuse him first.
Who'll dare assert your story is untrue,
if all the evidence shall speak for you;
your present grief, your past despair of mind,
the Prince's sword so luckily left behind?

Do you think Theseus will oppose his son's
second exile? He has consented once!
    PHAEDRA. How dare I take this murderous, plunging course?
    OENONE. I tremble, Lady, I too feel remorse.
If death could rescue you from infamy,
Madam, I too would follow you and die.
Help me by being silent. I will speak
in such a way the King will only seek
a bloodless exile to assert his rights.
A father is still a father when he smites,
You shudder at this evil sacrifice,
but nothing's evil or too high a price
to save your menaced honor from defeat.
Ah Minos, Minos, you defended Crete
by killing young men? Help us! If the cost
for saving Phaedra is a holocaust
of virtue, Minos, you must sanctify
our undertaking, or watch your daughter die.
I see the King.
    PHAEDRA. I see Hippolytus!

SCENE FOUR. PHAEDRA, THESEUS, HIPPOLYTUS, OENONE.

    THESEUS. Fate's heard me, Phaedra, and removed the bar
that kept me from your arms.
    PHAEDRA. Theseus, stop where you are!
Your raptures and endearments are profane.
Your arm must never comfort me again.
You have been wronged, the gods who spared your life
have used your absence to disgrace your wife,
unworthy now to please you or come near.
My only refuge is to disappear.

SCENE FIVE. THESEUS, HIPPOLYTUS.

    THESEUS. What a strange welcome! This bewildered me,
My son, what's happened?
    HIPPOLYTUS. Phaedra holds the key.

Ask Phaedra. If you love me, let me leave
this kingdom. I'm determined to achieve
some action that will show my strength. I fear
Phaedra. I am afraid of living here,
    THESEUS. My son, you want to leave me?
    HIPPOLYTUS. I never sought
her grace or favor. Your decision brought
her here from Athens. Your desires prevailed
against my judgment, Father, when you sailed
leaving Phaedra and Aricia in my care.
I've done my duty, now I must prepare
for sterner actions, I must test my skill
on monsters far more dangerous to kill
than any wolf or eagle in this wood.
Release me, I too must prove my manhood.
Oh Father, you were hardly half my age,
when herds of giants writhed before your rage—
you were already famous as the scourge
of insolence. Our people saw you purge
the pirates from the shores of Greece and Thrace,
the harmless merchantman was free to race
the winds, and weary Hercules could pause
from slaughter, knowing you upheld his cause.
The world revered you. I am still unknown;
even my mother's deeds surpass my own.
Some tyrants have escaped you; let me meet
with them and throw their bodies at your feet.
I'll drag them from their wolf-holes; if I die,
my death will show I struggled worthily.
Oh, Father, raise me from oblivion;
my deeds shall tell the universe I am your son.
    THESEUS. What do I see? Oh gods, what horror drives
my queen and children fleeing for their lives
before me? If so little warmth remains,
oh why did you release me from my chains?
Why am I hated, and so little loved?
I had a friend, just one. His folly moved
me till I aided his conspiracy
to ravish Queen Persephone.

The gods, tormented by our blasphemous
designs, befogged our minds and blinded us—
we invaded Epirus instead of hell.
There a diseased and subtle tyrant fell
upon us as we slept, and while I stood
by, helpless, monsters crazed for human blood
consumed Pirithoüs. I myself was chained
fast in a death-deep dungeon. I remained
six months there, then the gods had pity,
and put me in possession of the city.
I killed the tyrant; now his body feasts
the famished, pampered bellies of his beasts.
At last, I voyaged home, cast anchor, furled
my sails. When I was rushing to my world—
what am I saying? When my heart and soul
were mine again, unable to control
themselves for longing—who receives me? All run
and shun me, as if I were a skeleton.
Now I myself begin to feel the fear
I inspire. I wish I were a prisoner
again or dead. Speak! Phaedra says my home
was outraged. Who betrayed me? Someone come
and tell me. I have fought for Greece. Will Greece,
sustained by Theseus, give my enemies
asylum in my household? Tell me why
I've no avenger? Is my son a spy?
You will not answer. I must know my fate.
Suspicion chokes me, while I hesitate
and stand here pleading. Wait, let no one stir.
Phaedra shall tell me what has troubled her.

SCENE SIX. HIPPOLYTUS.

HIPPOLYTUS. What now? His anger turns my blood to ice.
Will Phaedra, always uncertain, sacrifice
herself? What will she tell the King? How hot
the air's becoming here! I feel the rot
of love seeping like poison through this house.
I feel the pollution. I cannot rouse

my former loyalties. When I try to gather
the necessary strength to face my father,
my mind spins with some dark presentiment . . .
How can such terror touch the innocent?
I LOVE ARICIA! Father, I confess
my treason to you is my happiness!
I LOVE ARICIA! Will this bring you joy,
our love you have no power to destroy?

act four

SCENE ONE. THESEUS, OENONE.

THESEUS. What's this, you tell me he dishonors me,
and has assaulted Phaedra's chastity?
Oh heavy fortune, I no longer know
who loves me, who I am, or where I go.
Who has ever seen such disloyalty
after such love? Such sly audacity!
His youth made no impression on her soul,
so he fell back on force to reach his goal!
I recognized this perjured sword; I gave
him this myself to teach him to be brave!
Oh Zeus, are blood-ties no impediment?
Phaedra tried to save him from punishment!
Why did her silence spare this parricide?

OENONE. She hoped to spare a trusting father's pride.
She felt so sickened by your son's attempt,
his hot eyes leering at her with contempt,
she had no wish to live. She read out her will
to me, then lifted up her arm to kill
herself. I struck the sword out of her hand.
Fainting, she babbled the secret she had planned
to bury with her in the grave. My ears
unwillingly interpreted her tears.

THESEUS. Oh traitor! I know why he seemed to blanch
and toss with terror like an aspen branch
when Phaedra saw him. Now I know why he stood
back, then embraced me so coldly he froze my blood.

Was Athens the first stage for his obscene
attentions? Did he dare attack the Queen
before our marriage?
　　OENONE. Remember her disgust
and hate then? She already feared his lust.
　　THESEUS. And when I sailed, this started up again?
　　OENONE. I've hidden nothing. Do you want your pain
redoubled? Phaedra calls me. Let me go,
and save her. I have told you what I know.

SCENE TWO. THESEUS, HIPPOLYTUS.

　　THESEUS. My son returns! Oh God, reserved and cool,
dressed in a casual freedom that could fool
the sharpest. Is it right his brows should blaze
and dazzle me with virtue's sacred rays?
Are there not signs? Should not ADULTERER
in looping scarlet script be branded there?
　　HIPPOLYTUS. What cares becloud your kingly countenance,
Father! What is this irritated glance?
Tell me! Are you afraid to trust your son?
　　THESEUS. How dare you stand here? May the great Zeus stone
me, if I let my fondness and your birth
protect you! Is my strength which rid the earth
of brigands paralysed? Am I so sick
and senile, any coward with a stick
can strike me? Am I a schoolboy's target? Oh God,
am I food for vultures? Some carrion you must prod
and poke to see if it's alive or dead?
Your hands are moist and itching for my bed,
Coward! Wasn't begetting you enough
dishonor to destroy me? Must I snuff
your perjured life, my own son's life, and stain
a thousand glories? Let the gods restrain
my fury! Fly! live hated and alone—
there are places where my name may be unknown.
Go, find them, follow your disastrous star
through filth; if I discover where you are,
I'll add another body to the hill

of vermin I've extinguished by my skill.
Fly from me, let the grieving storm-winds bear
your contagion from me. You corrupt the air.
I call upon Poseidon. Help me, Lord
of Ocean, help your servant! Once my sword
heaped crucified assassins on your shore
and let them burn like beacons. God, you swore
my first request would be fulfilled. My first!
I never made it. Even through the worst
torments of Epirus I held my peace;
no threat or torture brought me to my knees
beseeching favors; even then I knew
some greater project was reserved for you!
Poseidon, now I kneel. Avenge me, dash
my incestuous son against your rocks, and wash
his dishonor from my household; wave on wave
of roaring nothingness shall be his grave.

    HIPPOLYTUS. Phaedra accuses me of lawless love!
Phaedra! My heart stops, I can hardly move
my lips and answer. I have no defense,
if you condemn me without evidence.

    THESEUS. Oh coward, you were counting on the Queen
to hide your brutal insolence and screen
your outrage with her weakness! You forgot
something. You dropped your sword and spoiled your plot.
You should have kept it. Surely you had time
to kill the only witness to your crime!

    HIPPOLYTUS. Why do I stand this, and forbear to clear
away these lies, and let the truth appear?
I could so easily. Where would you be,
if I spoke out? Respect my loyalty,
Father, respect your own intelligence.
Examine me. What am I? My defense
is my whole life. When have I wavered, when
have I pursued the vices of young men?
Father, you have no scaffolding to rig
your charges on. Small crimes precede the big.
Phaedra accused me of attempting rape!
Am I some Proteus, who can change his shape?

Nature despises such disparities.
Vice, like virtue, advances by degrees.
Bred by Antiope to manly arms,
I hate the fever of this lust that warms
the loins and rots the spirit. I was taught
uprightness by Theramenes. I fought
with wolves, tamed horses, gave my soul to sport,
and shunned the joys of women and the court.
I dislike praise, but those who know me best
grant me one virtue—it's that I detest
the very crimes of which I am accused.
How often you yourself have been amused
and puzzled by my love of purity,
pushed to the point of crudeness. By the sea
and in the forests, I have filled my heart
with freedom, far from women.
   THESEUS. When this part
was dropped, could only Phaedra violate
the cold abyss of your immaculate
reptilian soul. How could this funeral urn
contain a heart, a living heart, or burn
for any woman but my wife?
   HIPPOLYTUS. Ah no!
Father, I too have seen my passions blow
into a tempest. Why should I conceal
my true offense? I feel, Father, I feel
what other young men feel. I love, I love
Aricia. Father, I love the sister of
your worst enemies. I worship her!
I only feel and breathe and live for her!
   THESEUS. You love Aricia? God! No, this is meant
to blind my eyes and throw me off the scent.
   HIPPOLYTUS. Father, for six months I have done my worst
to kill this passion. You shall be the first
to know . . . You frown still. Nothing can remove
your dark obsession. Father, what will prove
my innocence? I swear by earth and sky,
and nature's solemn, shining majesty. . . .
   THESEUS. Oaths and religion are the common cant

of all betrayers. If you wish to taunt
me, find a better prop than blasphemy.

HIPPOLYTUS. All's blasphemy to eyes that cannot see.
Could even Phaedra bear me such ill will?

THESEUS. Phaedra, Phaedra! Name her again, I'll kill
you! My hand's already on my sword.

HIPPOLYTUS. Explain
my terms of exile. What do you ordain?

THESEUS. Sail out across the ocean. Everywhere
on earth and under heaven is too near.

HIPPOLYTUS. Who'll take me in? Oh who will pity me,
and give me bread, if you abandon me?

THESEUS. You'll find fitting companions. Look for friends
who honor everything that most offends.
Pimps and jackals who praise adultery
and incest will protect your purity!

HIPPOLYTUS. Adultery! Is it your privilege
to fling this word in my teeth? I've reached the edge
of madness . . . No, I'll say no more. Compare
my breeding with Phaedra's. Think and beware . . .
She had a mother . . . No, I must not speak.

THESEUS. You devil, you'll attack the queen still weak
from your assault. How can you stand and face
your father? Must I drive you from this place
with my own hand. Run off, or I will flog
you with the flat of my sword like a dog!

SCENE THREE: THESEUS.

THESEUS. You go to your inevitable fate,
Child—by the river immortals venerate.
Poseidon gave his word. You cannot fly:
death and the gods march on invisibly.
I loved you once; despite your perfidy,
my bowels writhe inside me. Must you die?
Yes; I am in too deep now to draw back.
What son has placed his father on such a rack?
What father groans for such a monstrous birth?
Oh gods, your thunder throws me to the earth.

SCENE FOUR. THESEUS, PHAEDRA.

PHAEDRA. Theseus, I heard the deluge of your voice,
and stand here trembling. If there's time for choice,
hold back your hand, still bloodless; spare your race!
I supplicate you, I kneel here for grace.
Oh, Theseus, Theseus, will you drench the earth
with your own blood? His virtue, youth and birth
cry out for him. Is he already slain
by you for me—spare me this incestuous pain!
THESEUS. Phaedra, my son's blood has not touched my hand;
and yet I'll be avenged. On sea and land,
spirits, the swift of foot, shall track him down.
Poseidon owes me this. Why do you frown?
PHAEDRA. Poseidon owes you this? What have you done
in anger?
THESEUS. What! You wish to help my son?
No, stir my anger, back me to the hilt,
call for blacker colors to paint his guilt.
Lash, strike and drive me on! You cannot guess
the nerve and fury of his wickedness.
Phaedra, he slandered your sincerity,
he told me your accusation was a lie.
He swore he lover Aricia, he wants to wed
Aricia. . . .
PHAEDRA. What, my lord!
THESEUS. That's what he said.
Of course, I scorn his shallow artifice.
Help me, Poseidon, hear me, sacrifice
my son. I seek the altar. Come! Let us both
kneel down and beg the gods to keep their oath.

SCENE FIVE. PHAEDRA.

PHAEDRA. My husband's gone, still rumbling his own name
and fame. He has no inkling of the flame
his words have started. If he hadn't spoken,
I might have . . . I was on my feet, I'd broken
loose from Oenone, and had just begun

to say I know not what to save his son.
Who knows how far I would have gone? Remorse,
longing and anguish shook me with such force,
I might have told the truth and suffered death,
before this revelation stopped my breath:
Hippolytus is not insensible,
only insensible to me! His dull
heart chases shadows. He is glad to rest
upon Aricia's adolescent breast!
Oh thin abstraction! When I saw his firm
repugnance spurn my passion like a worm,
I thought he had some magic to withstand
the lure of any woman in the land,
and now I see a schoolgirl leads the boy,
as simply as her puppy or a toy.
Was I about to perish for this sham,
this panting hypocrite? Perhaps I am
the only woman that he could refuse!

SCENE SIX. PHAEDRA, OENONE.

PHAEDRA. Oenone, dearest, have you heard the news?
OENONE. No, I know nothing, but I am afraid.
How can I follow you? You have betrayed
your life and children. What have you revealed,
Madam?
PHAEDRA. I have a rival in the field,
Oenone.
OENONE. What?
PHAEDRA. Oenone, he's in love—
this howling monster, able to disprove
my beauty, mock my passion, scorn each prayer,
and face me like a tiger in its lair—
he's tamed, the beast is harnessed to a cart;
Aricia's found an entrance to his heart.
OENONE. Aricia?
PHAEDRA. Nurse, my last calamity
has come. This is the bottom of the sea.
All that preceded this had little force—

the flames of lust, the horrors of remorse,
the prim refusal by my grim young master,
were only feeble hints of this disaster.
They love each other! Passion blinded me.
I let them blind me, let them meet and see
each other freely! Was such bounty wrong?
Oenone, you have known this all along,
you must have seen their meetings, watched them sneak
off to their forest, playing hide-and-seek!
Alas, such rendezvous are no offence:
innocent nature smiles of innocence,
for them each natural impulse was allowed,
each day was summer and without a cloud.
Oenone, nature hated me. I fled
its light, as if a price were on my head.
I shut my eyes and hungered for my end.
Death was the only God my vows could bend.
And even while my desolation served
me gall and tears, I knew I was observed;
I never had security or leisure
for honest weeping, but must steal this pleasure.
Oh hideous pomp; a monarch only wears
the robes of majesty to hide her tears!

    OENONE. How can their folly help them? They will never
enjoy its fruit.

    PHAEDRA. Ugh, they will love forever—
even while I am talking, they embrace,
they scorn me, they are laughing in my face!
In the teeth of exile, I hear them swear
they will be true forever, everywhere.
Oenone, have pity on my jealous rage;
I'll kill this happiness that jeers at age.
I'll summon Theseus; hate shall answer hate!
I'll drive my husband to annihilate
Aricia—let no trivial punishment,
her instant death, or bloodless banishment . . .
What am I saying? Have I lost my mind?
I am jealous, and call my husband! Bind
me, gag me; I am frothing with desire.

My husband is alive, and I'm on fire!
For whom? Hippolytus. When I have said
his name, blood fills my eyes, my heart stops dead.
Imposture, incest, murder! I have passed
the limits of damnation; now at last,
my lover's lifeblood is my single good.
Nothing else cools my murderous thirst for blood.
Yet I live on! I live, looked down upon
by my progenitor, the sacred sun,
by Zeus, by Europa, by the universe
of gods and stars, my ancestors. They curse
their daughter. Let me die. In the great night
of Hades, I'll find shelter from their sight.
What am I saying? I've no place to turn:
Minos, my father, holds the judge's urn.
The gods have placed damnation in his hands,
the shades in Hades follow his commands.
Will he not shake and curse his fatal star
that brings his daughter trembling to his bar?
His child by Pasiphaë forced to tell
a thousand sins unclassified in hell?
Father, when you interpret what I speak,
I fear your fortitude will be too weak
to hold the urn. I see you fumbling for
new punishments for crimes unknown before.
You'll be your own child's executioner!
You cannot kill me; look, my murderer
is Venus, who destroyed our family;
Father, she has already murdered me.
I killed myself—and what is worse I wasted
my life for pleasures I have never tasted.
My lover flees me still, and my last gasp
is for the fleeting flesh I failed to clasp.

    OENONE. Madam, Madam, cast off this groundless terror!
Is love now an unprecedented error?
You love! What then? You love! Accept your fate.
You're not the first to sail into this strait.
Will chaos overturn the earth and Jove,
because a mortal woman is in love?

Such accidents are easy, all too common.
A woman must submit to being woman.
You curse a failure in the source of things.
Venus has feasted on the hearts of kings;
even the gods, man's judges, feel desire,
Zeus learned to live with his adulterous fire.

PHAEDRA. Must I listen and drink your poisoned breath?
My death's redoubled on the edge of death.
I'd fled Hippolytus and I was free
till your entreaties stabbed and blinded me,
and dragged me howling to the pit of lust.
Oenone, I was learning to be just.
You fed my malice. Attacking the young Prince
was not enough; you clothed him with my sins.
You wished to kill him; he is dying now,
because of you, and Theseus' brutal vow.
You watch my torture; I'm the last ungorged
scrap rotting in this trap your plots have forged.
What binds you to me? Leave me, go, and die,
may your punishment be to terrify
all those who ruin princes by their lies,
hints, acquiescence, filth, and blasphemies—
panders who grease the grooves of inclination,
and lure our willing bodies from salvation.
Go die, go frighten false flatterers, the worst
friends the gods can give to kings they've cursed!

OENONE. I have given all and left all for her service,
almighty gods! I have been paid my price!

act five
SCENE ONE. HIPPOLYTUS, ARICIA.

ARICIA. Take a stand, speak the truth, if you respect
your father's glory and your life. Protect
yourself! I'm nothing to you. You consent
without a struggle to your banishment.
If you are weary of Aricia, go;

at least do something to prevent the blow
that dooms your honor and existence—both
at a strike! Your father must recall his oath;
there is time still, but if the truth's concealed,
you offer your accuser a free field.
Speak to your father!

    HIPPOLYTUS. I've already said
what's lawful. Shall I point to his soiled bed,
tell Athens how his marriage was foresworn,
make Theseus curse the day that he was born?
My aching heart recoils. I only want
God and Aricia for my confidants.
See how I love you; love makes me confide
in you this horror I have tried to hide
from my own heart. My faith must not be broken;
forget, if possible, what I have spoken.
Ah Princess, if even a whisper slips
past you, it will perjure your pure lips.
God's justice is committed to the cause
of those who love him, and uphold his laws;
sooner or later, heaven itself will rise
in wrath and punish Phaedra's blasphemies.
I must not. If I rip away her mask,
I'll kill my father. Give me what I ask.
Do this! Then throw away your chains; it's right
for you to follow me, and share my flight.
Fly from this prison; here the vices seethe
and simmer, virtue has no air to breathe.
In the confusion of my exile, none
will even notice that Aricia's gone.
Banish and broken, Princess, I am still
a force in Greece. Your guards obey my will,
powerful intercessors wish us well:
our neighbors, Argos' citadel
is armed, and in Mycenae our allies
will shelter us, if lying Phaedra tries
to hurry us from our paternal throne,
and steal our sacred titles for her son.

The gods are ours, they urge us to attack.
Why do you tremble, falter and hold back?
Your interests drive me to this sacrifice.
While I'm on fire, your blood has changed to ice.
Princess, is exile more than you can face?
   ARICIA. Exile with you, my lord? What sweeter place
is under heaven? Standing at your side,
I'd let the universe and heaven slide.
You're my one love, my king, but can I hope
for peace and honor, Prince, if I elope
unmarried? This . . . I wasn't questioning
the decency of flying from the King.
Is he my father? Only an abject
spirit honors tyrants with respect.
You say you love me. Prince, I am afraid.
   HIPPOLYTUS. Aricia, you shall never be betrayed;
accept me! Let our love be sanctified,
then flee from your oppressor as my bride.
Bear witness, oh you gods, our love released
by danger, needs no temple or a priest.
It's faith, not ceremonial, that saves.
Here at the city gates, among these graves
the resting places of my ancient line,
there stands a sacred temple and a shrine.
Here, where no mortal ever swore in vain,
here in these shadows, where eternal pain
is ready to engulf the perjurer;
here heaven's scepter quivers to confer
its final sanction; here, my Love, we'll kneel,
and pray the gods to consecrate and seal
our love. Zeus, the father of the world will stand
here as your father and bestow your hand.
Only the pure shall be our witnesses:
Hera, the guarantor of marriages,
Demeter and the virgin Artemis.
   ARICIA. The King is coming. Fly. I'll stay and meet
his anger here and cover your retreat.
Hurry. Be off, send me some friend to guide
my timid footsteps, husband, to your side.

SCENE TWO. THESEUS, ISMENE, ARICIA.

THESEUS. Oh God, illuminate my troubled mind.
Show me the answer I have failed to find.
ARICIA. Go, Ismene, be ready to escape.

SCENE THREE. THESEUS, ARICIA.

THESEUS. Princess, you are disturbed. You twist your cape
and blush. The Prince was talking to you. Why
is he running?
ARICIA. We've said our last goodbye, my lord.
THESEUS. I see the beauty of your eyes
moves even my son, and you have gain a prize
no woman hoped for.
ARICIA. He hasn't taken on
your hatred for me, though he is your son.
THESEUS. I follow. I can hear the oaths he swore.
He knelt, he wept. He has done this before
and worse. You are deceived.
ARICIA. Deceived, my lord?
THESEUS. Princess, are you so rich? Can you afford
to hunger for this lover that my queen
rejected? Your betrayer loves my wife.
ARICIA. How can you bear to blacken his pure life?
Is kingship only for the blind and strong,
unable to distinguish right from wrong?
What insolent prerogative obscures
a light that shines in every eye but yours?
You have betrayed him to his enemies.
What more, my lord? Repent your blasphemies.
Are you not fearful lest the gods so loathe
and hate you they will gratify your oath?
Fear God, my lord, fear God. How many times
he grants men's wishes to expose their crimes.
THESEUS. Love blinds you, Princess, and beclouds your reason.
Your outburst cannot cover up his treason.
My trust's in witnesses that cannot lie.
I have seen Phaedra's tears. She tried to die.

ARICIA. Take care, your Highness. What your killing hand
drove all the thieves and reptiles from the land,
you missed one monster, one was left alive,
one . . . No, I must not name her, Sire, or strive
to save your helpless son; he wants to spare
your reputation. Let me go. I dare
not stay here. If I stayed I'd be too weak
to keep my promise. I'd be forced to speak.

SCENE FOUR. THESEUS.

THESEUS. What was she saying? I must try to reach
the meaning of her interrupted speech.
Is it a pitfall? A conspiracy?
Are they plotting together to torture me?
Why did I let the rash, wild girl depart?
What is this whisper crying in my heart?
A secret pity fills my soul with pain.
I must question Oenone once again.
My guards, summon Oenone to the throne.
Quick, bring her. I must talk with her alone.

SCENE FIVE. THESEUS, PANOPE.

PANOPE. The Queen's deranged, your Highness. Some accursed
madness is driving her; some fury stalks
behind her back, possesses her, and talks
its evil through her, and blasphemes the world.
She cursed Oenone. Now Oenone's hurled
herself into the ocean, Sire, and drowned.
Why did she do it. No reason can be found.
THESEUS. Oenone's drowned?
PANOPE. Her death has brought no peace.
The cries of Phaedra's troubled soul increase.
Now driven by some sinister unrest,
she snatches up her children to her breast,
pets them and weeps, till something makes her scoff
at her affection, and she drives them off.
Her glance is drunken and irregular,

she looks through us and wonders who we are;
thrice she has started letters to you, Sire,
thrice tossed the shredded fragments in the fire.
Oh call her to you. Help her!

THESEUS. The nurse is drowned? Phaedra wishes to die?
Oh gods! Summon my son. Let him defend
himself, tell him I'd ready to attend.
I want him!

(*Exit Panope*)

Neptune, hear me, spare my son!
My vengeance was too hastily begun.
Oh why was I so eager to believe
Oenone's accusation? The gods deceive
the victims they are ready to destroy!

SCENE SIX. THESEUS, THERAMENES.

THESEUS. Here is Theramenes. Where is my boy,
my first-born? He was yours to guard and keep.
Where is he? Answer me. What's this? You weep?

THERAMENES. Oh, tardy, futile grief, his blood is shed.
My lord, your son, Hippolytus, is dead.

THESEUS. Oh gods, have mercy!

THERAMENES. I saw him die. The most
lovely and innocent of men is lost.

THESEUS. He's dead? The gods have hurried him away
and killed him? . . . just as I began to pray . . .
What sudden thunderbolt struck him down?

THERAMENES. We'd started out, and hardly left the town.
He held the reins; a few feet to his rear,
a single, silent guard held up a spear.
He followed the Mycenae highroad, deep
in thought, reins dangling, as if half asleep;
his famous horses, only he could hold,
trudged on with lowered heads, and sometimes rolled
their dull eyes slowly—they seemed to have caught
their master's melancholy, and aped his thought.
Then all at once winds struck us like a fist,
we heard a sudden roaring through the mist;

from underground a voice in agony
answered the prolonged groaning of the sea.
We shook, the horses' manes rose on their heads,
and now against a sky of blacks and reds,
we saw the flat waves hump into a mountain
of green-white water rising like a fountain,
as it reached land and crashed with a last roar
to shatter like a galley on the shore.
Out of its fragments rose a monster, half
dragon, half bull; a mouth that seemed to laugh
drooled venom on its dirty yellow scales
and python belly, forking to three tails.
The shore was shaken like a tuning fork,
ships bounced on the stung sea like bits of cork,
the earth moved, and the sun spun round and round,
a sulphur-colored venom swept the ground.
We fled; each felt his useless courage falter,
and sought asylum at a nearby altar.
Only the Prince remained; he wheeled about,
and hurled a javelin through the monster's snout.
Each kept advancing. Flung from the Prince's arm,
dart after dart struck where the blood was warm.
The monster in its death-throes felt defeat,
and bounded howling to the horses' feet.
There it stretcherd gullet and its armor broke,
and drenched the chariot with blood and smoke,
and then the horses, terror-struck, stampeded.
Their master's whip and shouting went unheeded,
they dragged his breathless body to the spray.
Their red mouths bit the bloody surf, men say
Poseidon stood beside them, that the god
was stabbing at their bellies with a goad.
Their terror drove them crashing on a cliff,
the chariot crashed in two, they ran as if
the Furies screamed and crackled in their manes,
their fallen hero tangled in the reins,
jounced on the rocks behind them. The sweet light
of heaven never will expunge this sight:
the horses that Hippolytus had tamed,

now dragged him headlong, and their mad hooves maimed
his face past recognition. When he tried
to call them, calling only terrified;
faster and ever faster moved their feet,
his body was a piece of bloody meat.
The cliffs and ocean trembled to our shout,
at last their panic failed, they turned about,
and stopped not far from where those hallowed graves,
the Prince's fathers, overlook the waves.
I ran on breathless, guards were at my back,
my master's blood had left a generous track.
The stones were red, each thistle in the mud
was stuck with bits of hair and skin and blood.
I came upon him, called; he stretched his right
hand to me, blinked his eyes, then closed them tight.
"I die," he whispered, "it's the gods' desire.
Friend, stand between Aricia and my sire—
some day enlightened, softened, disabused,
he will lament his son, falsely accused;
then when at last he wishes to appease
my soul, he'll treat my lover well, release
and honor Aricia. . . ." On this word, he died.
Only a broken body testified
he'd lived and loved once. On the sand now lies
something his father will not recognize.

THESEUS. My son, my son! Alas, I stand alone
before the gods. I never can atone.

THERAMENES. Meanwhile Aricia, rushing down the path,
approached us. She was fleeing from your wrath,
my lord, and wished to make Hippolytus
her husband in God's eyes. Then nearing us,
she saw the signs of struggle in the waste,
she saw (oh what a sight) her love defaced,
her young love lying lifeless on the sand.
At first she hardly seemed to understand;
while staring at the body in the grass,
she kept on asking where her lover was.
At last the black and fearful truth broke through
her desolation! She seemed to curse the blue

and murdering ocean, as she caught his head
up in her lap; then fainting lay half dead,
until Ismene somehow summoned back her breath,
restored the child to life—or rather death.
I come, great King, to urge my final task,
your dying son's last outcry was to ask
mercy for poor Aricia, for his bride.
Now Phaedra comes. She killed him. She has lied.

SCENE SEVEN. THESEUS, PHAEDRA, PANOPE.

THESEUS. Ah Phaedra, you have won. He's dead. A man
was killed. Were you watching? His horses ran
him down, and tore his body limb from limb.
Poseidon struck him, Theseus murdered him.
I served you! Tell me why Oenone died?
Was it to save you? Is her suicide
A proof of your truth? No, since he's dead, I must
accept your evidence, just or unjust.
I must believe my faith has been abused;
you have accused him; he shall stand accused.
He's friendless even in the world below.
There the shades fear him! Am I forced to know
the truth? Truth cannot bring my son to life.
If fathers murder, shall I kill my wife
too? Leave me, Phaedra. Far from you, exiled
from Greece, I will lament my murdered child.
I am a murdered gladiator, whirled
in black circles. I want to leave the world;
my whole life rises to increase my guilt—
all those dazzled, dazzling eyes, my glory built
on killing killers. Less known, less magnified,
I might escape, and find a place to hide.
Stand back, Poseidon. I know the gods are hard
to please. I pleased you. This is my reward:
I killed my son. I killed him! Only a god
spares enemies, and wants his servants' blood!
    PHAEDRA. No, Theseus, I must disobey your prayer.
Hippolytus was innocent.

Listen to me. I'm dying. I declare
Hippolytus was innocent.

    THESEUS. Ah Phaedra, on your evidence, I sent
him to his death. Do you ask me to forgive
my son's assassin? Can I let you live?

    PHAEDRA. My time's too short, your highness. It was I,
who lusted for your son with my hot eye.
The flames of Aphrodite maddened me;
I loathed myself, and yearned outrageously
like a starved wolf to fall upon the sheep.
I wished to hold him to me in my sleep
and dreamt I had him. Then Oenone's tears,
troubled my mind; she played upon my fears,
until her pleading forced me to declare
I loved your son. He scorned me. In despair,
I ploted with my nurse, and our conspiracy
made you believe your son assaulted me.
Oenone's punished; fleeing from my wrath,
she drowned herself, and found a too easy path
to death and hell. Perhaps you wonder why
I still survive her, and refuse to die?
Theseus, I stand before you to absolve
your noble son. Sire, only this resolve
upheld me, and made me throw down my knife.
I've chosen a slower way to end my life—
Medea's poison; chills already dart
along my boiling veins and squeeze my heart.
A cold composure I have never known
gives me a moment's poise. I stand alone
and seem to see my outraged husband fade
and waver into death's dissolving shade.
My eyes at last give up their light, and see
the day they've soiled resume its purity.

    PANOPE. She's dead, my lord.

    THESEUS. Would God, all memory
of her and me had died with her! Now I
must live. This knowledge that has come too late
must give me strength and help me expiate
my sacrilegious vow. Let's go, I'll pay

my son the honors he has earned today.
His father's tears shall mingle with his blood.
My love that did my son so little good
asks mercy from his spirit. I declare
Aricia is my daughter and my heir.

POLITICS AND PASSION IN *PHÈDRE*

This essay examines *Phaedra* in terms of Racine's commitment to the tragedy of the tortured individual who is a great public figure, and who is therefore susceptible to both public and private agony.* This examination is accomplished in the analysis of the public, political world of the play, and the public and political awareness and action of the several characters. In the play, politics has on the one hand the function of furnishing a context outlining and circumscribing the play's social world; and on the other hand, the function of furnishing the crucial fulcrum against which the tragic action is levered from potentiality to actuality—politics furnishes the public frame and center within and around which the drama of private passion develops. From the first, Hippolytus assumes Phaedra's apparent animosity is a matter of dynastic ambition; and the major obstacle to Hippolytus' love for Aricia is that Theseus, who has just consolidated his take-over of Athens, has forbidden her to marry and produce heirs for the old royal line. Phaedra believes that Hippolytus is motivated by a desire for power. At the beginning of Act I, Scene 4, when the exposition has been completed, Panope enters with the news that Theseus is dead. Thus, Phaedra's tragic passion—which is until then secret and private—is given public space in which to develop: she is both a widow in love and a queen with power to offer. As far as the play world is concerned, and to a great extent as far as Oenone and Phaedra are concerned, it is not so much Theseus the man, as Theseus the king, who is dead. Problems of civil unrest in Athens and the succession to the throne begin to dominate the action. These problems become, for a while, paramount in Hippolytus' mind, if only for Aricia's sake; as for Phaedra and Oenone, politics and the succession become simultaneously a real concern and a convenient means to solve the heretoforce insoluble moral crisis of Phaedra's passion. Phaedra will act as if her love for Hippolytus is motivated by her concern for the political security of her young sons. At the same time, Hippolytus embraces the political

* Abstracted from Conny E. Nelson, "Politics and Passion in *Phèdre*," *French Review*, XXXIX (1965), 22-35.

interests of Aricia, and lovingly offers to support her cause against the apparently power hungry Phaedra—he will do this even at the expense of his own interests in Athens. After his misunderstanding with his father, Hippolytus for Aricia's sake proposes a civil war against Theseus, who has suspicions that Hippolytus has tried to usurp the throne. The play ends with Theseus and Aricia knitting together the rent fabric of the state. Between the false announcement of Theseus' death and his eventual reappearance, all the characters think about love and talk about power, or think about power and talk about love. Neither is a mask for the other; both love and power are inseparably bound together in the moral and emotional consciousness of all characters.

ERRORS AND INVENTION IN RACINE'S *PHÈDRE*

In *Phèdre*, Act IV, Scene ii, Hippolyte expresses surprise at Thesee's troubled mien.* This remark is strange in view of the fact that Thésée has already—and in Hippolyte's presence—shown his feeling of horror at the negative reactions which greeted his return after a long absence. After an examination of various possible explanations of this inconsistency, the one adopted is that Racine simply borrowed these lines from Euripides, even though he had significantly changed the context. The inconsistency of Hippolyte's speech arises above all from the unexpected return of Theseus, after the report of his death. It is this false death report, invented by Racine, which is behind the consternation which his return causes and which destroys the plausibility of the Euripidean borrowing. Thus, what must be termed an error on Racine's part has as its cause an innovation. This innovation in the long Hippolytus-Phaedra tradition turns out to be of great importance to the action; indeed, it may be Racine's most brilliant coup in this strongest of his tragedies. May it be that other errors or oversights in Racine (and many have been

* Abstracted from Abraham C. Keller, "Error and Invention in Racine's *Phèdre*," *Romanic Review*, IV (1959), 99-106.

found!) are, similarly, closely connected with moments of great originality, and might this not lead us, not merely to excuse, but even to take a very positive view of, "errors"—because they spring from invention?

READING RACINE

The English reader, attuned as he is to Shakespeare and the Jacobean dramatists, may find the plays of Racine lacking in breadth of scope and variety of theme; or their vocabulary too limited and repetitive, their speeches too long and rhetorical.* Nonetheless, Racine is more akin to Shakespeare than to the English classical dramatists. Yet an English reader of Racine encounters the same risks as a French reader of Shakespeare: regardless of how much either admires, he is likely to admire in the wrong way. As the conventions of Shakespearean theatre are liable to be an obstacle to the French reader, so the conventions of the Racinian theatre can be a stumbling block to English readers. Consider the matter of structure: Racine's plays are constructed to extract the greatest possible significance from not only the theme but from each particular situation as well. Each play is whole, complete; there seems nothing more to say to the audience. Further, Racine's gift of psychological insight is unequalled by any dramatist, past or present, and there is little dispute about the greatness, for example, of *Phaedra.* The classical mold does not render that play cold or marble-like; the last scene of the play, for instance, is one of Racine's great strokes. In that scene, where Phaedra confesses for the third and last time, Racine manages to evoke more pity for her than for either Hippolytus, her innocent victim, or her husband, whose life is ruined. It is unwarranted to view Racine's work as nothing more than orderly, eloquent, and moralizing; he is, rather, a terrifying dramatist. Despite their evenness of diction, his characters are frequently frenzied and violent, their violence and crimes often horrifying. The plays end less in the restoration of order than in the quiet of exhaustion. These character-

* Abstracted from Kenneth Muir, *Jean Racine,* New York, 1960, xi-xxviii.

istics of Racine's work—frenzy, rage, brutality, exaltation—are fused in the perfection of the classical form, a form which concentrates rather than diffuses the emotional content.

RACINE'S *PHÈDRE:* A SOPHOCLEAN AND SENECAN TRAGEDY

Though specific in acknowledgment of his debt to Euripides, Racine devotes to Seneca only a rapid allusion in the *Préface* to *Phèdre.** However, in his interpretation of the role of Phèdre and in shifting the *colère des dieux* from Hippolyte to Phèdre, Racine has so completely altered the concept and atmosphere of the legend that it can no longer be considered Euripidean in fundamental idea and execution. In basic concept, atmosphere, and execution, as well as in incident and detail, Racine's primary debt is to Seneca. Racine was able to avoid the errors of Seneca and to give his subject true tragic grandeur, more genuinely tragic in the Aristotelian definition, than Euripides' original dramatic version. In the psychological study of the character of Phèdre and in the treatment of the timeless problem of man's inability to overcome his evil inclinations by means of his own will power, Racine's Phèdre is informed by the Sophoclean dramatic canon. Assuming that Racine desired to concentrate on the study of the character of Phèdre, it became necessary for him to follow the version of Seneca, in which Phèdre remains the real protagonist until the end of the play. By the alteration of the *colère divine* from Hippolyte because of his *hubris* to Phèdre because she is a granddaughter of Apollo, the tragedy has been profoundly changed. Attention is centered on Phèdre, who exhibits the inner conflict which is the true tragic interest of the legend. Racine, treating a subject of Euripides, found difficulty in adapting it to the

* Abstracted from Julian E. White, "Racine's *Phèdre:* A Sophoclean and Senecan Tragedy," *Revue de Littérature Comparée*, XXXIX (1965), 605-613.

Aristotelian concept and consequently followed the example of
Seneca, whose tragedy more nearly fits the Aristotelian, and hence
Sophoclean, canon. Additionally, both Seneca and Racine heighten
the tragic effect and actually create true tragedy by having Phèdre
aware of Venus' curse. The tragic hero, in the Aristotelian concept,
must eventually be aware of his tragic situation. Neither Racine nor
his critics have done *complete* justice to the influence of Seneca. Yet
a careful comparison indicates that Racine follows Seneca more
closely than Euripides in detail, in general plot, and in the fundamental shifting of focus from Hippolyte to Phèdre. Racine has succeeded in creating a "Greek" tragic atmosphere and has broadened
and deepened the scope in order to deal with universal human
problems.

Ghosts

HENRIK IBSEN

CHARACTERS

TRANSLATED BY
MICHAEL MEYER

MRS. HELEN ALVING, *widow of Captain Alving, late Chamberlain to the King.*
OSWALD ALVING, *her son, a painter.*

PASTOR MANDERS.
ENGSTRAND, *a carpenter.*
REGINIA ENGSTRAND, *Mrs. Alving's maid.*

The action takes place on MRS. ALVING's country estate by a large fjord in Western Norway.

act one

A spacious garden-room, with a door in the left-hand wall and two doors in the right-hand wall. In the centre of the room is a round table with chairs around it; on the table are books, magazines and newspapers. Downstage left is a window, in front of which is a small sofa with a sewing-table by it. Backstage the room opens out into a slightly narrower conservatory, with walls of large panes of glass. In the right-hand wall of the conservatory is a door leading down to the garden. Through the glass wall a gloomy fjord landscape is discernible, veiled by steady rain.

ENGSTRAND, a carpenter, is standing at the garden door. His left leg is slightly crooked; under the sole of his boot is fixed a block of wood. REGINA, with an empty garden syringe in her hand, bars his entry.

REGINA (*keeping her voice low*). What do you want? Stay where you are! You're dripping wet!

ENGSTRAND. It is God's blessed rain, my child.

REGINA. The Devil's damned rain, more like.

ENGSTRAND. Why, Regina, the way you talk!

(*Limps a few steps into the room.*) What I wanted to say is—

REGINA. Here, you! Don't make such a noise with that foot. The young master's asleep upstairs.

Henrik Ibsen, "Ghosts," in *Ghosts and Three Other Plays,* translated by Michael Meyer. Copyright © 1962 by Michael Meyer. Used by permission of Doubleday & Company, Inc.

ENGSTRAND. In bed—at this hour? Why, the day's half gone.

REGINA. That's none of your business.

ENGSTRAND. I was out drinking last night—

REGINA. I'm sure.

ENGSTRAND. We are but flesh and blood, my child—

REGINA (*drily*). Quite.

ENGSTRAND. And the temptations of this world are manifold. But God is my witness; I was at my bench by half past five this morning.

REGINA. Yes, yes. Come on now, clear off. I don't want to be caught having a rendezvous with you.

ENGSTRAND. You don't what?

REGINA. I don't want anyone to see you here. Come on, go away, get out.

ENGSTRAND (*comes a few steps nearer*). Not before I've had a word with you. This afternoon I'll be through with the job down at the school house, and tonight I'm catching the steamer back to town.

REGINA (*mutters*). *Bon voyage.*

ENGSTRAND. Thank you, my child. They're dedicating the new Orphanage here tomorrow, and there'll be celebrations, with intoxicating liquor. And no one shall say of Jacob Engstrand that he can't turn his back on temptation. (REGINA *laughs scornfully.*) Yes, well, there'll be a lot of tiptop people coming here tomorrow. Pastor Manders is expected from town.

REGINA. He's arriving today.

ENGSTRAND. Well, there you are. And I'm damned if I'm going to risk getting into his bad books.

REGINA. Oh, so that's it.

ENGSTRAND. What do you mean?

REGINA (*looks knowingly at him*). What are you trying to fool the Pastor into this time?

ENGSTRAND. Hush! Are you mad? Me try to fool Pastor Manders? Oh no, Pastor Manders is much too good a friend to me for that. Now what I wanted to talk to you about is this. I'm going back home tonight.

REGINA. The sooner you go the better.

ENGSTRAND. Yes, but I want to take you with me, Regina.

REGINA (*her jaw drops*). You want to take me—? What are you talking about?

ENGSTRAND. I want to take you with me, I say.

REGINA (*scornfully*). Home with you? Not likely I won't!

ENGSTRAND. Oh, we'll see, we'll see.

REGINA. You bet your life we'll see. You expect me to go back and live with you? In that house? After Mrs. Alving's brought me up in her own home, treats me as though I was one of the family? Get out!

ENGSTRAND. What the hell's this? Are you setting yourself up against your father, my girl?

REGINA (*mutters without looking at him*). You've said often enough that I'm no concern of yours.

ENGSTRAND. Oh—you don't want to take any notice of that—

REGINA. What about all the times you've sworn at me and called me a—oh, *mon dieu!*

ENGSTRAND. May God strike me dead if I ever used such a vile word!

REGINA. Oh, I know what word you used.

ENGSTRAND. Yes, but that was only when I wasn't myself. Hm. The temptations of this world are manifold, Regina.

REGINA. Ugh!

ENGSTRAND. And when your mother was being difficult. I had to think up some way to nark her. She was always acting the fine lady. (*Mimics.*) "Let me go, Engstrand! Stop it! I've been in service for three years with Chamberlain Alving at Rosenvold, and don't you forget it!" (*Laughs.*) She never could forget the Captain had been made a Chamberlain when she was working for him.

REGINA. Poor Mother! You killed her soon enough with your bullying.

ENGSTRAND (*uncomfortably*). That's right, blame me for everything.

REGINA (*turns away and mutters beneath her breath*). Ugh! And that leg!

ENGSTRAND. What's that you said, my child?

REGINA. *Pied de mouton!*

ENGSTRAND. What's that, English?

REGINA. Yes.

ENGSTRAND. Ah, well. They've made a scholar of you out here anyway, and that'll come in handy now, Regina.

REGINA (*after a short silence*). And—what was it you wanted me for in town?

ENGSTRAND. Fancy asking such a question! What should a father want from his only child? Aren't I a lonely, forsaken widower?

REGINA. Oh, don't try to fool me with that rubbish. What do you want me up there for?

ENGSTRAND. Well, it's like this. I'm thinking of starting out on something new.

REGINA (*sniffs*). You've tried that often enough. And you've always made a mess of it.

ENGSTRAND. Yes, but this time, you'll see, Regina! God rot me if I don't—!

REGINA (*stamps her foot*). Stop swearing!

ENGSTRAND. Ssh, Ssh! How right you are, my child! Now what I wanted to say was this. I've put quite a bit of money aside out of the work I've been doing at this new Orphanage.

REGINA. Have you? Good for you.

ENGSTRAND. Well, there ain't much for a man to spend his money on out here in the country, is there?

REGINA. Well? Go on.

ENGSTRAND. Yes, well, you see, so I thought I'd put the money into something that might bring me in a bit. A kind of home for sailors—

REGINA (*disgusted*). Oh, my God!

ENGSTRAND. A real smart place, you understand—not one of those low waterfront joints. No, damn it, this is going to be for captains and officers and—tip-top people, you understand.

REGINA. And I'm to—?

ENGSTRAND. You're going to help me. Just for appearance's sake, of course. You won't have to work hard, my child. You can fix your own hours.

REGINA. I see!

ENGSTRAND. Well, we've got to have a bit of skirt on show, I mean that's obvious. Got to give them a little fun in the evenings—dancing and singing and so forth. You must remember these men are wandering mariners lost on the ocean of life. (*Comes closer.*) Now don't be stupid and make things difficult for yourself, Regina. What can you make of yourself out here? What good is it going to do you, all this fine education Mrs. Alving's given you? I hear you're going to look after the orphans down the road. Is that what you want to do? Are you so anxious to ruin your health for those filthy brats?

REGINA. No, if things work out the way I—Ah well, they might. They might.

ENGSTRAND. What are you talking about?

REGINA. Never you mind. This money you've managed to save out here—is it a lot?

ENGSTRAND. All told I'd say it comes to between thirty-five and forty pounds.

REGINA. Not bad.

ENGSTRAND. Enough to make a start with, my child.

REGINA. Aren't you going to give me any of it?

ENGSTRAND. Not damn likely I'm not.

REGINA. Aren't you even going to send me a new dress?

ENGSTRAND. You just come back to town and set up with me, and you'll get dresses enough.

REGINA (*laughs scornfully*). I could do *that* on my own, if I wanted to.

ENGSTRAND. No, Regina, you need a father's hand to guide you. There's a nice house I can get in Little Harbour Street. They don't want much cash on the nail; and we could turn it into a sort of— well—sailors' mission.

REGINA. But I don't want to live with *you!* I don't want anything to do with you. Come on, get out.

ENGSTRAND. You wouldn't need to stay with me for long, my child. More's the pity. If you play your card properly. The way you've blossomed out these last few years, you—

REGINA. Yes?

ENGSTRAND. You wouldn't have to wait long before some nice officer—perhaps even a captain—

REGINA. I don't want to marry any of them. Sailors haven't any *savoir vivre.*

ENGSTRAND. Haven't any what?

REGINA. I know sailors. There's no future in marrying them.

ENGSTRAND. All right then, don't marry them. You can do just as well without. (*Lowers his voice.*) The Englishman—him with the yacht—fifty pounds he paid out—and she wasn't any prettier than you.

REGINA (*goes towards him*). Get out!

ENGSTRAND (*shrinks*). Now, now, you wouldn't hit your own father!

REGINA. Wouldn't I? You say another word about mother, and you'll see! Get out, I tell you! (*Pushes him towards the garden door.*) And don't slam the door. Young Mr. Alving's—

ENGSTRAND. Yes, I know. He's asleep. Why do you fuss so much about him? (*More quietly.*) Ah-ha! You wouldn't be thinking of *him,* would you?

REGINA. Out, and be quick about it! You're out of your mind. No, not that way. Here's Pastor Manders. Go out through the kitchen.

ENGSTRAND (*goes right*). All right, I'll go. But you ask *him*— his Reverence. He'll tell you what a child's duty is to its father. I am your father, you know, whatever you say. I can prove it from the parish register.

(*He goes out through the second door, which* REGINA *has opened and closed behind him. She looks quickly at herself in the mirror, dusts herself with her handkerchief, and straightens her collar; then she begins to water the flowers.* PASTOR MANDERS, *in an overcoat and carrying an umbrella, and with a small travelling bag on a strap from his shoulder, enters through the garden door into the conservatory.*)

MANDERS. Good morning, Miss Engstrand.

REGINA (*turns in surprise and delight*). Why, Pastor Manders! Has the boat come already?

MANDERS. It arrived a few minutes ago. (*Enters the garden room.*) Very tiresome this rain we're having.

REGINA (*following him*). A blessing for the farmers, though, sir.

MANDERS. Yes, you are right. We city people tend to forget that. (*Begins to take off his overcoat.*)

REGINA. Oh, please let me help you! There. Oh, it's soaking! I'll hang it up in the hall. Oh, and the umbrella! I'll open it out to let it dry.

(*She takes the coat and umbrella out through the other door, right.* MANDERS *takes his bag from his shoulder and puts it and his hat on a chair. Meanwhile* REGINA *comes back.*)

MANDERS. Ah, it's good to be under a dry roof again. Well, I trust all is well here?

REGINA. Yes, thank you, sir.

MANDERS. Everyone very busy, I suppose, getting ready for to-morrow?

REGINA. Oh, yes, there are one or two things to be done.

MANDERS. Mrs. Alving is at home, I hope?

REGINA. Oh, dear me, yes, she's just gone upstairs to make a cup of chocolate for the young master.

MANDERS. Ah, yes. I heard when I got off the boat that Oswald had returned.

REGINA. Yes, he arrived the day before yesterday. We hadn't expected him until today.

MANDERS. In good health and spirits, I trust?

REGINA. Oh yes, thank you, I think so. He felt dreadfully tired after his journey, though. He came all the way from Paris in one go—*par rapide.* I think he's having a little sleep just now, so we'd better talk just a tiny bit quietly.

MANDERS. Ssh! We'll be like mice!

REGINA (*moves an armchair near the table*). Now sit down and make yourself comfortable, sir. (*He sits. She puts a footstool under his feet.*) There now. Are you quite comfortable?

MANDERS. Thank you, thank you; yes, very comfortable. (*Looks at her.*) Do you know, Miss Engstrand, I really believe you've grown since I last saw you.

REGINA. Do you think so? Madam says I've rounded out a bit too.

MANDERS. Rounded out? Well, yes, a little perhaps. Not too much. (*Short pause.*)

REGINA. Shall I tell madam you've come?

MANDERS. Thank you, there's no hurry, my dear child. Er—tell me now, Regina, how is your father getting on out here?

REGINA. Thank you, Pastor, he's doing very well.

MANDERS. He came to see me when he was last in town.

REGINA. No, did he really? He's always so happy when he gets a chance to speak to you, sir.

MANDERS. And you go down and see him quite often?

REGINA. I? Oh yes, of course—whenever I get the chance—

MANDERS. Your father hasn't a very strong character, Miss Engstrand. He badly needs a hand to guide him.

REGINA. Oh—yes, I dare say you're right there.

MANDERS. He needs to have someone near whom he is fond of,

and whose judgment he respects. He admitted it quite openly the last time he visited me.

REGINA. Yes, he said something of the sort to me too. But I don't know whether Mrs. Alving will want to lose me, especially now we've the new Orphange to look after. Besides, I'd hate to leave Mrs. Alving. She's always been so kind to me.

MANDERS. But my dear girl, a daughter's duty! Naturally we would have to obtain your mistress's permission first.

REGINA. But I don't know that it'd be right and proper for me to keep house for an unmarried man at my age.

MANDERS. What! But my dear Miss Engstrand, this is your own father we're talking about!

REGINA. Yes—but all the same—Oh yes, if it was a nice house, with a real gentleman—

MANDERS. But my dear Regina—!

REGINA. Someone I could feel affection for and look up to as a father—

MANDERS. But my dear good child—!

REGINA. Oh, I'd so love to go and live in the city. Out here it's so dreadfully lonely—and you know, don't you, sir, what it means to be all alone in the world? And I'm quick and willing—I think I can say that. Oh, Pastor Manders, don't you know of a place I could go to?

MANDERS. I? No, I'm afraid I don't know of anyone at all.

REGINA. Oh, but do please think of me if ever you should, dear, dear Pastor Manders.

MANDERS (*gets up*). Yes, yes, Miss Engstrand, I certainly will.

REGINA. You see, if only I—

MANDERS. Will you be so good as to call Mrs. Alving for me?

REGINA. Yes, sir. I'll call her at once.

(*She goes out left.* PASTOR MANDERS *walks up and down the room a couple of times, stands for a moment upstage with his hands behind his back and looks out into the garden. Then he comes back to the part of the room where the table is, picks up a book and glances at its title page, starts and looks at some of the others.*)

MANDERS. Hm! I see!

(MRS. ALVING *enters through the door left. She is followed by* REGINA, *who at once goes out through the door downstage right.*)

MRS. ALVING (*holds out her hand*). Welcome to Rosenvold, Pastor.

MANDERS. Good morning, Mrs. Alving. Well, I've kept my promise.

MRS. ALVING. Punctual as always.

MANDERS. But you know it wasn't easy for me to get away. All these blessed boards and committees. I sit on—

MRS. ALVING. All the kinder of you to arrive in such good time. Now we can get our business settled before lunch. But where's your luggage?

MANDERS (*quickly*). My portmanteau is down at the village store. I shall be sleeping there.

MRS. ALVING (*represses a smile*). I can't persuade you to spend a night in my house even now?

MANDERS. No, no, Mrs. Alving—it's very kind of you, but I'll sleep down there as usual. It's so convenient for when I go on board again.

MRS. ALVING. As you please. Though I really think two old people like you and me could—

MANDERS. Bless me, you're joking. But of course you must be very happy. The great day tomorrow—and you have Oswald home again.

MRS. ALVING. Yes, you can imagine how happy that makes me. It's over two years since he was home last. And now he's promised to stay with me the whole winter.

MANDERS. No, has he really? Well, that's nice of him. He knows his filial duty. I fancy life in Paris and Rome must offer altogether different attractions.

MRS. ALVING. Yes, but his home is here, and his mother. Ah, my dear boy; he loves his mother, God bless him.

MANDERS. It would be sad indeed if distance and dabbling in art and such things should blunt his natural affections.

MRS. ALVING. It certainly would. But luckily there's nothing wrong with him. I'll be amused to see whether you recognize him again. He'll be down later; he's upstairs now taking a little rest on the sofa. But please sit down, my dear Pastor.

MANDERS. Thank you. Er—you're sure this is a convenient moment—?

MRS. ALVING. Certainly.

(*She sits down at the table.*)

MANDERS. Good. Well, then— (*Goes over to the chair on which his bag is lying, takes out a sheaf of papers, sits down on the opposite side of the table and looks for a space to put down the papers.*) Well, to begin with, here are the— (*Breaks off.*) Tell me, Mrs. Alvin, how do *these* books come to be here?

MRS. ALVING. Those books? I'm reading them.

MANDERS. You read writings of this kind?

MRS. ALVING. Certainly I do.

MANDERS. And does this kind of reading make you feel better or happier?

MRS. ALVING. I think they make me feel more secure.

MANDERS. How extraordinary! In what way?

MRS. ALVING. Well, they sort of explain and confirm many things that puzzle me. Yes, that's what's so strange, Pastor Manders—there isn't really anything new in these books—there's nothing in them that most people haven't already thought for themselves. It's only that most people either haven't fully realized it, or they won't admit it.

MANDERS. Well, dear God! Do you seriously believe that most people—?

MRS. ALVING. Yes, I do.

MANDERS. But surely not in this country? Not people like us?

MRS. ALVING. Oh, yes. People like us, too.

MANDERS. Well, really! I must say—!

MRS. ALVING. But what do you object to in these books?

MANDERS. Object to? You surely don't imagine I spend my time studying such publications?

MRS. ALVIN. In other words, you've no idea what you're condemning?

MANDERS. I've read quite enough about these writings to disapprove of them.

MRS. ALVING. Don't you think you ought to form your own opinion—?

MANDERS. My dear Mrs. Alving, there are many occasions in life when one must rely on the judgment of others. That is the way things are and it is good that it should be so. If it were not so, what would become of society?

MRS. ALVING. Yes, yes. You may be right.

MANDERS. Of course I don't deny there may be quite a lot that is attractive about these writings. And I cannot exactly blame you for wishing to keep informed of these intellectual movements in the great world outside about which one hears so much. After all, you have allowed your son to wander there for a number of years. But—

MRS. ALVING. But—?

MANDERS (*lowers his voice*). But one does not have to talk about it, Mrs. Alving. One really does not need to account to all and sundry for what one reads and thinks within one's own four walls.

MRS. ALVING. No, of course not. I quite agree with you.

MANDERS. Remember the duty you owe to this Orphanage which you decided to found at a time when your attitude towards spiritual matters was quite different from what it is now—as far as *I* can judge.

MRS. ALVING. Yes, yes, that's perfectly true. But it was the Orphanage we were going to—

MANDERS. It was the Orphanage we were going to discuss, yes. But—be discreet, dear Mrs. Alving! And now let us turn to our business. (*Opens the packet and takes out some of the papers.*) You see these?

MRS. ALVING. Are those the deeds?

MANDERS. All of them. Ready and completed. As you can imagine, it's been no easy task to get them all through in time. I really had to get out my whip. The authorities are almost painfully conscientious when you want a decision from them. But here we have them nevertheless. (*Leafs through them.*) Here is the executed conveyance of the farmstead named Solvik in the Manor of Rosenvold, with its newly constructed buildings, schoolrooms, staff accommodation and chapel. And here is the settlement of the endowment and the trust deed of the institution. Look (*Reads.*) Deed of trust for the Captain Alving Memorial Home.

MRS. ALVING (*stares for a long while at the paper*). So there it is.

MANDERS. I thought I'd say Captain rather than Chamberlain. Captain looks less ostentatious.

MRS. ALVING. Yes, yes, as you think best.

MANDERS. And here is the bankbook for the capital which has been placed on deposit to cover the running expenses of the Orphanage.

MRS. ALVING. Thank you; but I think it would be more convenient if you kept that, if you don't mind.

MANDERS. Certainly, certainly. I think we may as well leave the money on deposit to begin with. Admittedly the interest isn't very attractive—four per cent with six months notice of withdrawal. If we could obtain a good mortgage later—of course it would have to be a first mortgage and of unimpeachable security—we might reconsider the matter.

MRS. ALVING. Yes, well, dear Pastor Manders, you know best about all that.

MANDERS. Anyway, I'll keep my eyes open. But now there's another matter I've several times been meaning to ask you about.

MRS. ALVING. And what is that?

MANDERS. Should the buildings of the Orphange be insured or not.

MRS. ALVING. Yes, of course they must be insured.

MANDERS. Ah, but wait a minute, Mrs. Alving. Let us consider this question a little more closely.

MRS. ALVING. Everything I have is insured—buildings, furniture, crops, livestock.

MANDERS. Naturally. On your own estate. I do the same, of course. But you see, this is quite a different matter. The Orphanage is, so to speak, to be consecrated to a higher purpose.

MRS. ALVING. Yes, but—

MANDERS. As far as I personally am concerned, I see nothing offensive in securing ourselves against all eventualities—

MRS. ALVING. Well, I certainly don't.

MANDERS. But what is the feeling among the local people out here? You can judge that better than I can.

MRS. ALVING. The feeling?

MANDERS. Are there many people with a right to an opinion—I mean, people who really have the right to hold an opinion—who might take offence?

MRS. ALVING. Well, what do you mean by people who have the right to hold an opinion?

MANDERS. Oh, I am thinking chiefly of people sufficiently independent and influential to make it impossible for one to ignore their opinions altogether.

MRS. ALVING. There are quite a few people like that who I suppose might take offence—

MANDERS. You see! In town, we have a great many such people. Followers of other denominations. People might very easily come to the conclusion that neither you nor I have sufficient trust in the ordinance of a Higher Power.

MRS. ALVING. But my dear Pastor, as long as you yourself—

MANDERS. I know, I know—my conscience is clear, that is true. But all the same, we couldn't prevent a false and unfavourable interpretation being placed on our action. And that might well adversely influence the purpose for which the Orphanage has been dedicated.

MRS. ALVING. If that were so I—

MANDERS. And I can't altogether close my eyes to the difficult— I might even say deeply embarrassing—position in which I might find myself. Among influential circles in town there is a great interest in the cause of the Orphanage. After all, it is to serve the town as well, and it is hoped that it may considerably ease the burden of the ratepayers in respect to the poor. But since I have acted as your adviser and been in charge of the business side I must admit I fear certain over-zealous persons might in the first place direct their attacks against me—

MRS. ALVING. Well, you mustn't lay yourself open to that.

MANDERS. Not to speak of the attacks which would undoubtedly be launched against me in certain newspapers and periodicals, and which—

MRS. ALVING. Enough, dear Pastor Manders. That settles it.

MANDERS. Then you do not wish the Orphanage to be insured?

MRS. ALVING. No. We will forget about it.

MANDERS (*leans back in his chair*). But suppose an accident should occur—you never can tell—would you be able to make good the damage?

MRS. ALVING. No, quite frankly I couldn't.

MANDERS. Well, but you know, Mrs. Alving, this is really rather a serious responsibility we are taking on our shoulders.

MRS. ALVING. But do you think we have any alternative?

MANDERS. No, that's just it. I don't think there is any real alternative. We must not lay ourselves open to misinterpretation. And we have no right to antagonize public opinion.

MRS. ALVING. At any rate you, as a clergyman, must not.

MANDERS. And I really think we must believe that such an institution will have luck on its side—nay, that it stands under special protection.

MRS. ALVING. Let us hope so, Pastor Manders.

MANDERS. Shall we take the risk, then?

MRS. ALVING. Yes, let us.

MANDERS. Good. As you wish. (*Makes a note.*) No insurance, then.

MRS. ALVING. It's strange you happened to mention this today—

MANDERS. I've often thought of raising the matter with you—

MRS. ALVING. Because yesterday we almost had a fire down there.

MANDERS. What!

MRS. ALVING. Well, it was nothing much really. Some shavings caught fire in the carpentry shop.

MANDERS. Where Engstrand works?

MRS. ALVING. Yes. They say he's very careless with matches.

MANDERS. He's got so many things to think about, poor man—so many temptations. Thank heaven I hear he has now resolved to lead a virtuous life.

MRS. ALVING. Oh? Who says so?

MANDERS. He has assured me so himself. And he's a good worker.

MRS. ALVING. Oh, yes—as long as he keeps sober—

MANDERS. Yes, that is a grievous weakness! But he is often compelled to yield to it because of his bad leg, he says. The last time he was in town I was quite touched. He came to see me and thanked me so sincerely because I had got him this job here, so that he could be near Regina.

MRS. ALVING. I don't think he sees her very often.

MANDERS. Oh yes, he told me himself. He talks to her every day.

MRS. ALVING. Oh, well. Possibly.

MANDERS. He is so conscious of his need to have someone who can restrain him when temptation presents itself. That is what is so lovable about Jacob Engstrand, that he comes to one like a child and accuses himself and admits his weakness. The last time he came up and talked to me—Tell me, Mrs. Alving, if it were absolutely vital for the poor man to have Regina back to live with him again—

MRS. ALVING. (*rises swiftly*). Regina!

MANDERS. You must not oppose it.

MRS. ALVING. I certainly shall. Anyway, Regina is going to work at the Orphanage.

MANDERS. But don't forget, he is her father—

MRS. ALVING. Oh, I know very well the kind of father he's been to her. No, I shall never consent to her going back to him.

MANDERS. (*rises*). But my dear Mrs. Alving, you mustn't get so emotional about it. You seem quite frightened. It's sad the way you misjudge this man Engstrand.

MRS. ALVING. (*more quietly*). Never mind that. I have taken Regina into my house, and here she shall stay. (*Listens*) Hush now, dear Pastor Manders, let's not say anything more about it. (*Happily.*) Listen! There's Oswald coming downstairs. Now we will think of nothing but him.

OSWALD ALVING, *in a light overcoat, with his hat in his hand and smoking a big meerschaum pipe, enters through the door left.*)

OSWALD (*stops in the doorway*). Oh, I'm sorry—I thought you were in the study. (*Comes closer.*) Good morning, Pastor.

MANDERS (*stares*). Why—! Most extraordinary!

MRS. ALVING. Well, Pastor Manders, what do you think of him?

MANDERS. I think—I think—! But is this really—?

OSWALD. Yes, this is the Prodigal Son, Pastor.

MANDERS. Oh, but my dear young friend—!

Well, the son, anyway.

MRS. ALVING. Oswald is thinking of the time when you used to be so strongly opposed to his becoming a painter.

MANDERS. Many a step which to human eyes seems dubious often turns out— (*Shakes his hand.*) Anyway, welcome, welcome! My dear Oswald—! I trust you will allow me to call you by your Christian name?

OSWALD. What else?

MANDERS. Excellent. Now, my dear Oswald, what I was going to say was this. You mustn't think I condemn the artistic profession out of hand. I presume there are many who succeed in keeping the inner man untarnished in that profession too.

OSWALD. Let us hope so.

MRS. ALVING (*happily*). I know one person who has remained pure both inwardly and outwardly. Just look at him. Pastor Manders.

OSWALD (*wanders across the room*). Yes, yes, Mother dear, please.

MANDERS. Unquestionably—there's no denying that. Besides, you have begun to acquire a name now. The newspapers often speak of you, and in most flattering terms. Well—that is to say, I don't seem to have read about you quite so much lately.

OSWALD (*by the flowers upstage*). I haven't done so much painting lately.

MRS. ALVING. Even painters have to rest now and then.

MANDERS. I suppose so. To prepare themselves and conserve their energies for some great work.

OSWALD. Yes. Mother, shall we be eating soon?

MRS. ALVING. In about half an hour. He still enjoys his food, thank heaven.

MANDERS. And his tobacco, I see.

OSWALD. I found Father's pipe upstairs in the bedroom, so I—

MANDERS. Of course!

MRS. ALVING. What do you mean?

MANDERS. When Oswald appeared in that doorway with that pipe in his mouth, it was just as though I saw his father alive again.

OSWALD. Oh? Really?

MRS. ALVING. Oh, how can you say that? Oswald takes after me.

MANDERS. Yes; but there's an expression at the corner of his mouth, something about his lips, that reminds me so vividly of Alving—at any rate now when he's smoking.

MRS. ALVING. How can you say that? Oswald has much more the mouth of a clergyman, I think.

MANDERS. True, true. Some of my colleagues have a similar expression.

MRS. ALVING. But put away that pipe, my dear boy. I don't want any smoke in here.

OSWALD (*obeys*). I'm sorry. I only wanted to try it. You see, I smoked it once when I was a child.

MRS. ALVING. What?

OSWALD. Yes. I was quite small at the time. I remember, I went upstairs to see Father in his room one evening. He was so happy and cheerful.

MRS. ALVING. Oh, you don't remember anything from that time.

OSWALD. Oh, yes, I remember very clearly, he picked me up and sat me on his knee and let me smoke his pipe. "Puff away, boy," he said, "puff hard." And I puffed as hard as I could. I felt myself go pale and the sweat broke out on my forehead in great drops. And that made him roar with laughter—

MANDERS. How very strange.

MRS. ALVING. My dear, it's just something Oswald has dreamed.

OSWALD. No, Mother, I didn't dream it. Surely you must remember —you came in and carried me back into the nursery. Then I was sick and I saw you crying. Did Father often play jokes like that?

MANDERS. In his youth he was an extremely gay young man—

OSWALD. And yet he managed to achieve so much. So much that was good and useful; although he died so young.

MANDERS. Yes, you have inherited the name of an industrious and worthy man, my dear Oswald Alving. Well, I hope this will spur you on.

OSWALD. Yes, it ought to, oughtn't it?

MANDERS. In any case it was good of you to come home and join us in honouring him.

OSWALD. It was the least I could do for Father.

MRS. ALVING. And the best thing of all is that I'm going to have him here for so long.

MANDERS. Yes, I hear you're staying the winter.

OSWALD. I am here for an indefinite period, Pastor. Oh, but it's good to be home!

MRS. ALVING. (*warmly*). Yes, Oswald. It is, isn't it?

MANDERS (*looks at him sympathetically*). Yes, you went out into the world early, my dear Oswald.

OSWALD. I did. Sometimes I wonder if it wasn't too early.

MRS. ALVING. Oh, nonsense. It's good for a healthy lad; especially if he's an only child. It's bad for them to stay at home with their mother and father and be pampered.

MANDERS. That is a very debatable point, Mrs. Alving. When all is said and done, the parental home is where a child belongs.

OSWALD. I agree with you there, Pastor.

MANDERS. Take your own son. Well, it will do no harm to talk about it in his presence. What has been the consequence for him? Here he is, twenty-six or twenty-seven years old, and he's never had the opportunity to know what a real home is like.

OSWALD. I beg your pardon, sir, but there you're quite mistaken.

MANDERS. Oh? I thought you had spent practically all your time in artistic circles.

OSWALD. I have.

MANDERS. Mostly among young artists.

OSWALD. Yes.

MANDERS. But I thought most of those people lacked the means to support a family and make a home for themselves.

OSWALD. Some of them can't afford to get married, sir.

MANDERS. Yes, that's what I'm saying.

OSWALD. But that doesn't mean they can't have a home. Several of them have; and very good and comfortable homes at that.

(MRS. ALVING *listens intently and nods, but says nothing.*)

MANDERS. But I'm not speaking about bachelor establishments. By a home I mean a family establishment, where a man lives with his wife and children.

OSWALD. Quite. Or with his children and their mother.

MANDERS (*starts and claps his hands together*). Merciful heavens! You don't—?

OSWALD. Yes?

MANDERS. Lives with—with the mother of his children?

OSWALD. Yes, would you rather be disowned the mother of his children?

MANDERS. So you are speaking of unlegalized relationships! These so-called free marriages!

OSWALD. I've never noticed anything particularly free about the way such people live.

MANDERS. But how is it possible that—that any reasonably well brought up man or young woman can bring themselves to live like that—openly, for everyone to see?

OSWALD. But what else can they do? A poor young artist—a poor young girl—It costs a lot of money to get married. What can they do?

MANDERS. What can they do? I'll tell you, Mr. Alving, what they can do. They should have kept away from each other in the first place—that's what they should have done.

OSWALD. That argument won't get you far with young people who are in love and have red blood in their veins.

MRS. ALVING. No, that won't get you very far.

MANDERS (*takes no notice*). And to think that the authorities tolerate such behaviour! That it is allowed to happen openly! (*Turns to* MRS. ALVING.) Wasn't I right to be so concerned about your son?

In circles where immorality is practised openly and is, one might almost say, accepted—

OSWALD. Let me tell you something, sir, I have been a regular Sunday guest in one or two of these irregular households—

MANDERS. On Sundays!

OSWALD. Yes, that's the day when one's meant to enjoy oneself. But I have never heard an offensive word there, far less ever witnessed anything which could be called immoral. No; do you know when and where I have encountered immorality in artistic circles?

MANDERS. No, I don't, thank heaven.

OSWALD. Well, I shall tell you. I have encountered it when one or another of our model husbands and fathers came down there to look around a little on their own—and did the artists the honour of visiting them in their humble bistros. Then we learned a few things. Those gentlemen were able to tell us about places and things of which we had never dreamed.

MANDERS. What! Are you suggesting that honourable men from this country—!

OSWALD. Have you never, when these honourable men returned home, have you never heard them hold forth on the rampancy of immorality in foreign countries?

MANDERS. Yes, of course—

MRS. ALVING. I've heard that, too.

OSWALD. Well, you can take their word for it. Some of them are experts. (*Clasps his head.*) Oh, that beautiful life of freedom—that it should be so soiled!

MR. ALVING. You mustn't get over-excited, Oswald. It isn't good for you.

OSWALD. No, you're right, Mother. It isn't good for my health. It's that damned tired-ness, you know. Well, I'll take a little walk before dinner. I'm sorry, Pastor. I know you can't see it from my point of view. But I had to say what I felt.

(*He goes out through the second door on the right.*)

MRS. ALVING. My poor boy—!

MANDERS. Yes, you may well say that. So it's come to this.

(MRS. ALVING *looks at him but remains silent.*)

MANDERS. (*walks up and down*). He called himself the prodigal son. Alas, alas!

(MRS. ALVING *still looks a him.*)

MANDERS. And what do you say to all this?

MRS. ALVING. I say that Oswald was right in every word he said.

MANDERS (*stops dead*). Right? Right! In expressing those principles!

MRS. ALVING. Here in my loneliness I have come to think like him, Pastor Manders. But I have never dared to bring up the subject. Now my son shall speak for me.

MANDERS. I feel deeply sorry for you, Mrs. Alving. But now I will have to speak to you in earnest. I am not addressing you now as your business manager and adviser, nor as your and your late husband's old friend. I stand before you now as your priest, as I did at the moment when you had strayed so far.

MRS. ALVING. And what has the priest to say to me?

MANDERS. First I wish to refresh your memory, Mrs. Alving. The occasion is appropriate. Tomorrow will be the tenth anniversary of your husband's death. Tomorrow the memorial to him who is no longer with us is to be unveiled. Tomorrow I shall address the whole assembled flock. But today I wish to speak to you alone.

MRS. ALVING. Very well, Pastor. Speak.

MANDERS. Have you forgotten that after barely a year of marriage you stood on the very brink of the abyss? That you abandoned your house and home—that you deserted your husband—yes, Mrs. Alving, deserted, deserted—and refused to return to him, although he begged and entreated you to do so?

MRS. ALVING. Have you forgotten how desperately unhappy I was during that first year?

MANDERS. Yes, that is the sign of the rebellious spirit, to demand happiness from this earthly life. What right have we to happiness? No, Mrs. Alving, we must do our duty! And your duty was to remain with the man you had chosen, and to whom you were bound by a sacred bond.

MRS. ALVING. You know quite well the kind of life Alving led at that time; the depravities he indulged in.

MANDERS. I am only too aware of the rumours that were circulating about him; and I least of anyone approve his conduct during his youthful years, if those rumours contained the truth. But a wife is not appointed to be her husband's judge. It was your duty humbly to bear that cross which a higher will had seen fit to assign to you. But instead you rebelliously fling down that cross, abandon the erring soul you should have supported, hazard your good name, and very nearly ruin the reputations of others.

MRS. ALVING. Others? Another's, you mean?

MANDERS. It was extremely inconsiderate of you to seek refuge with me.

MRS. ALVING. With our priest? With an old friend?

MANDERS. Exactly. Well, you may thank God that I was possessed the necessary firmness—that I was able to dissuade you from your frenzied intentions and that it was granted to me to lead you back on to the path of duty and home to your lawful husband.

MRS. ALVING. Yes, Pastor Manders, that was certainly your doing.

MANDERS. I was merely a humble tool in the hand of a higher purpose. And that I persuaded you to bow to the call of duty and obedience, has not that proved a blessing which will surely enrich the remainder of your days? Did I not foretell all this? Did not Alving turn from his aberrations, like a man? Did he not afterwards live a loving and blameless life with you for the remainder of his days? Did he not become a public benefactor, did he not inspire you so that in time you became his right hand in all his enterprises? And a very capable right hand—oh, yes, I know that, Mrs. Alving, I give you credit for that. But now I come to the next great error of your life.

MRS. ALVING. And what do you mean by that?

MANDERS. Once you disowned your duties as a wife. Since then, you have disowned your duties as a mother.

MRS. ALVING. Ah—!

MANDERS. All your days you have been ruled by a fatal spirit of wilfulness. You have always longed for a life unconstrained by duties and principles. You have never been willing to suffer the curb of discipline. Everything that has been troublesome in your life you have cast off ruthlessly and callously, as if it were a burden which you had the right to reject. It was no longer convenient to you to be a wife, so you left your husband. You found it tiresome to be a mother, so you put your child out to live among strangers.

MRS. ALVING. Yes, that is true. I did.

MANDERS. And in consequence you have become a stranger to him.

MRS. ALVING. No, no! That's not true!

MANDERS. It is. It must be. And how have you got him back?

Think well, Mrs. Alving! You have sinned greatly against your husband. You admit that by raising the monument to him down there. Confess too, now, how you have sinned against your son. There may still be time to bring him back from the paths of wantonness. Turn; and save what may still be saved in him. (*With raised forefinger.*) For verily, Mrs. Alving, as a mother you carry a heavy burden of guilt. This I have regarded as my duty to say to you.

(*Silence.*)

MRS. ALVING. (*slow and controlled*). You have had your say, Pastor; and tomorrow you will speak at my husband's ceremony. I shall not speak tomorrow. But now I shall say a few words to you, just as you have said a few words to me.

MANDERS. Of course. You wish to excuse your conduct—

MRS. ALVING. No. I simply want to tell you what happened.

MANDERS. Oh?

MRS. ALVING. Everything that you have just said about me and my husband and our life together after you, as you put it, had led me back on to the path of duty—all that is something of which you have no knowledge from your own observations. From that moment you, who used to visit us every day, never once set foot in our house.

MANDERS. You and your husband moved from town shortly afterwards.

MRS. ALVING. Yes. And you never came out here to see us while my husband was alive. It was only the business connected with the Orphanage that compelled you to visit me.

MANDERS (*quietly and uncertainly*). Helen—if this is intended as a reproach, I must beg you to consider the—

MRS. ALVING. The duty you owed to your position, yes. And then I was a wife who had run away from her husband. One can never be too careful with such unprincipled women.

MANDERS. My dear . . . Mrs. Alving, you exaggerate grotesquely.

MRS. ALVING. Yes, yes, well, let us forget it. What I wanted to say was that when you judge my conduct as a wife, you are content to base your judgment on common opinion.

MANDERS. Yes, well; what of it?

MRS. ALVING. But now, Manders, now I shall tell the truth. I have sworn to myself that one day you should know it. Only you.

MANDERS. And what is the truth?

MRS. ALVING. The truth is that my husband died just as dissolute as he had always lived.

MANDERS (*gropes for a chair*). What did you say?

MRS. ALVING. Just as dissolute, at any rate in his desires, after nineteen years of marriage, as he was before you wedded us.

MANDERS. You call these youthful escapades—these irregularities —excesses, if you like—evidence of a dissolute life!

MRS. ALVING. That is the expression our doctor used.

MANDERS. I don't understand you.

MRS. ALVING. I doesn't matter.

MANDERS. I cannot believe my ears. You mean your whole married life—all those years you shared with your husband—were nothing but a façade!

MRS. ALVING. Yes. Now you know.

MANDERS. But—but this I cannot accept! I don't understand—I cannot credit it! But how on earth is it possible—how could such a thing be kept secret?

MRS. ALVING. I had to fight, day after day, to keep it secret. After Oswald was born I thought things became a little better with Alving. But it didn't last long. And now I had to fight a double battle, fight with all my strength to prevent anyone knowing what kind of a man my child's father was. And you know what a winning personality Alving had. No one could believe anything but good of him. He was one of those people whose reputations remain untarnished by the way they live. But then, Manders—you must know this too—then came the most loathsome thing of all.

MANDERS. More loathsome than this!

MRS. ALVING. I had put up with him, although I knew well what went on secretly outside the house. But when he offended within our four walls—

MANDERS. What are you saying? Here!

MRS. ALVING. Yes, here in our own home. In there— (*Points to the first door on the right.*) —it was in the dining-room I first found out about it. I had something to do in there and the door was standing ajar. Then I heard our maid come up from the garden to water the flowers in there.

MANDERS. Oh, yes?

MRS. ALVING. A few moments later I heard Alving enter the room.

He said something to her. And then I heard— (*Gives a short laugh.*)
—I still don't know whether to laugh or cry—I heard my own
servant whisper: "Stop it, Mr. Alving! Let me go!"

MANDERS. What an unseemly frivolity! But it was nothing more
than a frivolity, Mrs. Alving. Believe me.

MRS. ALVING. I soon found out what to believe. My husband had
his way with the girl. And that relationship had consequences, Pastor
Manders.

MANDERS (*petrified*). And all this took place in this house! In
this house!

MRS. ALVING. I had endured much in this house. To keep him at
home in the evenings—and at night—I had to make myself his
companion in his secret dissipations up in his room. There I had
to sit alone with him, had to clink my glass with his and drink with
him, listen to his obscene and senseless drivelling, had to fight him
with my fists to haul him into bed—

MANDERS (*shocked*). I don't know how you managed to endure
it.

MRS. ALVING. I had to, for my little son's sake. But when the final
humiliation came—when my own servant—then I swore to myself:
"This must stop!" And so I took oved the reins of this house; both
as regards him and everything else. For now, you see, I had a weapon
against him; he dared not murmur. It was then that I sent Oswald
away. He was nearly seven and was beginning to notice things and
ask questions, the way children do. I couldn't bear that, Manders.
I thought the child could not help but he poisoned merely by breathing in this tainted home. That was why I sent him away. And so
now you know why he was never allowed to set foot in his home
while his father was alive. No one knows what it cost me.

MANDERS. You have indeed been sorely tried.

MRS. ALVING. I could never have borne it if I had not had my
work. Yes, for I think I can say that I have worked! All the addi-
tions to the estate, all the improvements, all the useful innovations
for which Alving was praised—do you imagine he had the energy
to initiate any of them? He, who spent the whole day lying on the
sofa reading old court circulars? No; let me tell you this too; I drove
him forward when he was in his happier moods; and I had to bear
the whole burden when he started again on his dissipations or collapsed in snivelling helplessness.

MANDERS. And it is to this man that you raise a memorial.

MRS. ALVING. There you see the power of a guilty conscience.

MANDERS. A guilty—? What do you mean?

MRS. ALVING. I always believed that some time, inevitably, the truth would have to come out, and that it would be believed. The Orphanage would destroy all rumours and banish all doubt.

MANDERS. You certainly made no mistake there, Mrs. Alving.

MRS. ALVING. And then I had another motive. I wanted to make sure that my own son, Oswald, should not inherit anything whatever from his father.

MANDERS. You mean it was Alving's money that—?

MRS. ALVING. Yes. The annual donations that I have made to this Orphanage add up to the sum—I have calculated it carefully—the sum which made Lieutenant Alving, in his day, "a good match."

MANDERS. I understand—

MRS. ALVING. It was the sum with which he bought me. I do not wish that money to come into Oswald's hands. My son shall inherit everything from me.

(OSWALD ALVING *enters through the second door on the right; he has removed his hat and overcoat outside.*)

MRS. ALVING (*goes towards him*). Are you back already? My dear, dear boy!

OSWALD. Yes; what's one to do outside in this eternal rain? But I hear we're about to have dinner. How splendid.

REGINA (*enters from the kitchen with a parcel*). A parcel has just come for you, madam. (*Hands it to her.*)

MRS. ALVING (*with a glance at* PASTOR MANDERS). Copies of the songs for tomorrow's ceremony, I suppose.

MANDERS. Hm—

REGINA. Dinner is served, madam.

MRS. ALVING. Good. We'll come presently. I just want to— (*Begins to open the parcel.*)

REGINA (*to* OSWALD). Shall it be white port or red port, Mr. Oswald?

OSWALD. Both, Miss Engstrand.

REGINA. *Bien*—very good, Mr. Oswald.

(*She goes into the dining-room.*)

OSWALD. I'd better help her open the bottles—(*Follows her into the dining-room. The door swings half open behind him.*)

MRS. ALVING. (*who has opened the parcel*). Yes, that's right. It's the copies of the songs, Pastor Manders.

MANDERS (*with folded hands*). How I am to make my address tomorrow with a clear conscience. I—!

MRS. ALVING. Oh, you'll find a way—

MANDERS (*quietly, so as not to be heard in the dining-room*). Yes, there musn't be any scandal.

MRS. ALVING (*firmly in a low voice*). No. But now this long, loathsome comedy is over. From the day after tomorrow, it will be as if the dead had never lived in this house. There will be no one here but my boy and his mother.

(*From the dining-room is heard the crash of a chair being knocked over. At the same time* REGINA *says sharply, but keeping her voice low:*)

REGINA. Oswald! Are you mad? Let me go!

MRS. ALVING (*starts in fear*): Ah!

(*She stares distraught at the half open door.* OSWALD *coughs and begins to hum. A bottle is uncorked.*)

MANDERS (*indignantly*). What is going on, Mrs. Alving? What was that?

MRS. ALVING (*hoarsely*). Ghosts. The couple in the conservatory —walk.

MANDERS. What are you saying! Regina—? Is she the child you—?

MRS. ALVING. Yes. Come. Not a word.

She grips PASTOR MANDERS' *arms and walks falteringly towards the door of the dining-room.*

act two

The same room. The mist still lies heavily over the landscape. PASTOR MANDERS and MRS. ALVING enter from the dining-room.

MRS. ALVING (*still in the doorway*). I'm glad you enjoyed it, Pastor Manders. (*Speaks into the dining-room.*) Aren't you joining us, Oswald?

OSWALD (*offstage*). No, thank you. I think I'll go out and take a walk.

MRS. ALVING. Yes, do. It's stopped raining now. (*Closes the door of the dining-room, goes over to the hall door and calls.*) Regina!

REGINA (*offstage*). Yes, madam.

MRS. ALVING. Go down to the wash-house and give them a hand with the garlands.

REGINA. Very good, madam.

(MRS. ALVING *makes sure that* REGINA *has gone, then closes the door.*)

MANDERS. He can't hear anything from in there, can he?

MRS. ALVING. Not when the door is shut. Anyway, he's going out.

MANDERS. I am still stunned. I don't understand how I managed to swallow a mouthful of that excellent meal.

MRS. ALVING (*restless but controlled, walks up and down*). Neither do I. But what is to be done?

MANDERS. Yes, what is to be done? Upon my word, I don't know. I'm so sadly inexperienced in matters of this kind.

MRS. ALVING. I am convinced that no harm has been done yet.

MANDERS. No, heaven forbid! Nevertheless, it's a most improper situation.

MRS. ALVING. It's only a casual whim of Oswald's. You can be certain of that.

MANDERS. Well, as I said, I don't know about these things; but I'm sure—

MRS. ALVING. She must leave the house. And at once. That's obvious—

MANDERS. Yes, naturally.

MRS. ALVING. But where to? We can't just—

MANDERS. Where to? Home to her father, of course.

MRS. ALVING. To whom, did you say?

MANDERS. To her—oh, no, Engstrand isn't her—! But, dear God, Mrs. Alving, how can this be possible? Surely you must be mistaken.

MRS. ALVING. Unfortunatley I know I'm not mistaken. In the end Johanna had to confess to me; and Alving couldn't deny it. So there was nothing to be done but hush the matter up.

MANDERS. Yes, I suppose that was the only thing to do.

MRS. ALVING. The girl left my service at once, and was given a considerable sum of money to keep her mouth shut. The remaining difficulties she solved for herself when she got to town. She renewed an old acquaintance with Engstrand, let it be known, I dare say, how much money she had, and spun him a story about some foreigner or other who'd been here with a yacht that summer. Then she and Engstrand got themselves married in a hurry. Well, you married them yourself.

MANDERS. But how can that be true? I remember clearly how Engstrand came to me to arrange the wedding. He was completely abject, and accused himself most bitterly of having indulged with his betrothed in a moment of weakness.

MRS. ALVING. Well, he had to take the blame on himself.

MANDERS. But to be so dishonest! And to me! I certainly would never have believed that of Jacob Engstrand. I'll speak to him seriously about this. He can be sure of that. And the immorality of it! For money! How much was it you gave the girl?

MRS. ALVING. Fifty pounds.

MANDERS. Just imagine! To go and marry a fallen woman for a paltry fifty pounds!

MRS. ALVING. What about me? I went and married a fallen man.

MANDERS. Good God Almighty, what are you saying? A fallen man!

MRS. ALVING. Do you think Alving was any purer when I accompanied him to the altar than Johanna was when Engstrand married her?

MANDERS. But the two things are utterly different—

MRS. ALVING. Not so different. Oh, yes, there was a big difference in the price. A paltry fifty pounds against an entire fortune.

MANDERS. But how can you compare two such different situations? After all, you were obeying the counsels of your heart, and of your family.

MRS. ALVING (*does not look at him*). I thought you understood the direction in which what you call my heart had strayed at that time.

MANDERS (*distantly*). If I had understood anything of the kind, I should not have been a daily guest in your husband's house.

MRS. ALVING. Anyway, I didn't follow my own counsel. That is certain.

MANDERS. Well then, you obeyed your nearest relatives. Your mother and your two aunts. As was your duty.

MRS. ALVING. Yes, that is true. The three of them worked out a balance-sheet for me. Oh, it's incredible how patly they proved that it would be utter madness for me to turn down such an offer. If my mother could look down now and see what all that promise of splendour had led to.

MANDERS. No one can be held responsible for the outcome. And this much at least is sure, that your marriage was celebrated in an ordinary fashion and in full accordance with the law.

MRS. ALVING (*by the window*). All this talk about law and order. I often think that is what causes all the unhappiness in the world.

MANDERS. Mrs. Alving, now you are being sinful.

MRS. ALVING. Yes, perhaps I am. But I can't stand being bound by all these obligations and petty considerations. I can't! I must find my own way to freedom.

MANDER. What do you mean by that?

MRS. ALVING (*taps on the window frame*). I should never have concealed the truth about Alving's life. But I dared not do otherwise —and it wasn't only for Oswald's sake. I was such a coward.

MANDERS. Coward?

MRS. ALVING. If people had known, they would have said: "Poor man, it isn't surprising he strays now and then. After all, his wife ran away from him."

MANDERS. Perhaps they would not have been altogether unjusti-fied.

MRS. ALVING (*looks hard at him*). If I were a real mother, I would take Oswald and say to him: "Listen, my boy. Your father was a degenerate—"

MANDERS. But great heavens above—!

MRS. ALVING. And I would tell him everything I have told you. The whole story.

MANDERS. You scandalize me, Mrs. Alving.

MRS. ALVING. Yes, I know. I know! I scandalize myself. (*Comes away from the window.*) That's how cowardly I am.

MANDERS. You call it cowardice to do your simple duty! Have you forgotten that a child shall love and honour its father and mother?

MRS. ALVING. Let us not generalize so. Let us ask: "Shall Oswald love and honour Captain Alving?"

MANDERS. Is there not a voice in your mother's heart which for-bids you to destroy your son's ideals?

MRS. ALVING. Yes, but what about the truth?

MANDERS. Yes, but what about the ideals?

MRS. ALVING. Oh, ideals, ideals! If only I weren't such a coward!

MANDERS. Don't despise our ideals, Mrs. Alving. Retribution will surely follow. Take Oswald in particular. He hasn't many ideals, I'm afraid. But this much I have discovered, that his father is to him an ideal.

MRS. ALVING. You are right there.

MANDERS. And you yourself have awakened and fostered these ideals of his, by your letters.

MRS. ALVING. Yes. I was bound by these obligations and considerations, so I lied to my son, year out and year in. Oh, what a coward, what a coward I have been!

MANDERS. You have established a happy illusion in your son, Mrs. Alving—and you should certainly not regard that as being of little value.

MRS. ALVING. Hm. I wonder. But I shan't allow him to use Regina as a plaything. He is not going to make that poor girl unhappy.

MANDERS. Good heavens, no! That would be dreadful.

MRS. ALVING. If I knew that he meant it seriously, and that it would make him happy—

MANDERS. But that's impossible. Unfortunately Regina isn't that type.

MANDERS. How do you mean?

MRS. ALVING. If only I weren't such an abject coward, I'd say to him: "Marry her, or make what arrangements you please. As long as you're honest and open about it—"

MANDERS. Merciful God! You mean a legal marriage! What a terrible idea! It's absolutely unheard of—!

MRS. ALVING. Unheard of, did you say? Put your hand on your heart, Pastor Manders, and tell me—do you really believe there aren't married couples like that to be found in this country—as closely as these two?

MANDERS. I simply don't understand you.

MRS. ALVING. Oh, yes you do.

MANDERS. You're thinking that by chance possibly—? Yes, alas, family life is indeed not always as pure as it should be. But in that kind of case, one can never be sure—at any rate, not absolutely— But in this case—! That you, a mother, could want to allow your own—

MRS. ALVING. But I don't *want* to. I wouldn't allow it for any price in the world. That's just what I'm saying.

MANDERS. No, because you are a coward, as you put it. But if you weren't a coward—! Great God in heaven, what a shocking relationship!

MRS. ALVING. Well, we all stem from a relationship of that kind, so we are told. And who was it who arranged things like that in the world, Pastor Manders?

MANDERS. I shall not discuss such questions with you, Mrs. Alving. You are not in the right spiritual frame of mind for that. But that you dare to say that it is cowardly of you—!

MRS. ALVING. I shall tell you what I mean. I am frightened, because there is in me something ghostlike from which I can never free myself.

MANDERS. What did you call it?

MRS. ALVING. Ghostlike. When I heard Regina and Oswald in there, it was as if I saw ghosts. I almost think we are all ghosts—all of us, Pastor Manders. It isn't just what we have inherited from our father and mother that walks in us. It is all kinds of dead ideas and all sorts of old and obsolete beliefs. They are not alive in us; but they remain in us none the less, and we can never rid ourselves of them. I only have to take a newspaper and read it, and I see ghosts between the lines. There must be ghosts all over the country. They lie as thick as grains of sand. And we're all so horribly afraid of the light.

MANDERS. Aha—so there we have the fruits of your reading. Fine fruits indeed! Oh, these loathsome, rebellious, freethinking books!

MRS. ALVING. You are wrong, my dear Pastor. It was you yourself who first spurred me to think; and I thank and bless you for it.

MANDERS. I?

MRS. ALVING. Yes, when you forced me into what you called duty; when you praised as right and proper what my whole spirit rebelled against as something abominable. It was then that I began to examine the seams of your learning. I only wanted to pick at a single knot; but when I had worked it loose, the whole fabric fell apart. And then I saw that it was machine-sewn.

MANDERS (*quiet, shaken*). Is this the reward of my life's hardest struggle?

MRS. ALVING. Call it rather your life's most pitiful defeat.

MANDERS. It was my life's greatest victory, Helen. The victory over myself.

MRS. ALVING. It was a crime against us both.

MANDERS. That I besought you, saying: "Woman, go home to your lawful husband," when you came to me distraught and cried: "I am here! Take me!" Was that a crime?

MRS. ALVING. Yes, I think so.

MANDERS. We two do not understand each other.

MRS. ALVING. No; not any longer.

MANDERS. Never—never even in my most secret moments have I thought of you except as another man's wedded wife.

MRS. ALVING. Oh? I wonder.

MANDERS. Helen—

MRS. ALVING. One forgets so easily what one was like.

MANDERS. I do not. I am the same as I always was.

MRS. ALVING (*changes the subject*). Well, well, well—let's not talk any more about the past. Now you're up to your ears in commissions and committees; and I sit here fighting with ghosts, both in me and around me.

MANDERS. I will help you to bring to heel the ghosts around you. After all the dreadful things you have told me today, my conscience will not permit me to allow a young and unprotected girl to remain in your house.

MRS. ALVING. Don't you think it would be best if we could get her taken care of? I mean—well, decently married.

MANDERS. Indubitably. I think it would be desirable for her in every respect. Regina is just now at the age when—well, I don't really understand these things, but—

MRS. ALVING. Regina matured early.

MANDERS. Yes, didn't she? I seem to remember that she was noticeably well developed from a physical point of view when I prepared her for confirmation. But for the present at any rate she must go home. To her father's care—no, but of course, Engstrand isn't—! That he—that *he* could conceal the truth from me like that!

(*There is a knock on the door leading to the hall.*)

MRS. ALVING. Who can that be? Come in.

ENGSTRAND (*appears in the doorway in his Sunday suit*). Begging your pardon, madam, but—

MANDERS. Aha! Hm!

MRS. ALVING. Oh, is it you, Engstrand?

ENGSTRAND. There weren't any of the servants about, so I took the liberty of giving a little knock.

MRS. ALVING. Yes, yes. Well, come in. Do you want to speak to me about something?

ENGSTRAND (*enters*). No, thank you, ma'am. It's the Pastor I really wanted to have a word with.

MANDERS (*walks up and down*). Hm; really? You want to speak to me? Do you indeed?

ENGSTRAND. Yes, I'd be so terribly grateful if—

MANDERS (*stops in front of him*). Well! May I ask what is the nature of your question?

ENGSTRAND. Well, it's like this, Pastor. We've been paid off down there now—a thousand thanks, Mrs. Alving—and now we're ready with everything—and so I thought it'd only be right and proper if we who have worked so well together all this time—I thought we might conclude with a few prayers this evening.

MANDERS. Prayers? Down at the Orphanage?

ENGSTRAND. Well, of course, sir, if you don't think it's the right thing to do—

MANDERS. Oh yes, yes, indeed I do, but—hm—

ENGSTRAND. I've been in the habit of holding a little service myself down there of an evening—

MANDERS. Have you?

ENGSTRAND. Yes, now and then. Just a little edification, as you might say. But I'm only a poor humble man and haven't the proper gifts, God forgive me—and so I thought, seeing as Pastor Manders happens to be out here—

MANDERS. Now look here, Engstrand, first I must ask you a question. Are you in the correct frame of mind for such a meeting? Do you feel your conscience is clear and free?

ENGSTRAND. Oh, God forgive us, let's not talk about conscience, Pastor.

MANDERS. Yes, that's just what we are going to talk about. Well? What is your answer?

ENGSTRAND. Well—a man's conscience can be a bit of a beggar now and then—

MANDERS. Well, at least you admit it. But now, will you tell me the truth! What's all this about Regina?

MRS. ALVING (*quickly*). Pastor Manders!

MANDERS (*soothingly*). Leave this to me—

ENGSTRAND. Regina? Good heavens, how you frighten me! (*Looks at* MRS. ALVING.) Surely nothing's happened to Regina?

MANDERS. Let us hope not. But what I meant was, what's all this about you and Regina? You call yourself her father, don't you? Hm?

ENGSTRAND (*uncertainly*). Well—hm—you know all about me and poor Johanna.

MANDERS. Now I want no more prevarication. Your late wife told the whole truth to Mrs. Alving before she left her service.

ENGSTRAND. Well, may the—! No, did she really?

MANDERS. So now you are unmasked, Engstrand.

ENGSTRAND. And she promised and swore on the Bible that she—

MANDERS. Swore on the Bible—!

ENGSTRAND. No, she only promised, but so sincerely.

MANDERS. And all these years you have concealed the truth from me. Concealed it from *me,* who trusted you so implicitly.

ENGSTRAND. Yes, I'm afraid I have, I suppose.

MANDERS. Have I deserved this from you, Engstrand? Haven't I always been ready to assist you with help, both spiritual and material, as far as lay within my power? Answer! Haven't I?

ENGSTRAND. Things would often have looked black for me if it hadn't been for your Reverence.

MANDERS. And this is how you reward me! You cause me to enter false statements in the parish register, and withhold from me over a period of years the information which you owed both to me and to the cause of truth! Your conduct has been completely indefensible, Engstrand. From now on, I wash my hands of you.

ENGSTRAND (*with a sigh*). Yes, of course, sir. I appreciate that.

MANDERS. I mean, how could you possibly justify yourself?

ENGSTRAND. But wouldn't it have made things even worse for poor Johanna if the truth had been allowed to come out? Now just imagine if your Reverence had been in the same situation as her—

MANDERS. I!

ENGSTRAND. Oh, for heaven's sake, I don't mean exactly the same. But I mean, suppose your Reverence had something to be ashamed of in the eyes of the world, as the saying goes. We men mustn't judge a poor woman too harshly, your Reverence.

MANDERS. But I'm not. It's you I'm reproaching.

ENGSTRAND. May I ask your Reverence a tiny question?

MANDERS. Yes, yes, what is it?

ENGSTRAND. Isn't it right and proper for a man to raise up the fallen?

MANDERS. Of course it is.

ENGSTRAND. And isn't it a man's duty to stand by his word?

MANDERS. Certainly it is: but—

ENGSTRAND. That time when Johanna fell into misfortune through that Englishman—or maybe he was an American, or a Russian, as they call them—well, she came up to town. Poor creature, she'd turned up her nose at me once or twice; for she only looked at what was handsome and fine, poor thing; and of course I had this thing wrong with my leg. Well, your Reverence will remember how I'd ventured into a dancing-hall where foreign sailors were indulging in drunkenness and excess, as the saying goes. And when I tried to exhort them to start leading a better life—

MRS. ALVING (*by the window*). Hm—

MANDERS. I know, Engstrand. The ruffians threw you down the stairs. You've told me about it before. Your injury is something to be proud of.

ENGSTRAND. Oh, I take no pride in it, your Reverence. But what I was going to say was, so she came along and poured out all her troubles to me amid weeping and gnashing of teeth. I'll be frank, your Reverence; it nearly broke my heart to listen to her.

MANDERS. Did it really, Engstrand? Well, go on.

ENGSTRAND. Yes, well, so I said to her: "This American is a vagrant on the sea of life," I said. "And you, Johanna, you've committed a sin and are a fallen creature. But Jacob Engstrand," I said, "he's got both feet firmly on the ground"—speaking figuratively, you understand—

MANDERS. I understand you perfectly. Go on.

ENGSTRAND. Well, that's how I raised her up and made an honest woman of her so that people shouldn't get to know the wanton way she'd behaved with foreigners.

MANDERS. You acted very handsomely. The only thing I can't understand is how you could bring yourself to accept money—

ENGSTRAND. Money? I? Not a penny!

MANDERS (*glances questioningly at* MRS. ALVING). But—!

ENGSTRAND. Oh yes, wait a moment—now I remember. Johanna

did have a few shillings with her. But I wouldn't have any of it. "Fie!" I said, "that's Mammon, that's the wages of sin. We'll throw that wretched gold—or notes, or whatever it was—back in the American's face," I said. But he'd taken his hook and disappeared across the wild sea, your Reverence.

MANDERS. Had he, my dear Engstrand?

ENGSTRAND. Oh yes. And so Johanna and I agreed that the money was to be used to bring up the child, and that's what happened; and I can account for every shilling of it.

MANDERS. But this puts quite a different face on things.

ENGSTRAND. That's the way it was, your Reverence. And I think I can say I've been a real father to Regina—as far as stood within my power—for unfortunately I'm an ailing man.

MANDERS. Now, now, my dear Engstrand—

ENGSTRAND. But this I can say, that I've brought up the child tenderly and been a loving husband to poor Johanna and ordered my household the way the good book says. But it would never have entered my head to go along to your Reverence in sinful pride and boast that for once I too had done a good deed. No, when anything of that kind happens to Jacob Engstrand, he keeps quiet about it. I don't suppose that's always the way, more's the pity. And when I do go to see Pastor Manders I've always more than enough of wickedness and weakness to talk to him about. For I said it just now and I say it again—a man's conscience can be a real beggar now and then.

MANDERS. Give me your hand, Jacob Engstrand.

ENGSTRAND. Why, good heavens, Pastor—!

MANDERS. No argument, now. (*Presses his hand.*) There!

ENGSTRAND. And if I was to go down on my bended knees and humbly to beg your Reverence's forgiveness—?

MANDERS. You? No, on the contrary. It is I who must ask your pardon—

ENGSTRAND. Oh no, really—

MANDERS. Indeed, yes. And I do so with all my heart. Forgive me that I could ever have misjudged you so. And if there is any way in which I can show the sincerity of my regrets and of my good-will towards you—

ENGSTRAND. Would your Reverence really do that?

MANDERS. Most gladly.

ENGSTRAND. Well, in that case there's a real opportunity just now. With the money I've managed to put aside through the blessed work here, I'm thinking of starting a kind of home for sailors in the city.

MANDERS. *You* are?

ENGSTRAND. Yes, a kind of refuge like the one here, in a manner of speaking. The temptations for a sailor wandering on shore are so manifold. But in this house, with me there, I't be like them having a father to take care of them, I thought.

MANDERS. What have you to say to that, Mrs. Alving!

ENGSTRAND. My means are rather limited, God knows. But if only someone would stretch out a helping hand—

MANDERS. Yes, well, let us consider the matter more closely. Your project interests me very deeply. But go along now and get every-thing in order and light candles so as to make the place cheerful, and we'll have a little edification together, my dear Engstrand. For now I think you're in the right frame of mind.

ENGSTRAND. Yes, I think I am. Well, goodbye, Mrs. Alving, and thank you for everything. And take good care of Regina for me. (*Wipes a tear from his eye.*) Poor Johanna's child!—it's strange, but—it's just as though she'd grown to be a part of me. It is really, yes. (*Touches his forehead and goes out through the door.*)

MANDERS. Well, what have you to say about that man now, Mrs. Alving? That was quite a different explanation we were given there.

MRS. ALVING. It was indeed.

MANDERS. You see how terribly careful one must be about con-demning one's fellows. But then, again, it is a deep joy to discover that one has been mistaken. Or what do you say?

MRS. ALVING. I say: you are a great baby, Manders. And you always will be.

MANDERS. I?

MRS. ALVING (*places both her hands on his shoulders*). And I say: I'd like to throw both my arms round your neck.

MANDERS (*frees himself quickly*). No, no, bless you! Such im-pulses—!

MRS. ALVING (*with a smile*). Oh, you needn't be frightened of me.

MANDERS (*by the table*). You have such an extravagant way of expressing yourself sometimes. Now let me just gather these docu-ments together and put them in my case. (*Does so.*) There! And now, *au revoir*. Keep your eyes open when Oswald comes back. I'll be with you again presently. (*Takes his hat and goes out through the hall.*)

MRS. ALVING (*sighs, looks out of the window for a moment, tidies the room a little and is about to go into the dining-room, but stops in the doorway and calls softly*). Oswald, are you still at table?

OSWALD (*offstage*). I'm just finishing my cigar.

MRS. ALVING. I thought you'd gone for a little walk.

OSWALD. In this weather?

(*There is the clink of a glass.* MRS. ALVING *leaves the door open and sits down with her sewing on the sofa by the window.*)

OSWALD (*still offstage*). Wasn't that Pastor Manders who left just now?

MRS. ALVING. Yes, he's gone down to the Orphanage.

OSWALD. Hm. (*Clink of decanter and glass again.*)

MRS. ALVING (*with a worried glance*). Oswald dear, you ought to be careful with that liqueur. It's strong.

OSWALD. It keeps out the damp.

MRS. ALVING. Won't you come in and talk to me?

OSWALD. I can't smoke in there.

MRS. ALVING. You know I don't mind cigars.

OSWALD. All right, I'll come, then. Just one tiny drop more. There. (*He enters with his cigar and closes the door behind him. Short silence.*)

OSWALD. Where's the Pastor gone?

MRS. ALVING. I told you, he went down to the Orphanage.

OSWALD. Oh yes, so you did.

MRS. ALVING. You oughtn't to sit at table so long, Oswald.

OSWALD (*holding his cigar behind his back*). But I think it's so nice, Mother. (*Strokes and pats her.*) To come home, and sit at my mother's own table, in my mother's dinning-room, and eat my mother's beautiful food.

MRS. ALVING. My dear, dear boy.

OSWALD (*walks and smokes a trifle impatiently*). And what else is there for me to do here? I can't work—

MRS. ALVING. Can't you?

OSWALD. In this weather? Not a glimmer of sunlight all day. (*Walks across the room.*) That's the worst thing about it—not to be able to work—

MRS. ALVING. Perhaps you shouldn't have come home.

OSWALD. Yes, Mother, I had to.

MRS. ALVING. I'd ten times rather sacrifice the happiness of having you with me than that you should—

OSWALD (*stops by the table*). Tell me, Mother. Does it really make you so happy to have me home?

MRS. ALVING. Does it make me happy?

OSWALD (*crumples a newspaper*). I think it must be almost the same for you whether I'm alive or not.

MRS. ALVING. How can you have the heart to say that to your mother, Oswald?

OSWALD. But you managed so well to live without me before.

MRS. ALVING. Yes. I have lived without you. That is true.

(*Silence. Dusk begins to gather slowly.* OSWALD *paces up and down the room. He has put down his cigar.*)

OSWALD (*stops beside* MRS. ALVING). Mother, may I sit down on the sofa with you?

MRS. ALVING (*makes room for him*). Yes, of course, my dear boy.

OSWALD (*sits*). There's something I have to tell you, Mother.

MRS. ALVING. (*tensely*). Yes?

OSWALD (*stares vacantly ahead of him*). I can't keep it to myself any longer.

MRS. ALVING. What? What do you mean?

OSWALD (*as before*). I couldn't bring myself to write to you about it; and since I came home I—

MRS. ALVING (*grips his arm*). Oswald, what is this?

OSWALD. Yesterday and today I've been trying to forget. To escape. But it's no good.

MRS. ALVING (*rises*). Tell me the truth, Oswald.

OSWALD (*pulls her down on to the sofa again*). Sit still and I'll try to tell you about it. I've complained so much about how tired I felt after the journey—

MRS. ALVING. Yes. Well?

OSWALD. But it isn't that that's wrong with me. It isn't any ordinary tiredness—

MRS. ALVING (*tries to rise*). You're not ill, Oswald!

OSWALD (*pulls her down again*). Sit still, Mother. Just keep calm. No, I'm not really ill; not what people usually call ill. (*Clasps his*

hands to his head.) Mother, I'm spiritually broken—my will's gone
—I shall never be able to work any more!

(*He throws himself into her lap, with his hands over his face,
and sobs.*)

MRS. ALVING. (*pale and trembling.*) Oswald! Look at me! No, no,
it isn't true!

OSWALD (*looks up at her despairingly*). Never to be able to work
again! Never. Never. To be dead while I'm still alive. Mother, can
you imagine anything so dreadful?

MRS. ALVING. My poor boy. How did this frightful thing happen
to you?

OSWALD (*sits upright again*). Yes, that's just what I can't understand. I've never lived intemperately. Not in any way. You mustn't
believe that of me, Mother. I've never done that.

MRS. ALVING. Of course I don't believe it, Oswald.

OSWALD. And yet it's happened to me. This dreadful thing.

MRS. ALVING. Oh, but my dear, dear boy, it'll be all right. You've
just overworked. You take my word for it.

OSWALD (*heavily*). That's what I thought at first. But it isn't that.

MRS. ALVING. Tell me the whole story.

OSWALD. I shall, yes.

MRS. ALVING. When did you first notice it?

OSWALD. It was soon after the last time I'd been home, and had
gone back again to Paris. I began to feel the most violent pains in
my head—mostly at the back of my head, it seemed. It was as though
a tight iron ring had been screwed round my neck and just above it.

MRS. ALVING. Yes?

OSWALD. At first I thought it was just the usual headaches I used
to have so often while I was a child.

MRS. ALVING. Yes, yes—

OSWALD. But it wasn't. I soon realized that. I couldn't work any
more. I wanted to begin on a new painting, but it was as though my
powers had failed me. It was as though I was paralysed—I couldn't
see anything clearly—everything went misty and began to swim
in front of my eyes. Oh, it was dreadful! In the end I sent for the
doctor. And he told me the truth.

MRS. ALVING. How do you mean?

OSWALD. He was one of the leading doctors down there. I had
to tell him how I felt. And he began to ask me a lot of questions,

which seemed to me to have absolutely nothing to do with it. I didn't
understand what the man was driving at—

MRS. ALVING. Yes!

OSWALD. In the end he said: "You've been worm-eaten from
birth." That was the word he used: *vermoulu.*

MRS. ALVING (*tensely*). What did he mean by that?

OSWALD. I didn't understand either, and asked him to explain
more clearly. And then the old cynic said— (*Clenches his fist.*)
Oh—!

MRS. ALVING. What did he say?

OSWALD. He said: "The sins of the fathers shall be visited on the
children."

MRS. ALVING (*rises slowly*). The sins of the fathers—!

OSWALD. I nearly hit him in the face—

MRS. ALVING (*walks across the room*). The sins of the fathers—

OSWALD (*smiles sadly*). Yes, what do you think of that? Of
course I assured him it was quite out of the question. But do you
think he gave in? No, he stuck to his opinion; and it was only when
I brought out your letters and translated to him all the passages that
dealt with Father—

MRS. ALVING. But then he—?

OSWALD. Yes, then of course he had to admit he was on the wrong
track. And then I learned the truth. The incredible truth! This wonderfully happy life with my comrades, I should have abstained from.
It had been too much for my strength. In other words, I have only
myself to blame.

MRS. ALVING. Oswald! Oh, no, you mustn't think that!

OSWALD. There was no other explanation possible, he said. That's
the dreadful thing. Beyond cure—ruined for life—because of my
own folly. Everything I wanted to accomplish in the world—not
even to dare to think of it—not to be *able* to think of it. Oh, if only
I could start my life over again, and undo it all!

(*Throws himself face down on the sofa.* MRS. ALVING *wrings her
hands and walks to and fro, fighting silently with herself.*)

OSWALD (*after a while, looks up and remains half-leaning on his
elbow*). If it had been something I'd inherited. Something I wasn't
myself to blame for. But this! To have thrown away in this shameful,
thoughtless, light-hearted way one's whole happiness and health,
everything in the world—one's future, one's life—

MRS. ALVING. No, no, my dear, blessed boy—this is impossible! (*Leans over him.*) Things are not as desperate as you think.

OSWALD. Oh, you don't know—! (*Jumps up.*) And then, Mother, that I should cause you all this grief! I've often almost wished and hoped that you didn't care very much about me.

MRS. ALVING. I, Oswald! My only son! The only possession I have in the world—the only thing I care about!

OSWALD (*seizes both her hands and kisses them*). Yes, yes, I know. When I am at home, of course I know it. And that's one of the hardest things to bear. But now you know. And now we won't talk about it any more today. I can't bear to think about it for long. (*Walks across the room.*) Get me something to drink, Mother.

MRS. ALVING. Drink? What do you want to drink now?

OSWALD. Oh, anything. You have some cold punch in the house, haven't you?

MRS. ALVING. Yes, but, my dear Oswald—

OSWALD. Oh, Mother, don't be difficult. Be nice now! I *must* have something to help me forget these worries. (*Goes into the conservatory.*) Oh, how—how dark it is in here! (MRS. ALVING *pulls a bell-rope, right.*) And this incessant rain. It goes on week after week; sometimes for months. Never to see the sun! In all the years I've been at home I don't remember ever having seen the sun shine.

MRS. ALVING. Oswald! You are thinking of leaving me!

OSWALD. Hm—(*Sighs deeply.*) I'm not thinking about anything. I *can't* think about anything. (*Softly.*) I take good care not to.

REGINA (*enters from the dining-room*). Did you ring, madam?

MRS. ALVING. Yes, bring in the lamp.

REGINA. Yes, madam, at once. I've already lit it. (*Goes.*)

MRS. ALVING (*goes over to* OSWALD). Oswald, don't hide anything from me.

OSWALD. I'm not, Mother. (*Goes over to the table.*) Haven't I told you enough?

(REGINA *enters with the lamp and puts it on the table.*)

MRS. ALVING. Oh, Regina, you might bring us half a bottle of champagne.

REGINA. Very good, madam. (*Goes.*)

OSWALD (*takes* MRS. ALVING'S *head in his hands*). That's the way. I knew my Mother wouldn't let her boy go thirsty.

MRS. ALVING. My poor, dear Oswald! How could I deny you anything now?

OSWALD (*eagerly*). Is that true, Mother? Do you mean it?

MRS. ALVING. Mean what?

OSWALD. That you wouldn't deny me anything?

MRS. ALVING. But, my dear Oswald—

OSWALD. Ssh!

REGINA (*brings a tray with a half-bottle of champagne and two glasses, and puts it down on the table*). Shall I open—?

OSWALD. No, thank you, I'll do it myself.

(REGINA *goes.*)

MRS. ALVING (*sits down at the table.*) What did you mean just now, when you said I mustn't deny you anything?

OSWALD (*busy trying to open the bottle*). Let's taste this first. (*The cork jumps out. He fills one glass and is about to do likewise with the other.*)

MRS. ALVING (*puts her hand over it*). Thank you, not for me.

OSWALD. Well, for me, then. (*Empties the glass, refills it and empties it again. Then he sits down at the table.*)

MRS. ALVING (*tensely*). Well?

OSWALD (*not looking at her*). Tell me, Mother—I thought you and Pastor Manders looked so strange—hm—quiet—at dinner.

MRS. ALVING. Did you notice?

OSWALD. Yes—hm. (*Short silence.*) Tell me—what do you think of Regina?

MRS. ALVING. What do I think?

OSWALD. Yes, isn't she splendid?

MRS. ALVING. Oswald dear, you don't know her as well as I do—

OSWALD. Oh?

MRS. ALVING. Regina spent too much time at home, I'm afraid. I ought to have brought her here to live with me sooner.

OSWALD. Yes, but isn't she splendid to look at, Mother? (*Fills his glass.*)

MRS. ALVING. Regina has many great faults—

OSWALD. Oh, what does that matter? (*Drinks again.*)

MRS. ALVING. But I'm fond of her all the same. And I am responsible for her. I'd rather anything in the world happened than that she should come to any harm.

OSWALD (*jumps up*). Mother, Regina's my only hope!

MRS. ALVING (*rises*). What do you mean by that?

OSWALD. I can't bear all this misery alone.

MRS. ALVING. But you have your mother to bear it with you.

OSWALD. Yes, that's what I thought. And that's why I came home to you. But it won't work. I can see it; it won't work. I can't bear this life here.

MRS. ALVING. Oswald!

OSWALD. Oh, I must live differently, Mother. That's why I have to leave you. I don't want you to see.

MRS. ALVING. My poor, sick boy! Oh, but Oswald, as long as you're not well—

OSWALD. If it was just the illness, I'd stay with you, Mother. You're the best friend I have in the world.

MRS. ALVING. Yes, I am, Oswald, aren't I?

OSWALD (*walks around restlessly*). But it's all the remorse, the gnawing, the self-reproach. And then the fear! Oh—this dreadful fear!

MRS. ALVING (*follow him*). Fear? What fear? What do you mean?

OSWALD. Oh, don't ask me any more about it. I don't know. I can't describe it.

(MRS. ALVING *crosses and pulls the bell-rope.*)

OSWALD. What do you want?

MRS. ALVING. I want my boy to be happy. He shan't sit here and brood. (*To* REGINA *who appears in the doorway.*) More champagne. A whole bottle.

(REGINA *goes.*)

OSWALD. Mother!

MRS. ALVING. Do you think we don't know how to live here, too?

OSWALD. Isn't she splendid to look at? The way she's made! And so healthy and strong!

MRS. ALVING (*sits at the table*). Sit down, Oswald, and let's talk calmly together.

OSWALD (*sits*). You don't know this, Mother, but I have done Regina a wrong. And I've got to put it right.

MRS. ALVING. A wrong?

OSWALD. Well, a little thoughtlessness—whatever you care to call it. Quite innocently, really. When I was home last—

MRS. ALVING. Yes?

OSWALD. She asked me so often about Paris, and I told her this and that about the life down there. And I remember, one day I happened to say: "Wouldn't you like to come there yourself?"

MRS. ALVING. Oh?

OSWALD. Well, she blushed violently, and then she said: "Yes, I'd like to very much." "Well, well," I replied, "that might be arranged" —or something of the sort.

MRS. ALVING. Yes?

OSWALD. Well, of course I forgot the whole thing. But the day before yesterday, when I asked her if she was glad that I was going to stay at home so long—

MRS. ALVING. Yes?

OSWALD. She gave me such a strange look and then she asked: "But then, what's going to become of my trip to Paris?"

MRS. ALVING. Her trip!

OSWALD. And then I got it out of her that she'd taken the whole thing seriously, that she'd been going around here thinking about me the whole time, and that she'd begun to learn French—

MRS. ALVING. I see—

OSWALD. Mother—when I saw that splendid, handsome, healthy girl standing there in front of me—well, I'd never really noticed her before—but now, when she stood there, so to speak, with open arms ready to receive me—

MRS. ALVING. Oswald!

OSWALD. Then I realized that in her I could find salvation; for I saw that she was full of the joy of life.

MRS. ALVING (*starts*). The joy of life! But how could that help?

REGINA (*enters from the dining-room with a bottle of champagne*). I'm sorry I was so long. I had to go down to the cellar— (*Puts the bottle on the table.*)

OSWALD. And fetch another glass.

REGINA (*looks at him, surprised*). There is Mrs. Alving's glass.

OSWALD. But fetch one for yourself, Regina.

(REGINA *starts and throws a quick glance at* MRS. ALVING.)

OSWALD. Well?

REGINA (*quietly, hesitantly*). Do you wish me to, madam?

MRS. ALVING. Fetch the glass, Regina.

(REGINA *goes into the dining-room.*)

OSWALD (*watches her go*). Do you see how she walks? With such purpose and gaiety!

MRS. ALVING. This must not happen, Oswald.

OSWALD. It's already decided. Surely you can see. It's not use trying to stop it.

(REGINA *enters with an empty glass, which she keeps in her hand.*)

OSWALD. Sit down, Regina. (*She glances questioningly at* MRS. ALVING.)

MRS. ALVING. Sit down.

(REGINA *sits on a chair by the dining-room door, with the empty glass still in her hand.*)

MRS. ALVING. Oswald, what was it you were saying about the joy of life?

OSWALD. Oh, yes—the joy of life, Mother—you don't know much about that here. I never feel it here.

MRS. ALVING. Not when you are with me?

OSWALD. Not when I'm at home. But you don't understand that.

MRS. ALVING. Oh, yes—I think I do now—almost.

OSWALD. The joy of life and the love of one's work. They're practically the same thing. But that you don't know anything about, either.

MRS. ALVING. No, I don't suppose we do. Oswald, tell me more about this.

OSWALD. Well, all I mean is that here people are taught to believe that work is a curse and a punishment, and that life is a misery which we do best to get out of as quickly as possible.

MRS. ALVING. A vale of tears, yes. And we do our best to make it one.

OSWALD. But out there, people don't feel like that. No one there believes in that kind of teaching any longer. They feel it's wonderful and glorious just to be alive. Mother, have you noticed how everything I've painted is concerned with the joy of life? Always, always, the joy of life. Light and sunshine and holiday—and shining, contented faces. That's what makes me afraid to be here at home with you.

MRS. ALVING. Afraid? What are you afraid of here with me?

OSWALD. I'm afraid that everything in me will degenerate into ugliness here.

MRS. ALVING (*looks hard at him*). You think that would happen?

OSWALD. I know it. Live the same life here as down there, and it wouldn't be the same life.

MRS. ALVING (*who has listened intently, rises, her eyes large and thoughtful*). Now I see.

OSWALD. What do you see?

MRS. ALVING. Now I understand for the first time. And now I can speak.

OSWALD (*rises*). Mother, I don't follow you.

REGINA (*who has also risen*). Shall I go?

MRS. ALVING. No, stay. Now I can speak. Now, my boy you shall know everything. And then you can choose. Oswald! Regina!

OSWALD. Ssh! The Pastor—!

MANDERS (*enters the hall*). Well, we've had a most splendid and profitable hour down there.

OSWALD. So have we.

MANDERS. We must assist Engstrand with this sailors' home. Regina must go and help him—

REGINA. No thank you, Pastor.

MANDERS (*notices her for the first time*). What! You here! And with a glass in your hand!

REGINA (*puts the glass down quickly*). Oh, *pardon*—

OSWALD. Regina is leaving with me, sir.

MANDERS. Leaving! With you!

OSWALD. Yes. As my wife. If she so wishes.

MANDERS. But, good heavens—!

REGINA. It isn't my doing, sir.

OSWALD. Or she will stay here, if I stay.

REGINA (*involuntarily*). Here?

MANDERS. I am petrified at you, Mrs. Alving.

MRS. ALVING. She will neither leave with you nor stay with you. Now I can speak the truth.

MANDERS. But you mustn't! No, no, no!

MRS. ALVING. I can and I will. And I shan't destroy any ideals, either.

OSWALD. Mother, what have you been hiding from me?

REGINA (*listens*). Madam! Listen! People are shouting outside! (*She goes into the conservatory and looks out.*)

OSWALD (*at the window, left*). What's going on? Where's that light coming from?

REGINA (*cries*). The Orphanage is on fire!

MRS. ALVING (*at the window*). On fire!

MANDERS. On fire? Impossible! I've only just left it.

OSWALD. Where's my hat? Oh, never mind! Father's Orphanage—! (*Runs out through the garden door.*)

MRS. ALVING. My shawl, Regina! The whole building's alight!

MANDERS. Terrible! Mrs. Alving, there blazes the judgment of God upon this sinful house!

MRS. ALVING. Perhaps you are right. Come, Regina. (*She and* REGINA *hurry out through the hall.*)

MANDERS (*clasps his hands*). And not insured either! (*He follows them.*)

act three

The same. All the doors are standing open. The lamp is still burning on the table. Outside it is dark, with only a faint glow from the fire in the background, left. MRS. ALVING, with a big shawl over her head, is standing in the conservatory, looking out. REGINA, also with a shawl round her, stands a little behind her.

MRS. ALVING. All burnt. Burnt to the ground.

REGINA. It's still burning in the basement.

MRS. ALVING. Why doesn't Oswald come back? There's nothing to save.

REGINA. Would you like me to go down and take him his hat?

MRS. ALVING. Hasn't he even got his hat?

REGINA (*points to the hall*). No, it's hanging there.

MRS. ALVING. Let it hang. He must come up now. I'll go and look for him myself. (*Goes out through the garden door.*)

MANDERS (*enters from hall*). Isn't Mrs. Alving here?

REGINA. She's just this minute gone into the garden.

MANDERS. This is the most terrible night I have ever experienced.

REGINA. Yes, sir, isn't it a dreadful tragedy?

MANDERS. Oh, don't talk about it! I hardly dare even to think about it.

REGINA. But how can it have happened—?

MANDERS. Don't ask me, Miss Engstrand. How can I know? Are you, too, going to—? Isn't it enough that your father—?

REGINA. What's he done?

MANDERS. Oh, he's completely confused me.

ENGSTRAND (*enters from the hall*). Your Reverence—

MANDERS (*turns, alarmed*). Are you still pursuing me?

ENGSTRAND. Yes, well, God rot me if—oh, good heavens! But this is a terrible business, your Reverence.

MANDERS (*walks up and down*). It is indeed, it is indeed.

REGINA. What is?

ENGSTRAND. Well, you see, it all began with this prayer service. (*Aside.*) Now we've got him, my girl! (*Aloud.*) Fancy me being to blame for Pastor Manders being to blame for something like this.

MANDERS. But I assure you, Engstrand—

ENGSTRAND. But there was no one except your Reverence mucking around with the candles down there.

MANDERS (*stops*). Yes, so you keep on saying. But I'm sure I don't remember ever having had a candle in my hand.

ENGSTRAND. And I saw as plain as plain could be your Reverence take the candle and snuff it with your fingers and throw the wick right down among the shavings.

MANDERS. And you saw this?

ENGSTRAND. Yes, with these eyes.

MANDERS. That I cannot understand. It's not usually my habit to snuff out candles with my fingers.

ENGSTRAND. Yes, it looked a bit careless, I thought. But it can't really be as bad as you say, can it, your Reverence?

MANDERS (*paces uneasily up and down*). Oh, don't ask me.

ENGSTRAND (*walks with him*). And of course you haven't insured it, either?

MANDERS (*still walking*). No, no, no. I've told you.

ENGSTRAND (*still with him*). Not insured. And then to go straight over and set fire to it all. Oh, good heavens, what a tragedy.

MANDERS (*wipes the sweat from his forehead*). Yes, Engstrand, you may well say that.

ENGSTRAND. And that such a thing should happen to a charitable institution which was to have served the city as well as the country-side. The newspapers won't be too gentle with your Reverence, I'm afraid.

MANDERS. No, that's just what I'm thinking. That's almost the worst part of it. All these hateful attacks and accusations—! Oh, it's frightful to think about.

MRS. ALVING (*enters from the garden*). I can't persuade him to come away from the fire.

MANDERS. Ah, it's you, Mrs. Alving.

MRS. ALVING. Well, now you won't have to make that speech after all, Pastor Manders.

MANDERS. Oh, I'd have been only too happy to—

MRS. ALVING (*in a subdued voice*). It was all for the best. Nothing good would have come of this Orphanage.

MANDERS. You think not?

MRS. ALVING. What do you think?

MANDERS. Nevertheless, it was a terrible tragedy.

MRS. ALVING. We'll discuss it simply as a business matter. Are you waiting for the Pastor, Engstrand?

ENGSTRAND (*in the doorway to the hall*). That's right, madam.

MRS. ALVING. Well, sit down, then.

ENGSTRAND. Thank you, I'm happy standing.

MRS. ALVING (*to* MANDERS). I suppose you'll be leaving with the steamer?

MANDERS. Yes. In an hour.

MRS. ALVING. Would you be kind enough to take all the papers along with you? I don't want to hear another word about this. Now I have other things to think about—

MANDERS. Mrs. Alving—

MRS. ALVING. I'll send you a power of attorney so that you can take any measures you think fit.

MANDERS. I shall be only too happy to shoulder that responsibility. I fear the original purpose of the endowment will now have to be completely changed.

MRS. ALVING. I appreciate that.

MANDERS. Yes, I'm provisionally thinking of arranging for the Solvik property to be handed over to the parish. The freehold cannot by any means be said to be without value. It can always be put to some purpose or other. And the interest from the capital in the savings bank I could perhaps most suitably employ in supporting some enterprise or other which could be said to be of benefit to the town.

MRS. ALVING. As you please. It's a matter of complete indifference to me.

ENGSTRAND. Remember my home for sailors, your Reverence.

MANDERS. Yes, indeed, you have a point there. We shall have to consider that possibility carefully.

ENGSTRAND. Consider? To hell with—oh, good heavens!

MANDERS (*with a sigh*). And I'm afraid I don't know how long these matters will remain in my hands. Public opinion may force me to withdraw. It all depends on the outcome of the enquiry into the cause of the fire.

MRS. ALVING. What are you saying?

MANDERS. And one cannot possibly predict the outcome.

ENGSTRAND (*comes closer*). Oh, yes one can. Don't I stand here, and isn't my name Jacob Engstrand?

MANDERS. Yes, yes, but—

ENGSTRAND (*more quietly*). And Jacob Engstrand isn't the man to fail his blessed benefactor in his time of need, as the saying goes.

MANDERS. But, my dear man, how—?

ENGSTRAND. Jacob Engstrand can be likened to an angel of deliverance, as you might say, your Reverence.

MANDERS. No, no, I really cannot accept this.

ENGSTRAND. Oh, that's the way it's going to be. I know someone who's taken the blame for another man's wickedness once before.

MANDERS. Jacob! (*Presses his hand.*) You are indeed a rare person. Well, you too shall receive a helping hand. For your seamen's home. That you can rely upon.

(ENGSTRAND *wants to thank him, but is too moved to speak.*)

MANDERS (*hangs his travelling bag on his shoulder*). Well, let's be off. We two shall go together.

ENGSTRAND (*at the dining-room door, says quietly to* REGINA). You come with me, my girl. You'll live as tight as the yolk in an egg.

REGINA (*tosses her head*). Merci! (*Goes into the hall and fetches* MANDERS' *overcoat.*)

MANDERS. Farewell, Mrs. Alving. And may the spirit of law and order soon enter into this house.

MRS. ALVING. Goodbye, Manders.

(*She goes towards the conservatory, as she sees* OSWALD *come in through the garden door.*)

ENGSTRAND (*while he and* REGINA *help* MANDERS *on with his overcoat*). Goodbye, my child. And if ever you find yourself in any trouble, you know where Jacob Engstrand is to be found. (*Quietly.*) Little Harbour Street—hm—! (*To* MRS. ALVING *and* OSWALD.) And the house for wandering sailors is going to be called Captain Alving's Home. And if I am allowed to run it according to my ideas, I think I can promise you it'll be a worthy memorial to him, God rest his soul.

MANDERS (*in the doorway*). Hm—hm! Come along, my dear Engstrand. Goodbye, goodbye. (*He and* ENGSTRAND *go out through the hall.*)

OSWALD (*goes over towards the table*). What was that he was talking about?

MRS. ALVING. Some kind of home that he and Pastor Manders are going to found.

OSWALD. It'll burn down just like this one.

MRS. ALVING. Why do you say that?

OSWALD. Everything will burn. There will be nothing left to remind people of Father. I, too, am burning.

(REGINA *starts and stares at him.*)

MRS. ALVING. Oswald! You ought not to have stayed down there so long, my poor boy.

OSWALD (*sits down at the table*). I think you're right.

MRS. ALVING. Let me wipe your face, Oswald. It's soaking wet. (*She dries him with her handkerchief.*)

OSWALD (*stares indifferently ahead of him*). Thank you, Mother.

MRS. ALVING. Aren't you tired, Oswald? Wouldn't you like to go upstairs and sleep?

OSWALD (*frightened*). No, no, I won't sleep. I never sleep. I only pretend to. (*Heavily.*) It'll come soon enough.

MRS. ALVING (*looks worried at him*). My dear boy, you really are ill.

REGINA (*tensely*). Is Mr. Alving ill?

OSWALD (*impatiently*). And shut all the doors! Oh, this fear that haunts me—!

MRS. ALVING. Close them, Regina.

(REGINA *closes the doors and remains standing by the hall door.* MRS. ALVING *takes off her shawl.* REGINA *does likewise.*)

MRS. ALVING (*brings a chair over to* OSWALD'S *and sits down beside him*). There now. I'll sit beside you—

OSWALD. Yes, do. And Regina must stay here too. Regina must always be near me. You'll save me, Regina. Won't you?

REGINA. I don't understand—

MRS. ALVING. Save you—?

OSWALD. Yes. When the time comes.

MRS. ALVING. But Oswald, you have your mother.

OSWALD. You? (*Smiles.*) No, Mother, you wouldn't do this for me. (*Laughs heavily.*) You? Ha, ha! (*Looks earnestly at her.*) Though really you're the one who ought to. (*Violently.*) Why don't you speak to me as though I was your friend, Regina? Why don't you call me Oswald?

REGINA (*quietly*). I don't think Mrs. Alving would like it.

MRS. ALVING. You may do so presently. Come over and sit down here with us. (REGINA *sits quietly and diffidently on the other side of the table.*) And now, my poor, tormented boy, now I shall remove the burden from your mind—

OSWALD. You, Mother?

MRS. ALVING (*continues*). All this remorse and self-reproach you speak of—

OSWALD. You think you can do that?

MRS. ALVING. Yes, Oswald, now I can. You spoke of the joy of life; and that seemed to throw a new light over everything that has happened to me in my life.

OSWALD (*shakes his head*). I don't understand.

MRS. ALVING. You should have known your father when he was a young lieutenant. He was full of the joy of life, Oswald.

OSWALD. Yes, I know.

MRS. ALVING. It was like a sunny morning just to see him. And the untamed power and the vitality he had!

OSWALD. Yes?

MRS. ALVING. And this happy, carefree child—for he was like a child, then—had to live here in a little town that had no joy to offer him, only diversions. He had to live here with no purpose in life; simply a position to keep up. He could find no work into which he could throw himself heart and soul—just keeping the wheels of business turning. He hadn't a single friend capable of knowing what the joy of life means; only idlers and drinking-companions—

OSWALD. Mother—!

MRS. ALVING. And in the end the inevitable happened.

OSWALD. The inevitable?

MRS. ALVING. You said yourself this evening what would happen to you if you stayed at home.

OSWALD. You mean that Father—?

MRS. ALVING. Your poor father never found any outlet for the excess of vitality in him. And I didn't bring any sunshine into his home.

OSWALD. You didn't?

MRS. ALVING. They had taught me about duty and things like that, and I sat here for too long believing in them. In the end everything became a matter of duty—*my* duty, and *his* duty, and—I'm afraid I made his home intolerable for your poor father, Oswald.

OSWALD. Why did you never write and tell me about this?

MRS. ALVING. Until now I never saw it as something that I could tell you, because you were his son.

OSWALD. And how did you see it?

MRS. ALVING (*slowly*). I only saw that your father was a depraved man before you were born.

OSWALD (*quietly*). Ah—! (*Gets up and goes over to the window.*)

MRS. ALVING. And day in and day out I thought of only one thing, that Regina really belonged here in this house—just as much as my own son.

OSWALD (*turns swiftly*). Regina—!

REGINA (*jumps up and asks softly*). I?

MRS. ALVING. Yes, now you both know.

OSWALD. Regina!

REGINA (*to herself*). So Mother was one of them.

MRS. ALVING. Your mother was in many ways a good woman, Regina.

REGINA. Yes, but still, she was one of them. Yes, I've sometimes wondered; but—! Well, madam, if you'll allow me I think I'd better leave. At once.

MRS. ALVING. Do you really want to, Regina?

REGINA. Yes, I certainly do.

MRS. ALVING. Of course you must do as you please, but—

OSWALD (*goes over to* REGINA). Go now? But you belong here.

REGINA. *Merci,* Mr. Alving—yes, I suppose I'm allowed to say Oswald now. But it certainly isn't the way I'd hoped.

MRS. ALVING. Regina, I haven't been open with you—

REGINA. I should say not. If I'd known that Oswald was ill like this, I—Now that there can never be anything serious between us—No, I'm not going to stay out here in the country and wear myself out looking after invalids.

OSWALD. Not even for someone who is so close to you?

REGINA. I should say not. A poor girl has got to make the best of her life while she's young. Otherwise she'll be left high and dry before she knows where she is. And I've got the joy of life in me too, Mrs. Alving.

MRS. ALVING. Yes, I'm afraid you have. But don't throw yourself away, Regina.

REGINA. Oh, what will be will be. If Oswald takes after his father, I shouldn't be surprised but what I'll take after my mother. May I ask, madam, does Pastor Manders know this about me?

MRS. ALVING. Pastor Manders knows everything.

REGINA (*begins to put on her shawl*). Well then, I'd better get down to the steamer as quick as I can. The Pastor's such a nice man to get along with. And I'm sure I've as much a right to a little of that money as he has—that awful carpenter.

MRS. ALVING. I'm sure you're very welcome to it, Regina.

REGINA (*looks spitefully at her*). You might have brought me up like the daughter of a gentleman. It'd have been more appropriate considering. (*Tosses her head.*) Oh, what the hell does it matter? (*With a bitter glance at the bottle, still unopened.*) I can still drink champagne with gentlemen.

MRS. ALVING. And if ever you need a home, Regina, come to me.

REGINA. No thank you, madam. Pastor Manders will take care of me. And if things go really wrong, I know a house where I belong.

MRS. ALVING. Where is that?

REGINA. In Captain Alving's home for sailors.

MRS. ALVING. Regina—I can see it. You will destroy yourself.

REGINA. Oh, rubbish, *Adieu!* (*Curtseys and goes out through the hall.*)

OSWALD (*stands by the window, looking out*). Has she gone?

MRS. ALVING. Yes.

OSWALD (*mumbles to himself*). I think it was wrong, all this.

MRS. ALVING (*goes over behind him and places her hands on his shoulders*). Oswald, my dear boy, has this news upset you very much?

OSWALD (*turns his face towards her*). All this about Father, you mean?

MRS. ALVING. Yes, about your poor father. I'm so afraid it may have been too much for you.

OSWALD. What on earth makes you think that? Of course it came as a great surprise to me. But I can't really feel it makes any difference.

MRS. ALVING (*takes her hands away*). No difference! That your father was so miserably unhappy!

OSWALD. I feel sorry for him of course, as I would for anyone, but—

MRS. ALVING. Nothing else? For your own father!

OSWALD (*impatiently*). Oh, Father, Father! I never knew anything about Father. I don't remember anything about him, except that once he made me sick.

MRS. ALVING. This is terrible! Surely a child ought to love its father whatever may happen?

OSWALD. Even when a child has nothing to thank its father for? Has never known him? Do you really cling to that old superstition —you, who are otherwise so enlightened?

MRS. ALVING. Do you really think it's only a superstition—?

OSWALD. Yes, Mother, surely you realize that. It's one of those truisms people hand down to their children—

MRS. ALVING (*shudders*). Ghosts!

OSWALD (*walks across the room*). Yes, that's not a bad word for them. Ghosts.

MRS. ALVING (*emotionally*). Oswald! Then you don't love me either!

OSWALD. At least I know you—

MRS. ALVING. Know me, yes. But is that all?

OSWALD. And of course I know how fond you are of me; and for that I must be grateful to you. And you can do so much for me now that I'm ill.

MRS. ALVING. Yes, Oswald, I can, can't I? Oh, I could almost bless your sickness for bringing you home to me. I realize it now. You aren't mine. I must win you.

OSWALD (*impatiently*). Yes, yes, yes. These are just empty phrases. You must remember I'm sick, Mother. I can't be expected to bother about others. I've enough worry thinking about myself.

MRS. ALVING (*quietly*). I shall be patient and undemanding.

OSWALD. And cheerful, Mother!

MRS. ALVING. Yes, my dear boy—I know. (*Goes over to him.*) Have I freed you from all your anxiety and self-reproach now?

OSWALD. Yes, you have. But who will take away the fear?

MRS. ALVING. The fear?

OSWALD (*walks across the room*). Regina would have done it for the asking.

MRS. ALVING. I don't understand you. What's all this about fear—and Regina?

OSWALD. Is it very late, Mother?

MRS. ALVING. It's early morning. (*Looks out into the conservatory.*) The dawn's beginning to show upon the mountains. It's going to be a fine day. Oswald. In a little while you'll be able to see the sun.

OSWALD. I'll look forward to that. Oh, there's still so much for me to look forward to and live for—

MRS. ALVING. Of course there is!

OSWALD. Even if I can't work, there's—

MRS. ALVING. Oh, you'll soon be able to work again, my dear boy. You haven't all these gnawing and oppressing thoughts to brood over any longer now.

OSWALD. No, it was a good thing you managed to rid me of all those ideas. Once I've got over this one thing—! (*Sits on the sofa.*) Let's sit down and talk, Mother.

MRS. ALVING. Yes, let's. (*Moves an armchair over to the sofa, and sits close to him.*)

OSWALD. And while we talk the sun will rise. And then you'll know. And then I won't have this fear any longer.

MRS. ALVING. What will I know?

OSWALD (*not listening to her*). Mother, didn't you say earlier tonight that there wasn't anything in the world you wouldn't do for me if I asked you?

MRS. ALVING. Certainly I did.

OSWALD. And you'll keep your promise, Mother?

MRS. ALVING. Of course I will, my dearest, my only boy. I've nothing else to live for. Only you.

OSWALD. Yes, well, listen then. Mother, you're brave and strong, I know that. Now you must sit quite still while I tell you.

MRS. ALVING. But what is this dreadful thing you—?

OSWALD. You mustn't scream. You hear? Promise me that. We'll sit and talk about it quite calmly. Do you promise me that, Mother?

MRS. ALVING. Yes, yes, I promise. Only tell me.

OSWALD. Well then, all that business about being tired—and not being able to think about work—that isn't the real illness—

MRS. ALVING. What is the real illness?

OSWALD. The illness which is my inheritance—(*Points to his forehead and says quite quietly.*) That's in here.

MRS. ALVING (*almost speechless*). Oswald! No! No!

OSWALD. Don't scream. I can't bear it. Yes, Mother, it sits in here, watching and waiting. And it may break out any time; any hour.

MRS. ALVING. Oh, how horrible—!

OSWALD. Now keep calm. That's the way it is—

MRS. ALVING (*jumps up*). It isn't true, Oswald! It's impossible! It can't be true!

OSWALD. I had one attack down there. It soon passed. But when I found out what I had been like, this raging fear began to hunt me; and that's why I came back home to you as quickly as I could.

MRS. ALVING. So that's the fear—

OSWALD. Yes—it's so unspeakably repulsive, you see. Oh, if only it had been an ordinary illness that would have killed me—! Because I'm not so frightened of dying; though I'd like to live as long as I can.

MRS. ALVING. Yes, yes, Oswald, you must!

OSWALD. But this is so revolting. To be turned back into a slobbering baby; to have to be fed, to have to be—! Oh—! I can't think about it—!

MRS. ALVING. The child has its mother to nurse it.

OSWALD (*jumps up*). No, never! That's just what I won't allow! I can't bear to think that I might stay like that for years, growing old and grey. And perhaps you might die and leave me. (*Sits in* MRS. ALVING'S *chair.*) It might not mean that I'd die at once, the doctor said. He called it a softening of the brain or something. (*Smiles sadly.*) I think that sounds so beautiful. I shall always think of cherry-coloured velvet curtains—something delicious to stroke.

MRS. ALVING (*screams*). Oswald!

OSWALD (*jumps up again and walks across the room*). And now you've taken Regina from me. If only I had her! She would have saved me. I know.

MRS. ALVING (*goes over to him*). What do you mean by that, my beloved boy? Is there anything I wouldn't do to save you?

OSWALD. When I had recovered from the attack down there, the doctor told me that when it comes again—and it will come again— then there's no more hope.

MRS. ALVING. How could he be so heartless as to—?

OSWALD. I made him tell me. I told him I had arrangements to make. (*Smiles cunningly.*) And so I had. (*Takes a small box from his inside breast pocket.*) Mother, do you see this?

MRS. ALVING. What's that?

OSWALD. Morphine powders.

MRS. ALVING (*looks at him in horror*). Oswald—my boy—!

OSWALD. I've managed to collect twelve capsules—

MRS. ALVING (*tries to take it*). Give that box to me, Oswald.

OSWALD. Not yet, Mother. (*Puts it back in his pocket.*)

MRS. ALVING. I can't bear this!

OSWALD. You must bear it. If Regina had been here now, I'd have told her how things were with me—and asked her to do me this last service. I'm sure she would have helped me.

MRS. ALVING. Never!

OSWALD. When the horror was on me and she saw me lying there like a new-born baby, helpless, lost—beyond all hope—

MRS. ALVING. Regina would never have done it.

OSWALD. She would have. Regina was so splendidly carefree. And she would soon have got bored with looking after an invalid like me.

MRS. ALVING. Then thank God that Regina is not here!

OSWALD. Yes, well, so now you will have to do this last service for me, Mother.

MRS. ALVING (*screams aloud*). I?

OSWALD. Who else?

MRS. ALVING. I! Your mother!

OSWALD. Exactly.

MRS. ALVING. I, who gave you life!

OSWALD. I didn't ask you for life. And what kind of a life have you given me? I don't want it. Take it back.

MRS. ALVING. Help Help! (*Runs out into the hall.*)

OSWALD (*goes after her*). Don't leave me! Where are you going?

MRS. ALVING (*in the hall*). To fetch the doctor, Oswald. Let me go!

OSWALD (*also offstage*). You're not going anywhere. And no one's coming here. (*A key is turned.*)

MRS. ALVING (*comes back*). Oswald! Oswald—my child!

OSWALD (*follows her*). If you have a mother's love for me, how can you see me suffer like this?

MRS. ALVING (*after a moment's silence, says in a controlled voice*). Very well. (*Takes his hand.*) I give you my word.

OSWALD. You promise?

MRS. ALVING. If it becomes necessary. But it won't be. No, no, it's impossible.

OSWALD. Yes, let us hope so. And let us live together as long as we can. Thank you, Mother.

(*He sits in the armchair, which* MRS. ALVING *has moved over to the sofa. The day breaks. The lamp continues to burn on the table.*)

MRS. ALVING (*approaches him cautiously*). Do you feel calm now?

OSWALD. Yes.

MRS. ALVING (*leans over him*). You've just imagined these dreadful things, Oswald. You've imagined it all. All this suffering has been too much for you. But now you shall rest. At home with your own mother, my own dear, blessed boy. Point at anything you want and you shall have it, just like when you were a little child. There, there. Now the attack is over. You see how easily it passed! Oh, I know it! And, Oswald, do you see what a beautiful day we're going to have? Bright sunshine. Now you can really see your home.

(*She goes over to the table and puts out the lamp. The sun rises. The glacier and the snow-capped peaks in the background glitter in the morning light.*)

OSWALD (*sits in the armchair facing downstage, motionless. Suddenly he says*). Mother, give me the sun.

MRS. ALVING (*by the table, starts and looks at him*). What did you say?

OSWALD (*repeats dully and tonelessly*). The sun. The sun.

MRS. ALVING (*goes over to him*). Oswald, how are you feeling? (OSWALD *seems to shrink small in his chair. All his muscles go slack. His face is expressionless. His eyes stare emptily.*)

MRS. ALVING (*trembles with fear*). What's this? (*Screams loudly.*) Oswald! What is it? (*Throws herself on her knees beside him and shakes him.*) Oswald! Oswald! Look at me! Don't you know me?

OSWALD (*tonelessly as before*). The sun. The sun.

MRS. ALVING (*jumps to her feet in despair, tears her hair with both hands and screams*). I can't bear this! (*Whispers as though numbed.*) I can't bear it! No! (*Suddenly.*) Where did he put them? (*Fumbles quickly across his breast.*) Here! (*Shrinks a few steps backwards and screams.*) No; no; no! Yes! No; no! (*She stands a few steps away from him with her hands twisted in her hair, speechless, and stares at him in horror.*)

OSWALD (*still motionless.*) The sun. The sun.

THE SUN ALWAYS RISES: IBSEN'S *GHOSTS* AS TRAGEDY

Many criticisms of Ibsen's *Ghosts,* although enlightening, have failed to clearly focus on the central action of the play; consequently, we have erroneous evaluations of the play's sense of the tragic.* However, Ibsen's life relates directly to the central action of *Ghosts* and provides insights into the play's tragic sense. Plagued by an early life without parents (by his choice), by fathering an illegitimate child, and by personal and artistic failures, Ibsen rose to an esteemed social and artistic level. In his later years he increased his airs of dignity and respectability through his external habits as if to make up for earlier failures. These difficulties and change in life-style are translated into Ibsen's dramatic expression. For example, characters such as Mrs. Alving strive to suppress guilt feelings which derive from a desire for values that are accepted by society, yet which are false to the character's inner nature. Certainly, Mrs. Alving evidences an awareness of inherited and old beliefs which lie dormant within individuals yet motivate their behavior when she comments, "There must be ghosts all over the world . . . And we are so miserably afraid of the light, all of us . . . and I am here, fighting with ghosts both without and within me." The central action of the play then becomes one of an internal conflict quite similar to Ibsen's personal life. Mrs. Alving, as a character capable of rational behavior, is motivated by an emotional life she has inherited, and she has no control of such motivation. Her actions, her decisions, are based on ghosts of the past life, not on rational deliberation: marrying Captain Alving to conform to parental desires; returning to her husband; reacting to the relationship between Oswald and Regina; accepting Manders in spite of recognizing hypocrisy in the Engstrand situation; and failing to tell the truth about Oswald's father. The clearest example is her reaction toward Regina: "Out of the house she shall go—and at once." That respectable emotional reaction is later balanced by an intellectual realiza-

* Abstracted from Robert W. Corrigan "The Sun Always Rises: Ibsen's *Ghosts* as Tragedy," *Educational Theatre Journal,* XI (1959), 172-180.

tion: "If I were not such a miserable coward I would say to him: 'Marry her, or make any arrangement you like with her—only let there be no deceit in the matter.'" Constantly plagued by "I ought" realizations, Mrs. Alving knows there is a dichotomy between what she is and what she should be, and she feels a resultant guilt since she is incapable of rectifying the schism within herself. Opening in the gloom of night, the play moves to the rising of the sun, and there is the constant hope that Mrs. Alving will undergo a paralleled enlightening, a facing of the truth, but there can be only one answer that she can give, "No!" The central action of the play becomes clear: She, unable to give the sun to Oswald, is also unable to be enlightened herself. The second concern in Ibsen's drama is thus: Is this central action a tragedy? Tragedy has traditionally shown man as victim, but as victim capable of victory through enlightenment, even during defeat. Traditional criticism of *Ghosts* has seen the play as one of reform through social protest, believing that social injustices can be cured, leaving man to enjoy life. Ibsen hints at the belief that the sun can rise and shine forever, but perhaps this is only lip service to an ideal. In a letter written during the writing of *Ghosts* Ibsen questioned, "Who is the man among us who has not now and then felt and acknowledged within himself a contradiction between word and action, between will and task, between life and teaching on the whole?" Based on the understanding of the play's central action (that Mrs. Alving is victimized by a conflict she cannot control), the logical interpretation in relation to tragedy is that, since Mrs. Alving not only fails to become enlightened but also cannot give her boy the sun and is left with futility, *Ghosts* is not tragic, not in any traditional sense of the term. It may well be that Mrs. Alving's tragedy exceeds that of Oedipus or Hamlet, but, if so, it exceeds it through a sunrise of futility, not a sunrise of joy.

IBSEN'S AIM AND ACHIEVEMENT IN *GHOSTS*

Ibsen wanted and thought he had achieved an objective dramatic form when he wrote *Ghosts.** Unfortunately, despite the play's considerable strengths, it is essentially subjective and undramatic in conception and execution. In conception, it is a play about the impossibility of action; in execution, it is a series of discussions about why action is impossible. Mrs. Alving wants to find a way of acting that will satisfy two contradictory desires: she wants to be emancipated, free to act as her reason tells her she should, yet without going against the laws, customs and traditions imposed on her by society. Her relationship with her son Oswald epitomizes and illustrates how absolutely irreconcilable these contradictory claims are for her. While she feels that tradition stifles individual happiness, and she would like to fight it, she also desires a traditional mother-son relationship. All she can do is interpret the events to others. She cannot act. She must interpret the events because her interpretations are based on experiences which she alone has had. None of the other characters has been so dominated by tradition or suffered such self-denial as she has. Convinced that her experience has taught her the truth about tradition, yet unable to alleviate her own suffering, she tries to point out the lesson of her own experience. Significantly, no one is much interested in her observations. Manders is too sanctimonious to understand, Regina and Engstrand too greedy, and Oswald too involved in his emotional and physical suffering. Her talk has little or no effect on anyone. It does not even help her in a moment of crisis. When she must decide whether or not to administer the poison to Oswald, she cannot reach any decision. Reason tells her that she should give Oswald the merciful way out of his hopeless situation. Tradition tells her that as a mother she cannot kill her son. Because she accepts both reason and tradition, she stands frozen, unable to act, as Oswald begs insanely for the sun, and the final

* Abstracted from Irving Deer, "Ibsen's Aim and Achievement in *Ghosts,*" *Speech Monographs,* XXIV (1957), 264-274.

curtain falls. By paring away inessentials, using broad strokes, selected images, and techniques for interspersing his explanations, Ibsen is able to gain consistency, concentration, and symbolic reinforcement for what is essentially an intriguing analysis of Mrs. Alving's predicament. But sophisticated as his methods and arguments are, they are still used in the service of an impossible cause. Like his protagonist, Ibsen was afflicted with an insoluable dilemma: how could he reveal through action the impossibility of action?

SOUTHERN CRITICS OF 1903 ON IBSEN'S *GHOSTS*

The disappearance of the small town dramatic critic is a great loss to American life.* Almost unnoticed the movies have taken over entertainment in the provinces, and they have no need for a literate journalist. But years ago every small town paper had its theatrical critic who after the spectators had sought their street cars and their carriages, sat down at his desk and gave an earnest appraisal of the evening's entertainment—often with a fine literary flavor. In 1903 Miss Alberta Gallatin made a tour of the South with Ibsen's *Ghosts* which was considered sensational at the time; indeed, it was a play rejected by Christianity and bitterly attacked by London critics. Bernard Shaw has collected in his *Quintessence of Ibsenism* some specimens of opinions from London critics which at the present date seem incredibly stupid. Their attitude, in part, can be explained by the fact that Ibsen employed syphilis as a motive comparable—inexorable and overwhelming—to fate in Greek drama. Here are some examples of what they wrote: "Ibsen's positively abominable play *Ghosts*"; "an open drain"; "a loathsome sore unbandaged"; "a dirty act done publicly"; "merely dull dirt long drawn out." I was fortunate in meeting in the Library of Congress a former actor, Mr. Claus Bogel, who had played the part of Oswald in Miss Gallatin's troupe. He had saved clippings of the reception of the

* Abstracted from A. E. Zucker, "Southern Critics of 1903 on Ibsen's *Ghosts*," *Philological Quarterly*, XIX (1940), 392-399.

drama in various towns and, knowing of my interest, placed them at my disposal. In the following I present typical examples.

> *Richmond, Virginia:* "Theatre-goers in the cities of the South are fortunate this year in that Alberta Gallatin and a strong supporting company are making a tour in Henrik Ibsen's powerful psychological study entitled *Ghosts.*"
>
> *Asheville, North Carolina:* "Drama well acted is not rare in Asheville, but such a drama, so acted as the production last night of *Ghosts* at the Auditorium, is rare here."
>
> *Columbia, South Carolina:* "The critic turns to Shakespeare for an adequate expression of his emotions at the scene of Banquo's Ghost:

> > Can such things be
> > And overcome us like a summer's cloud
> > Without our special wonder?

> *New Orleans, Louisiana:* "*Ghosts* must be taken as a play calling for a display of strong histrionic and dramatic talent, and when viewed in this light, the play presented last night is a treat—for the prurient it is a severe disapointment.

Both the assessments of Londoners and Americans, then, reveal the various ways in which Ibsen's *Ghosts* may be received by audiences and critics alike. Indeed, the artistry of the play allows for multifarious reactions.

SHAKESPEARE AND IBSEN

Although numerous studies have been made regarding the dramas of Henrik Ibsen, few of these have noted any connection between Ibsen and Shakespeare.* Since the European literary world of Ibsen's time held Shakespearean drama in high regard, the notable lack of direct references to Shakespeare's works can suggest the possibility of a deeper, concealed connection between the two dramatists. Such

---

* Abstracted from Halvdan Koht, "Shakespeare and Ibsen," *Journal of English and Germanic Philology,* XLIV (1945), 79-86.

an influential relationship does exist. Letters written by Ibsen in 1852 from Dresden and Copenhagen refer to his reactions at having first viewed performances of Shakespeare's plays. He especially praised *Hamlet,* commenting on having seen "*Hamlet* and other of Shakespeare's plays." More importantly, Ibsen reviewed a Norwegian drama in 1857 in which he openly alluded to *Hamlet,* more out of preoccupation than comparison: "In *Hamlet* it is just the lack of active energy of the hero that determines the dramatic effect of the whole work." Ibsen's apparent preoccupation with Shakespearean dramatics becomes especially insightful when related to other evidence provided by several Ibsen biographers. While in Copenhagen and Dresden, Ibsen read and was highly affected by Hermann Hettner's critical work, *Das moderne Drama.* The combined effect of that critical work and Shakespeare's genius served to liberate Ibsen. Hettner's criticisms granted literary merit only to those dramas which were strongly based on the dynamics of psychological drives; Shakespeare practiced such psychological drama. It has frequently been noted that Ibsen's life, and consequently his dramas, presented a constant attempt to express the personal drama of his own personality. It comes as no surpise, therefore, that Ibsen's satire, *St. John's Night,* has a goblin who parallels the character and function of Puck in *Midsummer Night's Dream.* Nor is it surprising to find that *Lady Inger* presents a strong resemblance to *Macbeth,* even though the connection is most probably unconscious. The character of Lady Inger delivers monologues remarkably similar to those in the final act of *Richard III.* In fact, the basic structure of *Lady Inger* depends on the psychology of the main character, a truly Shakespearean dramatic construction. Once it is realized that Shakespeare's influence on Ibsen is so deep-seated, other connections become obvious. Ibsen's historical tragedy, *The Pretenders,* is quite closely related to *Othello.* Ibsen's jealous character, bishop Nikolas, is virtually identical to Iago in both motivation and behavior. Skule's wanderings recall King Lear, and the structure of *The Pretenders,* presenting motivational forces from a character killed early in the drama, immediately recalls the structure of *Julius Caesar.* Ibsen even includes a ghost scene in the play. Yet, despite the discernible parallels to Shakespeare's works, Ibsen went beyond the psychology of the Elizabethan master. Whereas Shakespeare clearly explained his villains, Ibsen utilized the interplay of personalities to accomplish characterization. His characters remain highly complex, and their personalities and motivations go deeper than typical Shakespearean characters. This complexity of psychological motivation reflects Ibsen's own personal complexity, but Isben is deeply indebted to Shakespeare for liberating his dramatics so that such psychological depths could be dramatized.

mISS JULIE
AUGUST STRINDBERG

TRANSLATED BY
ELIZABETH SPRIGGE

CHARACTERS

MISS JULIE, *aged 25*
JEAN, *the valet, aged 30*
KRISTIN, *the cook, aged 35*

SCENE: The large kitchen of a Swedish manor house in a country district in the eighties.

Midsummer eve.

The kitchen has three doors, two small ones into Jean's and Kristin's bedrooms, and a large, glass-fronted double one, opening on to a courtyard. This is the only way to the rest of the house.

Through these glass doors can be seen part of a fountain with a cupid, lilac bushes in flower and the tops of some Lombardy poplars. On one wall are shelves edged with scalloped paper on which are kitchen utensils of copper, iron and tin.

To the left is the corner of a large tiled range and part of its chimney-hood, to the right the end of the servants' dinner table with chairs beside it.

The stove is decorated with birch boughs, the floor shrewn with twigs of juniper. On the end of the table is a large Japanese spice jar full of lilac.

There are also an ice-box, a scullery table and a sink. Above the double door hangs a big old-fashioned bell; near it is a speaking-tube.

A fiddle can be heard from the dance in the barn near-by. Kristin is standing at the stove, frying something in a pan. She wears a light-coloured cotton dress and a big apron.

Jean enters, wearing livery and carrying a pair of large riding-boots with spurs, which he puts in a conspicuous place.

JEAN. Miss Julie's crazy again to-night, absolutely crazy.

KRISTIN. Oh, so you're back, are you?

JEAN. When I'd taken the Count to the station, I came back and dropped in at the Barn for a dance. And who did I see there but our young lady leading off with the gamekeeper. But the moment she sets eyes on me, up she rushes and invites me to waltz with her.

And how she waltzed—I've never seen anything like it! She's crazy.

KRISTIN. Always has been, but never so bad as this last fortnight since the engagement was broken off.

JEAN. Yes, that was a pretty busines, to be sure. He's a decent enough chap, too, even if he isn't rich. Oh, but they're choosy! (*Sits down at the end of the table.*) In any case, it's a bit odd that our young—er—lady would rather stay at home with the yokels than go with her father to visit her relations.

KRISTIN. Perhaps she feels a bit awkward, after that bust-up with her fiancé.

JEAN. Maybe. That chap had some guts, though. Do you know the sort of thing that was going on, Kristin? I saw it with my own eyes, though I didn't let on I had.

KRISTIN. You saw them . . . ?

JEAN. Didn't I just! Came across the pair of them one evening in the stableyard. Miss Julie was doing what she called "training" him. Know what that was? Making him jump over her riding-whip —the way you teach a dog. He did it twice and got a cut each time for his pains, but when it came to the third go, he snatched the whip out of her hand and broke it into smithereens. And then he cleared off.

KRISTIN. What goings on! I never did!

JEAN. Well, that's how it was with that little affair . . . Now, what have you got for me, Kristin? Something tasty?

KRISTIN (*serving from the pan to his plate*). Well, it's just a little bit of kidney I cut off their joint.

JEAN (*smelling it*). Fine! That's my special delice. (*Feels the plate.*) But you might have warmed the plate.

KRISTIN. When you choose to be finicky you're worse than the Count himself. (*Pulls his hair affectionately.*)

JEAN (*crossly*). Stop pulling my hair. You know how sensitive I am.

KRISTIN. There, there! It's only love, you know.

(JEAN *eats.* KRISTIN *brings a bottle of beer.*)

JEAN. Beer on Midsummer Eve? No thanks! I've got something better than that. (*From a drawer in the table brings out a bottle of red wine with a yellow seal.*) Yellow seal, see! Now get me a glass. You use a glass with a stem, of course, when you're drinking it straight.

KRISTIN (*giving him a wine-glass*). Lord help the woman who gets you for a husband, you old fusser! (*She puts the beer in the ice-box and sets a small saucepan on the stove.*)

JEAN. Nonsense! You'll be glad enough to get a fellow as smart as me. And I don't think it's done you any harm people calling me your fiancé. (*Tastes the wine.*) Good. Very good indeed. But not quite warmed enough. (*Warms the glass in his hand.*) We bought this in Dijon. Four francs the litre without the bottle, and duty on top of that. What are you cooking now? It stinks.

KRISTIN. Some bloody muck Miss Julie wants for Diana.

JEAN. You should be more refined in your speech, Kristin. But why should you spend a holiday cooking for that bitch? Is she sick or what?

KRISTIN. Yes, she's sick. She sneaked out with the pug at the lodge and got in the usual mess. And that, you know, Miss Julie won't have.

JEAN. Miss Julie's too high-and-mighty in some respects, and not enough in others, just like her mother before her. The Countess was more at home in the kitchen and cowsheds than anywhere else, but would she ever go driving with only one horse? She went round with her cuffs filthy, but she had to have the coronet on the cuff-links. Our young lady—to come back to her—hasn't any proper respect for herself or her position. I mean she isn't refined. In the Barn just now she dragged the gamekeeper away from Anna and made him dance with her—no waiting to be asked. We wouldn't do a thing like that. But that's what happens when the gentry try to behave like the common people—they become common . . . Still, she's a fine girl. Smashing! What shoulders! And what—er etcetera!

KRISTIN. Oh come off it! I know what Clara says, and she dresses her.

JEAN. Clara? Pooh, you're all jealous! But I've been out riding with her . . . and as for her dancing!

KRISTIN. Listen, Jean. You will dance with me, won't you, as soon as I'm through?

JEAN. Of course I will.

KRISTIN. Promise?

JEAN. Promise? When I say I'll do a thing I do it. Well, thanks for the supper. It was a real treat. (*Corks the bottle.*)

(JULIE *appears in the doorway, speaking to someone outside.*)

JULIE. I'll be back in a moment. Don't wait.

(JEAN *slips the bottle into the drawer and rises respectfully.* JULIE *enters and joins* KRISTIN *at the stove.*)

Well, have you made it? (KRISTIN *signs that* JEAN *is near them.*)

JEAN (*gallantly*). Have you ladies got some secret?

JULIE (*flipping his face with her handkerchief*). You're very inquistive.

JEAN. What a delicious smell! Violets.

JULIE (*coquettishly*). Impertinence! Are you an expert of scent too? I must say you know how to dance. Now don't look. Go away. (*The music of a schottische begins.*)

JEAN (*with impudent politeness*). Is it some witches' brew you're cooking on Midsummer Eve? Something to tell your stars by, so you can see your future?

JULIE (*sharply*). If you could see that you'd have good eyes. (*To* KRISTIN.) Put it in a bottle and cork it tight. Come and dance this schottische with me, Jean.

JEAN (*hesitating*). I don't want to be rude, but I've promised to dance this one with Kristin.

JULIE. Well, she can have another, can't you, Kristin? You'll lend me Jean, won't you?

KRISTIN (*bottling*). It's nothing to do with me. When you're so condescending, Miss, it's not his place to say no. Go on, Jean, and thank Miss Julie for the honour.

JEAN. Frankly speaking, Miss, and no offence meant, I wonder if it's wise for you to dance twice running with the same partner, specially as those people are so ready to jump to conclusions.

JULIE (*flaring up*). What did you say? What sort of conclusions? What do you mean?

JEAN (*meekly*). As you choose not to understand, Miss Julie, I'll have to speak more plainly. It looks bad to show a preference for one of your retainers when they're all hoping for the same unusual favour.

JULIE. Show a preference! The very idea! I'm surprised at you. I'm doing the people an honour by attending their ball when I'm mistress of the house, but if I'm really going to dance, I mean to have a partner who can lead and doesn't make me look ridiculous.

JEAN. If those are your orders, Miss, I'm at your service.

JULIE (*gently*). Don't take it as an order. To-night we're all just people enjoying a party. There's no question of class. So now give me your arm. Don't worry, Kristin. I shan't steal your sweetheart.

(JEAN *gives* JULIE *his arm and leads her out.*

Left alone, KRISTIN *plays her scene in an unhurried, natural way, humming to the tune of the schottische, played on a distant violin. She clears* JEAN's *place, washes up and puts things away, then takes off her apron, brings out a small mirror from a drawer, props it against the jar of lilac, lights a candle, warms a small pair of tongs and curls her fringe. She goes to the door and listens, then turning back to the table finds* MISS JULIE's *forgotten handkerchief. She smells it, then meditatively smooths it out and folds it. Enter* JEAN.)

JEAN. She really *is* crazy. What a way to dance! With people standing grinning at her too from behind the doors. What's got into her, Kristin?

KRISTIN. Oh, it's just her time coming on. She's always queer then. Are you going to dance with me now?

JEAN. Then you're not wild with me for cutting that one?

KRISTIN. You know I'm not—for a little thing like that. Besides, I know my place.

JEAN (*putting his arm round her waist*). You're a sensible girl, Kristin, and you'll make a very good wife . . .

(*Enter* JULIE, *unpleasantly surprised.*)

JULIE (*with forced gaiety*). You're a fine beau—running away from your partner.

JEAN. Not away, Miss Julie, but as you see, back to the one I deserted.

JULIE (*changing her tone*). You really can dance, you know. But why are you wearing your livery on a holiday? Take it off at once.

JEAN. Then I must ask you to go away for a moment, Miss. My black coat's here. (*Indicates it hanging on the door to his room.*)

JULIE. Are you so shy of me—just over changing a coat? Go into your room then—or stay here and I'll turn my back.

JEAN. Excuse me then, Miss. (*He goes to his room and is partly visible as he changes his coat.*)

JULIE. Tell me, Kristin, is Jean your fiancé? You seem very intimate.

KRISTIN. My fiancé? Yes, if you like. We call it that.

JULIE. Call it?

KRISTIN. Well, you've had a fiancé yourself, Miss, and . . .

JULIE. But we really were engaged.

KRISTIN. All the same it didn't come to anything.

(JEAN *returns in his black coat.*)

JULIE. Très gentil, Monsieur Jean. Très gentil.

JEAN. Vous voulez plaisanter, Madame.

JULIE. Et vous voluez parler français. Where did you learn it?

JEAN. In Switzerland, when I was sommelier at one of the biggest hotels in Lucerne.

JULIE. You look quite the gentleman in that get-up. Charming. (*Sits at the table.*)

JEAN. Oh, you're just flattering me!

JULIE (*annoyed*). Flattering you?

JEAN. I'm too modest to believe you would pay real compliments to a man like me, so I must take it you are exaggerating—that this is what's known as flattery.

JULIE. Where on earth did you learn to make speeches like that? Perhaps you've been to the theatre a lot.

JEAN. That's right. And travelled a lot too.

JULIE. But you come from this neighbourhood, don't you?

JEAN. Yes, my father was a labourer on the next estate—the District Attorney's place. I often used to see you, Miss Julie, when you were little, though you never noticed me.

JULIE. Did you really?

JEAN. Yes. One time specially I remember . . . but I can't tell you about that.

JULIE. Oh do! Why not? This is just the time.

JEAN. No, I really can't now. Another time, perhaps.

JULIE. Another time means never. What harm in now?

JEAN. No harm, but I'd rather not. (*Points to* KRISTIN, *now fast asleep.*) Look at her.

JULIE. She'll make a charming wife, won't she? I wonder if she snores.

JEAN. No, she doesn't, but she talks in her sleep.

JULIE (*cynically*). How do you know she talks in her sleep?

JEAN (*brazenly*). I've heard her. (*Pause. They look at one another.*)

JULIE. Why don't you sit down?

JEAN. I can't take such a liberty in your presence.

JULIE. Supposing I order you to.

JEAN. I'll obey.

JULIE. Then sit down. No, wait a minute. Will you get me a drink first?

JEAN. I don't know what's in the icebox. Only beer, I expect.

JULIE. There's no only about it. My taste is so simple I prefer it to wine.

(JEAN *takes a bottle from the ice-box, fetches a glass and plate and serves the beer.*)

JEAN. At your service.

JULIE. Thank you. Won't you have some yourself?

JEAN. I'm not really a beer-drinker, but if it's an order . . .

JULIE. Order? I should have thought it was ordinary manners to keep your partner company.

JEAN. That's a good way of putting it. (*He opens another bottle and fetches a glass.*)

JULIE. Now, drink my health. (*He hesitates.*) I believe the man really is shy.

(JEAN *kneels and raises his glass with mock ceremony.*)

JEAN. To the health of my lady!

JULIE. Bravo! Now kiss my shoe and everything will be perfect. (*He hesitates, then boldly takes hold of her foot and lightly kisses it.*) Splendid. You ought to have been an actor.

JEAN (*rising*). We can't go on like this, Miss Julie. Someone might come in and see us.

JULIE. Why would that matter?

JEAN. For the simple reason that they'd talk. And if you knew the way their tongues were wagging out there just now, you . . .

JULIE. What were they saying? Tell me. Sit down.

JEAN (*sitting*). No offence meant, Miss, but . . . well, their language wasn't nice, and they were hinting . . . oh, you know quite well what. You're not a child, and if a lady's seen drinking alone at night with a man—and a servant at that then . . .

JULIE. Then what? Besides, we're not alone. Kristin's here.

JEAN. Yes, asleep.

JULIE. I'll wake her up. (*Rises.*) Kristin, are you asleep? (KRISTIN *mumbles in her sleep.*) Kristin! Goodness, how she sleeps!

KRISTIN (*in her sleep*). The Count's boots are cleaned—put the coffee on—yes, yes, at once . . . (*Mumbles incoherently.*)

JULIE (*tweaking her nose*). Wake up, can't you!

JEAN (*sharply*). Let her sleep.

JULIE. What?

JEAN. When you've been standing at the stove all day you're likely to be tired at night. And sleep should be respected.

JULIE (*changing her tone*). What a nice idea. It does you credit. Thank you for it. (*Holds out her hand to him.*) Now come out and pick some lilac for me.

(*During the following,* KRISTIN *goes sleepily into her bedroom.*)

JEAN. Out with you, Miss Julie?

JULIE. Yes.

JEAN. It wouldn't do. It really wouldn't.

JULIE. I don't know what you mean. You can't possibly imagine that . . .

JEAN. I don't, but others do.

JULIE. What? That I'm in love with the valet?

JEAN. I'm not a conceited man, but such a thing's been known to happen, and to these rustics nothing's sacred.

JULIE. You, I take it, are an aristocrat.

JEAN. Yes, I am.

JULIE. And I am coming down in the world.

JEAN. Don't come down, Miss Julie. Take my advice. No one will believe you came down of your own accord. They'll all say you fell.

JULIE. I have a higher opinion of our people than you. Come and put it to the test. Come on. (*Gazes into his eyes.*)

JEAN. You're very strange, you know.

JULIE. Perhaps I am, but so are you. For that matter everything is strange. Life, human beings, everything, just scum drifting about on the water until it sinks—down and down. That reminds me of a dream I sometimes have, in which I'm on top of a pillar and can't see any way of getting down. When I look down I'm dizzy; I have to get down but I haven't the courage to jump. I can't stay there and I long to fall, but I don't fall. There's no respite. There can't be any peace at all for me until I'm down, right down on the ground. And if I did get to the ground I'd want to be under the ground . . . Have you ever felt like that?

JEAN. No. In my dream I'm lying under a great tree in a dark wood. I want to get up, up to the top of it, and look out over the bright landscape where the sun is shining and rob that high nest of its golden eggs. And I climb and climb, but the trunk is so thick and smooth and it's so far to the first branch. But I know if I can once reach that first branch I'll go to the top just as if I'm on a ladder. I haven't reached it yet, but I shall get there, even if only in my dreams.

JULIE. Here I am chattering about dreams with you. Come on. Only into the park. (*She takes his arm and they go towards the door.*)

JEAN. We must sleep on nine midsummer flowers tonight; then our dreams will come true, Miss Julie. (*They turn at the door. He has a hand to his eye.*)

JULIE. Have you got something in your eye? Let me see.

JEAN. Oh, it's nothing. Just a speck of dust. It'll be gone in a minute.

JULIE. My sleeve must have rubbed against you. Sit down and let me see to it. (*Takes him by the arm and makes him sit down, bends his head back and tries to get the speck out with the corner of her handkerchief.*) Keep still now, quite still. (*Slaps his hand.*) Do as I tell you. Why, I believe you're trembling, big, strong man though you are! (*Feels his biceps.*) What muscles!

JEAN (*warning*). Miss Julie!

JULIE. Yes, Monsieur Jean?

JEAN. Attention. Je ne suis qu'un homme.

JULIE. Will you stay still! There now. It's out. Kiss my hand and say thank you.

JEAN (*rising*). Miss Julie, listen. Kristin's gone to bed now. Will you listen?

JULIE. Kiss my hand first.

JEAN. Very well, but you'll have only yourself to blame.

JULIE. For what?

JEAN. For what! Are you still a child at twenty-five? Don't you know it's dangerous to play with fire?

JULIE. Not for me. I'm insured.

JEAN (*bluntly*). No, you're not. And even if you are, there's still stuff here to kindle a flame.

JULIE. Meaning yourself?

JEAN. Yes. Not because I'm me, but because I'm a man and young and . . .

JULIE. And good-looking? What incredible conceit! A Don Juan perhaps? Or a Joseph? Good Lord, I do believe you are a Joseph!

JEAN. Do you?

JULIE. I'm rather afraid so.

(JEAN *goes boldly up and tries to put his arms round her and kiss her. She boxes his ears.*)

How dare you!

JEAN. Was that in earnest or a joke?

JULIE. In earnest.

JEAN. Then what went before was in earnest too. You take your games too seriously and that's dangerous. Anyhow, I'm tired of playing now and beg leave to return to my work. The Count will want his boots first thing and it's past midnight now.

JULIE. Put those boots down.

JEAN. No. This is my work, which it's my duty to do. But I never undertook to be your playfellow and I never will be. I consider myself too good for that.

JULIE. You're proud.

JEAN. In some ways—not all.

JULIE. Have you ever been in love?

JEAN. We don't put it that way, but I've been gone on quite a few girls. And once I went sick because I couldn't have the one I wanted. Sick, I mean, like those princes in the Arabian Nights who couldn't eat or drink for love.

JULIE. Who was she? (*No answer.*) Who was she?

JEAN. You can't force me to tell you that.

JULIE. If I ask as an equal, ask as a—friend? Who was she?

JEAN. You.

JULIE (*sitting*). How absurd!

JEAN. Yes, ludicrous, if you like. That's the story I wouldn't tell you before, see, but now I will . . . Do you know what the world looks like from below? No, you don't. No more than the hawks and falcons do whose backs one hardly ever sees because they're always soaring up aloft. I lived in a labourer's hovel with seven other children and a pig, out in the grey fields where there isn't a single tree. But from the window I could see the wall round the Count's park with apple-trees above it. That was the Garden of Eden, guarded by many terrible angels with flaming swords. All the same I and the other boys managed to get to the tree of life. Does all this make you despise me?

JULIE. Goodness all boys steal apples!

JEAN. You say that now, but all the same you do despise me. However, one time I went into the Garden of Eden with my mother to weed the onion beds. Close to the kitchen garden there was a Turkish pavilion hung all over with jasmine and honeysuckle. I hadn't any idea what it was used for, but I'd never seen such a beautiful building. People used to go in and then come out again, and one day the door was left open. I crept up and saw the walls covered with pictures of kings and emperors, and the windows had red curtains with fringes—you know now what the place was, don't you? I . . . (*Breaks off a piece of lilac and holds it for* JULIE *to smell. As he talks, she takes it from him.*) I had never been inside the manor, never seen anything but the church, and this was more beautiful. No matter where my thoughts went, they always came back—to that place. The longing went on growing in me to enjoy it fully, just once. Enfin, I sneaked in, gazed and admired. Then I heard someone coming. There was only one way out for the gentry, but for me there was another and I had no choice but to take it. (JULIE *drops the lilac on the table.*) Then I took to my heels, plunged through the raspberry canes, dashed across the strawberry beds and found myself on the rose terrace. There I saw a pink dress and a pair of white stockings—it was you. I crawled into a weed pile and lay there right under it among prickly thistles and damp rank earth. I watched you walking among the roses and said to myself: "If it's true that a thief can get to heaven and be with the angels, it's pretty strange that a labourer's child here on God's earth mayn't come in the park and play with the Count's daughter."

JULIE (*sentimentally*). Do you think all poor children feel the way you did?

JEAN (*taken aback, then rallying*). All poor children? . . . Yes, of course they do. Of course.

JULIE. It must be terrible to be poor.

JEAN (*with exaggerated distress*). Oh yes, Miss Julie, yes. A dog may lie on the Countess's sofa, a horse may have his nose stroked by a young lady, but a servant . . . (*change of tone*) well, yes, now and then you meet one with guts enough to rise in the world, but how often? Anyhow, do you know what I did? Jumped in the millstream with my clothes on, was pulled out and got a hiding. But the next Sunday, when Father and all the rest went to Granny's, I managed to get left behind. Then I washed with soap and hot water, put my best clothes on and went to church so as to see you. I did see you and went home determined to die. But I wanted to die beautifully and peacefully, without any pain. Then I remembered it was dangerous to sleep under an elder bush. We had a big one in full bloom, so I stripped it and climbed into the oatsbin with the flowers. Have you ever noticed how smooth oats are? Soft to touch as human skin . . . Well, I closed the lid and shut my eyes, fell asleep, and when they woke me I was very ill. But I didn't die, as you see. What I meant by all that, I don't know. There was no hope of winning you —you were simply a symbol of the hopelessness of ever getting out of the class I was born in.

JULIE. You put things very well, you know. Did you go to school?

JEAN. For a while. But I've read a lot of novels and been to the theatre. Besides, I've heard educated folk talking—that's what's taught me the most.

JULIE. Do you stand round listening to what we're saying?

JEAN. Yes, of course. And I've heard quite a bit too! On the carriage box or rowing the boat. Once I heard you, Miss Julie, and one of your young lady friends . . .

JULIE. Oh! Whatever did you hear?

JEAN. Well, it wouldn't be nice to repeat it. And I must say I was pretty startled. I couldn't think where you had learnt such words. Perhaps, at bottom, there isn't as much difference between people as one's led to believe.

JULIE. How dare you! We don't behave as you do when we're engaged.

JEAN (looking hard at her). Are you sure? It's no use making out so innocent to me.

JULIE. The man I gave my love to was a rotter.

JEAN. That's what you always say—afterwards.

JULIE. Always?

JEAN. I think it must be always. I've heard the expression several times in similar circumstances.

JULIE. What circumstances?

JEAN. Like those in question. The last time . . .

JULIE (rising). Stop. I don't want to hear any more.

JEAN. Nor did she—curiously enough. May I go to bed now, please?

JULIE (*gently*). Go to bed on Midsummer Eve?

JEAN. Yes. Dancing with that crowd doesn't really amuse me.

JULIE. Get the key of the boathouse and row me out on the lake. I want to see the sun rise.

JEAN. Would that be wise?

JULIE. You sound as though you're frightened for your reputation.

JEAN. Why not? I don't want to be made a fool of, nor to be sent packing without a character when I'm trying to better myself. Besides, I have Kristin to consider.

JULIE. So now it's Kristin.

JEAN. Yes, but it's you I'm thinking about too. Take my advice and go to bed.

JULIE. Am I to take orders from you?

JEAN. Just this once, for your own sake. Please. It's very late and sleepiness goes to one's head and makes one rash. Go to bed. What's more, if my ears don't deceive me, I hear people coming this way. They'll be looking for me, and if they find us here, you're done for.

(*The* CHORUS *approaches, singing. During the following dialogue the song is heard in snatches, and in full when the peasants enter.*)

> *Out of the wood two women came,*
> *Tridiri-ralla, tridiri-ra.*
> *The feet of one were bare and cold,*
> *Tridiri-ralla-la.*
>
> *The other talked of bags of gold,*
> *Tridiri-ralla, tridiri-ra.*
> *But neither had a sou to her name,*
> *Tridiri-ralla-la.*
>
> *The bridal wreath I give to you,*
> *Tridiri-ralla, tridiri-ra.*
> *But to another I'll be true,*
> *Tridiri-ralla-la.*

JULIE. I know our people and I love them, just as they do me. Let them come. You'll see.

JEAN. No, Miss Julie, they don't love you. They take your food, then spit at it. You must believe me. Listen to them, just listen to what they're singing . . . No, don't listen.

JULIE (*listening*). What are they singing?

JEAN. They're mocking—you and me.

JULIE. Oh no! How horrible! What cowards!

JEAN. A pack like that's always cowardly. But against such odds there's nothing we can do but run away.

JULIE. Run away? Where to? We can't get out and we can't go into Kristin's room.

JEAN. Into mine, then. Necessity knows no rules. And you can trust me. I really am your true and devoted friend.

JULIE. But supposing . . . supposing they were to look for you in there?

JEAN. I'll bolt the door, and if they try to break in I'll shoot. Come on. (*Pleading.*) Please come.

JULIE (*tensely*). Do you promise . . . ?

JEAN. I swear!

(*Julie goes quickly into his room and he excitedly follows her. Led by the fiddler, the peasants enter in festive attire with flowers in their hats. They put a barrel of beer and a keg of spirits, garlanded with leaves, on the table, fetch glasses and begin to carouse. The scene becomes a ballet. They form a ring and dance and sing and mime: "Out of the wood two women came," Finally they go out, still singing.*

JULIE *comes in alone. She looks at the havoc in the kitchen, wrings her hands, then takes out her powder puff and powders her face.*

JEAN *enters in high spirits.*)

JEAN. Now you see! And you heard, didn't you? Do you still think it's possible for us to stay here?

JULIE. No, I don't. But what can we do?

JEAN. Run away. Far away. Take a journey.

JULIE. Journey? But where to?

JEAN. Switzerland. The Italian lakes. Ever been there?

JULIE. No. Is it nice?

JEAN. Ah! Eternal summer, oranges, evergreens . . . ah!

JULIE. But what would we do there?

JEAN. I'll start a hotel. First-class accommodation and first-class customers.

JULIE. Hotel?

JEAN. There's life for you. New faces all the time, new languages

—no time for nerves or worries, no need to look for something to do—work rolling up of its own accord. Bells ringing night and day, trains whistling, buses coming and going, and all the time gold pieces rolling on to the counter. There's life for you!

JULIE. For *you*. And I?

JEAN. Mistress of the house, ornament of the firm. With your looks, and your style . . . oh, it's bound to be a success! Terrific! You'll sit like a queen in the office and set your slaves in motion by pressing an electric button. The guests will file past your throne and nervousely lay their treasure on your table. You've no idea the way people tremble when they get their bills. I'll salt the bills and you'll sugar them with your sweetest smiles. Ah, let's get away from here! (*Produces a time-table.*) At once, by the next train. We shall be at Malmö at six-thirty, Hamburg eight-forty next morning, Frankfurt-Basle the following day, and Como by the St. Gothard pass in—let's see—three days. Three days!

JULIE. That's all very well. But Jean, you must give me courage. Tell me you love me. Come and take me in your arms.

JEAN (*reluctantly*). I'd like to, but I daren't. Not again in this house. I love you—that goes without saying. You can't doubt that, Miss Julie, can you?

JULIE (*shyly, very feminine*). Miss? Call me Julie. There aren't any barriers between us now. Call me Julie.

JEAN (*uneasily*). I can't. As long as we're in this house, there *are* barriers between us. There's the past and there's the Count. I've never been so servile to anyone as I am to him. I've only got to see his gloves on a chair to feel small. I've only to hear his bell and I shy like a horse. Even now, when I look at his boots, standing there so proud and stiff, I feel my back beginning to bend. (*Kicks the boots.*) It's those old, narrow-minded notions drummed into us as children . . . but they can soon be forgotten. You've only got to get to another country, a republic, and people will bend themselves double before my porter's livery. Yes, double they'll bend themselves, but I shan't. I wasn't born to bend. I've got guts, I've got character, and once I reach that first branch, you'll watch me climb. Today I'm valet, next year I'll be proprietor, in ten years I'll have made a fortune, and then I'll go to Roumania, get myself decorated and I may, I only say *may*, mind you, end up as a Count.

JULIE (*sadly*). That would be very nice.

JEAN. You see in Roumania one can buy a title, and then you'll be a Countess after all. My Countess.

JULIE. What do I care about all that? I'm putting those things behind me. Tell me you love me, because if you don't . . . if you don't, what am I?

JEAN. I'll tell you a thousand times over—later. But not here. No sentimentality now or everything will be lost. We must consider this thing calmly like reasonable people. (*Takes a cigar, cuts and lights it.*) You sit down there and I'll sit here and we'll talk as if nothing has happened.

JULIE. My God, have you no feelings at all?

JEAN. Nobody has more. But I know how to control them.

JULIE. A short time ago you were kissing my shoe. And now . . .

JEAN (*harshly*). Yes, that was then. Now, we have something else to think about.

JULIE. Don't speak to me so brutally.

JEAN. I'm not. Just sensibly. One folly's been committed, don't let's have more. The Count will be back at any moment and we've got to settle our future before that. Now, what do you think of my plans? Do you approve?

JULIE. It seems a very good idea—but just one thing. Such a big undertaking would need a lot of capital. Have you got any?

JEAN (*chewing his cigar*). I certainly have. I've got my professional skill, my wide experience and my knowledge of foreign languages. That's capital worth having, it seems to me.

JULIE. But it won't buy even one railway ticket.

JEAN. Quite true. That's why I need a backer to advance some ready cash.

JULIE. How could you get that at a moment's notice?

JEAN. You must get it, if you want to be my partner.

JULIE. I can't. I haven't any money of my own. (*Pause.*)

JEAN. Then the whole thing's off.

JULIE. And . . . ?

JEAN. We go on as we are.

JULIE. Do you think I'm going to stay under this roof as your mistress? With everyone pointing at me? Do you think I can face my father after this? No. Take me away from here, away from this shame, this humiliation. Oh my God, what have I done? My God, my God! (*Weeps.*)

JEAN. So that's the tune now, is it? What have you done? Same as many before you.

JULIE (*hysterically*). And now you despise me. I'm falling, I'm falling.

JEAN. Fall as far as me and I'll lift you up again.

JULIE. Why was I so terribly attracted to you? The weak to the strong, the falling to the rising? Or was it love? Is that love? Do you know what love is?

JEAN. Do I? You bet I do. Do you think I never had a girl before?

JULIE. The things you say, the things you think!

JEAN. That's what life's taught me, and that's what I am. It's no good getting hysterical or giving yourself airs. We're both in the same boat now. Here, my dear girl, let me give you a glass of something special. (*Opens the drawer, takes out the bottle of wine and fills two used glasses.*)

JULIE. Where did you get that wine?

JEAN. From the cellar.

JULIE. My father's burgundy.

JEAN. Why not, for his son-in-law?

JULIE. And I drink beer.

JEAN. That only shows your taste's not so good as mine.

JULIE. Thief!

JEAN. Are you going to tell on me?

JULIE. Oh God! The accomplice of a petty thief! Was I blind drunk? Have I dreamt this whole night? Midsummer Eve, the night for innocent merrymaking.

JEAN. Innocent, eh?

JULIE. Is anyone on earth as wretched as I am now?

JEAN. Why should *you* be? After such a conquest. What about Kristin in there? Don't you think she has any feelings?

JULIE. I did think so, but I don't any longer. No. A menial is a menial . . .

JEAN. And a whore is a whore.

JULIE (*falling to her knees, her hands clasped*). O God in heaven, put an end to my miserable life! Lift me out of this filth in which I'm sinking. Save me! Save me!

JEAN. I must admit I'm sorry for you. When I was in the onion bed and saw you up there among the roses, I . . . yes, I'll tell you now . . . I had the same dirty thoughts as all boys.

JULIE. You, who wanted to die because of me?

JEAN. In the oats-bin? That was just talk.

JULIE. Lies, you mean.

JEAN (*getting sleepy*). More or less. I think I read a story in some paper about a chimney-sweep who shut himself up in a chest full of lilac because he'd been summonsed for not supporting some brat . . .

JULIE. So this is what you're like.

JEAN. I had to think up something. It's always the fancy stuff that catches the women.

JULIE. Beast!

JEAN. Merde!

JULIE. Now you have seen the falcon's back.

JEAN. Not exactly its *back*.

JULIE. I was to be the first branch.

JEAN. But the branch was rotten.

JULIE. I was to be a hotel sign.

JEAN. And I the hotel.

JULIE. Sit at your counter, attract your clients and cook their accounts.

JEAN. I'd have done that myself.

JULIE. That any human being can be so steeped in filth!

JEAN. Clean it up, then.

JULIE. Menial! Lackey! Stand up when I speak to you.

JEAN. Menial's whore, lackey's harlot, shut your mouth and get out of here! Are you the one to lecture me for being coarse? Nobody of my kind would ever be as coarse as you were tonight. Do you think any servant girl would throw herself at a man that way? Have you ever seen a girl of my class asking for it like that? I haven't. Only animals and prostitutes.

JULIE (*broken*). Go on. Hit me, trample on me—it's all I deserve. I'm rotten. But help me! If there's any way out at all, help me.

JEAN (*more gently*). I'm not denying myself a share in the honour of seducing you, but do you think anybody in my place would have dared look in your direction if you yourself hadn't asked for it? I'm still amazed . . .

JULIE. And proud.

JEAN. Why not? Though I must admit the victory was too easy to make me lose my head.

JULIE. Go on hitting me.

JEAN (*rising*). No. On the contrary, I apologise for what I've said. I don't hit a person who's down—least of all a woman. I can't deny there's a certain satisfaction in finding that what dazzled one below was just moonshine, that that falcon's back is grey after all, that there's powder on the lovely cheek, that polished nails can have black tips, that the handkerchief is dirty although it smells of scent. On the other hand, it hurts to find that what I was struggling to reach wasn't high and isn't real. It hurts to see you fallen so low you're far lower than your own cook. Hurts like when you see the last flowers of summer lashed to pieces by rain and turned to mud.

JULIE. You're talking as if you're already my superior.

JEAN. I am. I might make you a Countess, but you could never make me a Count, you know.

JULIE. But I am the child of a Count, and you could never be that.

JEAN. True, but I might be the father of Counts if . . .

JULIE. You're a thief. I'm not.

JEAN. There are worse things than being a thief—much lower. Besides, when I'm in a place I regard myself as a member of the family to some extent, as one of the children. You don't call it stealing when children pinch a berry from overladen bushes. (*His passion is roused again.*) Miss Julie, you're a glorious woman, far too good for a man like me. You were carried away by some kind of madness, and now you're trying to cover up your mistake by persuading yourself you're in love with me. You're not, although you may find me physically attractive, which means your love's no better than mine. But I wouldn't be satisfied with being nothing but an animal for you, and I could never make you love me.

JULIE. Are you sure?

JEAN. You think there's a chance? Of my loving you, yes, of course. You're beautiful, refined (*takes her hand*) educated, and you can be nice when you want to be. The fire you kindle in a man isn't likely to go out. (*Puts his arm round her.*) You're like mulled wine, full of spices, and your kisses . . . (*He tries to pull her to him, but she breaks away.*)

JULIE. Let go of me! You won't win me that way.

JEAN. Not that way, how then? Not by kisses and fine speeches, not by planning the future and saving you from shame? How then?

JULIE. How? How? I don't know. There isn't any way. I loathe you—loathe you as I loathe rats, but I can't escape from you.

JEAN. Escape with me.

JULIE (*pulling herself together*). Escape? Yes, we must escape. But I'm so tired. Give me a glass of wine. (*He pours it out. She looks at her watch.*) First we must talk. We still have a little time. (*Empties the glass and holds it out for more.*)

JEAN. Don't drink like that. You'll get tipsy.

JULIE. What's that matter?

JEAN. What's it matter? It's vulgar to get drunk. Well, what have you got to say?

JULIE. We've got to run away, but we must talk first—or rather, I must, for so far you've done all the talking. You've told me about your life, now I want to tell you about mine, so that we really know each other before we begin this journey together.

JEAN. Wait. Excuse my saying so, but don't you think you may be sorry afterwards if you give away your secrets to me?

JULIE. Aren't you my friend?

JEAN. On the whole. But don't rely on me.

JULIE. You can't mean that. But anyway, everyone knows my secrets. Listen. My mother wasn't well-born; she came of quite humble people, and was brought up with all those new ideas of sex-equality and women's rights and so on. She thought marriage was quite wrong. So when my father proposed to her, she said she would never become his *wife* . . . but in the end she did. I came into the world, as far as I can make out, against my mother's will, and I was left to run wild, but I had to do all the things a boy does—to prove women are as good as men. I had to wear boys' clothes; I was taught to handle horses—and I wasn't allowed in the dairy. She made me groom and harness and go out hunting; I even had to try to plough. All the men on the estate were given the women's jobs, and the women the men's, until the whole place went to rack and ruin and we were the laughing-stock of the neighbourhood. At last my father seems to have come to his senses and rebelled. He changed every-thing and ran the place his own way. My mother got ill—I don't know what was the matter with her, but she used to have strange attacks and hide herself in the attic or the garden. Sometimes she stayed out all night. Then came the great fire which you have heard people talking about. The house and the stables and the barns—the whole place burnt to the ground. In very suspicious circumstances. Because the accident happened the very day the insurance had to be renewed, and my father had sent the new premium, but through some carelessness of the messenger it arrived too late. (*Refills her glass and drinks.*)

JEAN. Don't drink any more.

JULIE. Oh, what does it matter? We were destitute and had to sleep in the carriages. My father didn't know how to get money to rebuild, and then my mother suggested he should borrow from an old friend of hers, a local brick manufacturer. My father got the loan and, to his surprise, without having to pay interest. So the place was rebuilt. (*Drinks.*) Do you know who set fire to it?

JEAN. Your lady mother.

JULIE. Do you know who the brick manufacturer was?

JEAN. Your mother's lover?

JULIE. Do you know whose the money was?

JEAN. Wait . . . no, I don't know that.

JULIE. It was my mother's.

JEAN. In other words, the Count's, unless there was a settlement.

JULIE. There wasn't any settlement. My mother had a little money of her own which she didn't want my father to control, so she invested it with her—friend.

JEAN. Who grabbed it.

JULIE. Exactly. He appropriated it. My father came to know all this. He couldn't bring an action, couldn't pay his wife's lover, nor prove it was his wife's money. That was my mother's revenge because he made himself master in his own house. He nearly shot himself then—at least there's a rumour he tried and didn't bring it off. So he went on living, and my mother had to pay dearly for what she'd done. Imagine what those five years were like for me. My natural sympathies were with my father, yet I took my mother's side, because I didn't know the facts. I'd learnt from her to hate and distrust men—you know how she loathed the whole male sex. And I swore to her I'd never become the slave of any man.

JEAN. And so you got engaged to that attorney.

JULIE. So that he should be my slave.

JEAN. But he wouldn't be.

JULIE. Oh yes, he wanted to be, but he didn't have the chance. I got bored with him.

JEAN. Is that what I saw—in the stable-yard?

JULIE. What did you see?

JEAN. What I saw was him breaking off the engagement.

JULIE. That's a lie. It was I who broke it off. Did he say it was him? The cad.

JEAN. He's not a cad. Do you hate men, Miss Julie?

JULIE. Yes . . . most of the time. But when that weakness comes, oh . . . the shame!

JEAN. Then, do you hate me?

JULIE. Beyond words. I'd gladly have you killed like an animal.

JEAN. Quick as you'd shoot a mad dog, eh?

JULIE. Yes.

JEAN. But there's nothing here to shoot with—and there isn't a dog. So what do we do now?

JULIE. Go abroad.

JEAN. To make each other miserable for the rest of our lives?

JULIE. No, to enjoy ourselves for a day or two, for a week, for as long as enjoyment lasts, and then—to die . . .

JEAN. Die? How silly! I think it would be far better to start a hotel.

JULIE (*without listening*) . . . die on the shores of Lake Como, where the sun always shines and at Christmas time there are green trees and glowing oranges.

JEAN. Lake Como's a rainy hole and I didn't see any oranges outside the shops. But it's a good place for tourists. Plenty of villas to be rented by—er—honeymoon couples. Profitable business, that. Know why? Because they all sign a lease for six months and all leave after three weeks.

JULIE (*naïvely*). After three weeks? Why?

JEAN. They quarrel, of course. But the rent has to be paid just the same. And then it's let again. So it goes on and on, for there's plenty of love although it doesn't last long.

JULIE. You don't want to die with me?

JEAN. I don't want to die at all. For one thing I like living and for another I consider suicide's a sin against the Creator who gave us life.

JULIE. You believe in God—*you?*

JEAN. Yes, of course. And I go to church every Sunday. Look here, I'm tired of all this. I'm going to bed.

JULIE. Indeed! And do you think I'm going to leave things like this? Don't you know what you owe the woman you've ruined?

JEAN (*taking out his purse and throwing a silver coin on the table*). There you are. I don't want to be in anybody's debt.

JULIE (*pretending not to notice the insult*). Don't you know what the law is?

JEAN. There's no law unfortunately that punishes a woman for seducing a man.

JULIE. But can you see anything for it but to go abroad, get married and then divorce?

JEAN. What if I refuse this mésalliance?

JULIE. Mésalliance?

JEAN. Yes, for me. I'm better bred than you, see! Nobody in my family commited arson.

JULIE. How do you know?

JEAN. Well, you can't prove otherwise, because we haven't any family records outside the Registrar's office. But I've seen your family tree in that book on the drawing-room table. Do you know who the founder of your family was? A miller who let his wife sleep with the King one night during the Danish war. I haven't any ancestors like that. I haven't any ancestors at all, but I might become one.

JULIE. This is what I get for confiding in someone so low, for sacrificing my family honour . . .

JEAN. Dishonour! Well, I told you so. One shouldn't drink, because then one talks. And one shouldn't talk.

JULIE. Oh, how ashamed I am, how bitterly ashamed! If at least you loved me!

JEAN. Look here—for the last time—what do you want? Am I to burst into tears? Am I to jump over your riding whip? Shall I kiss you and carry you off to Lake Como for three weeks, after which . . . What am I to do? What do you want? This is getting unbearable, but that's what comes of playing around with women. Miss Julie, I can see how miserable you are; I know you're going through hell, but I don't understand you. We don't have scenes like this; we don't go in for hating each other. We make love for fun in our spare time, but we haven't all day and all night for it like you. I think you must be ill. I'm sure you're ill.

JULIE. Then you must be kind to me. You sound almost human now.

JEAN. Well, be human yourself. You spit at me, then won't let me wipe it off—on you.

JULIE. Help me, help me! Tell me what to do, where to go.

JEAN. Jesus, as if I knew!

JULIE. I've been mad, raving mad, but there must be a way out.

JEAN. Stay here and keep quiet. Nobody knows anything.

JULIE. I can't. People do know. Kristin knows.

JEAN. They don't know and they wouldn't believe such a thing.

JULIE (*hesitating*). But—it might happen again.

JEAN. That's true.

JULIE. And there might be—consequences.

JEAN. (*in panic*). Consequences! Fool that I am I never thought of that. Yes, there's nothing for it but to go. At once. I can't come with you. That would be a complete giveaway. You must go alone—abroad—anywhere.

JULIE. Alone? Where to? I can't.

JEAN. You must. And before the Count gets back. If you stay, we know what will happen. Once you've sinned you feel you might as well go on, as the harm's done. Then you get more and more reckless and in the end you're found out. No. You must go abroad. Then write to the Count and tell him everything, except that it was me. He'll never guess that—and I don't think he'll want to.

JULIE. I'll go if you come with me.

JEAN. Are you crazy, woman? "Miss Julie elopes with valet." Next day it would be in the headlines, and the Count would never live it down.

JULIE. I can't go. I can't stay. I'm so tired, so completely worn out. Give me orders. Set me going. I can't think any more, can't act . . .

JEAN. You see what weaklings you are. Why do you give yourselves airs and turn up your noses as if you're the lords of creation? Very well, I'll give you your orders. Go upstairs and dress. Get money for the journey and come down here again.

JULIE (*softly*). Come up with me.

JEAN. To your room? Now you've gone crazy again. (*Hesitates a moment.*) No! Go along at once. (*Takes her hand and pulls her to the door.*)

JULIE (*as she goes*). Speak kindly to me, Jean.

JEAN. Orders always sound unkind. Now you know. Now you know.

(*Left alone,* JEAN *sighs with relief, sits down at the table, takes out a notebook and pencil and adds up figures, now and then aloud. Dawn begins to break.* KRISTIN *enters dressed for church, carrying his white dickey and tie.*)

KRISTIN. Lord Jesus, look at the state the place is in! What have you been up to? (*Turns out the lamp.*)

JEAN. Oh, Miss Julie invited the crowd in. Did you sleep through it? Didn't you hear anything?

KRISTIN. I slept like a log.

JEAN. And dressed for church already.

KRISTIN. Yes, you promised to come to Communion with me today.

JEAN. Why, so I did. And you've got my bib and tucker, I see. Come on then. (*Sits.* KRISTIN *begins to put his things on. Pause. Sleepily.*) What's the lesson today?

KRISTIN. It's about the beheading of John the Baptist, I think.

JEAN. That's sure to be horribly long. Hi, you're choking me! Oh Lord, I'm so sleepy, so sleepy!

KRISTIN. Yes, what have you been doing up all night? You look absolutely green.

JEAN. Just sitting here talking with Miss Julie.

KRISTIN. She doesn't know what's proper, that one. (*Pause.*)

JEAN. I say, Kristin.

KRISTIN. What?

JEAN. It's queer really, isn't it, when you come to think of it? Her.

KRISTIN. What's queer?

JEAN. The whole thing. (*Pause.*)

KRISTIN (*looking at the half-filled glasses on the table*). Have you been drinking together too?

JEAN. Yes.

KRISTIN. More shame you. Look me straight in the face.

JEAN. Yes.

KRISTIN. Is it possible? Is it possible?

JEAN (*after a moment*). Yes, it is.

KRISTIN. Oh! This I would never have believed. How low!

JEAN. You're not jealous of her, surely?

KRISTIN. No, I'm not. If it had been Clara or Sophie I'd have scratched your eyes out. But not of her. I don't know why; that's how it is, though, But it's disgusting.

JEAN. You're angry with her, then.

KRISTIN. No. With you. It was wicked of you, very very wicked. Poor girl. And, mark my words, I won't stay here any longer now— in a place where one can't respect one's employers.

JEAN. Why should one respect them?

KRISTIN. You should know since you're so smart. But you don't want to stay in the service of people who aren't respectable, do you? I wouldn't demean myself.

JEAN. But it's rather a comfort to find out they're no better than us.

KRISTIN. I don't think so. If they're no better there's nothing for us to live up to. Oh and think of the Count! Think of him. He's been through so much already. No, I won't stay in the place any longer. A fellow like you too! If it had been that attorney, now, or somebody of her own class . . .

JEAN. Why, what's wrong with . . .

KRISTIN. Oh, you're all right in your own way, but when all's said and done there is a difference between one class and another. No, this is something I'll never be able to stomach. That our young lady who was so proud and so down on men you'd never believe she'd let one come near her should go and give herself to one like you. She who wanted to have poor Diana shot for running after the lodge-keeper's pug. No, I must say . . . ! Well, I won't stay here any longer. On the twenty-fourth of October I quit.

JEAN. And then?

KRISTIN. Well, since you mention it, it's about time you began to look around, if we're ever going to get married.

JEAN. But what am I to look for? I shan't get a place like this when I'm married.

KRISTIN. I know you won't. But you might get a job as porter or caretaker in some public institution. Government rations are small but sure, and there's a pension for the widow and children.

JEAN. That's all very fine, but it's not in my line to start thinking at once about dying for my wife and children. I must say I had rather bigger ideas.

KRISTIN. You and your ideas! You've got obligations too, and you'd better start thinking about them.

JEAN. Don't *you* start pestering me about obligations. I've had enough of that. (*Listens to a sound upstairs.*) Anyway, we've plenty of time to work things out. Go and get ready, now, and we'll be off to church.

KRISTIN. Who's that walking about upstairs?

JEAN. Don't know—unless it's Clara.

KRISTIN (*going*). You don't think the Count could have come back without our hearing him?

JEAN (*scared*). The Count? No, he can't have. He'd have rung for me.

KRISTIN. God help us! I've never known such goings on.
(*Exit.*)

(*The sun has now risen and is shining on the treetops. The light gradually changes until it slants in through the windows.* JEAN *goes to the door and beckons.* JULIE *enters in travelling clothes, carrying a small bird-cage covered with a cloth which she puts on a chair.*)

JULIE. I'm ready.

JEAN. Hush! Kristin's up.

JULIE (*in a very nervous state*). Does she suspect anything?

JEAN. Not a thing. But, my God, what a sight you are!

JULIE. Sight? What do you mean?

JEAN. You're white as a corpse and—pardon me—your face is dirty.

JULIE. Let me wash, then. (*Goes to the sink and washes her face and hands.*) There. Give me a towel. Oh! The sun is rising!

JEAN. And that breaks the spell.

JULIE. Yes. The spell of Midsummer Eve . . . But listen, Jean. Come with me. I've got the money.

JEAN (*skeptically*). Enough?

JULIE. Enough to start with. Come with me. I can't travel alone today. It's Midsummer Day, remember. I'd be packed into a suffocating train among crowds of people who'd all stare at me. And it would stop at every station while I yearned for wings. No, I can't do that, I simply can't. There will be memories too; memories of Midsummer Days when I was little. The leafy church—birch and lilac—the gaily spread dinner table, relatives, friends—evening in the park

—dancing and music and flowers and fun. Oh, however far you run away—there'll always be memories in the baggage car—and remorse and guilt.

JEAN. I will come with you, but quickly now then, before it's too late. At once.

JULIE. Put on your things. (*Picks up the cage.*)

JEAN. No luggage, mind. That would give us away.

JULIE. No, only what we can take with us in the carriage.

JEAN (*fetching his hat*). What on earth have you got there? What is it?

JULIE. Only my greenfinch. I don't want to leave it behind.

JEAN. Well, I'll be damned! We're to take a bird-cage along, are we? You're crazy. Put that cage down.

JULIE. It's the only thing I'm taking from my home. The only living creature who cares for me since Diana went off like that. Don't be cruel. Let me take it.

JEAN. Put that cage down, I tell you—and don't talk so loud. Kristin will hear.

JULIE. No, I won't leave it in strange hands. I'd rather you killed it.

JEAN. Give the little beast here, then, and I'll wring its neck.

JULIE. But don't hurt it, don't . . . no, I can't.

JEAN. Give it here. I *can.*

JULIE (*taking the bird out of the cage and kissing it*). Dear little Serena, must you die and leave your mistress?

JEAN. Please don't make a scene. It's *your* life and future we're worrying about. Come on, quick now!

(*He snatches the bird from her, puts it on a board and picks up a chopper.* JULIE *turns away.*)

You should have learnt how to kill chickens instead of target-shooting. Then you wouldn't faint at a drop of blood.

JULIE (*screaming*). Kill me too! Kill me! You who can butcher an innocent creature without a quiver. Oh, how I hate you, how I loathe you! There is blood between us now. I curse the hour I first saw you. I curse the hour I was conceived in my mother's womb.

JEAN. What's the use of cursing? Let's go.

JULIE (*going to the chopping-block as if drawn against her will*). No, I won't go yet. I can't . . . I must look. Listen! There's a carriage. (*Listens without taking her eyes off the board and chopper.*)

You don't think I can bear the sight of blood. You think I'm so weak. Oh, how I should like to see your blood and your brains on a chopping-block! I'd like to see the whole of your sex swimming like that in a sea of blood. I think I could drink out of your skull, bathe my feet in your broken breast and eat your heart roasted whole. You think I'm weak. You think I love you, that my womb yearned for your seed and I want to carry your offspring under my heart and nourish it with my blood. You think I want to bear your child and take your name. By the way, what is your name? I've never heard your surname. I don't suppose you've got one. I should be "Mrs. Hovel" or "Madam Dunghill." You dog wearing my collar, you lackey with my crest on your buttons! I share you with my cook; I'm my own servant's rival! Oh! Oh! Oh! . . . You think I'm a coward and will run away. No, now I'm going to stay—and let the storm break. My father will come back . . . find his desk broken open . . . his money gone. Then he'll ring that bell—twice for the valet—and then he'll send for the police . . . and I shall tell everything. Everything. Oh how wonderful to make an end of it all— a real end! He has a stroke and dies and that's the end of all of us. Just peace and quietness . . . eternal rest. The coat of arms broken on the coffin and the Count's line extinct . . . But the valet's line goes on in an orphanage, wins laurels in the gutter and ends in jail.

JEAN. There speaks the noble blood! Bravo, Miss Julie. But now, don't let the cat out of the bag.

(KRISTIN *enters dressed for church, carrying a prayer-book.* JULIE *rushes to her and flings herself into her arms for protection.*)

JULIE. Help me, Kristin! Protect me from this man!

KRISTIN (*unmoved and cold*). What goings-on for a feast day morning! (*Sees the board.*) And what a filthy mess. What's it all about? Why are you screaming and carrying on so?

JULIE. Kristin, you're a woman and my friend. Beware of that scoundrel!

JEAN (*embarrassed*). While you ladies are talking things over, I'll go and shave. (*Slips into his room.*)

JULIE. You must understand. You must listen to me.

KRISTIN. I certainly don't understand such loose ways. Where are you off to in those travelling clothes? And he had his hat on, didn't he, eh?

JULIE. Listen, Kristin. Listen, I'll tell you everything.

KRISTIN. I don't want to know anything.

JULIE. You must listen.

KRISTIN. What to? Your nonsense with Jean? I don't care a rap about that; it's nothing to do with me. But if you're thinking of getting him to run off with you, we'll soon put a stop to that.

JULIE (*very nervously*). Please try to be calm, Kristin, and listen. I can't stay here, nor can Jean—so we must go abroad.

KRISTIN. Hm, hm!

JULIE (*brightening*). But you see, I've had an idea. Supposing we all three go—abroad—to Switzerland and start a hotel together . . . I've got some money, you see . . . and Jean and I could run the whole thing—and I thought you would take charge of the kitchen. Wouldn't that be splendid? Say yes, do. If you come with us everything will be fine. Oh do say yes! (*Puts her arms round* KRISTIN.)

KRISTIN (*coolly thinking*). Hm, hm.

JULIE (*presto tempo*). You've never travelled, Kristin. You should go abroad and see the world. You've no idea how nice it is travelling by train—new faces all the time and new countries. On our way through Hamburg we'll go to the zoo—you'll love that— and we'll go to the theatre and the opera too . . . and when we get to Munich there'll be the museums, dear, and pictures by Rubens and Raphael—the great painters, you know . . . You've heard of Munich, haven't you? Where King Ludwig lived—you know, the king who went mad. . . . We'll see his castles—some of his castles are still just like in fairy-tales . . . and from there it's not far to Switzerland—and the Alps. Think of the Alps, Kristin dear, covered with snow in the middle of summer . . . and there are oranges there and trees that are green the whole year round . . .

(JEAN *is seen in the door of his room, sharpening his razor on a strop which he holds with his teeth and his left hand. He listens to the talk with satisfaction and now and then nods approval.*

JULIE *continues, tempo prestissimo.*)

And then we'll get a hotel . . . and I'll sit at the desk, while Jean receives the guests and goes out marketing and writes letters . . . There's life for you! Trains whistling, buses driving up, bells ringing upstairs and downstairs . . . and I shall make out the bills—and I shall cook them too . . . you've no idea how nervous travellers are when it comes to paying their bills. And you—you'll sit like a queen in the kitchen . . . of course there won't be any standing at the stove for you. You'll always have to be nicely dressed and ready to be seen, and with your looks—no, I'm not flattering you—one fine day you'll catch yourself a husband . . . some rich Englishman, I shouldn't wonder—they're the ones who are easy (*slowing down*) to catch . . . and then we'll get rich and build ourselves a villa on Lake Como . . . of course it rains there a little now and then—but—(*dully*)—the sun must shine there too sometimes—even though it seems gloomy —and if not—then we can come home again—come back—(*pause*) —here or somewhere else . . .

KRISTIN. Look here, Miss Julie, do you believe all that yourself?

JULIE (*exhausted*). Do I believe it?

KRISTIN. Yes.

JULIE (*wearily*). I don't know. I don't believe anything any more. (*Sinks down on the bench; her head in her arms on the table.*) Nothing. Nothing at all.

KRISTIN. (*turning to* JEAN). So you meant to beat it, did you?

JEAN (*disconcerted, putting the razor on the table*). Beat it? What are you talking about? You've heard Miss Julie's plan, and though she's tired now with being up all night, it's a perfectly sound plan.

KRISTIN. Oh, is it? If you thought I'd work for that . . .

JEAN (*interrupting*). Kindly use decent language in front of your mistress. Do you hear?

KRISTIN. Mistress?

JEAN. Yes.

KRISTIN. Well, well, just listen to that!

JEAN. Yes, it would be a good thing if you did listen and talked less. Miss Julie is your mistress and what's made you lose your respect for her now ought to make you feel the same about yourself.

KRISTIN. I've always had enough self-respect——

JEAN. To despise other people.

KRISTIN. —not to go below my own station. Has the Count's cook ever gone with the groom or the swineherd? Tell me that.

JEAN. No, you were lucky enough to have a high-class chap for your beau.

KRISTIN. High-class all right—selling the oats out of the Count's stable.

JEAN. You're a fine one to talk—taking a commission on the groceries and bribes from the butcher.

KRISTIN. What the devil . . . ?

JEAN. And now you can't feel any respect for your employers. You, you!

KRISTIN. Are you coming to church with me? I should think you need a good sermon after your fine deeds.

JEAN. No, I'm not going to church today. You can go alone and confess your own sins.

KRISTIN. Yes, I'll do that and bring back enough forgiveness to cover yours too. The Saviour suffered and died on the cross for all our sins, and if we go to Him with faith and a penitent heart, He takes all our sins upon Himself.

JEAN. Even grocery thefts?

JULIE. Do you believe that, Kristin?

KRISTIN. That is my living faith, as sure as I stand here. The faith I learnt as a child and have kept ever since, Miss Julie. "But where sin abounded, grace did much more abound."

JULIE. Oh, if I had your faith! Oh, if . . .

KRISTIN. But you see you can't have it without God's special grace, and it's not given to all to have that.

JULIE. Who is it given to then?

KRISTIN. That's the great secret of the workings of grace, Miss Julie. God is no respecter of persons, and with Him the last shall be first . . .

JULIE. Then I suppose He does respect the last.

KRISTIN (*continuing*) . . . and it is easier for a camel to go through the eye of a needle than for a rich man to enter into the kingdom of God. That's how it is, Miss Julie. Now I'm going— alone, and on my way I shall tell the groom not to let any of the horses out, in case anyone should want to leave before the Count gets back. Goodbye.

(*Exit.*)

JEAN. What a devil! And all on account of a greenfinch.

JULIE (*wearily*). Never mind the greenfinch. Do you see any way out of this, any end to it?

JEAN (*pondering*). No.

JULIE. If you were in my place, what would you do?

JEAN. In your place? Wait a bit. If I was a woman—a lady of rank who had—fallen. I don't know. Yes, I do know now.

JULIE (*picking up the razor and making a gesture*). This?

JEAN. Yes. But *I* wouldn't do it, you know. There's a difference between us.

JULIE. Because you're a man and I'm a woman? What is the difference?

JEAN. The usual difference—between man and woman.

JULIE (*holding the razor*). I'd like to. But I can't. My father couldn't either, that time he wanted to.

JEAN. No, he didn't want to. He had to be revenged first.

JULIE. And now my mother is revenged again, through me.

JEAN. Didn't you ever love your father, Miss Julie?

JULIE. Deeply, but I must have hated him too—unconsciously. And he let me be brought up to despise my own sex, to be half woman, half man. Whose fault is what's happened? My father's, my mother's or my own? My own? I haven't anything that's my own. I haven't one single thought that I didn't get from my father, one emotion that didn't come from my mother, and as for this last idea—about all people being equal—I got that from him, my fiancé—that's why I call him a cad. How can it be my fault? Push the responsibility on to Jesus, like Kristin does? No, I'm too proud and—thanks to my father's teaching—too intelligent. As for all that about a rich person not being able to get into heaven, it's just a lie, but Kristin, who has money in the savings-bank, will certainly not get in. Whose fault is it? What does it matter whose fault it is? In any case I must take the blame and bear the consequences.

JEAN. Yes, but . . . (*There are two sharp rings on the bell.* JULIE *jumps to her feet.* JEAN *changes into his livery.*) The Count is back. Supposing Kristin . . . (*Goes to the speaking-tube, presses it and listens.*)

JULIE. Has he been to his desk yet?

JEAN. This is Jean, sir. (*Listens.*) Yes, sir. (*Listens.*) Yes, sir, very good, sir. (*Listens.*) At once, sir? (*Listens.*) Very good, sir. In half an hour.

JULIE (*in panic*). What did he say? My God, what did he say?

JEAN. He ordered his boots and his coffee in half an hour.

JULIE. Then there's half an hour . . . Oh, I'm so tired! I can't do anything. Can't be sorry, can't run away, can't stay, can't live—can't die. Help me. Order me, and I'll obey like a dog. Do me this last service—save my honour, save his name. You know what I ought to do, but haven't the strength to do. Use your strength and order me to do it.

JEAN. I don't know why—I can't now—I don't understand . . . It's just as if this coat made me—I can't give you orders—and now that the Count has spoken to me—I can't quite explain, but . . . well, that devil of a lackey is bending my back again. I believe if the Count came down now and ordered me to cut my throat, I'd do it on the spot.

JULIE. Then pretend you're him and I'm you. You did some fine acting before, when you knelt to me and played the aristocrat. Or . . . Have you ever seen a hypnotist at the theatre? (*He nods.*) He says to the person "Take the broom," and he takes it. He says "Sweep," and he sweeps . . .

JEAN. But the person has to be asleep.

JULIE (*as if in a trance*). I am asleep already . . . the whole room has turned to smoke—and you look like a stove—a stove like a man in black with a tall hat—your eyes are glowing like coals when the fire is low—and your face is a white patch like ashes. (*The sunlight has now reached the floor and lights up* JEAN.) How nice and warm it is! (*She holds out her hands as though warming them at a fire.*) And so light—and so peaceful.

JEAN (*putting the razor in her hand*). Here is the broom. Go now while it's light—out to the barn—and . . . (*Whispers in her ear.*)

JULIE (*waking*). Thank you. I am going now—to rest. But just tell me that even the first can receive the gift of grace.

JEAN. The first? No, I can't tell you that. But wait . . . Miss Julie, I've got it! You aren't one of the first any longer. You're one of the last.

JULIE. That's true. I'm one of the very last. I *am* the last. Oh! . . . But now I can't go. Tell me again to go.

JEAN. No, I can't now, either. I can't.

JULIE. And the first shall be last.

JEAN. Don't think, don't think. You're taking my strength away too and making me a coward. What's that? I thought I saw the bell move . . . To be so frightened of a bell! Yes, but it's not just a bell. There's somebody behind it—a hand moving it—and something else moving the hand—and if you stop your ears—if you stop your ears—yes, then it rings louder than ever. Rings and rings until you

answer—and then it's too late. Then the police come and . . . and
. . . (*The bell rings twice loudly.* JEAN *flinches, then straightens
himself up.*) It's horrible. But there's no other way to end it . . . Go!
   (JULIE *walks firmly out through the door.*)

CURTAIN

A CONTRIBUTION TO THE ORIGIN OF STRINDBERG'S MISS JULIE

August Strindberg, the Swedish dramatist who pioneered the presentation of psychopathology in literature, is indebted to J. L. Dubut de Laforest's French novel, *Mademoiselle Tantale,* as being either the source for or a direct influence on the drama *Miss Julie.* *
Strindberg is known to have studied French literature which used psychiatric research materials, and, since *Mademoiselle Tantale* was dedicated to Jean-Martin Charcot, the leading French psychiatrist, it is most likely that Strindberg had read the novel or else had founded *Miss Julie* on a true story which could have also served as the basis for *Mademoiselle Tantale.* In any event, the problem of sexual pathology which is central in *Miss Julie* is unmistakably related to the novel. Strindberg prefaced his play with an enumeration of the various motives which ultimately lead to the downfall of Miss Julie: inherited instincts; faulty upbringing by the male example (her father); the influence on her by her betrothed; the Midsummer Eve festivity; her physical state; animal parallels; the dance's excitement, dusk, aphrodisiac effect of flowers; and a chance meeting with an already excited man. Those motives are virtually identical, in both content and order, to the causes which developed Mademoiselle Tantale's fate. The sequence of events in *Mademoiselle Tantale* is as follows: the heroine, Miss Mary Folkestone, born an illegitimate child, is plagued by nervousness. Her own condition is exaggerated by the increasing illness of her father and his subsequent death. An orphan at eighteen, she toured Europe as an heiress to a fortune. At twenty-two she experienced an incompatability with her first lover that resulted in a neurotic condition characterized by nervous attacks and erotic dreams. She developed sexual cravings beyond her imagination, abused herself, suffered persecution mania, and eventually submitted herself to hydrotherapeutic treatment. After tempo-

---

* Abstracted from Emil Offenbruacher, "A Contribution to the Origin of Strindberg's *Miss Julie,*" *Psychoanalitical Review,* XXXI (1944), 81-87.

rary relief, she surprised her maid with a lover, dismissed the maid at a later date, and, a few days later, met the maid's lover by chance, desired and embraced him, and then became repulsed by her own desires. After trying lesbianism and also being persecuted by sodomitic desires, she, in the final scene, virtually suffocated herself with an aphrodisiac, was swarmed by insects while in a nymphomaniac state, and after receiving a final kiss from her lover, died. The parallels to *Miss Julie* are unquestionable. Another similarity between the two works exists in that both men acknowledged in their prefaces that the story was true, and Strindberg even went so far as to mention that someone had told it to him. Neither the truth of that statement nor the identity of the teller can be determined by textual evidence, but the common origin of both works is undeniable. Strindberg wrote that *Miss Julie* was a "theme from real life." *Mademoiselle Tantale* provides that theme. Dubut de Laforest thus deserves the distinction of being recognized as a pioneer in the literature of psychopathology, a trend which clearly stretches from Strindberg to D. H. Lawrence.

THE HISTORY OF *MISS JULIE*

A careful examination of the process used by Alf Sjoberg in adapting Strindberg's *Miss Julie* to the film industry can provide new insights into the motivation of Miss Julie, as well as into Strindberg's structural technique.* Although adaptations from stage to screen frequently leave much to be desired, Sjoberg has maintained the play's intellectual complexity and has even managed to clarify some critical problems. *Miss Julie* presented a filming problem in that film makers need multiple sets to make their medium most effective; Strindberg's play take place in the kitchen of Miss Julie's father's house. Most film adaptations of drama find it necessary to write in connective dialogue between scenes, but *Miss Julie* was an exception. As Strindberg stated in the preface: "I have tried

* Abstracted from Vernon Young, "The History of *Miss Julie*," *Hudson Review*, VII (Spring, 1955), 123-130.

to abolish the division into acts." Although Strindberg's dramatic
unity eliminated a typical problem in film adaptation, it created
others. By handling prehistory, background, personality insights, and
psychic atmosphere in the preface or in dialogue, Strindberg created
a drama which was too brief for filming. Sjoberg's technique was
to provide this information in numerous flashback episodes. For
example, in the primary plot of present time, Jean and Kristin
discuss Miss Julie's rejection by her suitor; the film then immediately
cuts back to that episode. Such a technique clearly demonstrates to
the audience how earlier events work toward the total climax of the
primary story. Strindberg explained Miss Julie's fate by citing many
factors: ". . . her mother's fundamental instincts; her father's mistaken upbringing of the girl; her own nature; . . . her preoccupation
with the animals; the excitation of the dance" etc. Sjoberg captures
these factors for us in such a manner that the climax of the play
becomes predictable. The screenplay brings us into an understanding
of Miss Julie's behavior as being the result of the internal war
between her own nature and her heritage. The play's subject, Miss
Julie's fall, shifts in the film to the history of Miss Julie. Sjoberg's
genius combines the dual time sequence in a limited space and thus
provides direct insight into Strindberg's structural technique.

FROM NATURALISM TO THE DREAM PLAY: A STUDY OF THE EVOLUTION OF STRINDBERG'S UNIQUE THEATRICAL FORM

Detailed analysis of Strindberg's *Miss Julie, There Are Crimes
and Crimes,* and *A Dream Play* reveals a distinct evolution of the
playwright's personal search for the proper theatrical form for his

own rather consistent world view.* Indeed, Strindberg's career
presents a perfect model of the history of modern drama: a rejection
of realism and a return to stylized theater. Moreover, his work
mirrors the kind of modern sensibility that has been the main
impetus of theatrical experiments in our century. Throughout
Strindberg's works there is a consistency of themes which recur with
a frightening and sometimes repelling repetition. Hence, together
they amount to his major theme. This insistence and reiteration is
an expression of the playwright's concept of repetition, recurrence,
and demonic design of the universe. Thus repetition was to become
one of his major theatrical devices—and when viewed in terms of
his total canon, it suggests that Strindberg's purpose was to plot the
path of self-search in his drama. This search is cast in tragic terms,
since the individual, in trying to assert his self, or will, is faced with
the fact that he lives in a world which at every moment thwarts his
purpose. Hence, the conflict is inevitable, since living in the world
implies the necessity of an involvement with the world. This modern
tragic view does not include the classical concepts of justice and
reconciliation. And this difficulty in combining older forms with
the new concepts in this genre may be seen as the impetus for his
further and continuing experimentation. *Miss Julie* is his complete
success in the Naturalistic mode, *There Are Crimes and Crimes* as
an evaluation to naturalistic symbolism, and, finally, *A Dream Play*
as his ultimate and most personally inventive form. In tapping the
universal experience of dreaming, he found a basis for connecting
the audience to his own subjective views. And by presenting his
plays in waking and sleeping dream terms, he achieves the correspondence between the artist's experience and the audience's experience necessary for artistic communication.

* Abstracted from Alice N. Benston, "From Naturalism to the Dream
Play: A Study of the Evolution of Strindberg's Unique Theatrical Form,"
Modern Drama, VII (1964-65), 382-404.

THE MANY HELLS
OF AUGUST STRINDBERG

Hell was a recurring theme in the works of August Strindberg because he regarded hell as a fitting metaphor for his own troubled life.* Not only did he describe his personal sufferings in terms of damnation, as in his autobiographical *Inferno,* but he also objectified his experiences into a series of theatrical images of hell. Since his concepts of hell, like most of his attitudes, changed radically at different stages of his life, as we look at his plays we find not one but many hells. *Crime and Crime* offers a Swedenborgian hell. Written shortly after the ordeals described in *Inferno,* this play explores the Swedenborgian theory of expiation which had sustained Strindberg through his crisis. According to Swedenborg, every evil deed carries in its commitment a corresponding punishment. Hell is therefore simply the state of mind wherein the crime and punishment coexist simultaneously. The protagonist of the play, Maurice, wishes the death of his child. When news comes of the child's sudden demise, he feels guilty, and undergoes a brief period of intense suffering. When his internal punishment is equivalent to his external crime, his expiation is complete and he is able to leave his private mental hell and return to normal life. *Dance of Death* presents an existential hell through an image of an eternal triangle, in a situation closely resembling Sartre's *No Exit.* In this existential view, the individual finds himself in hell when he discovers that the presence of Other People threatens to reduce his own identity to that of an Object. In this play, the Captain and his wife Alice are isolated with an old friend Kurt on an island called Little Hell. They torture one another psychologically until the Captain is rendered speechless and immobile, a mere Object; his wife cries out "This is hell;" and Kurt, a former lover of Alice, is trapped in the marital misery which now unites the three victims in mutual bondage. *The Great Highway* portrays a Biblical hell called Tophet, after an allusion in Isiah to

---

* Abstracted from Charlotte K. Spivack, "The Many Hells of August Strindberg," *Twentieth Century Literature,* IX (1963), 10-16.

the abode of the damned. Subtitled "A Wayfaring Drama with Seven Stations," the play is a pageant of seven scenes, based on the stations of the cross. The Protagonist, called simply The Hunter, is introduced at the symbolic crossroads, whence he must descend to hell before he begins the ascent to heaven. Tophet is satirically envisioned as an arcade of showy but fraudulent shops. The Hunter visits this Vanity Fair, exposing its evil and folly, and rejects the Tempter's offer of a high salary in Tophet in favor of continuing his search for the Country of Desires. These are but three of Strindberg's dramatic images of damnation. Many others appear in the remainder of his numerous plays.

the
cherry Orchard

ANTON CHEKOV

TRANSLATED BY
TYRONE GUTHRIE
and LEONID KIPNIS

CHARACTERS

MADAME RANEVSKAYA, Lyubov Andreyevna, *the owner of the cherry orchard*

ANYA, *her daughter, aged about eighteen*

VARYA, *her adopted daughter, somewhat older*

GAEV, Leonid Andreyevich, MADAME RANEVSKAYA's *brother*

LOPAHIN, Yermolai Alexeyevich, *a merchant*

TROFIMOV, Pyotr Sergeyevich, *a student*

SIMEONOFF-PISHCHIK, *owner of a neighboring estate*

CHARLOTTA IVANOVNA, *a governess*

YEPIHODOV, *a clerk on* MADAME RANEVSKAYA's *estate*

DUNYASHA, *a maid*

FIRS, *a servant, age eighty-seven*

YASHA, *a young servant*

A PASSER-BY

STATION MASTER

A POST OFFICE EMPLOYEE

GUESTS *and* SERVANTS

The action of the play takes place in Russia at the beginning of this century on MADAME RANEVSKAYA's estate.

act one

A room which is still called the nursery. One of the doors leads into ANYA's room. It is dawn: the sun will be up soon. It is May, the cherry trees are in flower, but it is cold in the garden, with early morning frost. All windows are closed.

From Minnesota Drama Editions, Stephen Porter, Ed., *The Cherry Orchard by Anton Chekhov*, translated by Tyron Guthrie and Leonid Kipnis. University of Minnesota Press, Mpls. © Copyright 1965 University of Minnesota. "The Cherry Orchard" © copyright 1965 by Tyrone Guthrie and Leonid Kipnis. *Remarks*: All inquiries concerning performing rights (professional, amateur, stock), should be addressed to the translators.

(*Enter* DUNYASHA *with a candle and* LOPAHIN *with a book.*)

LOPAHIN. The train's in, thank God. What time is it?

DUNYASHA. Almost four o'clock. (*Blows out candle.*) It's light already.

LOPAHIN. I wonder how late the train is. Two hours, anyway. (*Yawns and stretches.*) I'm a great one! I've made a fool of myself! I came here specially to meet them at the station and fell asleep, if you please, in my chair. Idiotic . . . you might have wakened me up.

DUNYASHA. I thought you'd gone away. Listen! They're coming!

LOPAHIN (*listens*). No . . . there's the luggage and that to see to . . . (*Pause.*) Lyubov Andreyevna's been abroad for five years. What will she be like now? She's a fine person—an easy, simple person! I remember when I was a boy about fifteen, my father, God rest him, he kept a store in the village then, cracked me in the face with his fist, made my nose bleed . . . We'd come here, the pair of us, for some reason or other. He'd had a few drinks. Lyubov Andreyevna, I remember it as if it was yesterday, she was just a girl, skinny, she brought me to the washstand in this very room, the nursery. "Don't cry, little boy," she said. "You'll be yourself again by your wedding day." (*Pause.*) "Little boy." It's true, my father just lived in the village and look at me now, white waistcoat, brown shoes—talk about a pig in clover . . . I'm rich, now, lots of money, but when you come to think of it, when you get right down to things, I'm just my father's son. (*Fluttering the pages of the book.*) Here I've been reading this and didn't take in a thing. I read it and fell asleep. (*Pause.*)

DUNYASHA. The dogs have been awake all night. They can feel their people are coming home.

LOPAHIN. What is it, Dunyasha? You are so . . .

DUNYASHA. I'm trembling. I believe I'm going to faint.

LOPAHIN. You act so refined, Dunyasha. Got up like a young lady too. And look at your hair. It's all wrong, you know. You're forgetting who you are.

(YEPIHODOV *comes in with a bunch of flowers; he is in his Sunday best, with shiny boots which squeak loudly. As he comes in he drops the flowers.*)

YEPIHODOV (*picking up the flowers*). The gardener sent these in. Put them in the dining room, he says. Here (*Gives the flowers to* DUNYASHA.)

LOPAHIN (*to* DUNYASHA). And bring me some kvass.

DUNYASHA. Very well. (DUNYASHA *goes.*)

YEPIHODOV. A frost this morning—three degrees, and the cherries all in flower. I can't say I approve of our climate (*sighs*). I really can't. Our climate is really rather unhelpful, if one is to be strictly accurate! And look, Yermolai Alexeyevich, if you'll please excuse my saying so: I bought myself a pair of boots the day before yesterday and I venture to assure you that they squeak in a totally impossible manner. What should I grease them with?

LOPAHIN. That's enough. That'll do.

YEPIHODOV. Each and every day something unlucky happens to me. But I don't complain. I am accustomed to it. I even smile at it.

(DUNYASHA *comes in and gives the kvass to* LOPAHIN.)

YEPIHODOV. Well, I'll be off. (*Bumps against a chair which falls.*) There! (*Triumphantly.*) What did I tell you? Misfortunes never come singly. (YEPIHODOV *goes.*)

DUNYASHA. Yermolai Alexeyevich, I want to tell you something: Yepihodov has proposed to me.

LOPAHIN. Mm?

DUNYASHA. I really don't know . . . He's all right. But sometimes he starts talking and you don't really understand a thing. It's beautiful, of course, and full of feeling—only you can't understand a thing. I sort of like him. He's wild for me. He's an unlucky fellow. Each and every day some misfortune happens to him. Everyone here calls him "Never come singly."

LOPAHIN (*listening*). Listen! There they are!

DUNYASHA. They're here! What's the matter with me? I'm trembling!

LOPAHIN. They're really here! Let's go and meet them. Will she recognize me—it's been five years.

DUNYASHA (*agitated*). I shall faint. I know I shall.

(*Carriages are heard approaching.* LOPAHIN *and* DUNYASHA *go out hurriedly. The stage is empty. Then the neighboring rooms begin to be alive, noisy.* FIRS, *leaning on a cane, hurriedly crosses the stage. He's been to meet* MADAME RANEVSKAYA *and still wears his old livery and top hat. He speaks to himself but one can't understand a word. The noise backstage is intensified. A voice: "Let's come in here . . ."* MADAME RANEVSKAYA, ANYA, *and* CHARLOTTA IVANOVNA, *with a dog on a chain, come in. All are dressed for travel.* VARYA *is in an overcoat and shawl.* GAEV, SIMEONOFF-PISHCHIK, LOPAHIN, DUNYASHA *with a bundle and parasol, servants with pieces of luggage—all go through.*)

ANYA. Let's come through here. You remember this room, mamma?

RANEVSKAYA (*through happy tears*). The nursery!

VARYA. Oh it's cold! My hands are numb. (*To* RANEVSKAYA.) Your rooms are just as they were, darling mamma, the white one and the lilac.

RANEVSKAYA. The nursery, my own dear nursery—what a sweet old room it is! . . . I used to sleep here when I was little . . . and now it's as if I were little again . . . (*Kisses* GAEV, VARYA, *then her brother again.*) And Varya is just the same as ever—like a nun. And of course I knew Dunyasha too. (*Kisses* DUNYASHA.)

GAEV. The train was two hours late. What about that? What kind of organization is that?

CHARLOTTA (*to* PISHCHIK). My dog eats nuts.

PISHCHIK (*astonished*). Just fancy that!

(*Everybody goes out except* ANYA *and* DUNYASHA.)

DUNYASHA. We've been waiting and waiting . . . (*Takes off* ANYA'S *coat and hat.*)

ANYA. What a journey! I haven't slept for four nights. Now I'm perishing.

DUNYASHA. You went away in Lent—there was snow then and frost, and now . . . Oh my dearest (*laughs, kisses her*). I've been waiting and waiting for you, my love, my angel . . . now I'll tell you at once. I can't wait another minute . . .

ANYA (*without enthusiasm*). Not again . . .

DUNYASHA. After Holy Week Yepihodov proposed to me.

ANYA. It's always the same with you . . . (*Tidying her hair.*) I've lost all my hairpins. (*She is very tired; she sways on her feet.*)

DUNYASHA. I don't know what to think, really I don't. He loves me—oh so very much.

ANYA (*looks at the door of her room*). My room. My windows. It's as if I'd never been away. I'm home. Tomorrow morning I'll get up and run out into the garden. Oh if I could only sleep! I didn't sleep on the journey at all. I was so worried.

DUNYASHA. Do you know who turned up the day before yesterday? Trofimov.

ANYA (*joyfully*). Petya!

DUNYASHA. He's sleeping in the bathhouse. Living there actually. I don't want to be a nuisance, he says. (*Looking at her watch.*) I ought to wake him up but your sister Varya told me not to. Don't wake him up, she said.

(VARYA *comes in, a bunch of keys at her waist.*)

VARYA. Dunyasha. Coffee. Quick . . . darling mamma wants her coffee.

DUNYASHA. This very minute. (DUNYASHA *goes.*)

VARYA. Thank God you're all here! You're home again (*lovingly*). My little darling has come home! My lovely little angel has come home.

ANYA. It's been awful.

VARYA. I can imagine!

ANYA. I left in Lent. It was cold then. Charlotta never stopped talking, doing her tricks. Why did you have to hang Charlotta round my neck?

VARYA. But, darling, you could not travel all alone. At seventeen!

ANYA. We got to Paris; it was cold there and snowy. My French is horrible. There was mamma way up on the fifth floor. When I got there the room was full of the oddest people, Frenchmen and ladies, an old priest with a book. They were all smoking. It was all so . . . Suddenly I felt terribly sorry for mamma. I felt so sorry for her, I hugged her and couldn't let her go. And mamma was at her nicest and sweetest. She cried.

VARYA (*weeping*). Don't tell me. Don't tell me.

ANYA. She had already sold the villa on the Rivera. She hadn't anything left. And I hadn't anything left either—not a thing. We only just managed to get there. And mamma doesn't realize! When we dine in a station restaurant she insists upon the most expensive things and leaves far too large a tip. Charlotta's just the same. Yasha insists upon having the same things as we do. It's simply awful. You know Yasha's mamma's footman now. We've brought him back with us.

VARYA. Yes. I've seen him—nasty thing.

ANYA. Well now, tell me: has the interest been paid?

VARYA. How could it?

ANYA. Oh dear! Oh dear!

VARYA. In August they're going to sell the estate.

ANYA. Oh dear!

LOPAHIN (*looking in at the door*). Baa!! (*He goes.*)

VARYA (*through tears*). That's what I'd like to do to him! (*Shakes her fist.*)

ANYA (*embracing* VARYA). Varya, has he asked you to marry him? (VARYA *shakes her head.*)

ANYA. But he loves you . . . Why don't you talk it over like two sensible people? What are you waiting for?

VARYA. Do you know what I think? Nothing's going to come of it. He's so busy. He has no time for me. He doesn't even notice me. I can't bear even to see him, God help him . . . Everyone's talking about our marriage, everyone offers congratulations, but really and truly there's nothing in it. It's all like a dream . . . You've got a little brooch like a bee.

ANYA (*sadly*). Mamma bought it. (*Goes toward her room speaking gaily, almost like a child.*) And in Paris I went up in a balloon!

VARYA. My little darling has come home. My lovely little angel has come home.

(DUNYASHA *comes in with the coffee tray.*)

VARYA (*near Anya's door*). All the time that I'm busy about the house, I keep on dreaming. If we could only marry you off to a rich man! What a weight it would take off my mind! Then I should set off as a pilgrim, first to Kiev . . . to Moscow. I should wander on from one holy place to another. On and on, it would be heavenly.

ANYA. The birds are singing in the garden. What time is it?

VARYA. It must be nearly five. Time you went to sleep, darling . . . (*They go toward Anya's room*) Heavenly!

(YASHA *comes in with a traveling rug and bag.*)

YASHA (*tiptoeing across the room*). May one go through here?

DUNYASHA. Yasha! I shouldn't have known you. How you've changed abroad!

YASHA. Hm! And who may you be?

DUNYASHA. When you went away I was only so high! I'm Dunyasha, Fyodor Koroyedov's daughter. You don't remember!

YASHA. Hm! . . . A nice little piece.

(YASHA *looks around and puts his arm around her: she screams, breaks a saucer.* YASHA *goes out quickly.*)

VARYA (*at door of Anya's room, vexed*). What is it?

DUNYASHA (*nearly in tears*). I broke a saucer . . .

VARYA. Oh well, that's good luck.

ANYA (*coming out of her room*). We should warn mamma that Petya's here.

VARYA. I told them he wasn't to be wakened.

ANYA (*thoughtfully*). Six years since father died. A month later my brother Grisha was drowned in the river. Such a sweet little boy, he was only seven. Mamma simply couldn't bear it. She went away, she went right away (*shuddering*). If she only knew how well I understand her. (*Pause.*) And Petya Trofimov was Grisha's tutor. Seeing him would bring it all back to her . . .

(FIRS *comes in, in a jacket and white waistcoat.*)

FIRS (*at the coffee tray*). The mistress will have her coffee in here. (*Puts on white gloves.*) Is the coffee ready? (*To* DUNYASHA, *vexed.*) You! Where's the cream?

DUNYASHA. Oh my God . . . (*rushes out*).

FIRS. Ech! Silly young cuckoo! (*Mumbles to himself.*) They're home from Paris . . . The old master—he went to Paris once . . . It was horses then (*laughs*).

VARYA. What is it, Firs?

FIRS. At your service. (*Joyfully.*) The mistress is home! I've lived to see it . . . now I can die (*weeps for joy*).

MADAME RANEVSKAYA, GAEV, *and* SIMEONOFF-PISHCHIK *come in.* SIMEONOFF-PISHCHIK *is in a peasant coat made of a very fine cloth and wide trousers tucked into the top of his boots.* GAEV's *movements—both his arms and body—suggest a person playing billiards.*)

RANEVSKAYA. How does it go? Let's see . . . One ball in the corner! And two in the middle.

GAEV. Cutting into the corner. Time was, sister, when you and I slept in this very room, and now—strange to relate, I'm fifty-one years old . . .

LOPAHIN. Yes. Time flies.

GAEV. What?

LOPAHIN. Time flies, I said.

GAEV. There's a smell of cheap scent.

ANYA. I'm going to sleep. Good night, mamma (*kisses her mother*).

RANEVSKAYA. You dear little thing (*kisses her hands*). Are you happy to be home? I still can't believe it.

ANYA. Good night, uncle.

GAEV (*kisses her cheeks and hands*). God be with you, darling! You're the image of your mother! At her age, Lyuba, you were exactly like this child.

(ANYA *shakes hands with* LOPAHIN *and* PISHCHIK, *goes out, and and closes the door behind her.*)

RANEVSKAYA. She's tired out.

PISHCHIK. I suppose it's been a long way.

VARYA (*to* LOPAHIN *and* PISHCHIK). It's about five, gentlemen, time's up!

RANEVSKAYA (*laughing*). The same old Varya (*hugs her*). I'll just finish my coffee, then we'll go. (FIRS *sets a cushion under her feet.*) Thank you, my dear. I simply can't do without my coffee. I drink it day and night. Thank you, you dear old thing (*kisses* FIRS).

VARYA. I must go see whether they've brought in all your things. (*Goes out.*)

RANEVSKAYA. Am I really sitting here? (*Laughs.*) I could dance about and wave my arms. (*Hides her face in her hands.*) Perhaps I am dreaming. God knows I love my home, I love it, I love it. I couldn't look out of the train; I was crying too much. (*Through tears.*) But I must have my coffee just the same. Thank you, Firs. Thank you, you dear old thing. It's so good that you are still alive.

FIRS. The day before yesterday.

GAEV. Deaf as a post.

LOPAHIN. I've got to catch the train to Kharkov at six. Isn't it annoying? I wanted so much just to look at you and have a talk . . . You're as splendid as ever.

PISHCHIK (*breathing heavily*). Even more so. Paris fashions. I'm knocked absolutely flat.

LOPAHIN. Your brother here is always saying what a coarse, money-grubbing fellow I am. Well, I don't care. Let him say what he likes. All I want is that you should trust me as you used to, that you should look at me in that wonderful, moving way of yours. God have mercy! My father was a serf of your father and your grand-father before him, but you—and no one but you—once did so much for me that I forgot the whole of that and I love you as if you were one of my own . . . more than one of my own.

RANEVSKAYA. I can't sit here another second. I really can't . . . (*Jumps up and walks about in great emotion.*) I can't live through

such happiness . . . Laugh at me if you like, I know I'm silly . . .
My dear bookcase (*kisses bookcase*), my little table.

GAEV. Nurse died while you were away.

RANEVSKAYA (*sit down and drinks coffee*). Yes, the Kingdom
of Heaven be hers. You wrote me.

GAEV. Anataysi is dead too. Petrushka Kosoy has left me—he
works in town now, for the captain of police (*takes a box of sweets
out of his pocket and begins to suck one*).

PISHCHIK. My daughter Dashenka . . . sends her love.

LOPAHIN. I've got something very pleasant to tell you, something
nice. (*Looks at watch*) But I have to go now. No time to talk . . .
Oh well, in a couple of words . . . You know that your whole estate
including the cherry orchard is going to be sold to pay your debts.
The sale is fixed for the twenty-second of August. But don't worry
my dear, you needn't lose any sleep over it. There's a way out . . .
Here's my plan: now listen. Your estate isn't more than fifteen miles
from town and now the railroad runs quite near and if the cherry
orchard and the land by the river were divided up into small lots
and rented out for summer cottages, it would bring you in a very
substantial annual income.

GAEV. Excuse me, but that's absolute rubbish!

RANEVSKAYA. I don't think I quite understand you, Yermolai
Alexeyevich.

LOPAHIN. You should get at least twenty-five rubles an acre each
year from the summer residents. And if you let it be known at once,
I'll absolutely guarantee that you won't have a single empty lot,
they'll all be taken up. In short, congratulations, the day is saved.
It's a wonderful situation, a deep river. But of course it would have
to be cleared up . . . all the old buildings would have to come down,
naturally—this house too, which is no good for anything. The old
cherry orchard would have to be cut down . . .

RANEVSKAYA. Cut down? My dear man, you don't know what
you're talking about. If there's one thing in the whole province
which is interesting, yes even remarkable, it's our cherry orchard.

LOPAHIN. The only remarkable thing about your orchard is that
it's very large. The trees only bear cherries every other year and even
so nobody buys them.

GAEV. Our cherry orchard is even mentioned in the *Encyclopedia*.

LOPAHIN (*looking at his watch*). If we don't think of anything and don't come to any decision, then the cherry orchard and the whole estate will be put up for sale on the twenty-second of August. So make up your minds! There's no other way out, I assure you, no other way out at all.

FIRS. In the old days, forty—fifty years ago they used to dry the cherries, or soak them in brine, preserve them, make them into jam and sometimes . . .

GAEV. That'll do, Firs.

FIRS. And the dried cherries used to be sent by the wagon load to Moscow and Kharkov. There was money in those days! And the dried cherries were soft and juicy and sweet. They smelled delicious . . . In those days they knew the way to . . .

RANEVSKAYA. And why don't they know now?

FIRS. Forgotten. Nobody remembers anymore.

PISHCHIK (to RANEVSKAYA). What's it like in Paris? Did you eat frogs?

RANEVSKAYA. I ate crocodiles.

PISHCHIK. Fancy that! . . .

LOPAHIN. Up till now there's been nobody in the country but gentry and peasants; but now summer residents have arrived upon the scene. All the cities, even quite small ones, are surrounded now by summer cottages. And it is safe ot say that in twenty years these summer people will multiply incredibly. Right now they just drink tea on the porch but who knows when they won't start cultivating their little plots and then your cherry orchard will become a useful place, rich and glorious.

GAEV (shocked). What rubbish!

VARYA. Mamma darling, two cables for you. (Chooses a key and opens the old bookcase, which creaks.) Here they are.

RANEVSKAYA. From Paris (tears them up). I've finished with Paris.

GAEV. Do you know, Lyuba, how old this bookcase is? Last week I pulled out the bottom drawer and looked—the date has been burnt into it. The bookcase was made exactly a hundred years ago. Just think of that! There should have been a celebration for its centenary. It's only an inanimate object, but all the same it is a bookcase.

PISHCHIK (astonished). A hundred years . . . just fancy that!

GAEV. Yes . . . it's a good old thing . . . (Patting it.) My dear and most esteemed bookcase. Hail to thee who, for more than a hundred years hast kept us in mind of the high ideals of goodness and justice; in a hundred years thy silent call to fruitful work has never faltered, supporting (*through tears*) through all our generations the belief in a better future, inculcating in us the notion of virtue and of our duty as citizens.

(*Pause.*)

LOPAHIN. Yes . . .

RANEVSKAYA. Leonid, you haven't changed a bit.

GAEV (*embarrassed*). Into right corner! Cannon off the cushion!

LOPAHIN (*looking at watch*). Time's up. I must go.

YASHA (*giving her medicine to* RANEVSKAYA). Will you take your pills now?

PISHCHIK. You shouldn't take stuff like that, my dear . . . Does you no harm and no good . . . Give them to me, adorable lady! (*Takes the pills, tips them into the palm of his hand, blows on them, puts them all into his mouth, and swallows them with a mouthful of kvass*) You see!

RANEVSKAYA (*alarmed*). You are out of your mind!

PISHCHIK. I've taken all the pills.

LOPAHIN. Greedy guts.

(*All laugh.*)

FIRS. They were here one Easter and ate half a bucket of cucumbers . . . (*Mumbles*)

RANEVSKAYA. What's he talking about?

VARYA. He's been mumbling like that for three years. We've got used to it.

YASHA. It's a matter of age, actually.

(CHARLOTTA IVANOVNA *comes in, in a white dress, very thin, tightly corseted with a lorgnette at her belt. She passes across.*)

LOPAHIN. Forgive me, Charlotta Ivanovna, I didn't have a chance to ask how you were (*attempts to kiss her hand*).

CHARLOTTA (*pulling her hand away*). If I let you kiss my hand, next thing you'll want to kiss my elbow, then my shoulder.

LOPAHIN. This isn't my lucky day! (*All laugh.*) Charlotta Ivanovna, do one of your tricks!

RANEVSKAYA. Oh yes, Charlotta, do.

CHARLOTTA. I shan't. I want to go to sleep. (*Goes out*).

LOPAHIN. See you in three weeks (*kisses* RANEVSKAYA'S *hand*). Farewell for now. Time's up. (*To* GAEV.) Good-bye. (*Kisses* PISH-

CHIK.) Good-bye. (*Shakes hands with* VARYA, *then* FIRS *and* YASHA.) I wish I didn't have to go. (*To* RANEVSKAYA.) Now think it over, about the summer cottages, and if you decide to sell, let me know. I'll get you a loan of fifty thousand. Now mind and think it over carefully.

VARYA (*angrily*). Oh do go.

LOPAHIN. Going, going. (*He goes*)

GAEV. Scum! Oh excuse me . . . Varya is going to marry him. He's Varya's "intended."

VARYA. Now, uncle dear, don't talk like that.

RANEVSKAYA. Well but, Varya, I should be very glad. He's a decent creature.

PISHCHIK. If we're going to be strictly truthful, it's an extremely worthy creature . . . and my Dashenka . . . she says . . . lot of things (*snores but wakes up again at once*). But all the same, adorable lady, just lend me two hundred and forty rubles . . . the interest on my mortage is due tomorrow.

VARYA (*in a panic*). We don't have it! We don't have it!

RANEVSKAYA. As a matter of fact I simply haven't a thing.

PISHCHIK. It'll turn up (*laughs*). I never give up hope. For instance, I thought that I was utterly ruined, when lo and behold they put the railroad right across my land and . . . paid me for it. Something'll turn up, if not today, tomorrow . . . Dashenka will win two hundred thousand . . . she has a ticket in the lottery.

RANEVSKAYA. Well, we've finished our coffee; let's retire, friends.

FIRS (*brushing at* GAEV's *coat; as to a child*). You're in the wrong trousers again! What shall I do with you!

VARYA (*in a low tone*). Anya's asleep. (*Softly opens the window.*) The sun is up. It isn't cold anymore . . . Look, mamma darling. Isn't it beautiful? So fresh. The birds are singing.

GAEV (*opening another window*). The whole orchard is white. You haven't forgotten it, Lyuba? Look down there—between the trees—straight, straight as far as the eye can see. On moonlight nights it shines like a ribbon of silver. Do you remember? You haven't forgotten?

RANEVSKAYA (*looks out of the window*). Oh my childhood! My innocence! I used to sleep in this very room. I looked out from here over the orchard. Happiness woke with me each morning. And here it is. The same as ever. (*Laughs with joy.*) All, all white! Oh my orchard! After the dark, wild autumn and the cold winter you are young again, full of joy; God's heavenly angels haven't forsaken you ... Oh if I could only cast off the millstone which is weighing me down; if I could only forget my past ...

GAEV. Yes. And the orchard's going to be sold to pay our debts. Strange as that may seem!

RANEVSKAYA. Oh look! Mamma—walking in the orchard in a white dress. (*Laughs happily.*) There she is!

GAEV. Where?

VARYA. Oh no, no!

RANEVSKAYA. There's no one there! I was just imagining it. Over there, just beside the arbor, there's a white tree leaning over like a little bent woman ... (TROFIMOV *comes in, in an old student uniform and glasses.*) What a heavenly orchard. Masses of white flowers, blue sky ...

TROFIMOV. Lyubov Andreyevna (*she looks at him*) I've just looked in to see you. I'll go again at once. (*Fervently kisses her hand.*) They told me to wait till tomorrow. But I just couldn't ...

(RANEVSKAYA *looks at him at a loss.*)

VARYA (*moved*). It's Petya Trofimov.

TROFIMOV. Petya Trofimov. I used to be your Grisha's tutor. Do I look so different?

(RANEVSKAYA *embraces him and weeps.*)

GAEV (*embarrassed*). That'll do, Lyuba, that'll do.

VARYA (*crying*). I told you, Petya, you should have waited.

RANEVSKAYA. My Grisha ... my boy ... Grisha ... my son ...

VARYA. It was God's will, mamma darling. What can we do?

TROFIMOV (*gently*). Don't cry. Don't cry ...

RANEVSKAYA (*crying*). The boy is lost. Drowned. Why? Why? Will somebody please tell me why? (*More quietly.*) Anya's asleep there, and here I am making all this noise ... and you, Petya, you look so plain. Why do you look so old?

TROFIMOV. A woman on the train called me a seedy-looking gent.

RANEVSKAYA. You were just a boy then, a nice little student. And now look at you! Your hair's getting thin, and glasses! And is it true that you're still a student? (*She goes to the door.*)

TROFIMOV. It looks as if I should be a perennial student.

RANEVSKAYA (*kisses her brother, then* VARYA). Well, go to sleep ... and you're old too, Leonid.

PISHCHIK (*following her*). All right. So we have to go to sleep . . . oh, my gout! . . . I'll stay, if you'll keep me . . . and tomorrow morning, my dear Lyubov Andreyevna, I've just got to have that two hundred and forty.

GAEV. Always the same old story.

PISHCHIK. Two hundred and forty. It's the interest on my mortgage.

RANEVSKAYA. But, my dear man, I haven't any money.

PISHCHIK. I'll pay it back, my dear . . . it's such an insignificant amount.

RANEVSKAYA. Oh very well. Leonid will give it to you . . . Give it to him, Leonid.

GAEV (*ironically*). Of course.

RANEVSKAYA. What else can we do? Give it to him . . . he needs it. He'll pay it back.

(RANEVSKAYA, PISHCHIK, *and* TROFIMOV *go out.* VARYA, GAEV, *and* YASHA *remain.*)

GAEV. Sister still throws her money about. (*To* YASHA.) Get out of the way, my man, you smell of tobacco.

YASHA (*with a grin*). And you, Leonid Andreyevich, you're just the same as ever.

GAEV. What's that? (*To* VARYA.) What did he say?

VARYA (*to* YASHA). Your mother's come up from the village. She's been waiting in the servants' quarters since yesterday. She wants to see you.

YASHA (*grimacing*). Oh . . .

VARYA. You ought to be ashamed of yourself.

YASHA. Well, why should I care? She could have come tomorrow. (*Goes.*)

VARYA. Darling mamma is just the same as ever. She hasn't changed a bit. If she could, she'd give away everything she has.

GAEV. Yes . . . (*Pause.*) When all kinds of cures are suggested for a disease, it means that the disease is incurable. Here have I been racking my brains in every possible way, in every possible way, which means that I've thought of nothing. It would be a nice thing if someone left us a fortune; it would be nice to marry Anya off to a very rich man. It would be good if I went to Yaroslav and tried my luck with my aunt, the countess—she's as rich as ever she can be.

VARYA (*crying*). If only God would help us.

GAEV. Don't blubber! The aunt is very rich but she doesn't like us. In the first place my sister married a lawyer, not a nobleman (ANYA *is at the door of her room*); she didn't marry a nobleman and one couldn't say that her behavior was entirely virtuous; she's a kind good soul, I love her very much, but no matter what allowances one tries to make, one has to admit that there's something, well—sort of loose about her.

VARYA. Ssh! (*Whispering.*) Anya at the door.

GAEV. What? (*Pause.*) Odd thing! I've got something in my right eye. I can't see properly. And on Thursday when I was in the District Court . . .

(ANYA *comes in.*)

VARYA. Why aren't you asleep, Anya?

ANYA. I can't sleep.

GAEV. My baby (*kisses her face and hands*). My child—you're not my niece, you're my angel. You're everything in the world to me. Believe me, believe me.

ANYA. I believe you, uncle dear. Everybody loves you, respects you . . . but uncle dear, you must not talk so much. You simply must hold your tongue. What were you saying about my mother—your sister? Why did you say it?

GAEV. I know. I know. (*Covers his face with* ANYA's *hand.*) It's really horrible! Oh my God! My God! Help me! And today I made a speech to the bookcase . . . So silly . . . It was only when I'd finished that I realized how silly it was.

VARYA. It's true, uncle dear, you really must not talk so much. Just don't talk so much.

ANYA. If only you wouldn't talk so much it would be so much better for you.

GAEV. I'll hold my tongue (*kisses* VARYA's *and* ANYA's *hands*), I really will. But this is business. On Thursday I was in the District Court, a group of us started chatting about this and that, and it seems as if it might be possible to arrange a loan which would take care of the bank interest.

VARYA. If only God would help us!

GAEV. I'll go there on Tuesday and we'll speak about it again. (*To* VARYA.) Don't blubber. (*To* ANYA.) Your mother will speak to Lopahin; he certainly won't refuse her . . . and as for you—after you're rested—you'll go to Yaroslav to your great-aunt, the countess. And so we'll attack it from three sides at once and we can't miss the target. (*Puts a candy in his mouth.*) I swear by my happiness. Here's my hand. Call me a cheat, call me a rogue, if I let the sale go through! I swear it with all my heart and soul.

ANYA (*happy and relieved.*) Uncle, how good you are! And how clever! (*Embraces him.*) What a relief! What a wonderful relief!

(FIRS *comes in.*)

FIRS (*reproachfully*). Leonid Andreyevich, have you no fear of God! When are you going to bed?

GAEV. Coming, coming. You go, Firs. Tonight I'll undress myself! Night night, children . . . bed now . . . plans tomorrow (*kisses them*). I'm a man of the eighties . . . some people have no use for the eighties, but I'm here to say that in my time I've got into plenty of trouble for my beliefs. It isn't for nothing that your peasant loves me. One has to know one's peasant! One has to know how to . . .

ANYA. Uncle, you're off again.

VARYA. Uncle dear, hold your tongue.

FIRS (*angrily*). Leonid Andreyevich!

GAEV. Coming. Coming . . .

(*He goes, followed by* FIRS.)

ANYA. I feel so relieved. I feel better about it all. I don't want to go to Yaroslav. I don't like my great-aunt. But still I feel better about it all. Thanks to uncle. (*Sits down.*)

VARYA. Time to go to sleep. I'm going. Anya, while you were away something rather unpleasant happened. As you know there are only old people in what used to be the servants' quarters: Ye-fimka, Polya, Evstigney, oh, and Karp too. They began to let all sorts of odd people in for the night—I didn't say a word, I pretended not to notice. But then I hear a rumor that I've given orders to feed them nothing but dried peas—out of stinginess, if you please . . . Well it all comes from Evstigney. Very well, I think to myself. If that's the case, I think, just you wait. I send for Evstigney. "Evstigney," I said (*yawns*), "how can you be such an idiot . . . (*Looks at* ANYA.) Anitchka! (*Pause.*) She's asleep. (*Takes her by the arm.*) Let's go to bed. Come (*takes her*). My own darling has fallen asleep. Come. (*They go.*)

(*Far off in the garden a shepherd plays a reed pipe.* TROFIMOV *crosses the stage, sees* VARYA *and* ANYA *and stops.*)

VARYA. Tss! She's asleep . . . asleep. Come darling.

ANYA (*half asleep*). So tired . . . all those little bells . . . uncle . . . dear mamma and uncle . . .

VARYA. Come, my darling, come.

(*Goes with* ANYA *into Anya's room.*)

TROFIMOV (*emotionally*). My sunshine! My spring!

act two

Out in the fields. A chapel, old and tumbledown, long abandoned; an old bench. A road to GAEV's estate can be seen. To one side is a dark group of tall poplars: there the cherry orchard begins. In the distance is a row of telegraph poles. And far, far away, on the horizon, the vague outline of a large city, visible only in very good and clear weather. It is almost sunset. CHARLOTTA, YASHA, and DUNYASHA are sitting on the bench. YEPIHODOV is near them, playing his guitar. Everyone is lost in his own thoughts. CHARLOTTA wears an old uniform cap. She has taken a rifle off her shoulders and adjusts the buckle on the strap.

CHARLOTTA (*dreamily*). I don't have a proper passport. I don't know how old I am. I think of myself as quite a young person. When I was a little girl, my father and mother used to travel from fairground to fairground, giving performances, and very good ones too. I used to do a trapeze act, amongst other things. When papa and mamma died a German lady took me into her home and started to give me lessons. Well, there you are! I grew up and became a governess. But where I come from and who I am—I don't know . . . Who my parents were—they weren't even married for all I know. (*Takes a cucumber out of her pocket and gnaws it.*) . . . I don't know anything. (*Pause.*) I long to have someone to talk to. But there's nobody. I haven't anyone.

YEPIHODOV (*plays his guitar and sings*).
        What is the whole world to you, love?
        You are not for friends or for foes.
        We will fly on the wings of our true love,
        To the land where the passion fruit grows.
How nice it is to play the mandolin.

DUNYASHA. That's a guitar, not a mandolin. (*Looks in a pocket mirror and powders her face.*)

YEPIHODOV. For a lunatic who is in love, this is a mandolin (*sighs*).

> When I am alone with you, darling,
> I'm timid, I'm speechless, it's true;
> But surely in spite of my silence
> You can feel all my passion for you.

(YASHA *joins in the song.*)

CHARLOTTA. Shocking! The way these people sing! Ugh! Howling jackals!

DUNYASHA (*to* YASHA). All the same, how heavenly to have been abroad!

YASHA. Well, naturally. You're absolutely right. (*Yawns, lights cigar.*)

YEPIHODOV. It's understandable. Abroad everything's been going in great style for ages.

YASHA. Well, naturally.

YEPIHODOV. I'm a thinking man. I've read a great many *extraordinary* books. But somehow I can't understand where things are going. What do I want? Am I to go on living or, to put it in a nutshell, shall I shoot myself? Just the same I always carry a gun. Look! (*Shows pistol.*)

CHARLOTTA (*referring to cucumber*). Finished! I'll go now. (*Slings rifle over her shoulder.*) As for you, Yepihodov, you're a very clever man and a very frightening one; the women must be wild about you. Brr! (*Moving off.*) These clever people are all so silly. There's no one for me to speak to . . . I'm all alone. Alone . . . There isn't anyone . . . And who I am, or why I am, nobody knows. (*Goes out slowly.*)

YEPIHODOV. To speak absolutely precisely and come straight to the point, I am bound to say that among other things Fate treats me without mercy, as a storm tosses a little boat . . . Now, if, for the sake of argument, I am wrong, then why was it that this morning when I woke up, and just to give you an instance, there on my chest sits a spider of gigantic proportions. (*Shows with both hands.*) Big as this. Another thing; I take a drink of kvass and what should there be at the bottom of the glass, if you please, but something indecent in the highest degree—such as a cockroach. (*Pause.*) Have you read Buckle's *Natural History?* (*Pause, then to* DUNYASHA.) May I please trouble you to let me have a word?

DUNYASHA. Go ahead.

YEPIHODOV. I would like to speak to you alone (*sighs*).

DUNYASHA (*embarrassed*). Oh very well . . . but first of all would you bring my shawl. It's hanging behind the door . . . It's a bit chilly.

YEPIHODOV. Certainly. I'll get it. Now I know what to do with my gun.

(*Takes his guitar, and goes out playing it.*)

YASHA. "Never come singly"! Between you and me, he's a fool. (*Yawns.*)

DUNYASHA. Please God he doesn't shoot himself. (*Pause.*) I'm all on edge. I'm just a bundle of nerves. I've been with the gentry since I was a little girl and now I've got out of the old ways; look at my hands—white, even so white, like a young lady's. I'm frightened of just everything . . . Everything's so terrifying. And Yasha, if you don't do the right thing by me, then I don't know what will happen to my nerves.

YASHA (*kisses her*). Sugar! But let me tell you one thing! A person mustn't forget herself. If there's one thing I just hate it's a girl who misbehaves herself.

DUNYASHA. I'm madly in love with you—passionately. You're such an educated person. There's nothing you can't talk about.

(*Pause.*)

YASHA (*yawning*). Well, if you want to know what I think, if a girl lets herself fall in love with a person it means she's no better than she should be. (*Pause.*) It's nice, smoking a cigar out of doors . . . (*Listening.*) They're coming this way . . . (DUNYASHA *kisses him fervently.*) Go home. Pretend you were having a swim in the river. Go this way—if they meet you what will they think about me? They'll think I'd arranged to meet you. I couldn't stand that.

DUNYASHA (*coughing a little bit*). Your cigar is giving me a headache.

(DUNYASHA *goes,* YASHA *stays, sits by the chapel;* RANEVSKAYA, GAEV, *and* LOPAHIN *come in.*)

LOPAHIN. Listen: a decision must be made. Time waits for no man. It's as simple as this: will you or won't you let the land go for summer cottages? Answer in one word: yes or no—just one single word!

RANEVSKAYA. Someone's smoking—a horrid cheap cigar. (*Sits down.*)

GAEV. Since they built the railroad, everything's so easy. (*Sits down.*) We went into town and had our lunch . . . The yellow ball in the center! . . . I think I should like to go indoors and just have one game . . .

RANEVSKAYA. There's plenty of time.

LOPAHIN. Just a single word! (*Imploring.*) Give me an answer!

GAEV (*yawning*). What's that?

RANEVSKAYA (*looking in her purse*). Yesterday there was quite a bit of money and today there's hardly any. My poor Varya scrimps and scrapes and gives us nothing but soup and in the servants' quarters the old people get nothing but dried peas. And here am I spending money like water . . . (*Drops the purse, gold pieces roll about; with irritation.*) Oh look at that!

YASHA. Allow me. I'll pick them up in a second. (*Picks up the money.*)

RANEVSKAYA. Oh do, Yasha. And why did I have to go out to lunch? That restaurant of yours was ghastly; the music! The table-cloths all smelling of soap . . . Need one drink so much, Leonid? Need one eat so much? Need one talk so much? Today in the restaurant you were talking away again—and quite unsuitably—about the seventies, about the Decadents—and to whom? I mean, imagine talking to waiters about the Decadents!

LOPAHIN. Yes!

GAEV (*flapping his hands*). I'm incorrigible, that's quite clear . . . (*To* YASHA, *with irritation.*) You're always underfoot!

YASHA (*laughing*). I just can't help laughing at your voice.

GAEV (*to his sister*). Look . . . either he goes or I.

RANEVSKAYA. Run along. Yasha; get away with you.

YASHA (*returns her purse*). Right away. (*Trying not to laugh.*) This very minute. (*Goes.*)

LOPAHIN. Deriganov is planning to buy your estate. He's enormously rich. They say he'll come to the sale himself.

RANEVSKAYA. And where did you hear that?

LOPAHIN. They were talking about it in town.

GAEV. Our aunt from Yaroslav promised to send help. But when, and how much, who knows?

LOPAHIN. How much will she send? A hundred thousand? Two hundred?

RANEVSKAYA. Oh . . . We'd be very grateful for ten thousand or fifteen.

LOPAHIN. Excuse me, but in all my life I never met such feckless, unbusinesslike, extraordinary people as you! I tell you in words of one syllable that your estate is going to be sold and you don't seem to take it in.

RANEVSKAYA. But what are we to do? Tell us that?

LOPAHIN. I tell you every blessed day. I tell you the same thing over and over again. All the land, including the cherry orchard, must be let by the year for summer cottages. And this must be done now—as soon as possible. The sale is right on top of us! Do get this into your heads; once you've made up your minds that it should be summer cottages, you'll get all the money you want. You'll be saved.

RANEVSKAYA. Oh, summer cottages—and summer people—forgive me, it's so common.

GAEV. I agree with you entirely.

LOPAHIN. I shall either start to cry or I'll scream or I'll faint. This is the end! I can't take any more. (*To* GAEV) You're a silly old woman.

GAEV. What's that?

LOPAHIN. A silly old woman I said. (LOPAHIN *starts to go*)

RANEVSKAYA. No. No. Don't go away . . . Somehow with you here, it's more amusing . . . (*Pause.*) I feel all the time as if something dreadful were going to happen . . . As if the house were going to tumble about our ears.

GAEV (*deep in thoughts*). Double in the corner . . . Cannon off the cushion . . .

RANEVSKAYA. What sinners we've been!

LOPAHIN. What sort of sins have you committed?

GAEV (*with candy in his mouth*). They say that I've gobbled up all my fortune in sweets! (*Laughs.*)

RANEVSKAYA. Oh my sins . . . All my life I have spent money like wildfire, like a mad woman. I married a man who did nothing but get into debt. My husband dies—of champagne, he drank hideously —and then, for my undoing, I fell in love with another man. We came together, and at that very time—it was the first punishment— a blow right to the heart—in this very river . . . drowned . . . my little boy. I went abroad. I went away for good and all—never to return, never to see this river again . . . I shut my eyes and fled. Fled without a single thought. But he—followed me . . . a coarse man without mercy. I bought a villa on the Riviera because he had fallen ill there; and for three years neither day nor night did I know a single moment of peace. That sick man literally tore me apart. My soul shriveled up. A year ago I sold the villa to pay my debts and went to Paris; and there he absolutely fleeced me, and then went off with another woman. I tried to take poison . . . so stupid, so shameful . . . but then suddenly I felt myself drawn back to Russia, to my own country . . . to my girl. (*Wiping her eyes.*) Oh God, God be merciful, forgive me my sins! Don't punish me any more. (*Takes a cable out of her pocket.*) From Paris. I've done with Paris . . . He asks me to forgive him, implores me to come back. (*Tears up the cable.*) Music, somewhere (*listening*).

GAEV. That's our celebrated Jewish Orchestra. Surely you remember—four violins, flute, and double bass.

RANEVSKAYA. Still going? They must come out here and play. We'll give a little evening.

LOPAHIN (*listening*). I can't hear them. (*Hums softly, laughs.*) Last night at the theatre I saw the funniest play.

RANEVSKAYA. I don't suppose it was the least bit funny. You shouldn't look at plays. You should just take a good look at yourself. Your life is dull! Such a lot of talk about unimportant things.

LOPAHIN. It's true. Better admit it frankly. Life here is stupid . . . (*Pause.*) My old father was a peasant, a complete idiot. He didn't know anything about anything; he didn't teach me anything—all he did was to knock me about when he was drunk, and always with a stick. And as a matter of fact I'm just such another idiot and dunce. I never learnt anything, my handwriting is no better than a pig's: I am ashamed for people to see it.

RANEVSKAYA. You should get married, my friend . . .

LOPAHIN. Yes, that's true.

RANEVSKAYA. To our Varya. She's a good girl.

LOPAHIN. Yes.

RANEVSKAYA. She's a simple girl; works all day long. But the important thing is that she loves you and you've liked her for a long time.

LOPAHIN. Well, what about it? I'm not against it. She's a good girl. (*Pause.*)

GAEV. I've been offered a position in a bank. The salary isn't bad . . . Had you heard?

RANEVSKAYA. You just stay right where you are.

FIRS *comes in with* GAEV'S *overcoat.*)

FIRS (*to* GAEV). Please, sir—your overcoat. It's chilly.

GAEV (*putting on coat*). I'm sick of you, my dear fellow.

FIRS. What next? . . . You left in the morning without a word. (*Looks him over.*)

RANEVSKAYA. How old you've got, Firs!

FIRS. What's that?

LOPAHIN. They say you've got very old!

FIRS. I've been living a long time. They were trying to marry me off even before your father was born (*laughs*). By the time the serfs were set free I was head footman. I didn't take my freedom; I stayed with the family . . . (*Pause.*) I remember how glad the people all were. But why? They didn't know why.

LOPAHIN. In the old days everything was just great. There were great floggings anyway.

FIRS (*not hearing*). Yes, indeed. We belonged to them and they belonged to us. But now no one belongs to anyone. No one knows where they are.

GAEV. That'll do, Firs, thank you. I must go to town tomorrow. I was promised an introduction to a general who can arrange a loan for me.

LOPAHIN. Nothing will come of it . . . and, anyway, you wouldn't be able to pay the interest.

RANEVSKAYA. He's out of his mind. There are no generals.

(TROFIMOV, ANYA, *and* VARYA *come in.*)

GAEV. Here come the children.

ANYA. Here's mamma.

RANEVSKAYA (*tenderly*). Well, darlings (embraces ANYA *and* VARYA). If only you two knew how I love you! Sit here beside me. (*Everybody sits down.*)

LOPAHIN. Our perennial student always with the young ladies . . .

TROFIMOV. Not your business.

LOPAHIN. Almost fifty and still a student.

TROFIMOV. Don't try to be so funny.

LOPAHIN. Why are you cranky?

TROFIMOV. Oh, leave me alone.

LOPAHIN (*laughs*). Listen, let me ask you a question: what do you think of me?

TROFIMOV. Well, this is what I think of you: you're a rich man; you'll soon be a millionaire, and just as a ravenous wild beast, which devours all before it, is a necessary part of the natural process—so, my dear Yermolai Alexeyevich, are you.

(*All laugh.*)

VARYA. Petya, why don't you tell us something about the planets?

RANEVSKAYA. No; let's go on with what we were talking about yesterday.

TROFIMOV. What were we talking about?

GAEV. About human dignity.

TROFIMOV. We talked and talked yesterday, but we didn't get far. You said you thought that there was something mystical about human dignity. Well, maybe in your own way you are right. But if you look at it in a simple, straightforward way, what is the sense of human dignity? Suppose a person is a poor specimen of the human race, suppose, as happens more often than not, he is crude, stupid, deeply unhappy. He'd better not be too pleased with himself. What we have to do is work.

GAEV. All the same one has to die.

TROFIMOV. Who knows? And what does it mean—to die? It may very well be that a person has a hundred senses, and when he dies, only the five die which are known to us, and the other ninety-five are still alive.

RANEVSKAYA. What a clever boy you are, Petya!

LOPAHIN (*ironically*). Oh incredibly!

TROFIMOV. Humanity is marching onward from strength to strength. What is unattainable now, one day we shall be able to achieve, able to understand. But now what we have to do is work; to give all the help we possibly can to those who seek the truth.

But now, here in Russia, only a handful of people are working. The vast majority of the intelligentsia—anyway of the ones I know —aren't seeking for anything, aren't doing anything. They aren't yet fit to work. Intelligentsia they call themselves. But they condescend to servants, treat the peasants like animals; they have no desire to learn; they don't read anything serious; they don't do a thing. They just chatter about science; and as to art—well, they hardly understand one thing about it. Oh, they're all intensely serious; they all go about with long faces; they only discuss the weightiest topics—philosophy and that. But, meantime, right under their noses, the working people are wretchedly fed, sleep on bare boards, thirty or forty to a room, which is verminous, stinking, damp, and morally squalid as well. So it looks as if all the grand talk is just a sop to our consciences.

Tell me this: what about all the care of children, which we're always hearing about? What about public libraries? Oh, they exist in novels all right; but not in reality. In reality all we have is degradation, barbarity, and filth. I'm afraid I have no patience with serious faces; they frighten me; and so does serious talk. Better be silent.

LOPAHIN. Do you know, I'm up and about at five o'lcock in the morning each and every day. I work from dawn till dusk. And I always have money in my pocket—my own and other people's. It doesn't take you long to find out how few decent, honest people there are. Sometimes at night when I can't sleep, I think to myself: Dear God, I think, You have given us these immense forests, endless fields, limitless horizons and we who live in all this should be giants.

RANEVSKAYA. Oh, giants! They're all very fine in fairy tales. In real life they'd frighten one to death. (YEPIHODOV *passes in the background playing the guitar.*) There goes Yepihodov (*absently*).

ANYA (*absently*). There goes Yepihodov.

GAEV. Ladies and gentlemen, the sun has set.

TROFIMOV. Yes.

GAEV (*gently declaiming*). Oh Nature, divine Nature, thou shinest with perpetual radiance, beautiful, indifferent. We call thee Mother. In thee are united Life and Death; by thee are we brought to life and by thee destroyed.

VARYA (*pleading*). Uncle dear!

ANYA. Uncle dear!

TROFIMOV. You'd better cannon off the cushion.

GAEV. I'll hold my tongue. I'll hold my tongue.

(*Pause. Only the low mumbling of* FIRS. *Suddenly from far off is heard an unearthly sound—the sound of a broken string, dying, sad.*)

RANEVSKAYA. What's that?

LODAPHIN. I don't know. Somewhere, far off, a bucket has fallen in the mine. But far off.

GAEV. A bird of some sort? A heron?

TROFIMOV. Or an owl?

RANEVSKAYA (*shuddering*). It's unpleasant; I don't know why.
(*Pause.*)

FIRS. It was just the same before the disaster; the owl hooted and
the samovar hummed and no one knew why.

GAEV. Before what disaster?

FIRS. Before the serfs were set free.
(*Pause.*)

RANEVSKAYA. Let's go, friends. It's beginning to get dark. (*To*
ANYA.) There are tears in your eyes ... what's the matter, darling?
(*Embraces her*).

ANYA. It's nothing, mamma.

TROFIMOV. Somebody's coming.
(*A passer-by appears in an old, battered white military cap and
overcoat. He is somewhat drunk.*)

PASSER-BY. Would you be good enough to tell me: is the way to
the railroad station?

GAEV. Yes it is. Through there.

PASSER-BY. Most grateful thanks (*coughs*). What glorious
weather! (*Declaiming.*) Oh my brother, my suffering brother ... go
to the Volga, whose constant murmur ... (*To* VARYA.) Mademoiselle, would you spare a little something for a hungry Russian?
(*VARYA is frightened and cries out.*)

LOPAHIN (*angrily*). This is outrageous.

RANEVSKAYA. There! ... Take this ... (*looks in purse*) ...
no silver ... never mind ... take this.

PASSER-BY. My most grateful thanks. (*He goes.*)

VARYA. I give up ... I just give up. Mamma darling. There's
nothing for the servants to eat and you gave him a gold piece!

RANEVSKAYA. What is to be done with me? I'm so silly. When we
get back into the house I'll give you all I've got. Yermolai Alexeyevich, you'll make me another loan, won't you?

LOPAHIN. At your service.

RANEVSKAYA. Come on, children; time to go home. Varya, while
you weren't looking, we made a match for you. Congratulations!

VARYA (*through tears*). Don't make a joke of it, mamma.

LOPAHIN. Get thee to a nunnery, Amelia!

GAEV. My hands are itching. I haven't had a game for ages (*indicates billiards*).

LOPAHIN. Amelia, Nymph in thy something or other, be all my sins remembered.

RANEVSKAYA. Come on, children, let's go. Nearly time for supper.

VARYA. That man simply terrified me. My heart's still pounding.

LOPAHIN. Now don't forget . . . On August the twenty-second your cherry orchard goes up for sale. Think it over. Just think it over.

(*They all go, except* TROFIMOV *and* ANYA.)

ANYA (*laughing*). We should be grateful to that man. He frightened Varya and now we're by ourselves.

TROFIMOV. Varya's afraid that we shall fall in love; so she never leaves us alone. Her narrow little mind can't comprehend that we're above love. To rise above petty unreal things which keep us from freedom and happiness—in that is the purpose of life, in that is its meaning. Onward! Undaunted, towards the brilliant star which shines far off! Onward! Let nothing hold you back, my friends.

ANYA (*clapping her hands*). You just speak wonderfully! (*Pause.*) It's so glorious today!

TROFIMOV. Yes, it's lovely weather.

ANYA. What have you done to me, Petya? Why don't I love the cherry orchard as I used? I loved it so much. I thought there was no better place on earth than our orchard.

TROFIMOV. All Russia is our orchard. The world is wide and wonderful and full of beautiful places. (*Pause.*) Think, Anya: your grandfather, your great-grandfather, and all your ancestors—they were slave owners. They owned living souls. Can't you see that from every cherry in this orchard, from every leaf, from the trunk of every tree, human creatures are looking at you? Can't you hear their voices? . . . To own living souls . . . it has done something to all of you, those who lived before and those who are living now. So that your mother and you, and your uncle, no longer realize that your lives are being lived at the expense of others, of the very people whom you don't let inside the door . . . We are at least two hundred years behind the times. As yet we have nothing; no definite attitude to our past; we do nothing but philosophize; we gamble and are discontented, or else we just drink vodka. But it's perfectly clear. Before we can begin to live in the present we must atone for our past; we must make a break with it. But such atonement can only be achieved by suffering, only by tremendous, unremitting effort. You must understand this, Anya.

ANYA. The house we live in doesn't belong to us any more. It hasn't been ours for ages. I'll leave it. I promise I will.

TROFIMOV. Throw the keys into a deep well and go. Be free as the wind.

ANYA (*exalted*). Oh, you said that so wonderfully!

TROFIMOV. Believe me, Anya, believe me! I'm not thirty yet. I'm young. I'm still a student, but I've been through a great deal. In the winter I am hungry, I am sick, I am anxious and as poor as a beggar. And wherever I go a cruel fate pursues me. Yet—always . . . at every minute, day or night, I feel a mysterious intimation. I feel an intimation of happiness, Anya. It's here . . .

ANYA (*dreamily*). The moon is rising.

(YEPIHODOV'S *guitar is heard—still the same song. The moon rises.* VARYA *is looking for* ANYA.)

VARYA (*offstage, calling*). Anya! Where are you?

TROFIMOV. Yes, the moon is rising. (*Pause.*) Here it is. Happiness. It's coming. Nearer and nearer. I can hear it. And if we can't see it, if we don't recognize it, what does it matter? Others will see it.

VARYA (*offstage*). Anya! Where are you?

TROFIMOV. Varya *again*! . . . (*Angrily.*) It's outrageous!

ANYA. Oh well. Let's go down to the river. It's nice there.

TROFIMOV. Yes, let's go.

(*They go.*)

VARYA (*offstage*). Anya! Anya!

act three

A drawing room and ballroom separated by an arch. A lighted chandelier. The Jewish Orchestra—previously mentioned in Act II—is playing. A quadrille is in progress. Voice of SIMEONOFF-PISHCHIK: *"Promenade à une paire!"* First couple to come into the drawing room is SIMEONOFF-PISHCHIK and CHARLOTTA IVANOVNA, TROFIMOV and MADAME RANEVSKAYA next, then ANYA and a post office employee, then VARYA with the station master. VARYA cries quietly, mopping her eyes as she dances. DUNYASHA is in the last couple. PISHCHIK shouts: *"Grand-rond, balancez"* and *"Les cavaliers à genoux et remerciez vos dames."*

(FIRS, *in a tailcoat, brings in soda water on a tray.* PISHCHIK *and* TROFIMOV *come into the drawing room.*)

PISHCHIK. Ouf! Let me tell you one thing: I'm apoplectic. Yes; two strokes already. I shouldn't be dancing. But as the saying goes: if you're one of the pack you can bark or not bark but you *must* wag your tail. I'm as strong as a horse. My late progenitor used to make a joke of it—God rest his soul—he used to say that the ancient family of Simeonoff-Pishchik was descended from that very horse which Caligula made a Senator . . . (*sits down*) . . . but the dreadful thing is that there's no money! A hungry dog dreams of nothing but meat . . . (*snores, but wakes again at once*) . . . and that's how it is with me—only it's money.

TROFIMOV. You know, you do look a bit like a horse.

PISHCHIK. Oh well . . . a horse is a good animal. You can sell a horse . . .

(*The noise of billiards is heard from another room.* VARYA *comes in.*)

TROFIMOV (*teasing*). Madame Lopahin! Madame Lopahin!

VARYA (*vexed*). Seedy gent!

TROFIMOV. Yes, I am a seedy gent and proud of it.

VARYA (*bitterly*). We've hired the musicians but how are we going to pay them? (*Goes out.*)

TROFIMOV. If your entire life's energy hadn't been spent in scratching money together for the interest on your debts, you could have put it to some sensible purpose. Do you know what? You could have changed the face of the earth.

PISHCHIK. Nietzsche . . . the philosopher, don't you know . . . the greatest, the most celebrated . . . a man of prodigious intellect . . . he says in one of his books . . . that it's all right apparently for a person to forge bank notes.

TROFIMOV. You've read Nietzsche?

PISHCHIK. Well—actually I got it from Dashenka. But now I'm in such a mess that there's no other way out but to forge bank notes . . . the day after tomorrow I have to pay three hundred and thirty rubles . . . I've saved up a hundred and . . . (*patting his pockets—in a panic*) the money's gone! . . . I've lost it! . . . (*Through tears.*) Where's the money? (*Relieved.*) Here it is! In the lining . . . do you know, I'm sweating.

(RANEVSKAYA *and* CHARLOTTA *come in.*)

RANEVSKAYA (*humming gaily with the orchestra*). Why is Leonid so late? What is he doing in town? (*To* DUNYASHA.) Dunyasha, do offer the musicians some tea.

TROFIMOV. I expect the sale has been called off.

RANEVSKAYA. What a moment to get the musicians here! What a moment to give a party! Oh well, it can't be helped. (*Sits down and hums quietly.*)

CHARLOTTA (*giving a deck of cards to* PISHCHIK). Here is a deck of cards. Think of a card.

PISHCHIK. I've thought of one.

CHARLOTTA. Now shuffle . . . Good. Give it to me, kind sir. *Ein, Zwei, Drei* . . . now look in your pocket . . .

PISHCHIK (*takes card out of pocket*). Eight of spades. Absolutely right (*astonished*). Just fancy that!

CHARLOTTA (*holding the deck on her palm, to* TROFIMOV). Quick! Which is the top card?

TROFIMOV. I don't know . . . Queen of spades?

CHARLOTTA. Queen of spades it is! (*To* PISHCHIK.) You! which is the top card?

PISHCHIK. Ace of hearts.

CHARLOTTA. Ace of hearts it is! (*Clasps her hand and the deck disappears.*) What glorious weather we're having! (*A mysterious female voice replies as if from beneath the floor.*) Yes, indeed, lovely lady, just glorious weather. (*In her own voice*) How captivating you are; you're my ideal! (*The voice.*) And I'm enchanted by you, lovely lady!

STATION MASTER (*applauding*). Bravo, the lady ventriloquist!

PISHCHIK (*astonished*). Just fancy that! Charming! Charming! I'm in love with you.

CHARLOTTA. In love? (*Shrugging.*) Can *you* fall in love? *Guter Mensch aber schlechter Musikant.*

TROFIMOV (*patting* PISHCHIK *on the shoulder*). Dear old horse!

CHARLOTTA. Attention, please. One last trick. (*Takes a rug off a chair.*) Now here's a thing, and a very pretty thing. I want to sell it . . . (*Shakes the rug.*) Does anyone want to buy it?

PISHCHIK (*astonished*). Oh just fancy that!

CHARLOTTA. *Ein, Zwei, Drei!* . . .

(*She whisks away the rug.* ANYA *is behind it. She curtseys, runs to her mother, and embraces her; runs back amidst general enthusiasm.*)

RANEVSKAYA (*applauding*). Bravo! Bravo!

CHARLOTTA. Once again! *Ein, Zwei, Drei!* . . .

(*She whisks away the rug.* VARYA *is behind it; she bows.*)

PISHCHIK (*astonished*). Oh, my goodness, just fancy that!

CHARLOTTA. That's all. (*Throws the rug over* PISHCHIK, *bows, and runs out*).

PISHCHIK (*rushing after her*). Rogue! Did you ever! . . . Rogue!

RANEVSKAYA. Still no sign of Leonid. Why is he so long in town? I can't understand it. It must be all over by now. The estate must be sold or else the sale never took place. Why must we be left in this suspense?

VARYA (*trying to comfort her*). Darling uncle has bought it. I'm positive.

TROFIMOV (*mocking*). Oh, of course.

VARYA. The great-aunt authorized him to buy the estate in her name—and to transfer the mortgage. She's doing it for Anya's sake. And I'm positive that, with God's help, darling uncle will buy it.

RANEVSKAYA. The great-aunt from Yaroslav has sent fifteen thousand to buy the estate in her name. She doesn't trust us. It's not even enough to pay the interest. (*Covers her face with her hands.*) My fate will be decided today. Today.

TROFIMOV (*teasing* VARYA). Madame Lopahin!

VARYA (*angry*). Perennial student! You've been sacked from the University twice!

RANEVSKAYA. Why are you so cross, Varya? He's only teasing you about Lopahin. What of it? Marry him, if you want to. Why not? He's a good, interesting man. And if you don't want to, don't. Nobody's making you, darling.

VARYA. Mamma darling, this is serious to me. And one must be honest about it. He *is* a good man. I like him.

RANEVSKAYA. Then marry him. What are you waiting for? I don't understand.

VARYA. Mamma darling, I can't be the one to propose. For two years now everyone's been talking about him and me, everybody talks but he . . . doesn't say a word or else makes jokes. I can understand it. He's getting richer and richer, he's busy, he can't be bothered about me; if I had some money—not even a lot, just a little—I'd leave everything and go far away. I'd go to a convent.

TROFIMOV. That would be heaven!

VARYA (*to* TROFIMOV). A student ought to be intelligent! (*Through tears.*) How plain you've got, Petya, and so old! (*To* RANEVSKAYA.) I've got to keep going, mamma darling. (*No longer crying.*) I feel I've got to be doing something every moment of the day.

(YASHA *comes in.*)

YASHA (*hardly able to contain his laughter*). Yepihodov has broken a billiard cue.

VARYA. Why is Yepihodov here? Who said he could play billiards? I simply cannot understand these people! (*She goes out.*)

RANEVSKAYA. Don't tease her, Petya. Can't you see she's an unhappy girl?

TROFIMOV. She's a busybody. Poking her nose into other people's business; the whole summer long Anya and I have never had a moment's peace . . . Forever suspecting we were having a love affair. What business is that of hers? Besides there was nothing in it. I'm not interested in that kind of nonsense. We're above love.

RANEVSKAYA. And I suppose I'm beneath love. (*Agitated.*) Why isn't Leonid here? If we only knew whether the estate had been sold, or no. The whole hideous business just seems beyond my comprehension. I don't know what to think. I'm just lost. At this moment, I could scream. I could do something idiotic. Save me, Petya, say something, anything.

TROFIMOV. What difference does it make whether the estate is sold today or not? It's all over. There's no turning back. It's the end of the road. Try not to worry. What's the good of deceiving yourself? For once in your life look the truth straight in the face.

RANEVSKAYA. But what is the truth? You can see what's true and what isn't. But I seem to be blind. I can't see anything. You take all sorts of important decisions so confidently. But tell me this, my dear; isn't that because you're young? Isn't it because you haven't had time to experience the agony which such decisions can cause? You look ahead so confidently. But isn't that because you can't see and you don't expect anything dreadful to happen? That's because you haven't come to grips with life—oh yes, you're more confident, more honest, more profound than we are. But look at it from my point of view and be as generous as ever you can. I was born here. My father and mother lived here; my grandfather. I love this house. I simply couldn't live without the cherry orchard. And if it has to be sold, you must sell me with it. (*She kisses* TROFIMOV *on the forehead.*) My son was drowned here. (*Cries.*) Have some pity for me, my dear man.

TROFIMOV. You know I feel for you with all my heart and soul.

RANEVSKAYA. But that's not the way to *say* it. (*Takes handkerchief out of her pocket; cable falls out.*) Do you know, today I simply feel—crushed. You can have no idea. It's so noisy here— every sound jars on my nerves. I'm trembling. But I can't go away by myself. The silence frightens me. Don't think too badly of me, Petya . . . I love you as if you were one of my own family. I'd be perfectly willing to let you marry Anya—I promise. But, my dear boy, you must finish your studies, you must get your degree. You don't do a thing. Fate tosses you about from place to place. It's so odd . . . isn't it? Isn't it odd? And you must do something about that beard. Make it grow. (*Laughs.*) You're so funny!

TROFIMOV (*picking up cable*). I don't claim to be a beauty.

RANEVSKAYA. This is from Paris. I get one every day—yesterday —today. That wild creature is ill again. He implores me to forgive him and begs me to come to him; and I really ought to run over to Paris to be near him. You look so shocked, Petya. But my dear, what is one to do? What *shall* I do? He's ill, he's all alone, unhappy, who's to look after him? Who'll make him behave sensibly? Give him his medicine at the right times? Oh . . . what's the point of pretending; why not be open about it? I love him. It's quite obvious. I love him. I love him. He's a millstone around my neck; he's dragging me with him down to the depths. But I love my millstone. I can't live without him. (*Pressing* TROFIMOV'S *hand.*) Don't think badly of me, Petya. No, don't say anything. Please.

TROFIMOV (*through tears*). Forgive me but I just must be honest. He fleeced you!

RANEVSKAYA. No. No. No. Don't say that . . . (*Puts her hands over her ears.*)

TROFIMOV. He's just a rat, and you're the only person who doesn't know it. He's just a little insignificant, no-good rat.

RANEVSKAYA (*angry, but controlled*). You're twenty-six years old—no, twenty-seven, but you sound like a schoolboy.

TROFIMOV. Very well. What of it?

RANEVSKAYA. It's time you grew up. At your age you ought to understand people who are in love. You ought to be in love yourself. You ought to fall in love. (*Angrily.*) Yes, you ought. It's not purity in you, it's just priggishness. You're a prig. You're an ugly, ridiculous prig; do you know what you are? You're a freak.

TROFIMOV (*horrified*). What is she saying?

RANEVSKAYA. "I'm above love." You're not above love. Ours Firs has the right word for it. You're a silly young cuckoo. At your age you ought to have a mistress.

TROFIMOV (*horrified*). This is frightful! What is she saying! (*Rushes to door of inner room, clutching his head.*) It's frightful . . . I just can't . . . I'll faint. (*Dashes out but comes right back.*) All is over between us! (*Dashes out of main door.*)

RANEVSKAYA (*shouting after him*). Petya! Wait! You silly, I was only joking! Petya!

(*In the hall are heard rushing feet on the stairs, then a crash. ANYA and VARYA cry out—then laugh.*) What is it? (ANYA *rushes in*)

ANYA (*laughing*). Petya has fallen downstairs! (*Rushes out.*)

RANEVSKAYA. What an old freak he is!

(*The station master comes to the middle of the inner room and starts to read "The Sinner" by Aleksei Konstantinovich Tolstoi. Everyone listens; but before he has read more than a few lines, a waltz starts up and the reading is broken off. Everyone dances. TROFIMOV, VARYA, ANYA, and RANEVSKAYA come back into the room.*)

RANEVSKAYA. Petya, darling, you're a dear, pure angel . . . Forgive me . . . let's dance. (*Dances with him.*)

(ANYA *and* VARYA *dance together.* FIRS *comes in, leaves his cane by the door.* YASHA *comes in too, watches the dancers.*)

YASHA. What's the matter, grandpa?

FIRS. I don't feel well. In the old days, when we had a reception, generals, barons, admirals would be dancing here. But now we have to send for young fellows from the post office, station masters—and even they aren't extra pleased to come. I feel sort of feeble. The old master—these people's grandfather—used to dose everyone with sealing wax, whatever was wrong with them. I've been taking sealing wax every day for twenty years at least—much longer maybe; maybe that's why I'm still alive.

YASHA. I'm sick of you, gramps (*yawns*). I wish you'd drop dead.

FIRS. Ech you . . . silly young cuckoo . . . (*Mumbles.*)

(TROFIMOV *and* RANEVSKAYA *dance in.*)

RANEVSKAY. *Merci!* I'll rest. (*Sits down.*) I'm tired.

(ANYA *comes in.*)

ANYA (*agitated*). Out in the kitchen someone's been saying that the cherry orchard has been sold.

RANEVSKAYA. To whom?

ANYA. He didn't say. He went away again. (*Dances out with* TROFIMOV.)

YASHA. It's just talk—some old man who came by—a stranger.

FIRS. Leonid Andreyevich still hasn't come back. And he's only got his light overcoat—his *demi-saison.* He'll catch a cold if he's not careful. Silly young fool!

RANEVSKAYA. I think I shall die. Yasha, go and find out who's bought it.

YASHA. The old man left hours ago. (*Laughs*)

RANEVSKAYA (*irritated*). What is there to laugh at? What's funny about it?

YASHA. That Yepihodov! He's a scream! Gasbag! Old "Never come singly."

RANEVSKAYA. Firs, if the estate is sold, where will you go?

FIRS. I'll go wherever you tell me.

RANEVSKAYA. Are you all right? You don't look well. You ought to be in bed.

FIRS. Oh yes. In bed. And then who'll see to things? Who'll manage? There's nobody else in the whole house.

YASHA. Lyubov Andreyevna, may I please ask you something? Do me a favor. If you're going back to Paris, take me with you. Do please. It's just out of the question for me to stay here. (*Looking around to see that nobody overhears.*) I mean! You can see for yourself, they're so ignorant here. They've no morals. And on top of it all, it's so boring. The food in the kitchen is simply uneatable. And, as if that weren't enough, this Firs—everywhere you go, always mumbling the stupidest things. Do take me with you. Please!

(PISHCHIK *comes in.*)

PISHCHIK. Permit me to ask you . . . a tiny waltz, my precious. (RANEVSKAYA *waltzes with him.*) Nevertheless, charming lady, I must get a hundred and eighty rubles out of you . . . I shall, you know . . . a hundred and eighty . . . (They dance into the inner room.)

YASHA (*sings quietly*). "Could you but know my heart's unrest". . . (*In the inner room a figure in a top hat and check trousers appears capering about; shouts are heard of* "Bravo, Charlotta Ivanovna, bravo!")

DUNYASHA (*stopping to powder her face, speaking to* FIRS). My young ladies say I'm to dance. There are so many gentlemen and not enough ladies to go round, but I feel giddy when I dance and my heart pounds. Do you know, just now the young man from the post office said something that simply took my breath away.

(*Music gradually fades.*)

FIRS. What did he say to you?

DUNYASHA. "You're like a flower," he said.

YASHA. (*yawning*). Such ignorance! (*Goes.*)

DUNYASHA. "Like a flower". . . I'm such a sensitive little thing. I just love pretty speeches. I love them just terribly.

FIRS. Your head's turned.

(YEPIHODOV *comes in.*)

YEPIHODOV (*to* DUNYASHA). So you don't want to see me. You look through me as if I were an insect of some kind. (*Sighs.*) Such is life.

DUNYASHA. What do you want?

YEPIHODOV. No question; you're probably right (*sighs*). One thing is certain, if one looks at it from a point view, so if you'll please excuse me for speaking very, very frankly, you've thrown me into a perfect state, actually. I know my luck, every day some kind of trouble happens to me. I've got used to it. It's been going on a long time. I can regard Destiny with a smile. You gave me your word, and although I . . .

DUNYASHA. Please. We'll talk about it later. Just now leave me alone. I want to daydream. (*Plays with her fan.*)

YEPIHODOV. You know me. Troubles every day. Never come singly. And, if you'll allow me to say so, I just smile. I laugh even. (VARYA *comes in from inner room.*)

VARYA (*to* YEPIHODOV). Still here? Such cheek! (*To* DUN-

YASHA.) Run along, Dunyasha. (*To* YEPIHODOV.) First of all you play billiards and break a cue, then you hang about the drawing room like one of the guests . . .

YEPIHODOV. Don't you carp at me. If I may say so, you can't do such a thing.

VARYA. I'm not carping at you, I'm just telling you. You do nothing but stroll around the place—not a stroke of work. I simply don't know why we keep you as a clerk.

YEPIHODOV (*offended*). Whether I work, or whether I stroll around, or whether I eat or play billiards is for people to discuss who have some sense and who are older . . .

VARYA. How dare you! How dare you speak like that to me! (*Flaring up.*) Do you mean that I have no sense? Get out of here! This very minute.

YEPIHODOV. I must ask you not to take that tone.

VARYA (*beside herself*). This very minute. Out you go! Out! (*He goes toward the door; she follows him.*) "Never come singly." Don't let me catch you coming back. I don't want to set eyes on you ever again! (YEPIHODOV *goes; his voice is heard offstage:* "I shall lodge a complaint about this.") Coming back are you? (*Seizes Fir's cane which is at the door.*) Very well. Come on then. Come on. I'll show you . . . Are you coming or aren't you? Well? All right. Take that! (*She lifts the cane and* LOPAHIN *comes in.*)

LOPAHIN. My most respectful thanks.

VARYA (*crossly and ironically*). Very sorry, I'm sure.

LOPAHIN. It's nothing. My most respectful thanks for a delightful welcome.

VARYA. Don't mention it. (*Moving away, then looking back and asking gently.*) I didn't hurt you, did I?

LOPAHIN. It's nothing. There's a huge bruise coming up, that's all.

(*Voices in the inner room:* "Lopahin has come," "Yermolai Alexeyevich is here.")

PISHCHIK. Here's himself as large as life and twice as natural. (*Hugs* LOPAHIN; *then sniffs.*) Hm! Cognac! We're having a high old time here too.

RANEVSKAYA. You, Yermolai Alexeyevich! What's kept you? Where is Leonid?

LOPAHIN (*embarrassed; trying not to show his excitement*). The

sale was over by four o'clock. We missed the train. We had to wait
till the nine thirty. (*Deep sigh.*) Ough! (*Hand to forehead.*) I feel
a bit dizzy.

(GAEV *comes in, packages in his right hand; he wipes his eyes
with the other hand.*)

RANEVSKAYA. Well, Leonid? What . . . ? For God's sake tell us.

(GAEV *does not answer; just gestures with his hand.*)

GAEV (*to* FIRS, *through tears*). Here take these . . . anchovies,
and Kertsch herrings. I haven't had a bite to eat all day . . . What
I've been through! (*From the billiard room the click of the balls
is heard.* YASHA's *voice:* "Seven and eighteen!" GAEV's *expression
changes; he stops crying.*) I'm tired out. Firs, come and help me
change. (*Goes out followed by* FIRS.)

PISHCHIK. What happened at the sale? Tell us.

RANEVSKAYA. Is the orchard sold?

LOPAHIN. Sold.

RANEVSKAYA. Who bought it?

LOPAHIN. I did. (*Pause.* RANEVSKAYA *is overwhelmed.* VARYA
*takes the keys from her belt, throws them into the middle of the
room, and goes out.*) I bought it! Wait a minute. I'm dizzy. I can't
speak . . . (*Laughs.*) When we got to the sale, Deriganov was there
already. Leonid Andreyevich had no more than fifteen thousand,
but Deriganov bid thirty thousand straight away, over and above
the mortgage. I saw how things were and jumped right in—forty
thousand. Forty-five, bids Deriganov. Fifty-five, I said. He goes to
sixty. Seventy, I said. Every time he went up by five I jumped him
ten. Suddenly it was all over. In the end it was knocked down to
me at ninety thousand. The cherry orchard is mine now! Mine!
(*Laughing uproariously.*) My God! . . . Dear God Almighty, the
cherry orchard is mine! Tell me I'm drunk, tell me I'm raving mad,
tell me it isn't really happening. (*Stamps his feet.*) Don't laugh at
me! If only my father, my grandfather, could rise from the dead
and could see all this, how their Yermolai, the little boy they used
to thrash, who could hardly read or write, how their Yermolai, who
went barefoot in winter, how this same Yermolai has bought the
finest estate in the whole world. I've bought the estate where my
father and grandfather were serfs; where they weren't even allowed
into the kitchen. I'm asleep . . . it hasn't really happened . . . You're
just imagining it. It's just part of the mysterious half-light in which

we live. (*Picks up the keys, smiling kindly.*) She threw down the keys. She wanted to show that she's no longer the mistress . . . (*Jingles keys.*) Well, what of it? (*Orchestra tunes up.*) Hey, musicians, play up. Let me hear you! You must come, all of you, and see how Yermolai Alexeyevich will take the axe to the cherry orchard. The trees will come crashing down! Up will go summer cottages; and our grandchildren and their grandchildren will see a new life . . . Music! Play up! (*Music.* RANEVSKAYA *has collapsed on a chair and is crying.*) Why, oh why didn't you listen to me? Too late now, my poor dear. (*Through tears.*) If only it could all be over soon. If only our muddled, unhappy lives could somehow be changed.

PISHCHIK (*taking him by the arm; in a low tone*). She's crying. Let's go into the other room. She'd rather be alone . . . Come. (*They move off.*)

LOPAHIN. What's the matter? Music! Louder! Everything must be as I wish it. (*Ironically.*) Here comes the new master, here comes the owner of the cherry orchard! (*Accidentally he upsets a table, almost throwing down the candelabra.*) I can pay for everything . . . (*He and* PISHCHIK *go out.*)

(*Nobody is left except* RANEVSKAYA *sitting in a crumpled heap, crying bitterly. The orchestra is heard offstage.* ANYA *goes to her mother and kneels.* TROFIMOV *stays near the door of the other room.*)

ANYA. Mamma . . . mamma, don't cry . . . My dear darling, sweet, kind mamma, I love you. God bless you, darling. The cherry orchard is sold; it's over; that's true, that's true. But don't cry, mamma. You still have your life ahead of you . . . You're still your dear, wonderful self . . . come with me, come dearest; we'll go away! We'll plant a new orchard, a lovelier one; you'll live to see it; you'll know what it means. And happiness, deep, peaceful happiness will be all around you like evening sunshine. You'll be able to smile again, my own dear mamma! Come along my darling! Come . . .

act four

Same as Act One, but no curtains on the windows, no pictures. A few pieces of furniture are left which have been pushed into corners as if ready for sale. An emptiness is felt. Near the outer door, luggage, bundles, and so

on. The inner door to the left is open and from there voices of VARYA and
ANYA can be heard. LOPAHIN is standing about. YASHA holds a tray with
filled champagne glasses. In the entrance hall YEPIHODOV ties a trunk. In the
background are heard voices of peasants, servants who have come to bid
good-bye. GAEV's voice is heard: *"Thank you, friends, thank you."*

YASHA. The people about the place have come to say good-bye.
Do you know what I think, Yermolai Alexeyevich? Our people are
good but they haven't any sense.
   (*Voices are heard; they die away;* RANEVSKAYA *and* GAEV *come
   in from outside. She is composed but pale, her face trembles, she
   can hardly speak.*)
GAEV. You gave them your purse. You shouldn't have done that,
you really shouldn't.
RANEVSKAYA. I couldn't help it. I just had to. (*They go.*)
LOPAHIN (*to their retreating figures*). Please. Just one glass—
just to say farewell. I didn't think of bringing it out from town and
I could only get one bottle at the station. Please! (*Pause.*) No? (*Returns from door.*) If I'd known you wouldn't accept it, I wouldn't
have bought it. Oh well, I won't have any either. (YASHA *carefully
places the tray on a chair.*) You have one, Yasha, anyway.
YASHA. Here's to those who are leaving and to those who are
staying behind! (*Drinks.*) This isn't proper champagne, I can tell
you that.
LOPAHIN. Eight rubles a bottle. (*Pause.*) It's as cold as the devil.
YASHA. The stoves weren't lit today. After all, we're going away.
(*Laughs.*)
LOPAHIN. What's the joke?
YASHA. I'm laughing for joy.
LOPAHIN. It's October already; but it's still and golden like sum-
mer. Just the weather for building. (*Looks at watch and speaks to-
ward the door.*) Please remember the train will leave in forty-six
minutes! We must leave for the station in twenty minutes. So
hurry up!
   (TROFIMOV *enters from main door in overcoat.*)
TROFIMOV. Isn't it time we were going? The carriage is ready.
The devil alone knows where my galoshes are. They've disappeared.
(*Shouts through inner door.*) Anya, my galoshes aren't here! I can't
find them anywhere!
LOPAHIN. I've got to go to Kharkov. I'll go in your train. I'll

spend all winter in Kharkov. I've just been hanging around here all this time. I'm sick of having no work to do. I can't bear not to be working. I don't even know what to do with my hands; they just flap at my sides, as if they were somebody else's hands.

TROFIMOV. Let's be off now. And you can get busy with useful work again.

LOPAHIN. Have some.

TROFIMOV. Not for me (*indicating champagne*).

LOPAHIN. You're off to Moscow, I suppose.

TROFIMOV. Yes, I'll go with them to town and on to Moscow to-morrow.

LOPAHIN. Yes; I imagine the professors will hardly begin their lectures until you get there.

TROFIMOV. Not your business.

LOPAHIN. How many years have you been up at the University?

TROFIMOV. Think of something new for a change. That's old and cheap. (*Looks for galoshes.*) You know very likely you and I won't see each other again. So let me give you a last piece of advice: don't keep flapping your hands about. Get out of the habit of flapping. And another thing: building summer cottages on the assumption that the summer visitors will eventually buy their houses and culti-vate their land—well, that's just flapping too . . . But never mind; in spite of everything I'm really quite fond of you. You have the hands of an artist. And I believe you have the soul of an artist.

LOPAHIN (*hugs him*). Good-bye, my dear man, thank you for everything. Look, you may need a little money on the journey . . .

TROFIMOV. What for? I don't need it.

LOPAHIN. But you don't have any.

TROFIMOV. Oh yes I do. Thank you. I've just been paid for a translation. It's here. (*Indicates money in pocket; worried.*) But I can't find my galoshes.

VARYA (*offstage*). Here! Take the filthy things! (*Throws them into the room.*)

TROFIMOV. Why are you so cross, Varya? Oh! These aren't mine!

LOPAHIN. Last spring I sowed a thousand acres of poppies, and now I've cleared forty thousand net. And when my poppies were in flower—what a picture that was! But what I mean was I cleared forty thousand so you see I can make you a loan. Why do you turn your nose up at it? I'm a plain peasant and I'm making a plain offer.

TROFIMOV. Your father was a peasant, mine was a pharmacist—what difference does it make? (LOPAHIN *takes out his wallet.*) Put it away, I wouldn't take it if you gave me two hundred thousand. I'd rather stand on my own feet. All the grandeur and importance which you people value so much, whether you're rich or not, all that doesn't mean anything more to me than—a feather blown about by the wind. I can do without you. I can afford to ignore you. I'm strong and proud. Humanity is marching towards the most exalted truth, the most exalted happiness possible on earth; and I'm in the front rank.

LOPAHIN. Will you get there?

TROFIMOV. Yes. I will. (*Pause.*) I'll get there and I'll show other people how to get there too.

(*Far away is heard the sound of axes cutting the trees.*)

LOPAHIN. Well, good-bye, my dear man. It's time. You and I look at each other down our noses: meantime life's passing by. When I'm really hard at work, I don't have time to feel tired or depressed. And then I seem to know the purpose of *my* existence too. How many people there are in Russia—don't you agree, my dear fellow?—and none of them has the least notion of why he exists. Oh well, what of it? They say that Leonid Andreyevich has taken that post at the bank. The salary's quite good . . . but he won't keep it. He's too lazy.

ANYA (*at the door*). Mamma says will you please not cut the trees down till after she's gone.

TROFIMOV. Yes, a little tact would have done no harm. (*Goes out through the main door.*)

LOPAHIN. Of course, of course . . . what fools! (*Follow* TROFIMOV.)

ANYA. Has Firs been taken to the hospital?

YASHA. I spoke about it this morning. I suppose he has.

ANYA (*to* YEPIHODOV, *who crosses the stage*). Will you please find out if Firs has been taken to the hospital.

YASHA (*offended*). I told Yepihodov to see to it this morning. Why do you have to ask ten times?

YEPIHODOV. Firs is such an old man that, if you want my last word on the subject, it's hopeless to try to patch him up. He'd better go the way of his forefathers. And, for my part, I can only envy him. (*Puts a heavy case on a hatbox and crushes it.*) There you are! (*Goes out.*)

YASHA (*in a superior tone*). "Never come singly."

VARYA (*offstage*). Has Firs been taken to the hospital?

ANYA (*with a letter in her hand*). Yes, he has.

VARYA. But why didn't they take the letter to the doctor?

ANYA. We'll have to send it after him. (ANYA *goes out.*)

VARYA (*offstage*). Where is Yasha? Tell him his mother has come to say good-bye to him.

YASHA (*with a gesture*). They make me tired.

(*During the foregoing* DUNYASHA *has been busy with the luggage. Now that* YASHA *is alone she comes to him.*)

DUNYASHA. If you'd only look at me, Yasha, just once. You are going away . . . You're leaving me. (*Cries and throws her arms round his neck.*)

YASHA. What's the use of crying? (*Drinks champagne.*) In six days I'll be in Paris again. Tomorrow we shall be in the Express. We'll be gone for good. It's almost too good to be true. I can hardly believe it. *Vive la France!* . . . This place is not for me. I can't live here. Oh well, it can't be helped. (*Drinks champagne.*) What's the use of crying? Behave yourself, you won't cry then.

DUNYASHA (*looking in the hand mirror and powdering herself*). Write to me from Paris. I loved you so much, Yasha, so much! I'm a sensitive little person, Yasha!

YASHA. They're coming.

(*Busies himself with luggage; hums.* RANEVSKAYA, GAEV, ANYA, *and* CHARLOTTA *come in.*)

GAEV. We should be going. Not much time left. (*Looking at* YASHA.) Who's smelling of herring?

RANEVSKAYA. In ten minutes we must be in the carriage . . . (*Looks around the room.*) Good-bye, my dear old house. Winter will end, spring will come, and you won't be there; you will have been torn down. How many things these wall have seen! (*Kisses* ANYA *fervently.*) My precious, you look radiant; your eyes are sparkling like diamonds. Are you happy? Are you so very happy?

ANYA. Very. A new life is beginning, mamma.

GAEV (*gaily*). Yes; everything's for the best. Before the cherry orchard was sold, we were all anxious, miserable, but then when

matters were settled, irrevocably, once and for all, everybody accepted the situation and became quite cheerful again . . . I'm an
employee in a bank, I'm a financier . . . yellow in the center . . .
and as for you, sister, don't know why, but there's no question that
you're looking better.

RANEVSKAYA. Yes. My nerves are better—I feel calmer, it's true.
(*Her overcoat and hat are passed to her.*) I'm sleeping well. Take
my things out, Yasha, it's time. (*To* ANYA.) We shall see one another soon, my dear child, but now I must go to Paris. We shall live
there on the money which your great-aunt at Yaroslav sent to buy
the estate—praise be to the great-aunt! But of course it won't last
long.

ANYA. Mamma, you'll come back soon, won't you? I'll work hard
and pass my exams and then I'll get something to do and be able to
help you. Mamma, we'll read all sorts of books together, you and I,
won't we . . . (*Kisses her mother's hands.*) We'll read in the long
autumn evenings, read and read, and a new wonderful world will
open up to us. (*In a dreamy tone.*) You will come back, mamma.

RANEVSKAYA. Yes, my treasure, I will. (*Hugs her.*)

(LOPAHIN *comes in with* CHARLOTTA, *who is humming a song.*)

GAEV. Listen to Charlotta! She's happy.

CHARLOTTA (*rolls up a rug to look like a baby*). Baby's gone
s'eepy byes! (*A baby is heard to cry* "Wah! Wah!") I'm so sorry
for you. You break my heart. (*Throws the rug aside and in her own
voice.*) Please, you simply must find me a situation, you simply must.

LOPAHIN. We will, Charlotta Ivanovna, don't worry.

GAEV. Everyone is leaving us. Varya's going away . . . Nobody
needs us any more.

CHARLOTTA. I don't know where I'm to stay in town. It's time we
were off . . . (*hums*). Oh well!

(PISHCHIK *comes in.*)

LOPAHIN. Behold, the Wonder of the World!

PISHCHIK (*out of breath*). Oh, just let me catch my breath . . .
I'm utterly finished . . . my dear friends . . . water, please.

GAEV. He's after money, we may be quite sure. Your obedient
servant will slip away from danger. (*He goes.*)

PISHCHIK. Haven't been here for quite a time, gracious lady . . .
(*To* LOPAHIN.) You here? Take this! (*Gives money to* LOPAHIN.)
Four hundred; and another eight hundred and forty to come.

LOPAHIN (*shrugging in astonishment*). It's like a dream . . . where did you get it?

PISHCHIK. Wait! It's not . . . an extraordinary occurrence. Some Englishmen came and found some kind of white clay on my land. (*To* RANEVSKAYA.) For you too, four hundred . . . delightful, gracious lady . . . (*Gives money.*) More, later. (*Drinks water.*) Just now a young man on the train said that some . . . great philosopher advises jumping off the roof . . . "Jump" he said. That's the way to solve every problem. (*Astonished.*) Just fancy that! Water, please.

LOPAHIN. What kind of Englishmen?

PISHCHIK. I rented them the piece of land with the clay for twenty-four years. But now, excuse me, I'm in a hurry, I must gallop . . . I've got further to go . . . I must go to Znoykov . . . to Kardamanov . . . I owe money all round. (*Drinks water.*) God bless you all . . . I'll drop in on Thursday.

RANEVSKAYA. But we're just off to town; and tomorrow I go abroad.

PISHCHIK. What? (*Greatly agitated.*) Why to town? Oh yes . . . just look at the furniture . . . luggage . . . well, it can't be helped (*through tears*) . . . can't be helped . . . gigantic intelligence, those people, those Englishmen . . . it can't be helped . . . all the very best to you . . . God will help you . . . it can't be helped . . . in this world everything has to come to an end. (*Kisses* RANEVSKAYA's *hand.*) If ever word should reach you that my end has come, remember this . . . horse, and say: once there lived a man called Simeonoff-Pishchik, the Kingdom of Heaven be his . . . what wonderful weather . . . yes. (*He goes in great embarrassment, but comes back at once and says at the door.*) My Dashenka sends her love. (*He goes.*)

RANEVSKAYA. We can go now. But there are two things: first, Firs being so ill. (*Looks at watch.*) We still have five minutes.

ANYA. Mamma, Firs has been taken to the hospital. Yasha saw to it.

RANEVSKAYA. The second thing is—Varya. She's used to being up early, to working all day long, and now with no work she's like a fish out of water. She's lost weight; she's pale; and cries, poor thing, all the time. (*Pause.*) You know perfectly well, Yermolai Alexeyevich, I always dreamed of . . . giving her to you, and it always looked as if you and she were going to get married. (*Whispers to* ANYA, *who makes a sign to* CHARLOTTA *and both go out.*) She loves you,

you like her, and I don't know, I simply do not know why you seem to avoid each other. I can't understand it.

LOPAHIN. I can't understand it myself, to be perfectly frank. It's all so strange . . . if there's still time, I'm quite ready . . . Let's get it over and done with. I don't feel that, after you've gone, I shall be able to ask her.

RANEVSKAYA. Splendid. It won't take more than a moment. I'll call her now.

LOPAHIN. And we've got the champagne here—so appropriate. (*Looks at the glasses.*) Empty . . . somebody's drunk it all up. (YASHA *coughs.*) Swilled it all down, rather.

RANEVSKAYA (*gaily*). Splendid! We'll go out . . . Yasha, *allez!* I'll call her. (*In doorway.*) Varya, drop everything. Come here. Come! (RANEVSKAYA *and* YASHA *go out.*)

LOPAHIN (*looking at watch.*) Yes . . .

(*Pause. Offstage one hears giggles, whispering, finally* VARYA *is pushed in.*)

VARYA (*searching about*). Funny, I can't find it.

LOPAHIN. What are you looking for? (*Pause.*) Where are you off to now?

VARYA. I? To the Ragulins . . . We've arranged that I shall look after things there—a sort of housekeeper, in a way.

LOPAHIN. The Ragulins? That's at least seventy miles away. (*Pause.*) Well, life in this house is over.

VARYA (*searching about again*). Where can it be? Perhaps I put it in a trunk . . . Yes, life in this house has come to an end . . . there'll be no more life here.

LOPAHIN. I'm just off to Kharkov on this train. I've a lot of business. I'm leaving Yepihodov to look after things. I've hired him.

VARYA. Oh yes?

LOPAHIN. This time last year we had snow by this time. Remember? And now it's still and golden . . . cold though . . . at least three degrees of frost.

VARYA. I didn't look. Besides our thermometer's broken . . .

(*Pause. A voice from out of doors is heard:* "Yermolai Alexeyevich!")

LOPAHIN (*as if he had been expecting this call all the time.*) Coming! (*Goes out quickly.*)

(VARYA *sits on the floor, puts her head on a bundle, and cries quietly. The door opens.* RANEVSKAYA *tiptoes in.*)

RANEVSKAYA. Well? (*Pause.*) Time we were leaving.

VARYA (*not crying any more*). Yes, it's time, mamma darling. I'll still get to the Ragulins today, if we don't miss the train.

RANEVSKAYA (*calling toward doorway*). Anya, get your coat on!

(ANYA *comes in, then* GAEV *and* CHARLOTTA, GAEV *in a heavy traveling coat. Servants come in.* YEPIHODOV *fusses around the luggage.*)

RANEVSKAYA. Now we can be on our way.

ANYA (*joyously*). On our way!

GAEV. My friends, my dear, kind friends! Can I leave this house forever and keep silent? Can I restrain myself? I must on this occasion give expression to the feelings which are welling up from the depth of my being . . .

ANYA (*pleadingly*). Uncle!

VARYA. Uncle dear, don't.

GAEV (*sadly*). Yellow to the center . . . I'll hold my tongue.

(TROFIMOV *comes in; then* LOPAHIN.)

TROFIMOV. Well, time we were leaving!

LOPAHIN. Yepihodov, my coat!

RANEVSKAYA. I'll sit a moment longer. It's as if I'd never noticed before what the walls are like and the ceiling. And now I look at them so hungrily, with such deep love.

GAEV. I remember when I was six years old, it was on Trinity Sunday; I sat in this window and watched father starting for church.

RANEVSKAYA. Has everything been taken out?

LOPAHIN. Looks like it. (*To* YEPIHODOV *as he puts on his coat.*) See that everything is in order, Yepihodov.

YEPIHODOV (*hoarse voice*). Certainly, certainly, Yermolai Alexeyevich.

LOPAHIN. What's happened to your voice?

YEPIHODOV. I just had a drink of water and something went down the wrong way.

YASHA. Such ignorance!

RANEVSKAYA. We shall go and there won't be a soul left behind.

LOPAHIN. Till the spring.

VARYA (*takes a parasol from a bundle and it looks as if she were going to hit* LOPAHIN *with it;* LOPAHIN *pretends to be afraid*). I'm not going to hurt you . . . I didn't even think of it.

TROFIMOV. Come on! It's time! The train will be in any minute.

VARYA. Petya! Here they are! Your galoshes! (*In tears.*) How old they are—and filthy!

TROFIMOV (*putting on the galoshes*). Let's go, people.

GAEV (*confused; trying not to weep*). Train . . . railroad station cannon off the cushion . . . red on the spot.

RANEVSKAYA. Let's go.

LOPAHIN. Everybody here? Nobody left behind? (*Closes door to inner part of house.*) Everything is stored in there. Better be locked up. Let's go!

ANYA. Good-bye, house! Good-bye, old life!

TROFIMOV (*goes out with* ANYA). Welcome, new life!

(VARYA *looks around the room; goes out without haste.* YASHA *and* CHARLOTTA, *with her dog, go out.*)

LOPAHIN. Well, till the spring. (*To* RANEVSKAYA *and* GAEV.) Don't be long . . . Bye-bye. (*Goes out.*)

(RANEVSKAYA *and* GAEV *are left alone. It is as if they had waited for this moment. They cling together and weep quietly as if afraid to be overheard.*)

GAEV (*in despair*). My sister! My sister!

RANEVSKAYA. My wonderful, wonderful, wonderful orchard. My life, my youth, my happiness—good-bye! . . . Goodbye!

(ANYA's *voice calling gaily:* "Mamma." TROFIMOV's *voice, gay and excited:* "A-OO!")

RANEVSKAYA. One last look at the walls, the windows . . . dear mother used to love this room . . .

GAEV. My sister . . . my sister . . .

(ANYA's *voice:* "Mamma." TROFIMOV's *voice:* "A-OO!")

RANEVSKAYA (*calling*). Coming! (*They go.*)

(*The stage is empty. The sound is heard of doors being slammed, then locked, then of the carriages leaving. Silence. In the silence, the dull thud of an axe upon a tree. Footsteps are heard.* FIRS *appears from the inner door. As always, he is in his jacket and white vest but he is in slippers. He is ill.*)

FIRS (*goes to main door and rattles the handle*). Locked. They've gone . . . (*Sits on sofa.*) They forgot me . . . oh well . . . I'll just rest here. One thing; Leonid Andreyevich didn't take his fur coat.

Bet you he's gone off in his light coat . . . (*Sighs, in a worried manner.*) I should have seen to it. Silly young . . . (*Mumbles unintelligibly.*) Life has passed by as if I hadn't lived . . . (*Lies down.*) I'll lie down . . . You've no strength left—you've nothing left—nothing . . . ech! You're a silly young cuckoo.

(*A sound is heard far off, as if the string of a violin were broken. A sad sound and a dying one. Silence. No sound except far away in the orchard the axes against the trees.*)

ALLEGORY AND MYTH
IN *THE CHERRY ORCHARD*

On the level of psychological realism, *The Cherry Orchard* is a dramatization of ineffectual, "job-lot" people whose futile lives are played out in a society experiencing the throes of change.* The Ranevsky estate, a microcosm of Russian society, is peopled by representatives of the social classes in conflict with each other as a result of the unsettling of the old order. Thus, as social allegory, the play illustrates the various responses of each class to social stress. In addition to the obvious representatives of the aristocracy, the middle, and the working classes, there is, for example, in Varya the embodiment of the conservative spiritual values of the Orthodox Church whose worldly obligations (carrying the keys of the household) are in conflict with its spiritual impulses (yearning for saintly vagabondage) and who recognizes in the landless Tramp of Marxist orientation its rival for authority. The dilemma of the liberal intellectual is objectified in Trophimof the tutor, as that of the Russian artist is in Charlotte the governess. On the mythical level of the play, below that of the psychological alienation of the characters and the social alienation of the classes, there is a pattern of action and characterization that suggests a theme of permanence in the midst of change. The temporal action of the play is fitted to the seasonal cycle of nature, with the four acts paralleling the succession of spring, summer, fall, and winter. This literal correspondence between the four acts of the play and the four seasons of the year implies the figurative significance of the cycle of nature as continuation and renewal of life. Madame Ranevsky, who, on the literal level of the play, occupies a position of central importance in each of the four acts, functions on the mythic level of characterization as a symbol of the continuity of human life in the cycle of nature. She is successively a Sorrowing Mother, a Goddess of Fertility, Love Goddess, and Queen of the Dead. The myth of Demeter and Persephone is relevant to an understanding of her function in the outer acts of

---

* Abstracted from John H. Kelson, "Allegory and Myth in *The Cherry Orchard*," *Western Humanities Review,* XIII (1959), 321-324.

the play, as the myth of Venus and Adonis is to her role in the two inner acts.

CHEKOV'S COMIC SPIRIT AND *THE CHERRY ORCHARD*

Anton Chekhov's letters reveal his artistic creed—a scientific method and a distaste for pretension.* His goal was the achievement of the role of free artist, which required, as he noted in 1899, a non-political role: "I am not a liberal, not a Conservative . . . I should have liked to have been a free artist, and nothing more—and I regret God has not given me the strength to be one." Hating hypocrisy and lying in all their forms, finding Pharisaism, stupidity and despotism "not among merchants only but also in science, in literature, and in the younger generation," he thought Dostoievsky's use of big themes indiscreet, saying several times that he is over-pretentious. Paul Bourget's work, the liberal rage of the last decade of the nineteenth century, Chekhov condemned as "a pretentious crusade against materialism." Although he was not strictly anti-religious, he stressed humanistic values: "My holy of holies," he wrote, "is the human body, health, intelligence, talent, love." He was against armies, in favor of Dreyfus, and a lover of *Anna Karenina.* He said that Ibsen cannot write a play and asked for tickets to the *Pillars of Society* because "you know Ibsen is my favorite writer." He revised his judgment of Mrs. Beecher Stowe after he reread her with a scientific aim and experienced the unpleasant sensation mortals experience when they have eaten too many raisins and currants. His subject matter may have been like Mrs. Stowe's, but his treatment of the commonplace was comic, evoking what Meredith called "thoughtful laughter." His opinions were not steadfast, but changed with circumstances, and as a comic artist Chekhov was the pin-pricker of pretension, the man who cures by mockery.

* Abstracted from Norman Silverstein, "Chekhov's Comic Spirit and *The Cherry Orchard*," *Modern Drama, I* (1958), 91-100.

The comic artist is part of the commonalty, but if he is great, he is able to justify and to dignify it. From 1901, when Chekhov wrote that he was "tempted to write a farce" until 1903 when he wrote he had completed "a comedy almost a farce," Chekhov worked out *The Cherry Orchard*. He joked that he had at last written a play in which there was no pistol shot. On September 26, 1903, he announced that the finished play "has turned out not a drama, but a comedy, in parts a farce indeed." Chekhov intended *The Cherry Orchard* as a group of vaudeville sketches in which each character performs his bit comically and self-consciously. The general disaster of an era's passing is a tragic overtone. It is true that Chekhov does pit class against class throughout the play. Yet his reason for these conflicts of class is to show the virtues of all classes. Each of the characters has greater vitality than the residents of the summer cottages who will replace him. Epihodov's two-and-twenty misfortunes are the frustrations of schemes unfulfilled. Yet Epihodov hatches new plans which have new opportunities to be undone. His creaking boots, one of his misfortunes, is a source of vaudeville comedy. Like Malvolio, he is the upstart, a counting house clerk who refuses to know his place. Varya attacks his intrusiveness in using Gaev's billiard table, but he goes unpunished. Gaev, a grown-up child of fifty-one who sucks caramels, evokes laughter with his billiard imagery, until the final image, in which he conceives of the train and the station as 'baulk lines" on a billiard table—a grief to come before he takes a job in a bank. Mme. Ranevsky returns to a gayer life in Paris. All leave Firs behind, but they are set free from the past. *The Cherry Orchard* shows men as isolated, concerned with small pleasures, living for the moment, going to a new freedom after a delay in an unproductive past, making small jokes at their own expense, being curious about everything in their future, and abandoning pretension. The means justify the means, not the end. The play is antiheroic and antitragic—a comedy reflecting Chekhov's comic spirit.

THE CHERRY ORCHARD AS COMEDY

Throughout his lifetime, Chekhov was constantly plagued by seeing his plays mishandled and misunderstood.* The errors which surrounded his plays are still being perpetuated, only now by critics. The greatest misunderstanding has revolved around the tragic qualities of *The Cherry Orchard,* for that play is actually a comedy since futility never achieves tragedy but rather becomes a comic gesture. Chekhov's play concerns the passing of a social era, yet he did not see such a change as tragic. Members of the passing society are not tragic; they are useless due to the futility of their lifestyle. Thus, through their divergence from the new norms of the incoming social order, the dying aristocracy becomes comic. Gayeff and Madame Ranevskaya are characterized by childishness. Gayeff sees life as an imaginary billiard game, and his ridiculous relationship to it is accentuated by his child-like habit of stuffing candies into his mouth. Both he and his sister demonstrate their childish qualities through their relationship to their crumbling financial security. They overspend as a means of self-deception and fail to take any practical steps to preserve their estate. Other characters in the play are similarly ridiculous. Lopahin, though successful in his business ventures, cannot control his private life. Characterized by two symbols, a stick and a watch, Lopahin is plagued by the stick as a servitude symbol and needs the watch as a security symbol. Unable to propose to Varya, to articulate his feelings, he is also an impossible character and, thus, comic. Fiers, the servant, experiences a similar uselessness in that, although freed, he remains in servitude by choice even though his masters are not worthy of him. Madame Ranevskaya's daughters, Anya and Varya, are equally futile individuals. Varya loves Lopahin, but she cannot initiate the relationship as such boldness would be unladylike. Anya is, like her mother, a captive of a dream world, and Anya's intellectual lover, Trofimoff, is comic through his in-

---

* Abstracted from Jacqueline E. M. Latham, "*The Cherry Orchard* As Comedy," *Educational Theatre Journal.* X (1958), 21-29.

ability to act on truth even though he perceives it. The seven central characters are thus mutually ineffectual. Chekhov's major comic theme is that of divergence from normality, and all major characters in *The Cherry Orchard* exhibit that futile lifestyle. Characterized by self-deception, ludicrous behavior, complacency, and ill-adjustment, each serves to perpetuate Chekhov's basic thematic intention. Even if one wishes to maintain that *The Cherry Orchard* is tragic futility, it must be conceded that comedy reveals that futility.

THE CHERRY ORCHARD AS A COMEDY

The usual critical approach toward *The Cherry Orchard* has been to regard the play as social commentary on dying aristocracy and therefore classify the dramatic intent as tragedy.* If, however, Chekhov's play is to be accurately interpreted, such an interpretation must concern the dramatic qualities of the play, not its quality of providing social data. Examining *The Cherry Orchard* as to its literary type can provide an understanding of some of the basic principles of dramatic comedy. Typical criticisms of the play point out that the plot contains unhappy events carried to unhappy resolutions which are in no way comic. The error in this reasoning is that the play does not present the sad life of Madame Ranévskaya; the central action concerns the futile efforts of property owners to save the property from an impending sale, and the history of the characters' lives is seen in retrospect. Viewing the actions and ideas of the characters in relation to the central conflict, it becomes obvious that the characters' behavior it totally inappropriate and unrealistic in terms of the gravity of the conflict. The daydreaming schemes are comic, and Chekhov reinforces their comic quality by surrounding them with insignificant trivia: foul cigar smoke, imaginary billiard games, lost galoshes, and incessant eating, to name a few. The effect of such inclusions is one of intensification of the comic qualities of behavior

* Abstracted from Daniel Charles Gerould, *"The Cherry Orchard* As a Comedy," *Journal of General Education, XI* (1958), 109-122.

exhibited by the characters. One of the basic sources of comedy lies in incongruous reactions to situations, for such inappropriate behavior rapidly removes any character's tragic dignity. A second element which often gains mention in tragic analyses of the play is the emotional level of the characters. Their emotions seem too serious to be comic, but these reactions must be viewed in relation to the central action. *The Cherry Orchard* covers a six-month time span, moving from a busy May household to a deserted October setting. Throughout the action, the characters' responses never change. The outbursts continue unchanged since the characters are learning nothing from their life experiences. They discuss the past, live in the past, and fail to change as life carries them into the present world. The failure of the characters to adapt their emotional responses creates comedy. A second quality of comedy is that the characters make the same errors, respond in the same manner, and undergo no major changes in behavior. Finally, most critics maintain that the effect of the drama on an audience creates sympathy and sadness, and, therefore, they assert that audience reaction demonstrates tragedy as the ultimate effect. Yet, perhaps the ending is not as unhappy as it may seem. Gaieff comments: "Yes, really, everything's all right now." Madame Ranévskaya asserts that her nerves are better and replies to Gaieff that she will go back to Paris and live off the money sent to save the estate. Her intentions are to continue living the same extravagant life to which she had become accustomed. Recalling her comment in the first act, "I'm through with Paris," it is obvious that she is in no way changed. Secondly, comedy does not generally have a happy ending. Usually comic characters are in some way frustrated as to their intentions, and *The Cherry Orchard* fulfills that axiom; no one is able to accomplish anything that was intended. Concerning the critical assertion that audiences feel sympathy for the characters, there is no reason why they shouldn't. Comedy differs from tragedy in that tragedy presents struggling nobility; comedy presents the difference between man as he should be and man as he is.

MAJOR BARBARA
GEORGE BERNARD SHAW

CHARACTERS

STEPHEN UNDERSHAFT

LADY BRITOMART

BARBARA UNDERSHAFT

SARAH UNDERSHAFT

ANDREW UNDERSHAFT

JENNY HILL

BILL WALKER

MORRISON

ADOLPHUS CUSINS

CHARLES LOMAX

RUMMY MITCHENS

SNOBBY PRICE

PETER SHIRLEY

BILTON

MRS BAINES

act one

It is after dinner in January 1906, in the library in Lady Britomart Undershaft's house in Wilton Crescent. A large and comfortable settee is in the middle of the room, upholstered in dark leather. A person sitting on it (it is vacant at present) would have, on his right, Lady Britomart's writing table, with the lady herself busy at it; a smaller writing table behind him on his left; the door behind him on Lady Britomart's side; and a window with a window seat directly on his left. Near the window is an armchair.

Lady Britomart is a woman of fifty of thereabouts, well dressed and yet careless of her dress, well bred and quite reckless of her breeding, well mannered and yet appallingly outspoken and indifferent to the opinion of her interlocutors, amiable and yet peremptory, arbitrary, and high-tempered to the last bearable degree, and withal a very typical managing matron of the upper class, treated as a naughty child until she grew into a scolding mother,

N.B. The Euripidean verses in the second act of Major Barbara are not by me, nor even directly by Euripides. They are by Professor Gilbert Murray, whose English version of *The Bacchae* came into our dramatic literature with all the impulsive power of an original work shortly before *Major Barbara* was begun. The play, indeed, stands indebted to him in more ways than one. G.B.S.

and finally settling down with plenty of practical ability and worldly experience, limited in the oddest way with domestic and class limitations, conceiving the universe exactly as if it were a large house in Wilton Crescent, though handling her corner of it very effectively on that assumption, and being quite enlightened and liberal as to the books in the library, the pictures on the walls, the music in the portfolios, and the articles in the papers.

Her son, Stephen, comes in. He is a gravely correct young man under 25, taking himself very seriously, but still in some awe of his mother, from childish habit and bachelor shyness rather than from any weakness of character.

STEPHEN. Whats the matter?

LADY BRITOMART. Presently, Stephen.

(*Stephen submissively walks to the settee and sits down. He takes up a Liberal weekly called* The Speaker).

LADY BRITOMART. Dont begin to read, Stephen. I shall require all your attention.

STEPHEN. It was only while I was waiting—

LADY BRITOMART. Dont make excuses, Stephen. (*He puts down* The Speaker). Now! (*She finishes her writing; rises; and comes to the settee*). I have not kept you waiting very long, I think.

STEPHEN. Not at all, mother.

LADY BRITOMART. Bring me my cushion. (*He takes the cushion from the chair at the desk and arranges it for her as she sits down on the settee*). Sit down. (*He sits down and fingers his tie nervously*). Dont fiddle with your tie, Stephen: there is nothing the matter with it.

STEPHEN. I beg your pardon. (*He fiddles with his watch chain instead*).

LADY BRITOMART. Now are you attending to me, Stephen?

STEPHEN. Of course, mother.

LADY BRITOMART. No: it's *not* of course. I want something much more than your everyday matter-of-course attention. I am going to speak to you very seriously, Stephen. I wish you would let that chain alone.

STEPHEN (*hastily relinquishes the chain*). Have I done anything to annoy you, mother? If so, it was quite unintentional.

LADY BRITOMART (*astonished*). Nonsense! (*With some remorse*) My poor boy, did you think I was angry with you?

STEPHEN. What is it, then, mother? You are making me very uneasy.

LADY BRITOMART (*squaring herself at him rather aggressively*).

Stephen: may I ask how soon you intend to realize that you are a grown-up man, and that I am only a woman?

STEPHEN (*amazed*). Only a—

LADY BRITOMART. Dont repeat my words, please: it is a most aggravating habit. You must learn to face life seriously, Stephen. I really cannot bear the whole burden of our family affairs any longer. You must advise me: you must assume the responsibility.

STEPHEN. I!

LADY BRITOMART. Yes, you, of course. You were 24 last June. Youve been at Harrow and Cambridge. Youve been to India and Japan. You must know a lot of things, now; unless you have wasted your time most scandalously. Well, *advise* me.

STEPHEN (*much perplexed*). You know I have never interfered in the household—

LADY BRITOMART. No: I should think not. I dont want you to order the dinner.

STEPHEN. I mean in our family affairs.

LADY BRITOMART. Well, you must interfere now; for they are getting quite beyond me.

STEPHEN (*troubled*). I have thought sometimes that perhaps I ought; but really, mother, I know so little about them; and what I do know is so painful! it is so impossible to mention some things to you— (*he stops, ashamed*).

LADY BRITOMART. I suppose you mean your father.

STEPHEN (*almost inaudibly*). Yes.

LADY BRITOMART. My dear: we cant go on all our lives not mentioning him. Of course you were quite right not to open the subject until I asked you to; but you are old enough now to be taken into my confidence, and to help me to deal with him about the girls.

STEPHEN. But the girls are all right. They are engaged.

LADY BRITOMART (*complacently*). Yes: I have made a very good match for Sarah. Charles Lomax will be a millionaire at 35. But that is ten years ahead; and in the meantime his trustees cannot under the terms of his father's will allow him more than £800 a year.

STEPHEN. But the will says also that if he increases his income by his own own exertions, they may double the increase.

LADY BRITOMART. Charles Lomax's exertions are much more likely to decrease his income than to increase it. Sarah will have to find at least another £800 a year for the next ten years; and even then they will be as poor as church mice. And what about Barbara? I thought Barbara was going to make the most brilliant career of all of you. And what does she do? Joins the Salvation Army; discharges her maid; lives on a pound a week; and walks in one evening with a professor of Greek whom she has picked up in the street, and who pretends to be a Salvationist, and actually plays the big drum for her in public because he has fallen head over ears in love with her.

STEPHEN. I was certainly rather taken aback when I heard they were engaged. Cusins is a very nice fellow, certainly: nobody would ever guess that he was born in Australia; but—

LADY BRITOMART. Oh, Adolphus Cusins will make a very good husband. After all, nobody can say a word against Greek: it stamps a man at once as an educated gentleman. And my family, thank Heaven, is not a pig-headed Tory one. We are Whigs, and believe in liberty. Let snobbish people say what they please: Barbara shall marry, not the man they like but the man *I* like.

STEPHEN. Of course I was thinking only of his income. However, he is not likely to be extravagant.

LADY BRITOMART. Dont be too sure of that, Stephen. I know your quiet, simple, refined, poetic people like Adolphus: quite content with the best of everything! They cost more than your extravagant people, who are always as mean as they are second rate. No: Barbara will need at least £2000 a year. You see it means two additional households. Besides, my dear, *you* must marry soon. I dont approve of the present fashion of philandering bachelors and late marriages; and I am trying to arrange something for you.

STEPHEN. It's very good of you, mother; but perhaps I had better arrange that for myself.

LADY BRITOMART. Nonsense! you are much too young to begin matchmaking: you would be taken in by some pretty little nobody. Of course I dont mean that you are not to be consulted: you know that as well as I do. (*Stephen closes his lips and is silent*). Now dont sulk, Stephen.

STEPHEN. I am not sulking, mother. What has all this got to do with—with—with my father?

LADY BRITOMART. My dear Stephen: where is the money to come from? It is easy enough for you and the other children to live on my income as long as we are in the same house; but I cant keep four families in four separate houses. You know how poor my father is: he has barely seven thousand a year now; and really, if he were not the Earl of Stevenage, he would have to give up society. He says, naturally enough, that it is absurd that he should be asked to provide for the children of a man who is rolling in money. You see, Stephen, your father must be fabulously wealthy, because there is always a war going on somewhere.

STEPHEN. You need not remind me of that, mother. I have hardly ever opened a newspaper in my life without seeing our name in it. The Undershaft torpedo! The Undershaft quick firers! The Undershaft ten inch! The Undershaft disappearing rampart gun! the Undershaft submarine; and now the Undershaft aerial battleship! At Harrow they called me the Woolwich Infant. At Cambridge it was the same. A little brute at King's who was always trying to get up revivals, spoilt my Bible—your first birthday present to me—by writing under my name, "Son and heir to Undershaft and Lazarus, Death and Destruction Dealers: address Christendom and Judea." But that was not so bad as the way I was kowtowed to everywhere because my father was making millions by selling cannons.

LADY BRITOMART. It is not only the cannons, but the war loans that Lazarus arranges under cover of giving credit for the cannons. You know, Stephen, it's perfectly scandalous. Those two men, Andrew Undershaft and Lazarus, positively have Europe under their thumbs. That is why your father is able to behave as he does. He is above law. Do you think Bismarck or Gladstone or Disraeli could have openly defied every social and moral obligation all their lives as your father has? They simply wouldnt have dared. I asked Gladstone to take it up. I asked The Times to take it up. I asked the Lord Chamberlain to take it up. But it was just like asking them to declare war on the Sultan. They *wouldnt.* They said they couldnt touch him. I believe they were afraid.

STEPHEN. What could they do? He does not actually break the law.

LADY BRITOMART: Not break the law! He is always breaking the law. He broke the law when he was born: his parents were not married.

STEPHEN. Mother! Is that true?

LADY BRITOMART. Of course it's true: that was why we separated.

STEPHEN. He married without letting you know this!

LADY BRITOMART (*rather taken aback by this inference*). Oh no.

To do Andrew justice, that was not the sort of thing he did. Besides, you know the Undershaft motto: Unashamed. Everybody knew.

STEPHEN. But you said that was why you separated.

LADY BRITOMART. Yes, because he was not content with being a foundling himself: he wanted to disinherit you for another foundling. That was what I couldnt stand.

STEPHEN (*ashamed*). Do you mean for—for—for—

LADY BRITOMART. Dont stammer, Stephen. Speak distinctly.

STEPHEN. But this is so frightful to me, mother. To have to speak to you about such things!

LADY BRITOMART. It's not pleasant for me, either, especially if you are still so childish that you must make it worse by a display of embarrassment. It is only in the middle classes, Stephen, that people get into a state of dumb helpless horror when they find that there are wicked people in the world. In our class, we have to decide what is to be done with wicked people; and nothing should disturb our self-possession. Now ask your question properly.

STEPHEN. Mother: have you no consideration for me? For Heaven's sake either treat me as a child, as you always do, and tell me nothing at all; or tell me everything and let me take it as best I can.

LADY BRITOMART. Treat you as a child! What do you mean? It is most unkind and ungrateful of you to say such a thing. You know I have never treated any of you as children. I have always made you my companions and friends, and allow you perfect freedom to do and say whatever you liked, so long as you liked what I could approve of.

STEPHEN (*desperately*). I dare say we have been the very imperfect children of a very perfect mother; but I do beg you to let me alone for once, and tell me about this horrible business of my father wanting to set me aside for another son.

LADY BRITOMART (*amazed*). Another son! I never said anything of the kind. I never dreamt of such a thing. This is what comes of interrupting me.

STEPHEN. But you said—

LADY BRITOMART (*cutting him short*). Now be a good boy, Stephen, and listen to me patiently. The Undershafts are descended from a foundling in the parish of St Andrew Undershaft in the city. That was long ago, in the reign of James the First. Well, this foundling was adopted by an armorer and gun-maker. In the course of time the foundling succeeded to the business; and from some notion of gratitude, or some vow or something, he adopted another foundling, and left the business to him. And that foundling did the same. Ever since that, the cannon business has always been left to an adopted foundling named Andrew Undershaft.

STEPHEN. But did they never marry? Were there no legitimate sons?

LADY BRITOMART. Oh yes: they married just as your father did; and they were rich enough to buy land for their own children and leave them well provided for. But they always adopted and trained some foundling to succeed them in the business; and of course they always quarrelled with their wives furiously over it. Your father was adopted in that way; and he pretends to consider himself bound to keep up the tradition and adopt somebody to leave the business to. Of course I was not going to stand that. There may have been some reason for it when the Undershafts could only marry women in their own class, whose sons were not fit to govern great estates. But there could be no excuse for passing over my son.

STEPHEN (*dubiously*). I am afraid I should make a poor hand of managing a cannon foundry.

LADY BRITOMART. Nonsense! you could easily get a manager and pay him a salary.

STEPHEN. My father evidently had no great opinion of my capacity.

LADY BRITOMART. Stuff, child! you were only a baby: it had nothing to do with your capacity. Andrew did it on principle, just as he did every perverse and wicked thing on principle. When my father remonstrated, Andrew actually told him to his face that history tells us of only two successful institutions: one the Undershaft firm, and the other the Roman Empire under the Antonines. That was because the Antonine emperors all adopted their successors. Such rubbish! The Stevenages are as good as the Antonines, I hope; and you are a Stevenage. But that was Andrew all over. There you have the man! Always clever and unanswerable when he was defending nonsense and wickedness: always awkward and sullen when he had to behave sensibly and decently!

STEPHEN. Then it was on my account that your home life was broken up, mother. I am sorry.

LADY BRITOMART. Well, dear, there were other differences. I really cannot bear an immoral man. I am not a Pharisee, I hope; and I should not have minded his merely *doing* wrong things: we are none of us perfect. But your father didnt exactly *do* wrong things: he said them and thought them: that was what was so dreadful. He really had a sort of religion of wrongness. Just as one doesnt mind men practising immorality so long as they own that they are in the wrong by preaching morality; so I couldnt forgive Andrew for preaching immorality while he practised morality. You would all have grown up without principles, without any knowledge of right and wrong, if he had been in the house. You know, my dear, your father was a very attractive man in some ways. Children did not dislike him; and he took advantage of it to put the wickedest ideas into their heads, and make them quite unmanageable. I did not dislike him myself: very far from it; but nothing can bridge over moral disagreement.

STEPHEN. All this simply bewilders me, mother. People may differ about matters of opinion, or even about religion; but how can they differ about right and wrong? Right is right; and wrong is wrong; and if a man cannot distinguish them properly, he is either a fool or a rascal: thats all.

LADY BRITOMART (*touched*). Thats my own boy (*she pats his cheek*)! Your father never could answer that: he used to laugh and get out of it under cover of some affectionate nonsense. And now that you understand the situation, what do you advise me to do?

STEPHEN. Well, what *can* you do?

LADY BRITOMART. I must get the money somehow.

STEPHEN. We cannot take money from him. I had rather go and live in some cheap place like Bedford Square or even Hampstead than take a farthing of his money.

LADY BRITOMART. But after all, Stephen, our present income comes from Andrew.

STEPHEN (*shocked*). I never knew that.

LADY BRITOMART. Well, you surely didnt suppose your grandfather had anything to give me. The Stevenages could not do everything for you. We gave you social position. Andrew had to contribute *something*. He had a very good bargain, I think.

STEPHEN (*bitterly*). We are utterly dependent on him and his cannons, then?

LADY BRITOMART. Certainly not: the money is settled. But he provided it. So you see it is not a question of taking money from him or not: it is simply a question of how much. I dont want any more for myself.

STEPHEN. Nor do I.

LADY BRITOMART. But Sarah does, and Barbara does. That is, Charles Lomax and Adolphus Cusins will cost them more. So I must put my pride in my pocket and ask for it, I suppose. That is your advice, Stephen, is it not?

STEPHEN. No.

LADY BRITOMART (*sharply*). Stephen!

STEPHEN. Of course if you are determined—

LADY BRITOMART. I am not determined: I ask your advice; and I am waiting for it. I will not have all the responsibility thrown on my shoulders.

STEPHEN (*obstinately*). I would die sooner than ask him for another penny.

LADY BRITOMART (*resignedly*). You mean that *I* must ask him. Very well, Stephen: It shall be as you wish. You will be glad to know that your grandfather concurs. But he thinks I ought to ask Andrew to come here and see the girls. After all, he must have some natural affection for them.

STEPHEN. Ask him here!!!

LADY BRITOMART. Do *not* repeat my words, Stephen. Where else can I ask him?

STEPHEN. I never expected you to ask him at all.

LADY BRITOMART. Now dont tease, Stephen. Come! you see that it is necessary that he should pay us a visit, dont you?

STEPHEN (*reluctantly*). I suppose so, if the girls cannot do without his money.

LADY BRITOMART. Thank you, Stephen: I knew you would give me the right advice when it was properly explained to you. I have asked your father to come this evening. (*Stephen bounds from his seat*). Dont jump, Stephen: it fidgets me.

STEPHEN (*in utter consternation*). Do you mean to say that my father is coming here tonight—that he may be here at any moment?

LADY BRITOMART (*looking at her watch*). I said nine. (*He gasps. She rises*). Ring the bell, please. (*Stephen goes to the smaller writing table; presses a button on it; and sits at it with his elbows on the table and his head in his hands, outwitted and overwhelmed*). It is ten minutes to nine yet; and I have to prepare the girls. I asked Charles Lomax and Adolphus to dinner on purpose that they might be here. Andrew had better see them in case he should cherish any delusions as to their being capable of supporting their wives. (*The butler enters: Lady Britomart goes behind the settee to speak to him*). Morrison: go up to the drawing room and tell everybody to come down here at once. (*Morrison withdraws. Lady Britomart turns to Stephen*). Now remember, Stephen: I shall need all your countenance and authority. (*He rises and tries to recover some vestige of these attributes*). Give me a chair, dear. (*He pushes a chair forward from the wall to where she stands, near the smaller writing table. She sits down; and he goes to the armchair, into which he throws himself*). I dont know how Barbara will take it. Ever since they made her a major in the Salvation Army she has developed a propensity to have her own way and order people about which quite cows me sometimes. It's not ladylike: I'm sure I dont know where she picked it up. Anyhow, Barbara shant bully me; but still it's just as well that your father should be here before she has time to refuse to meet him or make a fuss. Dont look nervous, Stephen: it will only encourage Barbara to make difficulties. *I* am nervous enough, goodness knows; but I dont shew it.

(*Sarah and Barbara come in with their respective young men, Charles Lomax and Adolphus Cusins. Sarah is slender, bored, and mundane. Barbara is robuster, jollier, much more energetic. Sarah is fashionably dressed: Barbara is in Salvation Army uniform. Lomax, a young man about town, is like many other young men about town. He is afflicted with a frivolous sense of humor which plunges him at the most inopportune moments into paroxysms of imperfectly suppressed laughter. Cusins is a spectacled student. slight, thin haired, and sweet voiced, with a more complex form of Lomax's complaint. His sense of humor is intellectual and subtle, and is complicated by an appalling temper. The lifelong struggle of a benevolent temperament and a high conscience against impulses of inhuman ridicule and fierce impatience has set up a chronic strain which has visibly wrecked his constitution. He is a most implacable, determined, tenacious, intolerant person who by mere force of character presents himself as—and indeed actually is—considerate, gentle, explanatory, even mild and apolo-*

*getic, capable possibly of murder, but not of cruelty or coarseness.
By the operation of some instinct which is not merciful enough
to blind him with the illusions of love, he is obstinately bent on
marrying Barbara. Lomax likes Sarah and thinks it will be rather
a lark to marry her. Consequently he has not attempted to resist
Lady Britomart's arrangements to that end.*

*All four look as if they had been having a good deal of fun in the
drawing room. The girls enter first, leaving the swains outside.
Sarah comes to the settee. Barbara comes in after her and stops at
the door).*

BARBARA. Are Cholly and Dolly to come in?

LADY BRITOMART (*forcibly*). Barbara: I will not have Charles
called Cholly: the vulgarity of it positively makes me ill.

BARBARA. It's all right, mother: Cholly is quite correct nowadays.
Are they to come in?

LADY BRITOMART. Yes, if they will behave themselves.

BARBARA (*through the door*). Come in, Dolly; and behave yourself.

(*Barbara comes to her mother's writing table. Cusins enters smiling, and wanders towards Lady Britomart.*)

SARAH (*calling*). Come in, Cholly. (*Lomax enters, controlling his
features very imperfectly, and places himself vaguely between
Sarah and Barbara*).

LADY BRITOMART (*peremptorily*). Sit down, all of you. (*They
sit. Cusins crosses to the window and seats himself there. Lomax
takes a chair. Barbara sits at the writing table and Sarah on the
settee*). I dont in the least know what you are laughing at, Adolphus.
I am surprised at you, though I expected nothing better from Charles
Lomax.

CUSINS (*in a remarkably gentle voice*). Barbara has been trying
to teach me the West Ham Salvation March.

LADY BRITOMART. I see nothing to laugh at in that; nor should
you if you are really converted.

CUSINS (*sweetly*). You were not present. It was really funny, I
believe.

LOMAX. Ripping.

LADY BRITOMART. Be quiet, Charles. Now listen to me, children.
Your father is coming here this evening.

(*General stupefaction. Lomax, Sarah, and Barbara rise: Sarah scared, and Barbara amused and expectant*).

LOMAX (*remonstrating*). Oh I say!

LADY BRITOMART. You are not called on to say anything, Charles.

SARAH. Are you serious, mother?

LADY BRITOMART. Of course I am serious. It is on your account, Sarah, and also on Charles's. (*Silence. Sarah sits, with a shrug. Charles looks painfully unworthy.*) I hope you are not going to object, Barbara.

BARBARA. I! why should I? My father has a soul to be saved like anyone else. He's quite welcome as far as I am concerned. (*She sits on the table, and softly whistles "Onward, Christian Soldiers"*).

LOMAX (*still remonstrant*). But really, dont you know! Oh I say!

LADY BRITOMART (*frigidly*). What do you wish to convey, Charles?

LOMAX. Well, you must admit that this is a bit thick.

LADY BRITOMART (*turning with ominous suavity to Cusins*): Adolphus: you are a professor of Greek. Can you translate Charles Lomax's remarks into reputable English for us?

CUSINS (*cautiously*). If I may say so, Lady Brit, I think Charles has rather happily expressed what we all feel. Homer, speaking of Autolycus, uses the same phrase. πνκινου δομου ελθειν means a bit thick.

LOMAX (*handsomely*). Not that I mind, you know, if Sarah dont. (*He sits*).

LADY BRITOMART (*crushingly*). Thank you. Have I *your* permis- Adolphus, to invite my own husband to my own house?

CUSINS (*gallantly*). You have my unhesitating support in everything you do.

LADY BRITOMART. Tush! Sarah: have you nothing to say?

SARAH. Do you mean that he is coming regularly to live here?

LADY BRITOMART. Certainly not. The spare room is ready for him if he likes to stay for a day or two and see a little more of you; but there are limits.

SARAH. Well, he cant eat us, I suppose. *I* dont mind.

LOMAX (*chuckling*). I wonder how the old man will take it.

LADY BRITOMART. Much as the old woman will, no doubt, Charles.

LOMAX (*abashed*). I didnt mean—at least—

LADY BRITOMART. You didnt *think,* Charles. You never do; and the result is, you never mean anything. And now please attend to me, children. Your father will be quite a stranger to us.

LOMAX. I suppose he hasnt seen Sarah since she was a little kid.

LADY BRITOMART. Not since she was a little kid, Charles, as you express it with that elegance of diction and refinement of thought that seem never to desert you. Accordingly—er—(*impatiently*) Now I have forgotten what I was going to say. That comes of your provoking me to be sarcastic, Charles. Adolphus: will you kindly tell me where I was.

CUSINS (*sweetly*). You were saying that as Mr Undershaft has not seen his children since they were babies, he will form his opinion of the way you have brought them up from their behavior tonight, and that therefore you wish us all to be particularly careful to conduct ourselves well, especially Charles.

LADY BRITOMART (*with emphatic approval*). Precisely.

LOMAX. Look here, Dolly: Lady Brit didnt say that.

LADY BRITOMART (*vehemently*). I did, Charles. Adolphus's recollection is perfectly correct. It is most important that you should be good; and I do beg you for once not to pair off into opposite corners and giggle and whisper while I am speaking to your father.

BARBARA. All right, mother. We'll do you credit. (*She comes off the table, and sits in her chair with ladylike elegance*).

LADY BRITOMART. Remember, Charles, that Sarah will want to feel proud of you instead of ashamed of you.

LOMAX. Oh I say! theres nothing to be exactly proud of, dont you know.

LADY BRITOMART. Well, try and look as if there was.

(*Morrison, pale and dismayed, breaks into the room in unconcealed disorder.*)

MORRISON. Might I speak a word to you, my lady?

LADY BRITOMART. Nonsense! Shew him up.

MORRISON. Yes, my lady. (*He goes*).

LOMAX. Does Morrison know who it is?

LADY BRITOMART. Of course. Morrison has always been with us.

LOMAX. It must be a regular corker for him, dont you know.

LADY BRITOMART. Is this a moment to get on my nerves, Charles, with your outrageous expressions?

LOMAX. But this is something out of the ordinary, really—

MORRISON (*at the door*). The—er—Mr Undershaft. (*He retreats in confusion*).

(*Andrew Undershaft comes in. All rise. Lady Britomart meets him in the middle of the room behind the settee. Andrew is, on the surface, a stoutish, easygoing elderly man, with kindly patient manners, and an engaging simplicity of character. But he has a watchful, deliberate, waiting, listening face, and formidable reserves of power, both bodily and mental, in his capacious chest and long head. His gentleness is partly that of a strong man who has learnt by experience that his natural grip hurts ordinary people unless he handles them very carefully, and partly the mellowness of age and success. He is also a little shy in his present very delicate situation*).

LADY BRITOMART. Good evening, Andrew.

UNDERSHAFT. How d'ye do, my dear.

LADY BRITOMART. You look a good deal older.

UNDERSHAFT (*apologetically*). I *am* somewhat older. (*Taking her hand with a touch of courtship*) Time has stood still with you.

LADY BRITOMART (*throwing away his hand*). Rubbish! This is your family.

UNDERSHAFT (*surprised*). Is it so large? I am sorry to say my memory is failing very badly in some things. (*He offers his hand with paternal kindness to Lomax*).

LOMAX (*jerkily shaking his hand*). Ahdedoo.

UNDERSHAFT. I can see you are my eldest. I am very glad to meet you again, my boy.

LOMAX (*remonstrating*). No, but look here dont you know— (*Overcome*) Oh I say!

LADY BRITOMART (*recovering from momentary speechlessness*). Andrew: do you mean to say that you dont remember how many children you have?

UNDERSHAFT. Well, I am afraid I—. They have grown so much—er. Am I making any ridiculous mistake? I may as well confess: I recollect only one son. But so many things have happened since, of course—er—

LADY BRITOMART (*decisively*). Andrew: you are talking nonsense. Of course you have only one son.

UNDERSHAFT. Perhaps you will be good enough to introduce me, my dear.

LADY BRITOMART. That is Charles Lomax, who is engaged to Sarah.

UNDERSHAFT. My dear sir, I beg your pardon.

LOMAX. Notatall. Delighted, I assure you.

LADY BRITOMART. This is Stephen.

UNDERSHAFT (*bowing*). Happy to make your acquaintance, Mr Stephen. Then (*going to Cusins*) *you* must be my son. (*Taking Cusins' hands in his*) How are you, my young friend? (*To Lady Britomart*) He is very like you, my love.

CUSINS. You flatter me, Mr Undershaft. My name is Cusins: engaged to Barbara. (*Very explicitly*) That is Major Barbara Undershaft, of the Salvation Army. That is Sarah, your second daughter. This is Stephen Undershaft, your son.

UNDERSHAFT. My dear Stephen, I *beg* your pardon.

STEPHEN. Not at all.

UNDERSHAFT. Mr Cusins: I am much indebted to you for explaining so precisely. (*Turning to Sarah*) Barbara, my dear—

SARAH (*prompting him*). Sarah.

UNDERSHAFT. Sarah, of course. (*They shake hands. He goes over to Barbara*) Barbara—I am right this time, I hope?

BARBARA. Quite right. (*They shake hands*).

LADY BRITOMART (*resuming command*). Sit down, all of you. Sit down, Andrew. (*She comes forward and sits on the settee. Cusins also brings his chair forward on her left. Barbara and Stephen resume their seats. Lomax gives his chair to Sarah and goes for another*).

UNDERSHAFT. Thank you, my love.

LOMAX (*conversationally, as he brings a chair forward between the writing table and the settee, and offers it to Undershaft*). Takes you some time to find out exactly where you are, dont it?

UNDERSHAFT (*accepting the chair, but remaining standing*). That is not what embarrasses me, Mr Lomax. My difficulty is that if I play the part of a father, I shall produce the effect of an intrusive stranger; and if I play the part of a discreet stranger, I may appear a callous father.

LADY BRITOMART. There is no need for you to play any part at all, Andrew. You had much better be sincere and natural.

UNDERSHAFT (*submissively*). Yes, my dear: I daresay that will be best. (*He sits down comfortably*). Well, here I am. Now what can I do for you all?

LADY BRITOMART. You need not do anything, Andrew. You are one of the family. You can sit with us and enjoy yourself.

(*A painfully conscious pause. Barbara makes a face at Lomax, whose too long suppressed mirth immediately explodes in agonized neighings*).

LADY BRITOMART (*outraged*). Charles Lomax: if you can behave yourself, behave yourself. If not, leave the room.

LOMAX. I'm awfully sorry, Lady Brit; but really you know, upon my soul! (*He sits on the settee between Lady Britomart and Undershaft, quite overcome*).

BARBARA. Why dont you laugh if you want to, Cholly? It's good for your inside.

LADY BRITOMART. Barbara: you have had the education of a lady. Please let your father see that; and dont talk like a street girl.

UNDERSHAFT. Never mind me, my dear. As you know, I am not a gentleman; and I was never educated.

LOMAX (*encouragingly*). Nobody'd know it, I assure you. You look all right, you know.

CUSINS. Let me advise you to study Greek, Mr. Undershaft. Greek scholars are privileged men. Few of them know Greek; and none of them know anything else; but their position is unchallengeable. Other languages are the qualifications of waiters and commercial travelers: Greek is to a man of position what the hallmark is to silver.

BARBARA. Dolly: dont be insincere. Cholly: fetch your concertina and play something for us.

LOMAX (*jumps up eagerly, but checks himself to remark doubtfully to Undershaft*). Perhaps that sort of thing isnt in your line, eh?

UNDERSHAFT. I am particularly fond of music.

LOMAX (*delighted*). Are you? Then I'll get it. (*He goes upstairs for the instrument*).

UNDERSHAFT. Do you play, Barbara?

BARBARA. Only the tambourine. But Cholly's teaching me the concertina.

UNDERSHAFT. Is Cholly also a member of the Salvation Army?

BARBARA. No: he says it's bad form to be a dissenter. But I dont despair of Cholly. I made him come yesterday to a meeting at the dock gates, and take the collection in his hat.

UNDERSHAFT (*looks whimsically at his wife*). !!

LADY BRITOMART. It is not my doing, Andrew. Barbara is old enough to take her own way. She has no father to advise her.

BARBABA. Oh yes she has. There are no orphans in the Salvation Army.

UNDERSHAFT. Your father there has a great many children and plenty of experience, eh?

BARBARA (*looking at him with quick interest and nodding*). Just so. How did *you* come to understand that? (*Lomax is heard at the door trying the concertina*).

LADY BRITOMART. Come in, Charles. Play us something at once.

LOMAX. Righto! (*He sits down in his former place, and preludes*).

UNDERSHAFT. One moment, Mr Lomax. I am rather interested in the Salvation Army. Its motto might be my own: Blood and Fire.

LOMAX (*shocked*). But not your sort of blood and fire, you know.

UNDERSHAFT. My sort of blood cleanses: my sort of fire purifies.

BARBARA. So do ours. Come down tomorrow to my shelter—the West Ham shelter—and see what we're doing. We're going to march to a great meeting in the Assembly Hall at Mile End. Come and see the shelter and then march with us: it will do you a lot of good. Can you play anything?

UNDERSHAFT. In my youth I earned pennies, and even shillings occasionally, in the streets and in public house parlors by my natural talent for stepdancing. Later on, I became a member of the Undershaft orchestral society, and performed passably on the tenor trombone.

LOMAX (*scandalized—putting down the concertina*). Oh I say!

BARBARA. Many a sinner has played himself into heaven on the trombone, thanks to the Army.

LOMAX (*to Barbara, still rather shocked*). Yes; but what about the cannon business, dont you know? (*To Undershaft*) Getting into heaven is not exactly in your line, is it?

LADY BRITOMART. Charles!!!

LOMAX. Well; but it stands to reason, dont it? The cannon business may be necessary and all that: we cant get on without cannons;

but it isn't right, you know. On the other hand, there may be a certain amount of tosh about the Salvation Army—I belong to the Established Church myself—but still you cant deny that it's religion; and you cant go against religion, can you? At least unless youre downright immoral, dont you know.

UNDERSHAFT. You hardly appreciate my position, Mr Lomax—

LOMAX (*hastily*). I'm not saying anything against you personally—

UNDERSHAFT. Quite so, quite so. But consider for a moment. Here I am, a profiteer in mutilation and murder. I find myself in a specially amiable humor just now because, this morning, down at the foundry, we blew twenty-seven dummy soldiers into fragments with a gun which formerly destroyed only thirteen.

LOMAX (*leniently*). Well, the more destructive war becomes, the sooner it will be abolished, eh?

UNDERSHAFT. Not at all. The more destructive war becomes the more fascinating we find it. No, Mr Lomax: I am obliged to you for making the usual excuse for my trade; but I am not ashamed of it. I am not one of those men who keep their morals and their business in watertight compartments. All the spare money my trade rivals spend on hospitals, cathedrals, and other receptacles for conscience money, I devote to experiments and researches in improved methods of destroying life and property. I have always done so; and I always shall. Therefore your Christmas card moralities of peace on earth and goodwill among men are of no use to me. Your Christianity, which enjoins you to resist not evil, and to turn the other cheek, would make me a bankrupt. *My* morality—*my* religion—must have a place for cannons and torpedoes in it.

STEPHEN (*coldly—almost sullenly*). You speak as if there were a dozen moralities and religions to choose from, instead of one true morality and one true religion.

UNDERSHAFT. For me there is only one true morality; but it might not fit you, as you do not manufacture aerial battleships. There is only one true morality for every man; but every man has not the same true morality.

LOMAX (*overtaxed*). Would you mind saying that again? I didnt quite follow it.

CUSINS. It's quite simple. As Euripides says, one man's meat is another man's poison morally as well as physically.

UNDERSHAFT. Precisely.

LOMAX. Oh, *that!* Yes, yes, yes. True. True.

STEPHEN. In other words, some men are honest and some are scoundrels.

BARBARA. Bosh! There are no scoundrels.

UNDERSHAFT. Indeed? Are there any good men?

BARBARA. No. Not one. There are neither good men nor scoundrels: there are just children of one Father; and the sooner they stop calling one another names the better. You neednt talk to me: I know them. Ive had scores of them through my hands: scoundrels, criminals, infidels, philanthropists, missionaries, county councillors, all sorts. Theyre all just the same sort of sinner; and theres the same salvation ready for them all.

UNDERSHAFT. May I ask have you ever saved a maker of cannons?

BARBARA. No. Will you let me try?

UNDERSHAFT. Well, I will make a bargain with you. If I go to see you tomorrow in your Salvation Shelter, will you come the day after to see me in my cannon works?

BARBARA. Take care. It may end in your giving up the cannons for the sake of the Salvation Army.

UNDERSHAFT. Are you sure it will not end in your giving up the Salvation Army for the sake of the cannons?

BARBARA. I will take my chance of that.

UNDERSHAFT. And I will take my chance of the other. (*They shake hands on it*). Where is your shelter?

BARBARA. In the West Ham. At the sign of the cross. Ask anybody in Canning Town. Where are your works?

UNDERSHAFT. In Perivale St Andrews. At the sign of the sword. Ask anybody in Europe.

LOMAX. Hadnt I better play something?

BARBARA. Yes. Give us Onward, Christian Soldiers.

LOMAX. Well, thats rather a strong order to begin with, dont you know. Suppose I sing Thou't passing hence, my brother. It's much the same tune.

BARBARA. It's too melancholy. You get saved, Cholly; and youll pass hence, my brother, without making such a fuss about it.

LADY BRITOMART. Really, Barbara, you go on as if religion were a pleasant subject. Do have some sense of propriety.

UNDERSHAFT. I do not find it an unpleasant subject, my dear. It is the only one that capable people really care for.

LADY BRITOMART (*looking at her watch*). Well, if you are determined to have it, I insist on having it in a proper and respectable way. Charles: ring for prayers.

(*General amazement. Stephen rises in dismay*).

LOMAX (*rising*). Oh I say!

UNDERSHAFT. (*rising*). I am afraid I must be going.

LADY BRITOMART. You cannot go now, Andrew: it would be most improper. Sit down. What will the servants think?

UNDERSHAFT. My dear: I have conscientious scruples. May I suggest a compromise? If Barbara will conduct a little service in the drawing room, with Mr Lomax as organist, I will attend it willingly. I will even take part, if a trombone can be procured.

LADY BRITOMART. Dont mock, Andrew.

UNDERSHAFT (*shocked—to Barbara*). You dont think I am mocking, my love, I hope.

BARBARA. No, of course not; and it wouldnt matter if you were: half the Army came to their first meeting for a lark. (*Rising*) Come along. (*She throws her arm round her father and sweeps him out, calling to the others from the threshold*) Come, Dolly. Come Cholly.

(*Cusins rises*).

LADY BRITOMART. I will not be disobeyed by everybody. Adolphus: sit down. (*He does not*). Charles: you may go. You are not fit for prayers: you cannot keep your countenance.

LOMAX. Oh I say! (*He goes out*).

LADY BRITOMART (*continuing*). But you, Adolphus, can behave yourself if you choose to. I insist on your staying.

CUSINS. My dear Lady Brit: there are things in the family prayer book that I couldnt bear to hear you say.

LADY BRITOMART. What things, pray?

CUSINS. Well, you would have to say before all the servants that we have done things we ought not to have done, and left undone things we ought to have done, and that there is no health in us. I cannot bear to hear you doing yourself such an injustice, and Barbara such an injustice. As for myself, I flatly deny it: I have done my best. I shouldnt dare to marry Barbara—I couldnt look you in the face—

if it were true. So I must go to the drawing room.

LADY BRITOMART (*offended*). Well, go. (*He starts for the door*). And remember this, Adolphus (*he turns to listen*): I have a very strong suspicion that you went to the Salvation Army to worship Barbara and nothing else. And I quite appreciate the very clever way in which you systematically humbug me. I have found you out. Take care Barbara doesnt. Thats all.

CUSINS (*with unruffled sweetness*). Dont tell on me. (*He steals out*).

LADY BRITOMART. Sarah: if you want to go, go. Anything's better than to sit there as if you wished you were a thousand miles away.

SARAH (*languidly*). Very well, mamma. (*She goes*).

(*Lady Britomart, with a sudden flounce, gives way to a little gust of tears*).

STEPHEN (*going to her*). Mother: whats the matter?

LADY BRITOMART (*swishing away her tears with her handkerchief*). Nothing. Foolishness. You can go with him, too, if you like, and leave me with the servants.

STEPHEN. Oh, you mustnt think that, mother. I—I dont like him.

LADY BRITOMART. The others do. That is the injustice of a woman's lot. A woman has to bring up her children; and that means to restrain them, to deny them things they want, to set them tasks, to punish them when they do wrong, to do all the unpleasant things. And then the father, who has nothing to do but pet them and spoil them, comes in when all her work is done and steals their affection from her.

STEPHEN. He has not stolen our affection from you. It is only curiosity.

LADY BRITOMART (*violently*). I won't be consoled, Stephen. There is nothing the matter with me. (*She rises and goes towards the door*).

STEPHEN. Where are you going, mother?

LADY BRITOMART. To the drawing room, of course. (*She goes out. Onward, Christian Soldiers, on the concertina, with tambourine accompaniment, is heard when the door opens*). Are you coming. Stephen?

STEPHEN. No. Certainly not. (*She goes. He sits down on the settee, with compressed lips and an expression of strong dislike*).

act two

The yard of the West Ham shelter of the Salvation Army is a cold place on a January morning. The building itself, an old warehouse, is newly white-washed. Its gabled end projects into the yard in the middle, with a door on the ground floor, and another in the loft above it without any balcony or ladder, but wtih a pulley rigged over it for hoisting sacks. Those who come from this central gable end into the yard have the gateway leading to the street on their left, with a stone horse-trough just beyond it, and, on the right, a penthouse shielding a table from the weather. There are forms at the table; and on them are seated a man and a woman, both much down on their luck, finishing a meal of bread (one thick slice each, with margarine and golden syrup) and diluted milk.

The man, a workman out of employment, is young, agile, a talker, a poser, sharp enough to be capable of anything in reason except honesty or altruistic considerations of any kind. The woman is a commonplace old bundle of poverty and hard-worn humanity. She looks sixty and probably is forty-five. If they were rich people, gloved and muffed and well wrapped up in furs and overcoats, they would be numbed and miserable; for it is a grindingly cold raw January day; and a glance at the background of grimy warehouses and leaden sky visible over the whitewashed walls of the yard would drive any idle rich person straight to the Mediterranean. But these two, being no more troubled with visions of the Mediterranean than of the moon, and being compelled to keep more of their clothes in the pawnshop, and less on their persons, in winter than in summer, are not depressed by the cold: rather are they stung into vivacity, to which their meal has just now given an almost jolly turn. The man takes a pull at his mug, and then gets up and moves about the yard with his hands deep in his pockets, occasionally break-ing into a stepdance.

THE WOMAN. Feel better arter your meal, sir?

THE MAN. No. Call that a meal! Good enough for you, praps; but wot is it to me, an intelligent workin man.

THE WOMAN. Workin man! What are you?

THE MAN. Painter.

THE WOMAN (*sceptically*). Yus, I dessay.

THE MAN. Yus, you dessay! I know. Every loafer that cant do nothink calls isself a painter. Well, I'm a real painter: grainer, finisher, thirty-eight bob a week when I can get it.

THE WOMAN. Then why dont you go and get it?

THE MAN. I'll tell you why. Fust: I'm intelligent—fffff! it's rotten cold here (*he dances a step or two*)—yes: intelligent beyond the station o life into which it has pleased the capitalists to call me; and they dont like a man that sees through em. Second, an intelligent bein needs a doo share of appiness; so I drink somethink cruel when I get the chawnce. Third, I stand by my class and do as little as I can so's to leave arf the job for me fellow workers. Fourth, I'm fly enough to know wots inside the law and wots outside it; and inside it I do as the capitalists do: pinch wot I can lay me ands on. In a proper state of society I am sober, industrious and honest: in Rome, so to speak, I do as the Romans do. Wots the consequence? When trade is bad—and it's rotten bad just now—and the employers az to sack arf their men, they generally start on me.

THE WOMAN. Whats your name?

THE MAN. Price. Bronterre O'Brien Price. Usually called Snobby Price, for short.

THE WOMAN. Snobby's a carpenter, aint it? You said you was a painter.

PRICE. Not that kind of a snob, but the genteel sort. I'm too uppish, owing to my intelligence and my father being a Charist and a reading, thinking man: a stationer, too. I'm none of your common hewers of wood and drawers of water; and dont you forget it. (*He returns to his seat at the table, and takes up his mug*). Wots your name?

THE WOMAN. Rummy Mitchens, sir.

PRICE (*quaffing the remains of his milk to her*). Your elth, Miss Mitchens.

RUMMY (*correcting him*). Missis Mitchens.

PRICE. Wot! Oh Rummy, Rummy! Respectable married woman, Rummy, gittin rescued by the Salvation Army by pretendin to be a bad un. Same old game!

RUMMY. What am I to do? I cant starve. Them Salvation lasses is dear good girls; but the better you are, the worse they likes to think you were before they rescued you. Why shouldnt they av a bit o credit, poor loves? theyre worn to rags by their work. And where would they get the money to rescue us if we was to let on we're no worse than other people? You know what ladies and gentlemen are.

PRICE. Thievin swine! Wish I ad their job, Rummy, all the same. Wot does Rummy stand for? Pet name praps?

RUMMY. Short for Romola.

PRICE. For wot!?

RUMMY. Romola. It was out of a new book. Somebody me mother wanted me to grow up like.

PRICE. We're companions in misfortune, Rummy. Both on us got names that nobody cawnt pronounce. Consequently I'm Snobby and youre Rummy because Bill and Sally wasnt good enough for our parents. Such is life!

RUMMY. Who saved you, Mr Price? Was it Major Barbara?

PRICE. No: I come here on my own. I'm going to be Bronterre O'Brien Price, the converted painter. I know wot they like. I'll tell em how I blasphemed and gambled and wopped my poor old mother—

RUMMY (*shocked*). Used you to beat your mother?

PRICE. Not likely. She used to beat me. No matter: you come and listen to the converted painter, and youll hear how she was a pious woman that taught me me prayers at er knee, an how I used to come home drunk and drag her out o bed be er snow white airs, an lam into er with the poker.

RUMMY. Thats whats so unfair to us women. Your confessions is jus as big lies as ours: you dont tell what you really done no more than us; but you men can tell your lies right out at the meetins and be made much of for it; while the sort o confessions we az to make az to be wispered to one lady at a time. It aint right, spite of all their piety.

PRICE. Right! Do you spose the Army 'd be allowed if it went and did right? Not much. It combs our air and makes us good little blokes to be robbed and put upon. But I'll play the game as good as any of em. I'll see sombody struck by lightnin, or hear a voice sayin "Snobby Price: where will you spend eternity?" I'll av a time of it, I tell you.

RUMMY. You wont be let drink, though.

PRICE. I'll take it out in gorspellin, then. I dont want to drink if I can get fun enough any other way.

(*Jenny Hill, a pale, overwrought, pretty Salvation lass of 18, comes in through the yard gate, leading Peter Shirley, a half hardened, half worn-out elderly man, weak with hunger*).

JENNY (*supporting him*). Come! pluck up. I'll get you something to eat. Youll be all right then.

PRICE (*rising and hurrying officiously to take the old man off*

Jenny's hands). Poor old man! Cheer up, brother: youll find rest and peace and appiness ere. Hurry up with the food, miss: e's fair done. (*Jenny hurries into the shelter*). Ere, buck up, daddy! she's fetchin y'a thick slice of breadn treacle, an a mug o skyblue. (*He seats him at the corner of the table*).

RUMMY (*gaily*). Keep up your old art! Never say die!

SHIRLEY. I'm not an old man. I'm only 46. I'm as good as ever I was. The grey patch come in my hair before I was thirty. All it wants is three pennorth o hair dye: am I to be turned on the streets to starve for it? Holy God! Ive worked ten to twelve hours a day since I was thirteen, and paid my way all through; and now am I to be thrown into the gutter and my job given to a young man that can do it no better than me because Ive black hair that goes white at the first change?

PRICE (*cheerfully*). No good jawrin about it. Youre ony a jumped-up, jerked-off, orspittle-turned-out incurable of an ole workin man: who cares about you? Eh? Make the thievin swine give you a meal: theyve stole many a one from you. Get a bit o your own back. (*Jenny returns with the usual meal*). There you are, brother. Awsk a blessin an tuck that into you.

SHIRLEY (*looking at it ravenously but not touching it, and crying like a child*). I never took anything before.

JENNY (*petting him*). Come, come! the Lord sends it to you: he wasnt above taking bread from his friends; and why should you be? Besides, when we find you a job you can pay us for it if you like.

SHIRLEY (*eagerly*). Yes, yes: thats true. I can pay you back: it's only a loan. (*Shivering*) Oh Lord! oh Lord! (*He turns to the table and attacks the meal ravenously*).

JENNY. Well, Rummy, are you more comfortable now?

RUMMY. God bless you, lovey! youve fed my body and saved my soul, havnt you? (*Jenny, touched, kisses her*). Sit down and rest a bit: you must be ready to drop.

JENNY. Ive been going hard since morning. But theres more work than we can do. I musnt stop.

RUMMY. Try a prayer for just two minutes. Youll work all the better after.

JENNY (*her eyes lighting up*). Oh isnt it wonderful how a few minutes prayer revives you! I was quite lightheaded at twelve o'clock, I was so tired; but Major Barbara just sent me to pray for five min-

utes; and I was able to go on as if I had only just begun. (*To Price*)
Did you have a piece of bread?

PRICE (*with unction*). Yes, miss; but Ive got the piece that I
value more; and thats the peace that passeth hall hannerstennin.

RUMMY (*fervently*). Glory Hallelujah!

(*Bill Walker, a rough customer of about 25, appears at the yard
gate and looks malevolently at Jenny*).

JENNY. That makes me so happy. When you say that, I feel
wicked for loitering here. I must get to work again.

(*She is hurrying to the shelter, when the new-comer moves
quickly up to the door and intercepts her. His manner is so
threatening that she retreats as he comes at her truculently, driving her down the yard*).

BILL. Aw knaow you. Youre the one that took awy maw girl.
Youre the one that set er agen me. Well, I'm gowin to ev er aht.
Not that Aw care a carse for er or you: see? Bat Aw'll let er
knaow; and Aw'll let *you* knaow. Aw'm gowing to give her a doin
thatll teach er to cat awy from me. Nah in wiv you and tell er to
cam aht afore Aw cam in and kick er aht. Tell er Bill Walker wants
er. She'll knaow wot thet means; and if she keeps me witin itll be
worse. You stop to jawr beck at me; and Aw'll stawt on you: d'ye
eah? Theres your wy. In you gow. (*He takes her by the arm and
slings her towards the door of the shelter. She falls on her hand and
knee. Rummy helps her up again*).

PRICE (*rising, and venturing irresolutely towards Bill*). Easy there,
mate. She aint doin you no arm.

BILL. Oo are you callin mite? (*Standing over him threateningly*)
Youre gowin to stend ap fer er, aw yer? Put ap your ends.

RUMMY (*running indignantly to him to scold him*). Oh, you great
brute— (*He instantly swings his left hand back against her face.
She screams and reels back to the trough, where she sits down, covering her bruised face with her hands and rocking herself and moaning
with pain*).

JENNY (*going to her*). Oh, God forgive you! How could you
strike an old woman like that?

BILL (*seizing her by the hair so violently that she also screams,
and tearing her away from the old woman*). You Gawd forgimme
again an Aw'll Gawd forgive you one on the jawr thetll stop you

pryin for a week. (*Holding her and turning fiercely on Price*) Ev you ennything to sy agen it?

PRICE (*intimidated*). No, matey: she aint anything to do with me.

BILL. Good job for you! Aw'd pat two meals into you and fawt you with one finger arter, you stawved cur. (*To Jenny*) Nah are you gowin to fetch aht Mog Ebbijem; or em Aw to knock your fice off you and fetch her meself?

JENNY (*writhing in his grasp*). Oh please someone go in and tell Major Barbara— (*She screams again as he wrenches her head down; and Price and Rummy flee into the shelter*).

BILL. You want to gow in and tell your Mijor of me, do you?

JENNY. Oh please dont drag my hair. Let me go.

BILL. Do you or downt you? (*She stifles a scream*). Yus or nao?

JENNY. God give me strength—

BILL (*striking her with his fist in the face*). Gow an shaow her thet, and tell her if she wants one lawk it to cam and interfere with me. (*Jenny, crying with pain, goes into the shed. He goes to the form and addresses the old man*). Eah: finish your mess; an git aht o maw wy.

SHIRLEY (*springing up and facing him fiercely, with the mug in his hand*). You take a liberty with me, and I'll smash you over the face with the mug and cut your eye out. Aint you satisfied—young whelps like you—with takin the bread out o the mouths of your elders that have brought you up and slaved for you, but you must come shovin and cheekin and bullyin in here, where the bread o charity is sickenin in our stummicks?

BILL (*contemptuously, but backing a little*). Wot good are you, you aold palsy mag? Wot good are you?

SHIRLEY. As good as you and better. I'll do a day's work agen you or any fat young soaker of your age. Go and take my job at Horrockses, where I worked for ten year. They want young men there: they cant afford to keep men over forty-five. Theyre very sorry—give you a character and happy to help you to get anything suited to your years—sure a steady man wont be long out of a job. Well, yet em try *you*. Theyll find the differ. What do *you* know? Not as much as how to beeyave yourself—layin your dirty fist across the mouth of a respectable woman!

BILL. Downt provowk me to ly it acrost yours: d'ye eah?

SHIRLEY (*with blighting contempt*). Yes: you like an old man to hit, dont you, when youve finished with the women. I aint seen you hit a young one yet.

BILL (*stung*). You loy, you aold soupkitchener, you. There was a yang menn eah. Did Aw offer to itt him or did Aw not?

SHIRLEY. Was he starvin or was he not? Was he a man or only a crosseyed thief an a loafer? Would you hit my son-in-law's brother?

BILL. Oo's ee?

SHIRLEY. Todger Fairmile o Balls Pond. Him that won £20 off the Japanese wrastler at the music hall by standin out 17 minutes 4 seconds agen him.

BILL (*sullenly*). Aw'm nao music awl wrastler. Ken he box?

SHIRLEY. Yes: an you cant.

BILL. Wot! Aw cawnt, cawnt Aw? Wots thet you sy (*threatening him*)?

SHIRLEY (*not budging an inch*). Will you box Todger Fairmile if I put him on to you? Say the word.

BILL (*subsiding with a slouch*). Aw'll stend ap to enny menn alawv, if he was ten Todger Fairmawls. But Aw dont set ap to be a perfeshnal.

SHIRLEY (*looking down on him with unfathomable disdain*). You box! Slap an old woman with the back o your hand! You hadn't even the sense to hit her where a magistrate couldnt see the mark of it, you silly young lump of conceit and ignorance. Hit a girl in the jaw and ony make her cry! If Todger Fairmile'd done it, she wouldnt a got up inside o ten minutes, no more than you would if he got on to you. Yah! I'd set about you myself if I had a week's feedin in me instead o two months' starvation. (*He turns his back on him and sits down moodily at the table*).

BILL (*following him and stooping over him to drive the taunt in*). You loy! youve the bread and treacle in you that you cam eah to beg.

SHIRLEY (*bursting into tears*). Oh God! It's true: I'm only an old pauper on the scrap heap. (*Furiously*) But youll come to it yourself; and then youll know. Youll come to it sooner than a teetotaller like me, fillin yourself with gin at this hour o the mornin!

BILL. Aw'm nao gin drinker, you oald lawr; bat wen Aw want to give my girl a bloomin good awdin Aw lawk to ev a bit o devil in me: see? An eah Aw emm, talkin to a rotten aold blawter like you sted o givin her wot for. (*Working himself into a rage*) Aw'm gowin in there to fetch her aht. (*He makes vengefully for the shelter door*).

SHIRLEY. Youre going to the station on a stretcher, more likely; and theyll take the gin and the devil out of you there when they get you inside. You mind what youre about: the major here is the Earl o Stevenage's granddaughter.

BILL (*checked*). Garn!

SHIRLEY. Youll see.

BILL (*his resolution oozing*). Well, Aw aint dan nathin to er.

SHIRLEY. Spose she said you did! who'd believe you?

BILL (*very uneasy, skulking back to the corner of the penthouse*). Gawd! theres no jastice in this cantry. To think wot them people can do! Aw'm as good as er.

SHIRLEY. Tell her so. It's just what a fool like you would do.

(*Barbara, brisk and businesslike, comes from the shelter with a note book, and addresses herself to Shirley. Bill, cowed, sits down in the corner on a form, and turns his back on them*).

BARBARA. Good morning.

SHIRLEY (*standing up and taking off his hat*). Good morning, miss.

BARBARA. Sit down: make yourself at home. (*He hesitates, but she puts a friendly hand on his shoulder and makes him obey*). Now then! since youve made friends with us, we want to know all about you. Names and addresses and trades.

SHIRLEY. Peter Shirley. Fitter. Chucked out two months ago because I was too old.

BARBARA (*not at all surprised*). Youd pass still. Why didnt you dye your hair?

SHIRLEY. I did. Me age come out at a coroner's inquest on me daughter.

BARBARA. Steady?

SHIRLEY. Teetotaller. Never out of a job before. Good worker. And sent to the knackers like an old horse!

BARBARA. No matter: if you did your part God will do his.

SHIRLEY (*suddenly stubborn*). My religion's no concern of anybody but myself.

BARBARA (*guessing*). I know. Secularist?

SHIRLEY (*hotly*). Did I offer to deny it?

BARBARA. Why should you? My own father's a Secularist, I think. Our Father—yours and mine—fulfils himself in many ways; and I daresay he knew what he was about when he made a Secularist of you. So buck up, Peter! we can always find a job for a steady man like you. (*Shirley, disarmed and a little bewildered, touches his hat. She turns from him to Bill*). Whats your name?

BILL (*insolently*). Wots thet to you?

BARBARA (*calmly making a note*): Afraid to give his name. Any trade?

BILL. Oo's afride to give is nime? (*Doggedly, with a sense of heroically defying the House of Lords in the person of Lord Stevenage*) If you want to bring a chawge agen me, bring it. (*She waits, unruffled*). Moy nime's Bill Walker.

BARBARA (*as if the name were familiar: trying to remember how*). Bill Walker? (*Recollecting*) Oh, I know: youre the man that Jenny Hill was praying for inside just now. (*She enters his name in her note book*).

BILL. Oo's Jenny Ill? And wot call as she to pry for me?

BARBARA. I don't know. Perhaps it was you that cut her lip.

BILL (*defiantly*). Yus, it *was* me that cat her lip. Aw aint afride o *you*.

BARBARA. How could you be, since youre not afraid of God? Youre a brave man, Mr Walker. It takes some pluck to do *our* work here; but none of us dare lift our hand against a girl like that, for fear of her father in heaven.

BILL (*sullenly*). I want nan o your kentin jawr. I spowse you think Aw cam eah to beg from you, like this demmiged lot eah. Not me. Aw downt want your bread and scripe and ketlep. Aw dont blieve in your Gawd, no more than you do yourself.

BARBARA (*sunnily apologetic and ladylike, as on a new footing with him*). Oh, I beg your pardon for putting your name down, Mr Walker. I didnt understand. I'll strike it out.

BILL (*taking this as a slight, and deeply wounded by it*). Eah! you let maw nime alown. Aint it good enaff to be in your book?

BARBARA (*considering*). Well, you see, theres no use putting down your name unless I can do something for you, is there? Whats your trade?

BILL (*still staring*). Thets nao concern o yours.

BARBARA. Just so. (*Very businesslike*) I'll put you down as (*writing*) the man who—struck—poor little Jenny Hill—in the mouth.

BILL (*rising threateningly*). See eah. Awve ed enaff o this.

BARBARA (*quite sunny and fearless*). What did you come to us for?

BILL. Aw cam for maw gel, see? Aw cam to tike her aht o this and to brike er jawr for er.

BARBARA (*complacently*). You see I was right about your trade. (*Bill, on the point of retorting furiously, finds himself, to his great shame and terror, in danger of crying instead. He sits down again suddenly*). Whats her name?

BILL (*dogged*). Er nime's Mog Ebbijem: thets wot her nime is.

BARBARA. Mog Habbijam! Oh, she's gone to Canning Town, to our barracks there.

BILL (*fortified by his resentment of Mog's perfidy*). Is she? (*Vindictively*) Then Aw'm gowin to Kennintahn arter her. (*He crosses to the gate; hesitates; finally comes back at Barbara*). Are you loyin to me to git shat o me?

BARBARA. I dont want to get shut of you. I want to keep you here and save your soul. Youd better stay: youre going to have a bad time today, Bill.

BILL. Oo's gowin to give it to me? You, preps?

BARBARA. Someone you dont believe in. But youll be glad afterwards.

BILL (*slinking off*). Aw'll gow to Kennintahn to be aht o reach o your tangue. (*Suddenly turning on her with intense malice*) And if Aw downt fawnd Mog there, Aw'll cam beck and do two years for you, selp me Gawd if Aw downt!

BARBARA (*a shade kindlier, if possible*). It's no use, Bill. She's got another bloke.

BILL. Wot!

BARBARA. One of her own converts. He fell in love with her when he saw her with her soul saved, and her face clean, and her hair washed.

BILL (*surprised*). Wottud she wash it for, the carroty slat? It's red.

BARBARA. It's quite lovely now, because she wears a new look in her eyes with it. It's a pity youre too late. The new bloke has put your nose out of joint, Bill.

BILL. Aw'll put his nowse aht o joint for him. Not that Aw care a carse for er, mawned thet. But Aw'll teach her to drop me as if Aw was dirt. And Aw'll teach him to meddle with maw judy. Wots iz bleedin nime?

BARBARA. Sergeant Todger Fairmile.

SHIRLEY (*rising with grim joy*). I'll go with him, miss. I want to see them two meet. I'll take him to the infirmary when it's over.

BILL (*to Shirley, with undissembled misgiving*). Is thet im you was speakin on?

SHIRLEY. Thats him.

BILL. I'm that wrastled in the music awl?

SHIRLEY. The competitions at the National Sportin Club was worth nigh a hundred a year to him. He's gev em up now for religion; so he's a bit fresh for want of the exercise he was accustomed to. He'll be glad to see you. Come along.

BILL. Wots is wight?

SHIRLEY. Thirteen four. (*Bill's last hope expires*).

BARBARA. Go and talk to him, Bill. He'll convert you.

SHIRLEY. He'll convert your head into a mashed potato.

BILL (*sullenly*). Aw aint afride of im. Aw aint afride of ennybody. Bat e can lick me. She's dan me. (*He sits down moodily on the edge of the horse trough*).

SHIRLEY. You aint going. I thought not. (*He resumes his seat*).

BARBARA (*calling*). Jenny!

JENNY (*appearing at the shelter door with a plaster on the corner of her mouth*). Yes, Major.

BARBARA. Send Rummy Mitchens out to clear away here.

JENNY. I think she's afraid.

BARBARA (*her resemblance to her mother flashing out for a moment*). Nonsense! she must do as she's told.

JENNY (*calling into the shelter*). Rummy: the Major says you must come.

(*Jenny comes to Barbara, purposely keeping on the side next Bill, lest he should suppose that she shrank from him or bore malice*).

BARBARA. Poor little Jenny! Are you tired? (*Looking at the wounded cheek*) Does it hurt?

JENNY. No: it's all right now. It was nothing.

BARBARA (*critically*). It was as hard as he could hit, I expect. Poor Bill! You dont feel angry with him, do you?

JENNY. Oh no, no, no: indeed I dont, Major, bless his poor heart! (*Barbara kisses her; and she runs away merrily into the shelter. Bill writhes with an agonizing return of his new and alarming symptoms. but says nothing. Rummy Mitchens comes from the shelter*).

BARBARA (*going to meet Rummy*). Now Rummy, bustle. Take in those mugs and plates to be washed; and throw the crumbs about for the birds.

(*Rummy takes the three plates and mugs; but Shirley takes back his mug from her, as there is still some milk left in it*).

RUMMY. There aint any crumbs. This aint a time to waste good bread on birds.

PRICE (*appearing at the shelter door*). Gentleman come to see the shelter, Major. Says he's your father.

BARBARA. All right. Coming. (*Snobby goes back into the shelter, followed by Barbara*).

RUMMY (*stealing across to Bill and addressing him in a subdued voice, but with intense conviction*). I'd av the lor of you, you flat eared pignosed potwalloper, if she'd let me. Youre no gentleman, to hit a lady in the face. (*Bill, with greater things moving in him, takes no notice*).

SHIRLEY (*following her*). Here! in with you and dont get yourself into more trouble by talking.

RUMMY (*with hauteur*). I aint ad the pleasure o being hintroduced to you, as I can remember. (*She goes into the shelter with the plates*).

SHIRLEY. Thats the—

BILL (*savagely*). Downt you talk to me, d'ye eah? You lea me alown, or Aw'll do you a mischief. Aw'm not dirt under *your* feet, ennywy.

SHIRLEY (*calmly*). Dont you be afeerd. You aint such prime company that you need expect to be sought after. (*He is about to go into the shelter when Barbara comes out, with Undershaft on her right*).

BARBARA. Oh, there you are, Mr Shirley! (*Between them*) This is my father: I told you he was a Secularist, didn't I? Perhaps youll be able to comfort one another.

UNDERSHAFT (*startled*). A Secularist! Not the least in the world: on the contrary, a confirmed mystic.

BARBARA. Sorry, I'm sure. By the way, papa, what *is* your religion? in case I have to introduce you again.

UNDERSHAFT. My religion? Well, my dear, I am a Millionaire. That is my religion.

BARBARA. Then I'm afraid you and Mr Shirley wont be able to comfort one another after all. Youre not a Millionaire, are you, Peter?

SHIRLEY. No; and proud of it.

UNDERSHAFT (*gravely*). Poverty, my friend, is not a thing to be proud of.

SHIRLEY (*angrily*). Who made your millions for you? Me and my like. Whats kep us poor? Keepin you rich. I wouldnt have your conscience, not for all your income.

UNDERSHAFT. I wouldnt have your income, not for all your conscience, Mr Shirley. (*He goes to the penthouse and sits down on a form*).

BARBARA (*stopping Shirley adroitly as he is about to retort*). You wouldn't think he was my father, would you, Peter? Will you go into the shelter and lend the lasses a hand for a while: we're worked off our feet.

SHIRLEY (*bitterly*). Yes: I'm in their debt for a meal, aint I?

BARBARA. Oh, not because youre in their debt, but for love of them, Peter, for love of them. (*He cannot understand, and is rather scandalized*). There! dont stare at me. In with you; and give that conscience of yours a holiday (*bustling him into the shelter*).

SHIRLEY (*as he goes in*). Ah! it's a pity you never was trained to use your reason, miss. Youd have been a very taking lecturer on Secularism.

(*Barbara turns to her father*).

UNDERSHAFT. Never mind me, my dear. Go about your work; and let me watch it for a while.

BARBARA. All right.

UNDERSHAFT. For instance, whats the matter with that outpatient over there?

BARBARA (*looking at Bill, whose attitude has never changed, and whose expression of brooding wrath has deepened*). Oh, we shall cure him in no time. Just watch. (*She goes over to Bill and waits.*

He glances up at her and casts his eyes down again, uneasy, but grimmer than ever). It *would* be nice to just stamp on Mog Habbijam's face, wouldnt it, Bill?

BILL *(starting up from the trough in consternation).* It's a loy: Aw never said so. *(She shakes her head).* Oo taold you wot was in moy mawnd?

BARBARA. Only your new friend.

BILL. Wot new friend?

BARBARA. The devil, Bill. When he gets round people they get miserable, just like you.

BILL *(with a heartbreaking attempt at devil-may-care cheerfulness).* Aw aint miserable. *(He sits down again, and stretches his legs in an attempt to seem indifferent).*

BARBARA. Well, if youre happy, why dont you look happy, as we do?

BILL *(his legs curling back in spite of him).* Aw'm eppy enaff, Aw tell you. Woy cawnt you lea me alown? Wot ev I dan to *you?* Aw aint smashed *your* fice, ev Aw?

BARBARA *(softly: wooing his soul).* It's not me thats getting at you, Bill.

BILL. Oo else is it?

BARBARA. Somebody that doesnt intend you to smash women's faces, I suppose. Somebody or something that wants to make a man of you.

BILL *(blustering).* Mike a menn o *me!* Aint Aw a menn? eh? Oo sez Aw'm not a menn?

BARBARA. Theres a man in you somewhere, I suppose. But why did he let you hit poor little Jenny Hill? That wasnt very manly of him, was it?

BILL *(tormented).* Ev dan wiv it, Aw tell you. Chack it. Aw'm sick o your Jenny Ill and er silly little fice.

BARBARA. Then why do you keep thinking about it? Why does it keep coming up against you in your mind? Youre not getting converted, are you?

BILL *(with conviction).* Not ME. Not lawkly.

BARBARA. Thats right, Bill. Hold out against it. Put out your strength. Dont lets get you cheap. Todger Fairmile said he wrestled for three nights against his salvation harder than he ever wrestled with the Jap at the music hall. He gave in to the Jap when his arm was going to break. But he didn't give in to his salvation until his heart was going to break. Perhaps youll escape that. You havnt any heart, have you?

BILL. Wot d'ye mean? Woy aint Aw got a awt the sime as ennybody else?

BARBARA. A man with a heart wouldnt have bashed poor little Jenny's face, would he?

BILL (*almost crying*). Ow, *will* you lea me alown? Ev Aw ever offered to meddle with *you,* that you cam neggin and provowkin me lawk this? (*He writhes convulsively from his eyes to his toes*).

BARBARA (*with a steady soothing hand on his arm and a gentle voice that never lets him go*). It's your soul thats hurting you, Bill, and not me. Weve been through it all ourselves. Come with us, Bill. (*He looks wildly round*). To brave manhood on earth and eternal glory in heaven. (*He is on the point of breaking down*). Come. (*A drum is heard in the shelter; and Bill, with a gasp, escapes from the spell as Barbara turns quickly. Adolphus enters from the shelter with a big drum*). Oh! there you are, Dolly. Let me introduce a new friend of mine, Mr Bill Walker. This is my bloke, Bill: Mr Cusins. (*Cusins salutes with his drumstick*).

BILL. Gowin to merry im?

BARBARA. Yes.

BILL (*fervently*). Gawd elp im! Gaw-aw-aw-awd elp im!

BARBARA. Why? Do you think he wont be happy with me?

BILL. Awve aony ed to stend it for a mawnin: e'll ev to stend it for a lawftawm.

CUSINS. That is a frightful reflection, Mr Walker. But I cant tear myself away from her.

BILL. Well, Aw ken. (*To Barbara*) Eah! do you knaow where Aw'm gowin to, and wot Aw'm gowin to do?

BARBARA. Yes: youre going to heaven; and youre coming back here before the week's out to tell me so.

BILL. You loy. Aw'm gowin to Kennintahn, to spit in Todger Fairmawl's eye. Aw beshed Jenny Ill's fice; an nar Aw'll git me aown fice beshed and cam beck and shaow it to er. Ee'll itt me ardern Aw itt her. Thatll mike us square. (*To Adolphus*) Is thet fair or is it not? Youre a genlmn: you oughter knaow.

BARBARA. Two black eyes wont make one white one, Bill.

BILL. Aw didn't awst *you*. Cawnt you never keep your mahth shat? Oy awst the genlmn.

CUSINS (*reflectively*). Yes: I think youre right, Mr Walker. Yes: I should do it. It's curious: it's exactly what an ancient Greek would have done.

BARBARA. But what good will it do?

CUSINS. Well, it will give Mr Fairmile some exercise; and it will satisfy Mr Walker's soul.

BILL. Rot! there aint nao sach a thing as a saoul. Ah kin you tell wevver Awve a saoul or not? You never seen it.

BARBARA. Ive seen it hurting you when you went against it.

BILL (*with compressed aggravation*). If you was maw gel and took the word aht o me mahth lawk thet, Aw'd give you sathink youd feel urtin, Aw would. (*To Adolphus*) You tike maw tip, mite. Stop er jawr; or youll doy afoah your tawm. (*With intense expression*) Wore aht: thets wot youll be: wore aht. (*He goes away through the gate*).

CUSINS (*looking after him*). I wonder!

BARBARA. Dolly! (*indignant, in her mother's manner*).

CUSINS. Yes, my dear, it's very wearing to be in love with you. If it lasts, I quite think I shall die young.

BARBARA. Should you mind?

CUSINS. Not at all. (*He is suddenly softened, and kisses her over the drum, evidently not for the first time, as people cannot kiss over a big drum without practice. Undershaft coughs*).

BARBARA. It's all right, papa, weve not forgotten you. Dolly: explain the place to papa: I havnt time. (*She goes busily into the shelter*).

(*Undershaft and Adolphus now have the yard to themselves. Undershaft, seated on a form, and still keenly attentive, looks hard at Adolphus. Adolphus looks hard at him*).

UNDERSHAFT. I fancy you guess something of what is in my mind, Mr Cusins. (*Cusins flourishes his drumsticks as if in the act of beating a lively rataplan, but makes no sound*). Exactly so. But suppose Barbara finds you out!

CUSINS. You know, I do not admit that I am imposing on Barbara. I am quite genuinely interested in the views of the Salvation Army. The fact is, I am a sort of collector of religions; and the curious thing is that I find I can believe them all. By the way, have you any religion?

UNDERSHAFT. Yes.

CUSINS. Anything out of the common?

UNDERSHAFT. Only that there are two things necessary to Salvation.

CUSINS (*disappointed, but polite*). Ah, the Church Catechism. Charles Lomax also belongs to the Established Church.

UNDERSHAFT. The two things are—

CUSINS. Baptism and—

UNDERSHAFT. No. Money and gunpowder.

CUSINS (*surprised, but interested*). That is the general opinion of our governing classes. The novelty is in hearing any man confess it.

UNDERSHAFT. Just so.

CUSINS. Excuse me: is there any place in your religion for honor, justice, truth, love, mercy and so forth?

UNDERSHAFT. Yes: they are the graces and luxuries of a rich, strong, and safe life.

CUSINS. Suppose one is forced to choose between them and money or gunpowder?

UNDERSHAFT. Choose money and gunpowder; for without enough of both you cannot afford the others.

CUSINS. That is your religion?

UNDERSHAFT. Yes.

(*The cadence of this reply makes a full close in the conversation. Cusins twists his face dubiously and contemplates Undershaft. Undershaft contemplates him*).

CUSINS. Barbara wont stand that. You will have to choose between your religion and Barbara.

UNDERSHAFT. So will you, my friend. She will find out that that drum of yours is hollow.

CUSINS. Father Undershaft: you are mistaken: I am a sincere Salvationist. You do not understand the Salvation Army. It is the army of joy, of love, of courage: it has banished the fear and remorse and despair of the old hell-ridden evangelical sects: it marches to fight the devil with trumpet and drum, with music and dancing, with banner and palm, as becomes a sally from heaven by its happy garrison. It picks the waster out of the public house and makes a

man of him: it finds a worm wriggling in a back kitchen, and lo!
a woman! Men and women of rank too, sons and daughters of the
Highest. It takes the poor professor of Greek, the most artificial
and self-suppressed of human creatures, from his meal of roots, and
lets loose the rhapsodist in him; reveals the true worship of Dionysos
to him; sends him down the public street drumming dithyrambs.
(*He plays a thundering flourish on the drum*).

UNDERSHAFT. You will alarm the shelter.

CUSINS. Oh, they are accustomed to these sudden ecstasies of piety.
However, if the drum worries you—(*He pockets the drumsticks;
unhooks the drum; and stands it on the ground opposite the gate-
way*).

UNDERSHAFT. Thank you.

CUSINS. You remember what Euripides says about your money
and gunpowder?

UNDERSHAFT. No.

CUSINS (*declaiming*).

> One and another
> In money and guns may outpass his brother;
> And men in their millions float and flow
> And seethe with a million hopes as leaven;
> And they win their will; or they miss their will;
> And their hopes are dead or are pined for still;
> But whoe'er can know
> As the long days go
> That to live is happy, has found his heaven.

My translation: what do you think of it?

UNDERSHAFT. I think, my friend, that if you wish to know, as the
long days go, that to live is happy, you must first acquire money
enough for a decent life, and power enough to be your own master.

CUSINS. You are damnably discouraging. (*He resumes his dec-
lamation*).

> Is it so hard a thing to see
> That the spirit of God—whate'er it be—
> The law that abides and changes not, ages long,
> The Eternal and Nature-born: these things be strong?
> What else is Wisdom? What of Man's endeavor,
> Or God's high grace so lovely and so great?

> To stand from fear set free? to breathe and wait?
> To hold a hand uplifted over Fate?
> And shall not Barbara be loved for ever?

UNDERSHAFT. Euripides mentions Barbara, does he?

CUSINS. It is a fair translation. The word means Loveliness.

UNDERSHAFT. May I ask—as Barbara's father—how much a year she is to be loved for ever on?

CUSINS. As Barbara's father, that is more your affair than mine. I can feed her by teaching Greek: that is about all.

UNDERSHAFT. Do you consider it a good match for her?

CUSINS (*with polite obstinacy*). Mr. Undershaft: I am in many ways a weak, timid, ineffectual person; and my health is far from satisfactory. But whenever I feel that I must have anything, I get it, sooner or later. I feel that way about Barbara. I dont like marriage: I feel intensely afraid of it; and I dont know what I shall do with Barbara or what she will do with me. But I feel that I and nobody else must marry her. Please regard that as settled.—Not that I wish to be arbitrary; but why should I waste your time in discussing what is inevitable?

UNDERSHAFT. You mean that you will stick at nothing: not even the conversion of the Salvation Army to the worship of Dionysos.

CUSINS. The business of the Salvation Army is to save, not to wrangle about the name of the pathfinder. Dionysos or another: what does it matter?

UNDERSHAFT (*rising and approaching him*). Professor Cusins: you are a young man after my own heart.

CUSINS. Mr Undershaft: you are, as far as I am able to gather, a most infernal old rascal; but you appeal very strongly to my sense of ironic humor.

(*Undershaft mutely offers his hand. They shake.*)

UNDERSHAFT (*suddenly concentrating himself*). And now to business.

CUSINS. Pardon me. We were discussing religion. Why go back to such an uninteresting and unimportant subject as business?

UNDERSHAFT. Religion is our business at present, because it is through religion alone that we can win Barbara.

CUSINS. Have you, too, fallen in love with Barbara?

UNDERSHAFT. Yes, with a father's love.

CUSINS. A father's love for a grown-up daughter is the most

dangerous of all infatuations. I apologize for mentioning my own pale, coy, mistrustful fancy in the same breath with it.

UNDERSHAFT. Keep to the point. We have to win her; and we are neither of us Methodists.

CUSINS. That doesnt matter. The power Barbara wields here—the power that wields Barbara herself—is not Calvinism, not Presbyterianism, not Methodism—

UNDERSHAFT. Not Greek Paganism either, eh?

CUSINS. I admit that. Barbara is quite original in her religion.

UNDERSHAFT (*triumphantly*). Aha! Barbara Undershaft would be. Her inspiration comes from within herself.

CUSINS. How do you suppose it got there?

UNDERSHAFT (*in towering excitement*). It is the Undershaft inheritance. I shall hand on my torch to my daughter. She shall make my converts and preach my gospel—

CUSINS. What! Money and gunpowder!

UNDERSHAFT. Yes, money and gunpowder; freedom and power; command of life and command of death.

CUSINS (*urbanely: trying to bring him down to earth*). This is extremely interesting, Mr Undershaft. Of course you know that you are mad.

UNDERSHAFT (*with redoubled force*). And you?

CUSINS. Oh, mad as a hatter. You are welcome to my secret since I have discovered yours. But I am astonished. Can a madman make cannons?

UNDERSHAFT. Would anyone else than a madman make them? And now (*With surging energy*) question for question. Can a sane man translate Euripides?

CUSINS. No.

UNDERSHAFT (*seizing him by the shoulder*). Can a sane woman make a man of a waster or a woman of a worm?

CUSINS (*reeling before the storm*). Father Colossus—Mammoth Millionaire—

UNDERSHAFT (*pressing him*). Are there two mad people or three in this Salvation shelter today?

CUSINS. You mean Barbara is as mad as we are?

UNDERSHAFT (*pushing him lightly off and resuming his equanimity suddenly and completely*). Pooh, Professor! let us call things by their proper names. I am a millionaire; you are a poet: Barbara is a savior of souls. What have we three to do with the common mob of slaves and idolators? (*He sits down again with a shrug of contempt for the mob*).

CUSINS. Take care! Barbara is in love with the common people. So am I. Have you never felt the romance of that love?

UNDERSHAFT (*cold and sardonic*). Have you ever been in love with Poverty, like St Francis? Have you ever been in love with Dirt, like St Simeon! Have you ever been in love with disease and suffering, like our nurses and philanthropists? Such passions are not virtues, but the most unnatural of all the vices. This love of the common people may please an earl's granddaughter and a university professor; but I have been a common man and a poor man; and it has no romance for me. Leave it to the poor to pretend that poverty is a blessing; leave it to the coward to make a religion of his cowardice by preaching humility: we know better than that. We three must stand together above the common people: how else can we help their children to climb up beside us? Barbara must belong to us, not to the Salvation Army.

CUSINS. Well, I can only say that if you think you will get her away from the Salvation Army by talking to her as you have been talking to me, you dont know Barbara.

UNDERSHAFT. My friend: I never ask for what I can buy.

CUSINS (*in a white fury*). Do I understand you to imply that you can buy Barbara?

UNDERSHAFT. No; but I can buy the Salvation Army.

CUSINS. Quite impossible.

UNDERSHAFT. You shall see. All religious organizations exist by selling themselves to the rich.

CUSINS. Not the Army. That is the Church of the poor.

UNDERSHAFT. All the more reason for buying it.

CUSINS. I dont think you quite know what the Army does for the poor.

UNDERSHAFT. Oh yes I do. It draws their teeth: that is enough for me as a man of business.

CUSINS. Nonsense! It makes them sober—

UNDERSHAFT. I prefer sober workmen. The profits are larger.

CUSINS. —honest—

UNDERSHAFT. Honest workmen are the most economical.

CUSINS. —attached to their homes—

UNDERSHAFT. So much the better: they will put up with anything sooner than change their shop.

CUSINS. —happy—

UNDERSHAFT. An invaluable safeguard against revolution.

CUSINS. —unselfish—

UNDERSHAFT. Indifferent to their own interests, which suits me exactly.

CUSINS. —with their thoughts on heavenly things—

UNDERSHAFT (*rising*). And not on Trade Unionism nor Socialism. Excellent.

CUSINS (*revolted*). You really are an infernal old rascal.

UNDERSHAFT (*indicating Peter Shirley, who has just come from the shelter and strolled dejectedly down the yard between them*). And this is an honest man!

SHIRLEY. Yes; and what av I got by it? (*He passes on bitterly and sits on the form, in the corner of the penthouse*).

(*Snobby Price, beaming sanctimoniously, and Jenny Hill, with a tambourine full of coppers, come from the shelter and go to the drum, on which Jenny begins to count the money*).

UNDERSHAFT (*replying to Shirley*). Oh, your employers must have got a good deal by it from first to last.

(*He sits on the table, with one foot on the side form. Cusins, overwhelmed, sits down on the same form nearer the shelter. Barbara comes from the shelter to the middle of the yard. She is excited and a little over-wrought*).

BARBARA. Weve just had a splendid experience meeting at the other gate in Cripp's Lane. Ive hardly ever seen them so much moved as they were by your confession, Mr Price.

PRICE. I could almost be glad of my past wickedness if I could believe that it would elp to keep hathers stright.

BARBARA. So it will, Snobby. How much, Jenny?

JENNY. Four and tenpence, Major.

BARBARA. Oh Snobby, if you had given your poor mother just one more kick, we should have got the whole five shillings!

PRICE. If she heard you say that, miss, she'd be sorry I didnt. But I'm glad. Oh what a joy it will be to her when she hears I'm saved!

UNDERSHAFT. Shall I contribute the odd twopence. Barbara? The millionaire's mite, eh? (*He takes a couple of pennies from his pocket*).

BARBARA. How did you make that twopence?

UNDERSHAFT. As usual. By selling cannons, torpedoes, submarines, and my new patent Grand Duke hand grenade.

BARBARA. Put it back in your pocket. You cant buy your salvation here for twopence: you must work it out.

UNDERSHAFT. Is twopence not enough? I can afford a little more, of you press me.

BARBARA. Two million millions would not be enough. There is bad blood on your hands; and nothing but good blood can cleanse them. Money is no use. Take it away. (*She turns to Cusins*). Dolly: you must write another letter for me to the papers. (*He makes a wry face*). Yes: I know you dont like it; but it must be done. The starvation this winter is beating us: everybody is unemployed. The General says we must close this shelter if we cant get more money. I force the collections at the meetings until I am ashamed: dont I, Snobby?

PRICE. It's a fair treat to see you work it, miss. The way you got them up for three-and-six to four-and-ten with that hymn, penny by penny and verse by verse, was a caution. Not a Cheap Jack on Mile End Waste could touch you at it.

BARBARA. Yes; but I wish we could do without it. I am getting at last to think more of the collection than of the people's souls. And what are those hatfuls of pence and halfpence? We want thousands! tens of thousands! hundreds of thousands! I want to convert people, not to be always begging for the Army in a way I'd die sooner than beg for myself.

UNDERSHAFT (*in profound irony*). Genuine unselfishness is capable of anything, my dear.

BARBARA (*unsuspectingly, as she turns away to take the money from the drum and put it in a cash bag she carries*). Yes, isnt it? (*Undershaft looks sardonically at Cusins*).

CUSINS (*aside to Undershaft*). Mephistopheles! Machiavelli!

BARBARA (*tears coming into her eyes as she ties the bag and pockets it*). How are we to feed them! I cant talk religion to a man with bodily hunger in his eyes. (*Almost breaking down*) It's frightful.

JENNY (*running to her*). Major, dear—

BARBARA (*rebounding*). No: dont comfort me. It will be all right. We shall get the money.

UNDERSHAFT. How?

JENNY. By praying for it, of course. Mrs Baines says she prayed for it last night; and she has never prayed for it in vain: never once. (*She goes to the gate and looks out into the street*).

BARBARA (*who has dried her eyes and regained her composure*). By the way, dad, Mrs Baines has come to march with us to our big meeting this afternoon; and she is very anxious to meet you, for some reason or other. Perhaps she'll convert you.

UNDERSHAFT. I shall be delighted, my dear.

JENNY (*at the gate: excitedly*). Major! Major! heres that man back again.

BARBARA. What man?

JENNY. The man that hit me. Oh, I hope he's coming back to join us.

(*Bill Walker, with frost on his jacket, comes through the gate, his hands deep in his pockets and his chin sunk between his shoulders, like a cleaned-out gambler. He halts between Barbara and the drum*).

BARBARA. Hullo, Bill! Back already!

BILL (*nagging at her*). Bin talkin ever sence, ev you?

BARBARA. Pretty nearly. Well, has Todger paid you out for poor Jenny's jaw?

BILL. Nao e aint.

BARBARA. I thought you jacket looked a bit snowy.

BILL. Sao it is snaowy. You want to knaow where the snaow cam from, downt you?

BARBARA. Yes.

BILL. Well, it came from orf the grahnd in Pawkinses Corner in Kennintahn. It got rabbed orf be maw shaoulders: see?

BARBARA. Pity you didnt rub some off with your knees, Bill! That would have done you a lot of good.

BILL (*with sour mirthless humor*). Aw was sivin anather menn's knees at the tawm. E was kneelin on moy ed, e was.

JENNY. Who was kneeling on your head?

BILL. Todger was. E was pryin for me: pryin camfortable wiv me as a cawpet. Sow was Mog. Sao was the aol bloomin meetin. Mog she sez "Ow Lawd brike is stabborn sperrit; bat downt urt is dear art." Thet was wot she said. "Downt urt is dear art"! An er blowk—

thirteen stun four!—kneelin wiv all is wight on me. Fanny, aint it?

JENNY. Oh no. We're so sorry, Mr Walker.

BARBARA (*enjoying it frankly*). Nonsense! of course it's funny.
Served you right, Bill! You must have done something to him first.

BILL (*doggedly*). Aw did wot Aw saidAw'd do. Aw spit in is eye.
E looks ap at the skoy and sez, "Ow that Aw should be fahnd worthy
to be spit upon for the gospel's sike!" e sez; and Mog sez "Glaory
Allelloolier!"; an then e called me Braddher, an dahned me as if Aw
was a kid and e was me mather worshin me a Setterda nawt. Aw
ednt jast nao shaow wiv im at all. Arf the street pryed; an the
tather arf larfed fit to split theirselves. (*To Barbara*) There! are you
settisfawd nah?

BARBARA (*her eyes dancing*). Wish I'd been there, Bill.

BILL. Yus: youd a got in a hextra bit o talk on me, wouldnt you?

JENNY. I'm so sorry, Mr Walker.

BILL (*fiercely*). Downt you gow being sorry for me: youve no
call. Listen eah. Aw browk your jawr.

JENNY. No, it didnt hurt me: indeed it didn't, except for a
moment. It was only that I was frightened.

BILL. Aw downt want to be forgive be you, or be ennybody. Wot
Aw did Aw'll py for. Aw trawd to gat me aown jawr browk to
settisfaw you—

JENNY (*distressed*). Oh no—

BILL (*impatiently*). Tell y' Aw did: cawnt you listen to wots bein
taold you? All Aw got be it was bein mide a sawt of in the pablic
street for me pines. Well, if Aw cawnt settisfaw you one wy, Aw
ken anather. Listen eah! Aw ed two quid sived agen the frost; an
Awve a pahnd of it left. A mite o mawn last week ed words with
the judy e's gowing to merry. E give er wot-for; an e's bin fawnd
fifteen bob. E ed a rawt to itt er cause they was gowin to be merrid;
but Aw ednt nao rawt to itt you; sao put anather fawv bob on an
call it a pahnd's worth. (*He produces a sovereign*). Eahs the manney. Tike it; and lets ev no more o your forgivin an prying and your
Mijor jawrin me. Let wot Aw dan be dan an pide for; and let there
be a end of it.

JENNY. Oh, I couldnt take it, Mr Walker. But if you would give
a shilling or two to poor Rummy Mitchens! you really did hurt her;
and she's old.

BILL (*contemptuously*). Not lawkly. Aw'd give her anather as

soon as look at er. Let her ev the lawr o me as she threatened! *She*
aint forgiven me: not mach. Wot Av dan to er is not on me mawnd
—wot she (*indicating Barbara*) mawt call on me conscience—no
more than stickin a pig. It's this Christian gime o yours that Aw
wownt ev plyed agen me: this bloomin forgivin an neggin an
jawrin that mikes a menn that sore that iz lawf's a burdn to im. Aw
wownt ev it, Aw tell you; sao tike your manney and stop thraowin
your silly beshed fice hap agen me.

JENNY. Major: may I take a little bit of it for the Army?

BARBARA. No: the Army is not to be bought. We want your soul,
Bill; and we'll take nothing less.

BILL (*bitterly*). Aw knaow. Me an maw few shillins is not good
enaff for you. Youre a earl's grendorter, you are. Nathink less than
a andered pahnd for you.

UNDERSHAFT. Come, Barbara! you could do a great deal of good
with a hundred pounds. If you will set this gentleman's mind at ease
by taking his pound, I will give the other ninety-nine.

(*Bill, dazed by such opulence, instinctively touches his cap*).

BARBARA. Oh, youre too extravagant, papa. Bill offers twenty
pieces of silver. All you need offer is the other ten. That will make
the standard price to buy anybody who's for sale. I'm not; and the
Army's not. (*To Bill*) Youll never have another quiet moment,
Bill, until you come round to us. You cant stand out against your
salvation.

BILL (*sullenly*). Aw cawnt stend aht agen music awl wrastlers
and awtful tangued women. Awve offered to py. Aw can do no more.
Tike it or leave it. There it is. (*He throws the sovereign on the
drum, and sits down on the horse-trough. The coin fascinates Snobby
Price, who takes an early opportunity of dropping his cap on it*).

(*Mrs Baines comes from the shelter. She is dressed as a Salvation
Army Commissioner. She is an earnest looking woman of about
40, with a caressing, urgent voice, and an appealing manner*).

BARBARA. This is my father, Mrs Baines. (*Undershaft comes from
the table, taking his hat off with marked civility*). Try what you
can do with him. He wont listen to me, because he remembers what
a fool I was when I was a baby. (*She leaves them together and chats
with Jenny*).

MRS BAINES. Have you been shewn over the shelter, Mr Undershaft? You know the work we're doing, of course.

UNDERSHAFT (*very civilly*). The whole nation knows it, Mrs Baines.

MRS BAINES. No, sir: the whole nation does not know it, or we should not be crippled as we are for want of money to carry our work through the length and breadth of the land. Let me tell you that there would have been rioting this winter in London but for us.

UNDERSHAFT. You really think so?

MRS BAINES. I know it. I remember 1886, when you rich gentlemen hardened your hearts against the cry of the poor. They broke the windows of your clubs in Pall Mall.

UNDERSHAFT (*gleaming with approval of their method*). And the Mansion House Fund went up next day from thirty thousand pounds to seventy-nine thousand! I remember quite well.

MRS BAINES. Well, wont you help me to get at the people? They wont break windows then. Come here, Price. Let me shew you to this gentleman (*Price comes to be inspected*). Do you remember the window breaking?

PRICE. My ole father thought it was the revolution, maam.

MRS BAINES. Would you break windows now?

PRICE. Oh no, maam. The windows of eaven av been opened to me. I know now that the rich man is a sinner like myself.

RUMMY (*appearing above at the loft door*). Snobby Price!

SNOBBY. Wot is it?

RUMMY. Your mother's askin for you at the other gate in Cripps's Lane. She's heard about your confession (*Price turns pale*).

MRS BAINES. Go, Mr Price; and pray with her.

JENNY. You can go through the shelter, Snobby.

PRICE (*to Mrs Baines*). I couldn't face her now, maam, with all the weight of my sins fresh on me. Tell her she'll find her son at ome, waitin for her in prayer. (*He skulks off through the gate, incidentally stealing the sovereign on his way out by picking up his cap from the drum*).

MRS BAINES (*with swimming eyes*). You see how we take the anger and the bitterness against you out of their hearts, Mr Undershaft.

UNDERSHAFT. It is certainly most convenient and gratifying to all large employers of labor, Mrs Baines.

MRS BAINES. Barbara: Jenny: I have good news: most wonderful news. (*Jenny runs to her*). My prayers have been answered. I told you they would, Jenny, didnt I?

JENNY. Yes, yes.

BARBARA (*moving nearer to the drum*). Have we got money enough to keep the shelter open?

MRS BAINES. I hope we shall have enough to keep all the shelters open. Lord Saxmundham has promised us five thousand pounds—

BARBARA. Hooray!

JENNY. Glory!

MRS BAINES. —if—

BARBARA. "If!" If what?

MRS BAINES. —if five other gentlemen will give a thousand each to make it up to ten thousand.

BARBABA. Who is Lord Saxmundham? I never heard of him.

UNDERSHAFT (*who has pricked up his ears at the peer's name, and is now watching Barbara curiously*). A new creation, my dear. You have heard of Sir Horace Bodger?

BARBARA. Bodger! Do you mean the distiller? Bodger's whisky!

UNDERSHAFT. That is the man. He is one of the greatest of our public benefactors. He restored the cathedral at Hakington. They made him a baronet for that. He gave half a million to the funds of his party: they made him a baron for that.

SHIRLEY. What will they give him for the five thousand?

UNDERSHAFT. There is nothing left to give him. So the five thousand, I should think, is to save his soul.

MRS BAINES. Heaven grant it may! Oh Mr Undershaft, you have some very rich friends. Cant you help us towards the other five thousand? We are going to hold a great meeting this afternoon at the Assembly Hall in the Mile End Road. If I could only announce that one gentleman had come forward to support Lord Saxmundham, others would follow. Dont you know somebody? couldnt you? wouldnt you? (*her eyes fill with tears*) oh, think of those poor people, Mr Undershaft: think of how much it means to them, and how little to be a great man like you.

UNDERSHAFT (*sardonically gallant*). Mrs Baines: you are irresistible. I cant disappoint you; and I cant deny myself the satisfaction of making Bodger pay up. You shall have your five thousand pounds.

MRS BAINES. Thank God!

UNDERSHAFT. You dont thank *me?*

MRS BAINES. Oh sir, dont try to be cynical: dont be ashamed of being a good man. The Lord will bless you abundantly; and our prayers will be like a strong fortification round you all the days of your life. (*With a touch of caution*) You will let me have the cheque to shew at the meeting, wont you? Jenny: go in and fetch a pen and ink. (*Jenny runs to the shelter door*).

UNDERSHAFT. Do not disturb Miss Hill: I have a fountain pen (*Jenny halts. He sits at the table and writes the cheque. Cusins rises to make room for him. They all watch him silently*).

BILL (*cynically, aside to Barbara, his voice and accent horribly debased*). Wot prawce selvytion nah?

BARBARA. Stop. (*Undershaft stops writing: they all turn to her in surprise*). Mrs Baines: are you really going to take this money?

MRS BAINES (*astonished*). Why not, dear?

BARBARA. Why not! Do you know what my father is? Have you forgotten that Lord Saxmundham is Bodger the whisky man? Do you remember how we implored the County Council to stop him from writing Bodger's Whisky in letters of fire against the sky; so that the poor drink-ruined creatures on the Embankment could not wake up from their snatches of sleep without being reminded of their deadly thirst by that wicked sky sign? Do you know that the worst thing I have had to fight here is not the devil, but Bodger, Bodger, Bodger, with his whisky, his distilleries, and his tied houses? Are you going to make our shelter another tied house for him, and ask me to keep it?

BILL. Rotten dranken whisky it is too.

MRS BAINES. Dear Barbara: Lord Saxmundham has a soul to be saved like any of us. If heaven has found the way to make a good use of his money, are we to set ourselves up against the answer to our prayers?

BARBARA. I know he has a soul to be saved. Let him come down here; and I'll do my best to help him to his salvation. But he wants to send his cheque down to buy us, and go on being as wicked as ever.

UNDERSHAFT (*with a reasonableness which Cusins alone perceives to be ironical*). My dear Barbara: alcohol is a very necessary article. It heals the sick—

BARBARA. It does nothing of the sort.

UNDERSHAFT. Well, it assists the doctor: that is perhaps a less questionable way of putting it. It makes life bearable to millions of people who could not endure their existence if they were quite sober. It enables Parliament to do things at eleven at night that no sane person would do at eleven in the morning. Is it Bodger's fault that this inestimable gift is deplorably abused by less than one per cent of the poor? (*He turns again to the table; signs the cheque; and crosses it*).

MRS BAINES. Barbara: will there be less drinking or more if all those poor souls we are saving come tomorrow and find the doors of our shelters shut in their faces? Lord Saxmundham gives us the money to stop drinking—to take his own business from him.

CUSINS (*impishly*). Pure self-sacrifice on Bodger's part, clearly! Bless dear Bodger! (*Barbara almost breaks down as Adolphus, too, fails her*).

UNDERSHAFT (*tearing out the cheque and pocketing the book as he rises and goes past Cusins to Mrs Baines*). I also, Mrs Baines, may claim a little disinterestedness. Think of my business! think of the widows and orphans! the men and lads torn to pieces with shrapnel and poisoned with lyddite! (*Mrs Baines shrinks; but he goes on remorselessly*) the oceans of blood, not one drop of which is shed in a really just cause! the ravaged crops! the peaceful peasants forced, women and men, to till their fields under the fire of opposing armies on pain of starvation! the bad blood of the fierce little cowards at home who egg on others to fight for the gratification of their national vanity! All this makes money for me: I am never richer, never busier than when the papers are full of it. Well, it is your work to preach peace on earth and good will to men. (*Mrs Baines's face lights up again*). Every convert you make is a vote against war. (*Her lips move in prayer*). Yet I give you this money to help you to hasten my own commercial ruin. (*He gives her the cheque*).

CUSINS (*mounting the form in an ecstasy of mischief*). The millennium will be inaugurated by the unselfishness of Undershaft and Bodger. Oh be joyful! (*He takes the drumsticks from his pocket and flourishes them*).

MRS BAINES (*taking the cheque*). The longer I live the more proof I see that there is an Infinite Goodness that turns everything to the work of salvation sooner or later. Who would have thought that any good could have come out of war and drink? And yet their profits are brought today to the feet of salvation to do its blessed work. (*She is affected to tears*).

JENNY (*running to Mrs Baines and throwing her arms round her*). Oh dear! how blessed, how glorious it all is!

CUSINS (*in a convulsion of irony*). Let us seize this unspeakable moment. Let us march to the great meeting at once. Excuse me just an instant. (*He rushes into the shelter. Jenny takes her tambourine from the drum head*).

MRS BAINES. Mr Undershaft: have you ever seen a thousand people fall on their knees with one impulse and pray? Come with us to the meeting. Barbara shall tell them that the Army is saved, and saved through you.

CUSINS (*returning impetuously from the shelter with a flag and a trombone, and coming between Mrs Baines and Undershaft*). You shall carry the flag down the first street, Mrs Baines (*he gives her the flag*). Mr Undershaft is a gifted trombonist, he shall intone an Olympian diapason to the West Ham Salvation March. (*Aside to Undershaft, as he forces the trombone on him*) Blow, Machiavelli, blow.

UNDERSHAFT (*aside to him, as he takes the trombone*). The trumpet in Zion! (*Cusins rushes to the drum, which he takes up and puts on. Undershaft continues, aloud*) I will do my best. I could vamp a bass if I knew the tune.

CUSINS. It is a wedding chorus from one of Donizetti's operas; but we have converted it. We convert everything to good here, including Bodger. You remember the chorus. "For thee immense rejoicing—immenso giubilo—immenso giubilo." (*With drum obbligato*) Rum tum ti tum tum, tum tum ti ta—

BARBARA. Dolly: you are breaking my heart.

CUSINS. What is a broken heart more or less here? Dionysos Undershaft has descended. I am possessed.

MRS BAINES. Come, Barbara: I must have my dear Major to carry the flag with me.

JENNY. Yes, yes, Major darling.

(*Cusins snatches the tambourine out of Jenny's hand and mutely offers it to Barbara*).

BARBARA (*coming forward a little as she puts the offer behind her with a shudder, whilst Cusins recklessly tosses the tambourine back to Jenny and goes to the gate*). I cant come.

JENNY. Not come!

MRS BAINES (*with tears in her eyes*). Barbara: do you think I am wrong to take the money?

BARBARA (*impulsively going to her and kissing her*). No, no: God help you, dear, you must: you are saving the Army. Go; and may you have a great meeting!

JENNY. But arnt you coming?

BARBARA. No. (*She begins taking off the silver S brooch from her collar*).

MRS BAINES. Barbara: what are you doing?

JENNY. Why are you taking your badge off? You cant be going to leave us, Major.

BARBARA (*quietly*). Father: come here.

UNDERSHAFT (*coming to her*). My dear! (*Seeing that she is going to pin the badge on his collar, he retreats to the penthouse in some alarm*).

BARBARA (*following him*). Dont be frightened. (*She pins the badge on and steps back towards the table, shewing him to the others*) There! It's not much for £5000, is it?

MRS BAINES. Barbara: if you wont come and pray *with* us, promise me you will pray *for* us.

BARBARA. I cant pray now. Perhaps I shall never pray again.

MRS BAINES. Barbara!

JENNY. Major!

BARBARA (*almost delirious*). I cant bear any more. Quick march!

CUSINS (*calling to the procession in the street outside*). Off we go. Play up, there! *Immenso giubilo*. (*He gives the time with his drum; and the band strikes up the march, which rapidly becomes more distant as the procession moves briskly away*).

MRS BAINES. I must go, dear. Youre overworked: you will be all right tomorrow. We'll never lose you. Now Jenny: step out with the old flag. Blood and Fire! (*She marches out through the gate with her flag*).

JENNY. Glory Hallelujah! (*flourishing her tambourine and marching*).

UNDERSHAFT (*to Cusins, as he marches out past him easing the slide of his trombone*). "My ducats and my daughter"!

CUSINS (*following him out*). Money and gunpowder!

BARBARA. Drunkenness and Murder! My God: why hast thou forsaken me?

(*She sinks on the form with her face buried in her hands. The march passes away into silence. Bill Walker steals across to her*).

BILL (*taunting*). Wot prawce selvytion nah?

SHIRLEY. Dont you hit her when she's down.

BILL. She itt me wen aw wiz dahn. Waw shouldnt Aw git a bit o me aown beck?

BARBARA (*raising her head*). I didnt take *your* money, Bill. (*She crosses the yard to the gate and turns her back on the two men to hide her face from them*).

BILL (*sneering after her*). Naow, it warnt enaff for you. (*Turning to the drum, he misses the money*) Ellow! If you aint took it sammun else ez. Weres it gorn? Bly me if Jenny Ill didnt tike it arter all!

RUMMY (*screaming at him from the loft*). You lie, you dirty blackguard! Snobby Price pinched it off the drum when he took up his cap. I was up here all the time an see im do it.

BILL. Wot! Stowl maw manney! Waw didnt you call thief on him, you silly aold macker you?

RUMMY. To serve you aht for ittin me acrost the fice. It's cost y'pahnd, that az. (*Raising a paen of squalid triumph*) I done you. I'm even with you. Uve ad it aht *oy*— (*Bill snatches up Shirley's mug and hurls it at her. She slams the loft door and vanishes. The mug smashes against the door and falls in fragments*).

BILL (*beginning to chuckle*). Tell us, aol menn, wot o'clock this mawnin was it wen im as they call Snobby Prawce was sived?

BARBARA (*turning to him more composedly, and with unspoiled sweetness*). About half past twelve, Bill. And he pinched your pound at a quarter to two. *I* know. Well, you cant afford to lose it. I'll send it to you.

BILL (*his voice and accent suddenly improving*). Not if Aw wiz to stawve for it. Aw aint to be bought.

SHIRLEY. Aint you? Youd sell yourself to the devil for a pint o beer; only there aint no devil to make the offer.

BILL (*unashamed*). Sao Aw would, mite, and often ev, cheerful. But she cawnt baw me. (*Approaching Barbara*) You wanted maw saoul, did you? Well, you aint got it.

BARBARA. I nearly got it, Bill. But weve sold it back to you for ten thousand pounds.

SHIRLEY. And dear at the money!

BARBARA. No, Peter: it was worth more than money.

BILL (*salvationproof*). It's nao good: you cawnt get rahnd me nah. Aw downt blieve in it; and Awve seen tody that Aw was rawt. (*Going*) Sao long, aol soupkitchener! Ta, ta, Mijor Earl's Grendorter! (*Turning at the gate*) Wot prawce selvytion nah? Snobby Prawce! Ha! ha!

BARBARA (*offering her hand*). Goodbye, Bill.

BILL (*taken aback, half plucks his cap off; then shoves it on again defiantly*). Git aht. (*Barbara drops her hand, discouraged. He has a twinge of remorse*). But thets aw rawt, you knaow. Nathink pasnl. Naow mellice. Sao long, Judy. (*He goes*).

BARBARA. No malice. So long, Bill.

SHIRLEY (*shaking his head*). You make too much of him, miss, in your innocence.

BARBARA (*going to him*). Peter: I'm like you now. Cleaned out, and lost my job.

SHIRLEY. Youve youth an hope. Thats two better than me.

BARBARA. I'll get you a job, Peter. Thats hope for you: the youth will have to be enough for me. (*She counts her money*). I have just enough left for two teas at Lockharts, a Rowton doss for you, and my tram and bus home. (*He frowns and rises with offended pride. She takes his arm*). Dont be proud, Peter: it's sharing between friends. And promise me youll talk to me and not let me cry. (*She draws him towards the gate*).

SHIRLEY. Well, I'm not accustomed to talk to the like of you—

BARBARA (*urgently*). Yes, yes: you must talk to me. Tell me about Tom Paine's book and Bradlaugh's lectures. Come along.

SHIRLEY. Ah, if you would only read Tom Paine in the proper spirit, miss! (*They go out through the gate together*).

act three

Next day after lunch Lady Britomart is writing in the library in Wilton Crescent. Sarah is reading in the armchair near the window. Barbara, in ordinary fashionable dress, pale and brooding, is on the settee. Charles Lomax enters. He starts on seeing Barbara fashionably attired and in low spirits.

LOMAX. Youve left off your uniform!

(*Barbara says nothing; but an expression of pain passes over her face*).

LADY BRITOMART (*warning him in low tones to be careful*). Charles!

LOMAX (*much concerned, coming behind the settee and bending sympathetically over Barbara*). I'm awfully sorry, Barbara. You know I helped you all I could with the concertina and so forth. (*Momentously*) Still, I have never shut my eyes to the fact that there is a certain amount of tosh about the Salvation Army. Now the claims of the Church of England—

LADY BRITOMART. Thats enough, Charles. Speak of something suited to your mental capacity.

LOMAX. But surely the Church of England is suited to all our capacities.

BARBARA (*pressing his hand*). Thank you for your sympathy, Cholly. Now go and spoon with Sarah.

LOMAX (*dragging a chair from the writing table and seating himself affectionately by Sarah's side*). How is my ownest today?

SARAH. I wish you wouldnt tell Cholly to do things, Barbara. He always comes straight and does them. Cholly: we're going to the works this afternoon.

LOMAX. What works?

SARAH. The cannon works.

LOMAX. What? your governor's shop!

SARAH. Yes.

LOMAX. Oh I say!

(*Cusins enters in poor condition. He also starts visibly when he sees Barbara without her uniform*).

BARBARA. I expected you this morning, Dolly. Didnt you guess that?

CUSINS (*sitting down beside her*). I'm sorry. I have only just breakfasted.

SARAH. But weve just finished lunch.

BARBARA. Have you had one of your bad nights?

CUSINS. No: I had rather a good night: in fact, one of the most remarkable nights I have ever passed.

BARBARA. The meeting?

CUSINS. No: after the meeting.

LADY BRITOMART. You should have gone to bed after the meeting. What were you doing?

CUSINS. Drinking.

LADY BRITOMART. ⎫   ⎧ Adolphus!
SARAH.   ⎪   ⎪ Dolly!
BARBARA.   ⎬   ⎨ Dolly!
LOMAX.   ⎭   ⎩ Oh I say!

LADY BRITOMART. What were you drinking, may I ask?

CUSINS. A most devilish kind of Spanish burgundy, warranted free from added alcohol: a Temperance burgundy in fact. Its richness in natural alcohol made any addition superfluous.

BARBARA. Are you joking, Dolly?

CUSINS (*patiently*). No. I have been making a night of it with the nominal head of this household: that is all.

LADY BRITOMART. Andrew made you drunk!

CUSINS. No: he only provided the wine. I think it was Dionysos who made me drunk. (*To Barbara*) I told you I was possessed.

LADY BRITOMART. Youre not sober yet. Go home to bed at once.

CUSINS. I have never before ventured to reproach you, Lady Brit; but how could you marry the Prince of Darkness?

LADY BRITOMART. It was much more excusable to marry him than to get drunk with him. That is a new accomplishment of Andrew's, by the way. He usent to drink.

CUSINS. He doesnt now. He only sat there and completed the wreck of my moral basis, the rout of my convictions, the purchase of my soul. He cares for you, Barbara. That is what makes him so dangerous to me.

BARBARA. That has nothing to do with it, Dolly. There are larger loves and diviner dreams than the fireside ones. You know that, dont you?

CUSINS. Yes: that is our understanding. I know it. I hold to it. Unless he can win me on that holier ground he may amuse me for a while; but he can get no deeper hold, strong as he is.

BARBARA. Keep to that: and the end will be right. Now tell me what happened at the meeting?

CUSINS. It was an amazing meeting. Mrs Baines almost died of emotion. Jenny Hill simply gibbered with hysteria. The Prince of Darkness played his trombone like a madman: its brazen roarings were like the laughter of the damned. 117 conversions took place then and there. They prayed with the most touching sincerity and gratitude for Bodger, and for the anonymous donor of the £5000. Your father would not let his name be given.

LOMAX. That was rather fine of the old man, you know. Most chaps would have wanted the advertisement.

CUSINS. He said all the charitable institutions would be down on him like kites on a battlefield if he gave his name.

LADY BRITOMART. Thats Andrew all over. He never does a proper thing without giving an improper reason for it.

CUSINS. He convinced me that I have all my life been doing improper things for proper reasons.

LADY BRITOMART. Adolphus: now that Barbara has left the Salvation Army, you had better leave it too. I will not have you playing that drum in the streets.

CUSINS. Your orders are already obeyed, Lady Brit.

BARBARA. Dolly: were you ever really in earnest about it? Would you have joined if you had never seen me?

CUSINS (*disingenuously*). Well—er—well, possibly, as a collector of religions—

LOMAX (*cunningly*). Not as a drummer, though, you know. You are a very clearheaded brainy chap, Dolly; and it must have been apparent to you that there is a certain amount of tosh about—

LADY BRITOMART. Charles: if you must drivel, drivel like a grown-up man and not like a schoolboy.

LOMAX (*out of countenance*). Well, drivel is drivel, dont you know, whatever a man's age.

LADY BRITOMART. In good society in England, Charles, men drivel at all ages by repeating silly formulas with an air of wisdom. Schoolboys make their own formulas out of slang, like you. When they reach your age, and get political private secretaryships and things of that sort, they drop slang and get their formulas out of the Spectator or The Times. *You* had better confine yourself to The Times. You will find that there is a certain amount of tosh about The Times; but at least its language is reputable.

LOMAX (*overwhelmed*). You are so awfully strong-minded, Lady Brit—

LADY BRITOMART. Rubbish! (*Morrison comes in*). What is it?

MORRISON. If you please, my lady, Mr Undershaft has just drove up to the door.

LADY BRITOMART. Well, let him in. (*Morrison hesitates*). Whats the matter with you?

MORRISON. Shall I announce him, my lady; or is he at home here, so to speak, my lady?

LADY BRITOMART. Announce him.

MORRISON. Thank you, my lady. You wont mind my asking, I hope. The occasion is in a manner of speaking new to me.

LADY BRITOMART. Quite right. Go and let him in.

MORRISON. Thank you, my lady. (*He withdraws*).

LADY BRITOMART. Children: go and get ready. (*Sarah and Barbara go upstairs for their out-of-door wraps*). Charles: go and tell Stephen to come down here in five minutes: you will find him in the drawing room. (*Charles goes*). Adolphus: tell them to send round the carriage in about fifteen minutes. (*Adolphus goes*).

MORRISON (*at the door*). Mr Undershaft. (*Undershaft comes in. Morrison goes out*).

UNDERSHAFT. Alone! How fortunate!

LADY BRITOMART (*rising*). Dont be sentimental, Andrew. Sit down. (*She sits on the settee: he sits beside her, on her left. She comes to the point before he has time to breathe*). Sarah must have £800 a year until Charles Lomax comes into his property. Barbara will need more, and need it permanently, because Adolphus hasnt any property.

UNDERSHAFT (*resignedly*). Yes, my dear: I will see to it. Anything else? for yourself, for instance?

LADY BRITOMART. I want to talk to you about Stephen.

UNDERSHAFT (*rather wearily*). Dont, my dear. Stephen doesnt interest me.

LADY BRITOMART. He does interest me. He is our son.

UNDERSHAFT. Do you really think so? He has induced us to bring him into the world; but he chose his parents very incongruously, I think. I see nothing of myself in him, and less of you.

LADY BRITOMART. Andrew: Stephen is an excellent son, and a most steady, capable, high-minded young man. You are simply trying to find an excuse for disinheriting him.

UNDERSHAFT. My dear Biddy: the Undershaft tradition disinherits him. It would be dishonest of me to leave the cannon foundry to my son.

LADY BRITOMART. It would be most unnatural and improper of

you to leave it to anyone else, Andrew. Do you suppose this wicked and immoral tradition can be kept up for ever? Do you pretend that Stephen could not carry on the foundry just as well as all the other sons of the big business houses?

UNDERSHAFT. Yes: he could learn the office routine without understanding the business, like all the other sons; and the firm would go on by its own momentum until the real Undershaft—probably an Italian or a German—would invent a new method and cut him out.

LADY BRITOMART. There is nothing that any Italian or German could do that Stephen could not do. And Stephen at least has breeding.

UNDERSHAFT. The son of a foundling! Nonsense!

LADY BRITOMART. My son, Andrew! And even you may have good blood in your veins for all you know.

UNDERSHAFT. True. Probably I have. That is another argument in favour of a foundling.

LADY BRITOMART. Andrew: dont be aggravating. And dont be wicked. At present you are both.

UNDERSHAFT. This conversation is part of the Undershaft tradition, Biddy. Every Undershaft's wife has treated him to it ever since the house was founded. It is mere waste of breath. If the tradition be ever broken it will be for an abler man than Stephen.

LADY BRITOMART (*pouting*). Then go away.

UNDERSHAFT (*deprecatory*). Go away!

LADY BRITOMART. Yes: go away. If you will do nothing for Stephen, you are not wanted here. Go to your foundling, whoever he is; and look after *him*.

UNDERSHAFT. The fact is, Biddy—

LADY BRITOMART. Dont call me Biddy. I dont call you Andy.

UNDERSHAFT. I will not call my wife Britomart: it is not good sense. Seriously, my love, the Undershaft tradition has landed me in a difficulty. I am getting on in years; and my partner Lazarus has at last made a stand and insisted that the succession must be settled one way or the other; and of course he is quite right. You see, I havnt found a fit successor yet.

LADY BRITOMART (*obstinately*). There is Stephen.

UNDERSHAFT. Thats just it: all the foundlings I can find are exactly like Stephen.

LADY BRITOMART. Andrew!!

UNDERSHAFT. I want a man with no relations and no schooling: that is, a man who would be out of the running altogether if he were not a strong man. And I cant find him. Every blessed foundling nowadays is snapped up in his infancy by Barnardo homes, or School Board officers, or Boards of Guardians; and if he shews the least ability he is fastened on by schoolmasters; trained to win scholarships like a racehorse; crammed with second-hand ideas; drilled and disciplined in docility and what they call good taste; and lamed for life so that he is fit for nothing but teaching. If you want to keep the foundry in the family, you had better find an eligible foundling and marry him to Barbara.

LADY BRITOMART. Ah! Barbara! You pet! You would sacrifice Stephen to Barbara.

UNDERSHAFT. Cheerfully. And you, my dear, would boil Barbara to make soup for Stephen.

LADY BRITOMART. Andrew: this is not a question of our likings or dislikings: it is a question of duty. It is your duty to make Stephen your successor.

UNDERSHAFT. Just as much as it is your duty to submit to your husband. Come, Biddy! these tricks of the governing class are of no use with me. I am one of the governing class myself; and it is waste of time giving tracts to a missionary. I have the power in this matter; and I am not to be humbugged into using it for your purposes.

LADY BRITOMART. Andrew: you can talk my head off; but you cant change wrong into right. And your tie is all on one side. Put it straight.

UNDERSHAFT (*disconcerted*). It wont stay unless it's pinned— (*He fumbles at it with childish grimaces*).

(*Stephen comes in*).

STEPHEN (*at the door*). I beg your pardon (*about to retire*).

LADY BRITOMART. No: come in, Stephen. (*Stephen comes forward to his mother's writing table*).

UNDERSHAFT (*not very cordially*). Good afternoon.

STEPHEN (*coldly*). Good afternoon.

UNDERSHAFT (*to Lady Britomart*). He knows all about the tradition, I suppose?

LADY BRITOMART. Yes. (*To Stephen*) It is what I told you last night, Stephen.

UNDERSHAFT (*sulkily*). I understand you want to come into the cannon business.

STEPHEN. *I* go into trade! Certainly not.

UNDERSHAFT (*opening his eyes, greatly eased in mind and manner*). Oh! in that case—

LADY BRITOMART. Cannons are not trade, Stephen. They are enterprise.

STEPHEN. I have no intention of becoming a man of business in any sense. I have no capacity for business and no taste for it. I intend to devote myself to politics.

UNDERSHAFT (*rising*). My dear boy: this is an immense relief to me. And I trust it may prove an equally good thing for the country. I was afraid you would consider yourself disparaged and slighted. (*He moves towards Stephen as if to shake hands with him*).

LADY BRITOMART (*rising and interposing*). Stephen: I cannot allow you to throw away an enormous property like this.

STEPHEN (*stiffly*). Mother: there must be an end of treating me as a child, if you please. (*Lady Britomart recoils, deeply wounded by his tone*). Until last night I did not take your attitude seriously, because I did not think you meant it seriously. But I find now that you left me in the dark as to matters which you should have explained to me years ago. I am extremely hurt and offended. Any further discussion of my intentions had better take place with my father, as between one man and another.

LADY BRITOMART. Stephen! (*She sits down again, her eyes filling with tears*).

UNDERSHAFT (*with grave compassion*). You see, my dear, it is only the big men who can be treated as children.

STEPHEN. I am sorry, mother, that you have forced me—

UNDERSHAFT (*stopping him*). Yes, yes, yes, yes: thats all right, Stephen. She wont interfere with you any more: your independence is achieved: you have won your latchkey. Dont rub it in; and above all, dont apologize. (*He resumes his seat*). Now what about your future, as between one man and another—I beg your pardon, Biddy: as between two men and a woman.

LADY BRITOMART (*who has pulled herself together strongly*). I quite understand, Stephen. By all means go your own way if you feel strong enough. (*Stephen sits down magisterially in the chair at the writing table with an air of affirming his majority*).

UNDERSHAFT. It is settled that you do not ask for the succession to the cannon business.

STEPHEN. I hope it is settled that I repudiate the cannon business.

UNDERSHAFT. Come, come! dont be so devilishly sulky: it's boyish. Freedom should be generous. Besides, I owe you a fair start in life in exchange for disinheriting you. You cant become prime minister all at once. Havnt you a turn for something? What about literature, art, and so forth?

STEPHEN. I have nothing of the artist about me, either in faculty or character, thank Heaven!

UNDERSHAFT. A philosopher, perhaps? Eh?

STEPHEN. I make no such ridiculous pretension.

UNDERSHAFT. Just so. Well, there is the army, the navy, the Church, the Bar. The Bar requires some ability. What about the Bar?

STEPHEN. I have not studied law. And I am afraid I have not the necessary push—I believe that is the name barristers give to their vulgarity—for success in pleading.

UNDERSHAFT. Rather a difficult case, Stephen. Hardly anything left but the stage, is there? (*Stephen makes an impatient movement*). Well, come! is there *anything* you know or care for?

STEPHEN (*rising and looking at him steadily*). I know the difference between right and wrong.

UNDERSHAFT (*hugely tickled*). You dont say so! What! no capacity for business, no knowledge of law, no sympathy with art, no pretension to philosophy; only a simple knowledge of the secret that has puzzled all the philosophers, baffled all the lawyers, muddled all the men of business, and ruined most of the artists: the secret of right and wrong. Why, man, youre a genius, a master of masters, a god! At twenty-four, too!

STEPHEN (*keeping his temper with difficulty*). You are pleased to be facetious. I pretend to nothing more than any honorable English gentleman claims as his birthright. (*He sits down angrily*).

UNDERSHAFT. Oh, thats everybody's birthright. Look at poor little Jenny Hill, the Salvation lassie! she would think you were laughing at her if you asked her to stand up in the street and teach grammar or geography or mathematics or even drawing room dancing; but it never occurs to her to doubt that she can teach morals and religion. You are all alike, you respectable people. You cant tell me the bursting strain of a ten-inch gun, which is a very simple matter; but you all think you can tell me the bursting strain of a man under temptation. You darent handle high explosives; but youre all ready to handle honesty and truth and justice and the whole duty of man, and kill one another at that game. What a country! What a world!

LADY BRITOMART (*uneasily*). What do you think he had better do, Andrew?

UNDERSHAFT. Oh, just what he wants to do. He knows nothing and he thinks he knows everything. That points clearly to a political career. Get him a private secretaryship to someone who can get him an Under Secretaryship; and then leave him alone. He will find his natural and proper place in the end on the Treasury Bench.

STEPHEN (*springing up again*). I am sorry, sir, that you force me to forget the respect due to you as my father. I am an Englishman and I will not hear the Government of my country insulted. (*He thrusts his hands in his pockets, and walks angrily across to the window*).

UNDERSHAFT (*with a touch of brutality*). The government of your country! *I* am the government of your country: I, and Lazarus. Do you suppose that you and half a dozen amateurs like you, sitting in a row in that foolish gabble shop, can govern Undershaft and Lazarus? No, my friend: you will do what pays *us*. You will make war when it suits us, and keep peace when it doesnt. You will find out that trade requires certain measures when we have decided on those measures. When I want anything to keep my dividends up, you will discover that my want is a national need. When other people want something to keep my dividends down, you will call out the police and military. And in return you shall have the support and applause of my newspapers, and the delight of imagining that you are a great statesman. Government of your country! Be off with you, my boy, and play with your caucuses and leading articles and historic parties and great leaders and burning questions and the rest of your toys. *I* am going back to my counting-house to pay the piper and call the tune.

STEPHEN (*actually smiling, and putting his hand on his father's shoulder with indulgent patronage*). Really, my dear father, it is impossible to be angry with you. You dont know how absurd all

this sounds to *me*. You are very properly proud of having been industrious enough to make money; and it is greatly to your credit
that you have made so much of it. But it has kept you in circles
where you are valued for your money and deferred to for it, instead
of in the doubtless very old-fashioned and behind-the-times public
school and university where I formed my habits of mind. It is
natural for you to think that money governs England; but you must
allow me to think I know better.

UNDERSHAFT. And what *does* govern England, pray?

STEPHEN. Character, father, character.

UNDERSHAFT. Whose character? Yours or mine?

STEPHEN. Neither yours nor mine, father, but the best elements
in the English national character.

UNDERSHAFT. Stephen: Ive found your profession for you. Youre
a born journalist. I'll start you with a high-toned weekly review.
There!

(*Before Stephen can reply Sarah, Barbara, Lomax, and Cusins
come in ready for walking. Barbara crosses the room to the window and looks out. Cusins drifts amiably to the armchair. Lomax
remains near the door, whilst Sarah comes to her mother.*

*Stephen goes to the smaller writing table and busies himself with
his letters*).

SARAH. Go and get ready, mamma: the carriage is waiting. (*Lady
Britomart leaves the room*).

UNDERSHAFT (*to Sarah*). Good day, my dear. Good afternoon,
Mr Lomax.

LOMAX (*vaguely*). Ahdedoo.

UNDERSHAFT (*to Cusins*). Quite well after last night, Euripides,
eh?

CUSINS. As well as can be expected.

UNDERSHAFT. That's right. (*To Barbara*) So you are coming to
see my death and devastation factory, Barbara?

BARBARA (*at the window*). You came yesterday to see my salvation factory. I promised you a return visit.

LOMAX (*coming forward between Sarah and Undershaft*). Youll
find it awfully interesting. Ive been through the Woolwich Arsenal;
and it gives you a ripping feeling of security, you know, to think of
the lot of beggars we could kill if it came to fighting. (*To Undershaft, with sudden solemnity*) Still, it must be rather an awful re-

flection for you, from the religious point of view as it were. Youre getting on, you know, and all that.

SARAH. You dont mind Cholly's imbecility, papa, do you?

LOMAX (*much taken aback*). Oh I say!

UNDERSHAFT. Mr Lomax looks at the matter in a very proper spirit, my dear.

LOMAX. Just so. Thats all I meant, I assure you.

SARAH. Are you coming, Stephen?

STEPHEN. Well, I am rather busy—er—(*Magnanimously*) Oh well, yes: I'll come. That is, if there is room for me.

UNDERSHAFT. I can take two with me in a little motor I am experimenting with for field use. You wont mind its being rather unfashionable. It's not painted yet; but it's bullet proof.

LOMAX (*appalled at the prospect of confronting Wilton Crescent in an unpainted motor*). Oh I say!

SARAH. The carriage for me, thank you. Barbara doesnt mind what she's seen in.

LOMAX. I say, Dolly, old chap: do you really mind the car being a guy? Because of course if you do I'll go in it. Still—

CUSINS. I prefer it.

LOMAX. Thanks awfully, old man. Come, my ownest. (*He hurries out to secure his seat in the carriage. Sarah follows him*).

CUSINS (*moodily walking across to Lady Britomart's writing table*). Why are we two coming to this Works Department of Hell? that is what I ask myself.

BARRARA. I have always thought of it as a sort of pit where lost creatures with blackened faces stirred up smoky fires and were driven and tormented by my father. Is it like that, dad?

UNDERSHAFT (*scandalized*). My dear! It is a spotlessly clean and beautiful hillside town.

CUSINS. With a Methodist chapel? Oh *do* say theres a Methodist chapel.

UNDERSHAFT. There are two: a Primitive one and a sophisticated one. There is even an Ethical Society; but it is not much patronized, as my men are all strongly religious. In the High Explosives Sheds they object to the presence of Agnostics as unsafe.

CUSINS. And yet they dont object to you!

BARBARA. Do they obey all your orders?

UNDERSHAFT. I never give them any orders. When I speak to one of them it is "Well, Jones, is the baby doing well? and has Mrs Jones made a good recovery?" "Nicely, thank you, sir." And thats all.

CUSINS. But Jones has to be kept in order. How do you maintain discipline among your men?

UNDERSHAFT. I dont. They do. You see, the one thing Jones wont stand is any rebellion from the man under him, or any assertion of social equality between the wife of the man with 4 shillings a week less than himself, and Mrs Jones! Of course they all rebel against me, theoretically. Practically, every man of them keeps the man just below him in his place. I never meddle with them. I never bully them. I dont even bully Lazarus. I say that certain things are to be done; but I dont order anybody to do them. I dont say, mind you, that there is no ordering about and snubbing and even bullying. The men snub the boys and order them about; the carmen snub the sweepers; the artisans snub the unskilled laborers; the foremen drive and bully both the laborers and artisans; the assistant engineers find fault with the foremen; the chief engineers drop on the assistants; the departmental managers worry the chiefs; and the clerks have tall hats and hymnbooks and keep up the social tone by refusing to associate on equal terms with anybody. The result is a colossal profit, which comes to me.

CUSINS (*revolted*). You really are a—well, what I was saying yesterday.

BARBARA. What was he saying yesterday?

UNDERSHAFT. Never mind, my dear. He thinks I have made you unhappy. Have I?

BARBARA. Do you think I can be happy in this vulgar silly dress? I! who have worn the uniform. Do you understand what you have done to me? Yesterday I had a man's soul in my hand. I set him in the way of life with his face to salvation. But when we took your money he turned back to drunkenness and derision. (*With intense conviction*) I will never forgive you that. If I had a child, and you destroyed its body with your explosives—if you murdered Dolly with your horrible guns—I could forgive you if my forgiveness would open the gates of heaven to you. But to take a human soul from me, and turn it into the soul of a wolf! that is worse than any murder.

UNDERSHAFT. Does my daughter despair so easily? Can you strike a man to the heart and leave no mark on him?

BARBARA (*her face lighting up*). Oh, you are right: he can never be lost now: where was my faith?

CUSINS. Oh, clever clever devil!

BARBARA. You may be a devil; but God speaks through you sometimes. (*She takes her father's hands and kisses them*). You have given me back my happiness: I feel it deep down now, though my spirit is troubled.

UNDERSHAFT. You have learnt something. That always feels at first as if you had lost something.

BARBARA. Well, take me to the factory of death; and let me learn something more. There must be some truth or other behind all this frightful irony. Come, Dolly. (*She goes out*).

CUSINS. My guardian angel! (*To Undershaft*) Avaunt (*He follows Barbara*).

STEPHEN (*quietly, at the writing table*). You must not mind Cusins, father. He is a very amiable good fellow; but he is a Greek scholar and naturally a little eccentric.

UNDERSHAFT. Ah, quite so. Thank you, Stephen. Thank you. (*He goes out*).

(*Stephen smiles patronizingly; buttons his coat responsibly; and crosses the room to the door. Lady Britomart, dressed for out-of-doors, opens it before he reaches it. She looks round for the others; looks at Stephen; and turns to go without a word*).

STEPHEN (*embarrassed*). Mother—

LADY BRITOMART. Dont be apologetic, Stephen. And dont forget that you have outgrown your mother. (*She goes out*).

Perivale St Andrews lies between two Middlesex hills, half climbing the northern one. It is an almost smokeless town of white walls, roofs of narrow green slates or red tiles, tall trees, domes, campaniles, and slender chimney shafts, beautifully situated and beautiful in itself. The best view of it is obtained from the crest of a slope about half a mile to the east, where the high explosives are dealt with. The foundry lies hidden in the depths between, the tops of its chimneys sprouting like huge skittles into the middle distance. Across the crest runs an emplacement of concrete, with a firestep, and a parapet which suggests a fortification, because there is a huge cannon of the obsolete Woolwich Infant pattern peering across it at the town. The cannon is mounted on an experimental gun carriage: possibly the original model of the Undershaft disappearing rampart gun alluded to by Stephen. The firestep, being a convenient place to sit, is furnished here and there with straw disc cushions; and at one place there is the additional luxury of a fur rug.

Barbara is standing on the firestep, looking over the parapet towards the town. On her right is the cannon; on her left the end of a shed raised on piles, with a ladder of three or four steps up to the door, which opens outwards and has a little wooden landing at the threshold, with a fire bucket in the corner of the landing. Several dummy soldiers more or less mutilated, with straw protruding from their gashes, have been shoved out of the way under the landing. A few others are nearly upright against the shed; and one has fallen forward and lies, like a grotesque corpse, on the emplacement. The parapet stops short of the shed, leaving a gap which is the beginning of the path down the hill through the foundry to the town. The rug is on the firestep near this gap. Down on the emplacement behind the cannon is a trolley carrying a huge conical bombshell with a red band painted on it. Further to the right is the door of an office, which, like the sheds, is of the lightest possible construction.

(Cusins arrives by the path from the town).

BARBARA. Well?

CUSINS. Not a ray of hope. Everything perfect! wonderful! real! It only needs a cathedral to be a heavenly city instead of a hellish one.

BARBARA. Have you found out whether they have done anything for old Peter Shirley?

CUSINS. They have found him a job as gatekeeper and timekeeper. He's frightfully miserable. He calls the timekeeping brainwork, and says he isnt uśed to it; and his gate lodge is so splendid that he's ashamed to use the rooms, and skulks in the scullery.

BARBARA. Poor Peter!

(Stephen arrives from the town. He carries a fieldglass).

STEPHEN *(enthusiastically)*. Have you two seen the place? Why did you leave us?

CUSINS. I wanted to see everything I was not intended to see; and Barbara wanted to make the men talk.

STEPHEN. Have you found anything discreditable?

CUSINS. No. They call him Dandy Andy and are proud of his

being a cunning old rascal; but it's all horribly, frightfully, immorally, unanswerably perfect.

(*Sarah arrives.*)

SARAH. Heavens! what a place! (*She crosses to the trolley*). Did you see the nursing home!? (*She sits down on the shell*).

STEPHEN. Did you see the libraries and schools!?

SARAH. Did you see the ball room and the banqueting chamber in the Town Hall!?

STEPHEN. Have you gone into the insurance fund, the pension fund, the building society, the various applications of cooperation!?

(*Undershaft comes from the office, with a sheaf of telegrams in his hand*).

UNDERSHAFT. Well, have you seen everything? I'm sorry I was called away. (*Indicating the telegrams*) Good news from Manchuria.

STEPHEN. Another Japanese victory?

UNDERSHAFT. Oh, I dont know. Which side wins does not concern us here. No: the good news is that the aerial battleship is a tremendous success. At the first trial it has wiped out a fort with three hundred soldiers in it.

CUSINS (*from the platform*). Dummy soldiers?

UNDERSHAFT (*striding across to Stephen and kicking the prostrate dummy brutally out of his way*). No: the real thing.

(*Cusins and Barbara exchange glances. Then Cusins sits on the step and buries his face in his hands. Barbara gravely lays her hand on his shoulder. He looks up at her in whimsical desperation*).

UNDERSHAFT. Well, Stephen, what do you think of the place?

STEPHEN. Oh, magnificent. A perfect triumph of modern industry. Frankly, my dear father, I have been a fool: I had no idea of what it all meant: of the wonderful forethought, the power of organization, the administrative capacity, the financial genius, the colossal capital it represents. I have been repeating to myself as I came through your streets "Peace hath her victories no less renowned than War." I have only one misgiving about it all.

UNDERSHAFT. Out with it.

STEPHEN. Well, I cannot help thinking that all this provision for every want of your workmen may sap their independence and weaken their sense of responsibility. And greatly as we enjoyed our tea at that splendid restaurant—how they gave us all that luxury

and cake and jam and cream for threepence I really cannot imagine!
—still you must remember that restaurants break up home life. Look
at the continent, for instance! Are you sure so much pampering is
really good for the men's characters?

UNDERSHAFT. Well you see, my dear boy, when you are organiz-
ing civilization you have to make up your mind whether trouble
and anxiety are good things or not. If you decide that they are, then,
I take it, you simply dont organize civilization; and there you are,
with trouble and anxiety enough to make us all angels! But if you
decide the other way, you may as well go through with it. However,
Stephen, our characters are safe here. A sufficient dose of anxiety is
always provided by the fact that we may be blown to smithereens at
any moment.

SARAH. By the way, papa, where do you make the explosives?

UNDERSHAFT. In separate little sheds, like that one. When one of
them blows up, it costs very little; and only the people quite close
to it are killed.

(*Stephen, who is quite close to it, looks at it rather scaredly, and
moves away quickly to the cannon. At the same moment the door
of the shed is thrown abruptly open; and a foreman in overalls
and list slippers comes out on the little landing and holds the door
for Lomax, who appears in the doorway*).

LOMAX (*with studied coolness*). My good fellow: you neednt
get into a state of nerves. Nothing's going to happen to you; and
I suppose it wouldnt be the end of the world if anything did. A
little bit of British pluck is what *you* want, old chap. (*He descends
and strolls across to Sarah*).

UNDERSHAFT (*to the foreman*). Anything wrong, Bilton?

BILTON (*with ironic calm*). Gentleman walked into the high explosives shed and lit a cigaret, sir: thats all.

UNDERSHAFT. Ah, quite so. (*Going over to Lomax*) Do you happen to remember what you did with the match?

LOMAX. Oh come! I'm not a fool. I took jolly good care to blow
it out before I chucked it away.

BILTON. The top of it was red hot inside, sir.

LOMAX. Well, suppose it was! I didn't chuck it into any of your
messes.

UNDERSHAFT. Think no more of it, Mr. Lomax. By the way,
would you mind lending me your matches.

LOMAX (*offering his box*). Certainly.

UNDERSHAFT. Thanks. (*He pockets the matches*).

LOMAX (*lecturing to the company generally*). You know, these high explosives dont go off like gunpowder, except when theyre in a gun. When theyre spread loose, you can put a match to them without the least risk: they just burn quietly like a bit of paper. (*Warming to the scientific interest of the subject*) Did you know that, Undershaft? Have you ever tried?

UNDERSHAFT. Not on a large scale, Mr. Lomax. Bilton will give -you a sample of gun cotton when you are leaving if you ask him. You can experiment with it at home. (*Bilton looks puzzled*).

SARAH. Bilton will do nothing of the sort, papa. I suppose it's your business to blow up the Russian and Japs; but you might really stop short of blowing up poor Cholly. (*Bilton gives it up and retires into the shed*).

LOMAX. My ownest, there is no danger. (*He sits beside her on the shell*).

(*Lady Britomart arrives from the town with a bouquet*).

LADY BRITOMART (*impetuously*). Andrew: you shouldnt have let me see this place.

UNDERSHAFT. Why, my dear?

LADY BRITOMART. Never mind why: you shouldnt have: thats all. To think of all that (*indicating the town*) being yours! and that you have kept it to yourself all these years!

UNDERSHAFT. It does not belong to me. I belong to it. It is the Undershaft inheritance.

LADY BRITOMART. It is not. Your ridiculous cannons and that noisy banging foundry may be the Undershaft inheritance; but all that plate and linen, all that furniture and those houses and orchards and gardens belong to us. They belong to *me:* they are a man's business. I wont give them up. You must be out of your senses to throw them all away; and if you persist in such folly, I will call in a doctor.

UNDERSHAFT (*stooping to smell the bouquet*). Where did you get the flowers, my dear?

LADY BRITOMART. Your men presented them to me in your William Morris Labor Church.

CUSINS. Oh! It needed only that. A Labor Church! (*He mounts the firestep distractedly, and leans with his elbows on the parapet, turning his back to them*).

LADY BRITOMART. Yes, with Morris's words in mosaic letters ten feet high round the dome. No MAN IS GOOD ENOUGH TO BE ANOTHER MAN'S MASTER. The cynicism of it!

UNDERSHAFT. It shocked the men at first, I am afraid. But now they take no more notice of it than of the ten commandments in church.

LADY BRITOMART. Andrew: you are trying to put me off the subject of the inheritance by profane jokes. Well, you shant. I dont ask it any longer for Stephen: he has inherited far too much of your perversity to be fit for it. But Barbara has rights as well as Stephen. Why should not Adolphus succeed to the inheritance? I could manage the town for him; and he can look after the cannons, if they are really necessary.

UNDERSHAFT. I should ask nothing better if Adolphus were a foundling. He is exactly the sort of new blood that is wanted in English business. But he's not a foundling; and theres an end of it. (*He makes for the office door*).

CUSINS (*turning to them*). Not quite. (*They all turn and stare at him*). I think— Mind! I am not committing myself in any way as to my future course—but I *think* the foundling difficulty can be got over. (*He jumps down to the emplacement*).

UNDERSHAFT (*coming back to him*). What do you mean?

CUSINS. Well, I have something to say which is in the nature of a confession.

SARAH.
LADY BRITOMART.   } Confession!
BARBARA.
STEPHEN.

LOMAX. Oh I say!

CUSINS. Yes, a confession. Listen, all. Until I met Barbara I thought myself in the main an honorable, truthful man, because I wanted the approval of my conscience more than I wanted anything else. But the moment I saw Barbara, I wanted her far more than the approval of my conscience.

LADY BRITOMART. Adolphus!

CUSINS. It is true. You accused me yourself, Lady Brit, of joining the Army to worship Barbara; and so I did. She bought my soul like a flower at a street corner; but she bought it for herself.

UNDERSHAFT. What! Not for Dionysos or another?

CUSINS. Dionysos and all the others are in herself. I adored what was divine in her, and was therefore a true worshipper. But I was romantic about her too. I thought she was a woman of the people, and that a marriage with a professor of Greek would be far beyond the wildest social ambitions of her rank.

LADY BRITOMART. Adolphus!

LOMAX. Oh I say!!!

CUSINS. When I learnt the horrible truth—

LADY BRITOMART. What do you mean by the horrible truth, pray?

CUSINS. That she was enormously rich; that her grandfather was an earl; that her father was the Prince of Darkness—

UNDERSHAFT. Chut!

CUSINS. —and that I was only an adventurer trying to catch a rich wife, then I stooped to deceive her about my birth.

BARBARA (rising). Dolly!

LADY BRITOMART. Your birth! Now Adolphus, dont dare to make up a wicked story for the sake of these wretched cannons. Remember: I have seen photographs of your parents; and the Agent General for South Western Australia knows them personally and has assured me that they are most respectable married people.

CUSINS. So they are in Australia; but here they are outcasts. Their marriage is legal in Australia, but not in England. My mother is my father's deceased wife's sister; and in this island I am consequently a foundling. (Sensation).

BARBARA. Silly! (She climbs to the cannon, and leans, listening, in the angle it makes with the parapet).

CUSINS. Is the subterfuge good enough, Machiavelli?

UNDERSHAFT (thoughtfully). Biddy: this may be a way out of the difficulty.

LADY BRITOMART. Stuff! A man cant make cannons any the better for being his own cousin instead of his proper self. (She sits down on the rug with a bounce that expresses her downright contempt for their casuistry).

UNDERSHAFT (to Cusins). You are an educated man. That is against the tradition.

CUSINS. Once in ten thousand times it happens that the schoolboy is a born master of what they try to teach him. Greek has not destroyed my mind: it has nourished it. Besides, I did not learn it at an English public school.

UNDERSHAFT. Hm! Well, I cannot afford to be too particular: you have cornered the foundling market. Let it pass. You are eligible, Euripides: you are eligible.

BARBARA. Dolly: yesterday morning, when Stephen told us all about the tradition, you became very silent; and you have been strange and excited ever since. Were you thinking of your birth then?

CUSINS. When the finger of Destiny suddenly points at a man in the middle of his breakfast, it makes him thoughtful.

UNDERSHAFT. Aha! You have had your eye on the business, my young friend, have you?

CUSINS. Take care! There is an abyss of moral horror between me and your accursed aerial battleships.

UNDERSHAFT. Never mind the abyss for the present. Let us settle the practical details and leave your final decision open. You know that you will have to change your name. Do you object to that?

CUSINS. Would any man named Adolphus—any man called Dolly! —object to be called something else?

UNDERSHAFT. Good. Now, as to money! I propose to treat you handsomely from the beginning. You shall start at a thousand a year.

CUSINS (*with sudden heat, his spectacles twinkling with mischief*). A thousand! You dare offer a miserable thousand to the son-in-law of a millionaire! No, by Heavens, Machiavelli! you shall not cheat *me*. You cannot do without me; and I can do without you. I must have two thousand five hundred a year for two years. At the end of that time, if I am a failure, I go. But if I am a success, and stay on, you must give me the other five thousand.

UNDERSHAFT. What other five thousand?

CUSINS. To make the two years up to five thousand a year. The two thousand five hundred is only half pay in case I should turn out a failure. The third year I must have ten per cent on the profits.

UNDERSHAFT (*taken aback*). Ten per cent! Why, man, do you know what my profits are?

CUSINS. Enormous, I hope: otherwise I shall require twenty-five per cent.

UNDERSHAFT. But, Mr Cusins, this is a serious matter of business. You are not bringing any capital into the concern.

CUSINS. What! no capital! Is my mastery of Greek no capital? Is my access to the subtlest thought, the loftiest poetry yet attained by humanity, no capital? My character! my intellect! my life! my career! what Barbara calls my soul are these no capital? Say another word; and I double my salary.

UNDERSHAFT. Be reasonable—

CUSINS (*peremptorily*). Mr Undershaft: you have my terms. Take them or leave them.

UNDERSHAFT (*recovering himself*). Very well. I note your terms; and I offer you half.

CUSINS (*disgusted*). Half!

UNDERSHAFT (*firmly*). Half.

CUSINS. You call yourself a gentleman; and you offer me half!!

UNDERSHAFT. I do not call myself a gentleman; but I offer you half.

CUSINS. This to your future partner! your successor! your son-in-law!

BARBARA. You are selling your own soul, Dolly, not mine. Leave me out of the bargain, please.

UNDERSHAFT. Come! I will go a step further for Barbara's sake. I will give you three fifths; but that is my last word.

CUSINS. Done!

LOMAX. Done in the eye! Why, *I* get only eight hundred, you know.

CUSINS. By the way, Mac, I am a classical scholar, not an arithmetical one. Is three fifths more than half or less?

UNDERSHAFT. More, of course.

CUSINS. I would have taken two hundred and fifty. How you can succeed in business when you are willing to pay all that money to a University don who is obviously not worth a junior clerk's wages! —well! What will Lazarus say?

UNDERSHAFT. Lazarus is a gentle romantic Jew who cares for nothing but string quartets and stalls at fashionable theatres. He will be blamed for your rapacity in money matters, poor fellow! as he has hitherto been blamed for mine. You are a shark of the first order, Euripides. So much the better for the firm!

BARBARA. Is the bargain closed, Dolly? Does your soul belong to him now?

CUSINS. No: the price is settled: that is all. The real tug of war is still to come. What about the moral question?

LADY BRITOMART. There is no moral question in the matter at all, Adolphus. You must simply sell cannons and weapons to people whose cause is right and just, and refuse them to foreigners and criminals.

UNDERSHAFT (*determinedly*). No: none of that. You must keep the true faith of an Armorer, or you dont come in here.

CUSINS. What on earth is the true faith of an Armorer?

UNDERSHAFT. To give arms to all men who offer an honest price for them, without respect of persons or principles: to aristocrat and republican, to Nihilist and Tsar, to Capitalist and Socialist, to Protestant and Catholic, to burglar and policeman, to black man, white man and yellow man, to all sorts and conditions, all nationalities, all faiths, all follies, all causes and all crimes. The first Undershaft wrote up in his shop IF GOD GAVE THE HAND, LET NOT MAN WITHHOLD THE SWORD. The second wrote up ALL HAVE THE RIGHT TO FIGHT: NONE HAVE THE RIGHT TO JUDGE. The third wrote up TO MAN THE WEAPON: TO HEAVEN THE VICTORY. The fourth had no literary turn; so he did not write up anything; but he sold cannons to Napoleon under the nose of George the Third. The fifth wrote up PEACE SHALL NOT PREVAIL SAVE WITH A SWORD IN HER HAND. The sixth, my master, was the best of all. He wrote up NOTHING IS EVER DONE IN THIS WORLD UNTIL MEN ARE PREPARED TO KILL ONE ANOTHER IF IT IS NOT DONE. After that, there was nothing left for the seventh to say. So he wrote up, simply, UNASHAMED.

CUSINS. My good Machiavelli, I shall certainly write something up on the wall; only, as I shall write it in Greek, you wont be able to read it. But as to your Armorer's faith, if I take my neck out of the noose of my own morality I am not going to put it into the noose of yours. I shall sell cannons to whom I please and refuse them to whom I please. So there!

UNDERSHAFT. From the moment when you become Andrew Undershaft, you will never do as you please again. Dont come here lusting for power, young man.

CUSINS. If power were my aim I should not come here for it. You have no power.

UNDERSHAFT. None of my own, certainly.

CUSINS. I have more power than you, more will. You do not drive this place: it drives you. And what drives the place?

UNDERSHAFT (*enigmatically*). A will of which I am a part.

BARBARA (*startled*). Father! Do you know what you are saying; or are you laying a snare for my soul?

CUSINS. Dont listen to his metaphysics, Barbara. The place is driven by the most rascally part of society, the money hunters, the pleasure hunters, the military promotion hunters; and he is their slave.

UNDERSHAFT. Not necessarily. Remember the Armorer's Faith. I will take an order from a good man as cheerfully as from a bad one. If you good people prefer preaching and shirking to buying my weapons and fighting the rascals, dont blame me. I can make cannons: I cannot make courage and conviction. Bah! You tire me, Euripides, with your morality mongering. Ask Barbara: *she* understands. (*He suddenly reaches up and takes Barbara's hands, looking powerfully into her eyes*). Tell him, my love, what power really means.

BARBARA (*hypnotized*). Before I joined the Salvation Army, I was in my own power; and the consequence was that I never knew what to do with myself. When I joined it, I had not time enough for all the things I had to do.

UNDERSHAFT (*approvingly*). Just so. And why was that, do you suppose?

BARBARA. Yesterday I should have said, because I was in the power of God. (*She resumes her self-possession, withdrawing her hands from his with a power equal to his own*). But you came and shewed me that I was in the power of Bodger and Undershaft. Today I feel—oh! how can I put it into words? Sarah: do you remember the earthquake at Cannes, when we were little children—how little the surprise of the first shock mattered compared to the dread and horror of waiting for the second? That is how I feel in this place today. I stood on the rock I thought eternal; and without a word of warning it reeled and crumbled under me. I was safe with an infinite wisdom watching me, an army marching to Salvation with me; and in a moment, at a stroke of your pen in a cheque book, I stood alone; and the heavens were empty. That was the first shock of the earthquake: I am waiting for the second.

UNDERSHAFT. Come, come, my daughter! dont make too much of your little tinpot tragedy. What do we do here when we spend years of work and thought and thousands of pounds of solid cash on a new gun or an aerial battleship that turns out just a hairs-breadth wrong after all? Scrap it. Scrap it without wasting another hour or another pound on it. Well, you have made for yourself something that you call a morality or a religion or what not. It doesn't fit the facts. Well, scrap it. Scrap it and get one that does fit. That is what is wrong with the world at present. It scraps its obsolete steam engines and dynamos; but it wont scrap its old prejudices and its old moralities and its old religions and its old political constitutions? Whats the result? In machinery it does very well; but in morals and religion and politics it is working at a loss that brings it nearer bankruptcy every year. Dont persist in that folly. If your old religion broke down yesterday, get a newer and a better one for tomorrow.

BARBARA. Oh how gladly I would take a better one to my soul! But you offer me a worse one. (*Turning on him with sudden vehemence*). Justify yourself: shew me some light through the darkness of this dreadful place, with its beautifully clean workshops, and respectable workmen, and model homes.

UNDERSHAFT. Cleanliness and respectability do not need justification, Barbara: they justify themselves. I see no darkness here, no dreadfulness. In your Salvation shelter I saw poverty, misery, cold and hunger. You gave them bread and treacle and dreams of heaven. I give from thirty shillings a week to twelve thousand a year. They find their own dreams; but I look after the drainage.

BARBARA. And their souls?

UNDERSHAFT. I save their souls just as I saved yours.

BARBARA (*revolted*). You saved my soul! What do you mean?

UNDERSHAFT. I fed you and clothed you and housed you. I took care that you should have money enough to live handsomely—more than enough; so that you could be wasteful, careless, generous. That saved your soul from the seven deadly sins.

BARBARA (*bewildered*). The seven deadly sins!

UNDERSHAFT. Yes, the deadly seven. (*Counting on his fingers*) Food, clothing, firing, rent, taxes, respectability and childen. Nothing can lift those seven millstones from Man's neck but money; and the spirit cannot soar until the millstones are lifted. I lifted them from your spirit. I enabled Barbara to become Major Barbara; and I saved her from the crime of poverty.

CUSINS. Do you call poverty a crime?

UNDERSHAFT. The worst of crimes. All the other crimes are virtues beside it: all the other dishonors are chivalry itself by comparison. Poverty blights whole cities; spreads horrible pestilences; strikes dead the very souls of all who come within sight, sound, or smell of it. What *you* call crime is nothing: a murder here and a theft there, a blow now and a curse then: what do they matter? they are only the accidents and illnesses of life: there are not fifty genuine professional criminals in London. But there are millions of poor people, abject people, dirty people, ill fed, ill clothed people. They poison us morally and physically: they kill the happiness of society: they force us to do away with our own liberties and to organize unnatural cruelties for fear they should rise against us and drag us down into their abyss. Only fools fear crime: we all fear poverty. Pah! (*turning on Barbara*) you talk of your half-saved ruffian in West Ham: you accuse me of dragging his soul back to perdition. Well, bring him to me here; and I will drag his soul back again to salvation for you. Not by words and dreams; but by thirty-eight shillings a week, a sound house in a handsome street, and a permanent job. In three weeks he will have a fancy waistcoat; in three months a tall hat and a chapel sitting; before the end of the year he will shake hands with a duchess at a Primrose League meeting, and join the Conservative Party.

BARBARA. And will he be the better for that?

UNDERSHAFT. You know he will. Dont be a hypocrite, Barbara. He will be better fed, better housed, better clothed, better behaved; and his children will be pounds heavier and bigger. That will be better than an American cloth mattress in a shelter, chopping firewood, eating bread and treacle, and being forced to kneel down from time to time to thank heaven for it: knee drill, I think you call it. It is cheap work converting starving men with a Bible in one hand and a slice of bread in the other. I will undertake to convert West Ham to Mahometanism on the same terms. Try your hand on *my* men: their souls are hungry because their bodies are full.

BARBARA. And leave the east end to starve?

UNDERSHAFT (*his energetic tone dropping into one of bitter and brooding remembrance*). I was an east ender. I moralized and starved until one day I swore that I would be a full-fed free man at all costs; that nothing should stop me except a bullet, neither reason nor morals nor the lives of other men. I said "Thou shalt starve ere I starve"; and with that word I became free and great. I was a dangerous man until I had my will: now I am a useful, beneficent, kindly person. That is the history of most self-made millionaires, I fancy. When it is the history of every Englishman we shall have an England worth living in.

LADY BRITOMART. Stop making speeches, Andrew. This is not the place for them.

UNDERSHAFT (*punctured*). My dear: I have no other means of conveying my ideas.

LADY BRITOMART. Your ideas are nonsense. You got on because you were selfish and unscrupulous.

UNDERSHAFT. Not at all. I had the strongest scruples about poverty and starvation. Your moralists are quite unscrupulous about both: they make virtues of them. I had rather be a thief than a pauper. I had rather be a murderer than a slave. I dont want to be either; but if you force the alternative on me, then, by Heaven, I'll choose the braver and more moral one. I hate poverty and slavery worse than any other crimes whatsoever. And let me tell you this. Poverty and slavery have stood up for centuries to your sermons and leading articles: they will not stand up to my machine guns. Dont preach at them: dont reason with them. Kill them.

BARBARA. Killing. Is that your remedy for everything?

UNDERSHAFT. It is the final test of conviction, the only lever strong enough to overturn a social system, the only way of saying Must. Let six hundred and seventy fools loose in the streets; and three policemen can scatter them. But huddle them together in a certain house in Westminster; and let them go through certain ceremonies and call themselves certain names until at last they get the courage to kill; and your six hundred and seventy fools become a government. Your pious mob fills up ballot papers and imagines it is governing its masters; but the ballot paper that really governs is the paper that has a bullet wrapped up in it.

CUSINS. That is perhaps why, like most intelligent people, I never vote.

UNDERSHAFT. Vote! Bah! When you vote, you only change the names of the cabinet. When you shoot, you pull down governments, inaugurate new epochs, abolish old orders and set up new. Is that historically true, Mr. Learned Man, or is it not?

CUSINS. It is historically true. I loathe having to admit it. I repudiate your sentiments. I abhor your nature. I defy you in every possible way. Still, it is true. But it ought not to be true.

UNDERSHAFT. Ought! ought! ought! ought! ought! Are you going to spend your life saying ought, like the rest of our moralists? Turn your oughts into shalls, man. Come and make explosives with me. Whatever can blow men up can blow society up. The history of the world is the history of those who had courage enough to embrace this truth. Have you the courage to embrace it, Barbara?

LADY BRITOMART. Barbara: I positively forbid you to listen to your father's abominable wickedness. And you, Adolphus, ought to know better than to go about saying that wrong things are true. What does it matter whether they are true if they are wrong?

UNDERSHAFT. What does it matter whether they are wrong if they are true?

LADY BRITOMART (*rising*). Children: come home instantly. Andrew: I am exceedingly sorry I allowed you to call on us. You are wickeder than ever. Come at once.

BARBARA (*shaking her head*). It's no use running away from wicked people, mamma.

LADY BRITOMART. It is every use. It shews your disapprobation of them.

BARBARA. It does not save them.

LADY BRITOMART. I can see that you are going to disobey me. Sarah: are you coming home or are you not?

SARAH. I daresay it's very wicked of papa to make cannons; but I dont think I shall cut him on that account.

LOMAX (*pouring oil on the troubled waters*). The fact is, you know, there is a certain amount of tosh about this notion of wickedness. It doesnt work. You must look at facts. Not that I would say a word in favor of anything wrong; but then, you see, all sorts of chaps are always doing all sorts of things; and we have to fit them in somehow, dont you know. What I mean is that you cant go cutting everybody; and thats about what it comes to. (*Their rapt attention to his eloquence makes him nervous*). Perhaps I dont make myself clear.

LADY BRITOMART. You are lucidity itself, Charles. Because Andrew is successful and has plenty of money to give to Sarah, you will flatter him and encourage him in his wickedness.

LOMAX (*unruffled*). Well, where the carcase is, there will the eagles be gathered, dont you know. (*To Undershaft*) Eh? What?

UNDERSHAFT. Precisely. By the way, may I call you Charles?

LOMAX. Delighted. Cholly is the usual ticket.

UNDERSHAFT (*to Lady Britomart*). Biddy—

LADY BRITOMART (*violently*). Dont dare call me Biddy. Charles Lomax: you are a fool. Adolphus Cusins: you are a Jesuit. Stephen: you are a prig. Barbara: you are a lunatic. Andrew: you are a vulgar tradesman. Now you all know my opinion; and my conscience is clear, at all events. (*She sits down with a vehemence that the rug fortunately softens*).

UNDERSHAFT. My dear: you are the incarnation of morality. (*She snorts*). Your conscience is clear and your duty done when you have called everybody names. Come, Euripides! it is getting late; and we all want to go home. Make up your mind.

CUSINS. Understand this, you old demon—

LADY BRITOMART. Adolphus!

UNDERSHAFT. Let him alone, Biddy. Proceed, Euripides.

CUSINS. You have me in a horrible dilemma. I want Barbara.

UNDERSHAFT. Like all young men, you greatly exaggerate the difference between one young woman and another.

BARBARA. Quite true, Dolly.

CUSINS. I also want to avoid being a rascal.

UNDERSHAFT (*with biting contempt*). You lust for personal righteousness, for self-approval, for what you call a good conscience, for what Barbara calls salvation, for what I call patronizing people who are not so lucky as yourself.

CUSINS. I do not: all the poet in me recoils from being a good man. But there are things in me that I must reckon with. Pity—

UNDERSHAFT. Pity! The scavenger of misery.

CUSINS. Well, love.

UNDERSHAFT. I know. You love the needy and the outcast: you love the oppressed races, the negro, the Indian ryot, the underdog everywhere. Do you love the Japanese? Do you love the French? Do you love the English?

CUSINS. No. Every true Englishman detests the English. We are the wickedest nation on earth; and our success is a moral horror.

UNDERSHAFT. That is what comes of your gospel of love, is it?

CUSINS. May I not love even my father-in-law?

UNDERSHAFT. Who wants your love, man? By what right do

you take the liberty of offering it to me? I will have your due heed and respect, or I will kill you. But your love! Damn your impertinence!

CUSINS (*grinning*). I may not be able to control my affections, Mac.

UNDERSHAFT. You are fencing, Euripides. You are weakening: your grip is slipping. Come! try your last weapon. Pity and love have broken in your hand: forgiveness is still left.

CUSINS. No: forgiveness is a beggar's refuge. I am with you there: we must pay our debts.

UNDERSHAFT. Well said. Come! you will suit me. Remember the words of Plato.

CUSINS (*starting*). Plato! *You* dare quote Plato to *me!*

UNDERSHAFT. Plato says, my friend, that society cannot be saved until either the Professors of Greek take to making gunpowder, or else the makers of gunpowder become Professors of Greek.

CUSINS. Oh, tempter, cunning tempter!

UNDERSHAFT. Come! choose, man, choose.

CUSINS. But perhaps Barbara will not marry me if I make the wrong choice.

BARBARA. Perhaps not.

CUSINS (*desperately perplexed*). You hear!

BARBARA. Father: do you love nobody?

UNDERSHAFT. I love my best friend.

LADY BRITOMART. And who is that, pray?

UNDERSHAFT. My bravest enemy. That is the man who keeps me up to the mark.

CUSINS. You know, the creature is really a sort of poet in his way. Suppose he is a great man, after all!

UNDERSHAFT. Suppose you stop talking and make up your mind, my young friend.

CUSINS. But you are driving me against my nature. I hate war.

UNDERSHAFT. Hatred is the coward's revenge for being intimidated. Dare you make war on war? Here are the means: my friend Mr Lomax is sitting on them.

LOMAX (*springs up*). Oh I say! You dont mean that this thing is loaded, do you? My ownest: come off it.

SARAH (*sitting placidly on the shelf*). If I am to be blown up, the more thoroughly it is done the better. Dont fuss, Cholly.

LOMAX (*to Undershaft, strongly remonstrant*). Your own daughter, you know!

UNDERSHAFT. So I see. (*To Cusins*) Well, my friend, may we expect you here at six tomorrow morning?

CUSINS (*firmly*). Not on any account. I will see the whole establishment blown up with its own dynamite before I will get up at five. My hours are healthy, rational hours: eleven to five.

UNDERSHAFT. Come when you please: before a week you will come at six and stay until I turn you out for the sake of your health. (*Calling*) Bilton! (*He turns to Lady Britomart, who rises*). My dear: let us leave these two young people to themselves for a moment. (*Bilton comes from the shed*). I am going to take you through the gun cotton shed.

BILTON (*barring the way*). You cant take anything explosive in here, sir.

LADY BRITOMART. What do you mean? Are you alluding to me?

BILTON (*unmoved*). No, maam. Mr Undershaft has the other gentleman's matches in his pocket.

LADY BRITOMART (*abruptly*). Oh! I beg your pardon. (*She goes into the shed*).

UNDERSHAFT. Quite right, Bilton, quite right: here you are. (*He gives Bilton the box of matches*). Come, Stephen. Come, Charles. Bring Sarah. (*He passes into the shed*).

(*Bilton opens the box and deliberately drops the matches into the fire-bucket*).

LOMAX. Oh! I say. (*Bilton stolidly hands him the empty box*). Infernal nonsense! Pure scientific ignorance! (*He goes in*).

SARAH. Am I all right, Bilton?

BILTON. Youll have to put on list slippers, miss: thats all. Weve got em inside. (*She goes in*).

STEPHEN (*very seriously to Cusins*). Dolly, old fellow, think. Think before you decide. Do you feel that you are a sufficiently practical man? It is a huge undertaking, an enormous responsibility. All this mass of business will be Greek to you.

CUSINS. Oh, I think it will be much less difficult than Greek.

STEPHEN. Well, I just want to say this before I leave you to yourselves. Dont let anything I have said about right and wrong prejudice you against this great chance in life. I have satisfied myself that the business is one of the highest character and a credit to our country. (*Emotionally*) I am very proud of my father. I— (*Unable to proceed, he presses Cusins' hand and goes hastily into the shed, followed by Bilton*).

(*Barbara and Cusins, left alone together, look at one another silently*).

CUSINS. Barbara: I am going to accept this offer.

BARBARA. I thought you would.

CUSINS. You understand, dont you, that I had to decide without consulting you. If I had thrown the burden of the choice on you, you would sooner or later have despised me for it.

BARBARA. Yes: I did not want you to sell your soul for me any more than for this inheritance.

CUSINS. It is not the sale of my soul that troubles me: I have sold it too often to care about that. I have sold it for a professorship. I have sold it for an income. I have sold it to escape being imprisoned for refusing to pay taxes for hangmen's ropes and unjust wars and things that I abhor. What is all human conduct but the daily and hourly sale of our souls for trifles? What I am now selling it for is neither money nor position nor comfort, but for reality and for power.

BARBARA. You know that you will have no power, and that he has none.

CUSINS. I know. It is not for myself alone. I want to make power for the world.

BARBARA. I want to make power for the world too; but it must be spiritual power.

CUSINS. I think all power is spiritual: these cannons will not go off by themselves. I have tried to make spiritual power by teaching Greek. But the world can never be really touched by a dead language and a dead civilization. The people must have power; and the people cannot have Greek. Now the power that is made here can be wielded by all men.

BARBARA. Power to burn women's houses down and kill their sons and tear their husbands to pieces.

CUSINS. You cannot have power for good without having power for evil too. Even mother's milk nourishes murderers as well as heroes. This power which only tears men's bodies to pieces has never been so horribly abused as the intellectual power, the imaginative power, the poetic, religious power that can enslave men's souls. As a teacher of Greek I gave the intellectual man weapons against the common man. I now want to give the common man weapons against the intellectual man. I love the common people. I want to arm them against the lawyers, the doctors, the priests, the literary men, the professors, the artists, and the politicians, who, once in authority, are more disastrous and tyrannical than all the fools, rascals, and impostors. I want a power simple enough for common men to use, yet strong enough to force the intellectual oligarchy to use its genius for the general good.

BARBARA. Is there no higher power than that (*pointing to the shell*)?

CUSINS. Yes; but that power can destroy the higher powers just as a tiger can destroy a man: therefore Man must master that power first. I admitted this when the Turks and Greeks were last at war. My best pupil went out to fight for Hellas. My parting gift to him was not a copy of Plato's Republic, but a revolver and a hundred Undershaft cartridges. The blood of every Turk he shot—if he shot any—is on my head as well as on Undershaft's. That act committed me to this place for ever. Your father's challenge has beaten me. Dare I make war on war? I must. I will. And now, is it all over between us?

BARBARA (*touched by his evident dread of her answer*). Silly baby Dolly! How could it be!

CUSINS (*overjoyed*). Then you—you—you— Oh for my drum! (*He flourishes imaginary drumsticks*).

BARBARA (*angered by his levity*). Take care, Dolly, take care. Oh, if only I could get away from you and from father and from it all! if I could have the wings of a dove and fly away to heaven!

CUSINS. And leave *me!*

BARBARA. Yes, you, and all the other naughty mischievous children of men. But I cant. I was happy in the Salvation Army for a moment. I escaped from the world into a paradise of enthusiasm and prayer and soul saving; but the moment our money ran short, it all came back to Bodger: it was he who saved our people: he, and the Prince of Darkness, my papa. Undershaft and Bodger: their hands stretch everywhere: when we feed a starving fellow creature, it is with their bread, because there is no other bread; when we tend the sick, it is in the hospitals they endow; if we turn from the churches they build, we must kneel on the stones of the streets they

pave. As long as that lasts, there is no getting away from them. Turning our backs on Bodger and Undershaft is turning our backs on life.

CUSINS. I thought you were determined to turn your back on the
wicked side of life.

BARBARA. There is no wicked side: life is all one. And I never
wanted to shirk my share in whatever evil must be endured, whether
it be sin or suffering. I wish I could cure you of middle-class ideas,
Dolly.

CUSINS (*gasping*). Middle cl—! A snub! A social snub to *me!*
from the daughter of a foundling!

BARBARA. That is why I have no class, Dolly: I come straight out
of the heart of the whole people. If I were middle-class I should turn
my back on my father's business; and we should both live in an
artistic drawing room with you reading the reviews in one corner,
and I in the other at the piano, playing Schumann: both very superior persons, and neither of us a bit of use. Sooner than that, I would
sweep out the gun-cotton shed, or be one of Bodger's barmaids. Do
you know what would have happened if you had refused papa's
offer?

CUSINS. I wonder!

BARBARA. I should have given you up and married the man who
accepted it. After all, my dear old mother has more sense than any of
you. I felt like her when I saw this place—felt that I must have it—
that never, never, never could I let it go; only she thought it was
the houses and the kitchen ranges and the linen and china, when it
was really all the human souls to be saved: not weak souls in starved
bodies, sobbing with gratitude for a scrap of bread and treacle, but
fulfed, quarrelsome, snobbish, uppish creatures, all standing on their
rights and dignities, and thinking that my father ought to be greatly
obliged to them for making so much money for him—and so he
ought. That is where salvation is really wanted. My father shall never
throw it in my teeth again that my converts were bribed with bread.
(*She is transfigured*). I have got rid of the bribe of bread. I have
got rid of the bribe of heaven. Let God's work be done for its own
sake: the work he had to create us to do because it cannot be done
except by living men and women. When I die, let him be in my
debt, not I in his; and let me forgive him as becomes a woman of
my rank.

CUSINS. Then the way of life lies through the factory of death?

BARBARA. Yes, through the raising of hell to heaven and of man to God, through the unveiling of an eternal light in the Valley of The Shadow. (*Seizing him with both hands*) Oh, did you think my courage would never come back? did you believe that I was a deserter? that I, who have stood in the streets, and taken my people to my heart, and talked of the holiest and greatest things with them, could ever. turn back and chatter foolishly to fashionable people about nothing in a drawing room? Never, never, never, never: Major Barbara will die with the colors. Oh! and I have my dear little Dolly boy still; and he has found me my place and my work. Glory Hallelujas! (*She kisses him*).

CUSINS. My dearest: consider my delicate health. I cannot stand as much happiness as you can.

BARBARA. Yes: it is not easy work being in love with me, is it? But it's good for you. (*She runs to the shed, and calls, childlike*) Mamma! Mamma! (*Bilton comes out of the shed, followed by Undershaft*). I want Mamma.

UNDERSHAFT. She is taking off her list slippers, dear. (*He passes on to Cusins*). Well? What does she say?

CUSINS. She has gone right up into the skies.

LADY BRITOMART (*coming from the shed and stopping on the steps, obstructing Sarah, who follows with Lomax. Barbara clutches like a baby at her mother's skirt*). Barbara: when will you learn to be independent and to act and think for yourself? I know as well as possible what that cry of "Mamma, Mamma," means. Always running to me!

SARAH (*touching Lady Britomart's ribs with her finger tips and imitating a bicycle horn*). Pip! pip!

LADY BRITOMART (*highly indignant*). How dare you say Pip! pip! to me, Sarah? You are both very naughty children. What do you want, Barbara?

BARBARA. I want a house in the village to live in with Dolly. (*Dragging at the skirt*) Come and tell me which one to take.

UNDERSHAFT (*to Cusins*). Six o'clock tomorrow morning, Euripides.

THE END

MAJOR BARBARA—
SHAW'S "DIVINE COMEDY"

Major Barbara, Shaw's most religious drama, contains most of the qualities of Shaw's earlier and later output.* It is the epitome of his dramatic talent and deservedly requires careful examination. A comparison to Dante's *Divine Comedy* can bring a greater understanding of *Major Barbara.* At the outset it must be acknowledged that, as comedies, the *Divine Comedy* and *Major Barbara* differ in technique. However, they both utilize the threefold structure of sin, repentance, and salvation, and that common structure makes the comparison valuable. Both Shaw's and Dante's works move from a picture of hell toward a vision of heaven; both are parables of the human condition. The parallel qualities of the two works are not, however, readily apparent until the second act of *Major Barbara,* as Shaw uses Act I for introduction of characters. Act I establishes, as a religious allegory, the conflict between Barbara and Undershaft. Undershaft, a merchant of weapons, challenges his daughter Barbara, a representative of the Christianity-focused Salvation Army, to a contest of ideologies. As his basic premise, Shaw operates from the belief that poverty is the ultimate in sin; whereas, Dante's beginning point was the justness of an omnipotent God. Shaw's viewpoint is thus a negative one, and Undershaft functions by trying to obliterate poverty at all costs. Act II serves a purpose similar to Dante's inferno and Purgatorio. Shaw must present the existence of sin, poverty, the need for repentance, and direction toward salvation, Undershaft's economic power. Bill Walker establishes the process through feeling remorse for his sin, striking a Salvation Army girl. Cusins serves as Undershaft's first antagonist, and, through Cusins, the contest with and ultimately for Barbara is waged. Undershaft's purchase of the Salvation Army does not provide immediate victory in the contest, for it is also necessary that Shaw's concept of revolution be under the leadership of the elite; Cusins and Barbara must be converted as Undershaft, because of his birth, is not elite. Bill Walker's conflict occurs parallel to the contest and reinforces the process of sin-

* Abstracted from Joseph Frank, *"Major Barbara*—Shaw's 'Divine Comedy,'" *PMLA, LXXI* (1956), 61-74.

repentance-salvation while demonstrating a loss of confidence in traditional modes of social justice, the charity of the Salvation Army which fosters poverty, submissiveness, and humility. At the end of Act II, Cusins, Barbara, and Bill Walker are rapidly moving toward Undershaftian salvation, toward wealth, rebellion, and pride. Act III presents a view of Undershaft's city of heaven, Perivale St. Andrews. As such, the act structurally parallels Dante's Paradiso, yet this heaven contains a paradox. As a Utopia, its center is a materialistic factory of death and destruction. In order for Undershaft to be victorious in the ideological contest, he must win Barbara's soul by spanning the moral abyss which Cusins recognizes. Shaw spans this abyss with a logic reminiscent of Dante's. Weapons are not an issue of morality since they are available to both good men and bad men. A good man, in order to achieve good, is willing to use any means and will destroy any tradition in order to reach a positive end. If poverty can only be destroyed by ruthlessness, then the good man, following in Undershaft's footsteps, must employ those means. Cusins and Barbara accept Undershaft's heaven, paralleling the multifoliate rose of Dante, and the tone of the drama soars to a religious level. Just as did Dante's pilgrim, Barbara joins with the Life Force, the Will, which transcends the death factory and reaches into the heavenly city of life. *Major Barbara* contains Shaw's socialism and his disillusionment with democracy. It involves the concept of Life Force, but to a lesser extent than earlier plays. Shaw's treatment of Undershaft, a mixture of reverence and mockery, exemplifies his later dramatic techniques. *Major Barbara* is central to Shaw's dramatic abilities, and, as such, is well-deserving of comparison to Dante's *Divine Comedy*.

THE DEVIL
AND *MAJOR BARBARA*

Although George Bernard Shaw generally sought stylistic clarity in his use of irony, exceptions do exist.* Unfortunately, the more subtle the use of irony, the more it tests the reader's abilities and the more likely the reader is to misinterpret the literary work. In the case of *Major Barbara,* Shaw's ironic technique, multi-dimensional in its vision, creates interpretation difficulties. The similarities between Shaw's preface to *Major Barbara* and Undershaft's views on money and power (gunpowder) are obvious. Such similarities have caused critics to assume that Shaw used Undershaft as a mouthpiece for political philosophy. Since presenting revolution as an expedient to socialism differs from such Shaw works as *Man and Superman* and *Arms and the Man,* critics have further suggested that *Major Barbara* represents a dramatic change in the evolution of Shaw's political-philosophical thought. In these respects, *Major Barbara* has been seriously misunderstood. Writing to Louis Calvert, an actor, Shaw described Undershaft as having "a most terribly wicked religion of his own, believing only in money and gunpowder. . . ." Although Undershaft seems to champion militarism as being moral, Shaw's reputation for ideas, established through his other creative works, does not coincide with Undershaft's morality. Examining the character of Jack Tanner in *Man and Superman,* Tanner obviously manifests a life style which is active and consistent. Shaw himself was known for this quality, and so is Undershaft. But there is a crucial difference between Tanner and Undershaft, just as there is a difference between Shaw and Undershaft. Tanner develops his life style while thriving under the freedom and power characteristic of the rich; Undershaft achieves his under the realistic pressure of poverty. For Undershaft the choice lies between poverty through pacifism or wealth through militarism. Undershaft therefore chose the aggressive trade since it provided for the active expression of his Life Force, a quality similar to Bergson's "élan vital," rather than

* Abstracted from Charles A. Berst, "The Devil and *Major Barbara.*" *PMLA,* LXXXIII (March, 1968), 71-79.

the alternative of a passive existence. Undershaft went into arma-
ments; Kitty Warren became a prostitute. Both chose a way of life
which permitted an active expression of their respective Life Forces.
Shaw is not promoting the morality of prostitution or revolution.
Rather, his concern lies with the portrayal of characters who do the
best they can in the situation society creates. Because these characters
act to fulfill their Life Force, their life style becomes a religion, a
total commitment. Within this process, the distinction between
character and conduct becomes important in Shaw's use of subtle
irony. In order to achieve this distinction between character and
conduct, Shaw portrays Undershaft's devil qualities against Barbara's
angelic qualities. Considering Undershaft as the main character aids
in the interpretation of the ironies involved in the counterpoint
structure of the drama. Undershaft is diabolical, for he reflects the
diabolical society which nurtured him. Moreover, Shaw portrays
Undershaft as a orphan in order to reinforce the man-as-product-
of-society relationship; Undershaft's orphan status means he is a
child of society alone. As such, he conducts himself as the Prince
of Darkness. His character is, however, more complex; Undershaft
should be considered as a character who honestly lives his Life
Force. Shaw and Undershaft are not one, for Shaw's own Life Force
did not gain fulfillment in destruction and death as does Undershaft's. *Major Barbara* should thus be viewed as a search for a religion which incorporates both the diabolical fact of society and the
altruistic ideal of individual integrity.

TOWARD AN INTERPRETATION OF *MAJOR BARBARA*

The fact that Andrew Undershaft seems to dominate *Major
Barbara,* plus the fact of Shaw's designation of him in the Preface
as the hero of the play, has been the cause of concern and puzzlement
among a variety of commentators.* The drama has been called "a

* Abstracted from Bernard F. Dukore, "Toward an Interpretation of
Major Barbara," Shaw Review, VI (May, 1963), 62-70.

dance of devils," "the triumph of the unmoral purpose," and, in the Marxist view, heresy ("the imperialist is canonized as St. Andrew Undershaft . . . Shaw's Fabianism made him choose the wrong hero, the capitalist himself"). Even Eric Bentley declared that Shaw's intention to make Cusins the synthesis of idealism and realism fails because Undershaft is a "monster so impressive that no good man can match him." However, examination of Shaw's revisions of *Major Barbara,* comparing the two basic editions of the play (1907 and the Standard Edition of 1931), can aid in determining the relative importance of Undershaft, Barbara, and Cusins. Shaw's revisions fall into two general categories: refinement of detail, and interpretation. Those of the first category concern such matters as stage business and characterization: the opening stage directions in the later edition are more specific; character is more sharply drawn in the later version; and there are more descriptive details to aid our perception of the characters' manner on the stage. By these revisions regarding detail, Shaw achieves in the Standard Edition greater clarity and apprehension of the stage "business" for the reader. The second category of changes, however, is significant in terms of the play's meaning: these changes build up in importance the roles of Barbara and Cusins, and provide evidence that Barbara may properly be regarded as the play's heroine. The revisions tend to make Barbara more prominent, and Undershaft consequently less prominent. Additionally, the revised version delineates an aspect of Undershaft's personality—his cruelty —that serves to greatly diminish the reader's admiration for him. And, finally, the revised play closes with the suggestion that it is the Professor of Greek who will take over the munitions works— suggesting to us the Platonic paraphrase: "society cannot be saved until either the Professors of Greek take to making gunpowder or else the makers of gunpowder become Professors of Greek." This serves to blunt the image of "Undershaft Triumphant" at the end of the play.

DIALECTICAL ACTION IN *MAJOR BARBARA*

Through its characters, plot, and dialogue, *Major Barbara* explores the problems of modern society and projects a solution to those problems.* It does so by means of a dialectic (thesis-antithesis-synthesis) that merges the spiritual and the physical, the poetic and the practical, and the emotional and the intellectual. The play moves from Sin (Act I) to Suffering (Act II) to Atonement (Act III); this may also be seen as a series of corollary movements: from Society to Poverty to Socialism, and from Hell to Purgatory to Heaven. Act One sets the characters, establishes their illusions and complacencies, and makes clear Shaw's view that "a soul that is no longer moving and growing is in Hell." Act Two reveals the reality under the library's surface and shows that Barbara, who is trying to convert others to her religion, is in fact being converted herself to a greater religion in the sense that her moral view is being expanded. In Act Three an ideal state is approached, the state wherein every man has time and self respect enough to cultivate his own moral view. Barbara ultimately sees the way toward a viable moral position; she is "transformed" in a basic synthesis which leads her to assert that "There is no wicked side: life is all one . . . Evil must be endured, whether it be sin or suffering." Shaw's optimism, not so inadequate or shallow as some believe, reflects not a simple ignorance of the darker side of life but instead a great and encompassing dream that, if attained, could treat the central neurosis of our times: the apparent evil in human existence, which Shaw refused to be overwhelmed by. Man could, in Shaw's view, be transformed, by means of a dialectic synthesis, into "a force of Nature instead of a feverish little clod of ailments and grievances complaining that the world will not devote itself to making him happy." The words are from Shaw's "Epistle Dedicatory" to *Man and Superman,* but they are equally applicable to *Major Barbara.*

* Abstracted from Daniel J. Leary, "Dialectical Action in *Major Barbara,*" *Shaw Review,* XII (May, 1969), 46-58.

Desire under the elms

EUGENE O'NEILL

CHARACTERS

EPHRAIM CABOT.

SIMEON
PETER } *his sons.*
EBEN

ABBIE PUTNAM.

Young GIRL, *two* FARMERS, *the* FIDDLER, *a* SHERIFF, *and other folk from the neighboring farms.*

The action of the entire play takes place in, and immediately outside of, the Cabot farmhouse in New England, in the year 1850. The south end of the house faces front to a stone wall with a wooden gate at center opening on a country road. The house is in good condition but in need of paint. Its walls are a sickly grayish, the green of the shutters faded. Two enormous elms are on each side of the house. They bend their trailing branches down over the roof. They appear to protect and at the same time subdue. There is a sinister maternity in their aspect, a crushing, jealous absorption. They have developed from their intimate contact with the life of man in the house an appalling humaneness. They brood oppressively over the house. They are like exhausted women resting their sagging breasts and hands and hair on its roof, and when it rains their tears trickle down monotonously and rot on the shingles.

There is a path running from the gate around the right corner of the house to the front door. A narrow porch is on this side. The end wall facing us has two windows in its upper story, two larger ones on the floor below. The two upper are those of the father's bedroom and that of the brothers. On the left, ground floor, is the kitchen—on the right, the parlor, the shades of which are always drawn down.

PART 1

SCENE ONE.

Exterior of the farmhouse. It is sunset of a day at the beginning of summer in the year 1850. There is no wind and everything is still. The sky above the roof is suffused with deep colors, the green of the elms glows, but the house is in shadow, seeming pale and washed out by contrast.

A door opens and EBEN CABOT comes to the end of the porch and stands looking down the road to the right. He has a large bell in his hand and this he swings mechanically, awakening a deafening clangor. Then he puts his hands on his hips and stares up at the sky. He sighs with a puzzled awe and blurts out with halting appreciation.

EBEN. God! Purty! (*His eyes fall and he stares about him frowningly. He is twenty-five, tall and sinewy. His face is well formed, good-looking, but its expression is resentful and defensive. His defiant, dark eyes remind one of a wild animal's in captivity. Each day is a cage in which he finds himself trapped but inwardly unsubdued. There is a fierce repressed vitality about him. He has black hair, mustache, a thin curly trace of beard. He is dressed in rough farm clothes.*

He spits on the ground with intense disgust, turns and goes back into the house.

SIMEON *and* PETER *come in from their work in the fields. They are tall men, much older than their half-brother (*SIMEON *is thirty-nine and* PETER *thirty-seven), built on a squarer, simpler model, fleshier in body, more bovine and homelier in face, shrewder and more practical. Their shoulders stoop a bit from years of farm work. They clump heavily along in their clumsy thick-soled boots caked with earth. Their clothes, their faces, hands, bare arms and throats are earth-stained. They smell of earth. They stand together for a moment in front of the house and, as if with the one impulse, stare dumbly up at the sky, leaning on their hoes. Their faces have a compressed, unresigned expression. As they look upward, this softens.*)

SIMEON (*grudgingly*). Purty.

PETER. Ay-eh.

SIMEON (*suddenly*). Eighteen year ago.

PETER. What?

SIMEON. Jenn. My woman. She died.

PETER. I'd fergot.

SIMEON. I rec'lect—now an' agin. Makes it lonesome. She'd hair long's a hoss' tail—an' yaller like gold!

PETER. Waal—she's gone. (*This with indifferent finality—then after a pause*) They's gold in the West, Sim.

SIMEON (*still under the influence of sunset—vaguely*). In the sky?

PETER. Waal—in a manner o' speakin'—that's the promise. (*Growing excited*) Gold in the sky—in the West—Golden Gate—Californi-a!—Goldest West!—fields o' gold!

SIMEON (*excited in his turn*). Fortunes layin' just atop o' the ground waitin' t' be picked! Solomon's mines, they says! (*For a moment they continue looking up at the sky—then their eyes drop.*)

PETER (*with sardonic bitterness*). Here—it's stones atop o' the ground—stones atop o' stones—makin' stone walls— year atop o' year—him 'n' yew 'n' me 'n' then Eben—makin' stone walls fur him to fence us in!

SIMEON. We've wuked. Give our strength. Give our years. Plowed 'em under in the ground—(*he stamps rebelliously*)—rottin'—makin' soil for his crops! (*A pause.*) Waal—the farm pays good for hereabouts.

PETER. If we plowed in Californi-a, they'd be lumps o' gold in the furrow!

SIMEON. Californi-a's t'other side o' earth, a'most. We got t' calc'late—

PETER (*after a pause*). 'Twould be hard fur me, too, to give up what we've 'arned here by our sweat. (*A pause,* EBEN *sticks his head out of the dining-room window, listening.*)

SIMEON. Ay-eh. (*A pause.*) Mebbe—he'll die soon.

PETER (*doubtfully*). Mebbe.

SIMEON. Mebbe—fur all we knows— he's dead now.

PETER. Ye'd need proof.

SIMEON. He's been gone two months—with no word.

PETER. Left us in the fields an evenin' like this. Hitched up an' druv off into the West. That's plum onnateral. He hain't never been off this farm 'ceptin' t' the village in thirty year or more, not since he married Eben's maw. (*A pause. Shrewdly*) I calc'late we might git him declared crazy by the court.

SIMEON. He skinned 'em too slick. He got the best o' all on 'em. They'd never b'lieve him crazy. (*A pause*) We got t' wait—till he's under ground.

EBEN (*with a sardonic chuckle*). Honor thy father! (*They turn, startled, and stare at him. He grins, then scowls.*) I pray he's died. (*They stare at him. He continues matter-of-factly*) Supper's ready.

SIMEON *and* PETER (*together*). Ay-eh.

EBEN (*gazing up at the sky*). Sun's downin' purty.

SIMEON *and* PETER (*together*). Ay-eh. They's gold in the West.

EBEN. Ay-eh. (*Pointing*) Yonder atop o' the hill pasture, ye mean?

SIMEON *and* PETER (*together*). In Californi-a!

EBEN. Hunh? (*Stares at them indifferently for a second, then drawls*) Waal—supper's gittin' cold. (*He turns back into kitchen.*)

SIMEON (*startled—smacks his lips*). I air hungry!

PETER (*sniffing*). I smells bacon!

SIMEON (*with hungry appreciation*). Bacon's good!

PETER (*in same tone*). Bacon's bacon! (*They turn, shouldering each other, their bodies bumping and rubbing together as they hurry clumsily to their food, like two friendly oxen toward their evening meal. They disappear around the right corner of house and can be heard entering the door.*)

CURTAIN

SCENE TWO.

The color fades from the sky. Twilight begins. The interior of the kitchen is now visible. A pine table is at center, a cook-stove in the right rear corner, four rough wooden chairs, a tallow candle on the table. In the middle of the rear wall is fastened a big advertising poster with a ship in full sail and the word "California" in big letters. Kitchen utensils hang from nails. Everything is neat and in order but the atmosphere is of a men's camp kitchen rather than that of a home.

Places for three are laid. EBEN takes boiled potatoes and bacon from the stove and puts them on the table, also a loaf of bread and a crock of water. SIMEON and PETER shoulder in, slump down in their chairs without a word. EBEN joins them. The three eat in silence for a moment, the two elder as naturally unrestrained as beasts of the field, EBEN picking at his food without appetite, glancing at them with a tolerant dislike.

SIMEON (*suddenly turns to* EBEN). Looky here! Ye'd oughtn't t' said that, Eben.

PETER. 'Twa'n't righteous.

EBEN. What?

SIMEON. Ye prayed he'd died.

EBEN. Waal—don't yew pray it? (*A pause.*)

PETER. He's our Paw.

EBEN (*violently*). Not mine!

SIMEON (*dryly*). Ye'd not let no one else say that about yer Maw! Ha! (*He gives one abrupt sardonic guffaw.* PETER *grins.*)

EBEN (*very pale*). I meant—I hain't his'n—I hain't like him—he hain't me!

PETER (*dryly*). Wait tell ye've growed his age!

EBEN (*intensely*). I'm Maw—every drop o' blood! (*A pause. They stare at him with indifferent curiosity.*)

PETER (*reminiscently*). She was good t' Sim 'n' me. A good Step-maw's scurse.

SIMEON. She was good t' everyone.

EBEN (*greatly moved, gets to his feet and makes an awkward bow to each of them—stammering*). I be thankful t'ye. I'm her—her heir. (*He sits down in confusion.*)

PETER (*after a pause—judicially*). She was good even t' him.

EBEN (*fiercely*). An' fur thanks he killed her!

SIMEON (*after a pause*). No one never kills nobody. It's allus somethin'. That's the murderer.

EBEN. Didn't he slave Maw t' death?

PETER. He slaved himself t' death. He's slaved Sim 'n' me 'n' yew t' death—on'y none o' us hain't died—yit.

SIMEON. It's somethin'—drivin' him—t' drive us!

EBEN (*vengefully*). Waal—I hold him t' jedgment! (*Then scornfully*) Somethin'! What's somethin'?

SIMEON. Dunno.

EBEN (*sardonically*). What's drivin' yew to Californi-a, mebbe? (*They look at him in surprise.*) Oh, I've heerd ye! (*Then, after a pause*) But ye'll never go t' the gold fields!

PETER (*assertively*). Mebbe!

EBEN. Whar'll ye git the money?

PETER. We kin walk. It's an a'mighty ways—Calforni-a—but if yew was t' put all the steps we've walked on this farm end t' end we'd be in the moon!

EBEN. The Injuns'll skulp ye on the plains.

SIMEON (*with grim humor*). We'll mebbe make 'em pay a hair fur a hair!

EBEN (*decisively*). But t'ain't that. Ye won't never go because ye'll wait here fur yer share o' the farm, thinkin' allus he'll die soon.

SIMEON (*after a pause*). We've a right.

PETER. Two-thirds belongs t' us.

EBEN (*jumping to his feet*). Ye've no right! She wa'n't yewr Maw! It was her farm! Didn't he steal it from her? She's dead. It's my farm.

SIMEON (*sardonically*). Tell that t' Paw—when he comes! I'll bet ye a dollar he'll laugh—fur once in his life. Ha! (*He laughs himself in one single mirthless bark.*)

PETER (*amused in turn, echoes his brother*). Ha!

SIMEON (*after a pause*). What've ye got held agin us, Eben? Year after year it's skulked in yer eye—somethin'.

PETER. Ay-eh.

EBEN. Ay-eh. They's somethin'. (*Suddenly exploding*) Why didn't ye never stand between him 'n' my Maw when he was slavin' her to her grave—t' pay her back fur the kindness she done t' yew?

(*There is a long pause. They stare at him in surprise.*)

SIMEON. Waal—the stock'd got t' be watered.

PETER. 'R they was woodin' t' do.

SIMEON. 'R plowin'.

PETER. 'R hayin'.

SIMEON. 'R spreadin' manure.

PETER. 'R weedin'.

SIMEON. 'R prunin'.

PETER. 'R milkin'.

EBEN (*breaking in harshly*). An' makin' walls—stone atop o' stone—makin' walls till yer heart's a stone ye heft up out o' the way o' growth onto a stone wall t' wall in yer heart!

SIMEON (*matter-of-factly*). We never had no time t' meddle.

PETER (*to EBEN*). Yew was fifteen afore yer Maw died—an' big fur yer age. Why didn't ye never do nothin'?

EBEN (*harshly*). They was chores t' do, wa'n't they? (*A pause—then slowly*) It was on'y arter she died I come to think o' it. Me cookin'—doin' her work—that made me know her, suffer her sufferin'—she'd come back t' help—come back t' bile potatoes—come back t' fry bacon—come back t' bake biscuits—come back all cramped up t' shake the fire, an' carry ashes, her eyes weepin' an' bloody with smoke an' cinders same's they used t' be. She still comes back—stands by the stove thar in the evenin'—she can't find it nateral sleepin' an' restin' in peace. She can't git used t' bein' free—even in her grave.

SIMEON. She never complained none.

EBEN. She'd got too tired. She'd got too used t' bein' too tired. That was what he done. (*With vengeful passion*) An' sooner 'r later, I'll meddle. I'll say the thin's I didn't say then t' him! I'll yell 'em at the top o' my lungs. I'll see t' it my Maw gits some rest an' sleep in her grave! (*He sits down again, relapsing into a brooding silence. They look at him with a queer indifferent curiosity.*)

PETER (*after a pause*). Whar in tarnation d'ye s'pose he went, Sim?

SIMEON. Dunno. He druv off in the buggy, all spick an' span, with the mare all breshed an' shiny, druv off clackin' his tongue an' wavin' his whip. I remember it right well. I was finishin' plowin', it was spring an' May an' sunset, an' gold in the West, an' he druv off into it. I yells "Whar ye goin', Paw?" an' he hauls up by the stone wall a jiffy. His old snake's eyes was glitterin' in the sun like he'd been drinkin' a jugful an' he says with a mule's grin: "Don't ye run away till I come back!"

PETER. Wonder if he knowed we was wantin' fur Californi-a?

SIMEON. Mebbe. I didn't say nothin' and he says, lookin' kinder queer an' sick: "I been hearin' the hens cluckin' an' the roosters crowin' all the durn day. I been listenin' t' the cows lowin' an' everythin' else kickin' up till I can't stand it no more. It's spring an' I'm feelin' damned," he says. "Damned like a old bare hickory tree fit on'y fur burnin'," he says. An' then I calc'late I must've looked a mite hopeful, fur he adds real spry and vicious: "But don't git no fool idee I'm dead. I've sworn t' live a hundred an' I'll do it, if on'y t' spite yer sinful greed! An' now I'm ridin' out t' learn God's message t' me in the spring, like the prophets done. An' yew git back t' yer plowin'," he says. An' he druv off singin' a hymn. I thought he was drunk—'r I'd stopped him goin'.

EBEN (*scornfully*). No, ye wouldn't! Ye're scared o' him. He's stronger—inside—than both o' ye put together!

PETER (*sardonically*). An' yew—be yew Samson?

EBEN. I'm gittin' stronger. I kin feel it growin' in me—growin' an' growin'—till it'll bust out—! (*He gets up and puts on his coat and a hat. They watch him, gradually breaking into grins. EBEN avoids their eyes sheepishly.*) I'm goin' out fur a spell—up the road.

PETER. T' the village?

SIMEON. T' see Minnie?

EBEN (*defiantly*). Ay-eh!

PETER (*jeeringly*). The Scarlet Woman!

SIMEON. Lust—that's what's growin' in ye!

EBEN. Waal—she's purty!

PETER. She's been purty fur twenty year!

SIMEON. A new coat o' paint'll make a heifer out of forty.

EBEN. She hain't forty!

PETER. If she hain't, she's teeterin' on the edge.

EBEN (*desperately*). What d'yew know—

PETER. All they is . . . Sim knew her—an' then me arter—

SIMEON. An' Paw kin tell yew somethin' too! He was fust!

EBEN. D'ye mean t' say he . . . ?

SIMEON (*with a grin*). Ay-eh! We air his heirs in everythin'!

EBEN (*intensely*). That's more to it! That grows on it! It'll bust soon! (*Then violently*) I'll go smash my fist in her face! (*He pulls open the door in rear violently.*)

SIMEON (*with a wink at* PETER—*drawlingly*). Mebbe—but the night's wa'm—purty—by the time ye get thar mebbe ye'll kiss her instead!

PETER. Sart'n he will! (*They both roar with coarse laughter.* EBEN *rushes out and slams the door—then the outside front door—comes around the corner of the house and stands still by the gate, staring up at the sky.*)

SIMEON (*looking after him*). Like his Paw.

PETER. Dead spit an' image!

SIMEON. Dog'll eat dog!

PETER. Ay-eh. (*Pause. With yearning*) Mebbe a year from now we'll be in Californi-a.

SIMEON. Ay-eh. (*A pause. Both yawn.*) Let's git t'bed. (*He blows out the candle. They go out door in rear.* EBEN *stretches his arms up to the sky—rebelliously.*)

EBEN. Waal—thar's a star, an' somewhar's they's him, an' here's me, an' thar's Min up the road—in the same night. What if I does kiss her? She's like t'night, she's soft 'n' wa'm, her eyes kin wink like a star, her mouth's wa'm, her arms're wa'm, she smells like a wa'm plowed field, she's purty . . . Ay-eh! By God A'mighty she's purty, an' I don't give a damn how many sins she's sinned afore mine or who she's sinned 'em with, my sin's as purty as any one on 'em! (*He strides off down the road to the left.*)

SCENE THREE.

It is the pitch darkness just before dawn. EBEN comes in from the left and goes around to the porch, feeling his way, chuckling bitterly and cursing half-aloud to himself.

EBEN. The cussed old miser! (*He can be heard going in the front door. There is a pause as he goes upstairs, then a loud knock on the bedroom door of the brothers.*) Wake up!

SIMEON (*startedly*). Who's that?

EBEN (*pushing open the door and coming in, a lighted candle in his hand. The bedroom of the brothers is revealed. Its ceiling is the sloping roof. They can stand upright only close to the center dividing wall of the upstairs.* SIMEON *and* PETER *are in a double bed, front.* EBEN'*s cot is to the rear.* EBEN *has a mixture of silly grin and vicious scowl on his face*). I be!

PETER (*angrily*). What in hell's-fire . . . ?

EBEN. I got news fur ye! Ha! (*He gives one abrupt sardonic guffaw.*)

SIMEON (*angrily*). Couldn't ye hold it 'til we'd got our sleep?

EBEN. It's nigh sunup. (*Then explosively*) He's gone an' married agen!

SIMEON *and* PETER (*explosively*). Paw?

EBEN. Got himself hitched to a female 'bout thirty-five—an' purty, they says . . .

SIMEON (*aghast*). It's a durn lie!

PETER. Who says?

SIMEON. They been stringin' ye!

EBEN. Think I'm a dunce, do ye? The hull village says. The preacher from New Dover, he brung the news—told it t'our preacher —New Dover, that's whar the old loon got himself hitched—that's whar the woman lived—

PETER (*no longer doubting—stunned*). Waal . . . !

SIMEON (*the same*). Waal . . . !

EBEN (*sitting down on a bed—with vicious hatred*). Ain't he a devil out o' hell? It's jest t' spite us—the damned old mule!

PETER (*after a pause*). Everythin'll go t' her now.

SIMEON. Ay-eh (*A pause—dully*) Waal—if it's done—

PETER. It's done us. (*Pause—then persuasively*) They's gold in the fields o' Californi-a, Sim. No good a-stayin' here now.

SIMEON. Jest what I was a-thinkin'. (*Then with decision*) S'well fust's last! Let's light out and git this mornin'.

PETER. Suits me.

EBEN. Ye must like walkin'.

SIMEON (*sardonically*). If ye'd grow wings on us we'd fly thar!

EBEN. Ye'd like ridin' better—on a boat, wouldn't ye? (*Fumbles in his pocket and takes out a crumpled sheet of fools-cap.*) Waal, if ye sign this ye kin ride on a boat. I've had it writ out an' ready in case ye'd ever go. It says fur three hundred dollars t' each ye agree yewr shares o' the farm is sold t' me. (*They look suspiciously at the paper. A pause.*)

SIMEON (*wonderingly*). But if he's hitched agen—

PETER. An' whar'd yew git that sum o' money, anyways?

EBIN (*cunningly*). I know whar it's hid. I been waitin'—Maw told me. She knew whar it lay fur years, but she was waitin' . . . It's her'n—the money he hoarded from her farm an' hid from Maw. It's my money by rights now.

PETER. Whar's it hid?

EBEN (*cunningly*). Whar yew won't never find it without me. Maw spied on him—'r she'd never knowed. (*A pause. They look at him suspiciously, and he at them.*) Waal, is it fa'r trade?

SIMEON. Dunno.

PETER. Dunno.

SIMEON (*looking at window*). Sky's grayin'.

PETER. Ye better start the fire, Eben.

SIMEON. An' fix some vittles.

EBEN. Ay-eh. (*Then with a forced jocular heartiness*) I'll git ye a good one. If ye're startin' t' hoof it t' Californi-a ye'll need somethin' that'll stick t' yer ribs. (*He turns to the door, adding meaningly*) But ye kin ride on a boat if ye'll swap. (*He stops at the door and pauses. They stare at him.*)

SIMEON (*suspiciously*). Whar was ye all night?

EBEN (*defiantly*). Up t' Min's. (*Then slowly*) Walkin' thar, fust I felt 's if I'd kiss her; then I got a-thinkin' o' what ye'd said o' him an' her an' I says, I'll bust her nose fur that! Then I got t' the village an' heerd the news an' I got madder'n hell an' run all the way t' Min's not knowin' what I'd do— (*He pauses—then sheepishly but more defiantly*) Waal—when I seen her, I didn't hit her—nor I didn't kiss her nuther—I begun t' beller like a calf an' cuss at the same time, I was so durn mad—an' she got scared—an' I jest grabbed holt an' tuk her! (*Proudly*) Yes, sirree! I tuk her. She may've been his'n—an' your'n, too—but she's mine now!

SIMEON (*dryly*). In love, air yew?

EBEN (*with lofty scorn*). Love! I don't take no stock in sech slop!

PETER (*winking at* SIMEON). Mebbe Eben's aimin' t' marry, too.

SIMEON. Min'd make a true faithful he'pmeet! (*They snicker.*)

EBEN. What do I care fur her—'ceptin' she's round an' wa'm? The p'int is she was his'n—an' now she belongs t' me! (*He goes to the door—then turns—rebelliously.*) An' Min hain't sech a bad un. They's worse'n Min in the world, I'll bet ye! Wait'll we see this cow the Old Man's hitched t'! She'll beat Min, I got a notion! (*He starts to go out.*)

SIMEON (*suddenly*). Mebbe ye'll try t' make her your'n, too?

PETER. Ha! (*He gives a sardonic laugh of relish at this idea.*)

EBEN (*spitting with disgust*). Her—here—sleepin' with him— stealin' my Maw's farm! I'd as soon pet a skunk 'r kiss a snake! (*He goes out. The two stare after him suspiciously. A pause. They listen to his steps receding.*)

PETER. He's startin' the fire.

SIMEON. I'd like t' ride t' Californi-a—but—

PETER. Min might o' put some scheme in his head.

SIMEON. Mebbe it's all a lie 'bout Paw marryin'. We'd best wait an 'see the bride.

PETER. An' don't sign nothin' till we does!

SIMEON. Nor till we've tested it's good money! (*Then with a grin*) But if Paw's hitched we'd be sellin' Eben somethin' we'd never git nohow!

PETER. We'll wait an' see. (*Then with sudden vindictive anger*) An' till he comes, let's yew 'n' me not wuk a lick, let Eben tend to thin's if he's a mind t', let's us jest sleep an' eat an' drink likker, an' let the hull damned farm go t' blazes!

SIMEON (*excitedly*). By God, we've 'arned a rest! We'll play rich fur a change. I hain't a-goin' to stir outa bed till breakfast's ready.

PETER. An' on the table!

SIMEON (*after a pause—thoughtfully*). What d' ye calc'late she'll be like—our new Maw? Like Eben thinks?

PETER. More'n likely.

SIMEON (*vindictively*). Waal—I hope she's a she-devil that'll make him wish he was dead an' living in the pit o' hell fur comfort!

PETER (*fervently*). Amen!

SIMEON (*imitating his father's voice*). "I'm ridin' out t' learn God's message t' me in the spring like the prophets done," he says. I'll bet right then an' thar he knew plumb well he was goin' whorin', the stinkin' old hypocrite!

SCENE FOUR.

Same as Scene Two—shows the interior of the kitchen with a lighted candle on table. It is gray dawn outside. SIMEON and PETER are just finishing their breakfast. EBEN sits before his plate of untouched food, brooding frowningly.

PETER (*glancing at him rather irritably*). Lookin' glum don't help none.

SIMEON (*sarcastically*). Sorrowin' over his lust o' the flesh!

PETER (*with a grin*). Was she yer fust?

EBEN (*angrily*). None o' yer business. (*A pause.*) I was thinkin' o' him. I got a notion he's gittin' near—I kin feel him comin' on like yew kin feel malaria chill afore it takes ye.

PETER. It's too early yet.

SIMEON. Dunno. He'd like t' catch us nappin'—jest t' have somethin' t' hoss us 'round over.

PETER (*mechanically gets to his feet. SIMEON does the same*). Waal—let's git t' wuk. (*They both plod mechanically toward the door before they realize. Then they stop short.*)

SIMEON (*grinning*). Ye're a cussed fool, Pete—and I be wuss! Let him see we hain't wukin'! We don't give a durn!

PETER (*as they go back to the table*). Not a damned durn! It'll serve t' show him we're done with him. (*They sit down again. EBEN stares from one to the other with surprise.*)

SIMEON (*grins at him*). We're aimin' t' start bein' lilies o' the field.

PETER. Nary a toil 'r spin 'r lick o' wuk do we put in!

SIMEON. Ye're sole owner—till he comes—that's what ye wanted. Waal, ye got t' be sole hand, too.

PETER. The cows air bellerin'. Ye better hustle at the milkin'.

EBEN (*with excited joy*). Ye mean ye'll sign the paper?

SIMEON (*dryly*). Mebbe.

PETER. Mebbe.

SIMEON. We're considerin'. (*Peremptorily*) Ye better git t' wuk.

EBEN (*with queer excitement*). It's Maw's farm agen! It's my farm! Them's my cows! I'll milk my durn fingers off fur cows o' mine! (*He goes out door in rear, they stare after him indifferently.*)

SIMEON. Like his Paw.

PETER. Dead spit 'n' image!

SIMEON. Waal—let dog eat dog! (EBEN *comes out of front door and around the corner of the house. The sky is beginning to grow flushed with sunrise.* EBEN *stops by the gate and stares around him with glowing, possessive eyes. He takes in the whole farm with his embracing glance of desire.*)

EBEN. It's purty! It's damned purty! It's mine! (*He suddenly throws his head back boldly and glares with hard, defiant eye at the sky.*) Mine, d'ye hear? Mine! (*He turns and walks quickly off left, rear, toward the barn. The two brothers light their pipes.*)

SIMEON (*putting his muddy boots up on the table, tilting back his chair, and puffing defiantly*). Waal—this air solid comfort—fur once.

PETER. Ay-eh. (*He follows suit. A pause. Unconsciously they both sigh.*)

SIMEON (*suddenly*). He never was much o' a hand at milkin', Eben wa'n't.

PETER (*with a snort*). His hands air like hoofs! (*A pause.*)

SIMEON. Reach down the jug thar! Let's take a swaller. I'm feelin' kind o' low.

PETER. Good idee! (*He does so—gets two glasses—they pour out drinks of whisky.*) Here's t' the gold in Californi-a!

SIMEON. An' luck t' find it! (*They drink—puff resolutely—sigh —take their feet down from the table.*)

PETER. Likker don't 'pear t' sot right.

SIMEON. We hain't used t' it this early. (*A pause. They become very restless.*)

PETER. Gittin' close in this kitchen.

SIMEON (*with immense relief*). Let's git a breath o' air. (*They arise briskly and go out rear—appear around house and stop by the gate. They stare up at the sky with a numbed appreciation.*)

PETER. Purty!

SIMEON. Ay-eh. Gold's t' the East now.

PETER. Sun's startin' with us fur the Golden West.

SIMEON (*staring around the farm, his compressed face tightened, unable to conceal his emotion*). Waal—it's our last mornin'—mebbe.

PETER (*the same*). Ay-eh.

SIMEON (*stamps his foot on the earth and addresses it desperately*). Waal—ye've thirty year o' me buried in ye—spread out over ye—blood an' bone an' sweat—rotted away—fertilizin' ye—richin' yer soul—prime manure, by God, that's what I been t' ye!

PETER. Ay-eh; An' me!

SIMEON. An' yew, Peter. (*He sighs—then spits.*) Waal—no use'n crying over spilt milk.

PETER. They's gold in the West—an' freedom, mebbe. We been slaves t' stone walls here.

SIMEON (*defiantly*). We hain't nobody's slaves from this out— nor no thin's slaves nuther. (*A pause—restlessly*) Speakin' o' milk, wonder how Eben's managin'?

PETER. I s'pose he's managin'.

SIMEON. Mebbe we'd ought t' help—this once.

PETER. Mebbe. The cows knows us.

SIMEON. An' likes us. They don't know him much.

PETER. An' the hosses, an' pigs, an' chickens. They don't know him much.

SIMEON. They knows us like brothers—an' likes us! (*Proudly*) Hain't we raised 'em t' be fust-rate, number one prize stock?

PETER. We hain't—not no more.

SIMEON (*dully*). I was fergittin'. (*Then resignedly*) Waal, let's go help Eben a spell an' git waked up.

PETER. Suits me. (*They are starting off down left, rear, for the barn when EBEN appears from there hurrying toward them, his face excited.*)

EBEN (*breathlessly*). Waal—har they be! The old mule an' the bride! I seen 'em from the barn down below at the turnin'.

PETER. How could ye tell that far?

EBEN. Hain't I as far-sight as he's near-sight? Don't I know the mare 'n' buggy, an' two people settin' in it? Who else . . . ? An' I tell ye I kin feel 'em a-comin', too! (*He squirms as if he had the itch.*)

PETER (*begining to be angry*). Waal—let him do his own un-hitchin'!

SIMEON (*angry in his turn*). Let's hustle in an' git our bundles an' be a-goin' as he's a-comin'. I don't want never t' step inside the door agen arter he's back. (*They both start back around the corner of the house.* EBEN *follows them.*)

EBEN (*anxiously*). Will ye sign it afore ye go?

PETER. Let's see the color o' the old skinflint's money an' we'll sign. (*They disappear left. The two brothers clump upstairs to get their bundles,* EBEN *appears in the kitchen, runs to the window, peers out, comes back and pulls up a strip of flooring in under stove, takes out a canvas bag and puts it on table, then sets the floorboard back in place. The two brothers appear a moment after. They carry old carpet bags.*)

EBEN (*puts his hand on bag guardingly*). Have ye signed?

SIMEON (*shows paper in his hand*). Ay-eh (*Greedily*) Be that the money?

EBEN (*opens bag and pours out pile of twenty-dollar gold pieces*). Twenty-dollar pieces—thirty on 'em. Count 'em. (PETER *does so, arranging them in stacks of five, biting one or two to test them.*)

PETER. Six hundred. (*He puts them in bag and puts it inside his shirt, carefully.*)

SIMEON (*handing paper to* EBEN). Har ye be.

EBEN (*after a glance, folds it carefully and hides it under his shirt —gratefully*). Thank yew.

PETER. Thank yew fur the ride.

SIMEON. We'll send ye a lump o' gold fur Christmas. (*A pause.* EBEN *stares at them and they at him.*)

PETER (*awkwardly*). Waal—we're a-goin'.

SIMEON. Comin' out 't the yard?

EBEN. No. I'm waitin' in here a spell. (*Another silence. The brothers edge awkwardly to the door in rear—then turn and stand.*)

SIMEON. Waal—good-by.

PETER. Good-by.

EBEN. Good-by. (*They go out. He sits down at the table, faces the stove and pulls out the paper. He looks from it to the stove. His face, lighted up by the shaft of sunlight from the window, has an expression of trance. His lips move. The two brothers come out to the gate.*)

PETER (*looking off toward barn*). Thar he be—unhitchin'.

SIMEON (*with a chuckle*). I'll bet ye he's riled!

PETER. An', thar she be.

SIMEON. Let's wait 'n' see what our new Maw looks like.

PETER (*with a grin*). An' give him our partin' cuss!

SIMEON (*grinning*). I feel like raisin' fun. I feel light in my head an' feet.

PETER. Me, too. I feel like laffin' till I'd split up the middle.

SIMEON. Reckon it's the likker?

PETER. No. My feet feel itchin' t' walk an' walk—an' jump high over thin's—an'. . . .

SIMEON. Dance? (*A pause.*)

PETER (*puzzled*). It's plumb onnateral.

SIMEON (*a light coming over his face*). I calc'late it's 'cause school's out. It's holiday. Fur once we're free!

PETER (*dazedly*). Free?

SIMEON. The halter's broke—the harness is busted—the fence bars is down—the stone walls air crumblin' an' tumblin'! We'll be kickin' up an' tearin' away down the road!

PETER (*drawing a deep breath—oratorically*). Anybody that wants this stinkin' old rock-pile of a farm kin hev it. 'T'ain't our'n, no sirree!

SIMEON (*takes the gate off its hinges and puts it under his arm*). We harby 'bolishes shet gates an' open gates, an' all gates, by thunder!

PETER. We'll take it with us fur luck an' let 'er sail free down some river.

SIMEON (*as a sound of voices comes from left, rear*). Har they comes! (*The two brothers congeal into two stiff grim-visaged statues.* EPHRAIM CABOT *and* ABBIE PUTNAM *come in.* CABOT *is seventy-five, tall and gaunt, with great, wiry, concentrated power, but stoop-shouldered from toil. His face is as hard as if it were hewn out of a boulder, yet there is a weakness in it, a petty pride in its own narrow strength. His eyes are small, close together, and extremely near-sighted, blinking continually in the effort to focus on objects, their stare having a straining, ingrowing quality. He is dressed in his dismal black Sunday suit.* ABBIE *is thirty-five, buxom, full of vitality. Her round face is pretty but marred by its rather gross sensuality. There is strength and obstinacy in her jaw, a hard determination in her eyes, and about her whole personality the same unsettled, untamed, desperate quality which is so apparent in* EBEN.)

CABOT (*as they enter—a queer strangled emotion in his dry cracking voice*). Har we be t' hum, Abbie.

ABBIE (*with lust for the word*). Hum! (*Her eyes gloating on the house without seeming to see the two stiff figures at the gate.*) It's purty—purty! I can't b'lieve it's r'ally mine.

CABOT (*sharply*). Yewr'n? Mine! (*He stares at her penetratingly. She stares back. He adds relentingly.*) Our'n—mebbe! It was lonesome too long. I was growin' old in the spring. A hum's got t' hev a woman.

ABBIE (*her voice taking possession*). A woman's got 't hev a hum!

CABOT (*nodding uncertainly*). Ay-eh. (*Then irritably*) Whar be they? Ain't thar nobody about—'r wukin'—'r nothin'?

ABBIE (*sees the brothers. She returns their stare of cold appraising contempt with interest—slowly*). Thar's two men loafin' at the gate an' starin' at me like a couple o' strayed hogs.

CABOT (*straining his eyes*). I kin see 'em—but I can't make out. . . .

SIMEON. It's Simeon.

PETER. It's Peter.

CABOT (*exploding*). Why hain't ye wukin'?

SIMEON (*dryly*). We're waitin' t' welcome ye hum—yew an' the bride!

CABOT (*confusedly*). Huh? Waal—this be yer new Maw, boys. (*She stares at them and they at her.*)

SIMEON (*turns away and spits contemptuously*). I see her!

PETER (*spits also*). An' I see her!

ABBIE (*with the conqueror's conscious superiority*). I'll go in an' look at my house. (*She goes slowly around to porch.*)

SIMEON (*with a snort*). Her house!

PETER (*calls after her*). Ye'll find Eben inside. Ye better not tell him it's *yewr* house.

ABBIE (*mouthing the name*). Eben. (*Then quietly*) I'll tell Eben.

CABOT (*with a contemptuous sneer*). Ye needn't heed Eben. Eben's a dumb fool—like his Maw—soft an' simple!

SIMEON (*with his sardonic burst of laughter*). Ha! Eben's a chip o' yew—spit 'n' image—hard 'n' bitter's a hickory tree! Dog'll eat dog. He'll eat ye yet, old man!

CABOT (*commandingly*). Ye git t' wuk!

SIMEON (*as* ABBIE *disappears in house—winks at* PETER *and says tauntingly*). So that thar's our new Maw, be it? Whar in hell did ye dig her up? (*He and* PETER *laugh.*)

PETER. Ha! Ye'd better turn her in the pen with the other sows. (*They laugh uproariously, slapping their thighs.*)

CABOT (*so amazed at their effrontery that he stutters in confusion*). Simeon! Peter! What's come over ye? Air ye drunk?

SIMEON. We're free, old man—free o' yew an' the hull damned farm! (*They grow more and more hilarious and excited.*)

PETER. An' we're startin' out fur the gold fields o' Californi-a!

SIMEON. Ye kin take this place an' burn it!

PETER. An' bury it—fur all we cares!

SIMEON. We're free, old man! (*He cuts a caper.*)

PETER. Free! (*He gives a kick in the air.*)

SIMEON (*in a frenzy*). Whoop!

PETER. Whoop! (*They do an absurd Indian war dance about the old man, who is petrified between rage and the fear that they are insane.*)

SIMEON. We're free as Injuns! Lucky we don't skulp ye!

PETER. An' burn yer barn an' kill the stock!

SIMEON. An' rape yer new woman! Whoop! (*He and* PETER *stop their dance, holding their sides, rocking with wild laughter.*)

CABOT (*edging away*). Lust fur gold—fur the sinful, easy gold o' Californi-a! It's made ye mad!

SIMEON (*tauntingly*). Wouldn't ye like us to send ye back some sinful gold, ye old sinner?

PETER. They's gold besides what's in Californi-a! (*He retreats back beyond the vision of the old man and takes the bag of money and flaunts it in the air above his head, laughing.*)

SIMEON. And sinfuller, too!

PETER. We'll be voyagin' on the sea! Whoop! (*He leaps up and down.*)

SIMEON. Livin' free! Whoop! (*He leaps in turn.*)

CABOT (*suddenly roaring with rage*). My cuss on ye!

SIMEON. Take our'n in trade fur it! Whoop!

CABOT. I'll hev ye both chained up in the asylum!

PETER. Ye old skinflint! Good-by!

SIMEON. Ye old blood sucker! Good-by!

CABOT. Go afore I . . . !

PETER. Whoop. (*He picks a stone from the road.* SIMEON *does the same.*)

SIMEON. Maw'll be in the parlor.

PETER. Ay-eh! One! Two!

CABOT (*frightened*). What air ye . . . ?

PETER. Three! (*They both throw, the stones hitting the parlor window with a crash of glass, tearing the shade.*)

SIMEON. Whoop!

PETER. Whoop!

CABOT (*in a fury now, rushing toward them*). If I kin lay hands on ye—I'll break yer bones fur ye! (*But they beat a capering retreat before him,* SIMEON *with the gate still under his arm.* CABOT *comes back, panting with impotent rage. Their voices as they go off take up the song of the gold-seekers to the old tune of "Oh, Susannah!"*)

"I jumped aboard the Liza ship,
And traveled on the sea,
And every time I thought of home
I wished it wasn't me!
Oh! Californi-a,
That's the land fur me!
I'm off to Californi-a!
With my wash bowl on my knee."

(*In the meantime, the window of the upper bedroom on right is raised and* ABBIE *sticks her head out. She looks down at* CABOT— *with a sigh of relief.*)

ABBIE. Waal—that's the last o' them two, hain't it? (*He doesn't answer. Then in possessive tones*) This here's a nice bedroom, Ephraim. It's a r'al nice bed. Is it my room, Ephraim?

CABOT (*grimly—without looking up*). Our'n! (*She cannot control a grimace of aversion and pulls back her head slowly and shuts the window. A sudden horrible thought seems to enter* CABOT'*s head.*) They been up to somethin'! Mebbe—mebbe they've pizened the stock—'r somethin'! (*He almost runs off down toward the barn. A moment later the kitchen door is slowly pushed open and* ABBIE *enters. For a moment she stands looking at* EBEN. *He does not notice her at first. Her eyes take him in penetratingly with a calculating appraisal of his strength as against hers. But under this her desire is dimly awakened by his youth and good looks. Suddenly he becomes conscious of her presence and looks up. Their eyes meet. He leaps to his feet, glowering at her speechlessly.*)

ABBIE (*in her most seductive tones, which she uses all through this scene*). Be you—Eben? I'm Abbie—(*She laughs.*) I mean, I'm yer new Maw.

EBEN (*viciously*). No, damn ye!

ABBIE (*as if she hadn't heard—with a queer smile*). Yer Paw's spoke a lot o' yew. . . .

EBEN. Ha!

ABBIE. Ye mustn't mind him. He's an old man. (*A long pause. They stare at each other.*) I don't want t' pretend playin' Maw t' ye, Eben. (*Admiringly*) Ye're too big an' strong fur that. I want t' be frens with ye. Mebbe with me fur a fren ye'd find ye'd like livin' here better. I kin make it easy fur ye with him, mebbe. (*With a scornful sense of power*) I calc'late I kin git him t' do most anythin' fur me.

EBEN (*with bitter scorn*). Ha! (*They stare again,* EBEN *obscurely moved, physically attracted to her—in forced stilted tones*) Yew kin go t' the devil!

ABBIE (*calmly*). If cussin' me does ye good, cuss all ye've a mind t'. I'm all prepared t' have ye agin me—at fust. I don't blame ye nuther. I'd feel the same at any stranger comin' t' take my Maw's place. (*He shudders. She is watching him carefully.*) Yew must've cared a lot fur yewr Maw, didn't ye? My Maw died afore I'd growed. I don't remember her none. (*A pause.*) But yew won't hate me long, Eben. I'm not the wust in the world—an' yew an' me've got a lot in common. I kin tell that by lookin' at ye. Waal—I've had a hard life, too—oceans o' trouble an' nuthin' but wuk fur reward. I was a orphan early an had t' wuk fur others in other folks' hums. Then I married an' he turned out a drunken spreer an' so he had to wuk fur others an' me too agen in other folks' hums, an' the baby died, an' my husband got sick an' died too, an' I was glad, sayin' now I'm free fur once, on'y I diskivered right away all I was free fur was t' wuk agen in other folks' hums, doin' other folks' wuk till I'd most give up hope o' ever doin' my own wuk in my own hum, an' then your Paw come. . . . (CABOT *appears returning from the barn. He comes to the gate and looks down the road the brothers have gone. A faint strain of their retreating voices is heard:*) "Oh, Californi-a!

That's the place for me." He stands glowering, his fist clenched, his face grim with rage.)

EBEN (*fighting against his growing attraction and sympathy—harshly*). An' bought yew—like a harlot! (*She is stung and flushes angrily. She has been sincerely moved by the recital of her troubles. He adds furiously:*) An' the price he's payin' ye—this farm—was my Maw's, damn ye!—an' mine now!

ABBIE (*with a cool laugh of confidence*). Yewr'n? We'll see 'bout that! (*Then strongly*) Waal—what if I did need a hum? What else'd I marry an old man like him fur?

EBEN (*maliciously*). I'll tell him ye said that!

ABBIE (*smiling*). I'll say ye're lyin' a-purpose—an' he'll drive ye off the place!

EBEN. Ye devil!

ABBIE (*defying him*). This be my farm—this be my hum—this be my kitchen—!

EBEN (*furiously, as if he were going to attack her*). Shut up, damn ye!

ABBIE (*walks up to him—a queer coarse expression of desire in her face and body—slowly*). An' upstairs—that be my bedroom—an' my bed! (*He stares into her eyes, terribly confused and torn. She adds softly:*) I hain't bad nor mean—'ceptin' fur an enemy—but I got t' fight fur what's due me out o' life, if I ever 'spect t' git it. (*Then putting her hand on his arm—seductively*) Let's yew 'n' me be frens, Eben.

EBEN (*stupidly—as if hypnotized*). Ay-eh. (*Then furiously flinging off her arm*) No, ye durned old witch! I hate ye! (*He rushes out the door.*)

ABBIE (*looks after him smiling satisfiedly—then half to herself, mouthing the word*). Eben's nice. (*She looks at the table, proudly.*) I'll wash up *my* dishes now. (EBEN *appears outside, slamming the door behind him. He comes around corner, stops on seeing his father, and stands staring at him with hate.*)

CABOT (*raising his arms to heaven in the fury he can no longer control*). Lord God o' Hosts, smite the undutiful sons with Thy wust cuss!

EBEN (*breaking in violently*). Yew 'n' yewr God! Allus cussin' folks—allus naggin' 'em!

CABOT (*oblivious to him—summoningly*). God o' the old! God o' the lonesome!

EBEN (*mockingly*). Naggin' His sheep t' sin! T' hell with yewr God! (CABOT *turns. He and* EBEN *glower at each other.*)

CABOT (*harshly*). So it's yew. I might've knowed it. (*Shaking his finger threateningly at him*) Blasphemin' fool! (*Then quickly*) Why hain't ye t' wuk?

EBEN. Why haint' yew? They've went. I can't wuk it all alone.

CABOT (*contemptuously*). Nor noways! I'm wuth ten o' ye yit, old's I be! Ye'll never be more'n half a man! (*Then, matter-of-factly*) Waal—let's git t' the barn. (*They go. A last faint note of the "Californi-a" song is heard from the distance.* ABBIE *is washing her dishes.*)

CURTAIN

pARt 11

SCENE ONE.

The exterior of the farmhouse, as in Part One—a hot Sunday afternoon two months later. ABBIE, dressed in her best, is discovered sitting in a rocker at the end of the porch. She rocks listlessly, enervated by the heat, staring in front of her with bored, half-closed eyes.

EBEN *sticks his head out of his bedroom window. He looks around furtively and tries to see—or hear—if anyone is on the porch, but although he has been careful to make no noise,* ABBIE *has sensed his movement. She stops rocking, her face grows animated and eager, she waits attentively.* EBEN *seems to feel her presence, he scowls back his thoughts of her and spits with exaggerated disdain—then withdraws back into the room.* ABBIE *waits, holding her breath as she listens with passionate eagerness for every sound within the house.*

EBEN *comes out. Their eyes meet. His falter, he is confused, he turns away and slams the door resentfully. At this gesture,* ABBIE *laughs tantalizingly, amused but at the same time piqued and irritated. He scowls, strides off the porch to the path and starts to walk past her to the road with a grand swagger of ignoring her existence. He is dressed in his store suit, spruced up, his face shines from soap and water.* ABBIE *leans forward on her chair, her eyes hard and angry now, and, as he passes her, gives a sneering, taunting chuckle.*)

EBEN (*stung—turns on her furiously*). What air yew cacklin' 'bout?

ABBIE (*triumphant*). Yew!

EBEN. What about me?

ABBIE. Ye look all slicked up like a prize bull.

EBEN (*with a sneer*). Waal—ye hain't so durned purty yerself, be ye? (*They stare into each other's eyes, his held by hers in spite of himself, hers glowingly possessive. Their physical attraction becomes a palpable force quivering in the hot air.*)

ABBIE (*softly*). Ye don't mean that, Eben. Ye may think ye mean it, mebbe, but ye don't. Ye can't. It's agin nature, Eben. Ye been fightin' yer nature ever since the day I come—tryin' t' tell yerself I hain't putty t'ye. (*She laughs a low humid laugh without taking her eyes from his. A pause—her body squirms desirously—she murmurs languorously.*) Hain't the sun strong an' hot? Ye kin feel it burnin' into the earth—Nature—makin' thin's grow—bigger 'n' bigger—burnin' inside ye—makin' ye want t' grow—into somethin' else—till ye're jined with it—an' it's your'n—but it owns ye, too—an' makes ye grow bigger—like a tree—like them elums—(*She laughs again softly, holding his eyes. He takes a step toward her, compelled against his will.*) Nature'll beat ye, Eben. Ye might's well own up t' it fust 's last.

EBEN (*trying to break from her spell—confusedly*). If Paw'd hear ye goin' on. . . . (*Resentfully*) But ye've made such a damned idjit out o' the old devil . . . ! (ABBIE *laughs.*)

ABBIE. Waal—hain't it easier fur yew with him changed softer?

EBEN (*defiantly*). No. I'm fightin' him—fightin' yew—fightin' fur Maw's rights t' her hum! (*This breaks her spell for him. He glowers at her.*) An' I'm onto ye. Ye hain't foolin' me a mite. Ye're aimin' t' swaller up everythin' an' make it your'n. Waal, you'll find I'm a heap sight bigger hunk nor yew kin chew! (*He turns from her with a sneer.*)

ABBIE (*trying to regain her ascendancy—seductively*). Eben!

EBEN. Leave me be! (*He starts to walk away.*)   ,

ABBIE (*more commandingly*). Eben!

EBEN (*stops—resentfully*). What d'ye want?

ABBIE (*trying to conceal a growing excitement*). Whar air ye goin'?

EBEN (*with malicious nonchalance*). Oh—up the road a spell.

ABBIE. T' the village?

EBEN (*airily*). Mebbe.

ABBIE (*excitedly*). T' see that Min, I s'pose?

EBEN. Mebbe.

ABBIE (*weakly*). What d'ye want t' waste time on her fur?

EBEN (*revenging himself now—grinning at her*). Ye can't beat Nature, didn't ye say? (*He laughs and again starts to walk away.*)

ABBIE (*bursting out*). An ugly old hake!

EBEN (*with a tantalizing sneer*). She's purtier'n yew be!

ABBIE. That every wuthless drunk in the county has. . . .

EBEN (*tauntingly*). Mebbe—but she's better'n yew. She owns up fa'r 'n' squar' t' her doin's.

ABBIE (*furiously*). Don't ye dare compare. . . .

EBEN. She don't go sneakin' an' stealin'—what's mine.

ABBIE (*savagely seizing on his weak point*). Your'n? Yew mean —my farm?

EBEN. I mean the farm yew sold yerself fur like any other old whore—my farm!

ABBIE (*stung—fiercely*). Ye'll never live t' see the day when even a stinkin' weed on it'll belong t' ye! (*Then in a scream*) Git out o' my sight! Go on t' yer slut—disgracin' yer Paw 'n' me! I'll git yer Paw t' horsewhip ye off the place if I want t'! Ye're only livin' here 'cause I tolerate ye! Git along! I hate the sight o' ye! (*She stops, panting and glaring at him.*)

EBEN (*returning her glance in kind*). An' I hate the sight o' yew! (*He turns and strides off up the road. She follows his retreating figure with concentrated hate. Old* CABOT *appears coming up from the barn. The hard, grim expression of his face has changed. He seems in some queer way softened, mellowed. His eyes have taken on a strange, incongruous dreamy quality. Yet there is no hint of physical weakness about him—rather he looks more robust and younger.* ABBIE *sees him and turns away quickly with unconcealed aversion. He comes slowly up to her.*)

CABOT (*mildly*). War yew an' Eben quarrelin' agen?

ABBIE (*shortly*). No.

CABOT. Ye was talkin' a'mighty loud. (*He sits down on the edge of porch.*)

ABBIE (*snappishly*). If ye heerd us they hain't no need askin' questions.

CABOT. I didn't hear what ye said.

ABBIE (*relieved*). Waal—it wa'n't nothin' t' speak on.

CABOT (*after a pause*). Eben's queer.

ABBIE (*bitterly*). He's the dead spit 'n' image o' yew!

CABOT (*queerly interested*). D'ye think so, Abbie? (*After a pause, ruminatingly*) Me 'n' Eben's allus fit 'n' fit. I never could b'ar him noways. He's so thunderin' soft—like his Maw.

ABBIE (*scornfully*). Ay-eh! 'Bout as soft as yew be!

CABOT (*as if he hadn't heard*). Mebbe I been too hard on him.

ABBIE (*jeeringly*). Waal—ye're gettin' soft now—soft as slop! That's what Eben was sayin'.

CABOT (*his face instantly grim and ominous*). Eben was sayin'? Waal, he'd best not do nothin' t' try me 'r he'll soon diskiver.... (*A pause. She keeps her face turned away. His gradually softens. He stares up at the sky.*) Purty, hain't it?

ABBIE (*crossly*). I don't see nothin' purty.

CABOT. The sky. Feels like a wa'm field up thar.

ABBIE (*sarcastically*). Air yew aimin' t' buy up over the farm too? (*She snickers contemptuously.*)

CABOT (*strangely*). I'd like t' own my place up thar. (*A pause.*) I'm gittin' old Abbie, I'm gittin' ripe on the bough. (*A pause. She stares at him mystified. He goes on.*) It's allus lonesome cold in the house—even when it's bilin' hot outside. Hain't yew noticed?

ABBIE. No.

CABOT. It's wa'm down t' the barn—nice smellin' an' warm—with the cows. (*A pause.*) Cows is queer.

ABBIE. Like yew?

CABOT. Like Eben. (*A pause.*) I'm gittin' t' feel resigned t' Eben —jest as I got t' feel 'bout his Maw. I'm gittin' t' learn to b'ar his softness—jest like her'n. I calc'late I c'd a'most take t' him—if he wa'n't sech a dumb fool! (*A pause.*) I s'pose it's old age a-creepin' in my bones.

ABBIE (*indifferently*). Waal—ye hain't dead yet.

CABOT (*roused*). No, I hain't, yew bet—not by a hell of a sight —I'm sound 'n' tough as hickory! (*Then moodily*) But arter three score and ten the Lord warns ye t' prepare. (*A pause.*) That's why

Eben's come in my head. Now that his cussed sinful brothers is gone their path t' hell, they's no one left but Eben.

ABBIE (*resentfully*). They's me, hain't they? (*Agitatedly*) What's all this sudden likin' ye tuk to Eben? Why don't ye say nothin' 'bout me? Hain't I yer lawful wife?

CABOT (*simply*). Ay-eh. Ye be. (*A pause—he stares at her desirously—his eyes grow avid—then with a sudden movement he seizes her hands and squeezes them, declaiming in a queer camp meeting preacher's tempo:*) Yew air my Rose o' Sharon! Behold, yew air fair; yer eyes aid doves; yer lips air like scarlet; yer two breasts air like two fawns; yet navel be like a round goblet; yer belly be like a heap o' wheat. . . . (*He covers her hand with kisses. She does not seem to notice. She stares before her with hard angry eyes.*)

ABBIE (*jerking her hands away—harshly*). So ye're plannin' t' leave the farm t' Eben, air ye?

CABOT (*dazedly*). Leave . . . ? (*Then with resentful obstinacy*) I hain't a-givin' it t' no one!

ABBIE (*remorselessly*). Ye can't take it with ye.

CABOT (*thinks a moment—then reluctantly*). No, I calc'late not. (*After a pause—with a strange passion*) But if I could, I would, by the Etarnal! 'R if I could, in my dyin' hour, I'd set it afire an' watch it burn—this house an' every ear o' corn an' every tree down t' the last blade o' hay! I'd sit an' know it was all a-dying with me an' no one else'd ever own what was mine, what I'd made out o' nothin' with my own sweat 'n' blood! (*A pause—then he adds with a queer affection.*) 'Ceptin' the cows. Them I'd turn free.

ABBIE (*harshly*). An' me?

CABOT (*with a queer smile*). Ye'd be turned free, too.

ABBIE (*furiously*). So that's the thanks I git fur marryin' ye—t' have ye change kind to Eben who hates ye, an' talk o' turnin' me out in the road.

CABOT (*hastily*). Abbie! Ye know I wa'n't. . . .

ABBIE (*vengefully*). Just let me tell ye a thing or two 'bout Eben. Whar's he gone? T' see that harlot, Min! I tried fur t' stop him. Disgracin' yew an' me—on the Sabbath, too!

CABOT (*rather guiltily*). He's a sinner—nateral-born. It's lust eatin' his heart.

ABBIE (*enraged beyond endurance— wildly vindictive*). An' his lust fur me! Kin ye find excuses fur that?

CABOT (*stares at her—after a dead pause*). Lust—fur yew?

ABBIE (*defiantly*). He was tryin' t' make love t' me—when ye heerd us quarrelin'.

CABOT (*stares at her—then a terrible expression of rage comes over his face—he springs to his feet shaking all over*). By the A'mighty God—I'll end him!

ABBIE (*frightened now for* EBEN). No! Don't ye!

CABOT (*violently*). I'll git the shotgun an' blow his soft brains t' the top o' them elums!

ABBIE (*throwing her arms around him*). No, Ephraim!

CABOT (*pushing her away violently*). I will, by God!

ABBIE (*in a quieting tone*). Listen, Ephraim. 'Twa'n't nothin' bad —on'y a boy's foolin'—'twa'n't meant serious—jest jokin' and teasin'. . . .

CABOT. Then why did ye say—lust?

ABBIE. It must hev sounded wusser'n I meant. An' I was mad at thinkin'—ye'd leave him the farm.

CABOT (*quieter but still grim and cruel*). Waal then, I'll horse-whip him off the place if that much'll content ye.

ABBIE (*reaching out and taking his hand*). No. Don't think o' me! Ye mustn't drive him off. 'Tain't sensible. Who'll ye get to help ye on the farm? They's no one hereabouts.

CABOT (*considers this—then nodding his appreciation*). Ye got a head on ye. (*Then irritably:*) Waal, let him stay. (*He sits down on the edge of the porch. She sits beside him. He murmurs contemptuously:*) I oughtn't git riled so—at that 'ere fool calf. (*A pause.*) But har's the p'int. What son o' mine'll keep on here t' the farm—when the Lord does call me? Simeon an' Peter air gone t' hell—an' Eben's follerin' 'em.

ABBIE. They's me.

CABOT. Ye're on'y a woman.

ABBIE. I'm yewr wife.

CABOT. That hain't me. A son is me—my blood—mine. Mine ought t'git mine. An' then it's still mine—even though I be six foot under. D'ye see?

ABBIE (*giving him a look of hatred*). Ay-eh. I see. (*She becomes*

very thoughtful, her face growing shrewd, her eyes studying CABOT
craftily.)

CABOT. I'm gittin' old—ripe on the bough. (*Then with a sudden forced reassurance*) Not but what I hain't a hard nut t' crack even yet—an' fur many a year t' come! By the Etarnal, I kin break most o' the young fellars' backs at any kind o' work any day o' the year!

ABBIE (*suddenly*). Mebbe the Lord'll give *us* a son.

CABOT (*turns and stares at her eagerly*). Ye mean—a son—t' me 'n' yew?

ABBIE (*with a cajoling smile*). Ye're a strong man yet, hain't ye? 'Tain't noways impossible, be it? We know that. Why d'ye stare so? Hain't ye never thought o' that afore? I been thinkin' o' it all along. Ay-eh—an' I been prayin' it'd happen, too.

CABOT (*his face growing full of joyous pride and a sort of religious ecstasy*). Ye been prayin', Abbie?—fur a son?—t' us?

ABBIE. Ay-eh. (*With a grim resolution*) I want a son now.

CABOT (*excitedly clutching both of her hands in his*). It'd be the blessin' o' God, Abbie—the blessin' o' God A'mighty on me—in my old age—in my lonesomeness! They hain't nothin' I wouldn't do fur ye then, Abbie. Ye'd hev on'y t' ask it—anythin' ye'd a mind t'!

ABBIE (*interrupting*). Would ye will the farm t' me then—t' me an' it . . . ?

CABOT (*vehemently*). I'd do anythin' ye axed, I tell ye! I swar it! May I be everlastin' damned t' hell if I wouldn't! (*He sinks to his knees, pulling her down with him. He trembles all over with the fervor of his hopes.*) Pray t' the Lord agen, Abbie. It's the Sabbath! I'll jine ye! Two prayers air better nor one. "An' God hearkened unto Rachel"! An' God hearkened unto Abbie! Pray, Abbie! Pray fur him to hearken! (*He bows his head, mumbling. She pretends to do likewise but gives him a side glance of scorn and triumph.*)

SCENE TWO.

About eight in the evening. The interior of the two bedrooms on the top floor is shown——EBEN is sitting on the side of his bed in the room on the left. On account of the heat he has taken off everything but his undershirt and pants. His feet are bare. He faces front, brooding moodily, his chin propped on his hands, a desperate expression on his face.

In the other room CABOT and ABBIE are sitting side by side on the edge of their bed, an old four-poster with feather mattress. He is in his night shirt, she in her nightdress. He is still in the queer, excited mood into which the notion of a son has thrown him. Both rooms are lighted dimly and flickeringly by tallow candles.

CABOT. The farm needs a son.

ABBIE. I need a son.

CABOT. Ay-eh. Sometimes ye air the farm an' sometimes the farm be yew. That's why I clove t' ye in my lonesomeness. (*A pause. He pounds his knee with his fist.*) Me an' the farm has got t' beget a son!

ABBIE. Ye'd best go t' sleep. Ye're gittin' thin's all mixed.

CABOT (*with an impatient gesture*). No, I hain't. My mind's clear's a well. Ye don't know me, that's it. (*He stares hopelessly at the floor.*)

ABBIE (*indifferently*). Mebbe. (*In the next room* EBEN *gets up and paces up and down distractedly.* ABBIE *hears him. Her eyes fasten on the intervening wall with concentrated attention.* EBEN *stops and stares. Their hot glances seem to meet through the wall. Unconsciously he stretches out his arms for her and she half rises. Then aware, he mutters a curse at himself and flings himself face downward on the bed, his clenched fists above his head, his face buried in the pillow.* ABBIE *relaxes with a faint sigh but her eyes remain fixed on the wall; she listens with all her attention for some movement from* EBEN.)

CABOT (*suddenly raises his head and looks at her—scornfully*). Will ye ever know me—'r will any man 'r woman? (*Shaking his head*) No. I calc'late 't wa'n't 't be. (*He turns away.* ABBIE *looks at the wall. Then, evidently unable to keep silent about his thoughts, without looking at his wife, he puts out his hand and clutches her knee. She starts violently, looks at him, sees he is not watching her, concentrates again on the wall and pays no attention to what he says.*) Listen, Abbie. When I come here fifty odd year ago—I was jest twenty an' the strongest an' hardest ye ever seen—ten times as strong an' fifty times as hard as Eben. Waal—this place was nothin' but fields o' stones. Folks laughed when I tuk it. They couldn't know what I knowed. When ye kin make corn sprout out o' stones, God's livin' in yew! They wa'n't strong enuf fur that! They reckoned God was easy. They laughed. They don't laugh no more. Some died hereabouts. Some went West an' died. They're all under ground—

fur follerin' arter an easy God. God hain't easy. (*He shakes his head slowly.*) An' I growed hard. Folks kept allus sayin' he's a hard man like 'twas sinful t' be hard, so's at last I said back at 'em: Waal then, by thunder, ye'll git me hard an' see how ye like it! (*Then suddenly*) But I give in t' weakness once. 'Twas arter I'd been here two year. I got weak—despairful—they was so many stones. They was a party leavin', givin' up, goin' West. I jined 'em. We tracked on 'n on. We come t' broad medders, plains, whar the soil was black an' rich as gold. Nary a stone. Easy. Ye'd on'y to plow an' sow an' then set an' smoke yer pipe an' watch thin's grow. I could o' been a rich man—but somethin' in me fit me an' fit me—the voice o' God sayin': "This hain't wuth nothin' t' Me. Get ye back t' hum!" I got afeerd o' that voice an' I lit out back t' hum here, leavin' my claim an' crops t' whoever'd a mind t' take 'em. Ay-eh. I actoolly give up what was righful mine! God's hard, not easy! God's in the stones! Build my church on a rock—out o' stones an' I'll be in them! That's what He meant t' Peter! (*He sighs heavily—a pause.*) Stones I picked 'em up an' piled 'em into walls. Ye kin read the years o' my life in them walls, every day a hefted stone, climbin' over the hills up and down, fencin' in the fields that was mine, whar I'd made thin's grow out o' nothin'—like the will o' God, like the servant o' His hand. It wa'n't easy. It was hard an' He made me hard fur it. (*He pauses.*) All the time I kept gittin' lonesomer. I tuk a wife. She bore Simeon an' Peter. She was a good woman. She wuked hard. We was married twenty year. She never knowed me. She helped but she never knowed what she was helpin'. I was allus lonesome. She died. After that it wa'n't so lonesome fur a spell. (*A pause.*) I lost count o' the years. I had no time t' fool away countin' 'em. Sim an' Peter helped. The farm growed. It was all mine! When I thought o' that I didn't feel lonesome. (*A pause.*) But ye can't hitch yer mind t' one thin' day an' night. I tuk another wife—Eben's Maw. Her folks was contestin' me at law over my deeds t' the farm—my farm! That's why Eben keeps a-talkin' his fool talk o' this bein' his Maw's farm. She bore Eben. She was purty—but soft. She tried t' be hard. She couldn't. She never knowed me nor nothin'. It was lonesomer 'n hell with her. After a matter o' sixteen odd years, she died. (*A pause.*) I lived with the boys. They hated me 'cause I was hard. I hated them 'cause they was soft. They coveted the farm without knowin' what it meant. It made me bitter 'n wormwood. It aged me—them coveting what I'd made fur mine. Then this spring the call come—the voice o' God cryin' in my wilderness, in my lonesomeness—t' go out an' seek an' find! (*Turning to her with strange passion*) I sought ye an' I found ye! Yew air my Rose o' Sharon! Yer eyes air like. . . . (*She has turned a blank face, resentful eyes to his. He stares at her for a moment—then harshly*) Air ye any the wiser fur all I've told ye?

ABBIE (*confusedly*). Mebbe.

CABOT (*pushing her away from him—angrily*). Ye don't know nothin'—nor never will. If ye don't hev a son t' redeem ye . . . (*This in a tone of cold threat.*)

ABBIE (*resentfully*). I've prayer, hain't I?

CABOT (*bitterly*). Pray agen—fur understandin'!

ABBIE (*a veiled threat in her tone*). Ye'll have a son out o' me, I promise ye.

CABOT. How kin ye promise?

ABBIE. I got second-sight mebbe. I kin foretell. (*She gives a queer smile.*)

CABOT. I believe ye have. Ye give me the chills sometimes. (*He shivers.*) It's cold in this house. It's oneasy. They's thin's pokin' about in the dark—in the corners. (*He pulls on his trousers, tucking in his night shirt, and pulls on his boots.*)

ABBIE (*surprised*). Whar air ye goin'?

CABOT (*queerly*). Down whar it's restful—whar it's warm—down t' the barn. (*Bitterly*) I kin talk t' the cows. They know. They know the farm an' me. They'll give me peace. (*He turns to go out the door.*)

ABBIE (*a bit frightenedly*). Air ye ailin' tonight, Ephraim?

CABOT. Growin'. Growin' ripe on the bough. (*He turns and goes, his boots clumping down the stairs.* EBEN *sits up with a start, listening.* ABBIE *is conscious of his movement and stares at the wall.* CABOT *comes out of the house around the corner and stands by the gate, blinking at the sky. He stretches up his hands in a tortured gesture*) God A'mighty, call from the dark! (*He listens as if expecting an answer. Then his arms drop, he shakes his head and plods off toward the barn.* EBEN *and* ABBIE *stare at each other through the wall.* EBEN *sighs heavily and* ABBIE *echoes it. Both become terribly nervous, uneasy. Finally* ABBIE *gets up and listens, her ear to the wall. He acts as if he saw every move she was making, he becomes resolutely*

*still. She seems driven into a decision—goes out the door in rear
determinedly. His eyes follow her. Then as the door of his room is
opened softly, he turns away, waits in an attitude of strained fixity.*
ABBIE *stands for a second staring at him, her eyes burning with
desire. Then with a little cry she runs over and throws her arms
about his neck, she pulls his head back and covers his mouth with
kisses. At first, he submits dumbly; then he puts his arms about
her neck and returns her kisses, but finally, suddenly aware of his
hatred, he hurls her away from him, springing to his feet. They stand
speechless and breathless, panting like two animals.)*

ABBIE (*at last—painfully.*) Ye shouldn't, Eben—ye shouldn't—I'd
make ye happy!

EBEN (*harshly*). I don't want t' be happy—from yew!

ABBIE (*helplessly*). Ye do, Eben! Ye do! Why d'ye lie?

EBEN (*viciously*). I don't take t' ye, I tell ye! I hate the sight o' ye!

ABBIE (*with an uncertain troubled laugh*). Waal, I kissed ye anyways—an' ye kissed back—yer lips was burnin'—ye can't lie 'bout
that! (*Intensely*) If ye don't care, why did ye kiss me back—why
was yer lips burnin'?

EBEN (*wiping his mouth*). It was like pizen on 'em (*Then
tauntingly*) When I kissed ye back, mebbe I thought 'twas someone
else.

ABBIE (*wildly*). Min?

EBEN. Mebbe.

ABBIE (*torturedly*). Did ye go t' see her? Did ye r'ally go? I
thought ye mightn't. Is that why ye throwed me off jest now?

EBEN (*sneeringly*). What if it be?

ABBIE (*raging*). Then ye're a dog, Eben Cabot!

EBEN (*threateningly*). Ye can't talk that way t' me!

ABBIE (*with a shrill laugh*). Can't I? Did ye think I was in love
with ye—a weak thin' like yew? Not much! I on'y wanted ye fur a
purpose o' my own—an' I'll hev ye fur it yet 'cause I'm stronger'n
yew be!

EBEN (*resentfully*). I knowed well it was on'y part o' yer plan t'
swaller everythin'!

ABBIE (*tauntingly*). Mebbe!

EBEN (*furious*). Git out o' my room!

ABBIE. This air my room an' ye're on'y hired help!

EBEN (*threateningly*). Git out afore I murder ye!

ABBIE (*quite confident now*). I hain't a mite afeerd. Ye want me, don't ye? Yes, ye do! An' yer Paw's son'll never kill what he wants! Look at yer eyes! They's lust fur me in 'em, burnin' 'em up! Look at yer lips now! They're tremblin' an' longin' t' kiss me, an' yer teeth t' bite (*He is watching her now with a horrible fascination. She laughs a crazy triumphant laugh.*) I'm a-goin' t' make all o' this hum my hum! They's one room hain't mine yet, but it's a-goin' t' be tonight. I'm a-goin' down now and light up! (*She makes him a mocking bow.*) Won't ye come courtin' me in the best parlor, Mister Cabot?

EBEN (*staring at her—horribly confused—dully*). Don't ye dare! It hain't been opened since Maw died an' was laid out thar! Don't ye . . . ! (*But her eyes are fixed on his so burningly that his will seems to wither before hers. He stands swaying toward her help-lessly.*)

ABBIE (*holding his eyes and putting all her will into her words as she backs out the door*). I'll expect ye afore long, Eben.

EBEN (*stares after her for a while, walking toward the door. A light appears in the parlor window. He murmurs*). In the parlor? (*This seems to arouse connotations for he comes back and puts on his white shirt, collar, half ties the tie mechanically, puts on coat, takes his hat, stands barefooted looking about him in bewilderment, mutters wonderingly:*) Maw! Whar air yew? (*Then goes slowly toward the door in rear.*)

SCENE THREE.

A few minutes later. The interior of the parlor is shown. A grim, repressed room like a tomb in which the family has been interred alive. ABBIE sits on the edge of the horsehair sofa. She has lighted all the candles and the room is revealed in all its preserved ugliness. A change has come over the woman. She looks awed and frightened now, ready to run away.

The door is opened and EBEN appears. His face wears an expression of obsessed confusion. He stands staring at her, his arms hanging disjointedly from his shoulders, his feet bare, his hat in his hand.

ABBIE (*after a pause—with a nervous, formal politeness*). Won't ye set?

EBEN (*dully*). Ay-eh. (*Mechanically he places his hat carefully on the floor near the door and sits stiffly beside her on the edge of the sofa. A pause. They both remain rigid, looking straight ahead with eyes full of fear.*)

ABBIE. When I fust came in—in the dark—they seemed somethin' here.

EBEN (*simply*). Maw.

ABBIE. I kin still feel—somethin'. . . .

EBEN. It's Maw.

ABBIE. At fust I was feerd o' it. I wanted t' yell an' run. Now—since yew come—seems like it's growin' soft an' kind t' me. (*Addressing the air—queerly*) Thank yew.

EBEN. Maw allus loved me.

ABBIE. Mebbe it knows I love yew too. Mebbe that makes it kind t' me.

EBEN (*dully*). I dunno. I should think she'd hate ye.

ABBIE (*with certainty*). No. I kin feel it don't—not no more.

EBEN. Hate ye fur stealin' her place—here in her hum—settin' in her parlor whar she was laid— (*He suddenly stops, staring stupidly before him.*)

ABBIE. What is it, Eben?

EBEN (*in a whisper*). Seems like Maw didn't want me t' remind ye.

ABBIE (*excitedly*). I knowed, Eben! It's kind t' me! It don't b'ar me no grudges fur what I never knowed an' couldn't help!

EBEN. Maw b'ars him a grudge.

ABBIE. Waal, so does all o' us.

EBEN. Ay-eh. (*With passion*) I does, by God!

ABBIE (*taking one of his hands in hers and patting it*). Thar! Don't git riled thinkin' o' him. Think o' yer Maw who's kind t' us. Tell me about yer Maw, Eben.

EBEN. They hain't nothin' much. She was kind. She was good.

ABBIE (*putting one arm over his shoulder. He does not seem to notice—passionately*). I'll be kind an' good t' ye!

EBEN. Sometimes she used t' sing fur me.

ABBIE. I'll sing fur ye!

EBEN. This was her hum. This was her farm.

ABBIE. This is my hum! This is my farm!

EBEN. He married her t' steal 'em. She was soft an' easy. He couldn't 'preciate her.

ABBIE. He can't 'preciate me!

EBEN. He murdered her with his hardness.

ABBIE. He's murderin' me!

EBEN. She died. (*A pause.*) Sometimes she used to sing fur me. (*He bursts into a fit of sobbing.*)

ABBIE (*both her arms around him—with wild passion*). I'll sing fur ye! I'll die fur ye! (*In spite of her overwhelming desire for him, there is a sincere maternal love in her manner and voice—a horribly frank mixture of lust and mother love.*) Don't cry, Eben! I'll take yer Maw's place! I'll be everythin' she wa t' ye! Let me kiss ye, Eben! (*She pulls his head around. He makes a bewildered pretense of resistance. She is tender.*) Don't be afeerd! I'll kiss ye pure, Eben —same 's if I was a Maw t' ye—an' ye kin kiss me back 's if yew was my son—my boy—sayin' good-night t' me! Kiss me, Eben. (*They kiss in restrained fashion. Then suddenly wild passion overcomes her. She kisses him lustfully aagin and again and he flings his arms about her and returns her kisses. Suddenly, as in the bedroom, he frees himself from her violently and springs to his feet. He is trembling all over, in a strange state of terror.* ABBIE *strains her arms toward him with fierce pleading.*) Don't ye leave me, Eben! Can't ye see it hain't enuf—lovin' ye like a Maw—can't ye see it's got t' be that an' more—much more—a hundred times more —fur me t' be happy—fur yew t' be happy?

EBEN (*to the presence he feels in the room*). Maw! Maw! What d'ye want? What air ye tellin' me?

ABBIE. She's tellin' ye t' love me. She knows I love ye an' I'll be good t' ye. Can't ye feel it? Don't ye know? She's tellin' ye t' love me, Eben!

EBEN. Ay-eh. I feel—mebbe she—but—I can't figger out—why —when ye've stole her place—here in her hum—in the parlor whar she was—

ABBIE (*fiercely*). She knows I love ye!

EBEN (*his face suddenly lighting up with a fierce triumphant grin*). I see it! I see why. It's her vengeance on him—so's she kin rest quiet in her grave!

ABBIE (*wildly*). Vengeance o' God on the hull o' us. What d'we give a durn? I love ye, Eben! God knows I love ye! (*She stretches out her arms for him.*)

EBEN (*throws himself on his knees beside the sofa and grabs her in his arms—releasing all his pent-up passion*). An' I love yew,

Abbie!—now I kin say it! I been dyin' fur want o' ye—every hour
since ye come! I love ye! (*Their lips meet in a fierce, bruising kiss.*)

SCENE FOUR.

Exterior of the farmhouse. It is just dawn. The front door at right is
opened and EBEN comes out and walks around to the gate. He is dressed
in his working clothes. He seems changed. His face wears a bold and confident expression, he is grinning to himself with evident satisfaction. As he
gets near the gate, the window of the parlor is heard opening and the shutters are flung back and ABBIE sticks her head out. Her hair tumbles over her
shoulders in disarray, her face is flushed, she looks at EBEN with tender,
languorous eyes and calls softly.

ABBIE. Eben. (*As he turns—playfully*) Jest one more kiss afore
ye go. I'm goin' to miss ye fearful all day.

EBEN. An' me yew, ye kin bet! (*He goes to her. They kiss several
times. He draws away, laughingly.*) Thar. That's enuf, hain't it? Ye
won't hev none left fur next time.

ABBIE. I got a million o' 'em left fur yew! (*Then a bit anxiously*)
D'ye r'ally love me, Eben?

EBEN (*emphatically*). I like ye better'n any gal I ever knowed!
That's gospel!

ABBIE. Likin' hain't lovin'.

EBEN. Waal then—I love ye. Now air yew satisfied?

ABBIE. Ay-eh, I be. (*She smiles at him adoringly.*)

EBEN. I beter git t' the barn. The old critter's liable t' suspicion
an' come sneakin' up.

ABBIE (*with a confident laugh*). Let him! I kin allus pull the wool
over his eyes. I'm goin' t' leave the shuters open and let in the sun
'n' air. This room's been dead long enuf. Now it's goin' t' be my
room!

EBEN (*frowning*). Ay-eh.

ABBIE (*hastily*). I meant—our room.

EBEN. Ay-eh.

ABBIE. We made it our'n last night, didn't we? We give it life—
our lovin' did. (*A pause.*)

EBEN (*with a strange look*). Maw's gone back t' her grave. She
kin sleep now.

ABBIE. May she rest in peace! (*Then tenderly rebuking*) Ye oughtn't t' talk o' sad thin's—this mornin'.

EBEN. It jest come up in my mind o' itself.

ABBIE. Don't let it. (*He doesn't answer. She yawns.*) Waal, I'm a-goin' t' steal a wink o' sleep. I'll tell the Old Man I hain't feelin' pert. Let him git his own vittles.

EBEN. I see him comin' from the barn. Ye better look smart an' git upstairs.

ABBIE. Ay-eh. Good-by. Don't fergit me. (*She throws him a kiss. He grins—then squares his shoulders and awaits his father confidently.* CABOT *walks slowly up from the left, staring up at the sky with a vague face.*)

EBEN (*jovially*). Mornin', Paw. Star-gazin' in daylight?

CABOT. Purty, hain't it?

EBEN (*looking around him possessively*). It's a durned purty farm.

CABOT. I mean the sky.

EBEN (*grinning*). How d'ye know? Them eyes o' your'n can't see that fur. (*This tickles his humor and he slaps his thigh and laughs.*) Ho-ho! That's a good un!

CABOT (*grimly sarcastic*). Ye're feelin' right chipper, hain't ye? Whar'd ye steal the likker?

EBEN (*good-naturedly*). 'Tain't likker. Jest life. (*Suddenly holding out his hand—soberly*) Yew 'n' me is quits. Let's shake hands.

CABOT (*suspiciously*). What's come over ye?

EBEN. Then don't. Mebbe it's jest as well. (*A moment's pause.*) What's come over me? (*Queerly*) Didn't ye feel her passin'—goin' back t' her grave?

CABOT (*dully*). Who?

EBEN. Maw. She kin rest now an' sleep content. She's quits with ye.

CABOT (*confusedly*). I rested. I slept good—down with the cows. They know how t' sleep. They're teachin' me.

EBEN (*suddenly jovial again*). Good fur the cows! Waal—ye better git t' work.

CABOT (*grimly amused*). Air ye bossin' me, ye calf?

EBEN (*beginning to laugh*). Ay-eh! I'm bossin' yew! Ha-ha-ha! see how ye like it! Ha-ha-ha! I'm the prize rooster o' this roost. Ha-ha-ha! (*He goes off toward the barn laughing.*)

CABOT (*looks after him with scornful pity*). Soft-headed. Like his Maw. Dead spit 'n' image. No hope in him! (*He spits with contemptuous disgust.*) A born fool! (*Then matter-of-factly*) Waal— I'm gittin' peckish. (*He goes toward door.*)

CURTAIN

pARt 111

SCENE ONE.

A night in late spring the following year. The kitchen and the two bedrooms upstairs are shown. The two bedrooms are dimly lighted by a tallow candle in each. EBEN is sitting on the side of the bed in his room, his chin propped on his fists, his face a study of the struggle he is making to understand his conflicting emotions. The noisy laughter and music from below where a kitchen dance is in progress annoy and distract him. He scowls at the floor.

In the next room a cradle stands beside the double bed.

In the kitchen all is festivity. The stove has been taken down to give more room to the dancers. The chairs, with wooden benches added, have been pushed back against the walls. On these are seated, squeezed in tight against one another, farmers and their wives and their young folks of both sexes from the neighboring farms. They are all chattering and laughing loudly. They evidently have some secret joke in common. There is no end of winking, of nudging, of meaning nods of the head toward CABOT who, in a state of extreme hilarious excitement increased by the amount he has drunk, is standing near the rear door where there is a small keg of whisky and serving drinks to all the men. In the left corner, front, dividing the attention with her husband, ABBIE is sitting in a rocking chair, a shawl wrapped about her shoulders. She is very pale, her face is thin and drawn, her eyes are fixed anxiously on the open door in rear as if waiting for someone.

The musician is tuning up his fiddle, seated in the far right corner. He is a lanky young fellow with a long, weak face. His pale eyes blink incessantly and he grins about him slyly with a greedy malice.

ABBIE (*suddenly turning to a young girl on her right*). Whar's Eben?

YOUNG GIRL (*eying her scornfully*). I dunno, Mrs. Cabot. I hain't seen Eben in ages. (*Meaningly*) Seems like he's spent most o' his time t' hum since yew come.

ABBIE (*vaguely*). I tuk his Maw's place.

YOUNG GIRL. Ay-eh. So I heerd. (*She turns away to retail this bit of gossip to her mother sitting next to her.* ABBIE *turns to her left to a big stoutish middle-aged man whose flushed face and staring eyes show the amount of "likker" he has consumed.*)

ABBIE. Ye hain't see Eben, hev ye?

MAN. No, I hain't. (*Then he adds with a wink*) If yew hain't, who would?

ABBIE. He's the best dancer in the county. He'd ought t' come an' dance.

MAN (*with a wink*). Mebbe he's doin' the dutiful an' walkin' the kid t' sleep. It's a boy' hain't it?

ABBIE (*nodding vaguely*). Ay-eh— born two weeks back—purty's a picter.

MAN. They all is—t' their Maws. (*Then in a whisper, with a nudge and a leer*) Listen, Abbie—if ye ever git tired o' Eben, remember me! Don't fergit now! (*He looks at her uncomprehending face for a second—then grunts disgustedly.*) Waal—guess I'll likker agin. (*He goes over and joins* CABOT, *who is arguing noisily with an old farmer over cows. They all drink.*)

ABBIE (*this time appealing to nobody in particular*). Wonder what Eben's a-doin'? (*Her remark is repeated down the line with many a guffaw and titter until it reaches the fiddler. He fastens his blinking eyes on* ABBIE.)

FIDDLER (*raising his voice*). Bet I kin tell ye, Abbie, what Eben's doin'! He's down t' the church offerin' up prayers o' thanksgivin'. (*They all titter expectantly.*)

MAN. What fur? (*Another titter.*)

FIDDLER. 'Cause unto him a—(*he hesitates just long enough*)— brother is born! (*A roar of laughter. They all look from* ABBIE *to* CABOT. *She is oblivious, staring at the door.* CABOT, *although he hasn't heard the words, is irritated by the laughter and steps forward, glaring about him. There is an immediate silence.*)

CABOT. What're ye all bleatin' about—like a flock o' goats? Why don't ye dance, damn ye? I axed ye here t' dance—t' eat, drink an' be merry—an' thar ye set cacklin' like a lot o' wet hens with the pip! Ye've swilled my likker an' guzzled my vittles like hogs, hain't ye? Then dance fur me, can't ye? That's fa'r an' squar', hain't it? (*A grumble of resentment goes around but they are all evidently in too much awe of him to express it openly.*)

FIDDLER (*slyly*). We're waitin' fur Eben. (*A suppressed laugh.*)

CABOT (*with a fierce exultation*). T'hell with Eben! Eben's done fur now! I got a new son! (*His mood switching with drunken suddenness*) But ye needn't t' laugh at Eben, none o' ye! He's my blood, if he be a dumb fool. He's better nor any o' yew! He kin do a day's work a'most up t' what I kin—an' that'd put any o' yew pore critters t' shame!

FIDDLER. An' he kin do a good night's work, too! (*A roar of laughter.*)

CABOT. Laugh, ye damn fools! Ye're right jist the same, Fiddler. He kin work day an' night too, like I kin, if need be!

OLD FARMER (*from behind the keg where he is weaving drunkenly back and forth—with great simplicity*). They hain't many t' touch ye, Ephraim—a son at seventy-six. That's a hard man fur ye! I be on'y sixty-eight an' I couldn't do it. (*A roar of laughter in which* CABOT *joins uproariously.*)

CABOT (*slapping him on the back*). I'm sorry fur ye, Hi. I'd never suspicion sech weakness from a boy like yew!

OLD FARMER. An' I never reckoned yew had it in ye nuther, Ephraim. (*There is another laugh.*)

CABOT (*suddenly grim*). I got a lot in me—a hell of a lot—folks don't know on. (*Turning to the* FIDDLER) Fiddle 'er up, darn ye! Give 'em somethin' t' dance t'! What air ye, an ornament? Hain't this a celebration? Then grease yer elbow an' go it!

FIDDLER (*seizes a drink which the* OLD FARMER *holds out to him and downs it*). Here goes! (*He starts to fiddle "Lady of the Lake."* Four young fellows and four girls form in two lines and dance a square dance. The FIDDLER shouts directions for the different movements, keeping his words in the rhythm of the music and interspersing them with jocular personal remarks to the dancers themselves. The people seated along the walls stamp their feet and clap their hands in unison, CABOT is especially active in this respect. Only ABBIE remains apathetic, staring at the door as if she were alone in a silent room.*)

FIDDLER. Swing your partner 't the right! That's it, Jim! Give her a b'ar hug! Her Maw hain't lookin'. (*Laughter.*) Change partners! That suits ye, don't it, Essie, now ye got Reub afore ye? Look at her redden up, will ye! Waal, life is short an' so's love, as the feller says. (*Laughter.*)

CABOT (*excitedly, stamping his foot*). Go it, boys! Go it, gals!

FIDDLER (*with a wink at the others*). Ye're the spryest seventy-six ever I sees, Ephraim! Now if ye'd on'y good eyesight . . . ! (*Suppressed laughter. He gives* CABOT *no chance to retort but roars.*) Promenade! Ye're walkin' like a bride down the aisle, Sarah! Waal, while they's life they's allus hope. I've heerd tell. Swing your partner to the left! Gosh A'mighty, look at Johnny Cook high-steppin'! They hain't goin' t' be much strength left fur hoein' in the corn lot t'morrow. (*Laughter.*)

CABOT. Go it! Go it! (*Then suddenly, unable to restrain himself any longer, he prances into the midst of the dancers, scattering them, waving his arms about wildly.*) Ye're all hoofs! Git out o' my road! Give me room! I'll show ye dancin'. Ye're all too soft! (*He pushes them roughly away. They crowd back toward the walls, muttering, looking at him resentfully.*)

FIDDLER (*jeeringly*). Go it, Ephraim! Go it! (*He starts "Pop Goes the Weasel," increasing the tempo with every verse until at the end he is fiddling crazily as fast as he can go.*)

CABOT (*starts to dance, which he does very well and with tremendous vigor. Then he begins to improvise, cuts incredibly grotesque capers, leaping up and cracking his heels together, prancing around in a circle with body bent in an Indian war dance, then suddenly straightening up and kicking as high as he can with both legs. He is like a monkey on a string. And all the while he intersperses his antics with shouts and derisive comments*). Whoop! Here's dancin' fur ye! Whoop! See that! Seventy-six, if I'm a day! Hard as iron yet! Beatin' the young 'uns like I allus done! Look at me! I'd invite ye t' dance on my hundredth birthday on'y ye'll all be dead by then. Ye're a sickly generation! Yer hearts air pink, not red! Yer veins is full o' mud an' water! I be the on'y man in the county! Whoop! See that! I'm a Injun! I've killed Injuns in the West afore ye was born—an' skulped 'em too! They's a arrer wound on my backside I c'd show ye! The hull tribe chased me. I outrun 'em all—with the arrer stuck in me! An' I tuk vengeance on 'em. Ten eyes fur an eye, that was my motter! Whoop! Look at me! I kin kick the ceilin' off the room! Whoop!

FIDDLER (*stops playing—exhaustedly*). God A'mighty, I got enuf. Ye got the devil's strength in ye.

CABOT (*delightedly*). Did I beat yew, too? Wa'al, ye played smart. Hev a swig. (*He pours whisky for himself and* FIDDLER.

They drink. The others watch CABOT *silently with cold, hostile eyes. There is a dead pause. The* FIDDLER *rests.* CABOT *leans against the keg, panting, glaring around him confusedly. In the room above,* EBEN *gets to his feet and tiptoes out the door in rear, appearing a moment later in the other bedroom. He moves silently, even frightenedly, toward the cradle and stands there looking down at the baby. His face is as vague as his reactions are confused, but there is a trace of tenderness, of interested discovery. At the same moment that he reaches the cradle,* ABBIE *seems to sense something. She gets up weakly and goes to* CABOT.)

ABBIE. I'm goin' up t' the baby.

CABOT (*with real solicitude*). Air ye able fur the stairs? D'ye want me t' help ye, Abbie?

ABBIE. No. I'm able. I'll be down agen soon.

CABOT. Don't ye git wore out! He needs ye, remember—our son does! (*He grins affectionately, patting her on the back. She shrinks from his touch.*)

ABBIE (*dully*). Don't—tech me. I'm goin'—up. (*She goes.* CABOT *looks after her. A whisper goes around the room.* CABOT *turns. It ceases. He wipes his forehead streaming with sweat. He is breathing pantingly.*)

CABOT. I'm a-goin' out t' git fresh air. I'm feelin' a mite dizzy. Fiddle up thar! Dance, all o' ye! Here's likker fur them as wants it. Enjoy yerselves. I'll be back. (*He goes, closing the door behind him.*)

FIDDLER (*sarcastically*). Don't hurry none on our account! (*A suppressed laugh. He imitates* ABBIE.) Whar's Eben? (*More laughter.*)

A WOMAN (*loudly*). What's happened in this house is plain as the nose on yer face! (ABBIE *appears in the doorway upstairs and stands looking in surprise and adoration at* EBEN, *who does not see her.*)

A MAN. Ssshh! He's li'ble t' be listenin' at the door. That'd be like him. (*Their voices die to an intensive whispering. Their faces are concentrated on this gossip. A noise as of dead leaves in the wind comes from the room.* CABOT *has come out from the porch and stands by the gate, leaning on it, staring at the sky blinkingly.* ABBIE *comes across the room silently.* EBEN *does not notice her until she is quite near.*)

EBEN (*starting*). Abbie!

ABBIE. Ssshh! (*She throws her arms around him. They kiss—*

then bend over the cradle together.) Ain't he purty?—dead spit 'n' image o' yew!

EBEN (*pleased*). Air he? I can't tell none.

ABBIE. E-zactly like!

EBEN (*frowningly*). I don't like this. I don't like lettin' on what's mine's his'n. I been doin' that all my life. I'm gittin' t' the end o' b'arin' it!

ABBIE (*putting her finger on his lips*). We're doin' the best we kin. We got t' wait. Somethin's bound t' happen. (*She puts her arms around him.*) I got t' go back.

EBEN. I'm goin' out. I can't b'ar it with the fiddle playin' an' the laughin'.

ABBIE. Don't git feelin' low. I love ye, Eben. Kiss me. (*He kisses her. They remain in each other's arms.*)

CABOT (*at the gate, confusedly*). Even the music can't drive it out—somethin'. Ye kin feel it droppin' off the elums, climbin' up the roof, sneakin' down the chimney, pokin' in the corners! They's no peace in houses, they's no rest livin' with folks. Somethin's always livin' with ye. (*With a deep sigh*) I'll go 't the barn an' rest a spell. (*He goes wearily toward the barn.*)

FIDDLER (*tuning up*). Let's celebrate the old skunk gittin' fooled! We kin have some fun now he's went. (*He starts to fiddle "Turkey in the Straw." There is real merriment now. The young folks get up to dance.*)

SCENE TWO

A half hour later—exterior—EBEN is standing by the gate looking up at the sky, an expression of dumb pain bewildered by itself on his face. CABOT appears, returning from the barn, walking wearily, his eyes on the ground. He sees EBEN and his whole mood immediately changes. He becomes excited, a cruel, triumphant grin comes to his lips, he strides up and slaps EBEN on the back. From within comes the whining of the fiddle and the noise of stamping feet and laughing voices.

CABOT. So har ye be!

EBEN (*startled, stares at him with hatred for a moment—then dully*). Ay-eh.

CABOT (*surveying him jeeringly*). Why hain't ye been in t' dance? They was all axin' fur ye.

EBEN. Let 'em ax!

CABOT. They's a hull passel o' purty gals.

EBEN. T' hell with 'em!

CABOT. Ye'd ought t' be marryin' one o' 'em soon.

EBEN. I hain't marryin' no one.

CABOT. Ye might 'arn a share 'o a farm that way.

EBEN (*with a sneer*). Like yew did, ye mean? I hain't that kind.

CABOT (*stung*). Ye lie! 'Twas yer Maw's folks aimed t' steal my farm from me.

EBEN. Other folks don't say so. (*After a pause—defiantly*) An' I got a farm, anyways!

CABOT (*derisively*). What?

EBEN (*stamps a foot on the ground*). Har!

CABOT (*throws his head back and laughs coarsely*). Ho-ho! Ye hev, hev ye? Waal, that's a good un!

EBEN (*controlling himself—grimly*). Ye'll see!

CABOT (*stares at him suspiciously, trying to make him out—a pause—then with scornful confidence*). Ay-eh. I'll see. So'll ye. It's ye that's blind—blind as a mole underground. (EBEN *suddenly laughs, one short sardonic bark: "Ha." A pause.* CABOT *peers at him with renewed suspicion.*) What air ye hawin' 'bout? (EBEN *turns away without answering.* CABOT *grows angry.*) God A'mighty, yew air a dumb dunce! They's nothin' in that thick skull o' your'n but noise—like a empty keg it be! (EBEN *doesn't seem to hear—* CABOT's *rage grows.*) Yewr farm! God A'mighty! If ye wa'n't a born donkey ye'd know ye'll never own stick nor stone on it, specially now arter him bein' born. It's his'n, I tell ye—his'n arter I die—but I'll live a hundred jest t' fool ye all—an' he'll be growed then—yewr age a'most! (EBEN *laughs again his sardonic "Ha." This drives* CABOT *into a fury.*) Ha? Ye think ye kin git 'round that someways, do ye? Waal, it'll be her'n, too—Abbie's—ye won't git 'round her—she knows yer tricks—she'll be too much fur ye—she wants the farm her'n—she was afeerd o' ye—she told me ye was sneakin' 'round tryin' t' make love t' her t' git her on yer side . . . ye . . . ye mad fool, ye! (*He raises his clenched fists threateningly.*)

EBEN (*is confronting him choking with rage*). Ye lie, ye old skunk! Abbie never said no sech thing!

CABOT (*suddenly triumphant when he sees how shaken* EBEN *is*). She did. An' I says, I'll blow his brains t' the top o' them elums—an' she says no, that hain't sense, who'll ye git t' help ye on the farm in his place—an' then she says yew'n me ought t' have a son—I know we kin, she says—an' I says, if we do, ye kin have anythin' I've got ye've a mind t'. An' she says, I wants Eben cut off so's this farm'll be mine when ye die! (*With terrible gloating*) An' that's what's happened, hain't it? An' the farm's her'n! An' the dust o' the road—that's you'rn! Ha! Now who's hawin'?

EBEN (*has been listening, petrified with grief and rage—suddenly laughs wildly and brokenly*). Ha-ha-ha! So that's her sneakin' game—all along!—like I suspicioned at fust—t' swaller it all—an' me, too . . . ! (*Madly*) I'll murder her! (*He springs toward the porch but* CABOT *is quicker and gets in between.*)

CABOT. No, ye don't!

EBEN. Git out o' my road! (*He tries to throw* CABOT *aside. They grapple in what becomes immediately a murderous struggle. The old man's concentrated strength is too much for* EBEN. CABOT *gets one hand on his throat and presses him back across the stone wall. At the same moment,* ABBIE *comes out on the porch. With a stifled cry she runs toward them.*)

ABBIE. Eben! Ephraim! (*She tugs at the hand on* EBEN'S *throat.*) Let go, Ephraim! Ye're chokin' him!

CABOT (*removes his hand and flings* EBEN *sideways full length on the grass, gasping and choking. With a cry,* ABBIE *kneels beside him, trying to take his head on her lap, but he pushes her away.* CABOT *stands looking down with fierce triumph*). Ye needn't t've fret, Abbie, I wa'n't aimin' t' kill him. He hain't wuth hangin' fur—not by a hell of a sight! (*More and more triumphantly*) Seventy-six an' him not thirty yit—an' look whar he be fur thinkin' his Paw was easy! No, by God, I hain't easy! An' him upstairs, I'll raise him t' be like me! (*He turns to leave them.*) I'm goin' in an' dance!—sing an' celebrate! (*He walks to the porch—then turns with a great grin.*) I don't calc'late it's left in him, but if he gits pesky, Abbie, ye jest sing out. I'll come a-runnin' an' by the Etarnal, I'll put him across my knee an' birch him! Ha-ha-ha! (*He goes into the house laughing. A moment later his loud "whoop" is heard.*)

ABBIE (*tenderly*). Eben. Air ye hurt? (*She tries to kiss him but he pushes her violently away and struggles to a sitting position.*)

EBEN (*gaspingly*). T'hell—with ye!

ABBIE (*not believing her ears*). It's me, Eben—Abbie—don't ye know me?

EBEN (*glowering at her with hatred*). Ay-eh—I know ye—now! (*He suddenly breaks down, sobbing weakly.*)

ABBIE (*fearfully*). Eben—what's happened t' ye—why did ye look at me 's if ye hated me ?

EBEN (*violently, between sobs and gasps*). I do hate ye! Ye're a whore—a damn trickin' whore!

ABBIE (*shrinking back horrified*). Eben! Ye don't know what ye're sayin'!

EBEN (*scrambling to his feet and following her—accusingly*). Ye're nothin' but a stinkin passel o' lies! Ye've been lyin' t' me every word ye spoke, day an' night, since we fust—done it. Ye've kept sayin' ye loved me. . . .

ABBIE (*frantically*). I do love ye! (*She takes his hand but he flings hers away.*)

EBEN (*unheeding*). Ye've made a fool o' me—a sick, dumb fool —a-purpose! Ye've been on'y playin' yer sneakin', stealin' game all along—gittin' me t' lie with ye so's ye'd hev a son he'd think was his'n, an' makin' him promise he'd give ye the farm and let me eat dust, if ye did git him a son! (*Staring at her with anguished, bewildered eyes*) They must be a devil livin' in ye! 'Tain't human t' be as bad as that be!

ABBIE (*stunned—dully*). He told yew . . . ?

EBEN. Hain't it true? It hain't no good in yew lyin'.

ABBIE (*pleadingly*). Eben, listen—ye must listen—it was long ago—afore we done nothin'—yew was scornin' me—goin' t' see Min —when I was lovin' ye—an' I said it t' him t' git vengeance on ye!

EBEN (*unheedingly. With tortured passion*). I wish ye was dead! I wish I was dead along with ye afore this come! (*Ragingly*) But I'll git my vengeance too! I'll pray Maw t' come back t' help me— t' put her cuss on yew an' him!

ABBIE (*brokenly*). Don't ye, Eben! Don't ye! (*She throws herself on her knees before him, weeping.*) I didn't mean t' do bad t'ye! Fergive me, won't ye?

EBEN (*not seeming to hear her—fiercely*). I'll git squar' with the old skunk—an' yew! I'll tell him the truth 'bout the son he's so proud o'! Then I'll leave ye here t' pizen each other—with Maw comin' out o' her grave at nights—an' I'll go t' the gold fields o' Californi-a whar Sim an' Peter be!

ABBIE (*terrified*). Ye won't—leave me? Ye can't!

EBEN (*with fierce determination*). I'm a-goin', I tell ye! I'll git rich thar an' come back an' fight him fur the farm he stole—an' I'll kick ye both out in the road—t' beg an' sleep in the woods—an' yer son along with ye—t' starve an' die! (*He is hysterical at the end.*)

ABBIE (*with a shudder—humbly*). He's yewr son, too, Eben.

EBEN (*torturedly*). I wish he never was born! I wish he'd die this minit! I wish I'd never sot eyes on him! It's him—yew havin' him—a-purpose t' steal—that's changed everythin'!

ABBIE (*gently*). Did ye believe I loved ye—afore he come?

EBEN. Ay-eh—like a dumb ox!

ABBIE. An' ye don't believe no more?

EBEN. B'lieve a lyin' thief! Ha!

ABBIE (*shudders—then humbly*). An' did ye r'ally love me afore?

EBEN (*brokenly*). Ay-eh—an' ye was trickin' me!

ABBIE. An' ye don't love me now!

EBEN (*violently*). I hate ye, I tell ye!

ABBIE. An' ye're truly goin' West—goin' t' leave me—all account o' him being born?

EBEN. I'm a-goin' in the mornin'—or may God strike me t' hell!

ABBIE (*after a pause—with a dreadful cold intensity—slowly*). If that's what his comin's done t' me—killin' yewr love—takin' yew away—my on'y joy—the on'y joy I've ever knowed—like heaven t' me—purtier'n heaven—then I hate him, too, even if I be his Maw!

EBEN (*bitterly*). Lies! Ye love him! He'll steal the farm fur ye! (*Brokenly*) But 'tain't the farm so much—not no more—it's yew foolin' me—gittin' me t' love ye—lyin' yew loved me—jest t' git a son t' steal!

ABBIE (*distractedly*). He won't steal! I'd kill him fust! I do love ye! I'll prove t' ye . . . !

EBEN (*harshly*). 'Tain't no use lyin' no more. I'm deaf t' ye! (*He turns away.*) I hain't seein' ye agen. Good-by!

ABBIE (*pale with anguish*). Hain't ye even goin' t' kiss me—not once—arter all we loved?

EBEN (*in a hard voice*). I hain't wantin' t' kiss ye never agen! I'm wantin' t' forgit I ever sot eyes on ye!

ABBIE. Eben!—ye mustn't—wait a spell—I want t' tell ye. . . .

EBEN. I'm a-goin' in t' git drunk. I'm a-goin' t' dance.

ABBIE (*clinging to his arm—with passionate earnestness*). If I could make it—'s if he'd never come up between us—if I could prove t' ye I wa'n't schemin' t' steal from ye—so's everythin' could be jest the same with us, lovin' each other jest the same, kissin' an' happy the same's we've been happy afore he come—if I could do it —ye'd love me agen, wouldn't ye? Ye'd kiss me agen! Ye wouldn't never leave me, would ye?

EBEN (*moved*). I calc'late not. (*Then shaking her hand off his arm—with a bitter smile*) But ye hain't God, be ye?

ABBIE (*exultantly*). Remember ye've promised! (*Then with strange intensity*) Mebbe I kin take back one thin' God does!

EBEN (*peeping at her*). Ye're gittin' cracked, hain't ye? (*Then going towards door*) I'm a-goin' t' dance.

ABBIE (*calls after him intensely*). I'll prove t' ye! I'll prove I love ye better'n. . . . (*He goes in the door, not seeming to hear. She remains standing where she is, looking after him—then she finishes desperately:*) Better'n everythin' else in the world!

SCENE THREE

Just before dawn in the morning—shows the kitchen and CABOT's bedroom. In the kitchen, by the light of a tallow candle on the table, EBEN is sitting, his chin propped on his hands, his drawn face blank and expressionless. His carpetbag is on the floor beside him. In the bedroom, dimly lighted by a small whale-oil lamp, CABOT lies asleep. ABBIE is bending over the cradle, listening, her face full of terror yet with an undercurrent of desperate triumph. Suddenly, she breaks down and sobs, appears about to throw herself on her knees beside the cradle; but the old man turns restlessly, groaning in his sleep, and she controls herself, and shrinking away from the cradle with a gesture of horror, backs swiftly toward the door in rear and goes out. A moment later she comes into the kitchen and, running to EBEN, flings her arms about his neck and kisses him wildly. He hardens himself, he remains unmoved and cold, he keeps his eyes straight ahead.

ABBIE (*hysterically*). I done it, Eben! I told ye I'd do it! I've proved I love ye—better'n everythin'—so's ye can't never doubt me no more!

EBEN (*dully*). Whatever ye done, it hain't no good now.

ABBIE (*wildly*). Don't ye say that! Kiss me, Eben, won't ye? I need ye t' kiss me arter what I done! I need ye t' say ye love me!

EBEN (*kisses her without emotion—dully*). That's fur good-by. I'm a-goin' soon.

ABBIE. No! No! Ye won't go—not now!

EBEN (*going on with his own thoughts*). I been a-thinkin'—an' I hain't goin' t' tell Paw nothin'. I'll leave Maw t' take vengeance on ye. If I told him, the old skunk'd jest be stinkin' mean enuf to take it out on that baby. (*His voice showing emotion in spite of him*) An' I don't want nothin' bad t' happen t' him. He hain't t' blame fur yew. (*He adds with a certain queer pride:*) An' he looks like me! An' by God, he's mine! An' some day I'll be a-comin' back an' . . . !

ABBIE (*too absorbed in her own thoughts to listen to him—pleadingly*). They's no cause fur ye t' go now—they's no sense—it's all the same's it was—they's nothin' come b'tween us now—arter what I done!

EBEN (*something in her voice arouses him. He stares at her a bit frightenedly*). Ye look mad, Abbie. What did ye do?

ABBIE. I—I killed him, Eben.

EBEN (*amazed*). Ye killed him?

ABBIE (*dully*). Ay-eh.

EBEN (*recovering from his astonishment—savagely*). An' serves him right! But we got t' do somethin' quick t' make it look s'if the old skunk'd killed himself when he was drunk. We kin prove by 'em all how drunk he got.

ABBIE (*wildly*). No! No! Not him! (*Laughing distractedly*) But that's what I ought t' done, hain't it? I oughter killed him instead! Why didn't ye tell me?

EBEN (*appalled*). Instead? What d'ye mean?

ABBIE. Not him.

EBEN (*his face grown ghastly*). Not—not that baby!

ABBIE (*dully*). Ay-eh!

EBEN (*falls to his knees as if he'd been struck—his voice trembling with horror*). Oh, God A'mighty! A'mighty God! Maw, whar was ye, why didn't ye stop her?

ABBIE (*simply*). She went back t' her grave that night we fust done it, remember? I hain't felt her about since. (*A pause. EBEN hides his head in his hands, trembling all over as if he had the ague. She goes on dully:*) I left the piller over his little face. Then he killed himself. He stopped breathin'. (*She begins to weep softly.*)

EBEN (*rage beginning to mingle with grief*). He looked like me. He was mine, damn ye!

ABBIE (*slowly and brokenly*). I didn't want t' do it. I hated myself fur doin' it. I loved him. He was so pretty—dead spit 'n' image
o' yew. But I loved yew more—an' yew was goin' away—far off
whar I'd never see ye agen, never kiss ye, never feel ye pressed agin
me agen—an' ye said ye hated me fur havin' him—ye said ye hated
him an' wished he was dead—ye said if it hadn't been fur him
comin' it'd be the same's afore between us.

EBEN (*unable to endure this, springs to his feet in a fury, threatening her, his twitching fingers seeming to reach out for her throat*).
Ye lie! I never said—I never dreamed ye'd—I'd cut off my head
afore I'd hurt his finger!

ABBIE (*piteously, sinking on her knees*). Eben, don't ye look at
me like that—hatin' me—not after what I done fur ye—fur us—
so's we could be happy agen—

EBEN (*furiously now*). Shut up, or I'll kill ye! I see yer game
now—the same old sneakin' trick—ye're aimin' t' blame me fur the
murder ye done!

ABBIE (*moaning—putting her hands over her ears*). Don't ye,
Eben! Don't ye! (*She grasps his legs.*)

EBEN (*his mood suddenly changing to horror, shrinks away from
her*). Don't ye tech me! Ye're pizen! How could ye—t' murder a
pore little critter—Ye must've swapped yer soul t' hell! (*Sudden
raging*) Ha! I kin see why ye done it! Not the lies ye jest told—
but 'cause ye wanted t' steal agen—steal the last thin' ye'd left me
—my part o' him—no, the hull o' him—ye saw he looked like me—
ye knowed he was all mine—an' ye couldn't b'ar it—I know ye! Ye
killed him fur bein' mine! (*All this has driven him almost insane.
He makes a rush past her for the door—then turns—shaking both
fists at her, violently.*) But I'll take vengeance now! I'll git the
Sheriff! I'll tell him everythin'! Then I'll sing "I'm off to Californi-
a!" an' go—gold—Golden Gate—gold sun—fields o' gold in the
West! (*This last he half shouts, half croons incoherently, suddenly
breaking off passionately.*) I'm a-goin' fur the Sheriff t' come an'
git ye! I want ye tuk away, locked up from me! I can't stand t' luk
at ye! Murderer an' thief 'r not, ye still tempt me! I'll give ye up t'
the Sheriff! (*He turns and runs out, around the corner of house,
panting and sobbing, and breaks into swerving sprint down the
road.*)

ABBIE (*struggling to her feet, runs to the door, calling after him*).

I love ye, Eben! I love ye! (*She stops at the door weakly, swaying, about to fall.*) I don't care what ye do—if ye'll only love me agen— (*She falls limply to the floor in a faint.*)

SCENE FOUR

About an hour later. Same as Scene Three. Shows the kitchen and CABOT's bedroom. It is after dawn. The sky is brilliant with the sunrise. In the kitchen, ABBIE sits at the table, her body limp and exhausted, her head bowed down over her arms, her face hidden. Upstairs, CABOT is still asleep but awakens with a start. He looks toward the window and gives a snort of surprise and irritation—throws back the covers and begins hurriedly pulling on his clothes. Without looking behind him, he begins talking to ABBIE, whom he supposes beside him.

CABOT. Thunder 'n' lightnin', Abbie! I hain't slept this late in fifty years! Looks 's if the sun was full riz a'most. Must've been the dancin' an' likker. Must be gittin' old. I hope Eben's t'wuk. Ye might've tuk the trouble t' rouse me, Abbie. (*He turns—sees no one there—surprised.*) Waal—whar air she? Gittin' vittles, I calc'-late. (*He tiptoes to the cradle and peers down—proudly*) Mornin', Sonny. Purry's picter! Sleepin' sound. He don't beller all night like most o' 'em. (*He goes quietly out the door in rear—a few moments later enters kitchen—sees ABBIE—with satisfaction*) So thar ye be. Ye got any vittles cooked?

ABBIE (*without moving*). No.

CABOT (*coming to her, almost sympathetically*). Ye feelin' sick?

ABBIE. No.

CABOT (*pats her on shoulder. She shudders*). Ye'd best lie down a spell. (*Half jocularly*) Yet son'll be needin' ye soon. He'd ought t' wake up with a gnashin' appetite, the sound way he's sleepin'.

ABBIE (*shudders—then in a dead voice*). He ain't never goin' to wake up.

CABOT (*jokingly*). Takes after me this mornin'. I ain't slept so late in . . .

ABBIE. He's dead.

CABOT (*stares at her—bewilderedly*). What . . .

ABBIE. I killed him.

CABOT (*stepping back from her—aghast*). Air ye drunk—'r crazy —'r . . . !

ABBIE (*suddenly lifts her head and turns on him—wildly*). I

killed him, I tell ye! I smothered him. Go up an' see if ye don't
b'lieve me! (CABOT *stares at her a second, then bolts out the rear
door, can be heard bounding up the stairs, and rushes into the bedroom and over to the cradle,* ABBIE *has sunk back lifelessly into her
former position.* CABOT *puts his hand down on the body in the crib.
An expression of fear and horror comes over his face.*)

CABOT (*shrinking away—tremblingly*). God A'mighty! God
A'mighty! (*He stumbles out the door—in a short while returns to
the kitchen—comes to* ABBIE, *the stunned expression still on his face
—hoarsely*) Why did ye do it? Why? (*As she doesn't answer, he
grabs her violently by the shoulder and shakes her.*) I ax ye why ye
done it! Ye'd better tell me 'r . . . !

ABBIE (*gives him a furious push which sends him staggering back
and springs to her feet—with wild rage and hatred*). Don't ye dare
tech me! What right hev ye t' question me 'bout him? He wa'n't
yewr son! Think I'd have a son by yew? I'd die fust! I hate the sight
o' ye an' allus did! It's yew I should've murdered, if I'd had good
sense! I hate ye! I love Eben. I did from the fust. An' he was Eben's
son—mine an' Eben's—not your'n.

CABOT (*stands looking at her dazedly—a pause—finding his
words with an effort—dully*). That was it—what I felt—pokin'
round the corners—while ye lied—holdin' yerself from me—sayin'
ye'd a'ready conceived— (*He lapses into crushed silence—then with
a strange emotion*) He's dead, sart'n. I felt his heart. Pore little
critter! (*He blinks back one tear, wiping his sleeve across his nose.*)

ABBIE (*hysterically*). Don't ye! Don't ye! (*She sobs unrestrain-
edly.*)

CABOT (*with a concentrated effort that stiffens his body into a
rigid line and hardens his face into a stony mask—through his teeth
to himself*). I got t' be—like a stone—a rock o' jedgment! (*A pause.
He gets complete control over himself—harshly*) If he was Eben's,
I be glad he air gone! An' mebbe I suspicioned it all along. I felt
they was somethin' onnateral—somewhars—the house got so lonesome—an' cold—drivin' me down t' the barn—t' the beasts o' the
field. . . . Ay-eh. I must've suspicioned—somethin'. Ye didn't fool
me—not altogether, leastways—I'm too old a bird—growin' ripe on
the bough. . . . (*He becomes aware he is wandering, straightens
again, looks at* ABBIE *with a cruel grin.*) So ye'd liked t' hev murdered me 'stead o' him, would ye? Waal, I'll live to a hundred! I'll

live t' see ye hung! I'll deliver, ye up t' the jedgment o' God an' the law! I'll git the Sheriff now. (*Starts for the door.*)

ABBIE (*dully*). Ye needn't. Eben's gone fur him.

CABOT (*amazed*). Eben—gone fur the Sheriff?

ABBIE. Ay-eh.

CABOT. T' inform agen ye?

ABBIE. Ay-eh.

CABOT (*considers this—a pause—then in a hard voice*). Waal, I'm thankful fur him savin' me the trouble. I'll git t' wuk. (*He goes to the door—then turns—in a voice full of strange emotion*) He'd ought t' been my son, Abbie. Ye'd ought t' loved me. I'm a man. If ye'd loved me, I'd never told no Sheriff on ye no matter what ye did, if they was t' brile me alive!

ABBIE (*defensively*). They's more to it nor yew know, makes him tell.

CABOT (*dryly*). Fur yewr sake, I hope they be. (*He goes out—comes around to the gate—stares up at the sky. His control relaxes. For a moment he is old and weary. He murmurs despairingly:*) God A'mighty, I be lonesomer'n ever! (*He hears running footsteps from the left, immediately is himself again.* EBEN *runs in, panting exhaustedly, wild-eyed and mad looking. He lurches through the gate.* CABOT *grabs him by the shoulder.* EBEN *stares at him dumbly.*) Did ye tell the sheriff?

EBEN (*nodding stupidly*). Ay-eh.

CABOT (*gives him a push away that sends him sprawling—laughing with withering contempt*). Good fur ye! A prime chip o' yer Maw ye be! (*He goes toward the barn, laughing harshly.* EBEN *scrambles to his feet. Suddenly* CABOT *turns—grimly threatening*) Git off this farm when the Sheriff takes her—or, by God, he'll have t' come back an' git me fur murder, too! (*He stalks off.* EBEN *does not appear to have heard him. He runs to the door and comes into the kitchen.* ABBIE *looks up with a cry of anguished joy.* EBEN *stumbles over and throws himself on his knees beside her—sobbing brokenly.*)

EBEN. Fergive me!

ABBIE (*happily*). Eben! (*She kisses him and pulls his head over against her breast.*)

EBEN. I love ye! Fergive me!

ABBIE (*ecstatically*). I'd fergive ye all the sins in hell fur sayin' that! (*She kisses his head, pressing it to her with a fierce passion of possession.*)

EBEN (*brokenly*). But I told the Sheriff. He's comin' fur ye!

ABBIE. I kin b'ar what happens t' me—now!

EBEN. I woke him up. I told him. He says, wait 'til I git dressed. I was waiting. I got to thinkin' o' yew. I got to thinkin' how I'd loved ye. It hurt like somethin' was bustin' in my chest an' head. I got t' cryin'. I knowed sudden I loved ye yet, an' allus would love ye!

ABBIE (*caressing his hair—tenderly*). My boy, hain't ye?

EBEN. I begun t' run back. I cut across the fields an' through the woods. I thought ye might have time t' run away—with me—an' . . .

ABBIE (*shaking her head*). I got t' take my punishment—t' pay fur my sin.

EBEN. Then I want t' share it with ye.

ABBIE. Ye didn't do nothin'.

EBEN. I put it in yer head. I wisht he was dead! I as much as urged ye t' do it!

ABBIE. No. It was me alone!

EBEN. I'm as guilty as yew be! He was the child o' our sin.

ABBIE (*lifting her head as if defying God*). I don't repent that sin! I hain't askin' God t' fergive that!

EBEN. Nor me—but it led up t' the other—an' the murder ye did, ye did 'count o' me—an' it's my murder, too, I'll tell the Sheriff— an' if ye deny it, I'll say we planned it t'gther—an' they'll all b'lieve me, fur they suspicion everythin' we've done, an' it'll seem likely an' true to 'em. An' it is true—way down. I did help ye—somehow.

ABBIE (*laying her head on his—sobbing*). No! I dont want yew t' suffer!

EBEN. I got t' pay fur my part o' the sin! An' I'd suffer wuss leavin' ye, goin' West, thinking' o' ye day an' night, bein' out when yew was in—(*lowering his voice*)—'r bein' alive when yew was dead. (*A pause.*) I want t' share with ye, Abbie—prison 'r death 'r hell 'r anythin'! (*He looks into her eyes and forces a trembling smile.*) If I'm sharin' with ye, I won't feel lonesome, leastways.

ABBIE (*weakly*). Eben! I won't let ye! I can't let ye!

EBEN (*kissing her—tenderly*). Ye can't he'p yerself. I got ye beat fur once!

ABBIE (*forcing a smile—adoringly*). I hain't beat—s'long's I got ye!

EBEN (*hears the sound of feet outside*). Ssshh! Listen! They've come t' take us!

ABBIE. No, it's him. Don't give him no chance to fight ye, Eben. Don't say nothin'—no mattter what he says. An' I won't neither. (*It is* CABOT. *He comes up from the barn in a great state of excitement and strides into the house and then into the kitchen.* EBEN *is kneeling beside* ABBIE, *his arm around her, hers around him. They stare straight ahead.*)

CABOT (*stares at them, his face hard. A long pause—vindictively*). Ye make a slick pair o' murderin' turtle doves! Ye'd ought t' be both hung on the same limb an' left thar t' swing in the breeze an' rot—a warnin' t' old fools like me t' ba'ar their lonesomeness alone—an' fur young fools like ye t' hobble their lust. (*A pause. The excitement returns to his face, his eyes snap, he looks a bit crazy.*) I couldn't work today. I couldn't take no interest. T' hell with the farm! I'm leavin' it! I've turned the cows an' other stock loose! I've druv 'em into the woods whar they kin be free! By freein' 'em, I'm freein' myself! I'm quittin' here today! I'll set fire t'house an' barn an' watch 'em burn, and I'll leave yer Maw t' haunt the ashes, an' I'll will the fields back t' God, so that nothin' human kin never touch 'em! I'll be a-goin' to Californi-a—t' jine Simeon an' Peter—true sons o' mine if they be dumb fools—an' the Cabots'll find Solomon's Mines t'gether! (*He suddenly cuts a mad caper*) Whoop! What was the song they sung? "Oh Californi-a! That's the land fur me." (*He sings this—then gets on his knees by the floorboard under which the money was hid.*) An' I'll sail thar on one o' the finest clippers I kin find! I've got the money! Pity ye didn't know whar this was hidden so's ye could steal . . . (*He has pulled up the board. He stares —feels—stares again. A pause of dead silence. He slowly turns, slumping into a sitting position on the floor, his eyes like those of a dead fish, his face the sickly green of an attack of nausea. He swallows painfully several times—forces a weak smile at last.*) So—ye did steal it!

EBEN (*emotionlessly*). I swapped it t' Sim an' Peter fur their share o' the farm—t' pay their passage t' Californi-a.

CABOT (*with one sardonic*) Ha! (*He begins to recover. Gets slowly to his feet—strangely*). I calc'late God give it to 'em—not yew! God's hard, not easy! Mebbe they's easy gold in the West but it hain't God's gold. It hain't fur me. I kin hear His voice warnin' me agen t' be hard an' stay on my farm. I kin see his hand usin' Eben t' steal t' keep me from weakness. I kin feel I be in the palm o' His hand, His fingers guidin' me. (*A pause—then he mutters sadly:*) It's a-goin' t' be lonesomer now than ever it war afore—an' I'm gittin' old, Lord—ripe on the bough. . . . (*Then stiffening*) Waal—what d'ye want? God's lonesome, hain't He? God's hard an' lonesome! (*A pause. The* SHERIFF *with two men comes up the road from the left. They move cautiously to the door. The* SHERIFF *knocks on it with the butt of his pistol.*)

SHERIFF. Open in the name o' the law! (*They start.*)

CABOT. They've come fur ye. (*He goes to the rear door.*) Come in, Jim! (*The three men enter.* CABOT *meets them in doorway.*) Jest a minit, Jim. I got 'em safe here. (*The* SHERIFF *nods. He and his companions remain in the doorway.*)

EBEN (*suddenly calls*). I lied this mornin', Jim. I helped her to do it. Ye kin take me, too.

ABBIE (*brokenly*). No!

CABOT. Take 'em both. (*He comes forward—stares at* EBEN *with a trace of grudging admiration*) Purty good—fur yew! Waal, I got t' round up the stock. Good-by.

EBEN. Good-by.

ABBIE. Good-by. (CABOT *turns and strides past the men—comes out and around the corner of the house, his shoulders squared, his face stony, and stalks grimly toward the barn. In the meantime the* SHERIFF *and men have come into the room.*)

SHERIFF (*embarrassedly*). Waal—we'd best start.

ABBIE. Wait. (*Turns to* EBEN.) I love ye, Eben.

EBEN. I love ye, Abbie. (*They kiss. The three men grin and shuffle embarassedly.* EBEN *takes* ABBIE'S *hand. They go out the door in rear, the men following, and come from the house, walking hand in hand to the gate.* EBEN *stops there and points to the sunrise sky.*) Sun's a-risin'. Purty, hain't it?

ABBIE. Ay-eh. (*They both stand for a moment looking up raptly in attitudes strangely aloof and devout.*)

SHERIFF (*looking around at the farm enviously—to his companion*). It's a jim-dandy farm, no denyin'. Wished I owned it!

CURTAIN

BIBLICAL PERVERSIONS IN
DESIRE UNDER THE ELMS

In *Desire Under the Elms* O'Neill establishes an ironic counterpoint between expectations of love and forgiveness aroused by religious allusions and the harsh realities of the actual religion practiced by the stone-hearted New Englanders he depicts.* When Simeon and Peter wish Ephraim dead and the farm theirs, Eben taunts them with "Honor thy father!" But when Eben makes explicit his half-brothers' wish—"I pray he's died!"—they hypocritically denounce his statement as not being righteous. Similarly, in Part III, Scene I, the townspeople mock the Cabots behind their backs, especially Ephraim, whom they dare not ridicule to his face: "Let's celebrate the old skunk gittin' fooled!" Saying that Eben is in church offering prayers of thanksgiving " 'Cause unto him a ———— brother is born" distorts the scripture and shows the lack of sympathy, charity, or morality. But Ephraim is as bad. He sanctions his ruthlessness by his harsh Puritanical religion, that worships toil, scorns ease and sentiment, or even the expression of affection. The objective correlative of the play is *stone,* hard, unyielding, impenetrable. Piled one on top of another, stones wall the farm like a prison, as Ephraim's values imprison him, his wives, and his sons. Two of the sons' names mean stone: Peter's in Greek, Eben's in Hebrew. And after the rocks have been cleared from the fields, the farm's chief crop is still the worst distortions of the Protestant ethic: greed, vengeance, incessant toil, and individual isolation. Ephraim uses the Song of Songs to encourage Abbie's fertility and to pray for a son; Abbie does pray for a son—Eben's. And Eben denounces his biological and spiritual fathers: ". . . Yew 'n' yewr God! Allus cussin' folks—allus naggin' 'em! . . . Naggin' His sheep t' sin! T' hell with yewr God." What unites and underscores this theme of Biblical expectation denied is the contrast between Ephraim and the prophet Hosea. By God's command (explicit in the Bible, assumed by Ephraim in the play), both journey forth and marry a prostitute (so Eben calls Abbie). When Hosea's wife deserts him, he is told to reclaim her as an alle-

---

* Abstracted from Peter L. Hays, "Biblical Perversions in *Desire Under the Elms," Modern Drama,* XI (1969), 423-428.

gory of the Lord's reaffirming His devotion to Israel, which had broken its covenant. Significantly, Hosea addresses Israel by the name of one of the twelve tribes, Ephraim.

> E'phraim has said, "Ah but I am rich
> I have gained wealth for myself:"
> but all his riches can never offset
> the guilt he has incurred. (Hos. 12:8)

By denying Hosea's message of love and forgiveness, Ephraim has perverted the Bible. He has killed his wives with work, driven off sons, mistakenly freed his animals, and been robbed by Eben. He has sown the wind and reaped the whirlwind (Hos. 8:7). Thus in *Desire* O'Neill shows that the harsh, loveless, and covetous Puritanism practiced by Ephraim is actually a perversion of religion that cripples love and destroys men.

DESIRE UNDER THE ELMS IN THE LIGHT OF STRINDBERG'S INFLUENCE

Desire Under the Elms (1924), O'Neill's first great tragedy, richly exploits a Strindbergian theme which was important in the lives and the works of both writers: the son's struggle with a selfish and domineering father-rival for the uncertain love of the mother.* Their larger ambivalence toward women generally (now the nourishing mother-goddess, now the evil temptress) derives from nineteenth-century feminism and its misogynist counter-current in Schopenhauer and Nietzsche. This ambivalence perhaps foredoomed their efforts to find substitute mothers in the women they married, and forms the leitmotiv behind *Desire*. Almost every plot element in the play can be traced to a work of Strindberg. The basic situation, where a youth has witnessed his mother worked to death by a hard

* Abstracted from Murray Hartman, *"Desire Under the Elms* in the Light of Strindberg's Influence," *American Literature,* XXX (1959), 360-369.

father and then has had to see her position usurped by the maid-turned-aggressive-stepmother, has its origin in Strindberg's autobiographical novel *The Son of a Servant.* The two older sons, like Simeon and Peter, were chagrined, but the youngest (like Eben) revolted against his father and conjured up his mother's shade. Later the stepmother bore a son and rival heir. O'Neill's intensification of this conflict in *Desire* is diabolical: Eben believes that his stepmother-mistress has betrayed him into begetting his own rival heir to the farm. O'Neill also retains the penury and prudential respectability of the father, reflecting the imperious James O'Neill. From Strindberg's *Gustavus Vasa* O'Neill borrows the ambivalence of a young man torn between his dead mother and his attractive stepmother; from *To Damascus* the idea of a cosmic mother who can reincarnate the dead to requite his love; from *The Father* the conflict in the wife of lust and motherlove. These situations are echoed in *Desire:* first in Eben's championing of his dead mother against his father; then in his carnal possession of Min, the paternal tart; and finally in his mastery of Abbie, the stepmother and nature-goddess who can give him both the maternal and sexual love he craves. The ironic celebration scene at the birth of the illegitimate child and its smothering by the mother are in debt to Strindberg's *The Bridal Crown,* as well as other works which deal with the murder of an unwanted child: *There Are Crimes and Crimes, The Confession of a Fool,* and *Inferno.* O'Neill's theme in *Desire* was the Strindbergian staple of man's tragic involvement in the toils of the umbilical cord —here the root of his desires for land and growth, for maternal and sexual love, and secretly for patricide and taintless rebirth in the mother.

O'NEILL'S USE OF THE *PHÈDRE* LEGEND IN *DESIRE UNDER THE ELMS*

Critics long have agreed that the form of classical tragedy under-lies O'Neill's modern tragedy, *Desire Under the Elms;* the unities of place and particularly of action influence the structural scheme, and the conception of the tragic hero who suffers a devastating fall because of *hamartia* provides the moral focus.* A strong case can be made for identifying the *Phèdre* legend as the direct source and Abbie Putman Cabot as the tragic heroine. Euripides and Racine have offered different perspectives on the story of a mother's in-cestuous love for her stepson and her death as a consequence. In *Hippolytus,* both Hippolytus and Phaedra are punished by Aphrodite for *hubris*—Phaedra for overweaning passion and Hippolytus for overweaning confidence. The moral of the play would seem to be the necessity for man to exercise restraint over his passions, though Euripides, with characteristic irony, shows the difficulty and even impossibility of attaining this result. Racine, in *Phèdre,* is not so concerned as Euripides with explaining and justifying the ways of the gods. For the French Jansenist the play studies the effect of guilt on a noble Christian. Love is "funeste poison," as the stricken mother declares her madness to her son: "Je m'égare/Seigneur, ma folle ardeur malgré moi se déclare." After admitting her guilt, Hip-polyte's denunciation coupled with her own shame overcome her. Learning that her husband has returned, she sees only one course of honor. In death she achieves expiation. O'Neill's most notable altera-tion of the *Phèdre* story in *Desire Under the Elms* is the moral view-point. Whereas Euripides and Racine clearly condemn the incestuous nature of *Phèdre's* love, O'Neill sanctions the immoral relationship. Abbie confesses to her stepson Eben that she has married Ephraim in

---

* Abstracted from Jay Ronald Meyers, "O'Neill's Use of the *Phèdre* Legend in *Desire Under the Elms,*" *Revue de Littérature Comparée,* XLI (1967), 120-125.

order to inherit his property. She provides him with an heir in order to insure her claim. But she discovers that her love for Eben is greater than her greed for the inheritance. She firmly declares her preference to Eben: "If that's what his comin's done t' me—killin' yewr love—takin' yew away—my on'y joy—the on'y joy I've ever knowed—like heaven t' me—purtier'n heaven—then I hate him, too, even if I be his Maw!" The infanticide is the one action that will demonstrate her love, and so it becomes an act of selflessness and even an expiation. To be sure, O'Neill uses an outrageous image with which to make his statement that the greed of the Cabots is base—baser even than incest and child-murder. We are made to sympathize with Abbie, and she attains tragic nobility in spite of and even through her illicit love. The play rises above the level of propaganda—on the evil of money worship and of the hardship of heart that afflicts those who become infatuated—to the grandeur of Aristotelian tragedy—its form compact and beautiful, its action pitiful and terrifying.

O'NEILL'S *DESIRE UNDER THE ELMS* AND SHAKESPEARE'S *KING LEAR*

Desire Under the Elms is nearly as close to *King Lear* in patterning, characterization, and mode as it is to its Greek models.* Once O'Neill chose, by coincidence or unconscious volition, the love-bargaining scene with which *Lear* begins for a play of his own, he was driven both by his personalized family-myth and by necessity imposed by the donnée (or initiatory pattern) to embody the play's development in similar archetypes and characters. In each play the action develops from initial bargaining scenes. A prime motive for the bargaining scenes is the archetypal competition between a young and an old man for a woman misused or coveted by an older man.

* Abstracted from Emil Roy, "O'Neill's *Desire Under the Elms* and Shakespeare's *King Lear*," *Die Neuren Sprachen*, XV (1967), 1-6.

Both Lear and Eben Cabot assume that love is measurable and quantifiable; both seize the godlike prerogatives of judgment; both are challenged by devil's advocates; both assume the future predictable and the present susceptible to manipulation; and both helplessly witness the murder of the most beloved child. As measure of their forcefulness, Lear and Ephraim Cabot receive the focus of the action even in their absence. They direct other's lives and hastily, egotistically, and selfishly attempt to anticipate the future as they controlled the past. Balked, they lose contact with the outside world; dishonored and dispossessed they identify their egos with the universe and seek to initiate the apocalypse. Thus, their utterances increasingly take on the character of a monologue. Despite their great age, Lear and Ephraim are forced to learn compassion, mercy, and forgiveness. Eben, like Edmund a younger son and self-proclaimed bastard, has a similar bent for deceptive loyalty, canny plotting, and lust. Like Edgar, Eben has lost home and inheritance and attempts to ameliorate his sense of dispossession by force. Abbie is a combination of Cordelia and Goneril-Regan, earth-mother and harlot, mindless sensualist and bitch. Although O'Neill's characters all feel the desire of the title in differing ways—for freedom, companionship, and property—a common mixture of sexual desire, greed, and religious devotion stirs each of them. Just as buying and selling, compassion and animalism are gauged in *Lear* by their place in nature, like motifs in *Desire* carrying primitive religious overtones sensed by the more intuitive characters. Both plays are studies in relationships of children to their parents, man to the state, and the gods to man. Characters appear good or bad, sane or mad, contemptible or dignified in terms of these relationships. Unlike the bad characters in *Lear,* however, Eben and Abbie discover integration in separation, life in death, achievement and permanence in loss and sacrifice. Similar conflicts of truth and illusion, reason and madness, chaos and stability reveal an underlying sickness in the body politic which aborts and poisons all the ceremonial affirmations of rebirth in both plays. The conclusions of both plays have a similar tragic import. Eben and Abbie, like Lear and Cordelia, must accept the tragic irony that their love has not come to fruition until the moment of inevitable loss, just as they accept without question the justice of fate.

the visit

FRIEDRICH DÜRRENMATT

TRANSLATED BY
MAURICE VALENCY

CHARACTERS

HOFBAUER, *First Man*

HELMESBERGER, *Second Man*

WECHSLER, *Third Man*

VOGEL, *Fourth Man*

PAINTER

STATION MASTER

BURGOMASTER

TEACHER

PASTOR

ANTON SCHILL

CLAIRE ZACHANASSIAN

CONDUCTOR

PEDRO CABRAL

BOBBY

POLICEMAN

FIRST GRANDCHILD

SECOND GRANDCHILD

MIKE

MAX

FIRST BLIND MAN

SECOND BLIND MAN

ATHLETE

FRAU BURGOMASTER

FRAU SCHILL

DAUGHTER

SON

DOCTOR NÜSSLIN

FRAU BLOCK, *First Woman*

TRUCK DRIVER

REPORTER

CAMERAMAN

TOWNSMAN

TOWNSMAN

(The action of the play takes place in and around the little town of Güllen, somewhere in Europe.)

(There are three acts.)

act one

(A railway-crossing bell starts ringing. Then is heard the distant sound of a locomotive whistle. The curtain rises.)

(The scene represents, in the simplest possible manner, a little town some-where in Central Europe. The time is the present. The town is shabby and

ruined, as if the plague had passed there. Its name, Güllen, is inscribed on
the shabby signboard which adorns the façade of the railway station. This
edifice is summarily indicated by a length of rusty iron paling, a platform
parallel to the proscenium, beyond which one imagines the rails to be, and a
baggage truck standing by a wall on which a torn timetable, marked *"Fahrplan,"* is affixed by three nails. In the station wall is a door with a sign:
"Eintritt Verboten." This leads to the Station Master's office.)

(Left of the station is a little house of gray stucco, formerly whitewashed.
It has a tile roof, badly in need of repair. Some shreds of travel posters still
adhere to the windowless walls. A shingle hanging over the entrance, left,
reads: *"Männer."* On the other side of the shingle reads: *"Damen."* Along
the walls of the little house there is a wooden bench, backless, on which four
men are lounging cheerlessly, shabbily dressed, with cracked shoes. A fifth
man is busied with paintpot and brush. He is kneeling on the ground, painting a strip of canvas with the words: *"Welcome, Clara."*)

(The warning signal rings uninterruptedly. The sound of the approaching
train comes closer and closer. The Station Master issues from his office, advances to the center of the platform and salutes.)

(The train is heard thundering past in a direction parallel to the footlights,
and is lost in the distance. The men on the bench follow its passing with a
slow movement of their heads, from left to right.)

FIRST MAN. The "Emperor." Hamburg-Naples.

SECOND MAN. Then comes the "Diplomat."

THIRD MAN. Then the "Banker."

FOURTH MAN. And at eleven twenty-seven the "Flying Dutchman." Venice-Stockholm.

FIRST MAN. Our only pleasure—watching trains. (*The station bell
rings again. The* STATION MASTER *comes out of his office and salutes
another train. The men follow its course, right to left.*)

FOURTH MAN. Once upon a time the "Emperor" and the "Flying
Dutchman" used to stop here in Güllen. So did the "Diplomat," the
"Banker" and the "Silver Comet."

SECOND MAN. Now it's only the local from Kaffigen and the
twelve-forty from Kalberstadt.

THIRD MAN. The fact is, we're ruined.

FIRST MAN. What with the Wagonworks shut down . . .

SECOND MAN. The Foundry finished . . .

FOURTH MAN. The Golden Eagle Pencil Factory all washed up . . .

FIRST MAN. It's life on the dole.

SECOND MAN. Did you say life?

THIRD MAN. We're rotting.

FIRST MAN. Starving.

SECOND MAN. Crumbling.

FOURTH MAN. The whole damn town. (*The station bell rings.*)

THIRD MAN. Once we were a center of industry.

PAINTER. A cradle of culture.

FOURTH MAN. One of the best little towns in the country.

FIRST MAN. In the world.

SECOND MAN. Here Goethe slept.

FOURTH MAN. Brahms composed a quartet.

THIRD MAN. Here Berthold Schwarz invented gunpowder.

PAINTER. And I once got first prize at the Dresden Exhibition of Contemporary Art. What am I doing now? Painting signs. (*The station bell rings. The* STATION MASTER *comes out. He throws away a cigarette butt. The men scramble for it.*)

FIRST MAN. Well, anyway, Madame Zachanassian will help us.

FOURTH MAN. If she comes . . .

THIRD MAN. If she comes.

SECOND MAN. Last week she was in France. She gave them a hospital.

FIRST MAN. In Rome she founded a free public nursery.

THIRD MAN. In Leuthenau, a bird sanctuary.

PAINTER. They say she got Picasso to design her car.

FIRST MAN. Where does she get all that money?

SECOND MAN. An oil company, a shipping line, three banks and five railways—

FOURTH MAN. And the biggest string of geisha houses in Japan.

(*From the direction of the town come the* BURGOMASTER, *the* PASTOR, *the* TEACHER *and* ANTON SCHILL. *The* BURGOMASTER, *the* TEACHER *and* SCHILL *are men in their fifties. The* PASTOR *is ten years younger. All four are dressed shabbily and are sad-looking. The* BURGOMASTER *looks official.* SCHILL *is tall and handsome, but graying and worn; nevertheless a man of considerable charm and presence. He walks directly to the little house and disappears into it.*)

PAINTER. Any news, Burogomaster? Is she coming?

ALL. Yes, is she coming?

BURGOMASTER. She's coming. The telegram has been confirmed. Our distinguished guest will arrive on the twelve-forty from Kalberstadt. Everyone must be ready.

TEACHER. The mixed choir is ready. So is the children's chorus.

BURGOMASTER. And the church bell, Pastor?

PASTOR. The church bell will ring. As soon as the new bell ropes are fitted. The man is working on them now.

BURGOMASTER. The town band will be drawn up in the market place and the Athletic Association will form a human pyramid in her honor—the top man will hold the wreath with her initials. Then lunch at the Golden Apostle. I shall say a few words.

TEACHER. Of course.

BURGOMASTER. I had thought of illuminating the town hall and the cathedral, but we can't afford the lamps.

PAINTER. Burgomaster—what do you think of this? (*He shows the banner.*)

BURGOMASTER. (*Calls.*) Schill! Schill!

TEACHER. Schill! (SCHILL *comes out of the little house.*)

SCHILL. Yes, right away. Right away.

BURGOMASTER. This is more in your line. What do you think of this?

SCHILL. (*Looks at the sign.*) No, no, no. That certainly won't do, Burgomaster. It's much too intimate. It shouldn't read: "Welcome, Clara." It should read: "Welcome, Madame . . ."

TEACHER. Zachanassian.

BURGOMASTER. Zachanassian.

SCHILL. Zachanassian.

PAINTER. But she's Clara to us.

FIRST MAN. Clara Wäscher.

SECOND MAN. Born here.

THIRD MAN. Her father was a carpenter. He built this. (*All turn and stare at the little house.*)

SCHILL. All the same . . .

PAINTER. If I . . .

BURGOMASTER. No, no, no. He's right. You'll have to change it.

PAINTER. Oh, well, I'll tell you what I'll do. I'll leave this and I'll put "Welcome, Madame Zachanassian" on the other side. Then if things go well, we can always turn it around.

BURGOMASTER. Good idea. (*To* SCHILL.) Yes?

SCHILL. Well, anyway, it's safer. Everything depends on the first impression. (*The train bell is heard. Two clangs. The* PAINTER *turns the banner over and goes to work.*)

FIRST MAN. Hear that? The ."Flying Dutchman" has just passed through Leuthenau.

FOURTH MAN. Eleven-twenty.

BURGOMASTER. Gentlemen, you know that the millionairess is our only hope.

PASTOR. Under God.

BURGOMASTER. Under God. Naturally. Schill, we depend entirely on you.

SCHILL. Yes, I know. You keep telling me.

BURGOMASTER. After all, you're the only one who really knew her.

SCHILL. Yes, I knew her.

PASTOR. You were really quite close to one another, I hear, in those days.

SCHILL. Close? Yes, we were close, there's no denying it. We were in love. I was young—good-looking, so they said—and Clara—you know, I can still see her in the great barn coming toward me—like a light out of the darkness. And in the Konradsweil Forest she'd come running to meet me—barefooted—her beautiful red hair streaming behind her. Like a witch. I was in love with her, all right. But you know how it is when you're twenty.

PASTOR. What happened?

SCHILL (Shrugs). Life came between us.

BURGOMASTER. You must give me some points about her for my speech. (He takes out his notebook.)

SCHILL. I think I can help you there.

TEACHER. Well, I've gone through the school records. And the young lady's marks were, I'm afraid to say, absolutely dreadful. Even in deportment. The only subject in which she was even remotely passable was natural history.

BURGOMASTER. Good in natural history. That's fine. Give me a pencil. (He makes a note.)

SCHILL. She was an outdoor girl. Wild. Once, I remember, they arrested a tramp, and she threw stones at the policeman. She hated injustice passionately.

BURGOMASTER. Strong sense of justice. Excellent.

SCHILL. And generous . . .

ALL. Generous?

SCHILL. Generous to a fault. Whatever little she had, she shared—

so good-hearted. I remember once she stole a bag of potatoes to give to a poor widow.

BURGOMASTER. (*Writing in notebook.*) Wonderful generosity—

TEACHER. Generosity.

BURGOMASTER. That, gentlemen, is something I must not fail to make a point of.

SCHILL. And such a sense of humor. I remember once when the oldest man in town fell and broke his leg, she said, "Oh, dear, now they'll have to shoot him."

BURGOMASTER. Well, I've got enough. The rest, my friend, is up to you. (*He puts the notebook away.*)

SCHILL. Yes, I know, but it's not so easy. After all, to part a woman like that from her millions—

BURGOMASTER. Exactly. Millions. We have to think in big terms here.

TEACHER. If she's thinking of buying us off with a nursery school—

ALL. Nursery school!

PASTOR. Don't accept.

TEACHER. Hold out.

SCHILL. I'm not so sure that I can do it. You know, she may have forgotten me completely.

BURGOMASTER. (*He exchanges a look with the* TEACHER *and the* PASTOR.) Schill, for many years you have been our most popular citizen. The most respected and the best loved.

SCHILL. Why, thank you . . .

BURGOMASTER. And therefore I must tell you—last week I sounded out the political opposition, and they agreed. In the spring you will be elected to succeed me as Burgomaster. By unanimous vote. (*The others clap their hands in approval.*)

SCHILL. But, my dear Burgomaster—!

BURGOMASTER. It's true.

TEACHER. I'm a witness. I was at the meeting.

SCHILL. This is—naturally, I'm terribly flattered—It's a completely unexpected honor.

BURGOMASTER. You deserve it.

SCHILL. Burgomaster! Well, well—! (*Briskly.*) Gentlemen, to business. The first chance I get, of course, I shall discuss our miserable position with Clara.

TEACHER. But tactfully, tactfully—

SCHILL. What do you take me for? We must feel our way. Everything must be correct. Psychologically correct. For example, here at the railway station, a single blunder, one false note, could be disastrous.

BURGOMASTER. He's absolutely right. The first impression colors all the rest. Madame Zachanassian sets foot on her native soil for the first time in many years. She sees our love and she sees our misery. She remembers her youth, her friends. The tears well up into her eyes. Her childhood companions throng about her. I will naturally not present myself like this, but in my black coat with my top hat. Next to me, my wife. Before me, my two grandchildren all in white, with roses. My God, if it only comes off as I see it! If only it comes off. (*The station bell begins ringing.*) Oh, my God! Quick! We must get dressed.

FIRST MAN. It's not her train. It's only the "Flying Dutchman."

PASTOR. (*Calmly.*) We have still two hours before she arrives.

SCHILL. For God's sake, don't let's lose our heads. We still have a full two hours.

BURGOMASTER. Who's losing their heads? (*To* FIRST *and* SECOND MAN.) When her train comes, you two, Helmesberger and Vogel, will hold up the banner with "Welcome Madame Zachanassian." The rest will applaud.

THIRD MAN. Bravo! (*He applauds.*)

BURGOMASTER. But, please, one thing—no wild cheering like last year with the government relief committee. It made no impression at all and we still haven't received any loan. What we need here is a feeling of genuine sincerity. That's how we greet with full hearts our beloved sister who has been away from us so long. Be sincerely moved, my friends, that's the secret; be sincere. Remember you're not dealing with a child. Next a few brief words from me. Then the church bell will start pealing—

PASTOR. If he can fix the ropes in time. (*The station bell rings.*)

BURGOMASTER.—Then the mixed choir moves in. And then—

TEACHER. We'll form a line down here.

BURGOMASTER. Then the rest of us will form in two lines leading from the station—(*He is interrupted by the thunder of the approaching train. The men crane their heads to see it pass. The Station Master advances to the platform and salutes. There is a sudden shriek of air brakes. The train screams to a stop. The four men jump up in consternation.*)

PAINTER. But the "Flying Dutchman" never stops!

FIRST MAN. It's stopping.

SECOND MAN. In Güllen!

THIRD MAN. In the poorest—

FIRST MAN. The dreariest—

SECOND MAN. The lousiest—

FOURTH MAN. The most God-forsaken hole between Venice and Stockholm.

STATION MASTER. It cannot stop! (*The train noises stop. There is only the panting of the engine.*)

PAINTER. It's stopped! (*The STATION MASTER runs out.*)

OFFSTAGE VOICE. What's happened? Is there an accident? (*A hubbub of offstage voices, as if the passengers on the invisible train were alighting.*)

CLAIRE. (*Offstage.*) Is this Güllen?

CONDUCTOR. (*Offstage.*) Here, here, what's going on?

CLAIRE. (*Offstage.*) Who the hell are you?

CONDUCTOR. (*Offstage.*) But you pulled the emergency cord, madame!

CLAIRE. (*Offstage.*) I always pull the emergency cord.

STATION MASTER. (*Offstage.*) I must ask you what's going on here.

CLAIRE. (*Offstage.*) And who the hell are you?

STATION MASTER. (*Offstage.*) I'm the Station Master, madame, and I must ask you—

CLAIRE. (*Enters.*) No!

(*From the right CLAIRE ZACHANASSIAN appears. She is an extraordinary woman. She is in her fifties, red-haired, remarkably dressed, with a face as impassive as that of an ancient idol, beautiful still, and with a singular grace of movement and manner. She is simple and unaffected, yet she has the haughtiness of a world power. The entire effect is striking to the point of the unbelievable. Behind her comes her fiancé, PEDRO CABRAL, tall, young, very handsome, and completely equipped for fishing, with creel and net, and with a rod case in his hand. An excited CONDUCTOR follows.*)

CONDUCTOR. But, madame, I must insist! You have stopped "The Flying Dutchman." I must have an explanation.

CLAIRE. Nonsense. Pedro.

PEDRO. Yes, my love?

CLAIRE. This is Güllen. Nothing has changed. I recognize it all. There's the forest of Konradsweil. There's a brook in it full of trout, where you can fish. And there's the roof of the great barn. Ha! God! What a miserable blot on the map.

(*She crosses the stage and goes off with* PEDRO.)

SCHILL. My God! Clara!

TEACHER. Claire Zachanassian!

BURGOMASTER. And the town band? The town band! Where is it?

TEACHER. The mixed choir! The mixed choir!

PASTOR. The church bell! The church bell!

BURGOMASTER. (*To the* FIRST MAN.) Quick! My dress coat. My top hat. My grandchildren. Run! Run! (FIRST MAN *runs off. The* BURGOMASTER *shouts after him.*) And don't forget my wife! (*General panic. The* THIRD MAN *and* FOURTH MAN *hold up the banner, on which only part of the name has been painted:* "Welcome Mad—" CLAIRE *and* PEDRO *re-enter, right.*)

CONDUCTOR. (*Mastering himself with an effort.*) Madame. The train is waiting. The entire international railway schedule has been disrupted. I await your explanation.

CLAIRE. You're a very foolish man. I wish to visit this town. Did you expect me to jump off a moving train?

CONDUCTOR. (*Stupefied.*) You stopped the "Flying Dutchman" because you wished to visit the town?

CLAIRE. Naturally.

CONDUCTOR. (*Inarticulate.*) Madame!

STATION MASTER. Madame, if you wished to visit the town, the twelve-forty from Kalberstadt was entirely at your service. Arrival in Güllen, one-seventeen.

CLAIRE. The local that stops at Loken, Beisenbach and Leuthenau? Do you expect me to waste three-quarters of an hour chugging dismally through this wilderness?

CONDUCTOR. Madame, you shall pay for this!

CLAIRE. Bobby, give him a thousand marks. (BOBBY, *her butler, a man in his seventies, wearing dark glasses, opens his wallet. The townspeople gasp.*)

CONDUCTOR. (*Taking the money in amazement.*) But, madame!

CLAIRE. And three thousand for the Railway Widows' Relief Fund.

CONDUCTOR. (*With the money in his hands.*) But we have no such fund, madame.

CLAIRE. Now you have. (*The* BURGOMASTER *pushes his way forward.*)

BURGOMASTER. (*He whispers to the* CONDUCTOR *and* TEACHER.) The lady is Madame Claire Zachanassian.

CONDUCTOR. Claire Zachanassian? Oh, my God! But that's naturally quite different. Needless to say, we would have stopped the train if we'd had the slightest idea. (*He hands the money back to Bobby.*) Here, please. I couldn't dream of it. Four thousand. My God!

CLAIRE. Keep it. Don't fuss.

CONDUCTOR. Would you like the train to wait, madame, while you visit the town? The administration will be delighted. The cathedral porch. The town hall—

CLAIRE. You may take the train away. I don't need it any more.

STATION MASTER. All aboard! (*He puts his whistle to his lips.* PEDRO *stops him.*)

PEDRO. But the press, my angel. They don't know anything about this. They're still in the dining car.

CLAIRE. Let them stay there. I don't want the press in Güllen at the moment. Later they will come by themselves. (*To* STATION MASTER.) And now what are you waiting for?

STATION MASTER. All aboard! (*The* STATION MASTER *blows a long blast on his whistle. The train leaves. Meanwhile, the* FIRST MAN *has brought the* BURGOMASTER's *dress coat and top hat. The* BURGOMASTER *puts on the coat, then advances slowly and solemnly.*)

CONDUCTOR. I trust madame will not speak of this to the administration. It was a pure misunderstanding. (*He salutes and runs for the train as it starts moving.*)

BURGOMASTER. (*Bows.*) Gracious lady, as Burgomaster of the town of Güllen, I have the honor—(*The rest of the speech is lost in the roar of the departing train. He continues speaking and gesturing, and at last bows amid applause as the train noises end.*)

CLAIRE. Thank you, Mr. Burgomaster. (*She glances at the beam-*

ing faces, and lastly at SCHILL, *whom she does not recognize. She turns upstage.*)

SCHILL. Clara!

CLAIRE. (*Turns and stares.*) Anton?

SCHILL. Yes. It's good that you've come back.

CLAIRE. Yes. I've waited for this moment. All my life. Ever since I left Güllen.

SCHILL. (*A little embarrassed.*) That is very kind of you to say, Clara.

CLAIRE. And have you thought about me?

SCHILL. Naturally. Always. You know that.

CLAIRE. Those were happy times we spent together.

SCHILL. Unforgettable. (*He smiles reassuringly at the* BURGO-MASTER.)

CLAIRE. Call me by the name you used to call me.

SCHILL. (*Whispers.*) My kitten.

CLAIRE. What?

SCHILL. (*Loudly.*) My kitten.

CLAIRE. And· what else?

SCHILL. Little witch.

CLAIRE. I used to call you my black panther. You're gray now, and soft.

SCHILL. But you are still the same, little witch.

CLAIRE. I am the same? (*She laughs.*) Oh, no, my black panther, I am not at all the same.

SCHILL. (*Gallantly.*) In my eyes you are. I see no difference.

CLAIRE. Would you like to meet my fiancé? Pedro Cabral. He owns an enormous plantation in Brazil.

SCHILL. A pleasure.

CLAIRE. We're to be married soon.

SCHILL. Congratulations.

CLAIRE. He will be my eighth husband. (PEDRO *stands by himself downstage, right.*) Pedro, come here and show your face. Come along, darling—come here! Don't sulk. Say hello.

PEDRO. Hello.

CLAIRE. A man of few words! Isn't he charming? A diplomat. He's interested only in fishing. Isn't he handsome, in his Latin way? You'd swear he was a Brazilian. But he's not—he's a Greek. His father was a White Russian. We were betrothed by a Bulgarian priest. We plan to be married in a few days here in the cathedral.

BURGOMASTER. Here in the cathedral? What an honor for us!

CLAIRE. No. It was my dream, when I was seventeen, to be married in Güllen cathedral. The dreams of youth are sacred, don't you think so, Anton?

SCHILL. Yes, of course.

CLAIRE. Yes, of course. I think so, too. Now I would like to look at the town. (*The mixed choir arrives, breathless, wearing ordinary clothes with green sashes.*) What's all this? Go away. (*She laughs.*) Ha! Ha! Ha!

TEACHER. Dear lady—(*He steps forward, having put on a sash also.*) Dear Lady, as Rector of the high school and a devotee of that noble muse, Music, I take pleasure in presenting the Güllen mixed choir.

CLAIRE. How do you do?

TEACHER. Who will sing for you an ancient folk song of the region, with specially amended words—if you will deign to listen.

CLAIRE. Very well. Fire away.

(*The* TEACHER *blows a pitch pipe. The mixed choir begins to sing the ancient folk song with the amended words. Just then the station bell starts ringing. The song is drowned in the roar of the passing express. The* STATION MASTER *salutes. When the train has passed, there is applause.*)

BURGOMASTER. The church bell! The church bell! Where's the church bell? (*The* PASTOR *shrugs helplessly.*)

CLAIRE. Thank you, Professor. They sang beautifully. The little blond bass—no, not that one—the one with the big Adam's apple—was most impressive. (*The* TEACHER *bows. The* POLICEMAN *pushes his way professionally through the mixed choir and comes to attention in front of* CLAIRE ZACHANASSIAN.) Now, who are you?

POLICEMAN. (*Clicks heels.*) Police Chief Schultz. At your service.

CLAIRE. (*She looks him up and down.*) I have no need of you at the moment. But I think there will be work for you by and by. Tell me, do you know how to close an eye from time to time?

POLICEMAN. How else could I get along in my profession?

CLAIRE. You might practice closing both.

SCHILL. (*Laughs.*) What a sense of humor, eh?

BURGOMASTER. (*Puts on the top hat.*) Permit me to present my grandchildren, gracious lady. Hermine and Adolphine. There's only my wife still to come. (*He wipes the perspiration from his brow, and replaces the hat. The little girls present the roses and elaborate curtsies.*)

CLAIRE. Thank you, my dears. Congratulations, Burgomaster. Extraordinary children. (*She plants the roses in* PEDRO's *arms. The* BURGOMASTER *secretly passes his top hat to the* PASTOR, *who puts it on.*)

BURGOMASTER. Our pastor, madame. (*The* PASTOR *takes off the hat and bows.*)

CLAIRE. Ah. The pastor. How do you do? Do you give consolation to the dying?

PASTOR. (*A bit puzzled.*) That is part of my ministry, yes.

CLAIRE. And to those who are condemned to death?

PASTOR. Capital punishment has been abolished in this country, madame.

CLAIRE. I see. Well, it could be restored, I suppose. (*The* PASTOR *hands back the hat. He shrugs his shoulders in confusion.*)

SCHILL. (*Laughs.*) What an original sense of humor! (*All laugh, a little blankly.*)

CLAIRE. Well, I can't sit here all day—I should like to see the town. (*The* BURGOMASTER *offers his arm.*)

BURGOMASTER. May I have the honor, gracious lady?

CLAIRE. Thank you, but these legs are not what they were. This one was broken in five places.

SCHILL. (*Full of concern.*) My kitten!

CLAIRE. When my airplane bumped into a mountain in Afghanistan. All the others were killed. Even the pilot. But as you see, I survived. I don't fly any more.

SCHILL. But you're as strong as ever now.

CLAIRE. Stronger.

BURGOMASTER. Never fear, gracious lady. The town doctor has a car.

CLAIRE. I never ride in motors.

BURGOMASTER. You never ride in motors?

CLAIRE. Not since my Ferrari crashed in Hong Kong.

SCHILL. But how do you travel, then, little witch? On a broom?

CLAIRE. Mike—Max! (*She claps her hands. Two huge bodyguards come in, left, carrying a sedan chair. She sits in it.*) I travel this way—a bit antiquated, of course. But perfectly safe. Ha! Ha! Aren't they magnificent? Mike and Max. I bought them in America. They were in jail, condemned to the chair. I had them pardoned. Now they're condemned to my chair. I paid fifty thousand dollars apiece for them. You couldn't get them now for twice the sum. The sedan chair comes from the Louvre. I fancied it so much that the President of France gave it to me. The French are so impulsive, don't you think so, Anton? Go! (MIKE *and* MAX *start to carry her off.*)

BURGOMASTER. You wish to visit the cathedral? And the old town hall?

CLAIRE. No. The great barn. And the forest of Konradsweil. I wish to go with Anton and visit our old haunts once again.

THE PASTOR. Very touching.

CLAIRE. (*To the butler.*) Will you send my luggage and the coffin to the Golden Apostle?

BURGOMASTER. The coffin?

CLAIRE. Yes. I brought one with me. Go!

TEACHER. Hip-hip—

ALL. Hurrah! Hip-hip, hurrah! Hurrah! (*They bear her off in the direction of the town. The Townspeople burst into cheers. The church bell rings.*)

BURGOMASTER. Ah, thank God—the bell at last.

(*The* POLICEMAN *is about to follow the others, when the two* BLIND MEN *appear. They are not young, yet they seem childish— a strange effect. Though they are of different height and features, they are dressed exactly alike, and so create the effect of being twins. They walk slowly, feeling their way. Their voices, when they speak, are curiously high and flutelike, and they have a curious trick of repetition of phrases.*)

FIRST BLIND MAN. We're in—

BOTH BLIND MEN. Güllen.

FIRST BLIND MAN. We breathe—

SECOND BLIND MAN. We breathe—

BOTH BLIND MEN. We breathe the air, the air of Güllen.

POLICEMAN. (*Startled.*) Who are you?

FIRST BLIND MAN. We belong to the lady.

SECOND BLIND MAN. We belong to the lady. She calls us—

FIRST BLIND MAN. Kobby.

SECOND BLIND MAN. And Lobby.

POLICEMAN. Madame Zachanassian is staying at the Golden Apostle.

FIRST BLIND MAN. We're blind.

SECOND BLIND MAN. We're blind.

POLICEMAN. Blind? Come along with me, then. I'll take you there.

FIRST BLIND MAN. Thank you, Mr. Policeman.

SECOND BLIND MAN. Thanks very much.

POLICEMAN. Hey! How do you know I'm a policeman, if you're blind?

BOTH BLIND MEN. By your voice. By your voice.

FIRST BLIND MAN. All policemen sound the same.

POLICEMAN. You've had a lot to do with the police, have you, little men?

FIRST BLIND MAN. Men he calls us!

BOTH BLIND MEN. Men!

POLICEMAN. What are you then?

BOTH BLIND MEN. You'll see. You'll see. (*The* POLICEMAN *claps his hands suddenly. The* BLIND MEN *turn sharply toward the sound. The* POLICEMAN *is convinced they are blind.*)

POLICEMAN. What's your trade?

BOTH BLIND MEN. We have no trade.

SECOND BLIND MAN. We play music.

FIRST BLIND MAN. We sing.

SECOND BLIND MAN. We amuse the lady.

FIRST BLIND MAN. We took after the beast.

SECOND BLIND MAN. We feed it.

FIRST BLIND MAN. We stroke it.

SECOND BLIND MAN. We take it for walks.

POLICEMAN. What beast?

BOTH BLIND MEN. You'll see—you'll see.

SECOND BLIND MAN. We give it raw meat.

FIRST BLIND MAN. And she gives us chicken and wine.

SECOND BLIND MAN. Every day—

BOTH BLIND MEN. Every day.

POLICEMAN. Rich people have strange tastes.

BOTH BLIND MEN. Strange tastes—strange tastes. (*The* POLICE-MAN *puts on his helmet.*)

POLICEMAN. Come along, I'll take you to the lady. (*The two* BLIND MEN *turn and walk off.*)

BOTH BLIND MEN. We know the way—we know the way.

(*The station and the little house vanish. A sign representing the Golden Apostle descends. The scene dissolves into the interior of the inn. The Golden Apostle is seen to be in the last stages of decay. The walls are cracked and moldering, and the plaster is falling from the ancient lath. A table represents the café of the inn. The* BURGOMASTER *and the* TEACHER *sit at this table, drinking a glass together. A procession of Townspeople, carrying many pieces of luggage, passes. Then comes a coffin, and last, a large box covered with a canvas. They cross the stage from right to left.*)

BURGOMASTER. Trunks. Suitcases. Boxes. (*He looks up apprehensively at the ceiling.*) The floor will never bear the weight. (*As the large covered box is carried in, he peers under the canvas, then draws back.*) Good God!

TEACHER. Why, what's in it?

BURGOMASTER. A live panther. (*They laugh. The* BURGOMASTER *lifts his glass solemnly.*) Your health, Professor. Let's hope she puts the Foundry back on its feet.

TEACHER. (*Lifts his glass.*) And the Wagonworks.

BURGOMASTER. And the Golden Eagle Pencil Factory. Once that starts moving, everything else will go. *Prosit.* (*They touch glasses and drink.*)

TEACHER. What does she need a panther for?

BURGOMASTER. Don't ask me. The whole thing is too much for me. The Pastor had to go home and lie down.

TEACHER. (*Sets down his glass.*) If you want to know the truth, she frightens me.

BURGOMASTER. (*Nods gravely.*) She's a strange one.

TEACHER. You understand, Burgomaster, a man who for twenty-two years has been correcting the Latin compositions of the students of Güllen is not unaccustomed to surprises. I have seen things to make one's hair stand on end. But when this woman suddenly appeared on the platform, a shudder tore through me. It was as though out of the clear sky all at once a fury descended upon us, beating its black wings—

(*The Policeman comes in. He mops his face.*)

POLICEMAN. Ah! Now the old place is livening up a bit!

BURGOMASTER. Ah, Schultz, come and join us.

POLICEMAN. Thank you. (*He calls.*) Beer!

BURGOMASTER. Well, what's the news from the front?

POLICEMAN. I'm just back from Schiller's barn. My God! What a scene! She had us all tiptoeing around in the straw as if we were in church. Nobody dared to speak above a whisper. And the way she carried on! I was so embarrassed I let them go to the forest by themselves.

BURGOMASTER. Does the fiancé go with them?

POLICEMAN. With his fishing rod and his landing net. In full marching order. (*He calls again.*) Beer!

BURGOMASTER. That will be her seventh husband.

TEACHER. Her eighth.

BURGOMASTER. But what does she expect to find in the Konradsweil forest?

POLICEMAN. The same thing she expected to find in the old barn, I suppose. The—the—

TEACHER. The ashes of her youthful love.

POLICEMAN. Exactly.

TEACHER. It's poetry.

POLICEMAN. Poetry.

TEACHER. Sheer poetry! It makes one think of Shakespeare, of Wagner, Of Romeo and Juliet. (*The* SECOND MAN *comes in as a waiter. The* POLICEMAN *is served his beer.*)

BURGOMASTER. Yes, you're right. (*Solemnly.*) Gentlemen, I would like to propose a toast. To our great and good friend, Anton Schill, who is even now working on our behalf.

POLICEMAN. Yes! He's really working.

BURGOMASTER. Gentlemen, to the best-loved citizen of this town. My successor, Anton Schill!

(*They raise their glasses. At this point an unearthly scream is heard. It is the black panther howling offstage. The sign of the Golden Apostle rises out of sight. The lights go down. The inn vanishes. Only the wooden bench, on which the four men were lounging in the opening scene, is left on the stage, downstage right. The procession comes on upstage. The two bodyguards carry in* CLAIRE's *sedan chair. Next to it walks* SCHILL. PEDRO *walks behind, with his fishing rod. Last come the two* BLIND MEN *and the butler.* CLAIRE *alights.*)

CLAIRE. Stop! Take my chair off somewhere else. I'm tired of looking at you (*The bodyguards and the sedan chair go off.*) Pedro darling, your brook is just a little further along down that path. Listen. You can hear it from here. Bobby, take him and show him where it is.

BOTH BLIND MEN. We'll show him the way—we'll show him the way.

(*They go off, left.* PEDRO *follows.* BOBBY *walks off, right.*)

CLAIRE. Look, Anton. Our tree. There's the heart you carved in the bark long ago.

SCHILL. Yes. It's still there.

CLAIRE. How it has grown! The trunk is black and wrinkled. Why, its limbs are twice what they were. Some of them have died.

SCHILL. It's aged. But it's there.

CLAIRE. Like everything else. (*She crosses, examining other trees.*) Oh, how tall they are. How long it is since I walked here, barefoot over the pine needles and the damp eaves. Look, Anton. A fawn.

SCHILL. Yes, a fawn. It's the season.

CLAIRE. I thought everything would be changed. But it's all just as we left it. This is the seat we sat on years ago. Under these branches you kissed me. And over there under the hawthorn, where the moss is soft and green, we would lie in each other's arms. It is all as it used to be. Only we have changed.

SCHILL. Not so much, little witch. I remember the first night we spent together, you ran away and I chased you till I was quite breathless—

CLAIRE. Yes.

SCHILL. Then I was angry and I was going home, when suddenly I heard you call and I looked up, and there you were sitting in a tree, laughing down at me.

CLAIRE. No. It was in the great barn. I was in the hayloft.

SCHILL. Were you?

CLAIRE. Yes. What else do you remember?

SCHILL. I remember the morning we went swimming by the waterfall, and afterwards we were lying together on the big rock in the sun, when suddenly we heard footsteps and we just had time to snatch up our clothes and run behind the bushes when the old pastor appeared and scolded you for not being in school.

CLAIRE. No. It was the schoolmaster who found us. It was Sunday and I was supposed to be in church.

SCHILL. Really?

CLAIRE. Yes. Tell me more.

SCHILL. I remember the time your father beat you, and you showed me the cuts on your back, and I swore I'd kill him. And the next day I dropped a tile from a roof top and split his head open.

CLAIRE. You missed him.

SCHILL. No!

CLAIRE. You hit old Mr. Reiner.

SCHILL. Did I?

CLAIRE. Yes. I was seventeen. And you were not yet twenty. You were so handsome. You were the best-looking boy in town. (*The two* BLIND MEN *begin playing mandolin music offstage, very softly.*)

SCHILL. And you were the prettiest girl.

CLAIRE. We were made for each other.

SCHILL. So we were.

CLAIRE. But you married Mathilde Blumhard and her store, and I married old Zachanassian and his oil wells. He found me in a whorehouse in Hamburg. It was my hair that entangled him, the old golden beetle.

SCHILL. Clara!

CLAIRE. (*She claps her hands.*) Bobby! A cigar. (BOBBY *appears with a leather case. He selects a cigar, puts it in a holder, lights it, and presents it to* CLAIRE.)

SCHILL. My kitten smoke cigars!

CLAIRE. Yes. I adore them. Would you care for one?

SCHILL. Yes, please. I've never smoked one of those.

CLAIRE. It's a taste I acquired from old Zachanassian. Among other things. He was a real connoisseur.

SCHILL. We used to sit on this bench once, you and I, and smoke cigarettes. Do you remember?

CLAIRE. Yes. I remember.

SCHILL. The cigarettes I bought from Mathilde.

CLAIRE. No. She gave them to you for nothing.

SCHILL. Clara—don't be angry with me for marrying Mathilde.

CLAIRE. She had money.

SCHILL. But what a lucky thing for you that I did!

CLAIRE. Oh?

SCHILL. You were so young, so beautiful. You deserved a far better fate than to settle in this wretched town without any future.

CLAIRE. Yes?

SCHILL. If you had stayed in Güllen and married me, your life would have been wasted, like mine.

CLAIRE. Oh?

SCHILL. Look at me. A wretched shopkeeper in a bankrupt town!

CLAIRE. But you have your family.

SCHILL. My family! Never for a moment do they let me forget my failure, my poverty.

CLAIRE. Mathilde has not made you happy?

SCHILL. (*Shrugs.*) What does it matter?

CLAIRE. And the children?

SCHILL. (*Shakes his head.*) They're so completely materialistic. You know, they have no interest whatever in higher things.

CLAIRE. How sad for you. (*A moment's pause, during which only the faint tinkling of the music is heard.*)

SCHILL. Yes. You know, since you went away my life has passed by like a stupid dream. I've hardly once been out of this town. A trip to a lake years ago. It rained all the time. And once five days in Berlin. That's all.

CLAIRE. The world is much the same everywhere.

SCHILL. At least you've seen it.

CLAIRE. Yes. I've seen it.

SCHILL. You've lived in it.

CLAIRE. I've lived in it. The world and I have been on very intimate terms.

SCHILL. Now that you've come back, perhaps things will change.

CLAIRE. Naturally. I certainly won't leave my native town in this condition.

SCHILL. It will take millions to put us on our feet again.

CLAIRE. I have millions.

SCHILL. One, two, three.

CLAIRE. Why not?

SCHILL. You mean—you will help us?

CLAIRE. Yes. (*A woodpecker is heard in the distance.*)

SCHILL. I knew it—I knew it. I told them you were generous. I told them you were good. Oh, my kitten, my kitten. (*He takes her hand. She turns her head away and listens.*)

CLAIRE. Listen! A woodpecker.

SCHILL. It's all just the way it was in the days when we were young and full of courage. The sun high above the pines. White clouds, piling up on one another. And the cry of the cuckoo in the distance. And the wind rustling the leaves, like the sound of surf on a beach. Just as it was years ago. If only we could roll back time and be together always.

CLAIRE. Is that your wish?

SCHILL. Yes. You left me, but you never left my heart. (*He raises her hands to his lips.*) The same soft little hand.

CLAIRE. No, not quite the same. It was crushed in the plane accident. But they mended it. They mend everything nowadays.

SCHILL. Crushed? You wouldn't know it. See, another fawn.

CLAIRE. The old wood is alive with memories.

(PEDRO *appears, right, with a fish in his hand.*)

PEDRO. See what I've caught, darling. See? A pike. Over two kilos.

(*The* BLIND MEN *appear onstage.*)

BOTH BLIND MEN. (*Clapping their hands.*) A pike! A pike! Hurrah! Hurrah!

(*As the* BLIND MEN *clap their hands,* CLAIRE *and* SCHILL *exit, and the scene dissolves. The clapping of hands is taken up on all sides. The townspeople wheel in the walls of the café. A brass band strikes up a march tune. The door of the Golden Apostle descends. The townspeople bring in tables and set them with ragged tablecloths, cracked china and glassware. There is a table in the center, upstage, flanked by two tables perpendicular to it, right and left. The* PASTOR *and the* BURGOMASTER *come in.* SCHILL *enters. Other townspeople filter in, left and right. One, the* ATHLETE, *is in gymnastic costume. The applause continues.*)

BURGOMASTER. She's coming! (CLAIRE *enters upstage, center, followed by* BOBBY.) The applause is meant for you, gracious lady.

CLAIRE. The band deserves it more than I. They blow from the heart. And the human pyramid was beautiful. You, show me your muscles. (*The* ATHLETE *kneels before her.*) Superb. Wonderful arms, powerful hands. Have you ever strangled a man with them?

ATHLETE. Strangled?

CLAIRE. Yes. It's perfectly simple. A little pressure in the proper place, and the rest goes by itself. As in politics.

(*The* BURGOMASTER'*s wife comes up, simpering.*)

BURGOMASTER. (*Presents her.*) Permit me to present my wife, Madame Zachanassian.

CLAIRE. Annette Dummermuth. The head of our class.

BURGOMASTER. (*He presents another sour-looking woman.*) Frau Schill.

CLAIRE. Mathilde Blumhard. I remember the way you used to follow Anton with your eyes, from behind the shop door. You've grown a little thin and dry, my poor Mathilde.

SCHILL. My daughter, Ottilie.

CLAIRE. Your daughter . . .

SCHILL. My son, Karl.

CLAIRE. Your son. Two of them!

(*The town* DOCTOR *comes in, right. He is a man of fifty, strong and stocky, with bristly black hair, a mustache and a saber cut on his cheek. He is wearing an old cutaway.*)

DOCTOR. Well, well, my old Mercedes got me here in time after all!

BURGOMASTER. Dr. Nüsslin, the town physician. Madame Zachanassian.

DOCTOR. Deeply honored, madame. (*He kisses her hand.* CLAIRE *studies him.*)

CLAIRE. It is you who signs the death certificates?

DOCTOR. Death certificates?

CLAIRE. When someone dies.

DOCTOR. Why certainly. That is one of my duties.

CLAIRE. And when the heart dies, what do you put down? Heart failure?

SCHILL. (*Laughing.*) What a golden sense of humor!

DOCTOR. Bit grim, wouldn't you say?

SCHILL. (*Whispers.*) Not at all, not at all. She's promised us a million.

BURGOMASTER. (*Turns his head.*) What?

SCHILL. A million!

ALL. (*Whisper.*) A million! (CLAIRE *turns toward them.*)

CLAIRE. Burgomaster.

BURGOMASTER. Yes?

CLAIRE. I'm hungry. (*The girls and the waiter fill glasses and bring food. There is a general stir. All take their places at the tables.*) Are you going to make a speech? (*The* BURGOMASTER *bows.* CLAIRE *sits next to the* BURGOMASTER. *The* BURGOMASTER *rises, tapping his knife on his glass. He is radiant with good will. All applaud.*)

BURGOMASTER. Gracious lady and friends. Gracious lady, it is now many years since you first left your native town of Güllen, which was founded by the Elector Hasso and which nestles in the green slope between the forest of Konradsweil and the beautiful valley of Pückenried. Much has taken place in this time, much that is evil.

TEACHER. That's true.

BURGOMASTER. The world is not what it was: it has become harsh and bitter, and we too have had our share of harshness and bitterness. But in all this time, dear lady, we have never forgotten our little Clara. (*Applause*) Many years ago you brightened the town with your pretty face as a child, and now once again you brighten it with your presence. (*Polite applause*) We haven't forgotten you, and we haven't forgotten your family. Your mother, beautiful and robust even in her old age—(*He looks for his notes on the table.*) —although unfortunately taken from us in the bloom of her youth by an infirmity of the lungs. Your respected father, Siegfried Wäscher, the builder, an example of whose work next to our railway station is often visited—(SCHILL *covers his face.*)—that is to say, admired—a lasting monument of local design and local workmanship. And you, gracious lady, whom we remember as a golden-haired—(*He looks at her.*)—little red-headed sprite romping about our peaceful streets—on your way to school—which of us does not treasure your memory? (*He pokes nervously at his notebook.*) We well remember your scholarly attainments—

TEACHER. Yes.

BURGOMASTER. Natural history . . . Extraordinary sense of justice . . . And, above all, your supreme generosity. (*Great applause.*) We shall never forget how you once spent the whole of your little savings to buy a sack of potatoes for a poor starving widow who was in need of food. Gracious lady, ladies and gentlemen, today our little Clara has become the world-famous Claire Zachanassian who has founded hospitals, soup kitchens, charitable institutes, art projects, libraries, nurseries and schools, and now that she has at last once more returned to the town of her birth, sadly fallen as it is, I say in the name of all her loving friends who have sorely missed her: Long live our Clara!

ALL. Long live our Clara! (*Cheers. Music. Fanfare. Applause. Claire rises.*)

CLAIRE. Mr. Burgomaster. Fellow townsmen. I am greatly moved by the nature of your welcome and the disinterested joy which you have manifested on the occasion of my visit to my native town. I was not quite the child the Burgomaster described in his gracious address . . .

BURGOMASTER. Too modest, madame.

CLAIRE. In school I was beaten—

TEACHER. Not by me.

CLAIRE. And the sack of potatoes which I presented to Widow Boll, I stole with the help of Anton Schill, not to save the old trull from starvation, but so that for once I might sleep with Anton in a real bed instead of under the trees of the forest. (*The townspeople look grave, embarrassed.*) Nevertheless, I shall try to deserve your good opinion. In memory of the seventeen years I spent among you, I am prepared to hand over as a gift to the town of Güllen the sum of one billion marks. Five hundred million to the town, and five hundred million to be divided per capita among the citizens. (*There is a moment of dead silence.*)

BURGOMASTER. A billion marks?

CLAIRE. On one condition. (*Suddenly a movement of uncontrollable joy breaks out. People jump on chairs, dance about, yell excitedly. The* ATHLETE *turns handsprings in front of the speaker's table.*)

SCHILL. Oh, Clara, you astonishing, incredible, magnificent woman! What a heart! What a gesture! Oh—my little witch! (*He kisses her hand.*)

BURGOMASTER. (*Holds up his arms for order.*) Quiet! Quiet, please! On one condition, the gracious lady said. Now, madame, may we know what that condition is?

CLAIRE. I will tell you. In exchange for my billion marks, I want justice. (*Silence.*)

BURGOMASTER. Justice, madame?

CLAIRE. I wish to buy justice.

BURGOMASTER. But justice cannot be bought, madame.

CLAIRE. Everything can be bought.

BURGOMASTER. I don't understand at all.

CLAIRE. Bobby, step forward. (*The butler goes to the center of the stage. He takes off his dark glasses and turns his face with a solemn air.*)

BOBBY. Does anyone here present recognize me?

FRAU SCHILL. Hofer! Hofer!

ALL. Who? What's that?

TEACHER. Not Chief Magistrate Hofer?

BOBBY. Exactly. Chief Magistrate Hofer. When Madame Zachanassian was a girl, I was presiding judge at the criminal court of Güllen. I served there until twenty-five years ago, when Madame Zachanassian offered me the opportunity of entering her service as butler. I accepted. You may consider it a strange employment for a member of the magistracy, but the salary—(CLAIRE *bangs the mallet on the table.*)

CLAIRE. Come to the point.

BOBBY. You have heard Madame Zachanassian's offer. She will give you a billion marks—when you have undone the injustice that she suffered at your hands here in Güllen as a girl. (*All murmur.*)

BURGOMASTER. Injustice at our hands? Impossible!

BOBBY. Anton Schill . . .

SCHILL. Yes?

BOBBY. Kindly stand. (SCHILL *rises. He smiles, as if puzzled. He shrugs.*)

SCHILL. Yes?

BOBBY. In those days, a bastardy case was tried before me. Madame Claire Zachanassian, at that time called Clara Wäscher, charged you with being the father of her illegitimate child. (*Silence.*) You denied the charge. And produced two witnesses in your support.

SCHILL. That's ancient history. An absurd business. We were children. Who remembers?

CLAIRE. Where are the blind men?

BOTH BLIND MEN. Here we are. Here we are. (MIKE *and* MAX *push them forward.*)

BOBBY. You recognize these men, Anton Schill?

SCHILL. I never saw them before in my life. What are they?

BOTH BLIND MEN. We've changed. We've changed.

BOBBY. What were your names in your former life?

FIRST BLIND MAN. I was Jacob Hueblein. Jacob Hueblein.

SECOND BLIND MAN. I was Ludwig Sparr. Ludwig Sparr.

BOBBY. (*To* SCHILL.) Well?

SCHILL. These names mean nothing to me.

BOBBY. Jacob Hueblein and Ludwig Sparr, do you recognize the defendant?

FIRST BLIND MAN. We're blind.

SECOND BLIND MAN. We're blind.

SCHILL. Ha-ha-ha!

BOBBY. By his voice?

BOTH BLIND MEN. By his voice. By his voice.

BOBBY. At that trial, I was the judge. And you?

BOTH BLIND MEN. We were the witnesses.

BOBBY. And what did you testify on that occasion?

FIRST BLIND MAN. That we had slept with Clara Wäscher.

SECOND BLIND MAN. Both of us. Many times.

BOBBY. And was it true?

FIRST BLIND MAN. No.

SECOND BLIND MAN. We swore falsely.

BOBBY. And why did you swear falsely?

FIRST BLIND MAN. Anton Schill bribed us.

SECOND BLIND MAN. He bribed us.

BOBBY. With what?

BOTH BLIND MEN. With a bottle of schnapps.

BOBBY. And now tell the people what happened to you. (*They hesitate and whimper.*) Speak!

FIRST BLIND MAN. (*In a low voice.*) She tracked us down.

BOBBY. Madame Zachanassian tracked them down. Jacob Hueblein was found in Canada. Ludwig Spaar in Australia. And when she found you, what did she do to you?

SECOND BLIND MAN. She handed us over to Mike and Max.

BOBBY. And what did Mike and Max do to you?

FIRST BLIND MAN. They made us what you see. (*The* BLIND MEN *cover their faces.* MIKE *and* MAX *push them off.*)

BOBBY. And there you have it. We are all present in Güllen once again. The plaintiff. The defendant. The two false witnesses. The judge. Many years have passed. Does the plaintiff have anything further to add?

CLAIRE. There is nothing to add.

BOBBY. And the defendant?

SCHILL. Why are you doing this? It was all dead and buried.

BOBBY. What happened to the child that was born?

CLAIRE. (*In a low voice.*) It lived a year.

BOBBY. And what happened to you?

CLAIRE. I became a whore.

BOBBY. Why?

CLAIRE. The judgment of the court left me no alternative. No one would trust me. No one would give me work.

BOBBY. So. And now, what is the nature of the reparation you demand?

CLAIRE. I want the life of Anton Schill. (FRAU SCHILL *springs to* ANTON'S *side. She puts her arms around him. The children rush to him. He breaks away.*)

FRAU SCHILL. Anton! No! No!

SCHILL. No— No— She's joking. That happened long ago. That's all forgotten.

CLAIRE. Nothing is forgotten. Neither the mornings in the forest, nor the nights in the great barn, nor the bedroom in the cottage, nor your treachery at the end. You said this morning that you wished that time might be rolled back. Very well—I have rolled it back. And now it is I who will buy justice. You bought it with a bottle of schnapps. I am willing to pay one billion marks. (*The* BURGO-MASTER *stands up, very pale and dignified.*)

BURGOMASTER. Madame Zachanassian, we are not in the jungle. We are in Europe. We may be poor, but we are not heathens. In the name of the town of Güllen, I decline your offer. In the name of humanity. We shall never accept. (*All applaud wildly. The applause turns into a sinister rhythmic beat. As* CLAIRE *rises, it dies away. She looks at the crowd, then at the* BURGOMASTER.)

CLAIRE. Thank you, Burgomaster. (*She stares at him a long moment.*) I can wait. (*She turns and walks off. Curtain.*)

act two

(*The façade of the Golden Apostle, with a balcony on which chairs and a table are set out. To the right of the inn is a sign which reads: "Anton Schill, Handlung." Under the sign the shop is represented by a broken counter. Behind the counter are some shelves with tobacco, cigarettes and liquor bottles. There are two milk cans. The shop door is imaginary, but each entrance is indicated by a doorbell with a tinny sound.*)

(*It is early morning.*)
(SCHILL *is sweeping the shop. The* SON *has a pan and brush and also sweeps. The* DAUGHTER *is dusting. They are singing "The Happy Wanderer."*)

SCHILL. Karl—(KARL *crosses with a dustpan.* SCHILL *sweeps dust into the pan. The doorbell rings. The* THIRD MAN *appears, carrying a crate of eggs.*)

THIRD MAN. 'Morning.

SCHILL. Ah, good morning, Wechsler.

THIRD MAN. Twelve dozen eggs, medium brown. Right?

SCHILL. Take them, Karl. (*The* SON *puts the crate in a corner.*) Did they deliver the milk yet?

SON. Before you came down.

THIRD MAN. Eggs are going up again, Herr Schill. First of the month. (*He gives* SCHILL *a slip to sign.*)

SCHILL. What? Again? And who's going to buy them?

THIRD MAN. Fifty pfennig a dozen.

SCHILL. I'll have to cancel my order, that's all.

THIRD MAN. That's up to you, Herr Schill. (SCHILL *signs the slip.*)

SCHILL. There's nothing else to do. (*He hands back the slip.*) And how's the family?

THIRD MAN. Oh, scraping along. Maybe now things will get better.

SCHILL. Maybe.

THIRD MAN. (*Going*) 'Morning.

SCHILL. Close the door. Don't let the flies in. (*The children resume their singing.*) Now, listen to me, children. I have a little piece of good news for you. I didn't mean to speak of it yet awhile, but well, why not? Who do you suppose is going to be the next Burgomaster? Eh? (*They look up at him.*) Yes, in spite of everything. It's settled. It's official. What an honor for the family, eh? Especially at a time like this. To say nothing of the salary and the rest of it.

SON. Burgomaster!

SCHILL. Burgomaster. (*The* SON *shakes him warmly by the hand. The* DAUGHTER *kisses him.*) You see, you don't have to be entirely ashamed of your father. (*Silence.*) Is your mother coming down to breakfast soon?

DAUGHTER. Mother's tired. She's going to stay upstairs.

SCHILL. You have a good mother, at least. There you are lucky. Oh, well, if she wants to rest, let her rest. We'll have breakfast together, the three of us. I'll fry some eggs and open a tin of the American ham. This morning we're going to breakfast like kings.

SON. I'd like to, only—I can't.

SCHILL. You've got to eat, you know.

SON. I've got to run down to the station. One of the laborers is sick. They said they could use me.

SCHILL. You want to work on the rails in all this heat? That's no work for a son of mine.

SON. Look, Father, we can use the money.

SCHILL. Well, if you feel you have to. (*The* SON *goes to the door. The* DAUGHTER *moves toward* SCHILL.)

DAUGHTER. I'm sorry, Father. I have to go too.

SCHILL. You too? And where is the young lady going, if I may be so bold?

DAUGHTER. There may be something for me at the employment agency.

SCHILL. Employment agency?

DAUGHTER. It's important to get there early.

SCHILL. All right. I'll have something nice for you when you get home.

SON AND DAUGHTER. (*Salute.*) Good day, Burgomaster.

(*The* SON *and* DAUGHTER *go out.*)

(*The* FIRST MAN *comes into* SCHILL'S *shop. Mandolin and guitar music are heard offstage.*)

SCHILL. Good morning, Hofbauer.

FIRST MAN. Cigarettes. (SCHILL *takes a pack from the shelf.*) Not those. I'll have the green today.

SCHILL. They cost more.

FIRST MAN. Put it in the book.

SCHILL. What?

FIRST MAN. Charge it.

SCHILL. Well, all right, I'll make an exception this time—seeing it's you, Hofbauer. (SCHILL *writes in his cash book.*)

FIRST MAN. (*Opening the pack of cigarettes*) Who's that playing out there?

SCHILL. The two blind men.

FIRST MAN. They play well.

SCHILL. To hell with them.

FIRST MAN. They make you nervous? (SCHILL *shrugs. The First Man lights a cigarette.*) She's getting ready for the wedding, I hear.

SCHILL. Yes. So they say.

(*Enter the* FIRST *and* SECOND WOMAN. *They cross to the counter.*)

FIRST WOMAN. Good morning, good morning.

SECOND WOMAN. Good morning.

FIRST MAN. Good morning.

SCHILL. Good morning, ladies.

FIRST WOMAN. Good morning, Herr Schill.

SECOND WOMAN. Good morning.

FIRST WOMAN. Milk please, Herr Schill.

SCHILL. Milk.

SECOND WOMAN. And milk for me too.

SCHILL. A liter of milk each. Right away.

FIRST WOMAN. Whole milk, please, Herr Schill.

SCHILL. Whole milk?

SECOND WOMAN. Yes. Whole milk, please.

SCHILL. Whole milk, I can only give you half a liter each of whole milk.

FIRST WOMAN. All right.

SCHILL. Half a liter of whole milk here, and half a liter of whole milk here. There you are.

FIRST WOMAN. And butter please, a quarter kilo.

SCHILL. Butter, I haven't any butter. I can give you some very nice lard?

FIRST WOMAN. No. Butter.

SCHILL. Goose fat? (*The* FIRST WOMAN *shakes her head.*) Chicken fat?

FIRST WOMAN. Butter.

SCHILL. Butter. Now, wait a minute, though. I have a tin of imported butter here somewhere. Ah. There you are. No, sorry, she asked first, but I can order some for you from Kalberstadt tomorrow.

SECOND WOMAN. And white bread.

SCHILL. White bread. (*He takes a loaf and a knife.*)

SECOND WOMAN. The whole loaf.

SCHILL. But a whole loaf would cost . . .

SECOND WOMAN. Charge it.

SCHILL. Charge it?

FIRST WOMAN. And a package of milk chocolate.

SCHILL. Package of milk chocolate—right away.

SECOND WOMAN. One for me, too, Herr Schill.

SCHILL. And a package of milk chocolate for you, too.

FIRST WOMAN. We'll eat it here, if you don't mind.

SCHILL. Yes, please do.

SECOND WOMAN. It's so cool at the back of the shop.

SCHILL. Charge it?

WOMEN. Of course.

SCHILL. All for one, one for all.

(*The* SECOND MAN *enters.*)

SECOND MAN. Good morning.

THE TWO WOMEN. Good morning.

SCHILL. Good morning, Helmesberger.

SECOND MAN. It's going to be a hot day.

SCHILL. Phew!

SECOND MAN. How's business?

SCHILL. Fabulous. For a while no one came, and now all of a sudden I'm running a luxury trade.

SECOND MAN. Good!

SCHILL. Oh, I'll never forget the way you all stood by me at the Golden Apostle in spite of your need, in spite of everything. That was the finest hour of my life.

FIRST MAN. We're not heathens, you know.

SECOND MAN. We're behind you, my boy; the whole town's behind you.

FIRST MAN. As firm as a rock.

FIRST WOMAN. (*Munching her chocolate.*) As firm as a rock, Herr Schill.

BOTH WOMEN. As firm as a rock.

SECOND MAN. There's no denying it—you're the most popular man in town.

FIRST MAN. The most important.

SECOND MAN. And in the spring, God willing, you will be our Burgomaster.

FIRST MAN. Sure as a gun.

ALL. Sure as a gun.

(*Enter* PEDRO *with fishing equipment ad a fish in his landing net.*)

PEDRO. Would you please weigh my fish for me?

SCHILL. (*Weighs it.*) Two kilos.

PEDRO. Is that all?

SCHILL. Two kilos exactly.

PEDRO. Two kilos!   (*He gives* SCHILL *a tip and exits.*)

SECOND WOMAN. The fiancé.

FIRST WOMAN. They're to be married this week. It will be a tremendous wedding.

SECOND WOMAN. I saw his picture in the paper.

FIRST WOMAN. (*Sighs.*) Ah, what a man!

SECOND MAN. Give me a bottle of schnapps.

SCHILL. The usual?

SECOND MAN. No, cognac.

SCHILL. Cognac? But cognac costs twenty-two marks fifty.

SECOND MAN. We all have to splurge a little now and again—

SCHILL. Here you are. Three Star.

SECOND MAN. And a package of pipe tobacco.

SCHILL. Black or blond?

SECOND MAN. English.

SCHILL. English! But that makes twenty-three marks eighty.

SECOND MAN. Chalk it up.

SCHILL. Now, look. I'll make an exception this week. Only, you will have to pay me the moment your unemployment check comes in. I don't want to be kept waiting. (*Suddenly.*) Helmesberger, are those new shoes you're wearing?

SECOND MAN. Yes, what about it?

SCHILL. You too, Hofbauer. Yellow shoes! Brand new!

FIRST MAN. So?

SCHILL. (*To the women.*) And you. You all have new shoes! New shoes!

FIRST WOMAN. A person can't walk around forever in the same old shoes.

SECOND WOMAN. Shoes wear out.

SCHILL. And the money. Where does the money come from?

FIRST WOMAN. We got them on credit, Herr Schill.

SECOND WOMAN. On credit.

SCHILL. On credit? And where all of a sudden do you get credit?

SECOND MAN. Everybody gives credit now.

FIRST WOMAN. You gave us credit yourself.

SCHILL. And what are you going to pay with? Eh? (*They are all silent.* SCHILL *advances upon them threateningly.*) With what? Eh? With what? With what?

(*Suddenly he understands. He takes his apron off quickly, flings it on the counter, gets his jacket, and walks off with an air of determination. Now the shop sign vanishes. The shelves are pushed off. The lights go up on the balcony of the Golden Apostle, and the balcony unit itself moves forward into the optical center. Claire and Bobby step out on the balcony.* CLAIRE *sits down.* BOBBY *serves coffee.*)

CLAIRE. A lovely autumn morning. A silver haze on the streets and a violet sky above. Count Holk would have liked this. Remember him, Bobby? My third husband?

BOBBY. Yes, madame.

CLAIRE. Horrible man!

BOBBY. Yes, madame.

CLAIRE. Where is Monsieur Pedro? Is he up yet?

BOBBY. Yes, madame. He's fishing.

CLAIRE. Already? What a singular passion!

(*Pedro comes in with the fish.*)

PEDRO. Good morning, my love.

CLAIRE. Pedro! There you are.

PEDRO. Look, my darling. Four kilos!

CLAIRE. A jewel! I'll have it grilled for your lunch. Give it to Bobby.

PEDRO. Ah—it is so wonderful here! I like your little town.

CLAIRE. Oh, do you?

PEDRO. Yes. These people, they are all so—what is the word?

CLAIRE. Simple, honest, hard-working, decent.

PEDRO. But, my angel, you are a mind reader. That's just what I was going to say—however did you guess?

CLAIRE. I know them.

PEDRO. Yet when we arrived it was all so dirty, so—what is the word?

CLAIRE. Shabby.

PEDRO. Exactly. But now everywhere you go, you see them busy as bees, cleaning their streets—

CLAIRE. Repairing their houses, sweeping—dusting—hanging new curtains in the windows—singing as they work.

PEDRO. But you astonishing, wonderful woman! You can't see all that from here.

CLAIRE. I know them. And in their gardens—I am sure that in their gardens they are manuring the soil for the spring.

PEDRO. My angel, you know everything. This morning on my way fishing I said to myself, look at them all manuring their gardens. It is extraordinary—and it's all because of you. Your return has given them a new—what is the word?

CLAIRE. Lease on life?

PEDRO. Precisely.

CLAIRE. The town was dying, it's true. But a town doesn't have to die. I think they realize that now. People die, not towns. Bobby! (BOBBY appears.) A cigar.

(*The lights fade on the balcony, which moves back upstage. Somewhat to the right, a sign descends. It reads: "Polizei." The* POLICE-MAN *pushes a desk under it. This, with the bench, becomes the police station. He places a bottle of beer and a glass on the desk, and goes to hang up his coat offstage. The telephone rings.*)

POLICEMAN. Schultz speaking. Yes, we have a couple of rooms for the night. No, not for rent. This is not the hotel. This is the Güllen police station. (*He laughs and hangs up.* SCHILL *comes in. He is evidently nervous.*)

SCHILL. Schultz.

POLICEMAN. Hello, Schill. Come in. Sit down. Beer?

SCHILL. Please. (*He drinks thirstily.*)

POLICEMAN. What can I do for you?

SCHILL. I want you to arrest Madame Zachanassian.

POLICEMAN. Eh?

SCHILL. I said I want you to arrest Madame Zachanassian.

POLICEMAN. What the hell are you talking about?

SCHILL. I ask you to arrest this woman at once.

POLICEMAN. What offense has the lady committed?

SCHILL. You know perfectly well. She offered a billion marks—

POLICEMAN. And you want her arrested for that? (*He pours beer into his glass.*)

SCHILL. Schultz! It's your duty.

SCHULTZ. Extraordinary! Extraordinary idea! (*He drinks his beer.*)

SCHILL. I'm speaking to you as your next Burgomaster.

POLICEMAN. Schill, that's true. The lady offered us a billion marks. But that doesn't entitle us to take police action against her.

SCHILL. Why not?

POLICEMAN. In order to be arrested, a person must first commit a crime.

SCHILL. Incitement to murder.

POLICEMAN. Incitement to murder is a crime. I agree.

SCHILL. Well?

POLICEMAN. And such a proposal—if serious—constitutes an assault.

SCHILL. That's what I mean.

POLICEMAN. But her offer can't be serious.

SCHILL. Why?

POLICEMAN. The price is too high. In a case like yours, one pays a thousand marks, at the most two thousand. But not a billion! That's ridiculous. And even if she meant it, that would only prove she was out of her mind. And that's not a matter for the police.

SCHILL. Whether she's out of her mind or not, the danger to me is the same. That's obvious.

POLICEMAN. Look, Schill, you show us where anyone threatens your life in any way—say, for instance, a man points a gun at you—and we'll be there in a flash.

SCHILL. (*Gets up.*) So I'm to wait till someone points a gun at me?

POLICEMAN. Pull yourself together, Schill. We're all for you in this town.

SCHILL. I wish I could believe it.

POLICEMAN. You don't believe it?

SCHILL. No. No, I don't. All of a sudden my customers are buying white bread, whole milk, butter, imported tobacco. What does it mean?

POLICEMAN. It means business is picking up.

SCHILL. Helmesberger lives on the dole; he hasn't earned anything in five years. Today he bought French cognac.

POLICEMAN. I'll have to try your cognac one of these days.

SCHILL. And shoes. They all have new shoes.

POLICEMAN. And what have you got against new shoes? I'm wearing a new pair myself. (*He holds out his foot.*)

SCHILL. You too?

POLICEMAN. Why not? (*He pours out the rest of his beer.*)

SCHILL. Is that Pilsen you're drinking now?

POLICEMAN. It's the only thing.

SCHILL. You used to drink the local beer.

POLICEMAN. Hogwash. (*Radio music is heard offstage.*)

SCHILL. Listen. You hear?

POLICEMAN. "The Merry Widow." Yes.

SCHILL. No. It's a radio.

POLICEMAN. That's Bergholzer's radio.

SCHILL. Bergholzer!

POLICEMAN. You're right. He should close his window when he plays it. I'll make a note to speak to him. (*He makes a note in his notebook.*)

SCHILL. And how can Bergholzer pay for a radio?

POLICEMAN. That's his business.

SCHILL. And you, Schultz, with your new shoes and your imported beer—how are you going to pay for them?

POLICEMAN. That's my business. (*His telephone rings. He picks it up.*) Police Station, Güllen. What? What? Where? Where? How? Right, we'll deal with it. (*He hangs up.*)

SCHILL. (*He speaks during the* POLICEMAN'*s telephone conversation.*) Schultz, listen. No. Schultz, please—listen to me. Don't you see they're all . . . Listen, please. Look, Schultz. They're all running up debts. And out of these debts comes this sudden prosperity. And out of this prosperity comes the absolute need to kill me.

POLICEMAN. (*Putting on his jacket.*) You're imagining things.

SCHILL. All she has to do is to sit on the balcony and wait.

POLICEMAN. Don't be a child.

SCHILL. You're all waiting.

POLICEMAN. (*Snaps a loaded clip into the magazine of a rifle.*) Look, Schill, you can relax. The police are here for your protection. They know their job. Let anyone, any time, make the slightest threat to your life, and all you have to do is let us know. We'll do the rest . . . Now, don't worry.

SCHILL. No, I won't.

POLICEMAN. And don't upset yourself. All right?

SCHILL. Yes. I won't. (*Then suddenly, in a low tone.*) You have a new gold tooth in your mouth!

POLICEMAN. What are you talking about?

SCHILL. (*Taking the* POLICEMAN's *head in his hands, and forcing his lips open*) A brand new, shining gold tooth.

POLICEMAN. (*Breaks away and involuntarily levels the gun at* SCHILL.) Are you crazy? Look, I've no time to waste. Madame Zachanassian's panther's broken loose.

SCHILL. Panther?

POLICEMAN. Yes, it's at large. I've got to hunt it down.

SCHILL. You're not hunting a panther and you know it. It's me you're hunting! (*The* POLICEMAN *clicks on the safety and lowers the gun.*)

POLICEMAN. Schill! Take my advice. Go home. Lock the door. Keep out of everyone's way. That way you'll be safe. Cheer up! Good times are just around the corner! (*The lights dim in this area and light up on the balcony.* PEDRO *is lounging in a chair.* CLAIRE *is smoking.*)

PEDRO. Oh, this little town oppresses me.

CLAIRE. Oh, does it? So you've changed your mind?

PEDRO. It is true, I find it charming, delightful—

CLAIRE. Picturesque.

PEDRO. Yes. After all, it's the place where you were born. But it is too quiet for me. Too provincial. Too much like all small towns everywhere. These people—look at them. They fear nothing, they desire nothing, they strive for nothing. They have everything they want. They are asleep.

CLAIRE. Perhaps one day they will come to life again.

PEDRO. My God—do I have to wait for that?

CLAIRE. Yes, you do. Why don't you go back to your fishing?

PEDRO. I think I will. (PEDRO *turns to go.*)

CLAIRE. Pedro.

PEDRO. Yes, my love?

CLAIRE. Telephone the president of Hambro's Bank. Ask him to transfer a billion marks to my current account.

PEDRO. A billion? Yes, my love.

(*He goes. The lights fade on the balcony. A sign is flown in. It reads:* "Rathaus." *The* THIRD MAN *crosses the stage, right to left,*

wheeling a new television set on a hand truck. The counter of
SCHILL's *shop is transformed into the* BURGOMASTER's *office. The*
BURGOMASTER *comes in. He takes a revolver from his pocket,*
examines it and sets it down on the desk. He sits down and starts
writing. SCHILL *knocks.*)

BURGOMASTER. Come in.

SCHILL. I must have a word with you, Burgomaster.

BURGOMASTER. Ah, Schill. Sit down, my friend.

SCHILL. Man to man. As your successor.

BURGOMASTER. But of course. Naturally. (SCHILL *remains stand-*
ing. He looks at the revolver.)

SCHILL. Is that a gun?

BURGOMASTER. Madame Zachanassian's black panther's broken
loose. It's been seen near the cathedral. It's as well to be prepared.

SCHILL. Oh, yes. Of course.

BURGOMASTER. I've sent out a call for all able-bodied men with
firearms. The streets have been cleared. The children have been kept
in school. We don't want any accidents.

SCHILL. (*Suspiciously.*) You're making quite a thing of it.

BURGOMASTER. (*Shrugs.*) Naturally. A panther is a dangerous
beast. Well? What's on your mind? Speak out. We're old friends.

SCHILL. That's a good cigar you're smoking, Burgomaster.

BURGOMASTER. Yes. Havana.

SCHILL. You used to smoke something else.

BURGEMASTER. Fortuna.

SCHILL. Cheaper.

BURGOMASTER. Too strong.

SCHILL. A new tie? Silk?

BURGOMASTER. Yes. Do you like it?

SCHILL. And have you also bought new shoes?

BURGOMASTER. (*Brings his feet out from under the desk.*) Why,
yes. I ordered a new pair from Kalberstadt. Extraordinary! However
did you guess?

SCHILL. That's why I'm here. (*The* THIRD MAN *knocks.*)

BURGOMASTER. Come in.

THIRD MAN. The new typewriter, sir.

BURGOMASTER. Put it on the table. (*The* THIRD MAN *sets it down*
and goes.) What's the matter with you? My dear fellow, aren't you
well?

SCHILL. It's you who don't seem well, Burgomaster.

BURGOMASTER. What do you mean?

SCHILL. You look pale.

BURGOMASTER. I?

SCHILL. Your hands are trembling. (*The* BURGOMASTER *involuntarily hides his hands.*) Are you frightened?

BURGOMASTER. What have I to be afraid of?

SCHILL. Perhaps this sudden prosperity alarms you.

BURGOMASTER. Is prosperity a crime?

SCHILL. That depends on how you pay for it.

BURGOMASTER. You'll have to forgive me, Schill, but I really haven't the slightest idea what you're talking about. Am I supposed to feel like a criminal every time I order a new typewriter?

SCHILL. Do you?

BURGOMASTER. Well, I hope you haven't come here to talk about a new typewriter. Now, what was it you wanted?

SCHILL. I have come to claim the protection of the authorities.

BURGOMASTER. Ei! Against whom?

SCHILL. You know against whom.

BURGOMASTER. You don't trust us?

SCHILL. That woman has put a price on my head.

BURGOMASTER. If you don't feel safe, why don't you go to the police?

SCHILL. I have just come from the police.

BURGOMASTER. And?

SCHILL. The chief has a new gold tooth in his mouth.

BURGOMASTER. A new—? Oh, Schill, really! You're forgetting. This is Güllen, the town of humane traditions. Goethe slept here. Brahms composed a quartet. You must have faith in us. This is a law-abiding community.

SCHILL. Then arrest this woman who wants to have me killed.

BURGOMASTER. Look here, Schill. God knows the lady has every right to be angry with you. What you did there wasn't very pretty. You forced two decent lads to perjure themselves and had a young girl thrown out on the streets.

SCHILL. That young girl owns half the world. (*A moment's silence.*)

BURGOMASTER. Very well, then, we'll speak frankly.

SCHILL. That's why I'm here.

BURGOMASTER. Man to man, just as you said. (*He clears his throat.*) Now—after what you did, you have no moral right to say a word against this lady. And I advise you not to try. Also—I regret to have to tell you this—there is no longer any question of your being elected Burgomaster.

SCHILL. Is that official?

BURGOMASTER. Official.

SCHILL. I see.

BURGOMASTER. The man who is chosen to exercise the high post of Burgomaster must have, obviously, certain moral qualifications. Qualifications which, unhappily, you no longer possess. Naturally, you may count on the esteem and friendship of the town, just as before. That goes without saying. The best thing will be to spread the mantle of silence over the whole miserable business.

SCHILL. So I'm to remain silent while they arrange my murder? (*The* BURGOMASTER *gets up.*)

BURGOMASTER. (*Suddenly noble.*) Now, who is arranging your murder? Give me the names and I will investigate the case at once. Unrelentingly. Well? The names?

SCHILL. You.

BURGOMASTER. I resent this. Do you think we want to kill you for money?

SCHILL. No. You don't want to kill me. But you want to have me killed.

(*The lights go down. The stage is filled with men prowling about with rifles, as if they were stalking a quarry. In the interval the* POLICEMAN's *bench and the* BURGOMASTER's *desk are shifted somewhat, so that they will compose the setting for the sacristy. The stage empties. The lights come up on the balcony.*)

(CLAIRE *appears.*)

CLAIRE. Bobby, what's going on here? What are all these men doing with guns? Whom are they hunting?

BOBBY. The black panther has escaped, madame.

CLAIRE. Who let him out?

BOBBY. Kobby and Lobby, madame.

CLAIRE. How excited they are! There may be shooting?

BOBBY. It is possible, madame.

(*The lights fade on the balcony. The sacristan comes in. He arranges the set, and puts the altar cloth on the altar. Then* SCHILL *comes on. He is looking for the* PASTOR. *The* PASTOR *enters, left. He is wearing his gown and carrying a rifle.*)

SCHILL. Sorry to disturb you, Pastor.

PASTOR. God's house is open to all. (*He sees that* SCHILL *is staring at the gun.*) Oh, the gun? That's because of the panther. It's best to be prepared.

SCHILL. Pastor, help me.

PASTOR. Of course. Sit down. (*He puts the rifle on the bench.*) What's the trouble?

SCHILL. (*Sits on the bench.*) I'm frightened.

PASTOR. Frightened? Of what?

SCHILL. Of everyone. They're hunting me down like a beast.

PASTOR. Have no fear of man, Schill. Fear God. Fear not the death of the body. Fear the death of the soul. Zip up my gown behind, Sacristan.

SCHILL. I'm afraid, Pastor.

PASTOR. Put your trust in heaven, my friend.

SCHILL. You see, I'm not well. I shake. I have such pains around the heart. I sweat.

PASTOR. I know. You're passing through a profound psychic experience.

SCHILL. I'm going through hell.

PASTOR. The hell you are going through exists only within yourself. Many years ago you betrayed a girl shamefully, for money. Now you think that we shall sell you just as you sold her. No, my friend, you are projecting your guilt upon others. It's quite natural. But remember, the root of our torment lies always within ourselves, in our hearts, in our sins. When you have understood this, you can conquer the fears that oppress you; you have weapons with which to destroy them.

SCHILL. Siemethofer has bought a new washing machine.

PASTOR. Don't worry about the washing machine. Worry about your immortal soul.

SCHILL. Stockers has a television set.

PASTOR. There is also great comfort in prayer. Sacristan, the bands. (SCHILL *crosses to the altar and kneels. The sacristan ties on the* PASTOR's *bands.*) Examine your conscience, Schill. Repent. Otherwise your fears will consume you. Believe me, this is the only way. We have no other. (*The church bell begins to peal.* SCHILL *seems relieved.*) Now I must leave you. I have a baptism. You may stay as long as you like. Sacristan, the Bible, Liturgy and Psalter. The child is beginning to cry. I can hear it from here. It is frightened. Let us make haste to give it the only security which this world affords.

SCHILL. A new bell?

PASTOR. Yes. Its tone is marvelous, don't you think? Full. Sonorous.

SCHILL. (*Steps back in horror.*) A new bell! You too, Pastor? You too? (*The* PASTOR *clasps his hands in horror. Then he takes* SCHILL *into his arms.*)

PASTOR. Oh, God, God forgive me. We are poor, weak things, all of us. Do not tempt us further into the hell in which you are burning. Go, Schill, my friend, go, my brother, go while there is time.

(*The* PASTOR *goes.*)

(SCHILL *picks up the rifle with a gesture of desperation. He goes out with it. As the lights fade, men appear with guns. Two shots are fired in the darkness. The lights come up on the balcony, which moves forward.*)

CLAIRE. Bobby! What was that shooting? Have they caught the panther?

BOBBY. He is dead, madame.

CLAIRE. There were two shots.

BOBBY. The panther is dead, madame.

CLAIRE. I loved him. (*Waves* BOBBY *away.*) I shall miss him.

(THE TEACHER *comes in with two little girls, singing. They stop under the balcony.*)

TEACHER. Gracious lady, be so good as to accept our heartfelt condolences. Your beautiful panther is no more. Believe me, we are deeply pained that so tragic an event should mar your visit here. But what could we do? The panther was savage, a beast. To him our human laws could not apply. There was no other way—(SCHILL *appears with the gun. He looks dangerous. The girls run off, frightened. The* TEACHER *follows the girls.*) Children—children— children!

CLAIRE. Anton, why are you frightening the children? (*He works the bolt, loading the chamber, and raises the gun slowly.*)

SCHILL. Go away, Claire—I warn you. Go away.

CLAIRE. How strange it is, Anton! How clearly it comes back to me! The day we saw one another for the first time, do you remember? I was on a balcony then. It was a day like today, a day in autumn without a breath of wind, warm as it is now—only lately I am always cold. You stood down there and stared at me without moving. I was embarrassed. I didn't know what to do. I wanted to go back into the darkness of the room, where it was safe, but I couldn't. You stared up at me darkly, almost angrily, as if you wished to hurt me, but your eyes were full of passion. (SCHILL *begins to lower the rifle involuntarily.*) Then, I don't know why, I left the balcony and I came down and stood in the street beside you. You didn't greet me, you didn't say a word, but you took my hand and we walked together out of the town into the fields, and behind us came Kobby and Lobby, like two dogs, sniveling and giggling and snarling. Suddenly you picked up a stone and hurled it at them, and they ran yelping back into the town, and we were alone. (SCHILL *has lowered the rifle completely. He moves forward toward her, as close as he can come.*) That was the beginning, and everything else had to follow. There is no escape. (*She goes in and closes the shutters.* SCHILL *stands immobile. The* TEACHER *tiptoes in. He stares at* SCHILL, *who doesn't see him. Then he beckons to the children.*)

TEACHER. Come, children, sing. Sing. (*They begin singing. He creeps behind* SCHILL *and snatches away the rifle.* SCHILL *turns sharply. The* PASTOR *comes in.*)

PASTOR. Go, Schill—go!

(SCHILL *goes out. The children continue singing, moving across the stage and off. The Golden Apostle vanishes. The crossing bell is heard. The scene dissolves into the railway-station setting, as in Act I. But there are certain changes. The timetable marked "Fahrplan" is now new, the frame freshly painted. There is a new travel poster on the station wall. It has a yellow sun and the words: "Reist in den Süden." On the other side of the Fahrplan is another poster with the words: "Die Passionsspiele Oberammergau." The sound of passing trains covers the scene change.* SCHILL *appears with an old valise in his hand, dressed in a shabby trench coat, his hat on his head. He looks about with a furtive air, walking slowly to the platform. Slowly, as if by chance, the townspeople enter, from all sides.* SCHILL *hesitates, stops.*)

BURGOMASTER. (*From upstage, center.*) Good evening, Schill.

SCHILL. Good evening.

POLICEMAN. Good evening.

SCHILL. Good evening.

PAINTER. (*Enters.*) Good evening.

SCHILL. Good evening.

DOCTOR. Good evening.

SCHILL. Good evening.

BURGOMASTER. So you're taking a little trip?

SCHILL. Yes. A little trip.

POLICEMAN. May one ask where to?

SCHILL. I don't know.

PAINTER. Don't know?

SCHILL. To Kalberstadt.

BURGOMASTER. (*With disbelief, pointing to the valise.*) Kalber-stadt?

SCHILL. After that—somewhere else.

PAINTER. Ah. After that somewhere else.

(*The* FOURTH MAN *walks in.*)

SCHILL. I thought maybe Australia.

BURGOMASTER. Australia!

ALL. Australia!

SCHILL. I'll raise the money somehow.

BURGOMASTER. But why Australia?

POLICEMAN. What would you be doing in Australia?

SCHILL. One can't always live in the same town, year in, year out.

PAINTER. But Australia—

DOCTOR. It's a risky trip for a man of your age.

BURGOMASTER. One of the lady's little men ran off to Australia . . .

ALL. Yes.

POLICEMAN. You'll be much safer here.

PAINTER. Much! (SCHILL *looks about him in anguish, like a beast at bay.*)

SCHILL. (*Low voice.*) I wrote a letter to the administration at Kaffigen.

BURGOMASTER. Yes? And? (*They are all intent on the answer.*)

SCHILL. They didn't answer. (*All laugh.*)

DOCTOR. Do you mean to say you don't trust your old friends? That's not very flattering, you know.

BURGOMASTER. No one's going to do you any harm here.

DOCTOR. No harm here.

SCHILL. They didn't answer because our postmaster held up my letter.

PAINTER. Our postmaster? What an idea.

BURGOMASTER. The postmaster is a member of the town council.

POLICEMAN. A man of the utmost integrity.

DOCTOR. He doesn't hold up letters. What an idea! (*The crossing bell starts ringing.*)

STATION MASTER. (*Announces*) Local to Kalberstadt! (*The townspeople all cross down to see the train arrive. Then they turn, with their backs to the audience, in a line across the stage.* SCHILL *cannot get through to reach the train.*)

SCHILL. (*In a low voice.*) What are you all doing here? What do you want of me?

BURGOMASTER. We don't like to see you go.

DOCTOR. We've come to see you off. (*The sound of the approaching train grows louder.*)

SCHILL. I didn't ask you to come.

POLICEMAN. But we have come.

DOCTOR. As old friends.

ALL. As old friends. (*The* STATION MASTER *holds up his paddle. The train stops with a screech of brakes. We hear the engine panting offstage.*)

VOICE. (*Offstage.*) Güllen!

BURGOMASTER. A pleasant journey.

DOCTOR. And long life!

PAINTER. And good luck in Australia!

ALL. Yes, good luck in Australia. (*They press around him jovially. He stands motionless and pale.*)

SCHILL. Why are you crowding me?

POLICEMAN. What's the matter now? (*The* STATION MASTER *blows a long blast on his whistle.*)

SCHILL. Give me room.

DOCTOR. But you have plenty of room. (*They all move away from him.*)

POLICEMAN. Better get aboard, Schill.

SCHILL. I see. I see. One of you is going to push me under the wheels.

POLICEMAN. Oh, nonsense. Go on, get aboard.

SCHILL. Get away from me, all of you.

BURGOMASTER. I don't know what you want. Just get on the train.

SCHILL. No. One of you will push me under.

DOCTOR. You're being ridiculous. Now, go on, get on the train.

SCHILL. Why are you all so near me?

DOCTOR. The man's gone mad.

STATION MASTER. 'Board! (*He blows his whistle. The engine bell clangs. The train starts.*)

BURGOMASTER. Get aboard, man. Quick. (*The following speeches are spoken all together until the train noises fade away.*)

DOCTOR. The train's starting.

ALL. Get aboard, man. Get aboard. The train's starting.

SCHILL. If I try to get aboard, one of you will hold me back.

ALL. No, no.

BURGOMASTER. Get on the train.

SCHILL. (*In terror, crouches against the wall of the* STATION MASTER'*s office.*) No—no—no. No. (*He falls on his knees. The others crowd around him. He cowers on the ground, abjectly. The train sounds fade away.*) Oh, no—no—don't push me, don't push me!

POLICEMAN. There. It's gone off without you. (*Slowly they leave him. He raises himself up to a sitting position, still trembling. A* TRUCK DRIVER *enters with an empty can.*)

TRUCK DRIVER. Do you know where I can get some water? My truck's boiling over. (SCHILL *points to the station office.*) Thanks. (*He enters the office, gets the water and comes out. By this time,* SCHILL *is erect.*) Missed your train?

SCHILL. Yes.

TRUCK DRIVER. To Kalberstadt?

SCHILL. Yes.

TRUCK DRIVER. Well, come with me. I'm going that way.

SCHILL. This is my town. This is my home. (*With strange new dignity.*) No, thank you. I've changed my mind. I'm staying.

TRUCK DRIVER. (*Shrugs.*) All right.

(*He goes out.* SCHILL *picks up his bag, looks right and left, and slowly walks off.* CURTAIN.)

act three

(Music is heard. Then the curtain rises on the interior of the old barn, a dim, cavernous structure. Bars of light fall across the shadowy forms, shafts of sunlight from the holes and cracks in the walls and roof. Overhead hang old rags, decaying sacks, great cobwebs. Extreme left is a ladder leading to the loft. Near it, an old haycart. Left, CLAIRE ZACHANASSIAN is sitting in her gilded sedan chair, motionless, in her magnificent bridal gown and veil. Near the chair stands an old keg.)

BOBBY. (*Comes in, treading carefully.*) The doctor and the teacher from the high school to see you, madame.

CLAIRE. (*Impassive.*) Show them in. (BOBBY *ushers them in as if they were entering a hall of state. The two grope their way through the litter. At last they find the lady, and bow. They are both well dressed in new clothes, but are very dusty.*)

BOBBY. Dr. Nüsslin and Professor Müller.

DOCTOR. Madame.

CLAIRE. You look dusty, gentlemen.

DOCTOR. (*Dusts himself off vigorously.*) Oh, forgive us. We had to climb over an old carriage.

TEACHER. Our respects.

DOCTOR. A fabulous wedding.

TEACHER. Beautiful occasion.

CLAIRE. It's stifling here. But I love this old barn. The smell of hay and old straw and axle grease—it is the scent of my youth. Sit down. All this rubbish—the haycart, the old carriage, the cask, even the pitchfork—it was all here when I was a girl.

TEACHER. Remarkable place. (*He mops his brow.*)

CLAIRE. I thought the pastor's text was very appropriate. The lesson a trifle long.

TEACHER. I Corinthians 13.

CLAIRE. Your choristers sang beautifully, Professor.

TEACHER. Bach. From the *St. Matthew Passion.*

DOCTOR. Güllen has never seen such magnificence! The flowers! The jewels! And the people.

TEACHER. The theatrical world, the world of finance, the world of art, the world of science . . .

CLAIRE. All these worlds are now back in their Cadillacs, speeding

9

toward the capital for the wedding reception. But I'm sure you didn't come here to talk about them.

DOCTOR. Dear lady, we should not intrude on your valuable time. Your husband must be waiting impatiently.

CLAIRE. No, no, I've packed him off to Brazil.

DOCTOR. To Brazil, madame?

CLAIRE. Yes. For his honeymoon.

TEACHER AND DOCTOR. Oh! But your wedding guests?

CLAIRE. I've planned a delightful dinner for them. They'll never miss me. Now what was it you wished to talk about?

TEACHER. About Anton Schill, madame.

CLAIRE. Is he dead?

TEACHER. Madame, we may be poor. But we have our principles.

CLAIRE. I see. Then what do you want?

TEACHER. (*He mops his brow again.*) The fact is, madame, in anticipation of your well-known munificence, that is, feeling that you would give the town some sort of gift, we have all been buying things. Necessities . . .

DOCTOR. With money we don't have. (*The* TEACHER *blows his nose.*)

CLAIRE. You've run into debt?

DOCTOR. Up to here.

CLAIRE. In spite of your principles?

TEACHER. We're human, madame.

CLAIRE. I see.

TEACHER. We have been poor for a long time. A long, long time.

DOCTOR. (*He rises.*) The question is, how are we going to pay?

CLAIRE. You already know.

TEACHER. (*Courageously.*) I beg you, Madame Zachanassian, put yourself in our position for a moment. For twenty-two years I've been cudgeling my brains to plant a few seeds of knowledge in this wilderness. And all this time, my gallant colleague, Dr. Nüsslin, has been rattling around in his ancient Mercedes, from patient to patient, trying to keep these wretches alive. Why? Why have we spent our lives in this miserable hole? For money? Hardly. The pay is ridiculous.

DOCTOR. And yet, the professor here has declined an offer to head the high school in Kalberstadt.

TEACHER. And Dr. Nüsslin has refused an important post at the

University of Erlangen. Madame, the simple fact is, we love our town. We were born here. It is our life.

DOCTOR. That's true.

TEACHER. What has kept us going all these years is the hope that one day the community will prosper again as it did in the days when we were young.

CLAIRE. Good.

TEACHER. Madame, there is no reason for our poverty. We suffer here from a mysterious blight. We have factories. They stand idle. There is oil in the valley of Pückenried.

DOCTOR. There is copper under the Konradsweil Forest. There is power in our streams, in our waterfalls.

TEACHER. We are not poor, madame. If we had credit, if we had confidence, the factories would open, orders and commissions would pour in. And our economy would bloom together with our cultural life. We would become once again like the towns around us, healthy and prosperous.

DOCTOR. If the Wagonworks were put on its feet again—

TEACHER. The Foundry.

DOCTOR. The Golden Eagle Pencil Factory.

TEACHER. Buy these plants, madame. Put them in operation once more, and I swear to you, Güllen will flourish and it will bless you. We don't need a billion marks. Ten million, properly invested, would give us back our life, and incidentally return to the investor an excellent dividend. Save us, madame. Save us, and we will not only bless you, we will make money for you.

CLAIRE. I don't need money.

DOCTOR. Madame, we are not asking for charity. This is business.

CLAIRE. It's a good idea . . .

DOCTOR. Dear lady! I knew you wouldn't let us down.

CLAIRE. But it's out of the question. I cannot buy the Wagonworks. I already own them.

DOCTOR. The Wagonworks?

TEACHER. And the Foundry?

CLAIRE. And the Foundry.

DOCTOR. And the Golden Eagle Pencil Factory?

CLAIRE. Everything. The valley of Pückenried with its oil, the forest of Konradsweil with its ore, the barn, the town, the streets, the houses, the shops, everything. I had my agents buy up this rubbish over the years, bit by bit, piece by piece, until I had it all. Your hopes were an illusion, your vision empty, your self-sacrifice a stupidity, your whole life completely senseless.

TEACHER. Then the mysterious blight—

CLAIRE. The mysterious blight was I.

DOCTOR. But this is monstrous!

CLAIRE. Monstrous. I was seventeen when I left this town. It was winter. I was dressed in a sailor suit and my red braids hung down my back. I was in my seventh month. As I walked down the street to the station, the boys whistled after me, and someone threw something. I sat freezing in my seat in the Hamburg Express. But before the roof of the great barn was lost behind the trees, I had made up my mind that one day I would come back . . .

TEACHER. But, madame—

CLAIRE. (*She smiles.*) And now I have. (*She claps her hands.*) Mike. Max. Take me back to the Golden Apostle. I've been here long enough. (MIKE *and* MAX *start to pick up the sedan chair. The* TEACHER *pushes* MIKE *away.*)

TEACHER. Madame. One moment. Please. I see it all now. I had thought of you as an avenging fury, a Medea, a Clytemnestra—but I was wrong. You are a warm-hearted woman who has suffered a terrible injustice, and now you have returned and taught us an unforgettable lesson. You have stripped us bare. But now that we stand before you naked, I know you will set aside these thoughts of vengeance. If we made you suffer, you too have put us through the fire. Have mercy, madame.

CLAIRE. When I have had justice. Mike! (*She signals to* MIKE *and* MAX *to pick up the sedan chair. They cross the stage. The* TEACHER *bars the way.*)

TEACHER. But, madame, one injustice cannot cure another. What good will it do to force us into crime? Horror succeeds horror, shame is piled on shame. It settles nothing.

CLAIRE. It settles everything. (*They move upstage toward the exit. The* TEACHER *follows.*)

TEACHER. Madame, this lesson you have taught us will never be forgotten. We will hand it down from father to son. It will be a monument more lasting than any vengeance. Whatever we have been, in the future we shall be better because of you. You have pushed us to the extreme. Now forgive us. Show us the way to a better life. Have pity, madame—pity. That is the highest justice. (*The sedan chair stops.*)

CLAIRE. The highest justice has no pity. It is bright and pure and clear. The world made me into a whore; now I make the world into a brothel. Those who wish to go down, may go down. Those who wish to dance with me, may dance with me. (*To her porters*) Go.

(*She is carried off.*)

(*The lights black out. Downstage, right, appears* SCHILL's *shop. It has a new sign, a new counter. The doorbell, when it rings, has an impressive sound.* FRAU SCHILL *stands behind the counter in a new dress. The* FIRST MAN *enters, left. He is dressed as a prosperous butcher, a few blood stains on his snowy apron, a gold watch chain across his open vest.*)

FIRST MAN. What a wedding! I'll swear the whole town was there. Cigarettes.

FRAU SCHILL. Clara is entitled to a little happiness after all. I'm happy for her. Green or white?

FIRST MAN. Turkish. The bridesmaids! Dancers and opera singers. And the dresses! Down to here.

FRAU SCHILL. It's the fashion nowadays.

FIRST MAN. Reporters! Photographers! From all over the world! (*In a low voice.*) They will be here any minute.

FRAU SCHILL. What have reporters to do with us? We are simple people, Herr Hofbauer. There is nothing for them here.

FIRST MAN. They're questioning everybody. They're asking everything. (*The* FIRST MAN *lights a cigarette. He looks up at the ceiling.*) Footsteps.

FRAU SCHILL. He's pacing the room. Up and down. Day and night.

FIRST MAN. Haven't seen him all week.

FRAU SCHILL. He never goes out.

FIRST MAN. It's his conscience. That was pretty mean, the way he treated poor Madame Zachanassian.

FRAU SCHILL. That's true. I feel very badly about it myself.

FIRST MAN. To ruin a young girl like that—God doesn't forgive it. (FRAU SCHILL *nods solemnly with pursed lips. The butcher gives her a level glance.*) Look, I hope he'll have sense enough to keep his mouth shut in front of the reporters.

FRAU SCHILL. I certainly hope so.

FIRST MAN. You know his character.

FRAU SCHILL. Only too well, Herr Hofbauer.

FIRST MAN. If he tries to throw dirt at our Clara and tell a lot of lies, how she tried to get us to kill him, which anyway she never meant—

FRAU SCHILL. Of course not.

FIRST MAN. —Then we'll really have to do something! And not because of the money—(*He spits.*) But out of ordinary human decency. God knows Madame Zachanassian has suffered enough through him already.

FRAU SCHILL. She has indeed.

(*The* TEACHER *comes in. He is not quite sober.*)

TEACHER. (*Looks about the shop.*) Has the press been here yet?

FIRST MAN. No.

TEACHER. It's not my custom, as you know, Frau Schill—but I wonder if I could have a strong alcoholic drink?

FRAU SCHILL. It's an honor to serve you. Herr Professor. I have a good Steinhäger. Would you like to try a glass?

TEACHER. A very small glass. (FRAU SCHILL *serves bottle and glass. The* TEACHER *tosses off a glass.*)

FRAU SCHILL. Your hand is shaking, Herr Professor.

TEACHER. To tell the truth, I have been drinking a little already.

FRAU SCHILL. Have another glass. It will do you good. (*He accepts another glass.*)

TEACHER. Is that he up there, walking?

FRAU SCHILL. Up and down. Up and down.

FIRST MAN. It's God punishing him.

(*The* PAINTER *comes in with the* SON *and the* DAUGHTER.)

PAINTER. Careful! A reporter just asked us the way to this shop.

FIRST MAN. I hope you didn't tell him.

PAINTER. I told him we were strangers here. (*They all laugh. The door opens. The* SECOND MAN *darts into the shop.*)

SECOND MAN. Look out, everybody! The press! They are across the street in your shop, Hofbauer.

FIRST MAN. My boy will know how to deal with them.

SECOND MAN. Make sure Schill doesn't come down, Hofbauer.

FIRST MAN. Leave that to me. (*They group themselves about the shop.*)

TEACHER. Listen to me, all of you. When the reporters come I'm

going to speak to them. I'm going to make a statement. A statement
to the world on behalf of myself as Rector of Güllen High School
and on behalf of you all, for all your sakes.

PAINTER. What are you going to say?

TEACHER. I shall tell the truth about Claire Zachanassian.

FRAU SCHILL. You're drunk, Herr Professor; you should be
ashamed of yourself.

TEACHER. I should be ashamed? You should all be ashamed!

SON. Shut your trap. You're drunk.

DAUGHTER. Please, Professor—

TEACHER. Girl, you disappoint me. It is your place to speak. But
you are silent and you force your old teacher to raise his voice. I am
going to speak the truth. It is my duty and I am not afraid. The
world may not wish to listen, but no one can silence me. I'm not
going to wait—I'm going over to Hofbauer's shop now.

ALL. No, you're not. Stop him. Stop him. (*They all spring at the*
TEACHER. *He defends himself. At this moment,* SCHILL *appears
through the door upstage. In contrast to the others, he is dressed
shabbily in an old black jacket, his best.*)

SCHILL. What's going on in my shop? (*The townsmen let go of
the* TEACHER *and turn to stare at* SCHILL.) What's the trouble, Professor?

TEACHER. Schill, I am speaking out at last! I am going to tell the
press everything.

SCHILL. Be quiet, Professor.

TEACHER. What did you say?

SCHILL. Be quiet.

TEACHER. You want me to be quiet?

SCHILL. Please.

TEACHER. But, Schill, if I keep quiet, if you miss this opportunity
—they're over in Hofbauer's shop now . . .

SCHILL. Please.

TEACHER. As you wish. If you too are on their side, I have no
more to say.

(*The doorbell jingles. A* REPORTER *comes in.*)

REPORTER. Is Anton Schill here? (*Moves to* SCHILL) Are you
Herr Schill?

SCHILL. What?

REPORTER. Herr Schill.

SCHILL. Er—no. Herr Schill's gone to Kalberstadt for the day.

REPORTER. Oh, thank you. Good day.

(*He goes out.*)

PAINTER. (*Mops his brow.*) Whew! Close shave.

(*He follows the* REPORTER *out.*)

SECOND MAN. (*Walking up to* SCHILL.) That was pretty smart of you to keep your mouth shut. You know what to expect if you don't.

(*He goes.*)

FIRST MAN. Give me a Havana. (SCHILL *serves him.*) Charge it. You bastard!

(*He goes.* SCHILL *opens his account book.*)

FRAU SCHILL. Come along, children—

(FRAU SCHILL, *the* SON *and the* DAUGHTER *go off, upstage.*)

TEACHER. They're going to kill you. I've known it all along, and you too, you must have known it. The need is too strong, the temptation too great. And now perhaps I too will join against you. I belong to them and, like them, I can feel myself hardening into something that is not human—not beautiful.

SCHILL. It can't be helped.

TEACHER. Pull yourself together, man. Speak to the reporters; you've no time to lose. (SCHILL *looks up from his account book.*)

SCHILL. No. I'm not going to fight any more.

TEACHER. Are you so frightened that you don't dare open your mouth?

SCHILL. I made Claire what she is, I made myself what I am. What should I do? Should I pretend that I'm innocent?

TEACHER. No, you can't. You are as guilty as hell.

SCHILL. Yes.

TEACHER. You are a bastard.

SCHILL. Yes.

TEACHER. But that does not justify your murder. (SCHILL *looks at him.*) I wish I could believe that for what they're doing—for what they're going to do—they will suffer for the rest of their lives. But it's not true. In a little while they will have justified everything and forgotten everything.

SCHILL. Of course.

TEACHER. Your name will never again be mentioned in this town. That's how it will be.

SCHILL. I don't hold it against you.

TEACHER. But I do. I will hold it against myself all my life. That's why—(*The doorbell jingles. The* BURGOMASTER *comes in. The* TEACHER *stares at him, then goes out without another word.*)

BURGOMASTER. Good afternoon, Schill. Don't let me disturb you. I've just dropped in for a moment.

SCHILL. I'm just finishing my accounts for the week. (*A moment's pause.*)

BURGOMASTER. The town council meets tonight. At the Golden Apostle. In the auditorium.

SCHILL. I'll be there.

BURGOMASTER. The whole town will be there. Your case will be discussed and final action taken. You've put us in a pretty tight spot, you know.

SCHILL. Yes. I'm sorry.

BURGOMASTER. The lady's offer will be rejected.

SCHILL. Possibly.

BURGOMASTER. Of course, I may be wrong.

SCHILL. Of course.

BURGOMASTER. In that case—are you prepared to accept the judgment of the town? The meeting will be covered by the press, you know.

SCHILL. By the press?

BURGOMASTER. Yes, and the radio and the newsreel. It's a very ticklish situation. Not only for you—believe me, it's even worse for us. What with the wedding, and all the publicity, we've become famous. All of a sudden our ancient democratic institutions have become of interest to the world.

SCHILL. Are you going to make the lady's condition public?

BURGOMASTER. No, no, of course not. Not directly. We will have to put the matter to a vote—that is unavoidable. But only those involved will understand.

SCHILL. I see.

BURGOMASTER. As far as the press is concerned, you are simply the intermediary between us and Madame Zachanassian. I have whitewashed you completely.

SCHILL. That is very generous of you.

BURGOMASTER. Frankly, it's not for your sake, but for the sake of your family. They are honest and decent people.

SCHILL. Oh—

BURGOMASTER. So far we've all played fair. You've kept your mouth shut and so have we. Now can we continue to depend on you? Because if you have any idea of opening your mouth at tonight's meeting, there won't be any meeting.

SCHILL. I'm glad to hear an open threat at last.

BURGOMASTER. We are not threatening you. You are threatening us. If you speak, you force us to act—in advance.

SCHILL. That won't be necessary.

BURGOMASTER. So if the town decides against you?

SCHILL. I will accept their decision.

BURGOMASTER. Good. (*A moment's pause.*) I'm delighted to see there is still a spark of decency left in you. But—wouldn't it be better if we didn't have to call a meeting at all? (*He pauses. He takes a gun from his pocket and puts it on the counter.*) I've brought you this.

SCHILL. Thank you.

BURGOMASTER. It's loaded.

SCHILL. I don't need a gun.

BURGOMASTER. (*He clears his throat.*) You see? We could tell the lady that we had condemned you in secret session and you had anticipated our decision. I've lost a lot of sleep getting to this point, believe me.

SCHILL. I believe you.

BURGOMASTER. Frankly, in your place, I myself would prefer to take the path of honor. Get it over with, once and for all. Don't you agree? For the sake of your friends! For the sake of our children, your own children—you have a daughter, a son—Schill, you know our need, our misery.

SCHILL. You've put me through hell, you and your town. You were my friends, you smiled and reassured me. But day by day I saw you change—your shoes, your ties, your suits—your hearts. If you had been honest with me then, perhaps I would feel differently toward you now. I might even use that gun you brought me. For the sake of my friends. But now I have conquered my fear. Alone. It was hard, but it's done. And now you will have to judge me. And I will accept your judgment. For me that will be justice. How it will be for you, I don't know. (*He turns away.*) You may kill me if you like. I won't complain. I won't protest, I won't defend myself. But I won't do your job for you either.

BURGOMASTER. (*Takes up his gun.*) There it is. You've had your chance and you won't take it. Too bad. (*He takes out a cigarette.*) I suppose it's more than we can expect of a man like you. (SCHILL *lights the* BURGOMASTER's *cigarette.*) Good day.

SCHILL. Good day. (*The* BURGOMASTER *goes.* FRAU SCHILL *comes in, dressed in a fur coat. The* DAUGHTER *is in a new red dress. The* SON *has a new sports jacket.*) What a beautiful coat, Mathilde!

FRAU SCHILL. Real fur. You like it?

SCHILL. Should I? What a lovely dress, Ottilie!

DAUGHTER. *C'est très chic, n'est-ce-pas?*

SCHILL. What?

FRAU SCHILL. Ottilie is taking a course in French.

SCHILL. Very useful. Karl—whose automobile is that out there at the curb?

SON. Oh, it's only an Opel. They're not expensive.

SCHILL. You bought yourself a car?

SON. On credit. Easiest thing in the world.

FRAU SCHILL. Everyone's buying on credit now, Anton. These fears of yours are ridiculous. You'll see. Clara has a good heart. She only means to teach you a lesson.

DAUGHTER. She means to teach you a lesson, that's all.

SON. It's high time you got the point, Father.

SCHILL. I get the point. (*The church bells start ringing.*) Listen. The bells of Güllen. Do you hear?

SON. Yes, we have four bells now. It sounds quite good.

DAUGHTER. Just like Gray's Elegy.

SCHILL. What?

FRAU SCHILL. Ottilie is taking a course in English literature.

SCHILL. Congratulations! It's Sunday. I should very much like to take a ride in your car. Our car.

SON. You want to ride in the car?

SCHILL. Why not? I want to ride through the Konradsweil Forest. I want to see the town where I've lived all my life.

FRAU SCHILL. I don't think that will look very nice for any of us.

SCHILL. No—perhaps not. Well, I'll go for a walk by myself.

FRAU SCHILL. Then take us to Kalberstadt, Karl, and we'll go to a cinema.

SCHILL. A cinema? It's a good idea.

FRAU SCHILL. See you soon, Anton.

SCHILL. Good-bye, Ottilie. Good-bye, Karl. Good-bye, Mathilde.

FAMILY. Good-bye.

(*They go out.*)

SCHILL. Good-bye. (*The shop sign flies off. The lights black out. They come up at once on the forest scene.*) Autumn. Even the forest has turned to gold. (SCHILL *wanders down to the bench in the forest. He sits.* CLAIRE's *voice is heard.*)

CLAIRE. (*Offstage.*) Stop. Wait here. (CLAIRE *comes in. She gazes slowly up at the trees, kicks at some leaves. Then she walks slowly down center. She stops before a tree, glances up the trunk.*) Bark-borers. The old tree is dying. (*She catches sight of* SCHILL.)

SCHILL. Clara.

CLAIRE. How pleasant to see you here. I was visiting my forest. May I sit by you?

SCHILL. Oh, yes. Please do. (*She sits next to him.*) I've just been saying good-bye to my family. They've gone to the cinema. Karl has bought himself a car.

CLAIRE. How nice.

SCHILL. Ottilie is taking French lessons. And a course in English literature.

CLAIRE. You see? They're beginning to take an interest in higher things.

SCHILL. Listen. A finch. You hear?

CLAIRE. Yes. It's a finch. And a cuckoo in the distance. Would you like some music?

SCHILL. Oh, yes. That would be very nice.

CLAIRE. Anything special?

SCHILL. "Deep in the Forest."

CLAIRE. Your favorite song. They know it. (*She raises her hand. Offstage, the mandolin and guitar play the tune softly.*)

SCHILL. We had a child?

CLAIRE. Yes.

SCHILL. Boy or girl?

CLAIRE. Girl.

SCHILL. What name did you give her?

CLAIRE. I called her Genevieve.

SCHILL. That's a very pretty name.

CLAIRE. Yes.

SCHILL. What was she like?

CLAIRE. I saw her only once. When she was born. Then they took her away from me.

SCHILL. Her eyes?

CLAIRE. They weren't open yet.

SCHILL. And her hair?

CLAIRE. Black, I think. It's usually black at first.

SCHILL. Yes, of course. Where did she die, Clara?

CLAIRE. In some family. I've forgotten their name. Meningitis, they said. The officials wrote me a letter.

SCHILL. Oh, I'm so very sorry, Clara.

CLAIRE. I've told you about our child. Now tell me about myself.

SCHILL. About yourself?

CLAIRE. Yes. How I was when I was seventeen in the days when you loved me.

SCHILL. I remember one day you waited for me in the great barn. I had to look all over the place for you. At last I found you lying in the haycart with nothing on and a long straw between your lips . . .

CLAIRE. Yes. I was pretty in those days.

SCHILL. You were beautiful, Clara.

CLAIRE. You were strong. The time you fought with those two railway men who were following me, I wiped the blood from your face with my red petticoat. (*The music ends.*) They've stopped.

SCHILL. Tell them to play "Thoughts of Home."

CLAIRE. They know that too. (*The music plays.*)

SCHILL. Here we are, Clara, sitting together in our forest for the last time. The town council meets tonight. They will condemn me to death, and one of them will kill me. I don't know who and I don't know where. Clara, I only know that in a little while a useless life will come to an end. (*He bows his head on her bosom. She takes him in her arms.*)

CLAIRE. (*Tenderly.*) I shall take you in your coffin to Capri. You will have your tomb in the park of my villa, where I can see you from my bedroom window. White marble and onyx in a grove of green cypress. With a beautiful view of the Mediterranean.

SCHILL. I've always wanted to see it.

CLAIRE. Your love for me died years ago, Anton. But my love for you would not die. It turned into something strong, like the hidden

roots of the forest; something evil, like white mushrooms that grow
unseen in the darkness. And slowly it reached out for your life.
Now I have you. You are mine. Alone. At last, and forever, a peaceful ghost in a silent house. (*The music ends.*)

SCHILL. The song is over.

CLAIRE. Adieu, Anton. (CLAIRE *kisses* ANTON, *a long kiss. Then
she rises.*)

SCHILL. Adieu.

(*She goes.* SCHILL *remains sitting on the bench. A row of lamps
descends from the flies. The townsmen come in from both sides,
each bearing his chair. A table and chairs are set upstage, center.
On both sides sits the townsmen. The* POLICEMAN, *in a new uniform, sits on the bench behind* SCHILL. *All the townsmen are in
new Sunday clothes. Around them are technicians of all sorts, with
lights, cameras and other equipment. The townswomen are absent.
They do not vote. The* BURGOMASTER *takes his place at the table,
center. The* DOCTOR *and the* PASTOR *sit at the same table, at his
right, and the* TEACHER *in his academic gown, at his left.*)

BURGOMASTER. (*At a sign from the radio technician, he pounds
the floor with his wand of office.*) Fellow citizens of Güllen, I call
this meeting to order. The agenda: there is only one matter before
us. I have the honor to announce officially that Madame Claire
Zachanassian, daughter of our beloved citizen, the famous architect
Siegfried Wäscher, has decided to make a gift to the town of one
billion marks. Five hundred million to the town, five hundred million to be divided per capita among the citizens. After certain
necessary preliminaries, a vote will be taken, and you, as citizens of
Güllen, will signify your will by a show of hands. Has anyone any
objection to this mode of procedure? The pastor? (*Silence.*) The
police? (*Silence.*) The town health official? (*Silence.*) The Rector
of Güllen High School? (*Silence.*) The political opposition? (*Silence.*) I shall then proceed to the vote—(*The* TEACHER *rises. The*
BURGOMASTER *turns in surprise and irritation.*) You wish to speak?

TEACHER. Yes.

BURGOMASTER. Very well. (*He takes his seat. The* TEACHER *advances. The movie camera starts running.*)

TEACHER. Fellow townsmen. (*The photographer flashes a bulb in
his face.*) Fellow townsmen. We all know that by means of this gift,

Madame Claire Zachanassian intends to attain a certain object. What is this object? To enrich the town of her youth, yes. But more than that, she desires by means of this gift to re-establish justice among us. This desire expressed by our benefactress raises an all-important question. Is it true that our community harbors in its soul such a burden of guilt?

BURGOMASTER. Yes! True!

SECOND MAN. Crimes are concealed among us.

THIRD MAN. (*He jumps up.*) Sins!

FOURTH MAN. (*He jumps up also.*) Perjuries.

PAINTER. Justice!

TOWNSMEN. Justice! Justice!

TEACHER. Citizens of Güllen, this, then, is the simple fact of the case. We have participated in an injustice. I thoroughly recognize the material advantages which this gift opens to us—I do not overlook the fact that it is poverty which is the root of all this bitterness and evil. Nevertheless, there is no question here of money.

TOWNSMEN. No! No!

TEACHER. Here there is no question of our prosperity as a community, or our well-being as individuals—The question is—must be—whether or not we wish to live according to the principles of justice, those principles for which our forefathers lived and fought and for which they died, those principles which form the soul of our Western culture.

TOWNSMEN. Hear! Hear! (*Applause.*)

TEACHER. (*Desperately, realizing that he is fighting a losing battle, and on the verge of hysteria.*) Wealth has meaning only when benevolence comes of it, but only he who hungers for grace will receive grace. Do you feel this hunger, my fellow citizens, this hunger of the spirit, or do you feel only that other profane hunger, the hunger of the body? That is the question which I, as Rector of your high school, now propound to you. Only if you can no longer tolerate the presence of evil among you, only if you can in no circumstances endure a world in which injustice exists, are you worthy to receive Madame Zachanassian's billion and fulfill the condition bound up with this gift. If not—(*Wild applause. He gestures desperately for silence.*) If not, then God have mercy on us! (*The townsmen crowd around him, ambiguously, in a mood somewhat between threat and congratulation. He takes his seat, utterly crushed, exhausted by his effort. The* BURGOMASTER *advances and takes charge once again. Order is restored.*)

BURGOMASTER. Anton Schill—(*The* POLICEMAN *gives* SCHILL *a shove.* SCHILL *gets up.*) Anton Schill, it is through you that this gift is offered to the town. Are you willing that this offer should be accepted? (SCHILL *mumbles something.*)

RADIO REPORTER. (*Steps to his side.*) You'll have to speak up a little, Herr Schill.

SCHILL. Yes.

BURGOMASTER. Will you respect our decision in the matter before us?

SCHILL. I will respect your decision.

BURGOMASTER. Then I proceed to the vote. All those who are in accord with the terms on which this gift is offered will signify the same by raising their right hands. (*After a moment, the* POLICEMAN *raises his hand. Then one by one the others. Last of all, very slowly, the* TEACHER) All against? The offer is accepted. I now solemnly call upon you, fellow townsmen, to declare in the face of all the world that you take this action, not out of love for worldly gain . . .

TOWNSMEN. (*In chorus.*) Not out of love for worldly gain . . .

BURGOMASTER. But out of love for the right.

TOWNSMEN. But out of love for the right.

BURGOMASTER. (*Holds up his hand, as if taking an oath.*) We join together, now, as brothers . . .

TOWNSMEN. (*Hold up their hands.*) We join together, now, as brothers . . .

BURGOMASTER. To purify our town of guilt . . .

TOWNSMEN. To purify our town of guilt . . .

BURGOMASTER. And to reaffirm our faith . . .

TOWNSMEN. And to reaffirm our faith . . .

BURGOMASTER. In the eternal power of justice.

TOWNSMEN. In the eternal power of justice. (*The lights go off suddenly.*)

SCHILL. (*A scream*) Oh, God!

VOICE. I'm sorry, Herr Burgomaster. We seem to have blown a fuse. (*The lights go on.*) Ah—there we are. Would you mind doing that last bit again?

BURGOMASTER. Again?

THE CAMERAMAN. (*Walks forward.*) Yes, for the newsreel.

BURGOMASTER. Oh, the newsreel. Certainly.

THE CAMERAMAN. Ready now? Right.

BURGOMASTER. And to reaffirm our faith . . .

TOWNSMEN. And to reaffirm our faith . . .

BURGOMASTER. In the eternal power of justice.

TOWNSMEN. In the eternal power of justice.

THE CAMERAMAN. (*To his assistant.*) It was better before, when he screamed "Oh, God." (*The assistant shrugs.*)

BURGOMASTER. Fellow citizens of Güllen, I declare this meeting adjourned. The ladies and gentlemen of the press will find refreshments served downstairs, with the compliments of the town council. The exits lead directly to the restaurant.

THE CAMERAMAN. Thank you. (*The newsmen go off with alacrity. The townsmen remain on the stage.* SCHILL *gets up.*)

POLICEMAN. (*Pushes* SCHILL *down.*) Sit down.

SCHILL. Is it to be now?

POLICEMAN. Naturally, now.

SCHILL. I thought it might be best to have it at my house.

POLICEMAN. It will be here.

BURGOMASTER. Lower the lights. (*The lights dim.*) Are they all gone?

VOICE. All gone.

BURGOMASTER. The gallery?

SECOND VOICE. Empty.

BURGOMASTER. Lock the doors.

THE VOICE. Locked here.

SECOND VOICE. Locked here.

BURGOMASTER. Form a lane. (*The men form a lane. At the end stands the* ATHLETE *in elegant white slacks, a red scarf around his singlet.*) Pastor. Will you be so good? (*The* PASTOR *walks slowly to* SCHILL.)

PASTOR. Anton Schill, your heavy hour has come.

SCHILL. May I have a cigarette?

PASTOR. Cigarette, Burgomaster.

BURGOMASTER. Of course. With pleasure. And a good one. (*He gives his case to the* PASTOR, *who offers it to* SCHILL. *The* POLICEMAN *lights the cigarette. The* PASTOR *returns the case.*)

PASTOR. In the words of the prophet Amos—

SCHILL. Please—(*He shakes his head.*)

PASTOR. You're no longer afraid?

SCHILL. No. I'm not afraid.

PASTOR. I will pray for you.

SCHILL. Pray for us all. (*The* PASTOR *bows his head.*)

BURGOMASTER. Anton Schill, stand up! (SCHILL *hesitates.*)

POLICEMAN. Stand up, you swine!

BURGOMASTER. Schultz, please.

POLICEMAN. I'm sorry. I was carried away. (SCHILL *gives the cigarette to the* POLICEMAN. *Then he walks slowly to the center of the stage and turns his back on the audience.*) Enter the lane.

(SCHILL *hesitates a moment. He goes slowly into the lane of silent men. The* ATHLETE *stares at him from the opposite end.* SCHILL *looks in turn at the hard faces of those who surround him, and sinks slowly to his knees. The lane contracts silently into a knot as the men close in and crouch over. Complete silence. The knot of men pulls back slowly, coming downstage. Then it opens. Only the* DOCTOR *is left in the center of the stage, kneeling by the corpse, over which the* TEACHER's *gown has been spread. The* DOCTOR *rises and takes off his stethoscope.*)

PASTOR. Is it all over?

DOCTOR. Heart failure.

BURGOMASTER. Died of joy.

ALL. Died of joy.

(*The townsmen turn their backs on the corpse and at once light cigarettes. A cloud of smoke rises over them. From the left comes* CLAIRE ZACHANASSIAN, *dressed in black, followed by* BOBBY. *She sees the corpse. Then she walks slowly to center stage and looks down at the body of* SCHILL.)

CLAIRE. Uncover him. (BOBBY *uncovers* SCHILL's *face. She stares at it a long moment. She sighs.*) Cover his face.

(BOBBY *covers it.* CLAIRE *goes out, up center.* BOBBY *takes the check from his wallet, holds it out peremptorily to the* BURGO-MASTER, *who walks over from the knot of silent men. He holds out his hand for the check. The lights fade. At once the warning bell is heard, and the scene dissolves into the setting of the railway station. The gradual transformation of the shabby town into a thing of elegance and beauty is now accomplished. The railway station glitters with neon lights and is surrounded with garlands, bright posters and flags. The townsfolk, men and women, now in brand new clothes, form themselves into a group in front of the station. The sound of the approaching train grows louder. The train stops.)*

STATION MASTER. Güllen-Rome Express. All aboard, please.

(The church bells start pealing. Men appear with trunks and boxes, a procession which duplicates that of the lady's arrival, but in inverse order. Then come the TWO BLIND MEN, then BOBBY, and MIKE and MAX carrying the coffin. Lastly CLAIRE. She is dressed in modish black. Her head is high, her face as impassive as that of an ancient idol. The procession crosses the stage and goes off. The people bow in silence as the coffin passes. When CLAIRE and her retinue have boarded the train, the STATION MASTER blows a long blast.)

'Bo—ard!

(He holds up his paddle. The train starts and moves off slowly, picking up speed. The crowd turns slowly, gazing after the departing train in complete silence. The train sounds fade. The curtain falls slowly.)

DÜRRENMATT'S *THE VISIT* AND *JOB*

The two principal characters in Dürrenmatt's *The Visit,* the vengeful old lady Claire Zachanassian and her victim Schill, are archetypical.* Reference to the names themselves, to clues in the text and to interpretations of the play by literary critics readily establishes that Dürrenmatt intended more than a realistic exposé of the havoc wrought in a middle-class community by the visitation of greed in the person of the richest woman in the world. She is less a character than a symbol, deliberately depersonalized by Dürrenmatt, who stresses the various prostheses she has undergone and, further to emphasize her unreality, uses the stage directions, which describe her climactically as an idol made of stone. As an agent (goddess, perhaps, with a Greek name) of the incomprehensible and, therefore, seemingly arbitrary forces which rule the lives of men, she appears in order to force them to acknowledge their guilt, their subservience to a divinity, ineffable and absurd. The object at which this bolt from the blue is hurled is Schill (cf. Fr. *il*), the complete bourgeoise, secure is his conviction that the walls of convention, the bastion of rationality and self-justification, cannot be breached. The pattern for this encounter between the inexplicable and the man called upon to admit it into his life has been set by the confrontation between God and Job. *The Visit* becomes in its second half a search for the resolution of the problem of man's acceptance of his fate: his finiteness in the face of the infinite, his sinfulness in the face of God's goodness. As Job solves the dilemma by submission to it, just by taking on the burden of not knowing, so Schill bows to the inevitable, the death sentence proclaimed by the omnipotent visitor at the Golden Apostle (St. Michael with the sword of justice), who is, indeed, also his first love Klara Wäscher, *clear washer,* and carried out by the people of his hometown in a final scene which is more ritualistic and abstract than violent and real. With Schill's yielding to the arbitrariness of death (and his brave dying) Claire and Schill are reconciled, as are God and Job. The unmistakable ambiguity which

* Abstracted from Kurt J. Fickert, "Dürrenmatt's *The Visit* and *Job*," *Books Abroad,* XLI (1967), 389-392.

hovers over any attempt to come to terms with the random destruction of the individual prevails in *The Visit*, as it does in at least two other literary works which have the theme of man summarily struck down by the blows of fate: MacLeish's *J.B.* and Shirley Jackson's "The Lottery." Perhaps the basic situation—the confrontation of man by God—precludes a pat denouement.

DÜRRENMATT'S *THE VISIT OF THE OLD LADY*

Dürrenmatt's *Der Besuch* gains its profound effects through ritualizing contemporary values and then presenting their subsequent breakdown within the framework of an ambiguous moral construct.* Durrenmatt ritualizes his play by directly relating it to a classical plot, Sophocles' *Oedipus Rex*. *Oedipus Rex* concerns the relationship between an ambitious, guilty, fear-ridden character, Oedipus, and the authority figure for Oedipus' cultural milieu, the Sphinx. Operating as a Sphinx symbol, Madame Zachanassian, as the dominating figure in *Der Besuch*, brings about the breakdown of traditional values on four major thematic levels: psychological, economic, political, and religious. Anton Schill is directly comparable to Oedipus, and Schill's ambition, guilt, and castration fears constitute the integral elements of the psychological theme. Oedipus' rise to command of the kingdom is paralleled by Anton Schill's designs on mayorship as the political theme. As the Sphinx directly influenced the economic and social development of Thebes, so too has Madame Zachanassian brought about the plight of the Gülleners. The ritualized downfall of Anton Schill, in fulfillment of the riddle, occurs not only through formally stylized actions but also through propriety of language. As ritualistic as Greek tragedy, action, style, language, and characterization convey the themes of *Der Besuch* while providing human values with a secure embodiment within the ritual construct. The impact of the play develops when traditional values and traditional gods are, within the secure ritual framework, replaced by materialism and a

* Abstracted from Melvin W. Askew, "Dürrenmatt's *The Visit of the Old Lady*," *Tulane Drama Review*, V (1961), 89-105.

vengeance-filled female billionaire. A new myth of Nature, a new
world view, established through Madame Zachanassian's financial
power, replaces traditional natural laws with the equation of profit
motivation and attendant technology. The fear, flight, and fate which
Anton Schill experiences become, therefore, the breakdown of humanity's traditional ideals. The religious level of the theme finds expression through the dissolution of dependence on God, replaced by
dependence on Madame Zachanassian as Providence since she pays
off, and through the dissolution of marriage as brought about by the
fear of castration. Accompanied by a coffin for the yet-living Schill, a
black panther, and two eunuchs, Madame Zachanassian's wealth challenges and subsequently defeats Anton as Everyman. The humanness
of humanity thus becomes castrated by money and its functions, and
the institutions developed as safe-guards for traditional human values
suffer a similar destruction. Since the play follows the classical pattern of a tragedy, the structure further adds to the ritualization of the
play. Anton Schill is reduced to the level of a purchasable item with a
billion dollar price tag, yet this dehumanization is of his own doing,
and he realizes it. As Everyman, Schill created that very system of
values which ultimately destroys him. True to the Aristotelian concept of tragedy, Schill's downfall arises from a tragic flaw, a weakness
within himself. The monetary system, arbitrarily created by man,
grown to uncontrollable proportions, subsequently strangles its
creator while reducing him to the level of another commodity. Thus
Der Besuch, while remaining within a ritualized framework of both
form and content, presents the ultimate decay of traditional values
and the subsequent rise of the monetary system as the new myth of
Nature.

JUSTICE IN THE WORKS OF
F. DÜRRENMATT

The works of the Swiss writer, Friedrich Dürrenmatt, one of the
most exciting and most important authors writing in Germany
today, present a panoramic vision of the world that is highly com-

plex, richly imaginative, and initially quite bewildering.* Part of the confusion surrounding him and his works results from his passion for experimenting with literary techniques and styles in a wide variety of forms: prose sketch, detective novel, comic novel, grotesque comic drama, radio play, literary essay, film scenario, and finally even opera. A methodical analysis of his writings, however, reveals that regardless of form, subject matter, or style, Dürrenmatt is primarily concerned with the problem of justice, which forms the most significant thematic unity of his works. Almost every plot is constructed of the triumvirate sinner, judge, and hangman and generally follows the progression: worldly injustice, acceptance of the principle of Divine justice, and hope for Divine grace. An understanding of Dürrenmatt's view of justice not only makes clear the interlocking nature of his works but also the larger rationale in which they operate in terms of his concept of the world. The matter of *Weltanschauung* is particularly important here, for it becomes ultimately the factor which determines form. Because Dürrenmatt conceives the world as a chaotic, unheroic, collective society, and devoid of individual responsibility and individual guilt, he believes that tragedy is no longer possible and that comedy is the only adequate means to portray contemporary life. Essentially, Dürrenmatt's works reflect his concern for society and for mankind, and represent his efforts to explore how justice can and does function in the dehumanizing modern context of computerized technology, big business, and tyrannical governments. Most often he shows that justice among men is virtually impossible. No matter how men strive to create a just society, their efforts are always defeated. Only the executioner remains a permanent entity in every system of human justice. In Dürrenmatt's new writings the confrontation of the individual with his executioner becomes a recurring archetypal situation. Nevertheless, Dürrenmatt rejects both despair and withdrawal from life as solutions to the problems of living. Life must be accepted as it is, enigmatic, threatening, and mysterious, and there must be no surrender. Don Quixote is Dürrenmatt's most frequently used symbol, and represents his view of the only attitude that man can take in life. Although one can never win in the unequal struggle, one must always strive for justice in God's name. Thus, by penetrating

* Abstracted from Donald G. Daviau, "Justice in the Works of F. Dürrenmatt," *Kentucky Foreign Language Quarterly,* IX (1962), 181-193.

the obscuring façade of Dürrenmatt's dazzling theatrical and prose techniques, which he utilizes to convey the complexity of the world, his works stand revealed as consistent expressions of moral, Christian, almost self-evident truths.

THE DIVINE PLAN BEHIND THE PLAYS OF FRIEDRICH DÜRRENMATT

Dürrenmatt is a religious thinker with a consistent Protestant orientation, and his basic dramatic theme is the proper relationship between three factors: (1) an absolute God; (2) a totally dependent individual; and (3) a chaotic world.* Dürrenmatt's heroes go from worldly chaos to awareness of their helplessness as individuals to faith in God. This change has been observed and commented on very ably by various critics. What has not been observed is that Dürrenmatt's dramatic production, as a whole, has gone in just the opposite direction; that is, from God to the aware individual to worldly chaos. To be sure, these three facets are present to some degree in every play; however, a definite pattern of emphasis does exist among them in the course of Dürrenmatt's dramatic production. Three different facets of the same central philosophy are highlighted over the years in a distinct chronological sequence. Thus the plays fall into three different units. The first two plays, *Es steht geschrieben* (1946) and *Der Blinde* (1947) are viewed as Christian tragedies in which the way of the individual to God is emphasized. They are both set in religious wars, their main inspiration is the Bible, and their primary action is the painful but triumphant way of the protagonist to God. The final scenes celebrate the victory of the protagonist over the chaos of the world and his enduring faith in God. The protagonists of the next three plays— *Romulus der Grosse* (1948 and 1956), *Die Ehe des Herrn Missis-*

* Abstracted from Robert Holzapfel, "The Divine Plan Behind the Plays of Friedrich Dürrenmatt," *Modern Drama*, XIII (1965), 236-246.

sippi (1950) and *Ein Engel kommt nach Babylon* (1953)—are no longer primarily interested in finding God, but in behaving courageously in the face of the chaos of the world and their own helplessness. At the end of these plays, we see them bravely but humbly maintaining a *modus vivendi* with the world. In the last group of three plays—*Der Besuch der alten Dame* (1955), *Frank der Funfte* (1958 and 1964), and *Die Physiker* (1962)—the chaotic nature of the world, which had always been present in the earlier dramas in subordinate role, is now stressed. The individual, although still capable of a proper relationship to God and the world, is shown as helpless in the face of the overpowering evil in the world. His role is reduced, and its Christian nature is not emphasized, if at all apparent. Chaos commands the last scenes of these three plays. There are two possibilities as to why this pattern of change should occur in Dürrenmatt's dramas: the pragmatic possibility that, after the critical reception of his first two Christian tragedies, the author desired a more universal theme, which he found first in his courageous individual, and later in the chaos of the modern world; secondly that the changes are the result of a parallel development in the author's life.